JOHN ALDEN CARPENTER

A Chicago Composer

Music in American Life

A list of books in the series appears at the end of this book.

JOHN ALDEN CARPENTER

A Chicago Composer

Howard Pollack

UNIVERSITY OF ILLINOIS PRESS
Urbana and Chicago

First Illinois paperback, 2001
© 1995 by Howard Pollack
Reprinted by arrangement with the author
All rights reserved
Manufactured in the United States of America
p 5 4 3 2 1

⊗ This book is printed on acid-free paper.

Previously published as *Skyscraper Lullaby: The Life and Music of
John Alden Carpenter* by the Smithsonian Institution Press.

Library of Congress Cataloging-in-Publication Data
Pollack, Howard.
[Skyscraper lullaby]
John Alden Carpenter : a Chicago composer / Howard Pollack.
— 1st Illinois pbk.
p. cm.— (Music in American life)
Includes bibliographical references (p.) and index.
ISBN 0-252-07014-3 (paper : acid-free paper)
1. Carpenter, John Alden, 1876–1951. 2. Composers—United
States—Biography. I. Title. II. Series.
ML410.C3278P6   2001
780'.92—dc21   2001033143
[B]

to

Darryl Wexler

When the misty shadows glide,
At the tranquil end of day,
Then let the soul of silence come,
And in our love abide.

Paul Verlaine, "En sourdine"
(trans. John Alden Carpenter)

If the day is done, if birds sing no
more, if the wind has flagged tired,
then draw the veil of darkness thick
upon me, even as thou hast wrapt the
earth with the coverlet of sleep and
tenderly closed the petals of the droop-
ing lotus at dusk.

Rabindranath Tagore, *Gitanjali*

When a Broadway baby says goodnight
It's early in the morning.
Manhattan babies don't sleep tight until the dawn.
Goodnight babies, goodnight,
The milkman's on his way.
Sleep tight, let's call it a day
Listen to the lullabye of old Broadway.

Al Dubin and Harry Warren, "Lullaby of Broadway"

It is pleasant to live over again the adventures of the
day. . . . It is pleasant to lie quite still and close my eyes,
and listen to the wheels of my perambulator. "How very
large the world is. How many things there are!"

John Alden Carpenter, program notes to
Adventures in a Perambulator

Contents

Contents

Acknowledgments

This book has many debts, but outstanding ones to William Austin, Alex Jeschke, Wayne Shirley, and Darryl Wexler, who corrected and edited my manuscript in various stages; Joan O'Connor, who provided me with a draft of her forthcoming bio-bibliography on the composer for Greenwood Press; Kay Stamey, who learned all of Carpenter's songs and recorded them with me; the University of Houston, whose grants allowed me to obtain copies of nearly all of Carpenter's publications, manuscripts and sketches, most recorded examples of his work, and photographs for duplication; and Martin Williams, who believed that John Alden Carpenter deserved a book.

In addition, John Alden Carpenter's granddaughter Rue H. Hubert gave me access to privately held materials relating to the composer as well as permission to copy Carpenter material housed in the Library of Congress and the New York Public Library. She also spoke with me about Carpenter, as did other family members, including Theodora Brown (a niece), Fairbank Carpenter (a grandnephew), Mary Carter (another niece), David Dangler (a cousin of Ellen Carpenter's), Patrick Hill (Carpenter's son-in-law), and Joan Leclerc, Robert Pirie, and Adlai Stevenson Jr. (his step-grandchildren). Otto Luening, Halina Rodzinski, Richard Rodzinski, Phil Kauffmann, William Santozzi, Milton Preves, Claudia Cassidy, and Robert Marsh also graciously consented to interviews.

I take pleasure in acknowledging John Canemaker for a xeroxed storyboard of Disney's *Adventures in a Perambulator*; Stuart Feder for bringing my attention to a relevant passage in Ives; Kevin Guess and Jimmy Lent for recording a four-hand arrangement of *The Birthday of the Infanta*; John H. Kirk, Edward Hunzinger, and Lionel C. Werhan for information about George B. Carpenter, Inc.; James W. Howlett and Sam Mozayani for material on Rush Street; Ronald M. Huntington for his exploration of Carpenter-Sowerby ties; Keith Lencho and Severine Neff for help on matters Ziehnian;

Acknowledgments

Thomas Pierson for a copy of a lecture on *Krazy Kat;* Marta Rodic for translating a Serbian document; Judith Tick for elucidating an Ellen Borden–Dane Rudhyar connection; Steven Tulin for making his home available to me in Washington, D.C.; and Louis Auchincloss, Rae Linda Brown, Richard Buckle, Lukas Foss, Evelyn Mein, Don Morris, Ned Rorem, Charles Schulz, Leonard Slatkin, Ron Wiecki, Tom Willis, and Linda Wolfe for answering my inquiries.

A number of institutions provided generous support. I am especially grateful to both Anita Anderson of the Park Ridge Historical Society and Betty Bandel of the Chittenden County Historical Society for extensive information about the Carpenters in Park Ridge and Charlotte; Frank R. Berger of the Bayerische Staatsoper for photographs of the 1928 Munich production of *Wolkenkratzer* (Skyscrapers); Linda Miles Coppens of Carmel's Harrison Memorial Library for articles from the local *Highland Piper;* Kendall L. Crilly of Yale University for responding to my inquiry about letters between E. Robert Schmitz and Carpenter and for checking the Carpenter-Thomson correspondence; and Sylvia Kenneck of Williams College for hunting through the Paul Whiteman scrapbooks on my behalf. The Newberry Library assisted my research with a fellowship.

I also appreciate the helpful assistance of Bridget Carr Blagbough (Boston Symphony Orchestra), Emily Clark (Chicago Historical Society), Robert L. Dean (Sarasota Department of Historical Resources), Julia Inouye (San Francisco Symphony), J. Morse (Beverly Historical Society), Paul Orlando (Philadelphia Orchestra), John Pennino (Metropolitan Opera), David R. Smith (Walt Disney Archives), and Brenda Nelson-Strauss and Frank Villella (Chicago Symphony). In addition, I would like to thank the staffs of Eastman's Sibley Library (especially Laura Snyder), G. Schirmer (especially Susan Feder), the Hollywood Bowl Museum, Harvard's Houghton Library, the Library of Congress (especially Gillian Anderson, Kate Rivers, and Wayne Shirley), the New York Public Library (especially Fran Barulich), the Newberry Library (especially Diana Haskell), the University of Arkansas Library, the University of Houston Library, and the University of Michigan Library.

I had excellent help from Aaron Appelstein, who edited my manuscript, Tom Clark, who designed the music examples, and Evelyn Lim, Aaminah Durrani, and Grace Baldridge, who prepared the index. I naturally take full responsibility for any misleading or erroneous content.

G. Schirmer has kindly permitted reproduction of music examples from the following copyrighted material:

SONG OF FAITH by John A. Carpenter
Copyright © 1931 (Renewed) G. Schirmer, Inc. (ASCAP)

SEA DRIFT by John A. Carpenter
Copyright © 1936 (Renewed) G. Schirmer, Inc. (ASCAP)

PIANO QUINTET, II and III by John A. Carpenter
Copyright © 1937 (Renewed) G. Schirmer, Inc. (ASCAP)

REST by John A. Carpenter
Copyright © 1936 (Renewed) G. Schirmer, Inc. (ASCAP)

DANZA by John A. Carpenter
Copyright © 1947 (Renewed) G. Schirmer, Inc. (ASCAP)

CONCERTO FOR VIOLIN AND ORCHESTRA (arranged for violin and piano) by John A. Carpenter
Copyright © 1939 (Renewed) G. Schirmer, Inc. (ASCAP)

THE ANXIOUS BUGLER by John A. Carpenter
Copyright © 1943 (Renewed) G. Schirmer, Inc. (ASCAP)

THE SEVEN AGES by John A. Carpenter
Copyright © 1945 (Renewed) G. Schirmer, Inc. (ASCAP)

International Copyright Secured. All Rights Reserved. Used by Permission.

Permission to reproduce photographs and illustrations is gratefully acknowledged as follows: the Bavarian State Opera for photographs of the 1928 Munich production of *Skyscrapers;* the Chicago Historical Society for a sketch of Rue Carpenter by Paul Thévenaz and a photograph of the William Borden mansion; the Chicago Symphony for photographs of Frederick Stock and the Chicago Symphony Orchestra; the Walt Disney Company for a storyboard sketch by Sylvia Moberly-Holland; J. W. Howlett for a photograph of the 700 block of Rush Street; Rue Hubert for photographs and portraits of her family; Joan Leclerc for a photograph of Carpenter and Ellen Borden; the Newberry Library for a photograph of Bernhard Ziehn; and Robert Tobin for Robert Edmond Jones's designs for *The Birthday of the Infanta* and *Skyscrapers.*

Introduction

In his lifetime John Alden Carpenter (1876–1951) won a success almost unparalleled for an American composer of concert music. The most acclaimed musicians performed his works regularly, including conductors of the stature of Walter Damrosch, Karl Muck, Frederick Stock, Leopold Stokowski, Serge Koussevitzky, Fritz Reiner, Artur Rodzinski, Fritz Busch, Pierre Monteux, Otto Klemperer, Bruno Walter, Eugene Ormandy, and Werner Janssen. Such legendary singers as Alma Gluck, John McCormack, Louise Homer, Ernestine Schumann-Heink, Maggie Teyte, Kirsten Flagstad, Conchita Supervia, Rose Bampton, Mina Hager, and Eleanor Steber sang his songs. Percy Grainger championed for decades Carpenter's Piano Concertino, and the Rosé, Budapest, and Pro Arte Quartets played the composer's String Quartet. The Chicago Opera and Metropolitan Opera mounted his ballets, one of which had been commissioned (though never produced) by Diaghilev and the Ballets Russes—a singular honor for an American composer.

Critics and colleagues warmly acknowledged Carpenter's originality, or at least his individuality. Walter Damrosch called him "the most American of our composers," and other composers as varied as Chadwick, Farwell, Mason, Sowerby, Luening, Hanson, Sessions, and Carter similarly emphasized the music's distinctiveness. If critics made connections with jazz or Debussy or Stravinsky—as many did—they usually meant no disparagement, but rather sought to highlight the composer's modernity and to applaud his sensitivity to new trends.

Critics admired, too, the music's craftsmanship—its polish, elegance, rhythmic ingenuity, harmonic sophistication, and expert writing for instruments. Olin Downes titled his 1930 article on the composer "J. A. Carpenter, American Craftsman."[1] Even Paul Rosenfeld, who early on became Carpenter's most distinguished detractor, admitted that "the Chicagoan's resources are coördinated to a degree approximated by no other young American composer. Neither Engel, Powell, Morris, nor any of our other hopefuls have themselves as well in hand as has he."[2] That Carpenter also was a businessman only added a certain glamor to his compositional skills.

Carpenter achieved prominence in less glorious ways as well. Students and amateurs around the country played his piano pieces and sang his songs. "The Home Road" and *Song of Faith* became popular with school and community choruses. G. Schirmer published most of his music, and sales were brisk.[3]

An accomplished pianist, Carpenter also occasionally performed and recorded his own music. Moreover, he was a well-known and highly respected patron of the arts.

Today's surveys of American music, like those by Charles Hamm and H. Wiley Hitchcock, remember Carpenter only as the composer of a handful of works that have some relation either to French music or to jazz. Despite his authorship of the Carpenter entry for the *New Grove Dictionary of American Music,* Gilbert Chase omitted Carpenter entirely from his last edition of *America's Music.*[4]

But Carpenter remains important over and above the fact that he loomed so large during his own lifetime. He is, for instance, a seminal figure: he epitomizes American music's transition from romanticism to modernism. At the start of his career, his name was linked to MacDowell and John Powell; later to Henry Gilbert and Deems Taylor; still later to Gershwin, Copland, and Sessions; and finally to Samuel Barber. He was the first American composer—or at least among the first—to recognize the importance of Debussy and Stravinsky and to experiment with rhythm, color, and harmony in the modernist fashion (creating, in the process, America's first significant ballet scores). Similarly, he argued for the importance of American popular music to high art, thus anticipating the music of Gershwin, Copland, Bernstein, Harbison, and many others, including a whole new generation of composers born in the 1950s and 1960s.

Moreover, Carpenter helped nurture modernist music—both native and European—in America and especially in his native Chicago. His enlightened and generous support of the arts, child welfare, and other civic and national causes also warrants our admiration and continued interest.

Above all, Carpenter's music stands up quite well, as many musicians, unencumbered by academic trends, well know. It is sophisticated, well-crafted music, alternately high-spirited, dreamily whimsical, and melancholy, but always full of personality. His best work deserves comparison with such contemporaries as Ravel, Holst, de Falla, and Janáček. It is time to welcome Carpenter back into the canon.

This book draws principally upon source material found at the Library of Congress, the Newberry Library, the New York Public Library, and G. Schirmer, as well as some in the possession of Rue Hubert, the composer's granddaughter. The largest collection of Carpenter material is at the Library of Congress, which houses nearly all of the composer's musical manuscripts; three enormous scrapbooks assembled by the composer (and, after his death, by his second wife) and crammed full of reviews, programs, and other memorabilia; and miscellaneous sketches, letters, photographs, awards, set and costume designs, and recordings. The Newberry Library contains a lesser, but still notable collection of manuscripts, letters, and photographs. The New York Public Library holds some music and recordings not available anywhere else, as well as a helpful clipping file. G. Schirmer's rental department handles a variety of both published and unpublished scores. And Rue Hubert's collection includes scrapbooks, letters, and other important material concerning the Carpenters and the Winterbothams.

Most secondary material about Carpenter dates from the composer's own lifetime, most notably, a 1930 survey by a fellow Chicagoan, Felix Borowski, who enjoyed access to the composer and his music.[5] Thomas Pierson's 1952 dissertation on the composer closes rather than opens a rich period of Carpenter criticism.[6] Over the last forty years, the Carpenter literature has consisted mostly of record reviews and master's theses on specialized topics.

This book offers the most ample biographical portrait of the composer to date, thanks, in part, to the discovery of the composer's letters to Ellen Borden, his mistress and second wife, at the Library of Congress. Most close friends and associates had died by the time I undertook this project, but I was able to interview his son-in-law, a niece, his grandchildren, and a few acquaintances.

This study further takes stock of Carpenter's entire oeuvre—published and unpublished, complete and incomplete alike—and considers such matters as compositional process, formal and stylistic analysis, critical reception, and performance history.

Carpenter's revisions pose a special challenge. The composer revised most of his major works at least once. Moreover, some of these revisions are quite extensive; a few even result in a virtually new piece. Because it seemed a questionable undertaking to include detailed discussions of all versions of a particular work, considering that many of these pieces are generally unknown, even unavailable, I decided to emphasize one version. But which?

Both the original and revised versions have their own claims: The earlier texts have historical interest, but the later ones represent the composer's mature view and tend to be stronger and more convincing. Most of the revisions, however, remain unpublished and are available only in holograph through G. Schirmer's rental department. Consequently, libraries tend to own original versions, whereas modern performers use the revised ones. Similarly, 78 rpm recordings use the originals, whereas LPs and CDs feature the revisions. (Fortunately, this problem applies mainly to the orchestral music, not to songs or chamber music.)

This study's historical and chronological approach favored, ultimately, the earlier over the later version. But I have studied all of the composer's revisions and generally report on them following the discussion of the original work. I hope this satisfies those readers interested in the composer's career as well as those more concerned about modern performance of his work.

The book usually refers to pitches in the abstract, but when the octave register seems called for, I use the common designation (in parentheses) of "c" for the C below middle C, "c¹" for middle C, and so forth.

CHAPTER ONE

The Carpenters of Chicago

1876–1893

John Alden Carpenter emerged against the background of the so-called Chicago Renaissance of 1890–1930, a time of imposing, indeed, unparalleled vibrancy in the cultural history of that city.

By 1890, after fifty years of population growth unmatched anywhere in the world, Chicago had become America's second largest city. "Chicago emerged as the colossus of the West," explains one historian, "because its hinterland contained the world's most productive agricultural area and because it was the terminus of the world's greatest internal waterway." Chicago led the nation in such areas as agricultural machinery, meatpacking, railroad car building, foundries, and piano and organ works.[1]

Chicago concurrently became an important cultural center (though "recent origin, an interior location, and early identification with heavy industry" would distinguish it from the older, more aristocratic cities of the eastern seaboard).[2] Even before 1890 Chicago had begun collecting contemporary French painting for its glamorous Art Institute, founded in 1882. In 1891 the city lured Theodore Thomas from New York and virtuosos from all over the world for a symphony orchestra. And in 1893, twenty-two years after a devastating fire, Chicago launched the World's Columbian Exposition and unveiled to an astounded international community that it had the wealth and determination to create a world of dazzling innovation and monumental beauty.

In the decades ahead, Chicago revolutionized architecture through the strikingly bold designs of Louis B. Sullivan and Frank Lloyd Wright, and transformed literature through the similarly hard-edged fiction of Henry Fuller, Hamlin Garland, Sherwood Anderson, and Theodore Dreiser and the hard-hitting journalism of George Ade and Eugene Field. Its little journals— *Poetry, Little Review, Dial*—introduced America to such local, distinctive poets as Edgar Lee Masters, Carl Sandburg, and Vachel Lindsay, as well as such international modernists as Yeats, Tagore, Pound, and Eliot.

1

This opulent, adventurous Chicago applauded Sarah Bernhardt, George Arliss, Mrs. Patrick Campbell, and Sophie Tucker at the theater; Amelita Galli-Curci, Enrico Caruso, John McCormack, and Mary Garden at the opera; and Ignace Paderewski, Josef Hofmann, Fritz Kreisler, and Joseph Lhevinne at the symphony, where Richard Strauss, Camille Saint-Saëns, Edward Elgar, and Serge Rachmaninoff came to perform their own works, and where Isadora Duncan danced to Gluck. The city's preeminent music theorist, Bernhard Ziehn, helped Busoni complete Bach's unfinished *Art of the Fugue,* and wealthy businessmen commissioned a concerto and opera from the young Prokofiev.

Chicago also attracted Southern blacks, who made the city a center of ragtime, blues, and, eventually, jazz. Such styles, in turn, helped local white songsters like Ben Jerome and Joseph E. Howard win national acclaim. Chicago further became a fledgling motion picture center (not yet superseded by Hollywood) that produced films by Charlie Chaplin, Gloria Swanson, and Wallace Beery. The Chicagoan artist John T. McCutcheon brought new distinction to the art of newspaper cartoons, and Irene Castle, having taught the world to tango and fox-trot, made Chicago her home.

Chicago also attracted progressive thinkers of every stripe, from Thorstein Veblen to Jane Addams; from John Dewey to Eugene Debs; from William Rainey Harper, who presided over the innovative University of Chicago, to Robert S. Abbott, whose *Defender* helped advance the cause of black civil rights in America.

It seemed that having overshadowed Boston and Philadelphia as a major cultural and economic center, Chicago would surpass its only serious rival nationally, New York. World War I and Prohibition, however, brought decline and stagnation. In the twilight of its glory, the city managed a final tour de force: the dissemination of the music of King Oliver, Louis Armstrong, and other Southern jazz musicians and the production of such local jazz talents as Bix Beiderbecke, Benny Goodman, and Gene Krupa. But the Great Depression of 1929 and the decline of the railroads further damaged the city's resiliency and ultimately proved more debilitating than the Great Fire of 1871.[3]

The career of John Alden Carpenter matched his city's fortunes. From a tentative, unprepossessing start followed an outpouring of beautiful songs, tone poems, and ballets that suggested a new meeting ground for high and popular art. By the 1930s Carpenter's prestige had begun to crumble. He lived long enough to see his work fade into fabled memory, but not long enough to see it, in the 1960s, demolished into almost total forgetfulness as a whole new Chicago took root.

Like the works of other great figures of the Chicago Renaissance, Carpenter's oeuvre was inextricably tied to the city itself. Carpenter grew up in Chicago and, though he traveled extensively, spent all of his life there. His most important teachers—Amy Fay and Bernhard Ziehn—were Chicagoans, as were his closest friends and his two wives. He patronized and helped guide a number of Chicago's arts institutions—symphony, opera, dance ensembles, museums, and the little journals. He belonged to various arts clubs, he knew the fashionable nightspots, and he was active in civic affairs. And in many ways his most notable accomplishment—a unique melding of European high art and American popular traditions—belonged very much to his time and place.

John Alden Carpenter was born into a prosperous, accomplished family on 28 February 1876 in the Chicago suburb of Park Ridge, Illinois. According to genealogical records unearthed by the composer himself, he may have descended from a John Carpenter of Hereford, England, who served in Parliament in 1323. The composer also found an Irish branch of the family, descended from one William Carpenter, who died in 1520. A later William Carpenter, esquire of Cobham, became messenger to Charles II, who in 1663 conferred upon him the Carpenter coat of arms—an argent, a greyhound passant, and a chief sable—and the family motto—Celeritas, Virtus, Fidelitas (Speed, Courage, Fidelity). Carpenters were in America by the 1600s, and the ancestral greyhound turned up on the tombstone of a Daniel Carpenter of Rehoboth, Massachusetts.[4]

Carpenter could also claim heir to those legendary Pilgrims John Alden (hence, his middle name) and Priscilla Mullins through his paternal great-grandmother, Charlotte Bartlett Alden, who married one Benjamin Carpenter. The composer's cousin Charlotte Brewster helped reconstruct this Alden family line for him—from John and Priscilla, to Jonathan and Abigail Alden, to Jonathan and Elizabeth Alden, to Seth and Lydia Alden, to Jonathan and Sarah Alden, the parents of his great-grandmother. The composer learned, too, about such famed seafaring relatives as Captain John Alden (b. 1770) and his son John (b. 1793), and about connections between such old American families as the Aldens, Brewsters, Bryants, Cushings, and so forth. He was especially intrigued by the possibility that Priscilla Mullins had a Huguenot background.[5]

The composer's grandfather, also named Benjamin, was born outside of Syracuse, New York, in the town of Manlius in 1806. He continued the family's westward trek, moving to eastern Ohio, where he married Abigail Hayes of Hartford, Ohio, in 1832. Benjamin and Abigail lived for a while in

3

Conneaut, Ohio, where a son, George Benjamin, was born in 1834. The Carpenters finally settled in Chicago in 1850.

In Chicago, Benjamin established the meatpacking house of Marsh and Carpenter and successfully entered politics, becoming an alderman of the Ninth Ward and one of the city's first commissioners of public works. He also helped found the New England Congregational Church. Such achievements, however, paled beside those of his son George, who built an enormous family enterprise, George B. Carpenter and Company.[6]

Carpenter and Company had its beginnings as Huginin and Pierce, a ship chandlery founded in 1839 that specialized in sail making. In 1840, apparently, George A. Robb, another chandlery, took over the business, which became Payson and Robb in 1843. In 1850 Gilbert Hubbard (for whom the composer's brother Hubbard was named) replaced Payson in the partnership. After Robb died in 1857, George Carpenter left his father's meatpacking firm and acquired a one-third interest in the chandlery.[7] Upon Hubbard's death in 1881, George became sole proprietor of the newly named George B. Carpenter and Company.[8]

Thanks in part to Hubbard's close ties to important Boston manufacturers, the company emerged as one of Chicago's leading wholesale and retail distributors of a wide variety of goods, including twine, cordage, sail duck, tar, paint, tents, banners, and flags. "This firm represents every article of cordage," wrote Isaac Guyer in 1862, "from the finest fishing line to the largest cable used, and every conceivable article used in rigging a vessel."[9] Located near a Chicago River marina on South Water Street (originally between Clark and LaSalle, but by the 1860s on the corner of Fifth Avenue), the company served hundreds of ships transporting lumber and other goods from Michigan and elsewhere, provided settlers and prospectors with tents, and, during the Civil War, helped supply federal troops with camp and naval articles. Although their building perished in the Chicago fire of 9 October 1871, the company set up shop the following day in a tent and erected a new building in 1872 at their South Water and Fifth Avenue location (now Wacker Drive and Wells Street).

With sole Carpenter proprietorship came continued prosperity and growth, as the company enjoyed the boom years of the 1880s and an expanded market that included railways, mills, and mining companies. Reported one source:

> Without question the success of Mr. [George B.] Carpenter, like that of all other leaders of business, lies in the fact that he never departed from clean-

cut and well-defined business principles; that promises were not made nor agreements entered into which could not be fulfilled to the letter. Being an excellent judge of men, he was able to surround himself with those who were not afraid to work and who by watching his interests furthered their own. Never a hard taskmaster, always considerate of the feelings of others, he inspired his assistants with vim and vigor by setting the example himself.[10]

An 1852 graduate of St. Mary's College, George Carpenter was also an educated man, whose library of more than one thousand volumes would form, after his death, the nucleus of the Park Ridge Public Library. These books included the memoirs of Ulysses S. Grant and those of Grant's sometime adversary, the German American reformist and anti-imperialist Carl Schurz; poems by Victor Hugo; many volumes of Alexandre Dumas; and a well-worn Bible.[11] George's son John Alden would inherit his father's love of literature and history, as well as his humanitarianism: in the years after the Chicago fire, George helped found the Chicago Christian Union, an aid society and employment agency.[12]

Described by the American violinist Maud Powell as "that charming and gifted woman," George's wife, Elizabeth Curtis Greene, was born in Pittsfield, New Hampshire, in 1838.[13] According to her granddaughter Katharine Bermingham, whose 1977 letter to Thomas Pierson constitutes the most extensive word on the subject, Elizabeth was distantly related to Daniel Webster.[14] Why or when she came to Chicago is not known, but she apparently arrived with her family; her niece Daisy Greene taught school in nearby Collinsville. In 1861 the twenty-three-year-old Elizabeth married the twenty-seven-year-old George, just starting out in the ship chandlery business. The Carpenters had four children: Benjamin (1865–1927), George Albert (1867–1944), Hubbard (1874–1953), and John Alden (1876–1951).

Elizabeth's great passion was music. She not only played organ and piano but "was gifted with a superb mezzo-soprano voice and was trained to become a professional," according to Bermingham. This training included lessons in London and Paris with two of the most celebrated voice teachers of the day: the singer and composer William Shakespeare, who wrote a popular manual, the *Art of Singing* (1901), and the German mezzo-soprano Mathilde Marchesi (1849–1931), who also authored a famed vocal method, and whose students included Calvé, Melba, and Garden.

Carpenter reminisced that his mother first pursued these European studies in her early thirties, when her two oldest boys "were about five and didn't need so much care. . . . Then she came back, and produced two more sons, and after a few years of bringing them up, she again went to Europe to study. That was a rare and courageous thing for a woman to do in the 1880s."[15] The boys sometimes accompanied her; John, for example, joined her in London in 1883, at which time she introduced Maud Powell to the first conductor of the Boston Symphony, George Henschel, and to "other distinguished musicians."[16]

Carpenter recalled that his father "had no awareness of music except through my mother, but he was so proud of her that he became a musical enthusiast."[17] So encouraged, Elizabeth became prominent in the musical life of both Park Ridge and Chicago.[18] In Park Ridge she played organ and sang in the local Congregational Church, taught Sunday school, and organized concerts, poetry readings, and exhibits.[19] She also sang with the Chicago Apollo Club (founded in 1875 and named after its Boston namesake), which specialized in sacred choral works by Bach, Handel, Mendelssohn, Gounod, Paine, and others.[20] One family story has her entertaining Jenny Lind on a trip to Chicago.

In 1877 Elizabeth and fourteen other women founded the Chicago Amateur Club, which met every two weeks on Monday afternoons for chamber music concerts. It soon became one of Chicago's leading arts organizations; by the 1890s its membership, which included Amy Fay and her sister Rose Fay (after 1890, Mrs. Theodore Thomas), had grown to more than six hundred.[21] Elizabeth also chaired the Women's Musical Congress in Chicago in July 1893, in which more than fifteen hundred people attended, including Maud Powell, the opera singer Lillian Nordica, and Rose Fay Thomas.[22]

We have only a few, scattered references to Elizabeth's singing. Minnie Haseman recalled evenings at Park Ridge in which Mrs. Carpenter would sing: "She had such a lovely voice people would walk back and forth on the sidewalk to hear her." A reporter, Martha Freeman Esmond, wrote in 1895 of hearing her sing Ethelbert Nevin's "O, That We Two Were Maying." And Bermingham related that Elizabeth once substituted at a Theodore Thomas concert and "received such an ovation that Thomas embraced her publicly before she left the stage." Bermingham could herself remember hearing her grandmother, quite ill before her death in 1905, honor a request to sing something; she chose one of her favorites, "For He Shall Feed His Flock," from Handel's *Messiah*.[23]

Carpenter only occasionally spoke about his mother: "[My mother was] one of the best musical amateurs that has ever come under my notice, and from her I got my inclination for music. When I use the word 'amateur' in speaking of my mother, I mean a true lover of music—one who could play and who could understand any kind of music."[24] At another time he further explained, "She had a beautiful soprano voice, and sang all the time, but not professionally."[25] If she lived in a later day, he told Madeleine Goss, she would have been a recitalist or an opera singer.[26]

Elizabeth's influence on Carpenter can be sensed most clearly in the composer's many lullabies, such as the finale of *Adventures in a Perambulator*, in which Elizabeth's soprano can almost be heard in the second violins. Her fondness for both popular and classical song presumably shaped the composer's temperament as well. Indeed, the following lines from some unpublished jottings titled "Foreword to the Wise" suggest that Elizabeth's voice stood at the core of her son's musical essence:

> Did you ever drop a stone in a quiet pond and watch the ripples spread out in a thousand broadening circles? When you listen—really listen, to a beautiful sound (perhaps your mother's voice) the same thing happens in your mind,—and the ripples go on spreading while you live. You may seem to forget them but you never really do. They are yours and no one can take them away. You may not care to talk about them, but every year they grow more precious, for they are timeless and never die.[27]

After losing a first home to the 1871 fire, the Carpenters built a house in Brickton, a little town about a thirty-minute train ride from Chicago.[28] The Carpenter home stood right by the railroad depot. In 1873 the town incorporated as a village, and George Carpenter Sr. was elected president of the village board. The board accepted his suggestion that Brickton be renamed Park Ridge.[29] The Carpenters, however, apparently spent only the springs and summers in Park Ridge; they remained in Chicago during the fall and winter.[30]

"My grandparents had unusual ideas about raising their sons," asserted Katharine Bermingham, referring to the fact that they first "paired" Benjamin and George and then Hubbard and John. They sent both pairs of boys to Harvard as roommates (Benjamin and George in 1884, Hubbard and John in 1893). And although they provided all four boys with musical instruction, they gave Benjamin and George violin lessons (both also sang), whereas they taught Hubbard and John to play the piano.[31]

In one childhood photograph, John, in bangs and curls, makes a striking contrast to his more masculinely shorn brother, Hubbard, who holds him protectively. Both look elegant in their lace collars and black slippers. John Alden remained a stylish dresser: in knickers and a polka-dotted shirt in the

1890s; in a three-piece suit, complete with studded cravat and pocket watch, at the turn of the century; sporting elegant bow ties in the 1910s; in a double-breasted blazer and straw hat in the 1920s; and casually relaxed in cardigans and ties in the 1930s and 1940s.

Grace Hibbard Reed, who grew up with the Carpenter boys, remembered the Carpenter home as a spacious, eighteen-room country estate furnished in walnut and mahogany, with colorful English wallpaper and a grand mahogany staircase. The grounds included gardens, a great variety of trees, an apple orchard, and a barn for two cows and chickens. In winter they all enjoyed toboggan rides and costume balls at the local hotel. In summer the children looked forward to Sunday school picnics with baked ham, potato salad, deviled eggs, marble cake, and ice cream and, for amusement, croquet, rope swings, bean bag, baseball, tag, and hayrides back home, with everyone singing "Aunt Dinah's Quilting Party," "My Bonnie Lies over the Ocean," "I'll Hang My Harp on a Weeping Willow Tree," and "Sweet Alice Ben Bolt" ("Oh, Don't You Remember Sweet Alice, Ben Bolt?").

Photographs from the period document the kind of midwestern idyll that Reed paints. In a photograph from 1887, John, his brother Hubbard, and three other boys lounge huddled together on a large hammock with their baseball bats. Another photo shows them lined up behind a volleyball net. In yet another snapshot, from the summer of 1889, a bunch of well-scrubbed, knickered youths pose at a Sunday school party at the Park Ridge First Congregational Church; Carpenter, his clear eyes peering out from his round, handsome face, leans on his bicycle.[32]

Life among the Illinois gentry was less idyllic for Minnie Haseman, the Carpenters' servant, or for the two German women already on staff when she was hired in the late 1880s or early 1890s. The Park Ridge home "was terrible." It had no gas, no electricity, no running water upstairs in the butler's pantry, and no dumbwaiter. Any time spent there during the winter was particularly rough, for they had to rely on wood stoves for heat and candles for light.

The Carpenters built a second home—a grand winter residence at 293 Dearborn, between Delaware and Walton Streets, across from Washington Park and the Newberry Library—about 1890. Haseman vividly recalled the Carpenters' first reception in this new home, with a black cook and butler in attendance, and the large dining room table set with yellow china, yellow candles, and yellow flowers, all set upon a white tablecloth. Following this reception came a whirlwind of other events—luncheons, dinners, card parties, and the visit of a Miss Hall, presumably the Marguerite Hall to whom

John dedicated some of his earliest songs, dated 1896. The Carpenters hosted no card parties during Lent, so the last took place on Shrove Tuesday and featured a dinner of fruit, sausage, potatoes, fried apples, rolls, and coffee, with pancakes and maple syrup served for dessert. After college John returned home to 293 Dearborn for three years (1897–1900) before marrying Rue Winterbotham.

According to Haseman the Carpenters sold the Dearborn house shortly thereafter, in response to Freemasons buying up the corner church and other property on the block. By this time Elizabeth was too ill to return to Park Ridge year-round, so the Carpenters wintered in Lake Geneva, Wisconsin, near their son Hubbard. It was about this time that Elizabeth's cousin Daisy Greene suspended her teaching position to help nurse Elizabeth and keep George company. After Elizabeth's death in 1905, George returned with Daisy and the staff to a renovated Park Ridge home that had gas and electricity. After George's death in 1912, the house changed hands, finally serving Park Ridge as City Hall from about 1935 to 1965. Soon after this, the town tore the house down, to the dismay of the local historical society.[33]

At age five John began piano lessons with his mother, and from age eleven to fifteen, he studied for four years (1887–90) with Amy Fay.[34] A native Mississippian, Fay (1844–1928) had studied piano in Berlin and Weimar with an imposing roster of teachers: Louis Ehlert, Carl Tausig, Theodor Kullak, Ludwig Deppe, and Franz Liszt. In 1881 she published an account of these lessons, titled *Music-Study in Germany*. The book became enormously popular, with sixteen editions by 1896, and inspired hundreds, perhaps thousands of Americans to study piano in Germany. The book is still valued, especially for its worshipful yet insightful portrait of Liszt, a portrait "naive and keen at the same time," in the words of Arthur Loesser.[35]

Deppe, however, was Fay's most important teacher. His method, which she introduced to many Americans, helped her achieve one of her principal objectives: the even, pure, round, soft, and penetrating tone produced by Liszt, Clara Schumann, and a few others. This necessitated giving up habits acquired under Kullak and learning a new method, one that involved curved, quiet fingers, light wrists, steady elbows, and low stools. The ideal was to let "the notes fall from the finger-tips like drops of water." Deppe also taught her to pedal "after the chord and not simultaneously with it." Whereas she had studied Chopin under Tausig, and Beethoven under Liszt, she gained, with Deppe, a new respect for Mozart and Haydn.[36]

On Fay's return to the States, she lived in Boston (1876–78), Chicago (1878–90), and New York (1890–1919). While in Chicago, she taught piano and concertized widely, eventually limiting such concerts to "piano conversations," in which, before playing a piece, she would discuss "what the work was intended to convey."[37] She also became active in the Amateur Musical Club and other local organizations; through such associations she undoubtedly saw Elizabeth Carpenter frequently.

At his piano lessons John presumably learned Deppe's method, which also influenced Leschetizky and, consequently, a whole generation of contemporary European pianists. Fay might also have transmitted to Carpenter something of Liszt's partiality toward lyricism and color over form, as well as something of the Hungarian composer's humility, generosity, and sense of adventure. Her descriptions of "what the work was intended to convey" might have predisposed Carpenter further to songs and program music. On the other hand, Fay undoubtedly helped nurture Carpenter's lifelong affection for Chopin and Mozart as well.

Under the tutelage of his mother, Fay, and later Seeboeck, Carpenter, who had long, delicate fingers, developed into a fine pianist. He expressed his appreciation to "Miss Amy Fay" with a dedication of an early song, the 1896 "Norse Lullaby."

During his last years with Fay, Carpenter enrolled in the University School (1889–93), not yet surpassed by the Chicago Latin School as the city's most prestigious private school. In the 1891 fall semester alone, he received grades for reading, spelling, penmanship, composition, declamation, history, Greek, Latin, German, algebra, gymnastics, and military drill. For his January 1892 examinations, he earned an "excellent" in spelling and Virgil and a "satisfactory" in German and anabasis.[38]

After Fay left Chicago for New York, John continued his musical studies, during his last two years at the University School (1891–93), with the pianist-composer William C. E. Seeboeck (1859–1907). Seeboeck belonged to that wave of German and Austrian immigration that gave Chicago its highly Teutonic complexion—its beer gardens and sausages, its rough stone walls and heavy arches, its resplendent Wagner and Richard Strauss. A native of Vienna, Seeboeck studied theory with the Beethoven scholar Gustav Nottebohm and piano with the Russian pianist Anton Rubinstein; he had some contact with Brahms as well. He settled in Chicago in 1881, working as the accompanist to the Apollo Club for a few years (during which time he surely became acquainted with Elizabeth Carpenter) and as a teacher at the Chicago Musical College.

Seeboeck had a good reputation as a pianist. An informed listener wrote: "[Seeboeck] is very musical, an extremely fluent reader and a most beautiful pianist. . . . Everything which Seeboeck plays sounds musical."[39] For one lecture series he discussed and performed concertos by Beethoven, Schumann, and Chopin. He also earned fame locally for his now-forgotten songs and operas, including *Gladiators*.[40]

John probably took his lessons not at the Chicago Musical College but at Seeboeck's apartment on Rush Street, close to John's home on Dearborn.[41] His studies included piano, music theory, and composition. He had previously done some "puttering" in composition: at age five he began to "fiddle around" at the piano, and by age ten he was writing down tunes.[42] But Seeboeck provided John with his first "definite instructions."[43] Seeboeck probably balanced Fay's enthusiasm for Liszt with a healthy regard for Bach and Brahms; one can certainly find traces of Brahms in all phases of Carpenter's work, especially in his late compositions.

During his high school years, Carpenter presumably took part in Chicago's exploding concert life: its symphony concerts, with Theodore Thomas conducting works by Beethoven, Wagner, Dvořák, Brahms, and Saint-Saëns; its opera, with memorable performances by Emma Calvé as Carmen, Lotte Lehmann as Elizabeth, and Adelina Patti as Violetta, in Sullivan's colossal Auditorium Theatre; and recitals of choral music by Rossini, Berlioz, and Mendelssohn sponsored by the Apollo Club, in which his mother played a prominent role.[44]

In all likelihood, however, the event that most impressed the young Carpenter was the great Columbian Exposition, which opened on 1 May 1893. Carpenter surely attended the exposition a number of times before leaving for Harvard in the fall of 1893.

The Columbian Exposition was among the most extraordinary events of its kind: more than twenty-seven million people attended this six-month world's fair in which fifty-one nations, thirty-nine colonies, and forty-seven states and territories participated. Sprawling thirty-one acres of land and sixty-one acres of waterways, the exposition featured more than 65,000 exhibits, including full-size replicas of Columbus's ships; the Yerkes telescope, the world's largest; Japanese and French impressionist painting; a greenhouse with more than sixteen thousand varieties of orchids; the kinetoscope, a precursor of the movie camera; keyboard instruments that belonged to Bach, Haydn, Mozart, and Beethoven; a huge collection of windmills; a display of women's literature and art; a thirty-five-foot tower containing fourteen thousand California oranges; and the world's first Ferris wheel, its enormous cars holding forty passengers, one of which contained a band that played the exposition's theme song, "After the Ball." No one could possibly attend all of these exhibits—not to mention the thousands of concerts and addresses—but most attendants visited the Midway Plaisance, described as follows:

> Traveling the length of the Midway Plaisance, the one mile-strip of land devoted to foreign and private exhibits, was like traveling the globe. In just a few hours, a fairgoer could pass through two Irish villages and kiss the Blarney Stone, stop for lunch in German Village, visit the bazaars of Algiers, walk through a Javanese encampment or a village of Laplanders and their reindeer, ride a donkey through a street of Cairo, view Samoans working in their grass huts or Central Africans dancing to unfamiliar rhythms, watch the thunderous eruption of Kilauea Volcano and brave a bumpy ride in a sedan chair.[45]

Carpenter would have naturally attended some of the musical events at the Music Hall, with its 300-piece Columbian Orchestra, and the Choral Hall, with its 2,500-person choir. Perhaps he took a special interest in Thomas's performances of such American composers as Chadwick, MacDowell, and Paine or in the arrival of John Philip Sousa, a last-minute replacement for Patrick Gilmore.[46] But one would have heard an incredible variety of music from all over the fairgrounds: gypsy bands from Hungary; musicians, snake charmers, jugglers, and dancing girls from North Africa; the songs of Samoan warriors; Bavarian bands; Chinese musicians and acrobats; the ragtime of African American pianists; a Moorish string band "playing monotonous repetitions"; exhibitions of American Indian music (that almost scared Frances Densmore to death); a rich assortment of music from Latin America, including daily performances by the Guatemala National Band; and the controversial "hootchy-kootchy" of Little Egypt that scandalized proper Victorians.[47]

The Columbian Exposition so anticipated Carpenter's career—his fascination with new technology and amusement parks, his sensitivity to popular music, his interest in world religions and non-Western cultures, his patriotic and utopian impulses—that one can view it as a seminal event in the composer's life, notwithstanding the absence of any concrete evidence as such. Indeed, many contemporaries thought of the exposition as marking a new aesthetic awareness not only for Chicagoans but for all Americans. Harry Thurston Peck, for example, credited the Columbian Exposition with revealing to "millions of Americans whose lives were necessarily colourless and narrow, the splendid possibilities of art, and the compelling power of the beautiful." William Dean Howells similarly claimed that the fair "evinced cooperation instead of competition, idealism instead of materialism, beauty instead of ugliness, social responsibility instead of individual avariciousness, and art instead of business."[48] "Here was a grand opportunity to proclaim America's greatness before the world," writes one historian, "to show the enormous strides in cultural achievement since the centennial, to set to rest forever the quibbles about American cultural inferiority, and, not incidentally, to foster patriotic harmony in a period of mounting domestic conflict."[49] A young man could even dream of becoming a composer.

CHAPTER TWO

Early Works

From "Love Whom I Have Never Seen" to
A Little Dutch Girl

1893–1900

Carpenter and his brother Hubbard arrived at Harvard in the fall of 1893. "You and I were fortunate in coming to Harvard as freshmen under the old regime," recalled Hubbard years later. "Bill Parks on Bosworth Place was still a going concern and it was possible to buy a table d'hote at Marlives with Red Ink at 80 cents."[1]

At the time, the Harvard faculty included such distinguished scholars as Charles Eliot Norton, Josiah Royce, George Santayana, and William James. Daniel Gregory Mason, Carpenter's senior by one year, later wrote of his alma mater:

> Any place where so large a number of such great individual teachers were gathered together as there were at Harvard in the nineties could not but have proved stimulating. But Harvard was more than stimulating, it was mellowing, ripening. This was because we students had not only the provocation of these contacts with truly great men, of a surprising diversity of interests, characters, and personalities, but, what is even more precious, liberty in the choosing of these influences, time to digest and assimilate them, leisure to grow from our centres as well as absorb at our points of contact. We were not regimented, standardized, herded and labelled.[2]

Unlike Mason, who studied philosophy with Royce, Santayana, and James, Carpenter elected courses in history, government and law, and economics. Perhaps he thought of becoming a lawyer, like his brother George, or of entering his father's business, like his brother Benjamin. In history and economics, as in physics, Hebrew, and fine arts, Carpenter earned average grades; he excelled in English, French, chemistry, and music, graduating summa cum laude in 1897.

In the 1890s Harvard averaged about fifty music students at any given time. These included, just before Carpenter's arrival, Frederick Converse, '93 (1871–1940), Edward Burlingame Hill, '94 (1872–1960), and Mason, '95 (1873–1953). John Knowles Paine (1839–1906) single-handedly supervised them all until 1895, when Walter Spalding, class of '87, joined the faculty, teaching freshmen and sophomores. Consequently, Paine taught all of Carpenter's music courses: harmony, counterpoint, canon and fugue, music history, instrumentation, and free composition.[3]

During these years John Knowles Paine's preeminence among American composers had not yet been overshadowed by the more original Edward MacDowell. Works like the melodramatic, post-Wagnerian overture *Oedipus Tyrannus* (1881), which Carpenter probably heard played by the Boston Symphony in 1894, arguably represented some of the loftiest American music of its time and revealed, for all its Victorian propriety and conventionality, an ardent sincerity.

Carpenter once discussed Paine with M. A. DeWolfe Howe for a 1939 tribute to his former teacher:

> I find that it is difficult to recapture anything of my contacts with "J. K." beyond rather vague impressions of a cheerful but reluctant teacher, full of pessimism as to his pupils, and filled with a fine defiance of the necessities which prevented him from getting on with his own creative work. I was fortunate to be under his guidance when he was in the throes of *delivering* the last pages of his opera [*Azara*]. . . . And these moments were sometimes followed by tea during which J. K. produced some of his favorite puns and pretended to be unaware of the sweet and peaceful presence of Mrs. J. K. whom we all, and he, adored.[4]

The last time Carpenter saw him, in June 1897, Paine "threw at me over his shoulder as a parting admonition: 'Better change your mind about going into that *business*,'" meaning the business of composition.

In the same tribute to Paine, Frederick Converse offered a similarly tactful remembrance of the self-absorbed, discouraging Paine, mentioning, further, his "sleepy lectures in musical history, in which he frequently bent forward over the desk until his nose almost touched it."[5] In his own recollections published about this same time, Mason was more outspoken in his criticism:

> Professor Paine struck me from the start as arbitrary, as lacking in that first and last gift of the teacher, the ability to see things from the angle of the

student. Typical, to give an example, was his blue-pencilling of a dissonance with which I had begun a song. He said it was "unprepared"—as undoubtedly it was; but to me it seemed seizing and exciting, and his prohibiting it merely cold-blanketed my enthusiasm without showing me the way to a wiser one.[6]

Carpenter composed chorales in a pseudo-Handelian style for Paine's counterpoint class, dutifully earning his A.

Whatever his limitations as a teacher, Paine suffered imposing restrictions: a mere two hundred volumes in the music library, inadequate space for lectures and for visiting chamber ensembles, and no faculty assistance. Paine made a desperate plea to the administration in 1895 for more resources, prompting, at least, the hiring of Walter Spalding the following year.

Paine was only the most senior of a number of Boston-based composers who helped make that city the principal center for new American concert music in the 1890s; these others included Arthur Foote (1853–1937), George Whitefield Chadwick (1854–1931), Charles Martin Loeffler (1861–1935), and Amy Beach (1867–1944). MacDowell (1860–1908) also lived in Boston from 1888 to 1896. Carpenter surely had some familiarity with their music, which he plausibly thought overly academic. He would not likely have shared Mason's enthusiasm for Chadwick, nor Hill's for MacDowell. After graduation Carpenter had minimal personal contact with the entire Boston scene, although he would have heard MacDowell and especially Chadwick at Chicago Symphony concerts with fair regularity up to World War II.

During Carpenter's Harvard years, the Boston Symphony was led by Emil Paur (1893–98), who programmed both the latest European and American works. Perhaps Carpenter heard Paur's 1896 performance of Brahms's Fourth Symphony, which won special praise for its "robustness and . . . sincerity."[7] Carpenter and his colleagues would have paid special attention to Dvořák's *New World* Symphony and its concomitant suggestion that American composers utilize native popular and folk traditions. In his own way Carpenter proved true to this most characteristic legacy of the 1890s.

In 1894, soon after entering Harvard, Carpenter began publishing songs and piano pieces. By 1898, one year after college graduation, his publications totaled nine songs—"Love Whom I Never Have Seen" (1894, words by the composer), "My Sweetheart" (1894, words by Griffith Alexander), "Alas, How Easily Things Go Wrong" (1896, words by George MacDonald, whose original title is "Sweet Peril"), "In Spring" (1896, words by Shakespeare), "Memory" (1896, words from the London *Atheneum*), "Norse Lullaby" (1896, words by Eugene Field), "Sicilian Lullaby" (1897, words by Eugene Field), "Little John's Song" (1897, words by Nora Hopper), and "Mistress Mine" (1897, words by Shakespeare)—and three piano pieces—*Minuet* (1894), *Twilight Reverie* (1894), and *Nocturne* (1898). Miles and Thompson published the 1894 songs and piano pieces, and H. B. Stevens published the later works.

Carpenter dedicated "In Spring" to Francis Fisher Powers and "Alas, How Easily Things Go Wrong" and "Memory" to Marguerite Hall. Powers and Hall were highly regarded song recitalists; Carpenter probably met them through his mother. We can assume that they sang the Carpenter songs dedicated to them, although we do not know where or when.

Richard Aldrich, music critic for the *New York Times,* described Marguerite Hall's singing as "a delight; it is sincere, intelligent, guided always by an artist's appreciation and a truly musical feeling, and though her voice is not in itself of the greatest beauty, she can make it expressive of widely diverse moods and emotions."[8] Carpenter apparently prized such voices, as is evident from the special regard with which he held, in later years, Maggie Teyte, Tom Dobson, Mina Hager, Eva Gauthier, and Marian Anderson. Maybe his mother had such a voice, too.

Carpenter's collegiate songs and piano pieces belong to the sentimental parlor tradition characteristic of American art music of the time. The songs, for example, are of a type found in Schirmer's representative *Anthology of American Song,* which, though published in 1911, consisted mostly of works originally published in the 1890s and early 1900s. The perfumed romance of Carpenter's "Memory" wafts through Charles Wakefield Cadman's "Moonlight Song" and any number of other selections with the word *rose* in the title (five out of twenty-five); the soothing moralizing of "Alas, How Easily Things Go Wrong" also informs C. B. Hawley's "Nightingale and the Rose"; the hey-nonny-no merriment of "Little John's Song" recalls Horatio Parker's "Milkmaid's Song"; and the fairy-tale sweetness of "Norse Lullaby" is comparable to Reginald de Koven's similarly titled "Norman Cradle Song." Moreover, for his two Shakespeare settings, Carpenter selected texts familiar to this repertory ("In Spring" is a setting of "It was a lover and his lass"), although neither text turns up in this particular *Anthology.*

Although recitalists like Powers and Hall programmed such songs alongside Gluck, Donizetti, and Wolf, Schirmer and other publishers often called such pieces "popular songs," rather than art songs, because they enjoyed, in fact, a certain popularity and were essentially intended for home use by America's musically literate middle classes—to be sung alongside popular songs, operetta airs, and folk-tune arrangements. Schirmer accordingly included Reginald de Koven in their *Anthology,* as they might have included Ethelbert Nevin or Carrie Jacobs Bond. Some art song anthologies of the period even found room for Stephen Foster and James Bland. Although such songs as those by MacDowell or Parker required a degree of musical training, their technical demands, for both singer and pianist, were modest. This popular strain in America's art songs quickly died out after World War I.

Although Europe produced an equivalent repertory, America's art songs of the period were often rather treacly and melodramatic compared even with Europe's minor song literature. David Perkins's description of such analogous American poets as Cawein and Markham suggests that such a distinction was to be found in other areas as well: "These poets were not striving to be different from their predecessors or contemporaries. They were not reacting against anybody. They were merely emulating what they understood to be poetry. In this they were not typical of all American poets. . . . But, collectively, they add a note that strongly differentiates American poetry at this time from that of England."[9]

Which composers did Americans "emulate" in order to create their "collective" style? The Schirmer *Anthology* suggests such diverse sources as Schubert, Gounod, Wagner, Grieg, and perhaps above all Thomas Moore, whose presence is felt in the pentatonic inflections, the emphasis on the subdominant harmony, the swaying $\frac{6}{8}$ meters, the dotted rhythms and Scotch snaps, the foursquare phraseology, the harplike rolled chords in the accompaniments, and the bardic, quasi-folkish tone. The slow songs seem direct descendants of "The Last Rose of Summer" and "Annie Laurie." American songsters possibly imagined themselves rather wildly romantic with their banks and braes, their hot tears and rose petals, their sea elfs and nightingales, their outdoor minstrelsy. But one can understand why many later listeners found such hackneyed sentimentality inane.

Carpenter's songs show an easy familiarity with this tradition. Their technical demands are modest, their vocal ranges small, their phrases fairly square, their melodies tuneful,[10] their rhythms and modes vaguely Irish or Scottish, and the prevailing mood restrained, dainty, sweet, and comforting. This orientation would faintly linger into the composer's vastly more interesting twentieth-century music; indeed, Carpenter admittedly struggled all his life to overcome a certain reserve he associated with his Puritan background.[11]

But even these college-aged songs anticipate Carpenter's mature output and differ from the typical art song of the 1890s in two important and somewhat contradictory respects. First, Carpenter's text settings show a special kind of sensitivity and control, as, for example, the way the descending melody for the line "Alas, how easily things go wrong" turns upward at the line "And yet how easily things go right" (ex. 1). These songs similarly reveal a refinement of harmony and voice leading, including polychordal touches derived from various uses of nonchordal tones, ninth and eleventh chords, and pedals. In example 1, note how a double appoggiatura and a passing tone at the words "sigh and" result in, enharmonically, an E♭ seventh chord over a B in the bass.

While such details disclose a natural elegance, nurtured by the composer's rarified upbringing, yet another distinction lies in quite another direction: in ties with popular music of a more humble nature. "Memory," for example, has the kind of close, chromatic, "barbershop" harmonies also found in Theodore Morse's "Dear Old Girl" or Paul Dresser's "On the Banks of the Wabash." "In Spring" opens with a syncopated figure not far removed from ragtime. "Alas, How Easily Things Go Wrong" and "Little John's Song" have the operetta-like lilt and verve of Victor Herbert's "Toyland." Nearly all of these songs begin by leaning into the submediant note on a strong beat, something found in Harry von Tilzer's "Mansion of Aching Hearts" and innumerable other contemporary popular songs.[12] Moreover, these songs have a direct and vigorous tone related to the American vernacular.

Carpenter's responsiveness to contemporary popular music probably had something to do with his Chicago provenance. The Midwest and particularly Chicago played a crucial role in forging the new, exciting popular music of

EXAMPLE I.   Carpenter, "Alas, How Easily Things Go Wrong," mm. 26–33.

the "gay nineties." Charles Harris, Paul Dresser, and Harry von Tilzer—three of the most important popular song composers of the decade—were all mid-westerners; their beer-garden waltzes and barbershop ballads set the stage for the emergence of modern popular song. At the same time, Chicago was in the forefront of the ragtime craze. Edward Berlin writes that "the city of Chicago . . . and specifically the vicinity of the 1893 World's Fair in Chicago, seems to have been the site of the initial unveiling of ragtime to a mass public and the beginning of its popularity."[13] Scott Joplin lived in Chicago between 1893 and 1896; the Chicagoan William Krell composed the first published rag, the "Mississippi Rag," in 1897; and the Chicagoan Joseph E. Howard wrote one of the first "ragtime" song hits, "Hello! Ma Baby" (which, like the Carpenter songs, favors falling *la-sol* appoggiaturas) in 1899.[14]

Popular music further gained the respect and affection of Chicago's educated and cultivated elite. "Upper-class activity in Chicago differed from Boston, New York, and Charleston in that . . . its leading cultural figures had a more democratic outlook," observes Frederic Cople Jaher.[15] Theodore Dreiser, for instance, took considerable interest in popular song (not least because his brother, Paul Dresser, wrote such music), and he viewed the genre sympathetically:

> [Popular songs] reach far out over land and water, touching the hearts of the nation. In mansion and hovel, by some blazing furnace of a steel mill, or through the open window of a farmland cottage, is trolled the simple story, written in halting phraseology, tuned as only a popular song is tuned. . . . All have heard the street hands and the organs, the street boys and the street loungers, all expressing a brief melody, snatched from the unknown by some process of the heart.
>
> Yes, here it is, wandering the land over like the sweet breath of summer, making for matings and partings, for happiness and pain. That it may not endure is also meet, going back into the soil, as it does, with those who hear it and those who create.[16]

Dreiser's phrase "mansion and hovel" suggests the acceptance of popular music among Chicago's upper crust, and in the tradition of midwestern populism, he sees this leveling as a desirable movement toward a stronger democracy.

Chicago's great humorist George Ade (1866–1944) responded less reverently to the vogue for popular music among Chicago's upper classes. In a "fable" from 1903, Ade depicted an evening "at the home of a Lady who invariably was first over the Fence in the Mad Pursuit of Culture":

In the course of time they got around to the Topic of Modern Music. All agreed that the Music which seemed to catch on with the low-browed public was exceedingly punk. They rather fancied "Parcifal" and were willing to concede that Vogner made good in Spots, but Mascagni they branded as a Crab. As for Victor Herbert and J. P. Sousa—back to the Water-Tanks!

A little later in the Game the Conversation began to sag and it was suggested that they have Something on the Piano. They gathered around the Stack of Music and then Vogner went into the Discard and Puccini fell to the floor unnoticed and the Classics did not get a Hand. But they gave a Yelp of Joy when they spotted a dear little Cantata about a Coon who carried a Razor and had trouble with his Wife. They sang the Chorus 38 times and the Young Lady wore out both Wrists doing Rag-time.

Moral: It is proper to enjoy the Cheaper Grades of Art, but they should not be formally Indorsed.[17]

Ade's career—like the careers of Eugene Field (1850–95), Finley Peter Dunne (1867–1936), John T. McCutcheon (1870–1949), and even Theodore Dreiser (1871–1945)—reminds us, too, that some of the city's most important critics worked for the local dailies, thus fomenting a certain populism in artistic and intellectual outlook.

Significantly, Carpenter's songs from the 1890s include two settings of Field. Moreover, Carpenter later collaborated with McCutcheon on a 1908 song, "The Debutante," subtitled "A Ka-Koon Song." Like so many Chicago critics, Carpenter was a lifelong friend of American popular music, and he showed more enthusiasm for George M. Cohan, Irving Berlin, Jerome Kern, George Gershwin, and Richard Rodgers than for any "serious" American composer.

Carpenter's three published piano pieces from the 1890s similarly combine the gentility of the salon and the vitality of the barbershop. Snatches of patriotic anthems, sentimental ballads, and beer-garden waltzes instinctively encroach on the basically Chopinesque idiom; the contrasting theme in *Twilight Reverie* even anticipates Irving Berlin's 1924 hit "Always." In a review of Denver Oldham's 1986 recording of Carpenter's collected piano works, Andrew Stiller found these pieces "well worth hearing." Kyle Gann, on the other hand, in reviewing the same recording, thought these pieces "stodgy and unimaginative," especially when compared with the composer's "delightful" later ones.[18]

Of the three pieces, the *Minuet* best fits Gann's description of "stodgy." Carpenter arranged it for the Harvard Pierian Sodality, who performed it on 18 December 1894; in this orchestral guise, the *Minuet* would have seemed even more like Elgar, with whom Carpenter would later study. Its form is utterly casual, with a B section in the dominant merely plopping into a C section in the subdominant. Of greater allure is *Nocturne;* its grace and elegance announce a composer who would be drawn, in time, to ballet.

Carpenter's early assimilation of popular music showed a determination to go his own way. In this respect he resembled Charles Ives, two years his senior and charting his own course at Yale. For both composers a strong attraction to the American vernacular betokened a nonconformity that similarly led them, perhaps, to business careers as a means of circumventing America's academic establishment. Andrew Stiller even discovered a resemblance between Carpenter's *Minuet* and an early Ives song, "Judges' Walk." According to Stiller this resemblance revealed "the essential identity of the starting conditions for both composers."[19]

Ives's First Symphony of 1898 and Carpenter's unpublished Piano Sonata in G Minor of 1897 accordingly make an interesting pair: both works attempt to come to terms with the great tradition by way of a graduation exercise. Carpenter's sonata, which he actually played at graduation, is in a conventional three-movement format (sonata, ABA slow movement, rondo finale), and, as in Ives's symphony, the handling of these forms seems rather strained. The development of the first movement, for instance, wanders aimlessly, and the return to G minor at the recapitulation sounds merely like the arrival of just another key. Carpenter backs away, sooner than Ives, from the constraints of formal development and counterpoint, however. His models are those of Schumann and Mendelssohn rather than Beethoven and Brahms. Voices come and go casually, subject to the inspiration of the improvising pianist. (In the introduction to the finale, such improvisation looks ahead, remarkably enough, to jazz styles of the latter twentieth century.) Further, Carpenter often simply repeats large blocks of material.

The sonata's slow movement—a sort of Mendelssohn out on the prairie—is, for all its loveliness, particularly repetitious; one can sympathize with Gann, who wanted to slit his wrists at the fifteenth return of the main theme. The last movement, in G minor and marked *feroce,* is plausibly related—perhaps intentionally—to the "Indianist" music of the period and points to later works, like *Skyscrapers,* that have some primitivist qualities (here the composer is about as savage as Schubert). Early on, this $\frac{4}{4}$ movement explores a few syncopated ideas that reveal some rhythmic ingenuity (especially two-bar phrases that form patterns of 1 + 2 + 2 + 3). Such inclinations lead eventually to a $\frac{5}{4}$ *cantando* episode in E♭ major that substitutes for a development section (ex. 2). Like Russian composers before him, Carpenter nat-

EXAMPLE 2.   Carpenter, Piano Sonata in G Minor, third movement, mm. 72–77.

urally gravitated toward meters of five, and he would explore these meters throughout his life. At the same time, the pentatonic inflections and sensuous harmonies of this *cantando* section forewarn of the composer's attraction to Debussy.

Gann found that the sonata's "undeniable melodic charm" compensated somewhat for the music's formal ineptitude.[20] Stiller similarly observed, "The themes of its three movements all prove attractive and memorable, and if their working-out does not (one's mind wanders a lot during the developments and excursions), at least one has no sense that one's time has been wasted."[21] In general, these themes tend toward pentatonic, modal shapes of a distinctively American variety.

Before leaving Carpenter's piano works from the 1890s, one might note here five unpublished piano pieces that probably date from this period: *Dutch Dance and Polka, Serenade, Petite Suite* (in three short movements), *Sehnsucht,* and *Animato.* The first three of these pieces are particularly rudimentary and possibly date from Carpenter's studies with Seeboeck. *Sehnsucht* and *Animato,* on the other hand, are more accomplished and possibly date as late as the early 1900s. *Serenade*'s main theme tellingly resembles Franz Léhar's hit tune "Vilia," from his 1905 operetta *The Merry Widow.* In addition to these five works, Carpenter's manuscripts at the Library of Congress include the first movement of a presumably unfinished early piano sonata in A major—probably a collegiate precursor of the Piano Sonata in G Minor.

While at Harvard, Carpenter served as president and conductor of the Harvard Glee Club. One mishap, like others in later years, reveals a certain absent-mindedness:

Rushing away from a tea, in town, to a Glee Club concert which he was to conduct, Mr. Carpenter discovered, to his dismay, that he had forgotten his evening clothes. A hasty search had to be made through the chorus for a person of Mr. Carpenter's build and the discomfited man was obliged to strip off his finery and to be clad in the president's afternoon "frock."[22]

Carpenter composed an alma mater, "Bright Truth Is Still Our Leader," for the club; the work's Elgarian sentiment anticipated Carpenter's World War I anthem "The Home Road." He also wrote a school song with H. T. Nichols—"Golden Hours"—which was performed at a Harvard class of '97 dinner as well as at a 1947 reunion.

In addition, Carpenter provided Harvard with *Strawberry Night Festival Music* in 1896, as well as music for Hasty Pudding Club shows: he wrote most of the music for *Branglebrink* (1896) and the entire score for *The Flying Dutchmen* (1897). By this time Hasty Pudding had become a family tradition: both George and Benjamin had taken part in their romps, Ben playing the Belle in the 1888 production *The Beau, the Belle and the Bandit*.[23] For Harvard composers a Hasty Pudding score was, moreover, something of a rite of passage: Mason and Hill each had written one, as would Leonard Bernstein and Irving Fine decades later. According to Mason, the experience was, in fact, "invaluable":

You had to produce so much copy, under conditions almost professional in their routine; there were no arbitrary prohibitions to be submitted to, of which you could not understand the reasons, as there were in the music courses given by Professor Paine; on the other hand, if what you wrote did not sound well, or hold the interest, you had to "face the music", or rather, recognize with salutary self-criticism that there wasn't any music.[24]

Mason only regretted that Hasty Pudding farmed out the orchestrations to "professional hacks" rather than having the students do the orchestrations themselves.

Harvard composers typically modeled such scores on Gilbert and Sullivan, spiced up by some borrowings from fin de siècle operetta and popular song. Carpenter probably profited in particular from a successful concert performance of *The Pirates of Penzance* by Harvard and Radcliffe students under Georg Fresé in 1896. The composer's "Cold Song" from *Branglebrink* (words by R. M. Townsend and E. G. Knoblauch),[25] while no exception, also showed a characteristic closeness to Christmas carols; the line "I dow this is the ed of be" (a stuffed-up version of "I know this is the end of me") is a musical pun on the opening phrase of "God Rest Ye Merry Gentlemen."

The Flying Dutchmen played on 29 and 30 April and 1 May 1897 in Cambridge, and on 3 and 4 May in Boston. Melville E. Stone Jr. wrote the libretto, and H. T. Nichols penned the lyrics. (Carpenter probably knew Stone, the son of a prominent Chicagoan publisher, before attending Harvard.) The story involved the quintessentially Anglo-American narrative of time travel: some bored "burgomasters" from New Amsterdam of 1650 (act 1) travel to modern-day Cambridge (act 2) and decide to return to New Amsterdam rather than suffer the "oligarchy of the Faculty" (act 3).

Carpenter's score was fairly accomplished and comparable to the operettas of Reginald de Koven (1859–1920) and Victor Herbert (1859–1924). Furthermore, the score's vigor and irony anticipated trends in popular music; the dance music for modern Cambridge in particular featured the kind of snappy rhythms later associated with, say, Zez Confrey (1895–1971), another Illinois composer. Even among the trappings of the turn-of-the-century operetta, Carpenter's individuality shone through.

Spalding claimed special distinction for the Hasty Pudding shows of the 1890s but pointed, above all, to the "true operetta" of Lewis Thompson, class of '92.[26] Spalding may well have detected a popular strain in Carpenter's work not necessarily to his liking.

After graduation Carpenter and Stone, back in Chicago, joined the Little Room, a lively, smart arts club, and collaborated on another show, *A Little Dutch Girl,* completed in 1900. This "pastoral play" in three acts adapted a story by the fashionable Ouida, the pseudonym of Marie Louise de la Ramée (1839–1908). The show was first performed at the home of Potter Palmer on 23 February 1900 as a benefit for the Women's Aid Society of the Passavant Hospital.

Like the composer's Hasty Pudding shows, the score stands midway between the operetta and modern musical comedy and features a Scotch-Irish dialect (especially in "I'll Be Waiting for Your Coming") somewhere between Victor Herbert's *Babes in Toyland* and Frederick Loewe's *Brigadoon.* Although a song like "Thou Wilt Surely Know" (ex. 3) reveals the work of a gifted melodist, the score's lovely tunes and tasteful accompaniments cannot overcome a certain musical dullness (not to mention the bathetic lyrics). Many of the songs are so rooted in the tonic that they fail to get off the ground. They lack, moreover, the rhythmic vigor of the earlier Hasty Pudding shows. One number, however—the modally chromatic "Prayer"—enjoyed a life of its own. The opera star Gladys Swarthout frequently performed it in the 1930s

EXAMPLE 3.   Carpenter, "Thou Wilt Surely Know," from *A Little Dutch Girl,*
mm. 5–12.

and received "innumerable requests from people as to where they could get a copy." She guessed that Carpenter had "forgotten that he ever wrote it."[27]

One can only wonder if Carpenter might have accomplished something truly noteworthy with the operetta, but he left this line to Rudolf Friml (1879–1972), Jerome Kern (1885–1945), and Sigmund Romberg (1887–1951) and sought his destiny elsewhere.

After graduation from Harvard, all four Carpenter brothers returned to Chicago and married women from the local gentry: George wed Harriet Isham, a doctor's daughter; Benjamin, Helen Graham Fairbank, who directed the first Girl Scouts of Chicago and who organized the Birth Control League; Hubbard, Rosalie Sturgis, a member of the Colonial Dames; and John, Rue Winterbotham, who led a distinguished career of her own.

In adulthood the Carpenter brothers were tall and fair: John had brown hair and blue eyes, stood 5'11", and kept himself trim (in 1923 he weighed 146 pounds, but later in life he filled out to 160 pounds). A 1911 reference book suggested that they shared interests and sensibilities as well. All were members—and in some cases active members—of the Republican Party. John and George listed their religious affiliation as Congregational. All except Hubbard cited philanthropic activities, in John's case a directorship of the Illinois Children's Home and Aid Society. All four belonged to numerous clubs, in all instances the Chicago Club, where Chicago's male elite gathered for martinis and good food, and the University Club, another favorite haunt for well-heeled businessmen. Only John did not list a membership in the Onwentsia Club, a country club famous for its polo matches. And only Benjamin mentioned belonging to the Cliff Dwellers, though, in fact, John belonged as well.[28] John had good but not particularly close relations with his brothers and their families; some letters indicated an occasional criticism of Benjamin and a special closeness to George.

George was the only brother not to enter the family business. Rather, he pursued a long and successful career in the law: He was admitted to the bar in 1890, became partner in a Chicago law firm in 1892, was elected circuit judge in 1906, and was appointed federal judge by President Taft in 1909. After resigning from this last position in 1933, he continued to serve as counsel for a private law firm until his death in 1944. Ben Hecht once told the following anecdote about George Carpenter: "Federal Judge Carpenter listened to evidence concluding that the 'Oceana Roll' was a piece of musical plagiarism. And he handed down the judgment that since the 'Oceana Roll,' to which he had listened with an open mind, was not music, it could not be a musical plagiarism. Case dismissed."[29]

The three other Carpenter brothers entered their father's business upon graduation. Benjamin became a partner in 1888, Hubbard and John in 1901. When the company was incorporated in 1909, George was named president; Benjamin, treasurer; Hubbard, secretary; and John, vice president. Benjamin took over as president upon their father's death on 11 December 1912. After Benjamin died in 1927, Hubbard became president; he and John both retired in 1936.

When John joined the firm in 1897, George B. Carpenter and Company had embarked on yet another boom period. Whether or not the Carpenters supported the 1898 Spanish-American War (and as liberal Republicans and readers of Carl Schurz, they might have been antipathetic toward the war, though most Chicagoan Republicans supported it), the military needed their products. In 1900 the company took advantage of a fire and, when rebuilding, added two stories to their South Water Street headquarters. By this time their employees numbered more than one hundred, and their catalog exceeded seven hundred pages.[30] "Our line was everything from a fishhook to a three inch hawser—or more specifically, twines, cordages, canvas goods, awnings, tents—lots of things," the composer once stated.[31]

In 1903 the firm opened branches in Seattle and South Chicago and acquired controlling interest in the Anniston Cordage Company (Anniston, Alabama) and the Chicago Net and Twine Company. The South Chicago branch—the Great Lakes Supply Company—helped distribute goods in the Calumet region. This branch included a warehouse equipped with five railroad tracks that permitted indoor transfer of materials from mill car to delivery truck.

In 1912 George B. Carpenter, Inc., relocated its headquarters to a new, large, eight-story building at 430-440 Wells Street (at the northwest corner of Wells and Hubbard), while retaining its property at South Water Street and Fifth. In addition, the company purchased some warehouses and barns at 340-356 West Grand Avenue near the new Wells Street office, apparently to stock merchandise. Growth continued throughout the decade as the firm once again helped equip the country in time of war. (In July 1917 the fifty-two-year-old Benjamin joined the army to help supervise the purchase of tents and tarpaulins. He retired from service in February 1919 with the rank of lieutenant colonel.)

By the late teens George B. Carpenter and Company had become a huge supplier of cordage, cotton, rubber, pipe, and other products to major contractors and manufacturers, mostly in naval and railroad construction. The company had six departments: marine supplies, hardware, cotton duck and awning stripes, mechanical rubber, and manufactured canvas goods. In 1918 Josiah Currey wrote that the company represented Chicago business at its best: "No concern in the United States carries a more diverse and comprehensive stock of cordage and twines than they do. No concern carries a larger stock or does a larger business, or tries harder to give its customers intelligent service, fair prices and a square deal." After similarly enthusiastic descriptions of the company's other departments (the marine department had a "good, old tarry smell" that suggested "all sorts of romantic associations"), Currey concluded: "Their roots are planted firmly in the very beginnings of historical Chicago, and they stand now, and will continue to stand, as one of the pillars of liberal and enlightened efficiency in the development of the Middle West."[32]

Benjamin Carpenter directed the company's affairs with vigor and success. A physical resemblance to Theodore Roosevelt probably inspired the following passage from a 1940 retrospective:

> A handsome, dynamic, Teddy Roosevelt type of man, he [Benjamin] seemed to have boundless stores of energy, and no detail of the business was ever too small to receive his personal attention. . . . He could crack the whip of discipline when necessary, but, no matter what happened, he always managed to keep the genuine respect and the affectionate regard of his employees. He had a great sense of humor. His buoyant laugh would often ring throughout the office.

This same source remembered Hubbard as "tall, slender, kindly—regarded by the employees as far and away the most polished gentleman in the organization," and John as "very exceptional because he was at once an astute businessman and a distinguished composer of music."[33]

In later years the composer stated that he joined his father's business "for two good reasons. . . . I wanted to get married and I wanted to keep on eating."[34] He mentioned a third reason to Madeleine Goss, namely, that he "felt that he had no choice. His father was expecting him to come into the firm."[35] "Those were the days," he explained further to Robert Pollak, "before male parents made it their custom to look with sympathetic eyes upon the artistic inclinations of their offspring."[36] Even more than the older American cities on the eastern seaboard, Chicago frowned on careers not only in the arts but in education and the ministry; the city favored, rather, law, medicine, and, above all, business.[37]

The degree of Carpenter's actual involvement with George B. Carpenter and Company over the years fluctuated depending on personal and business circumstances. In general, the responsibility for running the business fell mostly to Benjamin, who served first as company treasurer and later as president, and to Hubbard, who was company secretary. Both Benjamin and Hubbard "were intensely sympathetic and anxious to encourage him [John] to proceed in the career of a composer."[38]

Carpenter explained further: "I put in my years on the road and in the office. But it was a family business, and I was able to regulate my hours and vacations. If I needed a couple of extra weeks for composition, I could take them."[39] He worked mornings in his office and then devoted two hours in the afternoon to composition; he found that he could accomplish in two hours what he could in eight. He further devoted his weekends and holidays to composition. Moreover, he took at least two lengthy vacations during the winter and summer months, during which he also pursued music. Carpenter typically left Chicago after the Christmas holidays and returned in April. He left again in late June or early July (usually for summer retreats in Vermont or Massachusetts) and returned after Labor Day or as late as October. Thus, Carpenter often spent only three or four months in Chicago in the spring and three or four months in the fall. Recalled his son-in-law Patrick Hill, "He wasn't tied down to it [the company] terrifically."[40]

Consequently, Carpenter's schedule was less like that of a weekend composer like Ives than that of a teacher or professor who managed to compose a couple of hours every day and devote large blocks of time to composition over the summer. And these large blocks often consisted of six months or more! Little wonder—aside from everything else—he turned down an offer to teach music theory at the University of Minnesota in Minneapolis in 1913.[41]

Carpenter further made light of what business responsibilities he undertook, as in the following anecdote: In 1915, during a period of growth, the company hired an efficiency expert to help "straighten us out." Carpenter, who described the expert as "a bright, busy inquisitive little man, with the most piercing blue eyes I have ever seen," became his liaison and helped him "as well as I could."

> One day a professor from a downstate college called on me. He introduced himself as a student of bird calls and bird music and begged me to listen to his findings. I can resist nothing that pertains to music, and I listened. He reproduced bird music for me, all right. He whistled and he sang, he chirped and he hummed.
>
> In the midst of our interesting session, I could feel a steellike glance piercing me. It was the sharp, blue eye of our efficiency expert. His astonishment and disgust were boundless.
>
> "In heaven's name, what is going on here?" he demanded. I explained as best I could, but it was futile. I knew I had mortally offended our efficiency expert. He realized what a blow to efficiency I must be around George B. Carpenter & Co.[42]

Nonetheless, the widely held notion of the composer as independently wealthy—as put forth, say, by Virgil Thomson, who pegged Carpenter as a capitalist composer "whose chief revenue comes from invested capital" (like Magnard, Chausson, and Poulenc)—was misleading.[43] Carpenter worked most of his adult life in business. By his own admission he put in his years "on the road selling or in the office mulling over accounts and such matters."[44]

When he returned to work in October or April or whenever, he often needed to catch up on work and cover for one or another vacationing brother. In at least one instance—in the fall of 1923—both brothers left him in charge; commented Carpenter, "It will be my job to hold the fort in their absence."[45] Benjamin's stroke in 1924 and death in 1927, followed by the Depression, surely intensified John's own responsibilities. "I do not expect to ask you to publish any Chinoiseries by me," Carpenter wrote Carl Engel on returning from a trip to Asia, "at least not in the fiscal year of 1931, the balance of which I shall have to devote to 440 No. Wells St. to get myself out of that beautiful red ink."[46] On arriving back to work in April 1933, he found "many pressing questions in my office demanding solution."[47]

In short, Carpenter was an American entrepreneur—an "astute business-man" who, in his 1911 vita, identified himself as a "merchant," listing music as a "recreation" along with outdoor sports. Forty years in business gave him the candid, soft-spoken demeanor of a genteel businessman. At the same time, Chicago was widely aware of his musical career, and he himself made no secret of it, sometimes obtaining passes for his employees to hear a rehearsal or performance of one of his works.[48]

Over the years Carpenter offered varying thoughts on the subject of his double life. Sometimes he took a positive view: "I stole time for music, but I wouldn't give up now what I gained from business. Contacts with people I met there stimulated me and gave me new and richer musical ideas."[49] In 1918 he even counseled some such arrangement as advisable: "Every one should be interested in two things, as only when one is interested in more than a single thing can he hope to progress in life in general. There is a better chance of success when dividing attention, and this is true in art. . . . It would astound me if there were not many others like me."[50]

Sometimes Carpenter seemed merely resigned. "Circumstances have made it necessary for me to split up my life into several different chunks, as you know, and my time of producing [sic], as far as Music is concerned, is small," he stated matter-of-factly to Elizabeth Sprague Coolidge.[51] He took a similarly resigned tone with Madeleine Goss: "Even composers have to eat. . . . The majority of serious composers are forced to seek a living outside of composition. They teach, they write, they lecture—each according to his individual skill and opportunity—and compose when they can. The composer in business is fundamentally in much the same case."[52]

At still other times, he expressed regret. In 1929, when asked about young men going into music, he put his fist down on his desk ("more in firmness than in bitterness") and said, "Over my dead body would a son of mine try to be both musician and modern business man."[53] In 1940 he told a reporter: "I tried to pull my oar in business and do my duty to my music. But I wouldn't advise anyone to do likewise."[54] And an obituary from 1951 similarly quoted the composer as saying:

> My advice [to younger composers] would be 1) Never give up; 2) Do not expect to make any money out of it. During the early part of my life I engaged in both business and musical composition. My friends used to congratulate me on having two interests, but if I had it to do over again, I would only try one. A lifetime is not enough to devote to composing.[55]

In any case, Carpenter's career in business helped foster and shape the composer's individuality at a time when American composers still often aped European values and ideals. He shared this much, certainly, with Charles Ives, even if their work and lives ultimately proved very dissimilar. If a life in business allowed Charles Ives the independence to chart new and lonely terrain, it gave Carpenter the opportunity, quite often, to kick up his heels and have some fun, to be fashionably chic and entertaining, to take up popular and exotic cultures, and to look modern times squarely in the face. In all this the composer also owed much to his first wife, Rue Winterbotham.

CHAPTER THREE

Rue Winterbotham and Songs for Children

1901–1904

In 1899 John Alden Carpenter proposed marriage to Rue Winterbotham. The Winterbothams, who often traveled to Europe, suggested that Rue first take a trip abroad, including a tour of Cairo. Carpenter apparently joined them on this trip, meeting up with his own parents, who had left for Europe in May. They all returned home in May 1900.[1]

Like the Carpenters, the Winterbothams had emigrated from England to New York to Ohio to Chicago: Rue's great-grandfather, John, arrived in New York from England in 1811; her grandfather, Joseph, moved to Ohio; and her father, Joseph, born in Columbus, Ohio, in 1852, first settled in Joliet, Illinois (where Rue was born), and finally moved, in 1892, to Chicago. Also like the Carpenters, the Winterbothams were well-to-do Republicans with an interest in the arts (both families surely knew one another socially), but they belonged to the Episcopal, not the Congregational, Church.[2]

Joseph Winterbotham had made a fortune even larger than George Carpenter's by managing various business enterprises, including barrel and cask manufacturing and mortgage financing. He and his wife, Genevieve Fellows, granddaughter of U.S. Senator Abraham Baldwin, had four children: John, Rue, Joseph, and Genevieve. "By all accounts," says one source, "he was intelligent and witty, without pomposity or pretention."[3]

After graduating from Yale, Joseph's two sons established themselves successfully in business as well. His daughters he sent to the Farmington School and to Europe, where Rue became fluent in French and Italian. Even at Farmington, Rue made a stir. One schoolmate noted, "She has always been remarked as being independent and strong-minded, and does just as she wishes irrespective of what people say." When Rue and John married on 20 November 1900, Rue created a sensation by having her bridesmaids walk down the aisle singly, holding candles rather than flowers.[4]

Rue's unconventionality had become legendary among Chicagoans by the time of her death in 1931. "She was only a little over fifty when she died," wrote Arthur Meeker in 1955, "since then Chicago has seemed a greyer place."[5] Everyone in Chicago society of that time—and many celebrities from around the world—knew and admired (though not necessarily liked) her; in her social position she could be compared with such contemporary Parisian arbiters of taste and fashion as Misia Sert and Coco Chanel. Writes one historian, "She was avant-garde when the word was unknown in Chicago."[6]

Rue purposefully aimed to enlighten and beautify Chicago. She had inherited her intelligence and boldness from her father, and her sophistication and worldliness from years of European travel and education. Chicago carefully observed her friends, her interests, and perhaps above all her dress, whether her 1922 evening wear of "duchesse point lace over silver satin with a silver headress" or her "chic and springlike" 1926 attire at the annual meeting of the Arts Club: "Her small, unornamented hat was of woven, red straw. . . . Her frock looked as if it had just come from the Rue de la paix—a printed silk with great whirls and modernist figures in reds, greens, black and blues against a lemon yellow background. A large pink carnation was caught at the throat, just that last touch that so often finishes off a costume."[7]

Rue was best known professionally as an interior designer. She decorated not only many private homes but such public places as the Casino Club, the Fortnightly Club, the Auditorium Theatre, the Lewis Shop, and Elizabeth Arden's in New York. Some of this work was pictured in *Vogue* and *House & Garden*. As a decorator she led a crusade against the conventional, the saccharine, the cute—what she called "cheese." At Christmas she insisted that her daughter and niece—to their annual dismay—avoid the clichés and invent new, original decorations.[8]

Meeker named Rue, along with Elsie de Wolfe, among the greatest interior decorators of her time; Longstreet made the more modest claim that she was a designer with some taste and originality. Both agreed, however, that she ushered in a new period of interior decoration in Chicago, one that renounced uniformity of style in favor of eclecticism and mixing periods: she worked with various combinations of Biedermeier, Directoire, Empire, early American, and modern furnishings (the Casino introduced Chicago to a kind of early art deco), and she adorned her rooms with taffeta curtains, Aubusson rugs, polka-dotted or broad-striped wallpaper, Victorian wax flowers, opaline glass, and oriental and modern French painting. Rue took nothing for granted: tradition might dictate floral centerpieces, but she experimented with crystal baskets and a fantailed bird of red glass.[9]

Rue especially loved greens and reds; she dazzled Chicagoans with the

Casino's emerald greens, and New Yorkers with Elizabeth Arden's red doors (still their trademark). She selected a rich wine-red for a makeover of the Auditorium Theatre, and "for a season or two," wrote Meeker, "we had an opera house worthy of the troupe that sang in it."[10]

Rue occasionally wrote and lectured on the subject of interior decoration. In one such article, "Problems in Decoration," from 1930, she recommended that decorators consider details of architectural design, lighting, furniture, and color. She further made comparisons not only with painting but with musical composition: "Just as the composer may feel a significance in certain chance rhythms and combinations of sound, so the decorator may find his starting-point in the colour of a flower on a vase or in a figure in a carpet, the whole colour structure of the room then becomes a logical development of the original scheme, with perhaps a secondary related theme for variety with its own characteristic development, all these elements firmly fused into an organic whole." She warned against stylistic labels like "early American" or "modern." As for the latter, she stated:

> The modern period has much that is interesting and exciting to offer, but we need not swallow it all whole and run amuck. The best of its contributions are a new sense of simplicity based on necessity and a ruthless elimination of parasitic detail. The whole world has need of this vigorous sense, and the decorator can use it profitably every hour of his working day.[11]

She called for "fearlessness" as well; in matters of decor, "courage is the right choice between alternatives," she was quoted as saying.[12]

In an unpublished lecture, possibly from the same period, Rue again took up the subject of modernism in interior design. The modern movement, she explained, began as a "revolt against the romantic—the sentimental—the Victorian." The Great War intensified this revolt, and "I believe we are now on the verge of the final and most healthy debunking process of all, the deflation or debunking of the debunking pose itself. Any gesture when it loses its freedom becomes a pose as it seems plain there may yet be a place in life for a *moderate* amount of sentiment, romance and other discarded emotions." She quoted Picasso on the need for "essentials, beauty, suitability, balance."[13]

Rue was also well known socially as a founder of the Casino Club. In the midteens she joined Honoré Palmer, John McCutcheon, Lucy Blair, Eames MacVeagh, Nancy (Mrs. Joseph) Coleman—all imposing figures in the Chicago of their time—in establishing a club that would offer fine French food and "an attractive and convenient place for tea, bridge, dancing and supper after the play."[14] According to Arthur Meeker, the establishment of the Casino Club presupposed "an entirely new principle, that of providing a social club in town for both men and women." Built on East Delaware Street on land owned by the Palmers, and decorated by Rue, the Casino Club featured "the best food in town" and for many years became one of high society's favorite stomping grounds.[15] (Carpenter grew weary of his wife's love of haute cuisine; he preferred broiled lobster to lobster thermidor, a Casino favorite.)

Rue's greatest triumph and most enduring legacy, however, was her stewardship over the Chicago Arts Club, which she helped found in 1916, and over which she presided from 1918 to her death. Under Rue's leadership the Arts Club became a hugely ambitious and highly daring enterprise, one that attempted, in Rue's own words, "to present . . . the very highest in the fields of contemporary art, literature, and music."[16]

Initially located at 610 South Michigan Avenue (in 1924 the club moved to the second floor of the Wrigley Building at 410 Michigan),[17] the Arts Club owned two galleries, a concert stage, a lounge, and a dining room and regularly featured exhibitions, concerts, dance recitals, plays, poetry readings, and lectures. (In addition, the club maintained, until 1927, its own room at the Art Institute.)[18] The Arts Club also sponsored honorary luncheons and dinners for visiting artists, dignitaries, philanthropists, and even, on one occasion, Indian chiefs from various tribes. Club members included artists and art lovers alike; most events—including many of the honorary luncheons—were free to members, who paid a modest annual fee of twenty-five to fifty dollars.

Assisted by the architect Arthur Heun, Rue designed the club rooms herself. Her view of the club, writes James M. Wells,

> was marked by clarity, elegance, and style. Exhibitions were to be mounted in galleries with the best possible lighting and with no distractions. The lounge, open only to members, would be adaptable to lectures and concerts as well as teas, receptions, and parties. The dining room was to be simple, comfortable, and uncrowded, the food and drink of the highest possible standard. To this day the facilities and furnishings [of the Arts Club] include well cared-for antiques she selected for the club rooms at 610 South Michigan Avenue and the Wrigley Building, mixed with modern pieces. An air of discreet elegance has always been the hallmark of the Club.[19]

Parisians regarded Rue as one of the few Americans who knew how to exhibit artwork.

On behalf of the Arts Club, Rue brilliantly marshaled Chicago's resources. She turned to Alice Roullier, "a well-connected, sophisticated connoisseur," for help supervising the exhibitions.[20] She consulted Harriet Monroe, John McCutcheon, and Edgar Lee Masters on literature, Adolph Bolm on dance, and her husband and Frederick Stock on music. At the same time, she recruited the support of Chicago's wealthiest citizenry—the Palmers, the McCormicks (notably, Edith Rockefeller), and many others. Some years the restaurant service took the club into the red, but more typically the club showed a profit.

Under Rue's leadership, "the Arts Club became the leading voice for modern art in the city."[21] Although Chicagoans like Martin Ryerson and Frederic Bartlett (both of whom supported the Arts Club) had already begun their extraordinary collection of contemporary French art (including Bartlett's acquisition of Seurat's *Sunday Afternoon on the Island of La Grande Jatte*), and the city had hosted the Armory Show in 1913–14, the Arts Club established a public forum for modern art—probably the first of its kind in America (New York's Museum of Modern Art opened in 1929).[22] The Arts Club organized the first Chicago showings of drawings by Picasso; sculpture by Rodin, Lachaise, and Brancusi; and paintings by Davies, Marin, Schamberg, Sheeler, Stella, Braque, and Laurencin. It also launched one-man exhibitions of Miró, Rouault, Villon, and Léger.[23] Rue spearheaded all this, moreover, at a time when such art was little known and controversial, to say the least: in 1918 she felt compelled to argue that modernist painting did not promote Bolshevism.[24]

Rue also commissioned artwork. In 1928 she contacted the club from Munich (where she was attending the European premiere of her husband's *Skyscrapers*), directing Roullier to commission a screen from Nathalie Goncharova: "I thought a screen of spring would be lovely—flowers—cubist of course."[25] (Goncharova nobly realized Rue's conception.) Over the years artists such as Mary Foote, Harrington Mann, Paul Thévenaz, and Ambrose McEvoy painted or sketched Rue in appreciation of her support. Or they painted family members: Glyn Philpot painted John in a single sitting of around three hours in about 1917, and Marie Laurencin and Constantin Brancusi painted and sketched Ginny.[26]

The Arts Club not only exhibited modern art, including the work of local artists, but the old and exotic as well: Greek art, Chinese bronzes, African sculpture, medieval tapestries, and Persian and Turkish rugs valued, in 1926, at more than a million dollars (this last exhibit, along with visits by Bakst and Stravinsky, proved one of the club's most highly publicized events).

The club's activities in the other arts were less monumental but similarly sophisticated, daring, and central to Chicago's cultural life. Aside from the fine arts, music was most extensively represented, in large part owing to Carpenter's personal involvement. (Because Carpenter guided these activities not only during Rue's regime but throughout the 1930s as well, I will discuss the club's musical activities in a later chapter.)

Under Rue's leadership the Arts Club further presented poetry readings by Tagore, Lowell, Frost, Sandburg, and Millay; dance recitals by Kreutzberg, Graham, and Massine; and plays by Aristophanes, Schnitzler, Shaw, Strindberg, Wilde, and Philip Barry. The nonmusical lectures included Phyllis Ackerman on gothic tapestries, Thomas Whittemore on Byzantine art, A. V. Pope on Persian architecture, Stella Campbell on speech and acting, and Archibald MacLeish on contemporary poetry.

Upon the arrival of the Moscow Arts Theater in Chicago in 1923, with productions of Chekhov and Gorky in Russian, Rue revealed the breadth of her interests—as well as her personal clout—in various exhortations to the Arts Club and the community at large that they attend these performances. A newspaper article titled "See Moscow Players and Keep Up City's Reputation, Plea to Art Lovers" quoted her at length:

> Owing to the perfection of the art of these players a knowledge of Russian is not necessary to insure understanding and enjoyment of the play. Every one who fails to attend these performances forfeits a unique opportunity to broaden and enrich their knowledge of the art of the theater and its possibilities. Chicago is not patronizing the Moscow Theater as it should and in its failure to do so runs the grave risk of losing prestige as an art center and of being omitted from future itineraries whenever productions of great artistic quality are booked for the road.[27]

After Rue's death in 1931, the Arts Club established a $20,000 Carpenter–Arts Club Memorial "for Lectures on all the Living Arts in their *contemporary* aspects." The club's minutes stated:

> If the cities west of New York have attained to some knowledge of what has been happening in the world of the Living Arts within the past fifteen years, it is largely due to the efforts of the Arts Club of Chicago and its distinguished President. . . . Those who had the privilege of her intimate acquaintance were alive to the special quality with which she invested all social contact; a rare gift of adorning such moments with gayety, and animation,

and somehow this precious quality carried through to the larger world of Arts Club affairs and gave them their special flavor.[28]

Fernand Léger published a poem, "Chicago," in memoriam.[29]

Rue's interest in providing Chicago with a public forum for contemporary art led to the creation, in 1921, of the Art Institute's Joseph Winterbotham Collection. Encouraged by his daughter, Joseph donated $50,000 to the Art Institute, with the interest to be set aside to buy contemporary European painting. Another unusual stipulation demanded that after the institute purchased an initial thirty-five paintings, these paintings could be—and should be—periodically replaced by other, preferably newer works. This would enable the collection both to upgrade its holdings and to preserve its mission of bringing new art to Chicago (as of this writing, the collection has been more successful in the former than in the latter). Frederic Bartlett, who served as a trustee, supervised many of the early acquisitions, which included paintings by Matisse, Braque, Toulouse-Lautrec, and Gauguin. Rue herself selected André Dunoyer de Segonzac's 1926 *Summer Garden,* a painting resplendent with reds and greens and still a treasured part of the collection. Her daughter Ginny eventually donated another painting Rue had acquired, namely, Fernand Léger's vibrant *Follow the Arrow* from 1919.[30]

Rue also carved a special role for herself as a socialite. She loved throwing parties and earned a reputation as a brilliant and unconventional hostess. The dancer Ruth Page recalled "with such pleasure the brilliant parties she used to give. These were glamorous days in Chicago."[31] "When [Rue] walked in, the party began!" remembered Meeker.

> A resourceful amateur actress, she had besides an inexhaustible skill at getting up charades and circuses, dramatic entertainment of all sorts. Her sense of fun was delicious. Have you who heard them forgotten her monologues—particularly that wonderful one about her trip to Europe with "Mr. C."? ("Florence is a beautiful city, but so decayed.") . . . . She showed her friends how to be informal; how to sit on the floor; how to dress up . . . on the spur of the moment, using any materials that came to hand. I saw her once devise a romantic Persian outfit in ten minutes out of a handful of tinsel and a strip of pink leopard-spotted cloth.[32]

Harriett Welling recalled that they also "did a lot of black-face."[33] The atmosphere was fun loving: "It was not an earnest seeking after truth," remarked Theodora Brown.[34]

Rue especially liked entertaining visiting artists, who, in turn, enjoyed staying with her and John when in Chicago. Meeker attributed her success with celebrities to her ability to make them feel at home: "They'd not be fussed over tiresomely or placed on a pedestal. Like as not they'd be sitting on the cushion next to yours, sipping gin-and-lemon-juice, eating casserole of veal, guessing charades, or playing musical chairs—just *not* being celebrities."[35] Artists surely enjoyed the company of a wealthy, sophisticated woman who despised upper-class timidity and pretentiousness and who often got along better with working women than with society matrons. She astounded friends and guests by repeatedly calling for her maid, Margaret McNulty, without any response; finally, Margaret would show up, saying, "Yes, Mrs. Carpenter, wha'd'ya want now? You're always wanting something!"[36] She spoke candidly of such taboo subjects as the kept mistresses of Chicago's "well-off citizens."

Over the years Rue and John thus established a varied circle of friends and acquaintances, including famous actors (Stella Campbell, Sarah Bernhardt, Marie Tempest, Charlie Chaplin, George Arliss, John Drew, and Douglas Fairbanks), painters (John Singer Sargent, Pablo Picasso, Marie Laurencin, Leon Bakst, Fernand Léger, Marcel Duchamp, Gerald Murphy), musicians (Mary Garden, Maggie Teyte, Josef Hofmann, Jascha Heifetz, Arthur Rubinstein), composers (Igor Stravinsky, Serge Prokofiev), dancers (Irene Castle, Léonide Massine, Tamara Karsavina, Ruth Draper, Adolph Bolm), and writers (Victoria Sackville-West, Sir Hugh Walpole, Gertrude Stein, Vachel Lindsay, Archibald MacLeish).

A few letters and memoirs suggest that many of these artists were truly fond of Rue. Cole Porter arranged that Ginny sit for Marie Laurencin as a surprise for Rue, and on hearing that Rue was not feeling well, he offered to visit her and cheer her up. George Arliss similarly wrote Ginny that he was "much distressed to hear that your mother has had to undergo an operation."[37] Arthur Rubinstein, who remembered Rue as "a remarkably artistically inclined person," signed one photograph, "with intense wishes and deepest friendship"; Stella Campbell called her, "Rue, the loving giver"; Maggie Teyte addressed her as "Darling Rue"; Hugh Walpole signed one letter, "Your faithful friend."[38] On a trip to London, Rue found flowers sent to her by Victoria Sackville-West with the note, "It is only a trifle, but I send it with much love."[39]

Carpenter did not have Rue's charisma, but his congeniality, offbeat wit, and, of course, musical sophistication made for an attractive complement. Cole Porter respected and even envied him, and the Murphys loved him.[40]

John established particularly close friendships with Bolm, Stravinsky, Mac-Leish, and Frederic Bartlett. Robert Edmond Jones perhaps best summed up the feelings of many artist-friends when he wrote to Carpenter, upon hearing of Rue's death, "What magical hours you two have given to me and to all those who have known you."[41]

Rue made enemies as well. "Like most dictators of style to willing victims," comments Longstreet, "[Rue] was at times bad-tempered, ruthless with fools and bores, unless they flattered. She was jealous of rivals, and could be unfair in destroying social standings."[42] She often fought "tooth-and-nail" with men, including her father and husband,[43] who eventually sought romance out of the marriage. Even Meeker, who admired, among other things, "her heart-shaped face, white skin, and jewel-like eyes," and "her voice, high and elfin, lilting without being affected," admitted, "I don't suppose for a moment she was easy to live with."[44] Her daughter and only child, Genevieve ("Ginny"), born in 1904, admired her and inherited a good deal of her charisma; but she inherited something of her father's more gentle qualities as well. Rue passed on her tremendous resolve more directly to her niece, Rue Shaw, who, though possibly the most important figure in the Chicago art world during the decades after World War II, was still no match for her extraordinary aunt.

The Carpenters lived the charmed life of the American upper classes of the early twentieth century. Their staff included maids, cooks, and governesses. They often traveled abroad, where they bought paintings, musical instruments, and objets d'art.

They mostly resided in Chicago's Rush Street area: 32 Delaware (1901), 181 Rush (1902–5), 156 Rush (1906–9), 710 Rush (1910–21), 147 E. Ontario (1922–23), and 700 Rush (1924–31). For most of their married life, they lived on the 700 block of Rush, between Chicago Avenue and Ontario Street, in Chicago's Near North. Meeker remembered the area, long known as "McCormickville" because so many of the McCormicks had residences there, as a "quaintly shabby neighborhood,"[45] but only, perhaps, over time and only in distinction to the grandeur of Chicago's "Gold Coast" on Lake Shore Drive, where the Palmers and the Bordens lived. Shabby was hardly the word for Cyrus McCormick's "sumptious brownstone" at 675 Rush, built in the late 1870s and inspired by the Louvre's Pavillon Richelieu.[46] The neighborhood's other residences, less grand, consisted nonetheless of elegant and substantial brick or brownstone homes that dated to the years following the 1871 fire.

A rather long and narrow brownstone, 710 Rush, the site of so many of

Rue's memorable parties, was apparently built by one W. K. Nixon in the 1870s. It originally consisted of three floors and a basement (where the kitchen would be located), but the Nixons added a fourth floor "to accommodate the entourage of the Duke of Newcastle, when he visited the Nixons, in the early Nineties."[47] Carpenter reportedly had his music room on the first floor overlooking the tree-filled garden in the lot due south.[48] The attached duplex, 712 Rush, was the home of the hardware tycoon Joseph Coleman and his wife, Nancy, who for many years presided over the Casino Club and the Friends of Opera.[49]

After leaving Rush Street for two years, the Carpenters moved to 700 Rush, the home next door to 710, on the northwest corner of Rush and Huron Streets. This detached, redbrick house—originally built by George F. Rumsey after the 1871 fire but McCormick property for many years—had only two stories but was larger than 710 Rush; Carpenter made "the sunny kitchen in the high basement his music room."[50]

The Carpenters liked the Rush Street area for its artiness and because various Winterbothams lived thereabouts, including Rue's father, who took an apartment in the Virginia Hotel at the intersection of Ohio and Rush after the death of his wife in 1906. The Winterbothams led, in fact, what Meeker called a "tribal existence." They met every Sunday for breakfast at the Virginia Hotel; took trips together, including a 1926–27 world tour that included Thailand; and summered in Vermont.[51]

Early in his marriage, Joseph Winterbotham Sr. began spending summers in Charlotte, Vermont, a small town on Lake Champlain near Burlington, in part because his wife's family lived in Brattleboro. He eventually bought the McNeil Mansion that had been built about 1810 by Charles McNeil; it was located on a bluff, McNeil's Cove, out of which McNeil had run his ferry service to Essex, New York (a service still in operation). Rue inherited the home, and she and John summered there regularly until her death in 1931, at which time John gave the house to Ginny.

McNeil built his spacious home in a Georgian style that featured a Palladian window, formal entrance, and neat, symmetrical window arrangements. Although not as large as Joseph Winterbotham Jr.'s twenty-room Roman Revival home in Burlington, McNeil's house offered a spectacular view of the lake. Rue's interior decor made tasteful homage to its early American origins.[52]

Soon after their marriage, the Carpenters collaborated on twenty-four children's songs, most if not all of which were written in 1901 and 1902. John composed the music, Rue drew the illustrations, and both—or just John—wrote the words. The couple intended these songs as household music for the enjoyment and edification of children, in the tradition of such French song-books as *La Civilité* and *Puérile et honnête,* which the composer's mother had sung to him as a child.[53] The songs also resembled Yvette Guilbert's *Chansons de la vieille France* (illustrations by A. Roubille), which the composer kept in his library.

A. C. McClurg published twelve of the Carpenters' songs ("About My Garden," "Red Hair," "Aspiration," "The Thunderstorm," "A Plan," "Practicing," "Brother," "Contemplation," "Happy Heathen," "To Cross the Street," "Making Calls," and "When the Night Comes") as *When Little Boys Sing* (dedicated "To the Solemn Thoughts of Little Boys") in 1904 and another twelve ("For Careless Children," "Stout," "The Liar," "A Reproach," "Humility," "A Wicked Child," "Vanity," "Maria-Glutton," "Good Ellen," "War," "Spring," and "Lullaby") as *Improving Songs for Anxious Children* in 1907. (In 1913 G. Schirmer obtained the rights and published seventeen of these songs as *Improving Songs for Anxious Children.*)

Although somewhat coy and precious, these children's songs exhibit a gentle irony free from the more conventional sentimentality of Carpenter's earlier music. Some of the songs even register a mild sort of anti-Victorian protest, for instance, the arbitrariness of gender roles ("Red Hair") or the agony of being seen and not heard—or fed ("Making Calls"). Others—"A Plan," "Aspiration," and "Happy Heathen" among them—project a dreamy, visionary utopia where "little boys / Can hop and play / the whole long day / And never be scolded for noise." These songs do not represent the mature composer—Carpenter's studies with Bernhard Ziehn still lay ahead—but they mark a fresh beginning, a new slate devoid of "parasitic details."

The charmingly deadpan humor of *Improving Songs* also strikes a distinctly American note, making the collection a turn-of-the-century precursor to the world of *Our Gang* and *Peanuts.* The music contains many trademarks not only of the contemporary vernacular but of popular American music yet to come. The poignant "Making Calls" (ex. 4), for instance, has the sweet yearning of a late Gershwin tune, while the childlike bravado of "A Plan" (ex. 5) anticipates Richard Rodgers. Even the simple lullaby "When the Night Comes" has a slightly jazzy flavor, including a final major triad with an added sixth, a chord whose unusual spacing emphasizes the music's modal ambiguity. At the same time, these songs exhibit Carpenter's characteristic refinement, in particular the beautifully Schumannesque "Spring."

Rue's elegantly cartoonish illustrations perfectly match the music and

EXAMPLE 4.   Carpenter, "Making Calls," from *Improving Songs for Anxious Children,* mm. 18–21.

texts. The little girl who wants to get rid of her red curls and have straight black hair "like other boys and not like silly girls" has enormous bows on her shoes, her dress, and her hair; even her dog has bows! And the virtuous Ellen (who "never said an ugly word") wears a long, severe dress strapped together by a few too many buttons.

The Carpenters' honest, sensitive, and amusing depiction of a child's world—the tediousness of practicing piano, the joys of solitary springtime walks, the anxiety of being too fat, the fear of thunderstorms and street wagons—touched a responsive chord. *Current Opinion* stated: "Absolutely unqualified is Carpenter's triumph in the realm of children's songs. . . . Both verses and music are by Mr. Carpenter, it is understood. They reveal a subtle

EXAMPLE 5.   Carpenter, "A Plan," from *Improving Songs for Anxious Children,* mm. 1–8.

insight into child psychology and an intangible something we may call the comic spirit in music. These songs are as vivid and colorful as the drawings of Kate Greenaway or Bernard Boutet de Monvel."[54] The poet Louis Untermeyer, whose wife sang these songs at home, wrote the composer: "If your other work has half the originality and strength of these children's songs we [Untermeyer and his wife] both believe (we were trained and fed on Schumann, Franz, Hugo Wolf and Grieg) that no writer that America has yet produced can equal you in eloquence and sincerity."[55]

The songs were sung not only at home but in concert by the likes of Kitty Cheatham and Tom Dobson. (Carpenter even orchestrated seven of the songs for the Chicago Symphony.) Reviewing a Cheatham concert of 28 December 1906, Richard Aldrich wrote in the *New York Times* that "her hearers were delighted with a descriptive bit, 'Practicing,' in which the horrors of the five-finger exercise were explained by a little boy, whose sufferings were by no means so uncommon as not to find plenty of sympathetic listeners."[56] Cheatham continued to feature Carpenter's children's songs in her highly popular concerts, and during the period 1906–12 almost single-handedly established the composer's reputation in New York with her renditions of these settings.

In 1916 and 1917, during the height of his brief but memorable career, Tom Dobson also scored a hit with these children's songs. Invited to participate in an all-Carpenter tribute in 1917, Dobson delighted his audience with four of the *Improving Songs:* "Mr. Dobson sings these charming naïve bits of child philosophy to his own accompaniment with as much apparent effort as it takes to flick the ashes from one's cigarette. He provoked chuckles and peals of real laughter with his excruciatingly funny facial expressions and unique treatment of these songs."[57] And in a memorial tribute to Dobson, Kate Douglas Wiggin asked, "Who will ever forget his singing of John Carpenter's 'Improving Songs for Anxious Children'—among the wittiest of their kind in all musical literature?"[58]

In later years some of Carpenter's greatest successes, including *Adventures in a Perambulator, Gitanjali, The Birthday of the Infanta,* and even *Sea Drift,* similarly concerned children in one way or another. "I've always been a pushover for children's things," Carpenter confessed to a reporter impressed with the composer's own "disarming friendliness and youthful zest." "I've always been fond of children," he remarked on another occasion.[59]

Children, in turn, liked Carpenter: "Dogs, cats, servants and children are attracted to him," wrote Carleton Sprague Smith.[60] His daughter and granddaughter adored him. The latter remembered that he treated her almost conspiratorially, like a grown-up, offering her her first drink and cigarette and collaborating with her on a little "Sunset Waltz," named after Sunset Hill, his summer home in Beverly: he wrote the first half, and she was to finish it.

Carpenter's sensitivity to children was part a worldwide trend that culminated in the decades just preceding World War I. In music this trend included European composers as varied as Humperdinck, Tchaikovsky, Debussy, and Ravel, not to mention a long list of American popular composers who wrote songs from the point of view of children (e.g., H. W. Petrie's "I Don't Want to Play in Your Yard" or Harry von Tilzer's "BL-ND and P-G Spells Blind Pig").[61] Carpenter seemed, in fact, as close to this American popular tradition as to the more exalted European styles, in that he did not so much glorify or romanticize children (he hardly ever spoke about his own childhood) as take an amused, ironic interest in them. This sensibility attracted him in time to Blake, Carroll, Stevenson, Wilde, and newspaper comics. It also bespoke his efforts on behalf of child welfare, in particular, the Illinois Children's Home and Aid Society (ICHAS).[62]

For most of his adult life, Carpenter was a director of ICHAS, a nonprofit organization that located homes or otherwise cared for orphaned, delinquent, disabled, and other needy children.[63] The society had twenty-four directors in 1898, fifty-one in 1925, and sixty-three in 1930. "Composed of men and women prominent in the business and social life of the community," these directors approved appointments and bylaws, formed standing committees, and mostly helped raise funds. Automatically elected by the nominating committee, the board of directors tended to be "somewhat self-perpetuating," which explains Carpenter's lifelong membership.[64]

Carpenter's involvement with the ICHAS confirms the impression left by the *Improving Songs,* namely, that he neither patronized nor idealized children but viewed them as young adults—perhaps in need of guidance but also deserving of respect and understanding. Indeed, Carpenter frequently intended his music—even his "serious" works—for children as much as for adults. He would not only improvise stories at the piano for his grandchild and step-grandchildren—often animal stories, like "Swans on the Lake in Peking"—but actually play excerpts from his latest compositions for their approval.[65] Little wonder that works like *Adventures in a Perambulator* and *Krazy Kat* easily crossed over from subscription to children's concerts, or that *The Birthday of the Infanta* should turn up at a special children's matinee, where, reported James Gibbons Huneker, "The numerous kiddies in the holiday audience were in the seventh heaven."[66]

Carpenter's writings—whether his whacky, tongue-in-cheek limericks and children's poems or his humorous program notes for *Adventures in a Perambulator,* in which he viewed the world from an infant's perspective—often seemed similarly predisposed to both children and adults.[67] Such humor even informed his occasional music criticism, such as the time he agreed to fill in for Frederick Donaghey and review a Chicago Symphony concert in 1918:

> When the news was broken to him that his number had been drawn, the Draft Musical Critic was to buy a quart of champagne, a pocket compass, and a music box guaranteed to play "Joan of Arc" under water, and with these to walk due east to Michigan Ave. until my hat should be picked up in the harbor of St. Joe. Oh, how I wished not to be drafted! But the system is inexorable. The system is in New York enjoying himself—on the Lexington Avenue Front.[68]

Rue's hand can be discerned in some of this. Certainly, it seems significant that Carpenter should first unveil his inimitable humor in the *Improving Songs* and that the sentimentality that marred his juvenilia from the 1890s should evaporate practically in one stroke.

Friends and supporters later claimed Rue as the guiding genius behind her husband's work. "Without the active co-operation of his wife," wrote Meeker, "his artistic career would have been much less successful than it was. She knew how to push him as he couldn't push himself, and was largely instrumental in having the ballets staged at the Munich Opera and the Metropolitan." Meeker asserted that Carpenter "never composed another vital bar of music" after her death.[69]

Such statements went too far. Even before Rue's death, and certainly afterward, Carpenter promoted his music with vigor. As for the alleged decline in the music's quality, that, too, can be argued. But Rue clearly helped shape the composer's tastes and ideals: his mature music—its stylish attention to European trends, its incorporation of popular idioms, its verve, its fun—have qualities that she obviously nurtured. Rue helped bring Carpenter—literally and figuratively—into the twentieth century.

CHAPTER FOUR

From the *Berceuse* to the Violin Sonata

1908–1912

███ Aside from the two volumes of children's songs, Carpenter composed
virtually nothing in the period 1901–7. Some further incentive apparently came with Edward Elgar's arrival in Chicago in the spring of 1907.

Elgar (1857–1934) came to Chicago to conduct the Chicago Symphony
on 5 and 6 April in a concert of his own music, including *In the South,* the
Enigma Variations, and *Pomp and Circumstance* no. 1. His conducting received only lukewarm notices in the press, but the composer himself lavished
praise on the orchestra, telling the players: "I have never been in Japan or
South Africa. Maybe they have better orchestras there, but in Europe they
have none better than the Theodore Thomas Orchestra. I have never heard
my works played so well."[1] In all likelihood the Carpenters not only attended
one or both of these performances but met the composer and possibly entertained him at their home.

The Carpenters subsequently spent the following winter (1907–8) in
Rome, so that John could study with Elgar. They probably arrived in December 1907, at which time Elgar presented them with an inscribed photograph of himself.

Elgar was at his peak: the *Enigma Variations* (1899), *Dream of Gerontius*
(1900), and *Pomp and Circumstance* no. 1 (1902) had established him as the
foremost English composer of his time. Whatever the merits of his later
accomplishments, none would achieve greater acclaim than these works. Apparently while in Rome, Carpenter undertook a detailed study of the *Enigma
Variations.*

We can imagine that Carpenter liked Elgar's direct, individual, and modern voice and that he recognized something in it akin to the kind of "eloquence and sincerity" that Untermeyer admired in Carpenter's own children's
songs. One source reported that Carpenter was particularly impressed with
Elgar's "dry precisionism."[2] Moreover, Carpenter's own English background

might have warmed him to Elgar's nationalism. Finally, Elgar had a notable command of orchestration, and Carpenter might have felt that this, in particular, was an area in which he could profit from more instruction. Indeed, he very possibly composed his first original orchestral work, the *Berceuse,* under Elgar's supervision.

Carpenter, however, did not rate his brief time with Elgar a success. After four months of study, he decided that Elgar was "a fine man but a poor teacher."[3] In fact, Elgar had little teaching experience and rarely accepted pupils. Why he took on Carpenter as a student in the first place remains something of a mystery. Certainly, he felt bitter and desperate about his financial situation, despite his recent successes, and here was a pleasant, wealthy American who could pay well for his lessons and who had, further, a charming wife who could entertain him in style.[4] Perhaps he admired certain features in Carpenter's music. In any case, Elgar's financial concerns and his preoccupation with *Wand of Youth* and the First Symphony apparently undermined his effectiveness as a teacher.

Many listeners over the years detected Elgar's influence on Carpenter's music, nonetheless. "Elgar may not have been a great teacher," wrote Percy Young,

> but his finger prints occasionally show up in Carpenter unmistakably. There is, for instance, the American's use of the orchestra, spacious, brassy, and percussively eloquent, his blunt melodic diatonicism in moments of large effort, his elliptical modulations to remote keys (Franckian, but less long-winded!) and his almost pre-Raphaelite attention to details of illustration.[5]

Young also felt Elgar's influence in two Carpenter songs, namely, "Les Silhouettes" and "The Green River" (settings of Oscar Wilde and Lord Alfred Douglas, respectively). Richard Aldrich and Paul Snook similarly espied Elgarisms in the First Symphony and *Sea Drift.*[6] Indeed, one generally noted the influence of Elgar in Carpenter's more patriotic, solemn, and "nobilmente" music. But like his English contemporary, Gustav Holst, Carpenter subjected Elgar's influence to a more modern sensibility.

Carpenter completed the *Berceuse* for chamber orchestra in March 1908, probably during his last month with Elgar or just after his return to Chicago. He sketched it originally for piano and then scored the work for flutes, oboes, clarinets, bassoons, horns, and strings; he apparently wanted to try out his orchestral abilities with a relatively small ensemble. Although Carpenter did not specify the actual number of woodwinds and brass, the score seems to require two flutes, two oboes, four clarinets, two bassoons, and three horns.

The orchestral writing in the *Berceuse* betrays pianistic habits, with long melodies in the violins supported by arpeggiated figures in the lower strings, the woodwind choir reserved for contrast. Harmonically, the work favors simple triads with added sixths or with some occasional chromaticism that recalls Borodin and Grieg. The whole is not too far removed from the salon pieces of the 1890s; Elgar apparently did not inspire any notable daring on Carpenter's part. One can nonetheless detect inklings of the mature Carpenter in the work's rippling string writing, its luminous pentatonic harmonies, its surprisingly prescient blue notes in the cello and clarinet (p. 12 of the unpublished manuscript), and its main theme, which looks ahead to the lullaby from the 1931 *Song of Faith:* "Sounds a sweet lullaby, Sounds an old song my mother knew."

Soon after Carpenter returned home, he continued his studies with the German American theorist Bernhard Ziehn, on the recommendation of Frederick Stock, the recently appointed conductor of the Chicago Symphony (perhaps after Carpenter showed Stock some of his music). Carpenter thus began lessons with the man who would become his most important teacher.[7]

Ziehn came from Bach territory. Born in Erfurt, Thuringia, on 20 January 1845, he taught mathematics in Mühlhausen before lining up a job in a Lutheran school in Chicago, where he immigrated in 1868.[8] A brilliant theorist and musicologist, Ziehn felt restricted in his native country—he had no advanced degree, and his combative temperament offended such established figures as the eminent Bach scholar Philipp Spitta. After the 1871 fire Ziehn became a private teacher of piano, organ, theory, and composition and a freelance organist (he played, among other places, at a Chicago synagogue, "where . . . he was greatly impressed by the sonority of the Hebrew language").[9] He died after a long and painful battle with throat cancer on 18 September 1912.

Ziehn's students included the McCormick children as well as a number of distinguished pedagogues: the organist Wilhelm Middelschulte, who taught Otto Luening; Thorvald Otterström and Glenn Dillard Gunn, who taught Ernst Bacon; and the theorist Julius Gold, who taught Isaac Stern, Winthrop Sargeant, and Meredith Willson. Ziehn also became a close friend and adviser to conductors Theodore Thomas and Frederick Stock. According to Gold, Thomas changed the way he conducted Beethoven after knowing Ziehn; indeed, Thomas was quoted as saying, "I have met one man from whom I can always learn—Bernhard Ziehn."[10] This network of Ziehn, his associates, and his students made Chicago the "most musical" city in America, according to Ferruccio Busoni.[11]

Ziehn had a knowledge of music that, for depth and breadth, was probably unmatched in the United States, if not Europe. "In all his articles," wrote Otterström, "he spares no pain to ransack the entire literature in order to prove his contention, having for a basis always this: our great masters, our living music are the only laws and rules we have."[12] Winthrop Sargeant reported that Ziehn once cited some allegedly unique harmony by Bruckner in works of Henry VI, Pergolesi, Friedemann Bach, Beethoven, Wagner, d'Albert, and others.[13] Ziehn's article "Über die Kirchentöne" further showed familiarity with such Renaissance masters as Josquin and Lassus. At the same time, he introduced Helen Rudolph Heller to the harmonic novelties of Debussy and Strauss.[14]

Ziehn admired, above all, Bach, Beethoven, Schubert, Wagner, and Bruckner. (He named his two children Robert Sebastien and Isolde.) He also had a special fondness for the music of Eugen d'Albert and Robert Franz, both personal friends. His adulation of Bruckner was unusual for the times, and he took a concurrently hard view of Brahms, partly because he suspected that Brahms and Hanslick had thwarted Bruckner's career, and partly because conductors often played Brahms (and Schumann) and ignored, to his mind, the superior Bruckner. On hearing of Bruckner's death on 28 October 1896, Ziehn wrote a long piece that criticized Brahms as much as it praised Bruckner: "Had the less important Brahms died, our great conductors would already have given us memorial programs. . . . Brahms was not the man to imbue the ecclesiastical modes with new life. . . . Everyone who has truly studied the polyphony of Bach, Wagner and Beethoven will readily admit that Bruckner is a master of polyphony, and not Brahms—that matter is settled."[15] (Ziehn, who revised Hanslick's "three Bs" to read "Bach, Beethoven, and Bruckner," also accused Brahms of plagiarism.)[16] In appreciation Bruckner's friends sent Ziehn the manuscript of the Adagio to the unfinished Ninth Symphony.

"A man of strong opinions" and "brusque in speech,"[17] Ziehn took on not only Brahms and Hanslick from faraway Chicago but other prominent musicians: he derided Hans von Bülow's Beethoven editions (calling for urtext editions), clashed with Spitta over the authenticity of Bach's *St. Luke Passion* (deducing the work's spuriousness by comparing its chorales with other Bach chorales), and kept up a running feud with the theorist Hugo Riemann.

In addition to his own editions of baroque music and his extensive journalism (mostly in German), Ziehn published five theoretical treatises on keyboard playing and composition—*System der Übungen für Clavierspieler* (Hamburg, 1876), *Ein Lehrgang für den ersten Clavierunterricht* (Hamburg, 1881), *Harmonie- und Modulationslehre* (Berlin, 1888; an expanded English translation was published in Milwaukee in 1907 as *Manual of Harmony*), *Five- and Six-Part Harmonies: How to Use Them* (Milwaukee and Berlin, 1911), and *Canonical Studies: A New Technic of Composition* (Milwaukee and Berlin, 1912)—remarkable for their exhaustive exploration of chromatic harmony and counterpoint. His discussions of nine distinct chromatic seventh chords, for example, helped classify and explain the harmonic language of Wagner, Franck, Bruckner, Strauss, and Debussy. Further, his ideas about such matters as enharmonic equivalence, twelve-tone melody, and symmetrical inversion anticipated the work of Schoenberg and Bartók.[18] Julius Gold accordingly described him as "a singular blend of the strict pedant and the ultra-modern progressive."[19]

In tracing Ziehn's influence on the music of Otto Luening and Ernst Bacon, Severine Neff distinguished five "operations" that Ziehn employed to create "tonally ambiguous chord progressions": (1) "plurisignificance" (Ziehn's translation of the German *Mehrdeutigkeit*), in which a single pitch can be reinterpreted in numerous triadic contexts; (2) "'irregular' cadence," which features an unresolved dissonant pitch, a nonfunctional cadence, or some other irregularity such as modal ambiguity; (3) "order permutation," in which melodic fragments are reordered (this looks ahead to Webern and to Milton Babbitt's "derived sets"); (4) "figuration," defined by Neff as "the creation of surface ornamentation through local dissonance"; and (5) "symmetrical inversion," the use of simultaneously inverted motives. Such concepts helped spur Luening and Bacon to new ways of thinking about harmony, even leading, in Bacon's case, to nontonal explorations.[20]

Ziehn's progressiveness attracted the Italian-German composer Ferruccio Busoni when he visited Chicago in January 1910. "I am studying counterpoint again, for which Chicago has greatly stimulated me," he wrote to his wife.[21] Busoni found Ziehn something of a revelation. In an article titled "Die 'Gotiker' von Chicago, Illinois," written in New York in January 1910, Busoni praised the diligence, seriousness, and purity of Ziehn's and Middelschulte's work, as opposed to the more familiar and trivial aspects of American culture that Europeans aped.[22] Using a string of architectural metaphors, Busoni compared Ziehn's achievement to a Gothic cathedral: his work likewise created "a bridge between heaven and earth." Busoni defined such Gothic art as "that art in which delight in delicacy combines with the possibilities of power, feeling combines with fantasy, strict calculation with mystical belief."[23] In music, Gothic art arose from strict contrapuntal thinking; in contrast to the "Fantasie-Gotik" of Mendelssohn and Wagner, the true Gothic was best represented by Bach and César Franck. Ziehn and Middelschulte extended this tradition by arriving, contrapuntally, at harmonies even more novel than Franck's. Whatever their own limitations, they were "creating Columbuses" who might bring their work to full fruition.

Under Ziehn's guidance Busoni figured out a solution to the unfinished fugue from Bach's *Art of the Fugue,* which he subsequently incorporated into his own *Fantasia contrappuntistica.* More important, his study of the Ziehnian principle of symmetrical inversion—in which unusual harmonies arose from strict inversions of chromatic lines—led Busoni, by his own admission, to "quite surprising sounds and . . . one step further."[24] Otto Luening goes so far as to state that Ziehn's theories "completely changed Busoni's concept of composing techniques."[25]

Carpenter was the only major composer to have studied with Ziehn for any extended period. Beginning in the fall of 1908, he worked with Ziehn for four years, enrolling each fall and spring trimester. (In 1909 Ziehn charged thirty-five dollars per term.) Carpenter took his last lessons on 13 and 17 July 1912, shortly before the theorist's death.

Carpenter wrote hundreds of harmonic and contrapuntal exercises under Ziehn. Most of the harmonic exercises involved short progressions; starting from a given triad or seventh chord, he would quickly move to some distant triad via passing tones, a whole-tone bass, or some other designated way. Some of the results sounded like Wagner or Franck, some like Reger or Busoni, some like modern jazz, and some like nothing easily recognizable.

Carpenter's contrapuntal work consisted primarily of chromatic canons, ranging from simple two-voice canons at the octave to "symmetrical" canons (canons in inversion) to eight-voice double canons. Many revealed some study of the *Art of the Fugue,* although nearly all were ultrachromatic and freely dissonant. Ziehn actually published some of Carpenter's canons in his *Canonical Studies,* including a four-voice canon (ex. 6a) and its contrapuntal melodic inversion (ex. 6b).

Carpenter also wrote free compositions under Ziehn. One such work— the Prelude and Fugue (for piano)—resembled his academic exercises for Ziehn, showing an impressive command of an ultrachromatic idiom. Unlike

EXAMPLE 6.   Carpenter, "Frei erfundener Canon Thema von 8 Takten" (Freely invented canon theme of eight measures), in Bernhard Ziehn, *Canonical Studies: A New Technic of Composition* (Milwaukee: Kaun, 1912), 200–201.

a. Four-voice canon, mm. 5–8.

b. Contrapuntal melodic inversion of *(a)*, mm. 5–8.

Reger and Busoni, Carpenter never brought music like the four-voice Fugue to light, but the $\frac{5}{8}$ Prelude provided the basis for the last movement of the composer's Piano Concertino.

This Prelude and Fugue possibly dates from the composer's later years with Ziehn, since Carpenter's other compositions from the period 1909–10 (e.g., the 1909 Suite for Orchestra) do not exhibit the same level of maturity. Indeed, the Suite for Orchestra more closely resembles the *Berceuse,* including its scoring for (two) flutes, (two) oboes, two clarinets, two bassoons, two horns, timpani, and strings. Further, its two movements are somewhat rudimentary. The first movement, Andantino, puts forth yet another lullaby-like movement with singsong rhythms and static harmonies; the faster second movement, Allegro con moto, combines waltzlike and pastoral elements.

The suite represents an advance over the *Berceuse,* nonetheless. The more subtle orchestration features interesting blends, rather than the simple alternation of choirs. Further, the violins do not monopolize the principal themes, which here move along from instrument to instrument. Other aspects similarly reveal a growing sophistication: the occasional appearance of chromatic and augmented harmonies; the changes of tempo within a movement; the use of *dolce, grazioso, delicato,* and other expressive markings; the revamping of recapitulations to create a climax; and the attention paid to inner parts and bass lines.

Carpenter's *Two Little Pieces* for violin and piano possibly date from 1909 or 1910 as well, for they strongly resemble the two-movement Suite for Orchestra: the first number is similarly lullaby-like (Carpenter titled an early sketch of its main idea "Negro Berceuse"), and the second—later retitled Impromptu—is similarly waltzlike. Further, they recall some of Carpenter's contemporaneous songs: the first movement is like the 1909 "Looking-Glass River," and the second is like the (presumably) 1910 "Triste était mon âme." They are charming pieces, more melodically winning than the suite, though still not so compelling as the songs. Carpenter reached maturity as a songwriter sooner than as a composer of instrumental music.

We also find an undated movement from an apparently unfinished work for piano—cataloged simply as "I" by the Library of Congress—that possibly dates from these years. It is a waltz and might have been intended as the first movement of yet another suite. The music's blend of Chopin and American operetta smacks of Carpenter's work from the 1890s, but a few features point to Ziehn's influence: The main idea features symmetrical inversion, and the harmonies become, at times, rather chromatic. One episode, in particular, strongly recalls Sibelius's 1903 *Valse triste*. The music, in short, suggests a Ziehnian adaptation of the composer's salon style.

During his years with Ziehn, Carpenter also may have written the incidental music for a play titled *The Heart of Nature,* alternately referred to by the composer as *The Faun,* the title of a 1911 play by his old friend and collaborator Edward Knoblock. Carpenter scored *The Heart of Nature* / *The Faun* for two flutes, two oboes, two clarinets, two bassoons, two horns, cornet, trombone, percussion, and strings. The extant score includes an entr'acte "Suffragette March," a pantomime for Pan and the Nymphs in act 2, and a "Silvain Dance" in act 3. In the pantomime, especially, Carpenter uses the whole-tone scale extensively and somewhat crudely, as if he were discovering this resource for the first time and not sure what to do with it.

One can safely guess that an untitled, operatic fragment dates from this time as well. Only a part of one scene survives. The plot concerns a spoiled, bored princess and her suitor, Narcisse Apollo. Other characters include the King, the Herald, the Dancing Master, the Court Ladies, and Courtiers. The instrumentation calls for piccolo, two flutes, two oboes, two clarinets, two bassoons, four horns, trumpet, three trombones, percussion, harp, and strings. The composer's vocal writing in this excerpt is recitative-like; some of the music looks ahead to the colorful waltz (minus the jazzy breaks) found in the first movement of the Piano Concertino (five after 8).

Despite the apparent unpretentiousness, even naïveté—for a composer over thirty—of such works, the growing sophistication of Carpenter's music from 1909 and 1910 can be attributed to his work with Ziehn. The 1911 Violin Sonata documents Ziehn's influence better than any one work, however. Dedicated to Ziehn, the sonata represents something of a graduation piece, with some passages reminiscent of Carpenter's harmonic exercises for Ziehn. Consider the tonally ambiguous sequence at the first key change in the third movement (ex. 7). This third movement, in fact, derives from a short, unpublished Largo for piano that, although apparently the first movement of a larger work, seems very much an academic exploration of Ziehnian ideas (Carpenter added a tuneful middle section for the Violin Sonata).[26]

Moreover, the five aforementioned techniques that Neff associates with Ziehn's theoretical work inform the Violin Sonata as well: plurisignificance (ex. 8a, in which a D♯-major triad resolves into an E-minor triad, the enharmonically common tone being F✗/G; for another example, see the return of Tempo I in the second movement, in which the root of an A♭ dominant seventh chord becomes the G♯ of an A major-seventh chord); irregular cadence (ex. 8b, in which the F♯-minor cadence, which does not resolve the preceding E♭ dissonance, is unusually deceptive); order permutation (ex. 8c, in which the opening motive, A♭–F–E, is transformed in the secondary theme to E–F–A♭); figuration (ex. 8d, the chromatic tenor line); and symmetrical inversion (ex. 8e, in which the principal motive of three rising semitones is simultaneously inverted in the bass).

The music's tone—earnest, somber, reflective, sometimes grim, though sometimes sweetly nostalgic—also seems related to Ziehn and to his love for Bruckner and Franck. For many listeners the connection with Franck seems particularly strong.[27] Certainly the lilting, elegant melodies; the rich, rolled harmonies; and the cyclic finale place the Violin Sonata in the tradition of Franck. Indeed, the work perfectly fits Busoni's description of Chicago Gothic: it combines, like Franck, "delicacy" and "power," "feeling" and "fantasy," "calculation" and "mystical belief."

EXAMPLE 7.   Carpenter, Violin Sonata, third movement, mm. 23–26.

EXAMPLE 8.   Carpenter's use of Ziehnian techniques in the Violin Sonata.

a. Plurisignificance

b. Irregular cadence

c. Order permutation

EXAMPLE 8.   (*Continued*)

d. Figuration

e. Symmetrical inversion

At the same time, the Violin Sonata has its own distinctive, inventive, and even daring profile. Reviewing its 1912 premiere, the *New York Times* stated, "Mr. Carpenter is determined to be modern at any cost."[28]

Perhaps the work shows greatest originality in terms of texture. Instead of the brilliant, sensuous figuration that gives much romantic music its coloring, one finds fairly severe and sharply etched strokes of tremendous clarity and, at times, angularity. Even the work's sweetness is of the most delicate kind. In 1913 Albert Cotsworth could read such severity in the composer's face:

> At first glance Mr. Carpenter has a bit of severity in his face, as though he had inherited some of the austerity we invariably picture as belonging to his namesake of Old Plymouth. There is not much suggestion of the dreamer or the rapt enthusiast in this smooth visaged young man, with his firm jaw and high cheek and smoothly brushed brown hair. The lips are not full and do not smile easily. The eyes are bright, very bright, but cold until the relaxing

moment comes, when they light up the intelligent face and make it warm and cordial.[29]

Carpenter's astringencies look forward to the kind of textures favored by such later American composers as Copland, Thomson, and Piston. In fact, the sonata's textures sometimes suggest a distinctly neoclassical bent. Deems Taylor's comment that "the prevailing mood" of Carpenter's music "is that of eighteenth-century France, although the idiom is utterly contemporary," seems particularly pertinent here.[30]

The work's harmony is also distinctive and original: one finds open, parallel fifths and fourths, chromatic modality (the slow movement makes interesting use of the Dorian mode), polychordal and bitonal inflections, whole-tone sonorities, dissonant pedals, pandiatonicism, and one of the composer's trademarks, the French augmented sixth chord, now released from any traditional function.

The individual movements form unusual and evocative designs as well. The opening movement (in G major) reinvents the sonata as a large arch, with a tension between two motives (the first at m. 5 and the second, a three-note motive, at m. 17) taking the place of the traditional tonic-dominant struggle. The second movement scherzo (in D minor) is highly rhapsodic and full of intricate cross-rhythms and syncopations; its D♭-major "trio" sounds more like an episode than like some structural central point. The slow third movement proves just the opposite, a ternary form in which the long, lyrical E♭-major middle section overwhelms the F-minor outer sections. The last movement (in G major) wanders spontaneously through keys, tempos, and reminiscences of previous movements until it reaches a climactic return of the main theme and slowly subsides, unpredictably, into a quiet ending.[31]

The work, in short, resembles modern, so-called transitional styles of the period 1900–1910. The possible influence of Busoni himself cannot be dismissed. Carpenter presumably met and possibly entertained Busoni when the composer came to Chicago in early 1910. In any case, Carpenter gained some familiarity with Busoni's music, for in 1915 he called Busoni "one of the greatest living artists and composers" (while at the same time expressing reservations about the composer's *Indian Fantasy*). Certainly the Violin Sonata's neoclassical textures, unusual harmonies, and novel formal procedures suggest an aesthetic akin to Busoni's.

Carpenter spent much time and energy on the Violin Sonata, as evidenced by numerous versions of the work: sketches, pencil draft, fair copy (1911), revised version for the premiere (1912), and further revisions for the

Schirmer publication (1913). Consequently, the Violin Sonata that Carpenter wrote under Ziehn was not the same, in all particulars, as the one either premiered or published. This would prove typical, only in later years Carpenter would often revise a work after publication as well.

Aside from the slow movement, which remained for the most part intact, the most substantial revisions occurred about two-thirds into the individual movements, as the composer attempted to find a smoother and more interesting way to return to that particular movement's main theme and tonality. More generally, the revisions tended to add harmonic interest or extend tonal tension, especially through the use of harmonic sequence.

Between the fair copy and the published edition, Carpenter sent the score to the violinist Dorothy Swainson, who sent letters back from Paris and London, counseling against the use of octave doubling in certain passages in the second and third movements as contrary to "the spirit of the rest of the movement." Carpenter apparently ignored this criticism (and, as if to demonstrate his independence, even added octave doublings at the quiet conclusion of the finale), but he took her advice and removed some tremolos. He also revised the fourth-movement cadenza, it seems, in response to Swainson's request for "something more interesting" at that point. Unfortunately, he did not shorten the finale as she advised, although he may have lengthened the first movement partly in the hopes that this would rectify the work's obvious imbalance.[32]

Carpenter premiered the Violin Sonata with Russian violinist Mischa Elman at a Schola Cantorum concert at Aeolian Hall in New York on 11 December 1912. The reviews were negative: "more pretentious than impressive" *(Evening World)*, "slight melodies" *(Evening Sun)*, and, as noted, "determined to be modern at any cost" *(New York Times)*. Only the *Herald Tribune* liked the music, at least in part: "The last movement of the sonata contained considerable body and beauty, but the other three were less effective."[33]

In the ensuing years the work nonetheless enjoyed an extraordinary success for an American violin sonata: subsequent performances included those by Ludwig Becker and the composer in Chicago in January 1913; David and Clara Mannes in Boston in February 1913; Leon Sametini and Rudolph Reuter in Chicago in March 1913; Adolph Hahn and Theodor Bohlmann in Cincinnati in January 1914; André de Ribaupierre and Rudolph Ganz in London in 1914; Albert Spalding and André Benoist in New York in January 1915 and in Boston in November 1915; Gaylord Yost and Charles Gabriel in Indianapolis in February 1915; William MacPhail and Margaret Gilmore

MacPhail in Minneapolis in December 1915; and David Hochstein and Lester Donahue in New York in February 1917 at an all-Carpenter concert sponsored by the MacDowell Club.[34] Carpenter attended many of these performances and reported to Julius Gold in 1915: "I have found that there is a tendency to take the last movement of my sonata at too great a speed to permit of a clear and well accented accompaniment by the pianist. As a matter of fact the piano part is rather more difficult than that for the violin."[35]

Chicago and Boston proved vastly more receptive to the Violin Sonata than New York had been. The Mannes's Boston premiere brought raves from critics Henry Taylor Parker and Philip Hale; indeed, the *Chicago Evening Post* reported that this performance "had the aspect of one of those musical triumphs which are more possible in Germany than they are in our own unaesthetic nation."[36] Reviewing the Sametini-Reuter performance in Chicago, Eric De Lamarter wrote: "At no moment can it be said honestly that he [Carpenter] has not an exalted ideal of musical beauty. His sincerity can no more be questioned than his technical mastery."[37]

Carpenter's Violin Sonata found friends in other quarters as well. After hearing Spalding rehearse the sonata, the Irish tenor John McCormack told the *Chicago Musical Leader:* "If this was the work of any but an American, it would be one of the sensations. Every musician would be raving about it. It is immense in its bigness of thought and working out." "The violin sonata in its themes, its strikingly individual harmonic intuitions, and its structure generally, is of great beauty and interest," wrote Arthur Farwell, who also told Dorothy Swainson that he found the work "delightful." And Charles Wakefield Cadman wrote the composer that he had spent "many pleasant hours over your sonata for violin and piano. . . . You are reaching the heights where many have failed, and are planting an ideal worthy of emulation."[38]

That such notable "Indianist" composers as Farwell and Cadman praised the Violin Sonata deserves emphasis, for the work has a somber restraint and bold vigor related to the Indianist movement. Indeed, Carpenter's musical development may have derived something from the Indianist movement; not only would his Chicagoan provenance make such a connection plausible, but in the years ahead he would speak of Indian music as a potential source for American composers and would write explicitly Indianist music himself.

In the meantime the New York press remained, on balance, unimpressed with the work—whether played by Spalding and Benoist or by Hochstein and Donahue. Whatever the reason, this distinction established a pattern, and in future years Boston and Chicago (and other midwestern cities like Minneapolis, Cincinnati, Cleveland, and Detroit) would hold the composer in higher regard than New York or Philadelphia (despite Carpenter's friendship with Walter Damrosch, Leopold Stokowski, Bruno Walter, and Artur Rodzinski).

The sonata's limitations—its occasional monotony, formal imperfections, and uncertain balance between romantic rhetoric and modern daring (especially in the cadenza to the finale)—became more evident with time. Upon hearing in 1923 that Spalding was still playing "my ancient Violin Sonata," Carpenter himself admitted that the work "sounds pretty old-fashioned now."[39] By 1930 even sympathetic writers like Felix Borowski and John Tasker Howard found some of it dated.[40] Soon after the composer's death, Rudolph Ganz, who performed the sonata and who knew Carpenter's output quite well, declared, simply, that the Violin Sonata was not representative of its composer.[41]

After the Violin Sonata had fallen into obscurity for many years, a 1977 recording of the work (paired with Arthur Foote's Sonata in G Minor, op. 20) by Eugene Gratovich and Regis Benoit allowed an opportunity for its reevaluation.[42] Writing for both the *American Record Guide* and *New Records,* C. Thomas Veilleux found that unlike Foote's sonata, Carpenter's Violin Sonata warranted revival: it had "a little more to sink our teeth into. It is more refreshingly complex than Foote's travesty, with some fine moments for violin." On the other hand, Irving Lowens, in *High Fidelity,* found Foote's sonata "the more fascinating of the two." Paul Turok, in the *Music Journal,* called both works "real American finds."[43]

The Violin Sonata represents a personal victory for its composer: a triumph over the timidity that had informed his previous work, especially in the area of instrumental music. And it documents, better than any other piece, the role that Ziehn played in his development.

Carpenter remained devoted to the memory of Ziehn in the years following the theorist's death. "Ziehn was undoubtedly one of the greatest musical minds we have ever had in the Country," he wrote to Victor Lichtenstein in 1915, "and his death is a very distinct loss coming as it did before his methods and theories had time to acquire greater currency among teachers capable of perpetuating them."[44]

"In the short period that I worked with him," Carpenter stated in 1916, "I learned more and received more inspiration than from all other previous sources."[45] In 1918 he called Ziehn "a unique man who had a marvelous scientific grasp besides an open mind, who did not think music written by a

German was better than music written by an American, or music by a French-man was better than that by an Italian."[46]

In 1914 the theorist Julius Gold, who had studied with Ziehn during the same years Carpenter had (though they had never met), wrote a letter of introduction to Carpenter, who replied: "I remember just missing you one afternoon at Mr. Ziehn's house during the last year before he died. He spoke to me several times of you and your work and I know you held a very high place in his esteem. If you are carrying on his work and ideas in any form, you are doing the music world a service."[47] A short time later Carpenter provided Gold with a brief reminiscence of Ziehn. He recalled, above all, the theorist's struggle against throat cancer and likened Ziehn's spiritual resolve to that of the Italian actress Eleonora Duse:

> I have a curious feeling that a true record of my own contact with this ex-traordinary man would deal only incidentally with his contribution to musi-cal theory. I think of him more than anything else as embodying the triumph of the spiritual over the material. I had exactly the same impression the other day from Duse. The obvious fact that she is probably the greatest living actress seemed unimportant in the light of the power of her tremen-dous spirit over her physical infirmities.
>
> To have had the privilege of coming into frequent contact with Ziehn during the last year of his life when he had literally nothing left to go on but his will and his artistic integrity meant for me something much more important than the immediate technical problem involved in my studies with him.[48]

The respect Carpenter and Gold shared for Ziehn created a bond, reflected in more than ten years of correspondence. In 1916 Carpenter reported to Gold about Stock's performance of Strauss's *Alpine* Symphony: "If Ziehn could have lived, I am sure he would have found it 'kolossal,'—to use one of his favorite expressions." And discussing his own ballet, *Skyscrapers,* in 1929, Carpenter wrote to Gold, "I am afraid there are some moments in the score that would cause our late honored Master to shudder in his present resting place and for those moments I can only hope for his kind absolution."[49]

CHAPTER FIVE

From "Treat Me Nice" to "Terre promise"

1905–1913

In the years 1912 and 1913, Carpenter published a number of songs that immediately established him as one of America's foremost art song composers. He wrote most of these songs before 1912 but had not published anything since "Treat Me Nice," a 1905 setting of the poem "A Plea," by the black poet Paul Lawrence Dunbar.

Felix Borowski reported that the composer, rightly in his opinion, wanted to see "Treat Me Nice" suppressed. According to Borowski the song did not "stand upon the loftiest plane of art."[1] Far from being "lofty," the setting reflects, as does Dunbar's poem itself, something of the "coon song" tradition, though in its less offensive guise, as represented, for example, by Will Marion Cook's own 1898 collaboration with Dunbar, *Clorindy* (featuring such songs as "Darktown Is Out Tonight" and "Who Dat Say 'Chicken' in Dis Crowd?"), or, even more so, Bob Cole's sweet "Under the Bamboo Tree" (1902). In "A Plea" Dunbar's lovesick minstrel asks "Miss Mandy Jane," in comic Negro dialect, to "treat him nice." Carpenter's music, with its dotted rhythms suggesting the shuffling triplets of the American soft-shoe, seems grounded somewhere between the old schottische and newer styles associated with the term *ragtime*. The song's tunefulness brings it, in fact, in range of Tin Pan Alley. Perhaps some friend of the Carpenters'—like Harry Harvey— sang it at one of their blackface parties (the Carpenters apparently also knew Al Jolson). George Ade, after all, had a Chicago salon in mind when he wrote his aforementioned satirical fable of 1903 (see chap. 2), complete with its "dear little Cantata about a Coon."[2]

At the same time, "Treat Me Nice" contains features that distinguish it from much popular music, such as the varied accompaniment for each of its three stanzas. The melody itself contains some unusual inflections, for instance, its rise to the major seventh at the word "love" in the second phrase (ex. 9). Further, Carpenter's choice of a Dunbar text foreshadows his re-

EXAMPLE 9.   Carpenter, "Treat Me Nice," mm. 5–8.

markable receptivity to strong, if sometimes little-known, contemporary poetry.

Carpenter's unpublished settings of three poems by the late German romantic Karl Florenz (1865–1939)—"Die vier Jahreszeiten" (The four seasons), "Endlose Liebe" (Endless love), and "Schifferlied" (Boatman's song)—possibly date from about the same time as "Treat Me Nice." They might perhaps have been written as early as the 1890s, for Harvard students often wrote songs to German romantic verse. But American composers quite generally set German verse in the years before World War I, and these songs seem more mature than Carpenter's collegiate music.

In any case, Carpenter cast these songs in a Straussian idiom unlike anything else he wrote. Indeed, one possible clue to the dating of these songs is that Pauline Strauss sang "Morgen" with the Theodore Thomas Orchestra in April 1904, under her husband's baton.[3] Carpenter's songs—in particular, "Die vier Jahreszeiten"—are enough like "Morgen" to suggest that the composer wrote his Florenz songs under the stimulus of that performance.

On the other hand, a "sketch" of "Endlose Liebe" in the Library of Congress would suggest a date of composition after 1906, since the manuscript has Carpenter's 156 Read Street address at the top (Carpenter lived on Read Street from 1906 to 1909). This "sketch," however, is actually a revision of the original: it adds dynamics, expression marks, and pedal indications; changes the slow $\frac{4}{4}$ into cut time; provides a metronome marking; and transposes the song up a whole step, from Db major to Eb major, so that the lowest note is a more accessible Bb (bb), rather than Ab (ab). Carpenter also revises the concluding vi–V–IV–I progression, so that the IV chord now has an augmented sixth, which takes the edge off its modal character (which, especially in the original, was more redolent of a rock song than a romantic lied). In terms of dating, all this means is that Carpenter originally wrote the song sometime before 1909; perhaps he composed it in 1908 or early 1909, soon after beginning his studies with Ziehn.

A few versions of "Die vier Jahreszeiten" also exist, but their order is less clear. This highly episodic song has four large sections in different keys and meters, each depicting a season. In one version Carpenter modulates from D major (spring) to A major (summer) to D♭ major (autumn) to E minor (winter) before ending in F major—one hardly knows the piece has ended. In another version "winter" is a minor third lower, moving from C♯ minor to D major, which provides greater tonal symmetry. Carpenter probably composed this more symmetrical version first and revised it, once again, to avoid low notes, in this case A's below middle C. This would explain why the move from D♭ major to E minor in the first-mentioned version sounds like a patch-up job.

"Endlose Liebe" is the most charming of the Florenz settings. It blends German romantic and vernacular elements in a way close to American operetta, especially Romberg. Its depiction of rain by means of repeated notes at once looks back to Chopin's so-called raindrop Prelude in D♭ Major and ahead to other Carpenter songs with rain imagery, such as "Il pleure dans mon coeur." "Die vier Jahreszeiten" seems a more gauche attempt at Straussian elegance. The little ditty "Schifferlied" evokes a brusque and hearty kind of German humor; its primary interest resides in the composer's use of a German folk idiom.

In 1908 Carpenter wrote the earliest of his acclaimed "1912" songs: "The Cock Shall Crow," "Go, Lovely Rose," and "May, the Maiden." All three texts concern spring and its transience. In "The Cock Shall Crow," to words by Robert Louis Stevenson (1850–94), the dead narrator jauntily observes spring from a nearby cemetery. Carpenter originally titled the song "Ditty," after the poem's real title, "Ditty (to an Air from Bach)." In his setting he appropriately evokes a style somewhere between a British drinking song and a Bach gavotte. Although the song captures Stevenson's buccaneer romanticism nicely, Borowski found "The Cock Shall Crow" only slightly less embarrassing than "Treat Me Nice." Had he known it, Borowski probably would have dismissed "Schifferlied" as well, but all three songs document the composer's cosmopolitan interest in popular, folkish idioms.

Whereas "The Cock Shall Crow" and these other ditties are in a fairly straightforward strophic form (notwithstanding certain changes from strophe to strophe), "Go, Lovely Rose" and "May, the Maiden" are both in ternary (ABA) form. There are notable differences between them in this regard, however. In "Go, Lovely Rose" Carpenter sets off the middle section by key, tempo, melody, and so forth; whereas in "May, the Maiden," the music is more through-composed, with the middle section representing more an intensification of feeling than a wholly new mood. Carpenter subsequently used one or the other of these two kinds of ternary designs for the majority of his mature songs and for many of his shorter instrumental compositions as well.

Given his strong inclination toward ternary form, Carpenter naturally was attracted to poetry that had some kind of tripartite shape. But the composer frequently cast his songs in ternary form no matter what the original structure of the poem. This is the case with both "Go, Lovely Rose" and "May, the Maiden."

"Go, Lovely Rose" by Edmund Waller (1606–87) comprises four stanzas. In the first stanza, the poet compares a beautiful maiden to a rose; in the second and third stanzas, he chides the girl's modesty and reticence; and in the fourth stanza, he commands the rose to die, so that the maiden may appreciate beauty's ephemeral nature. Carpenter sets only stanzas 1, 2, and 4, which is understandable, given the redundancy of stanza 3. Whereas a piling up of metaphors works perfectly well in the Waller poem, it could possibly drag down a song, which requires concision and a minimum of poetic flourish.

Theoretically, Carpenter might have created an ABA form out of stanzas 1, 2, and 4, respectively. But Carpenter wants the poem's dramatic highlight, the death of the rose, at the song's midpoint, not at its end. Consequently, he returns to the opening stanza after the fourth stanza, so that stanzas 1 and 2 comprise the first part (A), stanza 4 offers dramatic contrast (B), and stanza 1 provides an abbreviated return (A). Many other Carpenter songs similarly use this method of repeating an opening stanza, couplet, or line in order to create a rounded design.

"May, the Maiden" is simpler. The original poem already comprises three stanzas, but the structure is flat: it is a love song set against the backdrop of the arrival of spring and dawn (stanza 1), twilight (stanza 2), and night-time (stanza 3), with imagery and mood remaining very much the same from stanza to stanza. But whereas Carpenter provides stanzas 1 and 3 with similar music, he intensifies the music for stanza 2 with chromatic harmonies, louder dynamics, and a climactic note on the name Marie, to whom the poem is addressed. The resultant feeling that the poem itself is rounded is purely illusory.

In both songs, then, Carpenter imposes a ternary form on the poetry, but convincingly so, not only because the demands of song are different from those of poetry but because rounded forms serve the images of cyclical time that underlie the poetry. Significantly, the passage of time is a theme that often recurs in Carpenter's work, both in his songs and in his instrumental work, and thus the composer's predilection for ternary and rounded forms seems related, at least in part, to certain extramusical preoccupations.

For all this, "Go, Lovely Rose" and "May, the Maiden" are very different—variety is surely among the most obvious assets of Carpenter's song output. "Go, Lovely Rose" is an attractive and sweet confection. In his landmark study *Art-Song in America,* William Treat Upton calls it one of Carpenter's "most ingratiating songs."[4] The opening stanza (ex. 10) immediately unfolds a number of nice touches: the luminous D♭-major accompaniment, close, in spirit, to the Wagnerian forest murmurs of "Die vier Jahreszeiten" but here with distinctively pentatonic inflections; the anticipation of the words "lovely rose" in the piano accompaniment's tenor voice; the surprisingly irregular division of the vocal line into three-, seven-, and five-measure phrases; the melody's one chromatic note, a jazzy, flatted seventh on the word "her" (m. 13); and the relaxed harmonic language, here featuring a V–IV–I progression that works splendidly.

Moreover, the B section nicely sets off the lovely A section: the tempo is slower; the melody, thoroughly pentatonic; the rhythm, more of an unmetrical parlando; the tonality, not a clear D♭ major but an ambiguous A major (it always cadences on D); and the texture, full of parallel chords, also pentatonic in makeup.

Carpenter returns to the opening strophe by means of a short and skillful modulating sequence of the kind he would use time and again. Because such sequences recall Carpenter's Ziehnian exercises, one can assume that he wrote this particular song in late 1908, after he had begun lessons with Ziehn. Upton draws particular attention to this section's "weirdly conceived harmonies" (although it is not clear what he found "weird": the pentatonic harmonies or this chromatic transition).[5] The return of the A section characteristically sounds thoroughly new and inspired.

"May, the Maiden," a serenade addressed to "Marie," is in a leisurely, almost hypnotic three, more like a barcarole than a slow waltz. Upton claims, with reason, that this is not as fine a song as "Go, Lovely Rose." Surely, the sentimental text by Sidney Lanier (1842–81) is not the equal of Waller's. But Carpenter's attempt to capture Lanier's spring, basked in violet, brings him in range, for the first time, of an "impressionist" style that characterizes some of his best songs. Such impressionist devices include the use of little arched motives to depict the pervasive "hovering" imagery, the rocking back and

EXAMPLE 10.   Carpenter, "Go, Lovely Rose," mm. 6–20.

forth between the mediant and the dominant ninth in the instrumental interlude to evoke the violet seascape, and the use of the extreme ranges of the
piano at the very end to describe the immensity of the stars.

About this time Carpenter probably attempted his other Lanier setting,
"The Marshes of Glynn," which he apparently left unfinished. The unfinished
sketches afford an especially good glimpse into Carpenter's compositional
methods, which often involved writing a melodic phrase, finding a suitable
harmonic accompaniment, writing a second phrase, providing more harmonies, and so on. (In other songs, however, he would write a fairly long
melodic line before composing harmonies.) Such compositional procedures
help explain the composer's freshness and spontaneity—as well as some of his
music's disjointed, episodic qualities.[6]

The sketches to "The Marshes of Glynn" also point to another aspect of the composer's style. Sometimes, as in such later songs as "The Green River," "Le Ciel," or "En sourdine," the composer arrives at a strong, internal cadence that practically brings the music to a halt. This typically occurs just before the middle, contrasting section. Carpenter seems to have reached such a juncture at the end of his sketches to "The Marshes of Glynn," suggesting that in this song the juncture became an impasse.

Carpenter wrote another unpublished and undated song (this one complete) during these years, namely, "Dawn in India" to words by Laurence Hope (1865–1904). Laurence Hope was a pseudonym for Adela Florence Nicholson, best known for her children's poetry. In this poem she portrays an Indian dawn, with cool breezes and morning larks "whose plaintive murmurs seem to say, I wait the sorrows of the day." Carpenter's setting, which combines the bright diatonicism of "Go, Lovely Rose" and the lilting rhythm of "May, the Maiden," points to a date of 1908 or thereabouts. Indeed, two versions of the song seem to document the composer's evolution from the Straussian "Die vier Jahreszeiten" to the more individual "Go, Lovely Rose" and "May, the Maiden": the second version overhauls the Wagnerian middle section, with its modulations by third, in favor of a restrained diatonicism colored gently by augmented triads and secondary dominants. In any case, the revised "Dawn in India" is every bit as good as Carpenter's other songs of 1908. Further, the song unveils the composer's interest in the Orient, although the exotic element here consists simply of little pentatonic ripples that depict the breezes of India.

In a lighter vein Carpenter wrote in 1908 the unpublished song "The Debutante" with his friend John T. McCutcheon for McCutcheon's Social and Pleasure Club. The club met in the cartoonist's studio in Chicago's Fine Arts Building, "for so many years the center of the city's artistic and cultural life."[7] Other members of the McCutcheon Social and Pleasure Club included the composer's wife, Rue, Ethel Hooper, Henry Blodgett ("Harry") Harvey, Laurance Ray, and Hazel Martyn Trudeau, a celebrated beauty and wife of the painter Sir John Lavery. In reminiscing about the club, McCutcheon recalled an anecdote that he felt captured the tone of the group: at a formal reception, Hazel had given her name, "Lady Lavery," to the announcer, who in return whispered to her, "Two doors to the left, madam." McCutcheon himself scandalized a "futurist" party in honor of the traveling Armory Show by turning up as a Matisse nude in lumpy, pink underwear. For the Social and Pleasure Club meetings, he rolled in a piano: "To hear John Carpenter accompany Harry Harvey in 'Gypsy John,' or Laurance Ray in 'Rolling Down to Rio,' was worth five dollars a ticket any day."[8]

McCutcheon and Carpenter wrote "The Debutante" (subtitled "A Ka-Koon Song") for a special party in honor of the debutantes of 1908. They sent copies of the song "to five different buds, Lucy Blair, Marion and Barbara Deering, Harriot Houghteling and Peggy Ayer, better known nowadays as Margaret Ayer Barnes, the novelist. I am afraid I let each girl assume what she would!"[9] In the song's verse the debutante "bids her doll goodbye" and "spreads her little butterfly wings"; in the chorus she emerges from her cocoon, her heart "full of sentiment for you, and you, and you!" Carpenter sets the verse as a slow waltz "to be sung with extreme languour," then shifts to a ragtime-flavored $\frac{4}{4}$ for the chorus (hence, the pun on "cocoon" and "coon"). The song resembles early Kern and Berlin, both of whom Carpenter, in later years, would praise highly; at the same time, the music's closeness to McCutcheon's ironic sophistication distinguishes it from popular musical comedy.

By the time Henry Harvey performed the song (presumably at the Social and Pleasure Club), McCutcheon had written some additional verses, each one growing more antic and satirical. He also had added a series of exclamations for both the debutante ("I wonder who'll be there," "Oh, what had I better wear," etc.) and her mother ("Put something around your neck," "Ask papa to give you a check," etc.). The song appeared in a program as "To the Debutantes of 1908 (A Co-Coon Song): Song for Baritone, Opus 1." In 1927 Carpenter sent a copy of "The Debutante" to McCutcheon, writing: "I thought you might like to file among your own archives the original copy of our masterpiece. I am ready to dare any other pair of collaborators to write a better song."[10]

A certain ironic detachment not unrelated to "The Debutante" emerges in the composer's four art songs from 1909—"Little Fly," "The Heart's Country," "Looking-Glass River," and "The Green River." Although like the earlier "Go, Lovely Rose," these songs reflect nature's rightness, they contain a greater sense of romantic alienation. In "Little Fly," one of William Blake's (1757–1827) *Songs of Experience,* the poet faces death with some equanimity by comparing his lot to that of a fly, but the childlike analogy only heightens the poet's bleakly humorous tone. In "The Heart's Country," by Florence Wilkinson, the poet "cries out" for an inner freedom comparable to the openness of hill, sea, and sky. (Carpenter probably knew Wilkinson, a Chicago poet and a member of Harriet Monroe's inner circle.) Robert Louis Stevenson's

"Looking-Glass River" presents a utopian mirror world: "How a child wishes to live down there!" And in Lord Alfred Douglas's "Green River," the poet hopes to "awake from this uneasy night" and find "some voice of music manifold." As a group the feeling suggested by these songs is, simply, one of paradise lost.

Carpenter's four 1909 art songs also show musical advances that stem from the composer's continuing study with Ziehn. Their new sense of harmonic daring in particular reveal Ziehn-like permutations: many progressions, for instance, retain one or two stationary voices, while the others move chromatically. In the first phrase of "Little Fly" (ex. 11), the fly's buzzing inspires such writing in the piano accompaniment; each of the phrase's two-measure groups chromatically slinks from I to V, in the process creating such fearless sonorities as Ab, Bbb, B, Eb (see the second beat of "play," m. 4). "Looking-Glass River" and "The Green River" are even richer harmonically, with such novelties as secondal, quartal, and quintal chords and such modally conceived ideas as the rocking back and forth between I and vi° ("Looking-Glass River") and I^{13} and VII ("The Green River"), both over a tonic pedal. These songs further use traditional harmonies, like the French augmented sixth chord, in unusual spacings and contexts. Such harmonies often anticipate sophisticated popular music of the later twentieth century.

EXAMPLE 11.   Carpenter, "Little Fly," mm. 1–6.

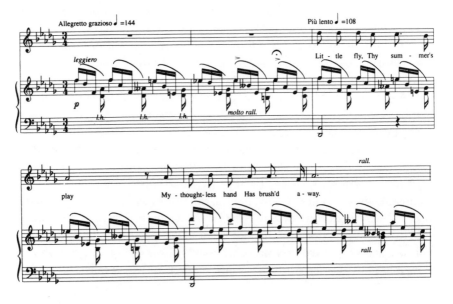

The vocal parts similarly show a growing maturity; they are less conventionally tuneful, more poetically conversational than the earlier songs. The singer Mina Hager emphasized this particular feature of "The Green River": "What he uses is not Sprechstimme; it is rather what one critic called Glorified Speech, because it sings almost as one would speak it."[11] As it happens, the "Glorified Speech" of "The Green River" is not all that representative: the composer writes the word *recitando* at the top of the score, and the speechlike melody serves a specific poetic function, which is to depict Lord Alfred Douglas's silent landscape (ex. 12). But in general Carpenter's mature songs frequently have the conversational intimacy that Hager finds epitomized in "The Green River."

Carpenter's new melodic plasticity accommodates all kinds of subtle word painting. In "Little Fly," at the end of the line "My thoughtless hand Has brush'd away," the melody moves upward to depict the act of brushing

EXAMPLE 12.   Carpenter, "The Green River," mm. 1–11.

away a fly, even though, given the previous phrase, we expect the line to move downward. Similarly, in "Looking-Glass River" and "The Green River," the vocal line embodies two kinds of waterways: one smooth and gleaming, the other twisted and quiet. The finely wrought, highly economical piano accompaniments similarly show greater refinement than before, whether it be the gentle buzzing of Blake's "Little Fly" or the extreme delicacy of Douglas's "Green River." The pentatonic ostinato in the "Looking-Glass River" is particularly noteworthy; Upton calls the song "rich in carillon effects of great attractiveness."[12]

"The Green River" and "Looking-Glass River" became Carpenter's first songs to gain real repertory status—as opposed to the fleeting popularity of some of the earlier songs. Over time critics and musicians often cited "The Green River" in discussions of the composer, as in Mina Hager's 1970 reminiscence. Upton's survey, in fact, devoted more attention to "The Green River" than to any other single American song written between 1750 and 1930. For its part, "Looking-Glass River" became one of the composer's few early songs to be recorded commercially.

With their rich harmonies, fluid vocal lines, and exquisite piano writing, "The Green River" and "Looking-Glass River" suggest the influence of Debussy. In later years Carpenter himself named Debussy—along with Bach, Mozart, Beethoven, Wagner, Brahms, and Stravinsky—as his favorite composers.[13] But he disavowed any knowledge of Debussy at the time he wrote "The Green River," stating, during World War I:

> I do admire intensely certain phases of the modern Gallic manner. Its subtlety, its rare restraint and economy, its power to evoke atmosphere. And for me it is the school that could least be spared from present-day musical literature. But I have never consciously allowed my pen to be directed by what the Frenchmen are doing. My music is myself. The song, "Green River," was written some thirteen years ago, before—strange as the admission must sound—I had even heard or seen a note of Debussy's music.[14]

Carpenter's disclaimer raises many questions, however. If the composer made these statements about 1917, as it appears, and composed "The Green River" in 1909, how does he arrive at a figure of "some thirteen years ago"? Did he actually write "The Green River" about 1904? And revise it in 1909? Is the reference to "thirteen years" a mistake? In any case there seems no reason to doubt the essential point that the composer was not familiar with Debussy when he wrote "The Green River" and "Looking-Glass River."[15]

How, then, do we account for the parallel chords and pentatonicism of "Go, Lovely Rose"? the "carillon" sounds of "Looking-Glass River"? the whole-tone shimmers of "The Green River"? Something of Debussy's influence might have been passed on secondhand: Leon R. Maxwell suggested Cyril Scott as one such source.[16] Another possibility might have been Puccini; Elgar, in fact, was studying *Madama Butterfly* at about the same time that Carpenter worked with him.

Quite simply, Carpenter's music, under Ziehn's guidance, was moving toward a style that would naturally incline him to Debussy when he did encounter him. Maxwell notes a similar phenomenon in the career of England's John Ireland (1879–1962); he could just as well have mentioned Spain's Manuel de Falla (1876–1946), Austria's Alexander von Zemlinsky (1872–1942), or any number of figures born in the 1870s (Carpenter and Zemlinsky shared the unusual distinction of writing works inspired by Wilde, Tagore, and Langston Hughes).

Carpenter probably discovered Debussy the following year, in 1910. He could hardly have avoided him: in February, Frederick Stock performed Debussy *(La Mer)* for the first time with the Chicago Symphony, and in November, Mary Garden launched the memorable Chicago premiere of *Pelléas et Mélisande*.[17] In fact, the establishment of the Chicago Grand Opera in 1910 by soprano Mary Garden and conductor Cleofonte Campanini signaled a new era in the city's musical life. During the previous decade Chicagoan taste in opera had changed swiftly and dramatically from Wagner to Italian opera,[18] but the Chicago Grand Opera now popularized the French repertoire, which, except for *Faust,* had never found a receptive audience in Chicago.

Mary Garden pointedly made her Chicago debut on 5 November 1910 as Mélisande, a role for which she had been selected and coached by Debussy himself.[19] According to Robert Marsh, the production, under Campanini's direction, spared no expense, as the Grand Opera hired a French stage director to bring the opera's "full artistic significance" to light. "While the public was confused," writes Ronald L. Davis, "at the same time it was intrigued. And after a few more hearings, the *Tribune* pronounced it 'the success of the season.'"[20]

In the remainder of the 1910–11 season, Mary Garden similarly conquered Chicago audiences as Louise, Thaïs, and Salome (sung in French to the original Oscar Wilde text). Her Salome, which included some impassioned lovemaking with the severed head of John the Baptist, left the first-night Auditorium audience literally speechless. The city's police chief later reported back to the citizens of Chicago: "It was disgusting. Miss Garden wallowed around like a cat in a bed of catnip."[21] (Even the sympathetic Alson J. Smith remarked, "It must be admitted that Mary put a little more of herself into the thing than the script called for.")[22] The following season Garden triumphed in two Massenet operas, *Le Jongleur* and *Cendrillon*. In the latter she shared the stage with Maggie Teyte, another famed Debussyan (leaving Arthur Meeker to recall how "even as a child I thought the rival Mélisandes looked at each other queerly").[23] This performance possibly marked the beginnings of Carpenter's long association with Teyte.

Carpenter's music supports the notion that he discovered Debussy in 1910. First, the ungainly whole-tone writing in *The Faun* suggests an immediate, undigested discovery. Second, 1910 witnessed five Verlaine settings ("Chanson d'automne," "Le Ciel," "Dansons la gigue!" "Il pleure dans mon coeur," and "When the Misty Shadows Glide" ["En sourdine"]) and possibly two others (the unpublished "Triste était mon âme" and the incomplete "Chevaux de bois"). (Carpenter composed all seven songs in French, although the five published ones included English translations as well.)[24]

The Verlaine songs, moreover, conspicuously exhibit a few distinctive Debussy trademarks: richly spaced ninth chords (especially on secondary dominants), open intervals in the high reaches of the piano (for the bell imagery in "Le Ciel"), whole-tone passages (more explicit here than the whole-tone inflections that arose from Carpenter's earlier use of French augmented sixth chords), modal and tonal ambiguities, and secondal harmonies (evoking some popular French music making in "Dansons la gigue!"). In fact, Arthur Farwell remarked that Carpenter's Verlaine songs remembered Debussy too well, "even to the point of forgetting his own characteristic manner."[25]

Carpenter actually retains a high degree of individuality in his Verlaine songs. One could hardly confuse, say, Carpenter's setting of "En sourdine" (ex. 13a) with Debussy's (ex. 13b). Carpenter's slow, barcarole-like three derives, for example, from such earlier landscapes as "May, the Maiden" and "Dawn in India." The steady, unhurried, almost monotonous rhythm of the melody line has a thoroughly American cast, showing a closer affinity with a Gershwin song like "Love Walked In" than to any song by Debussy. The song is also characteristic in its rounded ternary form; the lucid, diatonic harmonies; the widely spaced seventh chords; the restrained textures; the slow-moving harmonic rhythm; the jazzy, flatted sevenths on the words "vagues langueurs" ("langorous breath"); the similarly jazzy sequence at the phrase "Ferme tes yeux à demi" ("Close then thine eyes, my beloved"); and the gloriously sweet final cadence on "chantera" ("shall sing").

"En sourdine," "Le Ciel," and "Dansons la gigue!" seem the most inspired of the Verlaine songs. "Le Ciel" resembles "The Green River" but has a greater intimacy and poignance; indeed, it counts as one of the composer's finest songs. The first section of this ternary setting paints a serene landscape whose delicacy and economy look ahead not only to the composer's exquisite settings of Chinese poetry but to the opening of Copland's *Appalachian Spring*. The second section wavers uncertainly between augmented, diminished, and seventh chords as the poem contrasts the serene landscape with the murmuring of the distant town. In the third section, when the poet sadly asks what has happened to his youth, Carpenter sequentially moves to a climactic outburst that points, for the first time, to the song's key of B major. A resigned decrescendo, a ritardando, and an appoggiatura on the final word, "jeunesse" ("youth"), brings the song to an end, as the piano echoes the bell-like sonorities heard earlier in the piece.

EXAMPLE 13

a. Carpenter, "When the Misty Shadows Glide (En sourdine)," mm. 3–6.

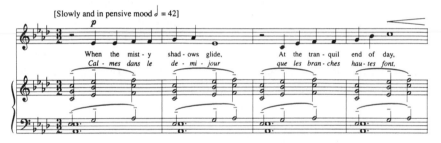

b. Claude Debussy, "En sourdine," mm. 3–5.

The bittersweet "Dansons la gigue!" has some polymetrical high jinks, with the voice part in a waltzlike $\frac{3}{4}$ and the piano part in a bolero-like $\frac{3}{2}$. Upton thought highly of the music's rhythmic ingenuity.[26] The song at once recalls the Spanish-French style of Bizet and Lalo and points to the Hispanic American style of Porter and Bernstein. Although hardly a ditty, it belongs in the same category as "Schifferlied," "The Cock Shall Crow," and other Carpenter songs that evoke popular foreign styles.

The three other Verlaine songs—"Il pleure dans mon coeur," "Chanson d'automne," and "Triste était mon âme"—interpret their melancholy texts not only through the use of the minor mode and fairly low registers but through ostinatos that give the impression of a heavy heart. "Il pleure dans mon coeur," for instance, uses a one-note pedal, D, throughout, reflecting the poem's rain imagery as well as its sadness. Borowski thought Carpenter's handling of such a technique "worthy of all praise" and superior to Cornelius's similar "Ein Ton."[27] All three songs show interesting modal propensities as well. In "Il pleure dans mon coeur," for instance, Carpenter does not define the D-minor tonality by way of the dominant (indeed, the song does not contain a single dominant harmony) but rather through an ambiguous chord with an E♭ that can be considered either a IV chord with an added sixth or a Neapolitan sixth with an added seventh. Similarly, in "Triste était mon âme," prominent A-minor triads give the G-minor tonality a Dorian coloring. And, finally, the four-chord ostinato at the opening of "Chanson d'automne" looks ahead to the modalities of rock music; in fact, this harmonic progression is identical to the opening of Eric Burdon's 1964 rock setting of the traditional "House of the Rising Sun," also recorded by Bob Dylan.

All in all the Verlaine songs mark yet another advance; they cast aside the genteel provincialism that had limited some of Carpenter's earlier work. At the same time, they do not ape European modernism but rather find their own way. More than the occasional appropriation of a certain chord or scale, this advance constitutes the real significance of Debussy to Carpenter.

In 1911 Carpenter reestablished contact with classic English poetry through settings of Robert Herrick's (1591–1674) "Bid Me to Live," William Blake's "Cradle Song," and William Barnes's (1820–86) "Don't Ceäre."

For the Herrick setting the composer selected three stanzas (out of six) amenable to a ternary musical design: the outer stanzas swear fealty to the beloved, while the middle stanza describes the lover's feelings. (In the printed score the text appears with a French translation by Maurice Maeterlinck.) Although not as ecstatic as such later love songs as "Light, My Light" or "Serenade," "Bid Me to Live" strikes a new, impassioned note unheard before. Its thick chords in the piano make it the richest of Carpenter's early songs. Bold enharmonics serve dramatic modulations from D♭ major (stanza 1) to D major (stanza 2) and back to D♭ major, this time with sweeping arpeggios (stanza 3). The melody itself, while true to Herrick's meter, is at the same time closer to American popular song than to European art song: a trenchant, four-note idea fills out four-measure phrases with almost complete regularity. The combination of square phrases, overripe harmonies, and sweeping arpeggios makes for a rather dated sentimentality. Even so, the song has an alluring, distinctive elegance.

"A Cradle Song" could hardly be more different—a reserved, thinly textured, limpidly diatonic lullaby, with a vaguely pentatonic ostinato that gives the whole a delicate, oriental coloring. Although Carpenter adapts the Blake poem to create a ternary design, like "Bid Me to Live," he does so by using only two stanzas and by repeating the first stanza at the end, as in his settings of "Go, Lovely Rose" and "Looking-Glass River." Carpenter seems inclined toward this kind of structure—with a literal repeat—when the mood is idyllic.

This "Cradle Song" is not the popular one from *Songs of Innocence,* however, but rather a later, darker, and less well known poem of the same name. The infant is no longer Jesus but a mortal baby; the poet detects "soft desires" rather than a "holy image" in the baby's face; and the infant himself weeps, not the watchful Nurse/Virgin Mary. As with "Little Fly," the music's bemused tone nicely captures Blake's irony.

"Don't Ceäre" is among Carpenter's most delightful, high-spirited efforts. It even charmed Upton, who admitted no liking for humorous songs. Using a poem in Dorsetshire dialect (which looks a good deal stranger on the written page than it sounds), Carpenter once again explores a folk culture: the use of dialect recalls "Treat Me Nice," while the vigorous hemiola looks back to "Dansons la gigue!" The music has its own profile, with drones and a *Ländler*-like lilt; its Nordic coolness reminds one of Nielsen in particular. Carpenter's inimitable wit comes to real maturity with this song, especially at the refrain, in which the young Jeäne, beleaguered by interfering relatives, cries out, with a kind of prefeminist defiance, "I don't ceäre if they do." Carpenter discovers in this defiance an especially authentic voice. Jeäne, after all, reminds one very much of his wife, Rue.

Carpenter's four songs from 1912—"Les Silhouettes" and "Her Voice" (both Oscar Wilde, 1854–1900), "Fog Wraiths" (Mildred Howells, b. 1872), and "To One Unknown" (Helen Dudley)—reveal a stature even more commanding than the songs of 1910 and 1911. "Her Voice" and "To One Unknown," in particular, represent Carpenter's biggest, most grand songs to that date. All four, however, show an expansiveness and spontaneity that illustrate, as Upton observed, the composer's growth as a songwriter.

"Les Silhouettes," for example, derives from the impressionist tone painting of "May, the Maiden" but is much more evocative (Largo mistico, writes the composer), with quartal harmonies, chromatic triads, and diatonic passages representing, respectively, the crying curlews, the billowing sky, and the happy sailor boy. The composer uses a dotted rhythm to skillfully interweave all three elements, "a striking instance of the economy of means to which, when he wishes, Carpenter is able to confine himself; and naturally the song is unified thereby as would scarcely be possible in any other way."[28] The music leads, eventually, to the gentlest of climaxes, the wonderful arrival, finally, of E♭ major on the word "pass" (ex. 14). The composer's understatement neatly matches Wilde's haikulike verse. Little wonder "Les Silhouettes" proved a favorite for Maggie Teyte, who, in selecting songs, was "very fond of trying to convey to the public the ethereal, mysterious quality that Debussy has put into the part of Mélisande."[29] Carpenter himself especially liked this song and arranged it for voice and orchestra in 1943.

The second Wilde setting, "Her Voice," like "Dansons la gigue!" reflects nostalgically on the end of a love affair. This time, however, the narrator is not the artist but the artist's lover: "I have my beauty, you your Art," the lover says consolingly. Carpenter creates a ternary design by using three of Wilde's six stanzas, in the course of which he freely interweaves, as in "Les Silhouettes," three principal ideas: jocular, dancelike music to depict the metaphor of the bee darting promiscuously from flower to flower; more somber *più lento* music as the lover sensitively addresses the artist; and dramatic, *recitando* music that recalls the love vows now broken. The composer's interplay of these ideas catches the shifting emotions of Wilde's poem.

In "Fog Wraiths" by Mildred Howells (daughter of novelist William Dean Howells), the "lost at sea" roll in with the fog to visit their old homes and seek their gravestones. Again, Carpenter plays down the three-stanza form in favor of a more subtle, through-composed design. Each phrase is similar but different enough to give the impression of one long, almost improvised line. This organic approach nicely reflects the poem's shape, as the fog rolls in and then recedes. The rich, modal harmonies in the piano's low range suggest the possible influence of Debussy's "Engulfed Cathedral" (1910), but the song is ultimately more like John Ireland's successful setting of John Masefield's "Sea-Fever," composed a short time later. Given its very modest means, "Fog Wraiths" proves more effective than the eye might

EXAMPLE 14.   Carpenter, "Les Silhouettes," mm. 32–43.

assume and makes a somewhat disturbing impression, not least due to the lingering D♯ over the final E-minor triad.

"To One Unknown" is also melancholy and set in a minor mode (B minor). The poet has communed with nature and art but not with the lover for whom she yearns. The rhetoric—both poetic and musical—harkens back to Tchaikovsky, but some melodic turns in both the voice and the accompaniment provide fresh, modern touches.

In May 1913 Carpenter began a lovely setting of Ernest Dowson's (1867–1900) "Ad Domnulam Suam," which he left unfinished. In June, however, he completed another Dowson song, "Terre promise." A song of sexual desire and release, "Terre promise" moves, like "Le Ciel" and "Les Silhouettes," from tonal ambiguity to tonal revelation. Surprisingly, Carpenter never published this exquisite setting, perhaps because he felt the song's languid eroticism was too personal. In any case, "Terre promise" remains one of Carpenter's most haunting songs.

The Carpenter songs from "Treat Me Nice" to "Terre promise" are amazingly varied but do not presuppose anything more than modest technical abilities. The vocal lines move typically by step, their ranges usually encompass nothing greater than an eleventh, and their tessitura lies comfortably in midregister. Mina Hager commented that Carpenter "used to hum . . . when he was composing—an octave below the melody line! I have often wondered if that might not be the reason that practically none of his songs go below B flat or higher than G."[30] Similarly, the piano parts have none of the flashy brilliance characteristic of the late romantic art song. What the composer demands from both vocalist and pianist is clarity, elegant phrasing, rich tone, and a thoughtful response to the poetry.

Indeed, these songs were distinguished by the excellence and suitability of their texts. The choice of poets—Herrick and Blake, Verlaine, the English "decadents" of the 1890s, contemporary Americans—reflected a songwriter of sophisticated and cultivated literary tastes; while the choice of poems—sonorous, lyrical, trenchant in their imagery—revealed a sensitivity to verse that can well accommodate music. Carpenter further helped transform these poems into good songs through skillful deletion and repetition of words, lines, and stanzas.

Carpenter's literary sophistication was related to his milieu. By 1900 novelists like Henry Blake Fuller, Hamlin Garland, and Theodore Dreiser and journalists like Eugene Field, John McCutcheon, and Finley Peter Dunne had already made Chicago a literary center to rival any in the country. But in the years just before World War I—the period of Carpenter's most active songwriting—poetry found an equally important voice in Chicago, as documented by the careers of Edgar Lee Masters (1869–1950), Carl Sandburg (1878–1967), and Vachel Lindsay (1879–1931); the growing popularity of the *Dial*, under Francis Fisher Browne; and the launching of Harriet Monroe's *Poetry: A Magazine of Verse* in 1912 and Margaret Anderson's *Little Review* in 1914. These and other activities established Chicago as one of the world's preeminent centers for poetry.

Carpenter was aware of these developments; indeed, he had his finger very much on the pulse of Chicago's literary life. A member of the Little

Room and the Cliff Dwellers, he set to music the verse of such local poets as McCutcheon, Field, and Wilkinson. According to Ralph Berton, Carpenter also frequented North Clark Street's Dill Pickle Club, a trendy literary saloon (before it became a speakeasy in the 1920s), where Ben Hecht wrote his *Daily News* column and where Jane Heap and Margaret Anderson ("openly and militantly living as husband & wife") edited the *Little Review*.[31] Carpenter also knew Harriet Monroe and helped finance *Poetry*. Monroe's literary tastes—which favored French symbolists, English decadents, Japanese and Chinese verse, and the delicate, vivid, modern verse she would label "imagist"—accorded with his own.[32] In fact, Carpenter found Dudley's "To One Unknown" in the first issue of *Poetry*. In the years ahead Carpenter set other poets favored by Monroe, including Tagore, Yeats, Teasdale, Li Po, and Vachel Lindsay, who stayed with the Carpenters for a few days in March 1917 (Lindsay sent ahead his poem "The Conscientious Deacon" for Carpenter's consideration).[33]

The authenticity and naturalness of Carpenter's songs derive at least in part from Chicago's responsiveness to poetry, especially to symbolist and imagist poetry from around the world. Significantly, as interest in poetry waned in Chicago toward the end of World War I, so did Carpenter's productivity as a song composer.[34]

In 1912 G. Schirmer published two sets of songs that Carpenter had written between 1908 and 1911: *Eight Songs for a Medium Voice,* consisting of "The Green River," "Don't Ceäre," "Looking-Glass River," "Bid Me to Live," "Go, Lovely Rose," "The Cock Shall Crow," "Little Fly," and "A Cradle Song"; and *Four Songs for a Solo Voice and Piano Accompaniment,* consisting of four Verlaine settings: "Chanson d'automne," "Le Ciel," "Dansons la gigue!" and "Il pleure dans mon coeur." In the same year Oliver Ditson published another three songs—"May, the Maiden," "The Heart's Country," and "When the Misty Shadows Glide (En sourdine)"—individually. In 1913 Schirmer published the four 1912 songs as *Four Songs for a Medium Voice.* Thus, in a mere two years nineteen major Carpenter songs came to light.

Carpenter explained that he had tried publishing his songs earlier but without success. Finally, in 1912,

I got through the door of the big Schirmer publishing house. I received an invitation from Mr. Schirmer himself. He listened to my songs and piano works.

"We'll publish them," he said. "Why haven't we heard from you before?" I politely told him that I had been sending him things for years. He called for the records, and they bore me out. He waved his hand in apology.[35]

Rudolph Schirmer (1859–1919) remained a Carpenter enthusiast. In 1914 he expressed to the composer "unbounded admiration for your work, the beauty of which is greatly enhanced by the repeated hearings," and he became one of the first of many admirers to suggest that Carpenter write an opera, something the composer would attempt but never accomplish.[36]

Carpenter's success with Schirmer owed no small debt to Kurt Schindler, the firm's consultant. In a letter dated 16 August 1912, Schindler told Carpenter that he had played the proofs of his songs "again and again for Mr. Schirmer and his associates. I believe it would give you great pleasure to see how your songs are being appreciated by each member of the staff, and how they are valued like priceless jewels. . . . I am simply entranced by them, and I can scarcely wait for the moment, when they will be appreciated by the great public."[37] In subsequent years Schindler continued to act vigorously on the composer's behalf.

A composer and conductor, Schindler (1882–1935), born in Berlin, settled in New York in 1905. He conducted at the Metropolitan Opera (1905–8) and then, in 1909, founded the MacDowell Chorus (renamed, in 1912, the Schola Cantorum, which, though still primarily a choral society, occasionally sponsored concerts of songs and instrumental music). In 1912 Schindler became choirmaster of Temple Emanu-El as well. His Carnegie Hall concerts introduced New Yorkers to new and little-known music; he championed the choral music of Musorgsky, Debussy, Busoni, Pizzetti, and Holst, among others. He also had an expert knowledge of European folk musics. Like Oscar Sonneck, he advised Schirmer in publication matters; Charles Griffes and others sought his friendship and counsel.[38]

Consequently, readers surely sat up when Schindler announced in a 12 October 1912 article for *Musical America* (titled "Composer Who'll Stir the World") that he had discovered an American composer "of such unusual accomplishments and culture, such gifts of melody and harmony that, to my mind, his success all over the world is already a matter of certainty."[39] Writing in a Schirmer *Bulletin,* Schindler subsequently identified this "great hope for American music" as Carpenter.[40] (Carpenter gratefully dedicated the publication of "Little Fly" to his new friend.)

As critics acquired their own copies of the songs, they, too, responded favorably. Arthur Farwell, whose opinion also carried considerable weight, wrote in *Musical America:*

> The essence of the composer's thought is concentrated in "The Green River," on the superlatively beautiful poem of Lord Alfred Douglas. . . . Modernity, ultra-modernity, if you will, animates this song from the first bar to the last, but it has authentic originality and timeliness. Each successive thought is crystal clear, and expressed with a simplicity and lucidity which are among the composer's happiest characteristics.[41]

Albert Cotsworth agreed: "The songs are all beautiful, all individual, all thoughtful, all aboundingly sincere."[42]

Philip Greeley Clapp, fresh from his Harvard doctorate, his own symphonies soon to be played by Muck and the Boston Symphony, wrote an extensive and warmly appreciative review of the songs for the *Boston Evening Transcript* of 13 November 1912: "Among recent outcroppings of maturity in American music, none can be more interesting than the twelve new songs by John A. Carpenter." Clapp argued that the composer displayed a healthy indifference to both "European theories and tendencies" and "artificial 'nationalism' of the restricted sort" and that his music was distinctly American only because it was "so thoroughly imbued with the American point of view and attitude toward life" and composed by "a person of strongly American ideals coupled with broadly cosmopolitan culture."[43] In the ensuing decades many would echo and restate Clapp's assessment of Carpenter's nationalism.

Others opined that Carpenter's songs had, in fact, some connection to European—and especially French—"tendencies," but that ultimately the music was American and individual just the same. The singer Alma Gluck, for example, stated in 1912: "He [Carpenter] has the force and originality of Strauss and the charm and refinement of Chausson. But more than that, he is himself."[44] In a 1919 discussion on Carpenter, Maxwell specifically distinguished Carpenter from the modern French style:

> It might once have been possible to pass Carpenter by with the remark that his songs were really French. . . . Whatever the source of Carpenter's style, it has long since become extremely individual and it has always been very beautiful. If a love of refined detail, of closely united and very expressive melodic phrases, of color, of atmosphere, is French and only French, then of course Carpenter's work is French; but I think I hear a beautiful American work when I listen to a Carpenter song which has these qualities, just as I feel that

John Ireland is none the less a worthy English composer because his songs also exhibit similar qualities. One may easily find a French prototype for songs like "Green River," "When the misty shadows glide," and the songs with texts by Verlaine, because the verses demand the uncertain atmosphere which we associate with French songs.[45]

Deems Taylor noted, "His music sounds French until you analyze it, when you discover that it sounds like Carpenter."[46]

Arthur Farwell similarly commented that Carpenter's published songs of 1912 and 1913 recalled "Minerva springing full-grown from the head of Jove." Even the earliest songs revealed the composer's "unique personality":

It is Carpenter's distinction, in a sense, to have begun where others have left off. He is a personality of the new musical time with its new and trans-formed outlook upon the art. The margin of advance gained by the most recent developments of modernity, more especially from the French stand-point, becomes his main territory, while it would be well-nigh impossible, from his work, to suspect that the old ground of tradition and formula had ever existed. Far from his modernity meaning complexity, it is attained gen-erally by means of a veritably startling simplicity. It is the *principles* of mo-dernity which interest him, and he seeks the simplest means of their exemplification. Above all, he takes high rank in the sensitive perception of beauty.[47]

Carpenter dedicated three of the 1908–13 songs to individual singers: "May, the Maiden" to Maggie Teyte, "The Green River" to Mrs. Samuel Wright, and "Bid Me to Live" to Henry Harvey (who had premiered "The Debu-tante"). These singers performed the songs even before publication. Maggie Teyte, for instance, sang some of the songs in Albert Hall, London, in October 1912, possibly the first public performance of the pieces; Mrs. Wright sang "Her Voice," "Don't Ceäre," "Les Silhouettes," and "Looking-Glass River" on 11 December 1912 at the same Schola Cantorum concert in which Elman and Carpenter premiered the Violin Sonata; and at the least, Henry Harvey would have sung these songs at informal gatherings in Chicago.

Carpenter further won endorsements from America's two most famous song recitalists—Alma Gluck and John McCormack. In October 1912 Gluck hurriedly put aside new discoveries of Rimsky-Korsakov and Ravel to tell a *New York Times* reporter about "the songs of a man who has just come to the fore as a serious song writer, and who will, I think, take the laurels away from every other American engaged in that occupation. I mean John Alden Carpenter."[48] She sang two Carpenter songs in Carnegie Hall on 2 November 1912, including "The Green River," which had to be repeated.[49] As for Mc-Cormack, given his high regard for Carpenter's Violin Sonata (see chap. 4), he almost certainly would have known the songs but apparently included only "Go, Lovely Rose" in his repertoire.[50]

Another renowned recitalist, the Dutch contralto Julia Culp, sang "Go, Lovely Rose" and "The Cock Shall Crow," as well as two *Gitanjali* songs, in Carnegie Hall on 24 February 1914. Culp discovered Carpenter while touring the States in 1914: "I found a wonderful American composer that ranks among the best of the modern European composers," she told a reporter. "He is John Alden Carpenter, a young Chicago banker [*sic*], who writes wonderful, wonderful music."[51] In the meantime, Lucille Stevenson and Frank Parker promoted Carpenter in Chicago. Stevenson, whose adventurous repertoire included Debussy, Strauss, and Cyril Scott, performed "The Cock Shall Crow"; Parker sang nine Carpenter songs on 22 May 1913 in Chicago with the composer at the piano.

Other early interpreters of the Carpenter songs included Tom Dobson, who sang "Le Ciel" and "A Cradle Song," and Louise Homer and Christine Miller, both of whom sang "Don't Ceäre." Homer's recording of "Don't Ceäre," in fact, was the only recording of a 1908–13 song made during the composer's lifetime. Unfortunately, the accompaniment, transcribed for wind band, marred her spirited rendition.

The 1908–13 songs found numerous other friends all across the country. In 1914 one singer wrote to the editors of *Opera Magazine* to say that the Carpenter songs were performed "as far west as Missouri."[52] Louis Untermeyer, who received a copy of the 1912 Schirmer volume from Carpenter, informed the composer that after his wife sang "The Green River" at a small musicale, "one intensely critical friend was actually dumb for the first time in many talkative years, and there was the suspicion of tears in the eyes of the less hardened trio." Untermeyer further wrote that "The Green River" had, unlike Debussy, "the surge of life beneath the thin veil of atmosphere"; that "Le Ciel" was "deeper" than Ravel; that "Go, Lovely Rose" (which Untermeyer would, in time, anthologize) "has haunted me for days." "I cannot get over the verve in the Stevenson ditty ['The Cock Shall Crow']—and the merry naïveté of the Dorset 'Don't Ceäre' (especially your treatment of the second verse) fairly waltzes through my none-too-roomy brain."[53]

As late as 1930 William Upton recognized the importance of Carpenter's early Schirmer/Ditson songs: "Surely, 1912 was a memorable year in American Song, for during this year appeared John Alden Carpenter's first published songs."[54] After World War II, however, these songs slipped into obscurity. Performances and recordings—like Donald Gramm's 1963 recording of "Looking-Glass River"—proved few and far between.[55] Historians tended to view Carpenter's songs as part of a Debussy trend in America. In 1952 Lucille Mendenhall, for example, wrote, "Carpenter's songs have tints rather than solid colors, and . . . show a strong kinship to Debussy."[56] In more recent times such comparisons occasionally evolved into dismissals like Hans Nathan's 1960 assessment: "The songs of John Alden Carpenter . . . fall entirely under the influence of Debussy's concepts, around 1910, and adhere to them for more than ten years. Their delicate sonorities and evocative poetic atmosphere reveal a musician of taste and craftsmanship but only within the limits of a style that was not sufficiently his own."[57]

Even in Carpenter's own time, all the songs from "Treat Me Nice" to "Terre promise" were quickly overshadowed by the publication of *Gitanjali* in 1914. But these settings represent the bulk of Carpenter's vocal output and have, moreover, an elegance and simplicity not superseded by the composer's later, more demanding songs. They are, quite simply, compositions of great beauty and offer one of the best hopes for a renewed appreciation of Carpenter.

CHAPTER SIX

From *Polonaise américaine* to *Gitanjali*

1912–1913

In 1914 Carpenter wrote to the woman who had recently become his mistress, Ellen Borden, that he had sent to Schirmer "a queer raggy Polonaise and another queer thing without any name," both for piano.[1] The following year Schirmer published them as *Polonaise américaine* and *Impromptu*.

Composed in December 1912, *Polonaise américaine* evokes the rhythm (a $\frac{3}{4}$ meter with a strong, dotted rhythm on the first beat), form (ternary), and grandeur of the traditional polonaise, but mixed with features that derive from American popular music (ex. 15). Carpenter's own description—"queer raggy"—alludes to the influence of ragtime, and one detects as much in the music's syncopations. The work's relation to the tango also led Thomas Pierson to cite the *Polonaise américaine* as Carpenter's first piano piece to use Hispanic elements.[2]

The music's bass line, a relentless ostinato (marked *marcato*) that involves some erratic movement, including leaping tritones, provides another "queer" touch. Below the carefree polonaise tune, this bass churns on and on like an engine, finally grinding to a crashing halt at the very end. Like Dukas's *Sorcerer's Apprentice* or Debussy's "Mouvement" (from *Images* 1), it anticipates the postwar *style mécanique*. Indeed, the music's hard edge looks ahead to the composer's own 1924 *Skyscrapers* and gives further resonance to the title's self-proclaimed nationalism.

In contrast, the *Impromptu*, composed in June 1913, is a billowy, impressionistic piece, with delicate splashes of color and sensitive changes of mood in the course of its ternary design. Its alternation of doleful, pastoral, and romantic elements resembles the composer's setting of Wilde's "Les Silhouettes" (see ex. 14 in chap. 5). It has an improvisatory quality but none of the fleet virtuosity associated with the traditional impromptu; rather, it weighs each note slowly and carefully. Although not advertised as such in its title, the

EXAMPLE 15.   Carpenter, *Polonaise américaine*, mm. 5–10.

Impromptu also seems very American, not least in its subdued and eloquent intimacy, a feature that looks ahead to the Copland of *Quiet City*.

Allen Spencer gave one of the earliest performances—perhaps the premiere—of these pieces on 21 February 1914. In later years concert artists performed them only occasionally, but the works found their way into the homes of thousands of amateurs and students. In 1947 Schirmer still sold more than six hundred copies of the *Polonaise américaine*, more than any other work of Carpenter's except "When I Bring to You Colour'd Toys" and "The Sleep That Flits on Baby's Eyes" from *Gitanjali*.

Since 1947, however, the *Impromptu* has overtaken the *Polonaise* in popularity to become Carpenter's only piano piece recorded as many as three times: by Grant Johannesen in 1963 (Golden Crest CRS-4065), by Roger Shields in volume 2 of his three-record anthology *Piano Music in America* (Vox SVBX-5303), and by Denver Oldham in the *Collected Piano Works* (New World NW 328/329). All three recordings ignore the composer's metronome indication, ♩ = 72, in favor of both faster and slower tempos: Johannesen and Oldham play the work at a brisk ♩ = 92 and 82, respectively, while Shields opts for a slow ♩ = 60. Oldham's rendition (which contains a few mistakes, including a repeated measure in the B section) is not as polished as Johannesen's, but their conception of the work is basically the same. Shields's reading is more probing and personal. He refrains from blurring the Debussyan filigree with pedal, and he carefully observes the composer's markings, including staccatos, dashes, and the subito piano at the B section's midpoint. Indeed, this recording is among the most inter-esting and compelling in the entire Carpenter discography, its too-slow tempo notwithstanding.

When, in the summer of 1913, Carpenter began work on *Gitanjali,* a setting of six poems by Rabindranath Tagore (1861–1941), the Indian poet had only recently arrived on the Western literary scene. In many respects Tagore's background resembled Carpenter's: He came from one of Calcutta's wealth-iest and most artistic families and grew up in the Anglo-Indian environment of colonial India's native elite. After studying literature in England for two years (1878–80), he returned to Calcutta, where he earned considerable local fame as an editor, teacher, playwright, short-story writer, musician, and, above all, poet, even as he managed the family estate.[3]

As late as 1912 few outside the Indian province of Bengal knew anything about Tagore: his work was rarely translated from its original Bengali. In 1911, however, an English painter, Sir William Rothenstein, met Tagore while in Calcutta and became taken with both the man and the few English transla-tions of his work that he could track down. Tagore accepted Rothenstein's invitation to visit England and translated some of his own poems into En-glish prose on the trip over.

After reading through these prose translations, Rothenstein wrote to his friend William Butler Yeats, "It looks as though we have at last a great poet among us again."[4] Yeats, equally impressed, agreed to help edit the transla-tions for publication (the extent of Yeats's editing remains controversial). In November 1912 a collection of 103 of these translations, under the title *Gi-tanjali (Song Offerings),* was published in a limited edition.

Tagore's prose-poems created a sensation, especially in England. Yeats explained in his introduction to the collection that he felt like an Englishman in the time of Richard II discovering translations of Petrarch or Dante. "I have carried the manuscript of these translations about with me for days, reading it in railway trains, or on the top of omnibuses and in restaurants, and I have often had to close it lest some stranger would see how much it moved me."[5] Yeats read some of these poems in "his musical ecstatic voice" to a gathering that included poets May Sinclair and Ezra Pound and the mission-ary Charles Freer Andrews. "Carried . . . completely away" by the "haunting melody of the English, so simple, like all the beautiful sounds of my child-hood," Andrews "remained out under the sky far into the night, almost till dawn was breaking." Sinclair immediately wrote to Tagore: "May I say now that as long as I live, even if I were never to hear them again, I shall never forget the impression they made. . . . You have put into English which is absolutely transparent in its perfection things it is despaired of ever seeing written in English at all or in any Western language."[6] And Pound would later state, "When I leave Mr. Tagore I feel exactly as if I were a barbarian clothed in skins, and carrying a stone warclub." To Pound, Tagore's poems offered "a sort of ultimate common sense, a reminder of one thing and of forty things of which we are over likely to lose sight in the confusion of our Western life, in the racket of our cities, in the jabber of manufactured literature, in the vortex of advertisement."[7]

Pound recommended the collection to Harriet Monroe, who published six selections in the December 1912 issue of *Poetry*. Much to her surprise, Monroe soon after received a request for some copies of the journal from Tagore's son, who indicated that he and his father were in Urbana! (Tagore had left London for Urbana in the fall of 1912 with his son, who was completing a doctorate in agriculture at the University of Illinois.) Delighted at their proximity, Monroe arranged for a few visits during the winter of 1912–13 at the home of Mrs. William Vaughan Moody. Since the Carpenters very likely attended these gatherings, Monroe's recollection warrants full quotation:

> Tagore was a patriarchal figure in his gray Bengali robe, with a long gray beard fringing his chin. His features were regular and Aryan, his skin scarcely darker than a Spaniard's. The Hendersons and I—and others—used to gather around Mrs. Moody's hearth fire, listening to his chanting of his lyrics, or to his talk of Oriental creeds, which made us feel as if we were sitting at the feet of Buddha. His English was more perfect than ours, but we loved best to analyze the formal Bengali rhythms and rhymes as his high tenor voice sang them. And we were interested in his satirical-humorous observations of Western civilization, his surprise over its utter separation of religion from life. He was bitter about the British subjection of his country. "India has been conquered more than once," he would say, "but when the conquest was over life would go on much as before. But this conquest is different; it is like a great steel hammer, crushing persistently the spirit of the people."[8]

Tagore's own poetry made no separation between religion and art. His poems, though universalist in intent, had deep roots in the Upanishads and in Vedantist spirituality, especially (1) the belief in Brahman, a nonpersonal Supreme One, the Ultimate Reality that lies behind all appearances (when the poems say "God," Tagore essentially means Brahman); (2) the striving for union with Brahman while on earth (because the soul and Brahman are one and the same); (3) a belief in the divinity of nature; and (4) the concept of time as cyclic.

In November 1913 Tagore became the first Asian to win the Nobel Prize. The Western success of *Gitanjali* came when it did, writes an Indian observer, because it carried "a message of peace and love in a divided and embittered world."[9]

Tagore immediately struck a responsive chord in Carpenter, who spent June to December 1913 setting six of the *Gitanjali* poems. Carpenter clearly loved song texts that had Tagore's kind of lyric simplicity. He could readily sympathize with the poet's delight in children as expressions of God's goodness, his yearning for spiritual union with nature, and his resolve to live a full and rich life, sentiments that had already attracted Carpenter to the poetry of Blake, Verlaine, and Wilde. Furthermore, Ziehn might have encouraged some inclination toward mysticism; indeed, in his 1911 Violin Sonata, Carpenter titled the very Ziehnian slow movement Largo mistico.

Carpenter may even have had prior interest in Hindu philosophy. Certainly, Chicago's elite had long been intrigued with Hinduism—at least since Swami Vivekananda's memorable appearance there in 1893.[10] Like London and Vienna, Chicago showed, during these years, a pronounced inclination toward Theosophy, a religious movement that combined features of Hinduism and Judeo-Christianity. Judith Tick has written about the influence of Theosophy on such younger Chicagoan composers as Otto Luening and Ruth Crawford in the 1920s.[11] Closer to home, Carpenter's mistress, Ellen, was active in the Theosophical movement.[12]

Significantly, Carpenter composed *Gitanjali* shortly after falling in love with Ellen; she undoubtedly would have shared his interest in Tagore. One imagines that the concluding number of *Gitanjali*, "Light, My Light," specifically expresses Carpenter's exhilarating love for Ellen, and in 1914 or 1915 he began work on another *Gitanjali* song, "Pluck This Little Flower and Take It" (no. 6), that he ostensibly intended to present to Ellen as a private love song.[13]

Carpenter selected a different six Tagore poems from the six published in *Poetry*—he must have obtained a copy of the complete *Gitanjali*. Calling his own work *Gitanjali*, Carpenter arranged the songs as follows: "When I Bring to You Colour'd Toys" (no. 62), "On the Day When Death Will Knock at Thy Door" (no. 90), "The Sleep That Flits on Baby's Eyes" (no. 61), "I Am Like a Remnant of a Cloud of Autumn" (no. 80), "On the Seashore of Endless Worlds" (no. 60), and "Light, My Light" (no. 57).

In "When I Bring to You Colour'd Toys," an infant enhances the poet's love of nature. The poem's four stanzas compare a child's reactions to colored toys, music, sweet things, and kisses to the poet's own appreciation of clouds, water, flowers; leaves and waves; honey and fruit; and morning warmth and summer breezes, respectively. The poet implies that much as man pleases a child with toys and kisses, so God pleases man with the beauties of nature.

Carpenter sets only the first three stanzas, omitting the stanza about the kiss. Characteristically, he creates a ternary musical design, with the middle stanza as his climax (indeed, the stanza's imagery of crashing waves provides a natural high point). The first and third stanzas are in a very rich F♯ major; the second stanza begins in D major but moves back to F♯ major at its climax on the word "earth." Carpenter actually anticipates the move to D major in the middle of the first stanza, adding formal elegance to the song.

The melody is in a lilting three but has a plasticity that befits Tagore's prose-poetry and captures the rich melodiousness of Indian speech (ex. 16). Carpenter must have thought of Ginny when he wrote this melody; even as late as the 1940s, he would quote its first phrase (the music for the words "When I bring to you colour'd toys, my child") on letters, cards, and packages that he sent her. The opening motto, a broken triad that is repeated quite often in the course of the song, suggests the European pastoral tradition but also prefigures George M. Cohan's World War I song "Over There." The tinkling piano accompaniment evokes the nursery.

The second song, "On the Day When Death Will Knock at Thy Door," expresses the poet's determination to lead a full life even in the face of death. In the first stanza, the poet asks, "On the day when death will knock at thy door what will thou offer to him?" His subsequent answer takes the form of two more stanzas: the poet offers death "the full vessel of my life" (in one stanza) and "all the sweet vintage of all my autumn days and summer nights" (in the other stanza).

Carpenter sets this text in its entirety and then, characteristically, repeats the opening question at the very end to round out the song. The musical rendering of the opening question evokes traditional romantic rhetoric: for the voice, a repeated-note melody like a funeral march; for the piano, repeated minor chords and a four-note motive (perhaps related to the "fate" motive of Beethoven's Fifth Symphony) to depict death's knocking. The mood of this opening is very much that of Brünnhilde's tidings of death ("Todesverkündigung") from *Die Walküre*.

Whereas the song's first stanza is in D minor, the second stanza ("I will set before my guest the full vessel of my life") is in F major, although the

EXAMPLE 16.   Carpenter, "When I Bring to You Colour'd Toys," from *Gitanjali*, mm. 4–12.

tonic never actually appears. Rather, the music rocks back and forth between ii and V, reaching a fortissimo climax on the words "I will never let him go with empty hands," after which he subsides into silence.

The third stanza in like manner suggests, at first, F minor and then A♭ major, though, again, only elliptically. This stanza ends with a dominant seventh chord that functions both as V of V in A♭ major and a German augmented sixth chord in D minor, allowing Carpenter to return to the opening phrase in its original tonality.

The subtle tonal play only outlined here shows a significant advance over Carpenter's earlier music that aims for a similarly dramatic tonal scheme, for example, the slow movement of the Violin Sonata. Here the composer manages smooth and artful modulations through individual and poetic use of deceptive cadence, augmented chords, and modal ambiguity.[14]

In "The Sleep That Flits on Baby's Eyes," Tagore asks and then answers the following three questions, each in a separate stanza: from where comes (1) "the sleep that flits on baby's eyes"? (2) "the smile that flickers on baby's lips when he sleeps"? and (3) "the sweet, soft freshness that blooms on baby's limbs"? Carpenter sets only the first stanza. He casts the opening question in

$\frac{3}{2}$ time, whereas he sets the answer—the baby's sleeping eyes are "two timid buds of enchantment" from the "fairy village among shadows of the forest dimly lit with glowworms"—in $\frac{4}{4}$. The song's thoroughly diatonic melody is memorable, with an exquisitely soft climax on the syllable "glow." The piano's richly spaced diminished, augmented, and seventh chords, often supported by pedal points, provide a shimmering, fairy-tale delicacy.

Carpenter sets the next song, "I Am Like a Remnant of a Cloud of Autumn," in its entirety. The poem contains some of the themes and imagery that attracted the composer to certain poems of Verlaine and Lord Alfred Douglas: the poet compares himself to an aimless cloud longing to unite with the sun (stanza 1); he asks the sun to "take this fleeting emptiness of mine, paint it with colours, gild it with gold" (stanza 2); and when night comes he accepts that he will fade into darkness or perhaps appear as "a smile of the white morning, in a coolness of purity transparent" (stanza 3). Tagore's poem, however, is more prayerlike than the verses by Verlaine and Douglas that Carpenter set: the poet, acknowledging his fragmentary, useless existence, prays for the sun, clearly a symbol for God, to bring "varied wonders" to his life and "a coolness of purity transparent" to his death.

Carpenter's setting follows the shape of the poem: each of the three stanzas ends with a fermata. The first stanza moves from B♭ minor to E♭ minor; the second, climactic stanza modulates to D♭ major at its climax; and the third stanza begins, like the first stanza, in B♭ minor but ends in D♭ major. The vocal line exemplifies the kind of writing Mina Hager termed "Glorified Speech," a style that the composer often cultivated in his sad and confessional songs, although the tone here is unusually stentorian and bardic. The piano's tolling, rich chords, and the exotic augmented seconds, are also somewhat atypical—the net effect is a bit like MacDowell on the Ganges. The song contains, nonetheless, some distinctive features, especially the surprising conclusion in D♭ major, which wonderfully captures the poet's subtle and mystic suggestions of reincarnation.

The cycle's next poem, "On the Seashore of Endless Worlds," was the one that sent Charles Freer Andrews reeling into the London night. Yeats similarly singled it out at the end of his introduction to *Gitanjali* (for Yeats this poem spoke not only of children but of such "saints" as Tagore himself). The poem describes children at play "on the seashore of endless worlds." Their sea is not the sea of fishermen, pearl divers, and merchants, a sea of struggle and conquest and tempests, but rather a sea that "surges up with laughter." Its cosmic vision of worldwide joy, oblivious to greed and death, naturally spoke strongly to a world poised on the edge of cataclysm.

Carpenter ambitiously sets all five of the poem's stanzas, making this song the longest in the cycle and among the longest in his entire oeuvre. The poem's shifting perspectives—from the children to the pearl fishers to the "death-dealing waves"—inspires musical shifts of some richness and complexity, involving, among other things, changing key and meter signatures. The composer achieves unity, however, through the piano accompaniment's two basic motives: a singsong ditty that depicts the children (especially the motive *la–ti–do–la–sol*) and the broken figuration that represents the sea.

Carpenter exploits a ternary design only vaguely inherent in the poem (stanzas 1–3 and 5 mostly describe the activities of children, whereas stanza 4 emphasizes the personified sea) and casts the song in a rounded form, with the first and fifth stanzas in A♭ major and the fourth stanza providing a climax in terms of dynamics, tempo, high notes, and harmonic instability. The fifth stanza, however, contains some smaller climaxes of its own: the high, fortissimo F♭ (f♭^{2}), against the piano's B♭ octave in the bass, for the concluding phrase, "death is abroad" (ex. 17); and the sublime and surprising E (e^2), instead of B♭ (b♭^{1}), at the final mention of "worlds."

Carpenter's cycle concludes with a setting of "Light, My Light," in which the poet compares his inner joy to a world ablaze in a "sea of light." This poem, too, contains five stanzas, but short ones that Carpenter can smoothly fashion into a ternary form: an introduction over a dominant pedal (stanza 1); the main theme, in C major (stanza 2); a slightly slower middle section (stanzas 3 and 4); and a return to C major (stanza 5).

"Light, My Light" is among the most dramatic songs Carpenter ever wrote. Much of the vocal writing is forceful and high (often sitting between c^2 and g^2), and the piano part contains crashing chords and thunderous octaves and tremolos. The song concludes with a high G (g^2) for the soprano, with both voice and piano triple fortissimo. Upton was impressed:

> Here is no slender threadlike melodic line, but great bursts of golden tone like the full-throated voice of the orchestra. It is no song in the true sense of the word, but a flaming forth of elemental ecstasy. I know of nothing like it. It is written for no mortal voice. Perhaps archangelic voices might cope with its long-drawn trumpet-like phrases, but no earthly voice should attempt these soaring flights![15]

"These soaring flights" betrayed—perhaps more than anything else composed by Carpenter—the composer's admiration for Wagner; indeed, *Gitanjali* over time attracted some of the world's greatest dramatic sopranos.

EXAMPLE 17.   Carpenter, "On the Seashore of Endless Worlds," from *Gitanjali*, mm. 99–104.

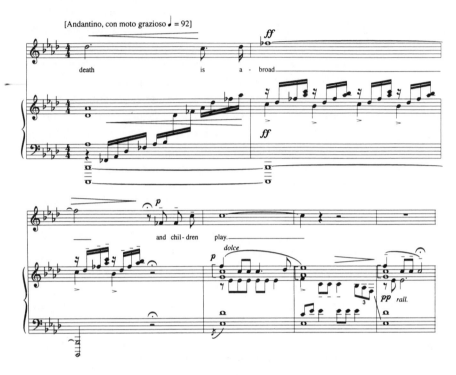

The song's main theme features a pentatonic, waltzlike idea in the piano, stylistically suspended somewhere between Schumann and Gershwin. Throughout, the music features fast-moving triads (including parallel augmented triads) and seventh chords. Whatever such harmonies owe to Debussy or Puccini, Carpenter fashions them in his own way; the middle section's repeated string of seventh chords (F^7–E^7–D^7–E^7 for the "butterflies" and the "lilies and jasmines"), for instance, exudes a decidedly jazzy flavor.

Gitanjali alternates three songs of childhood with three songs of adulthood—songs of innocence with songs of experience. Musical and poetic allusions often connect one song with another, though in subtle ways: the second and third songs begin with questions; the fifth song portrays a flood of water in which "death is abroad," whereas the sixth song depicts a flood of light in which "joy is abroad." Tonally, the music moves smoothly (usually by major or minor third) from the F♯-major opening to its distant C-major conclusion.

Do Carpenter's settings possibly reflect Tagore's own musical render-ings, which the composer may have heard in Chicago? Although Carpenter's music, as mentioned, captures something of the musical inflections of Indian speech, transcriptions of Tagore's music by A. H. Fox Strangways and later writers do not suggest a close—if any—connection.[16] And yet Fox Strang-ways himself admitted that such transcriptions could not capture the impres-sion of Tagore's singing:

> To hear him sing them is to realize the music in a way that it is seldom given to a foreigner to do. The notes of the song are no longer their mere selves, but the vehicle of a personality, and as such they go behind this or that system of music to that beauty of sound which all systems put out their hands to seize.[17]

In any case, Carpenter's exoticism is of a subtle kind. "There is warmth in his coloring," explains James Hall, "but no straining after the oriental."[18] *Gitan-jali*'s personal response to Indian culture deserves comparison with such works as Holst's *Savitri,* Roussel's *Padmâvatî,* and Zemlinsky's *Lyric Sym-phony;* indeed, *Gitanjali* represents their American counterpart. Whatever relation these varied Western styles have to the noble tradition of Indian classical music, Carpenter's sweet, ingratiating music is, significantly, clearly the closest to Indian popular song.

Schirmer's 1914 publication of *Gitanjali* featured an art nouveau border on every page. In addition, Carpenter framed the six songs with a prologue ("Credo") and an epilogue. The prologue quoted an unnamed Chinese source that, consistent with *Gitanjali,* declared the author's love for the eter-nal beauty of nature and, above all, for the "Source of my belief and my love." The epilogue quoted the following excerpt from Tagore's song number 13:

> The song that I came to sing remains unsung to this day. I have spent my days in stringing and unstringing my instrument.
> The time has not come true, the words have not been rightly set; only there is the agony of wishing in my heart.

The remainder of the poem—not given in the Schirmer edition—suggests that the "wishing" is for the face and voice of God: "I live in the hope of meeting with him; but this meeting is not yet."

Gitanjali was a critical and popular success. Shortly after its publication, Julius Gold wrote the composer: "I can honestly say that your songs appeal to me no less than do some of the best songs in the musical literature, not excepting even Hugo Wolf's! . . . In closing, I should say of your song-writing, what Rossetti in 1868 said of Walt Whitman's poetry—that it is 'incomparably the largest performance of our period.'"[19] In 1920 Henriette Weber referred to *Gitanjali* as the Carpenter work that "first stirred attention," writing, "Carpenter's tonal translations not only interpreted but illuminated. The words shone as through a prism. His music was more than anything else colorful, and yet it was controlled by a curious sense of fitness that resulted in a skilful blending of the Occidental with the Oriental."[20]

Julia Culp and Lucille Stevenson were among the first singers to include some of *Gitanjali* on their recitals, as was the American tenor George Hamlin, who sang "When I Bring to You Colour'd Toys" and "Light, My Light" in Berlin on 1 April 1914. Anne Thursfield performed "When I Bring to You Colour'd Toys" in London in 1920 (prompting Ezra Pound's dismissal of its "pseudo-Debussy accompaniment" and "mediocre" musicianship).[21] In the decades ahead *Gitanjali* attracted such outstanding singers as Eva Gauthier, Conchita Supervia, Rose Bampton, Kirsten Flagstad, and Eleanor Steber.

Flagstad's patronage of *Gitanjali* in the late 1940s represented, perhaps, the height of the cycle's prestige. The great Wagnerian soprano sang these songs on her American tour of 1949, including performances in Chicago on 13 November and New York on 11 December. After the Chicago performance she wrote Carpenter from Kansas City, "I was most happy to have the opportunity to sing your wonderful songs and your presence added greatly to the joy I felt." She assured him, too, that she would sing them better in New York.[22]

Carpenter hoped Flagstad would record the whole cycle,[23] but she recorded only "When I Bring to You Colour'd Toys" and "The Sleep That Flits on Baby's Eyes." Indeed, beginning as early as Culp and Stevenson, singers often sang just these two songs (notwithstanding Upton's claim that the first four songs were merely "preliminary to the supreme achievement of the last two songs"),[24] a predilection that became somewhat ingrained as the two settings became familiar anthology items. Because they were the sweetest, most ingratiating numbers, this surely left many musicians and listeners with a misleading impression of the work as a whole.

"When I Bring to You Colour'd Toys" was recorded as many as eight times: by Conchita Supervia, Rose Bampton, and Glenn Darwin in the days of 78 rpm; and in more recent times by Camilla Williams, Alice Mock, Kirsten Flagstad, John Hanks, and Alexandra Hunt on LP. One notable and questionable feature of these otherwise distinguished performances (Andrew Porter, in a recent lament on the singing of English, held up the Supervia recording as a model of sung English) is their degree of rhythmic laxity.[25] Apparently encouraged by Carpenter's occasional use of rallentando and melodic dashes, these recordings virtually forgo any regularity of pulse or beat. Moreover, they disregard the composer's metronome marking of ♩ = 144 and tempo marking, Animato, in favor of slower tempos that average ♩ = 106 (Flagstad's tempo, ♩ = 116, is the fastest; Williams's ♩ = 96, the slowest). At the third stanza, headed by Carpenter's admittedly vague direction *a tempo ma poco più lento,* nearly all the singers knock off exactly twenty points (Bampton shaves off thirty) to reach an average of ♩ = 86. Then, again in all the recordings, the final phrase slows practically to a dead halt, without any such suggestion on the composer's part.

The numerous recordings of "The Sleep That Flits on Baby's Eyes," on the other hand, take the $\frac{4}{4}$ section not ♩ = ♩, as indicated in the score, but considerably faster (nearly fifty points faster in the Flagstad recording!), until the approach of the word "glowworms," at which point every singer slows into a tempo somewhat like the original.

Apparently, both "When I Bring to You Colour'd Toys" and "The Sleep That Flits on Baby's Eyes" have long enjoyed an oral tradition at some disparity from the composer's written intent. In addition, this practice of slowing down "When I Bring to You Colour'd Toys" and speeding up "The Sleep That Flits on Baby's Eyes" has the unfortunate effect of making these two songs sound more alike than they are. The former should have something of the ecstasy of "Light, My Light," thereby balancing the entire cycle; the former should have the calm of a lullaby.

In 1914, at the request of Glenn Dillard Gunn, assistant conductor of the Chicago Symphony (and music critic for the *Chicago Tribune*), Carpenter orchestrated *Gitanjali* for an all-American Chicago Symphony concert. The composer made a number of changes for this orchestral version; most strikingly, he concluded "On the Day When Death Will Knock at Thy Door" with a single pitch on the dominant, rather than with a tonic triad.

Gunn and Stevenson premiered this orchestral version on 27 April 1914. Karleton Hackett reported that the songs "were delightful, and most appreciatively sung by Miss Stevenson, who was heartily applauded after each one, with several recalls at the end."[26] Carpenter, however, listened to his orchestration with "a great deal of depression" and "determined some day to make a new setting for these songs"—which he did in 1934.[27]

Carpenter approached the 1934 orchestration with much more experience in this area than he had in 1914. The 1934 orchestration is simpler and leaner than the original, with fewer glissandi and doublings. This later orchestration uses harp arpeggios, as in "I Am Like a Remnant of a Cloud of Autumn," or a piano, absent in the original orchestration, when a particularly rich effect is desired. Similarly, the sounds of the vibraphone and celesta are added to that of the glockenspiel for "The Sleep That Flits on Baby's Eyes." The 1934 orchestration also restores the triadic conclusion to "On the Day When Death Will Knock at Thy Door."

Carpenter revised the orchestration specifically for Mina Hager, who performed the work with Stock and the Chicago Symphony on 14 January 1936. Despite the fact that Hager had a bad cold, the press received the work enthusiastically. Wrote Claudia Cassidy, "The result is exquisite, pervaded with oriental languor, caught in the calm that is less resignation than understanding, filled with the most subtle pictorial effects, spilling out brief yet acutely tangible sounds of the surging sea, the rocking cradle, the full sweep of the poet's imagery."[28]

Carpenter hoped to interest Koussevitzky in the newly orchestrated *Gitanjali,* but to no avail.[29] Koussevitzky's nephew Fabien Sevitzky performed three of the songs, however, with Rose Bampton and the Indianapolis Symphony on 13 March 1943. Bampton had recorded, ten years earlier, not only "When I Bring to You Colour'd Toys" but "Light, My Light," proving that a "mortal voice" can, indeed, "cope with its long-drawn trumpet-like phrases."

CHAPTER SEVEN

From *Adventures in a Perambulator* to "The Day Is No More"

1914

On 29 April 1914 Carpenter informed Ellen Borden that he wanted to write "a little suite for orchestra" titled "From a Perambulator." "It would be all about the frightfully exciting things that a child sees when he is out with his nurse," he explained. He imagined a six-movement work: "The Little Rolly-Polly Perambulator," "The Policeman," "The Organ Grinder," "The Lake," "The Zoo," and "The Stars."[1]

As he wrote the work in the spring and summer of 1914, Carpenter apprised Ellen of his progress. He seemed particularly excited about the organ-grinder movement—now called "The Hurdy Gurdy": "I've been working at the Hurdy Gurdy since 9 this morning until 7 tonight—it's getting wilder and wilder." In another letter he identified the popular tunes he had used in this movement and confessed, "Sometimes I think it's going to be an awful mess—but it will be something new anyway."[2]

Carpenter composed "The Lake" while vacationing at Lake Geneva in Wisconsin. "The perambulator is on the edge of the lake with the big waves and the little waves rushing up to the very wheels," he wrote Ellen. Later, he told her, "I'm just finishing up the 'Lake.' It has taken longer than the others because the waves get so big."

During the summer, Carpenter visited the conductor of the Chicago Symphony, Frederick Stock, in Highland Park to show him his as yet unfinished score. "He reassured me a lot on the general question of balance and structure," Carpenter wrote Ellen.[3] Years later, Carpenter recalled this consultation with Stock: "After a quick 'lookover' his first question was: 'When will you finish this piece?' I answered, 'Oh, I hope in another month.' 'Hurry it up,' said he, 'get it done, and we will play it over. I think you have something there!'"[4]

Frederick Stock (1872–1942) would subsequently become Carpenter's greatest champion. During his thirty-seven years with the Chicago Symphony (1905–42), he played Carpenter more often than any other American composer aside from himself—fourteen works performed more than sixty times.[5] Stock, in turn, inherited the mantle of Theodore Thomas, founder and first conductor of the Chicago Symphony Orchestra. Thus, the line from Thomas to Carpenter, who grew up watching Thomas on the podium at the Auditorium Theatre, was a direct one.

Born in Germany, Theodore Thomas (1835–1905) came to the United States with his family at the age of ten. In his thirties he led the Brooklyn Philharmonic and an orchestra named after himself; in his forties he took over the New York Philharmonic. In 1891, somewhat daunted by personal problems and by the rivalry of Anton Seidl and Walter Damrosch, the fifty-six-year-old conductor left New York to found the Chicago Orchestra, which he directed until his death.[6]

Backed by Chicago's great wealth, Thomas "created a responsive and brilliant orchestra."[7] In 1902 the visiting Richard Strauss "was amazed" that *Also sprach Zarathustra* required only a single rehearsal. Elgar similarly stated in 1907, as mentioned, that "in Europe they have none better than the Theodore Thomas [Chicago] Orchestra."[8] According to Ezra Schabas, Thomas had a distinctive elegance and reserve: he conducted "with economy of motion, quiet control, and with no choreographic embellishments."[9]

For most of his tenure, Thomas conducted the Chicago Orchestra in Sullivan and Adler's acoustical and architectural marvel, the 4,200-seat Auditorium Theatre. But Thomas led a drive for a smaller theater, partly because the Auditorium was too big to fill, and partly because it rendered Mozart and Beethoven ineffective.[10] In 1904, shortly before Thomas's death, the new 2,566-seat Orchestra Hall opened. Thomas himself had attended to the acoustics of the new hall, designed by his friend Daniel H. Burnham, insisting on a short, sloped ceiling, curved walls, thinly carpeted aisles, and raised platforms for brass and percussion. Stunned by the recent Iroquois Theater fire, however, Chicagoan inspectors vetoed his recommendation for wood in favor of plaster and iron.[11]

In the meantime, Thomas's years in the colossal Auditorium helped nurture what would become the characteristic Chicago sound: resonant, massive, and blended. The Auditorium setting also matched the conductor's predilection for the grander works of Berlioz, Liszt, Wagner, Brahms, Bruckner, Dvořák, and Tchaikovsky. But Thomas continued to perform Beethoven more often than any other composer, whatever the theater. He showed, too, an adventurous side by introducing the new music of such young composers as Strauss, Elgar, Sibelius, and a number of Americans, including Chadwick and Paine. His tastes, if anything, grew more cosmopolitan during his Chicago years: only 64 percent of his Chicago programs, as opposed to 82 percent of his New York programs, consisted of Austro-German music.[12]

After moving to Chicago, Thomas became good friends with Bernhard Ziehn, who encouraged the conductor to take an interest in the entire community. One wonders how much Thomas's People's Concerts, at which Chicagoans could hear the orchestra for a dime, owed to Ziehn's idealism.[13]

Frederick (b. Friedrich August) Stock, in the meantime, had studied composition in his native Germany with Humperdinck and played violin in the Cologne Municipal Orchestra under the leadership of Franz Wüllner, a champion of Wagner, Brahms, and the young Richard Strauss. (Stock probably played the Brahms symphonies under the composer as well.)[14] In 1895 Thomas auditioned Stock in Cologne and invited him to join the Chicago Orchestra (as a violist). Stock's familiarity with modern music came in handy, and in 1899 Thomas appointed him assistant conductor.

After Thomas's death and some abortive attempts to interest Mottl, Weingartner, and Nikisch in the job,[15] the orchestra's board selected Stock as conductor (the orchestra did not change its name from the Theodore Thomas Orchestra to the Chicago Symphony Orchestra until 1912). Like Thomas, Stock remained the orchestra's conductor until his death in 1942 (except from October 1918 through February 1919, when he agreed, as a German citizen, to hand his baton over temporarily to Eric De Lamarter, the assistant conductor; he returned to the stage a naturalized citizen).[16]

Stock remained loyal to the traditions of Franz Wüllner and Theodore Thomas. "As Thomas's successor," writes Philip Hart, "Stock carried on the German tradition of the Chicago Symphony, both in its repertory and in retaining and building its basically German personnel."[17] Richard Strauss thought him a worthy successor to Thomas, and Busoni grouped him with Thomas and Ziehn as part of the triumvirate that had made Chicago a brilliant city musically.[18] In 1941 Charles Norman Fay, the utilities magnate (and brother of Amy and Rose Fay) who had helped bring Thomas to Chicago fifty years earlier, heard the Chicago Symphony in Boston and recognized Stock's "masterly continuation of the Thomas tradition." The Boston Symphony, he observed, might have "brilliance" and "unsurpassable technic," but not the quality, the tenderness, the balance and reserved emotion of our orchestra."[19]

New Yorkers similarly admired these qualities on those rare occasions—in 1911, 1921, and 1940—that Stock and the Chicago Symphony came east.[20] In 1921 Richard Aldrich reported that Stock "has put his orchestra in a position second to none in this country," praising especially the orchestra's sound: "Its tone as a whole is beautiful in quality, in mellowness and richness, in balance. The strings have a golden beauty and transparency of tone. The wood winds are delicious in their purity, their finish and finesse; especially the flutes and clarinets." Stock's performance of Brahms's Third Symphony, continued Aldrich, "was deeply musical in its conception, beautifully finished in the execution. . . . The conductor went hand in hand with the composer, seeking no 'effects,' but by skillful balancing, subordination and emphasis of the several choirs showing forth the depth and richness of Brahms's instrumentation as it should sound."[21] After hearing Stock conduct the Brahms Third Symphony nearly twenty years later, in 1940, Virgil Thomson similarly wrote: "Mr. Stock won his audience last night, as he has won audiences for thirty-five years, by playing them music very beautifully, not by wowing them. . . . The Brahms third symphony was a dream of loveliness and equilibrium . . . one of those rare and blessed readings in which the music seems to play itself . . . pastoral, poetic and effortlessly convincing."[22] And in appraising Stock's successor, Thomson complained that Désiré Defauw had "none of the dreamy quality that made Stock's playing of the same music so lovely and enveloping."[23]

Like Thomas, Stock enjoyed big, romantic scores, especially Wagner and Strauss. He frequently opened a concert with a Wagner excerpt (moreover, he chose *Siegfried* for his operatic debut with the Chicago Lyric Opera in 1923 and *Tristan und Isolde* for a return engagement in 1934).[24] He played some Strauss every year: *Death and Transfiguration* and *Don Juan* in his first season; *Also sprach Zarathustra* and *Macbeth* in his second; *Ein Heldenleben* and the Violin Concerto (as well as Mahler's Fifth Symphony) in his third; and so on. (Stock's successors, especially Reiner and Solti, continued this tradition of the Chicago Symphony as a great Wagner and Strauss orchestra into the second half of the twentieth century.)

Furthermore, Stock often edited the standard repertory for greater richness and color, frequently doubling woodwind parts. This included reorchestrations of the Schumann symphonies, adopted by Monteux and others.[25] But Stock did not stop with Schumann. Chicago critic Robert Marsh heard that at a rehearsal during Stock's tenure, guest conductor Sir Hamilton Harty stopped a few bars into Brahms's First Symphony and asked the orchestra, "What are you playing?" "We play Stock's version," responded one player. "Oh, I'm so terribly sorry," said Harty, "I always play Brahms's version." Marsh also remembered a reorchestrated Chausson symphony with organ.

Stock, however, regarded Mozart and perhaps Beethoven as sacrosanct in this regard.[26]

Stock shared Thomas's commitment to the community. He retained Popular Concerts at reduced prices; he instituted children's concerts, which he himself conducted; he established, in 1920, the Chicago Civic Orchestra as a training ensemble under Chicago Symphony supervision; and he promoted local composers.

Stock not only continued but surpassed Thomas's commitment to new music, to the point that only East Coast provincialism would preclude comparison with Koussevitzky and Stokowski in this particular area. Indeed, in discussing the repertories of Mengelberg, Damrosch, Koussevitzky, Stokowski, and Stock in the mid-1920s, Daniel Gregory Mason concluded that Stock's programming was the "most stimulating and adventurous," and that it showed "catholicity of taste and wide artistic range."[27] Alson J. Smith pointed out, for instance, that whereas "Thomas had had little use for Russian music," Stock "presented the works of Glazounoff and Miaskowsky, displaying particular affection for the latter. Nine of Miaskowsky's symphonies were programmed in Chicago and his Sixth Symphony was given nine performances!"[28] Miaskovsky dedicated his Tenth Symphony to Stock, writing to the conductor, "I wish to thank you for the attention you give to my music and, if I may speak for others, to express the gratitude that we, Russian composers, owe you for the frequent performances of our compositions."[29]

In the course of his career, Stock introduced Chicago not only to Glazunov and Miaskovsky but to works by Mahler, Debussy, Scriabin, Schoenberg, Stravinsky, Casella, Hindemith, Honegger, Milhaud, Bloch, Shostakovich, and others. According to Otto Luening, Stock often said, "You cannot hate a piece if you haven't heard it." He accordingly would sometimes repeat a new work at a given performance.[30] He also invited such composers as Glazunov, Rachmaninoff, Respighi, Ravel, Stravinsky, and Prokofiev to conduct their own music with the Chicago Symphony.

Stock also strongly supported American contemporary music, as documented by Howard Hanson's 1938 survey of new American works played by American orchestras, in which the Chicago Symphony Orchestra headed the list "with 272 compositions by 85 composers."[31] Stock's repertory included works by Barber, Bloch, Chadwick, Copland, Griffes, Harris, and Still, although he showed a special commitment to local Chicagoans, including not only Carpenter but Felix Borowski, Edward Collins, Eric De Lamarter, Henry Eichheim, Rudolph Ganz, Leo Sowerby, and Adolph Weidig.

Stock held American music in high regard. In 1930, for instance, he claimed: "For the first time in history, Americans are writing better symphonic music than Europeans. I refer to such composers as Carpenter and Sowerby of Chicago, and to Copland, Sessions, Ruggles, and the League of Composers group in New York." According to Luening, Stock would advise American composers "not to try to top" Bruckner, Mahler, and Strauss, but to look to their own world for inspiration.[32]

For their part composers often praised Stock, including Mason ("It will never be known how much American music owes to Mr. Frederick Stock alone . . . who for years has given it his great skill and his tireless loyalty"), Deems Taylor ("You can count on the fingers of one hand the men who have done as much for the cause of music in America as Fred Stock; and you might have a finger or two left over"), and Leo Sowerby ("I realized that here was a man from which I was to receive, not harsh criticism, but encouragement . . . so he is to everyone, kindly, genial, courteous, more than anxious to be helpful").[33] Carpenter himself observed that Stock had "a way of encouraging American composers."[34]

Indeed, no composer gave Stock more adulation than Carpenter—perhaps no composer had more reason to. In 1940 Carpenter even quipped, "I'm just a rabbit that Dr. Stock pulled out of his hat!" and went on to explain: "The great conductor's pushing and encouraging helped me to success. . . . I went to him for . . . advice like you would go to your father."[35] Such a father-son relationship (though Stock was Carpenter's senior by only four years) underscored a dream Carpenter had in 1922, in which he told Stock, "Goodbye, I'm on my way," and Stock responded, "All right, all right, just so you *know* your way."[36]

Carpenter's most extended tribute to Stock came in a speech given at a dinner in the conductor's honor at the Drake Hotel on 5 February 1924 (see app. A). He emphasized Stock's importance to American music, describing him as "the nurse, the doctor, and the godfather" of that "incubator baby" with "narrow shoulders and long, meager legs" and "subject to all the inhibitions that float out in all directions from New England."

> He picks it up when it falls out of its cradle, and he gives it the proper food and the proper stimulant that it needs, and it may be that eventually, if it can get over a slight tendency to kleptomania, it may achieve a physiognomy of its own. It has one thing to help it. It has the tremendous and deep-seated love and admiration of its godfather.

Carpenter further informed his audience that Stock, who founded the student Civic Orchestra, ran it without "one penny of reward, on top of an already tremendously full schedule." When the directors of the Civic Music Association awarded Stock one thousand dollars for his first year's work with the Civic Orchestra, Stock returned the check with the suggestion that the money be used to start a fund for the publication of American music. "Now, that, ladies and gentlemen, represents Mr. Stock."[37]

After the conductor's death, Claudia Cassidy wrote: "Simplicity itself, quiet, silver-haired, with a friendly twinkle that could be quickly quenched by frosty asperity, he had a native dignity no one challenged." Chicago Symphony violinist Phillip Kauffman similarly remembered: "He wasn't flamboyant, and he didn't play to the gallery. He had come out of the ranks, and he understood musicians."[38]

After World War II, posterity remembered Stock merely as an old-fashioned, competent conductor. "Papa Stock," recalled Arthur Meeker, was "a fine musician in the safe, comfortably spacious, German classical-romantic tradition." Stock hardly figured in Harold C. Schonberg's popular 1967 study *The Great Conductors*. And Michael Steinberg concluded that the recordings Stock left behind "do not appear to justify the esteem in which he was held as an interpreter."[39]

On the other hand, in 1991 Cassidy still put Stock in a class with Toscanini, Stokowski, and Koussevitzky. "You heard something individual," she claimed. "You felt richer on leaving the concert hall." According to Cassidy, Stock cultivated the kind of rich, dark tone that she had heard in only one other orchestra, the Berlin Philharmonic. Moreover, the bigger works had a commanding, cumulative quality. "When he did a big work," remembered Cassidy, "you would go somewhere." But she also recalled "wonderful" Bach, especially the Brandenburg Concertos, and superlative Mozart, in particular when he accompanied soprano Claire Dux: "I have never heard anything to equal it."[40]

Others remembered that Stock's performances were uneven, however. Otto Luening preferred his Beethoven, Schumann, Brahms, Tchaikovsky, and Strauss to his Mozart, Haydn, Schubert, Rimsky-Korsakov, and Debussy. Robert Marsh and Phillip Kauffman agreed that much depended on the conductor's physical and emotional health.[41]

Stock's recording of Schubert's Ninth Symphony, for example, has a finesse, a dignity, a relaxed warmth, and a tempered romanticism reminiscent of his German contemporary Bruno Walter.[42] The conductor freely changes tempo within movements, but in such a way as to help delineate form; for instance, he takes development and trio sections at noticeably slower tempos. Such practices might have influenced Carpenter, whose music often calls for changes of tempo from section to section. Stock's slower tempo after the grand pause in the second movement, for example, reminds one of the slow section toward the end of Carpenter's Piano Concertino. At the same time, Stock's performance has a rhythmic crispness and clarity that possibly constitutes a particularly American trait, as it points to Leonard Bernstein (much as Carpenter's music itself looks ahead to Bernstein's music).

Stock's own music possibly influenced Carpenter as well, since hardly a season went by that Stock did not play one of his own compositions. The incorporation of such popular tunes as "Old Folks at Home," "Yankee Doodle," and "Dixie" in his Festival March of 1910, for example, anticipated Carpenter's use of these same materials.[43] Carpenter thought Stock's Overture to a *Romantic Comedy,* first performed on 15 March 1918, a "joy." "I sat on the very edge of my seat and boiled and chuckled like a kettle on a stove of red hot coals. . . . I think you're right—'Sunshine' is the thing now that counts."[44] Greater familiarity with Stock's music might clarify this relation.

In any case, the composer's *Adventures in a Perambulator,* completed in 1914, responded to Stock's abilities and ideals: it was at once massive and tender, romantic and reserved. And although indebted to Strauss, the work did not try to "top" him; rather, it took its inspiration from the composer's own world and contained a distinctive personality of its own.

Carpenter decided on six movements somewhat different from those mentioned to Ellen in April 1914: (1) "En Voiture!" (2) "The Policeman," (3) "The Hurdy-Gurdy," (4) "The Lake," (5) "Dogs," and (6) "Dreams." He expanded the title to read *Adventures in a Perambulator* possibly in response to Lewis Carroll's *Alice's Adventures in Wonderland* (only Carpenter's "wonder" was not fantastical but rather mundane, evidence of his inimitable blend of mystic spiritualism and urban realism). (The use of "Adventures" possibly also involved a private joke with Ellen, whose husband, John, had just built a ship, *The Adventuress,* in order to explore sea mammals in Alaska.) Rather than a "little suite," the work turned out to be large in its scope and scored for a very full orchestra, including timpani, bass drum, snare drum, cymbals, bells, tambourine, triangle, castanets, xylophone, celesta, and piano. Carpenter dedicated the work to Rue's father, Joseph Winterbotham, here referred to as "my friend."

From the time of its premiere, critics have often noted similarities between *Adventures in a Perambulator* and Strauss's *Sinfonia Domestica* (1903), sometimes referring to the work as the "American Domestica." But unlike Strauss, Carpenter composed his music—as well as his program notes (see app. B)—from a baby's point of view (as opposed to the artist-husband's). The composer imagines the sights and sensations of the world through the eyes of a baby, the sort of imaginative act that, only the year before, he had explored in his Tagore settings. He comes before us not only as a child but as an infant, a conceit often encountered in children's literature and newspaper cartoons but rather unusual in music.

Much of the work's inspiration derived specifically from Carpenter's daughter Ginny, who played an important role in the composer's creative life. Ginny's governess, Margaret McNulty, remembered that the composer and his daughter were "inseparable"; they played tennis, croquet, and backgammon and took long walks together.[45] Mina Hager reports that "he [Carpenter] wrote many of his songs" for his "adorable" daughter.[46] Significantly, in the aforementioned dream about Stock, Carpenter also dreamed of Ginny, who "went to a fortune teller, who told her—Your father has been working on an unfinished piece of music—and he will go back to it and change it and finish it and it will be by far the best he has done."[47] (In the year subsequent to this dream, Carpenter, indeed, began his monumental *Skyscrapers*.) Even in his later years, Carpenter turned to Ginny for advice, as he would to Rue or Ellen: in a letter dated 1949, for instance, he asked Ginny what she thought of his "Jungle idea" for a ballet.[48]

Carpenter's oeuvre is in large part a lifelong chronicle of his feelings and thoughts about Ginny—as the infant in *Gitanjali* and *Adventures in a Perambulator,* as the twelve-year-old heroine of *The Birthday of the Infanta,* and as the Mary Pickfordish Herself in *Skyscrapers*. Ginny's love for jazz and comics contributed further to *Krazy Kat,* and her grief over her mother's death led to "Gentle Jesus, Meek and Mild." True, Carpenter had been inspired by children even before Ginny (the story of *Adventures in a Perambulator* reads very much, in fact, like his texts for the *Improving Songs*), but Ginny gave such inclinations focus and shape.

In the first movement of *Adventures in a Perambulator,* "En voiture!" (All aboard!), the Baby introduces us to his morning routine, in which his "very powerful" and "cheerful" Nurse straps him into his perambulator and takes him for an outing. Although Carpenter's music for this and the subsequent movements is highly picturesque ("Berlioz himself was rarely more realistic," noted one critic),[49] the actual relation between the composer's program notes and his music is somewhat oblique. Carpenter apparently does not mean to depict each and every image (nothing, for example, clearly suggests the line "A door opens and shuts"); nor does the music's form necessarily reflect the text's narrative structure. Rather, the written text suggests, essentially, the general mood and shape of the music.

This first movement, Larghetto, opens with a *giocoso* theme in parallel fifths, played by cellos, divisi. Innocent, joyful, with delicate flourishes of triplets, this theme represents the Baby waking up to a new day (ex. 18a). Next we hear the Perambulator theme, a delicate ostinato for violin, piano, celesta, and harp that vividly depicts the turning of baby carriage wheels. The slightly limping syncopation is said to have been inspired by a minor defect in one of the wheels of Ginny's perambulator (ex. 18b). Against this ostinato, Carpenter introduces the Nurse's theme, which resembles the opening phrase of *Hänsel und Gretel*'s "Brüderchen, komm' tanz mit mir," recast in an appropriately "powerful" guise (ex. 18c). (Carpenter thus suggests that, like the nannies of his own youth, the Nurse is German.)

"En voiture!" functions as a sort of prologue: it is short and never ventures away from its E♭-major tonality. The loose form varies, alternates, and combines its three principal ideas: the Baby's theme, the Perambulator theme, and the Nurse's theme. Vaguely resembling a rondo, the movement's main articulation consists of the four statements, slightly varied and rescored each time, of the Nurse's theme (although the Baby, anxious to get going, has the last word!).

The second movement, "The Policeman," opens with a brisk restatement of the Nurse and Perambulator themes, which leads into the main theme proper: the Policeman's theme, a $\frac{4}{4}$ march in A♭ major (ex. 19). Whereas the Nurse embodies maternal care, the Policeman stands for paternal strength (he is "taller than my father") and, as the next movement makes clear, repressive authority ("He walks like Doom"). His march is slightly pompous and stern, but its syncopated grace notes and stressed second beats lend a certain whimsy as well, somewhat recalling the toyland marches of Elgar and Herbert, but with a droll, exaggerated, almost cartoonlike humor of its own. (Such music surely fits the popular stereotype of the early twentieth-century Irish American policeman.) At ⑧ the Baby's "fascination" with the Policeman becomes visceral as the Policeman and Baby themes fuse.

The Nurse, too, feels the Policeman's fearful appeal; "she becomes less firm, less powerful" at ⑩, Poco più lento. A conversation ensues between the Policeman and the Nurse in a slightly slower middle section in D♭ major; the chromatic, *giocoso* bass instruments depict the Policeman, and the diatonic, *grazioso* violins portray the Nurse. Carpenter might have derived this passage from a similar one in *Ein Heldenleben,* but he depicts this seduction with a

EXAMPLE 18.   Carpenter, *Adventures in a Perambulator,* first movement.

a. Baby's theme, mm. 1–5.

b. Perambulator theme, ☐, mm. 1–2.

c. Nurse's theme, ☐, mm. 3–6.

distinctively dry and ironic wit. As the violins grow more and more animated, the bass instruments begin a chromatic ascent at four measures before ⑫. The violins answer in kind, until, in the Baby's words, "When I feel that they have gone far enough, I signal to my Nurse, a private signal." The "private signal" is the Nurse's theme, bawled out in a rude E major, triple fortissimo. "The Policeman resumes his Enormous Blue March," conveyed by a reprise of the A♭-major march.

In the third movement, "The Hurdy-Gurdy," the Nurse and Baby set off

EXAMPLE 19.   Carpenter, *Adventures in a Perambulator,* second movement, ⑦, mm. 1–4. Policeman's theme.

once more to a brisk version of the Nurse's theme in E major. Once again this serves as an introduction to the movement proper, in which a "dark man" and a "dark lady" (here Carpenter looks ahead to the Italian schemers in *Der Rosenkavalier*) grind out tunes on a hurdy-gurdy to the wild delight of the Baby—until the reappearance of the Policeman scares them off.

For this movement Carpenter uses snatches of popular melodies that an organ-grinder would have played in contemporary Chicago: the Miserere from *Il trovatore* (⑭), a sentimental waltz by the likes of de Koven or Herbert (⑮), Irving Berlin's "Alexander's Ragtime Band" (six measures after ⑯; see ex. 20), and Eduardo Di Capua's "Oh, Marie" (⑰).[50] Carpenter ingeniously depicts the hurdy-gurdy by means of two xylophones (the second optional), piano, harp, and occasionally celesta and glockenspiel. The tune fragments move from key to key, punctuated by the Baby's delighted reaction, represented principally by a sweeping waltz tune that uses hemiola and, at seven before ⑱, by the Baby's theme itself. At the climax, when the Baby has "a wild thought of dancing with my nurse and my perambulator," the Perambulator theme is heard in conjunction with the Baby waltz and "Oh, Marie."

The third movement celebrates music ("the most insidious form of noise," the Baby notes) in one of its more spontaneous, elemental forms—the popular songs of the streets. Carpenter suggests music's potential for uninhibited rapture not only through the Baby's waltzlike responses but through the jagged collage of tunes that wildly traverse foreign keys. The Policeman's brief entrance quickly puts an end to the whole business—law and order assert themselves. All that remains is a wistful remembrance of "Oh, Marie" and a haunting statement of the Nurse's theme.

As we know from the aforementioned letter to Ellen Borden, the "Lake" of the fourth movement takes its inspiration from Lake Geneva, though possibly Lake Michigan as well. This movement essentially has no other form but the flow and ebb of the lake's tide; the music breathes in regular two-measure intervals that never stray from Db major. Nonetheless, the movement contains something of a climax at ㉔, at which point Carpenter shows his tone-painting abilities to particularly good advantage: the surf comes crashing in with an arched melody in the strings doubled by the woodwinds (fortissimo), aided, at the last moment, by a harp glissando, and recedes with a soft and sustained minor harmony decorated with bits of clarinet and flute figuration. Other noteworthy details include the flute motive in measure 10, which presumably is the "white-seagull" mentioned in the program notes (it is somewhat like Wagner's Forest Bird), and occasional, subtle appearances of the Nurse and Perambulator themes.

EXAMPLE 20. Carpenter, *Adventures in a Perambulator,* third movement, ⟨16⟩, mm. 6–9.

The textures and colors of this movement owe a considerable debt to Debussy, especially "Sirènes" from *Nocturnes,* and as if by way of homage, a subsidiary theme shortly before ⟨25⟩ practically quotes the opening of *Prelude to the Afternoon of a Faun*. "The Lake," more than any other movement in the work, warrants the clichéd comparison with Debussy. But even here, Carpenter puts forth his own kind of clarity and sweetness.

Carpenter might have intended the fifth movement, "Dogs," as a symbolic portrayal of the vastness and confusion of society ("Little dogs, with sisters; big dogs, with aged parents. Kind dogs, brigand dogs, sad dogs and gay. They laugh, they fight, they flirt, they run"). The movement begins in a jaunty G major, as Nurse and Baby resume their stroll. At ⟨30⟩ Carpenter introduces the dogs, whose barking he depicts by major seconds, staccato. A

B pedal points to E minor, but whole-tone passages bring the music to a fermata on V of C minor. (These secondal and whole-tone harmonies also owe something to Debussy.)

Carpenter casts the main theme proper, played by the flutes against the "barks" in the strings, in an unexpected E♭ major. The melody shows some kinship to Arthur Pryor's popular "Whistler and His Dog," which itself derives from Septimus Winner's "Where, Oh Where Has My Little Dog Gone." Carpenter actually quotes the Winner song at [33], where it appears in a whole-tone context, again cartoonlike in its sense of distortion.

At two after [34] Carpenter returns to E♭ major and the main theme, which now provides the subject of a fugue ("And at last, in order to hold my interest, the very littlest brigand starts a game of 'Follow the Leader,' followed by all the others"). The dog barks provide counterpoint to the fugue theme, as does the tune "Ach, du lieber Augustin." As the fugue subsides, a solo violin states the Nurse's theme. The movement ends with a whimsical flourish in the piccolo.

In the last movement, "Dreams," Baby shuts his eyes and dreams of his Mother and of the day's adventures—a programmatic excuse, it would seem, for a cyclic finale. The movement opens with the Baby's theme in a yawning Larghetto in E♭ major, followed by an even drowsier Largo in D major. Carpenter modulates to D♭ major for the Mother's theme, which is a lullaby similar to "Dodo, l'enfant do," and which subtly incorporates the first phrase of the Nurse's theme (ex. 21); this explains Baby's statement, "Most of the time my Mother and my Nurse have but one identity in my mind, but at night or when I close my eyes, I can easily tell them apart, for my Mother has the greater charm." Carpenter accompanies the Mother's theme with a gossamer transformation of the Perambulator theme, which now resembles the twinkling of a music box or a nursery mobile.

Motives from, principally, "The Lake" and "The Policeman" bring the music to rest in D major at [46]. A Presto section recalls themes from "Dogs" and "The Hurdy-Gurdy." Baby's drowsy Largo leads once again to the Moth-

EXAMPLE 21. Carpenter, *Adventures in a Perambulator,* last movement, [41], mm. 3–6. Mother's theme.

er's lullaby, this time in D major and even more exquisitely scored. A final remembrance of "The Lake" brings the work to an end.

As a whole *Adventures in a Perambulator* forms a day cycle—from morning to night, from waking to sleeping, in the course of which the Baby experiences, symbolically, the world: the Nurse, domesticity; the Policeman, authority; the hurdy-gurdy, art; the lake, nature; dogs, society; and Mother, love. Not only do the various themes reappear throughout the work, but they often interconnect; says Baby twice in the course of the program notes, "It is confusing, but it is Life!" Carpenter also suggests this confusion by the work's colorful proliferation of tonal centers: from E♭ to A♭ to D to D♭ to E♭ to D♭ (all major).

Adventures in a Perambulator was an instant success, much greater than the composer could have reasonably expected given his inexperience in writing for orchestra. Reporting on the premiere by Stock and the Chicago Symphony on 19 March 1915, Eric De Lamarter told Boston readers, "Unquestionably, *Adventures in a Perambulator* is the cleverest score by an American composer we have heard in the history of the resident symphony orchestra."[51] Karleton Hackett wrote in the *Evening Post:* "There was wit, humor and tenderness, and through it all the feeling that Mr. Carpenter had something to say, something that he had actually felt and wished to express. The suite has distinction, and we are all proud that it came out of Chicago."[52] Excited by such success, Chicago society turned out to honor Carpenter at a repeat performance. Rue appeared in a short, fluffy, black chiffon gown and small high-heeled slippers. In another box sat the composer's brother, Judge George Carpenter, with his wife and in-laws.[53]

The work became so popular that one Chicago daily even ran a large cartoon by Carpenter's friend John McCutcheon that depicted Stock conducting a policeman, a governess, and other characters from the work. This cartoon tribute helped underscore the music's cartoonish wit and its ties with the popular humor of such Chicago journalists as McCutcheon, George Ade, and Finley Peter Dunne. Indebted to Twain, theirs was an urbanized frontier humor full of caricature, slang, and sarcasm, a Chicago tradition that would later inform the work of Ben Hecht, Studs Terkel, and Saul Bellow.

After Chicago, Stock brought *Adventures in a Perambulator* to Detroit and Cleveland. In the meantime, Walter Damrosch and Karl Muck vied for the East Coast premiere. Damrosch prevailed, performing the work with the Symphonic Society of New York on 5 November 1915. Carpenter traveled to New York for this performance, later thanking Damrosch for his "kindness and patience and enthusiasm"; the experience had been "wonderful."[54] Damrosch (1862–1950), like Stock, remained a loyal friend, and over the years he conducted many of the composer's works. He uttered, further, a statement that commanded the attention of all: "Carpenter is among the most American of our composers."[55] Looking back over his career in 1947, Carpenter wrote of his gratitude for all Damrosch had done: "Your generous willingness to place a bet on me in the early days, and your neverending encouragement and kindness ever since I can never forget."[56]

The New York press received the work with much greater enthusiasm than they had hitherto shown Carpenter. Their reviews singled out the aspect of surprise and novelty, as illustrated by such headlines as "Baby's Ideas of Park Trip Described in Novel Music," "Business Man Writes Season's Music Novelty," and "Surprise at Symphony." Another simply stated, "'Baby' Music by Carpenter Scores Hit."[57] Much like De Lamarter, Oscar Zeigler admired the music's pictorial realism and orchestral piquancy. He concluded, "No American work has been found so amusing and at the same time so musical in a long time."[58] Other reviews attested to the work's "ingenuity" *(New York Times),* "gentle lyric beauty" *(New York Sun),* and "lively fancy" *(New York Herald Tribune).* Reviewing the same performance a week or so later, *Musical America* questioned the music's mixture of "Debussy, Charpentier, Strauss, Ravel, even Puccini" but admitted that "the score, through its very complexity . . . demonstrated that Mr. Carpenter's technique is equal to that of all but a few contemporaries. Let the importance of this factor not be underestimated."[59]

Lawrence Gilman penned a particularly long and ambitious critique for the *North American Review.* "This baby," the review began, "was a confirmed hedonist." For Gilman the music suggested Walter Pater's query, "How can we pass most swiftly from point to point, and be present always at the focus where the greatest number of vital forces unite in their purest energy?" Gilman contended that Carpenter's answer offered something other than the dreamlike fantasy of Charles Lamb and Edward Elgar—"Mr. Carpenter's juvenile is of a clamorous and persistent actuality." Gilman concluded:

> We can think of no music dealing with the psychological stuff of childhood that we would so gladly hear again as this winsome and subjugating suite. It is conceived and accomplished with unfailing tact. How easily, in the hands of a less scrupulous and reticent artist,—above all, in the hands of a sentimentalist with a defective sense of humor,—it might have turned into something merely saccharine and absurd. But Mr. Carpenter has a mellow and

delicate humor, fine taste, a right and sure instinct in these treacherous matters. Moreover, he is witty, poetic, imaginative. . . . Looking back upon that dim and miraculous world, which is at once so near and personal yet so strange and incredible and remote,—which is even sometimes wholly shut away by forests and cities or by clouds and mists,—he has contrived to share with us the memory of his vision; so that, if only for a moment, we, too, remember those enchanted heights.[60]

Walter Damrosch and the New York Symphonic Society brought *Perambulator* to Boston on 16 November 1915. The composer George Chadwick immediately wrote Carpenter: "Although I have not the pleasure of your acquaintance, I enjoyed your Baby-wagon piece so much last night that I cannot resist the temptation to congratulate you upon it. It has both humor and sentiment, and while delightfully picturesque and vivid, never approaches the vulgar or commonplace."[61] (In a 1920 letter to Isabella Stewart Gardner, Charles Martin Loeffler, another Boston composer, expressed his fondness for *Perambulator,* adding, "I have always had a predilection for Carpenter's gift as a musician and I am delighted at his great success.")[62]

The Boston Symphony Orchestra first performed the work under Muck at a special pair of Christmas concerts on 24 and 25 December 1915. Carpenter attended these performances, reported Olin Downes, "but with the distaste for public attention which is one of his characteristics, refrained from acknowledging in person the applause of his work."[63] Once again, the reviews were excellent: "American Composer Triumphs" read one headline.[64] When Muck played the score again in 1916, one reviewer praised specifically the work's "instrumentation and manipulation of themes."[65]

Throughout the late teens premieres of *Adventures in a Perambulator* continued to make headlines and win praise around the country and eventually the world. On 3 March 1916 Max Zach conducted the work with the St. Louis Symphony; on 10 November 1916 Ernst Kunwald performed it with the Cincinnati Symphony; and on 30 March 1917 Emil Oberhoffer conducted it with the Minneapolis Symphony. In St. Louis one headline read, "Tonal Riot Heard in 'Adventures in Perambulator,'" suggesting some comparison with Stravinsky's contemporaneous *The Rite of Spring.* (Is it mere coincidence that Walt Disney considered both works suitable for his purposes?) And a knowledgeable Cincinnati reviewer identified the work as having "all the harmonic and contrapuntal originality with which Ziehn and, consequently his élèves overflow. . . . The interest never flags and new effects ever bring fascinating surprises."[66]

Perambulator had to wait for the end of World War I to travel abroad.

A 1918 performance in Rome possibly constituted its European premiere. Subsequently, Francis Casadesus conducted *Aventures dans une voiture d'enfant* (only "En voiture!" "The Policeman," and "Dogs") in Paris on 27 March 1919; Georg Schnéevoigt introduced *Äventyr i en barnvagn* in Stockholm on 23 October 1919; and Paul Scheinpflug performed *Abenteuer eines Kindes* in Berlin on 14 May 1920. More than twenty years later, Carlos Chávez conducted three movements—interestingly, the slower ones, "En coche," "El lago," and "Ensueños"—in Mexico City on 26 June 1942. The work also made its way to the Soviet Union, where, in 1946, a journalist cited it, along with Carpenter's *Skyscrapers* and music by Gershwin, Kern, Grofé, and Bloch, as among the most popular American music there.[67]

Back in the States, *Perambulator* became a repertory staple. Stock performed it for the rest of his career, enchanting such listeners as the young George Perle. After Muck both Monteux and Koussevitzky played it with the Boston Symphony Orchestra. (Koussevitzky performed the work better than Damrosch, Muck, or Monteux, wrote one well-seasoned critic in 1927: "Unlike his predecessors . . . the conductor neither pointed the humors, sharpened the characterization, nor enlivened the fancies. Instead, he was engrossed with the matter and manner of Mr. Carpenter's music as such." These same virtues, this critic continued, also characterized Koussevitzky's reading of Ravel's *Mother Goose Suite*.)[68] Fritz Reiner conducted the score with the Cincinnati Orchestra in 1926. And in 1934 Eugene Ormandy and the Minneapolis Symphony recorded it for Victor (in what is probably the best recording to date).[69]

About 1940 the *Chicago Herald Tribune* reported that Walt Disney (1901–66) was considering *Adventures in a Perambulator* for a sequel to his animated feature *Fantasia* (1937–40), and that Carpenter and Disney were going to meet to discuss the project. The article further stated that this seemed "like a wonderful idea, for what could lend itself better to the Disney magic than the private thoughts of a baby, expressed in the endearing Carpenter score." Carpenter, who by this time had worked with Serge Diaghilev and Paul Whiteman, would have happily collaborated with Disney, whose visionary ambitions and experimental populism also attracted the likes of Stravinsky, Prokofiev, Hindemith, and William Grant Still.[70]

Disney possibly first heard about Carpenter during a three-week conference in 1937 with Leopold Stokowski and Deems Taylor "at which hundreds of recordings were played and the concert feature program [for *Fantasia*] was picked."[71] Carpenter's name seemed destined to come up: both Stokowski and Taylor admired him and his cartoon-ballet *Krazy Kat*. That particular score's association with George Herriman's cartoons, however, would have put it out of the running for *Fantasia;* further, Disney would have needed to hear a recording of the work, and none then existed. Attention surely turned, instead, to Carpenter's two other picturesque hits already recorded: *Adventures in a Perambulator* and *Skyscrapers.* Disney might have given the latter due consideration—after hearing Shostakovich's *Age of Steel,* he envisioned "a montage effect of a building being erected"[72]—but he apparently preferred the adorableness of the former.

Although Disney passed over Carpenter for the original *Fantasia,* he planned, even before the movie's release in November 1940, to enlarge the *Fantasia* repertory: "He hoped that, in 1988, half a century after the film's debut, movie-goers would ask 'not only where and when *Fantasia* is playing, but *what Fantasia* is playing.'"[73] For this purpose Disney selected *Adventures in a Perambulator* along with mostly European music as one of nine new segments he would have incorporated into the original *Fantasia* or else released as a *Fantasia II.* From mid-1940 to mid-1941, the Disney studio completed preliminary work on most of these segments before dwindling European receipts, a crippling 1941 employees' strike, entry into World War II, and a disappointing public response to the original *Fantasia* forced Disney to abandon the project.[74] On 18 December 1941 Carpenter wrote Felix Borowski, "It has developed . . . that the Disney plans have changed, for whatever reason, and he has apparently returned to his first love, the realm of pure Disney fantasy, and I must say that *Dumbo* goes far to convince me that he is right."[75]

Work on the Carpenter segment progressed as far as a storyboard sketched out by Sylvia Moberly-Holland (1900–1974), who had worked on *Bambi* and on the "Nutcracker" episode in the original *Fantasia.* The animated version would have encapsulated Carpenter's story—a morning stroll, the policeman, the dogs, and so on—all seen from the baby's perspective, with overlarge faces and hands. John Canemaker called Holland's completed sketches "loose and bold in execution, reminding one of today's fine children's book illustration, particularly the work of Maurice Sendak," and he singled out for "great imagination and economy" two drawings, including one in which Mother attempts to soothe Baby's nightmarish recollection of the dogs.[76]

During the spring of 1941, Carpenter revised the score in anticipation of its use by Disney: "I . . . thought that it would be well to do a little house cleaning on this old score in honor of the occasion," he wrote Borowski. (Some of these revisions actually dated years earlier; Ormandy's 1934 recording, for instance, had already incorporated a few of them.) This particular revision, rather restrained compared with others that Carpenter undertook during these years, suggests that he regarded the work with few misgivings. Of course, the music's great popularity would have prevailed against extensive rewriting. In any case, Carpenter himself noted, "There are no essential changes in the score but I have made some minor corrections which I hoped would add to its clearness and effectiveness."[77]

Carpenter actually made a few significant cuts in the slower movements: he removed 22 to 23 and nine after 23 to 24 in "The Lake" and two before 45 to five after 46 in "Dreams." These cuts highlighted the casualness of Carpenter's formal procedures, for the music retained its sense of continuity without requiring any special stitching on the composer's part. On the other hand, the climax of "The Lake" now arrived, perhaps, unaccountably early.

Another noticeable revision involved a jig fragment at the very end of "The Policeman" that confirmed his Irishness. Other revisions addressed small details, especially added pickups and countermelodies for greater rhythmic energy. In the first measure the addition of a cymbal crash on the offbeat specifically recalled the composer's jazz-flavored works.

The most extensive changes concerned the orchestration, however. Years of experience led Carpenter to rescore the work in numerous ways. Overall, he emphasized the delicacy that characterized the piece from the start by making greater and more effective use of harp, triangle, glockenspiel, cymbals, snare drum, piccolo, oboe, English horn, and clarinet. Such changes resulted in sharper, clearer, and more brilliant sounds. At the same time, he occasionally enriched the music with added woodwind doublings.

A rather dramatic example of such rescoring—dramatic in part because accompanied by changed harmonies and textures—can be found at the Largo in the last movement (fifteen after 40, and 49 in the revised score). Originally, Carpenter scored this melody for cellos (muted and divisi) and bassoons, doubled and in open fifths: a soft, dark sound. In the revision the first-desk violas (muted) and the English horn (picked up by the first bassoon) state the tune, the first-chair cellos (pizzicato) and the harp provide accompaniment, and the glockenspiel and timpani offer additional rhythmic and color interest. The new scoring suggests a nursery even more vividly than the original.

The reorchestration of the hurdy-gurdy deserves special comment. In the original Carpenter scored a grace-note figure, suggestive of the creaking of the hurdy-gurdy, for the piano (two after 14), whereas in the revision he rewrote it for flutes and celesta (two after 17), an unabashed borrowing from Stravinsky's similar depiction of an organ-grinder in *Petrushka*. In fairness to

Carpenter, however, he apparently wrote his original hurdy-gurdy music without any knowledge of the Stravinsky score; presumably, he could not resist this slight touch-up after getting to know it.

Stock premiered the revised version on 26 December 1941. Other early performers of the revised score included Izler Saloman and the Columbus Symphony Orchestra in 1945; Karl Krueger and the Detroit Symphony in 1947, where it still "delighted the audience"; and Werner Janssen and the Portland Symphony Orchestra in 1949.[78] The revised *Adventures in a Perambulator* presumably served as well choreographer Thelma Biracee, who staged it under the title *Central Park* at the Fourteenth Annual Festival of American Music in Rochester, New York, on 28 April 1944. One critic thought "the whole thing was charming."[79]

During its first thirty years, *Adventures in a Perambulator* won not only numerous performances but the praise of such informed critics as Olin Downes (the work describes "with humor and astonishing ingenuity the adventures of baby in a perambulator"), Felix Borowski ("The music in 'Adventures in a Perambulator' is, in some respects, among the most attractive that its composer has given to the world"), and John Tasker Howard ("it is all exquisite fun, accomplished with simple means, vividly").[80] After hearing the work on WQXR in 1943, Abram Chasins wrote the composer, "Never have I loved this music so much, and I feel compelled to write you my deep thanks for the joy which your music always brings to me, and for the beauty and sanity of your creative gifts."[81]

Not all critics and listeners were so sanguine. Paul Rosenfeld sounded an early alarm:

> The suite, "In a Perambulator" . . . is not so much the world of the child felt directly as it is the adult comment on the sensations of the baby carriage. You have but to compare it with "The Children's Corner" of Debussy and "Ma Mère l'Oye" of Ravel to perceive its pseudo-realism. The two Frenchmen managed to coincide intuitively with the child. The American, with all his charming talent for light orchestration, his wit and musical good manners, causes us more to smile at a world made miniature and playfully ironic than feel the terror, the buzz and glow of the universe of the nursery. There is no poetry in the work. It moves us not.[82]

Charles Ives took more oblique but sharper aim at Carpenter and his *Perambulator* in that part of the *Essays before a Sonata* (part 5 of the "Epilogue") that upbraided Strauss, Dukas, and other "amusing" and "entertaining" composers:

> Magnifying the dull into the colossal, produces a kind of "comfort"—the comfort of a woman who takes more pleasure in the fit of fashionable clothes than in a healthy body—the kind of comfort that has brought so many "adventures of baby-carriages at county fairs"—"the sensation of Teddy bears, smoking their first cigarette"—on the program of symphony orchestras of one hundred performers,—the lure of the media—the means—not the end—but the finish,—thus the failure to perceive that thoughts and memories of childhood are too tender, and some of them too sacred to be worn lightly on the sleeve.[83]

Carpenter probably figured as well in Ives's subsequent rebuke of "technique" (including the oft-quoted remark, "My God! what has sound got to do with music!"), "wit," "talent," "manner," and, finally, the notion that ragtime represents the "true American music."

Rosenfeld and Ives agreed on "talent," "wit," and "manners" as disparaging code words for Carpenter. Moreover, both critiques suggested a shared aesthetic perspective—a solemn reverence for the innocence of childhood. While they expressed a minority view, they spoke for a large segment of America's burgeoning avant-garde, for instance, Carl Ruggles, who in 1922 stated, "I thought that music had reached the lowest possible point when I heard the works of John Alden Carpenter. Now, however, I have been examining the scores of Mr. Henry Hadley."[84]

This perspective gained after World War II as tastes changed. In 1946, for instance, Hugo Leichtentritt admitted that *Adventures in a Perambulator* "is itself not—and undoubtedly has not been—without charms," but he cited lapses of taste not found in comparable works by Strauss and Stravinsky; the music's "ingenuity and musical skill" had been "wasted on an improper theme."[85] Just the title seemed silly, and orchestras dropped *Perambulator* from the repertory because, as Andrew Stiller claimed, it "was subjected to so much ridicule."[86]

Denied the opportunity to hear the work in the concert hall, critics accordingly shifted attention to postwar recordings of the (revised) work by Henry Swoboda and the Vienna State Opera Orchestra (1952) and Howard Hanson and the Eastman-Rochester Orchestra (1957).[87]

The Swoboda recording helped reinforce the perspective of Leichtentritt, if not Rosenfeld and Ives. In one review, for instance, Irving Fine wrote:

> *Adventures in a Perambulator* leans heavily on Strauss for its style and subject matter (it is a kind of American *Sinfonia Domestica*). But it also pays its respects to Elgar and Debussy. The characteristic orchestral sound is one of

opulent *Gemütlichkeit*. The harmonies and melodic material are in the same vein. What connection the music has with the composer's own program is a moot point. The listener had best ignore the program as well as the other notes accompanying the recording. In the latter occurs the observation that *Adventures in a Perambulator* is one of Carpenter's lighter works and is "tremendously funny." It is neither light nor funny. Nor is it even cute. But it is skilfully made orchestral music, and pleasant, if somewhat soporific, listening.[88]

Peter Hugh Reed, also reviewing the Swoboda recording, similarly admired Carpenter's "workmanship" but opined that "enjoyment would seem contingent on acceptance of the program which is a bit implausible." Arthur Berger added, "If one cares to look for it, there is an American quality too. Since 1914, when Carpenter wrote his tone-poem, this Americanism, such as it is, has found its 'niveau' in the scores for the smart, fluffy films that were the vogue in Myrna Loy's hey-day." Postwar opinion, in short, viewed the work as hopelessly dated.[89]

The reviews of the Eastman-Rochester release proved somewhat more appreciative, perhaps because of the superiority of Hanson's conducting and Mercury's sound engineering. Hanson's "zestful performance," wrote R. D. Darrell, "and the breeziest of stereo recording reveals more piquantly than ever before the warmth and buoyancy which keep Carpenter's heart-warming masterpiece alive." The work "may not sound daringly modern," stated John Conly, but it "still can enchant." "The music itself is on the insubstantial side," commented Alfred Frankenstein, but Hanson's "deft and illuminating" touch make it "seem like a companion-piece to Ravel's *Mother-Goose*." *Musical America* gave the recording its top rating of four stars; the music "loses nothing for suggesting, at times, the music of Ravel and Debussy." And Trevor Harvey, writing in *Gramophone*, admitted that he "quite enjoyed it"; his only complaint was that "each piece was too long and ambitious for its slender idea, especially the final one, which takes a long time to come to an end."[90]

Even as late as the mid-1970s, retrospective reviews of the Hanson recording were surprisingly positive for a work that apparently had been laughed out of the concert hall. James Goodfriend wrote in *Stereo Review*, "*Adventures in a Perambulator* is a piece of American impressionism, pleasant, mildly whimsical, eminently listenable—*light* music." William D. Curtis agreed that the work was "lightweight in character" but claimed that "there is certainly nothing trivial about any of it."[91]

The continued enthusiasm of record reviewers gives one pause. If a long, whimsical orchestral fantasy detailing a baby's worldview could still provide pleasure when listened to on a recording, there seems no reason why it could not be successfully revived in the concert hall as well.

The year 1914 also witnessed five new Carpenter songs, including two contributions to *Kitty Cheatham: Her Book—A Collection of Songs from the Repertoire of Miss Kitty Cheatham, Written, with Four Exceptions, Expressly for Her and Heretofore Only in Manuscript Form* (published in 1915 by Schirmer).

Born in Nashville, Kitty Cheatham (1864?–1946) became the toast of New York in the decade before World War I by performing children's songs in a childlike way (her forty-some-odd-years notwithstanding).[92] And as mentioned earlier, her performances of Carpenter's *Improving Songs* had helped establish his reputation in New York (see chap. 3). At a Christmas concert on 25 December 1910, Cheatham sang some of the *Improving Songs* "wearing Mme. Paquin's idea of what a shepherdess might affect, something very sweet in pink and blue with ribbons and flowers and a wonderful hat tied under the chin with a blue bow." At this same concert, she surprised her audience by leaving the stage and returning with the visiting Engelbert Humperdinck, who accompanied her in his "Wiegenlied" and selections from *Hänsel und Gretel*. The *New York Times* reported that the audience "crowded the theater and applauded every number rapturously"; the renowned soprano Geraldine Farrar leaned from her box "to toss a large bouquet of pink roses at Miss Cheatham's feet."[93]

Cheatham's concerts were not exercises in frivolity, as might appear; her singing of lullabies and Negro spirituals deeply touched her audiences. A Christian Scientist and a self-styled mystical optimist, Cheatham even earned a certain notoriety for her controversial politics. During World War I, she argued for "a spiritual relationship between America and Russia" and led an impassioned campaign against "The Star-Spangled Banner," citing its militaristic imagery, its anti-English sentiments, and its tavern origins.[94]

Cheatham's spirituality led Carpenter to write two prayers for her: "The Little Prayer of I (I)," to words by the children's poet Archibald Sullivan, and "The Little Prayer of I (II)," to words by the composer. Both are short, simple songs in the style of the *Improving Songs*. The Archibald text reads:

> I think of all the nicest things
> The best one it would be
> For God to make a little star
> And call it after me.

Carpenter's "Little Prayer of I (II)" similarly consists of four phrases: God, who unfurls the red rose (1), teaches the baby lark to sing (2), and paints the maple trees scarlet (3), is asked to "call me there to see" (4). Here, in a song whose imagery evokes the passing seasons, the composer's characteristic preoccupation with the time cycle, put forth on a grand scale in *Adventures in a Perambulator,* takes its most encapsulated form.

In 1914 Carpenter further wrote "The Player Queen" (words by William Butler Yeats), "Wull Ye Come in Eärly Spring" (words by William Barnes), and "The Day Is No More" (words by Rabindranath Tagore). "The Player Queen" was surely inspired by Yeats's visit to Chicago in early 1914 for some lecture engagements. On 1 March, John and Rue, as part of a contingent of "guarantors," even attended a banquet sponsored in Yeats's honor by Harriet Monroe's *Poetry.* "The whole town rose to it in a manner unprecedented for an affair celebrating one of the arts," recalled Monroe. Yeats lectured on the need for American poets "to strive to become very simple, very humble." If Americans still indulged in sentimental rhetoric, it was "not because you are too far from England, but because you are too far from Paris." He suggested Villon as a model, praised the Chicago poet Vachel Lindsay, and read some poems exemplifying his ideals, including two by Ezra Pound. Then Lindsay himself capped off the evening with a successful reading of his own "The Congo."[95]

Carpenter subsequently set Yeats's five-stanza "The Player Queen" ("My Mother Dandled Me"), which had been published in *Poetry,* for voice and piano. Yeats intended to use the poem in a play-in-progress of the same name, a play that occupied him from about 1907 to 1919. (A reference to the song first appears in the poet's nineteenth draft, dating somewhere between 1910 and 1914.)[96] Although Yeats never used the entire lyric in any version of the play, all five verses turn up in one or another draft.

The Player Queen is about a queen who yearns to be a nun, and a lowborn actress, Decima, who aspires to be a queen; when given the opportunity to substitute for the ineffectual queen, Decima performs brilliantly. "A good actress will make a better queen than one born to the purple without, so to speak, a true vocation," wrote Yeats in an early scenario; "thus, the mask can have more power than the face it conceals." About the same time, Yeats wrote in another context, "I think all happiness depends on having the energy to assume the mask of some other self."[97]

Decima sings "My Mother Dandled Me" in act 2 as she comes out of hiding in the queen's throne room. She describes the song as "the old country ballad that was made by the mad [in another version, 'blind'] singing daughter of the harlot."[98] In this ballad the daughter recalls how her mother sorrowfully regretted that her baby did not wear a crown, "the golden top of care." Decima sings the song at that moment when she realizes her own aspirations to be a queen.

Carpenter casts the five verses in AABA form, with verse 5 constituting a coda. The song is an expressive (slightly "mad"?) remembrance of a mother's lullaby, depicted in the piano by the left hand's rocking ostinato and the right hand's suggestions of "Dodo, l'enfant do." The mixture of Dorian, Phrygian, Aeolian, and pentatonic modalities is haunting. Indeed, the song is unusually theatrical for Carpenter. The coda, in particular, with its chromatic descent followed by a final ascent to a high F on a fermata (left unresolved!), turns the setting into a little dramatic scene. More than any other song, "The Player Queen" suggests the kind of opera Carpenter might have written.

After completing the song, Carpenter proudly told Ellen: "I *know* you'll like it! That's boasting—but I feel too sure."[99] Maggie Teyte gave the song's premiere, or at least one of the earliest performances, on 4 April 1915. The piece naturally suited this famous Mélisande and became, along with "Les Silhouettes," one of Teyte's favorite Carpenter songs. When Claudia Cassidy heard her sing both songs more than thirty years later, in 1946, she wrote, "Aside from the French songs, I like Miss Teyte best in John Alden Carpenter's 'The Player Queen' and 'Silhouettes,' because they, too, are on the fabulous side, and they welcome a silver voice with immaculate respect for the composer's intentions."[100]

Carpenter wrote "Wull Ye Come in Eärly Spring" in June 1914, apparently for his fellow Cliff Dweller, the musical comedian Marion Green, who sang it that summer in Pride's Crossing, Massachusetts. Carpenter encouraged Ellen to attend this performance, writing, "My too handsome friend Mr. Green will sing several of my very worst works—including the 'Come' song that I did but three weeks ago—and wrote you about."[101] Green also sang "Wull Ye Come" in Boston on 26 March 1915.

The composer possibly intended the song as a companion piece to his earlier Barnes setting, "Don't Ceäre" of 1911, for both courtship songs make an attractive pair. Whereas "Don't Ceäre" jovially recalls a successful courtship, "Wull Ye Come" is full of romantic yearning: the lover eagerly awaits the beloved's arrival in the spring; at the song's end the beloved promises to come. Ellen apparently inspired this song, for Carpenter's letters to her reveal a similar urgency. Considering further that Carpenter composed "Wull Ye Come" while Ellen was summering in Massachusetts, and then arranged for her to hear it there, the song seems more specifically to have been a kind of musical missive.

Carpenter creates a ternary design out of the song's two verses, while retaining something of the original bipartite form as well: an A section puts forth the first verse; a contrasting B section presents the first half of the second verse; and the remainder of the second verse returns to the music of A, though it retains the soft dynamics of B. The beloved's one-line response at the poem's end, which functions as a sort of coda in the original poem (titled "Come"), receives a *quasi ad lib.* musical treatment.

Like Carpenter's other songs from 1914, "Wull Ye Come" reveals a growing sense of harmonic adventurousness. Note, for example, the prominent modal colorings (mostly Mixolydian) and the alternating C-major and C♯-minor triads just before the B section. In the B section itself, the chromatic ambiguities, combined with the arcane Dorsetshire dialect,[102] assume a particularly opaque quality. But this makes the song's marvelous ending—with its strong authentic cadence and the vocal sweep of an eleventh at the words "I wull come!"—all the more effective. (As with such earlier songs as "The Heart's Country" and "Little Fly," Carpenter originally wrote a shorter and simpler ending; he often elaborated endings on reflection.)

In September 1914, one month after war broke out in Europe, Carpenter returned to Tagore for one final setting from *Gitanjali*, "The Day Is No More" (no. 74). The poem is about death, but unlike the death poems Carpenter chose for the 1913 cycle, this one is full of dread and uncertainty. He surely selected it in response to the war: "the wind is up, the ripples are rampant in the river. . . . I know not if I shall come back home."

Tagore's poem has three stanzas. In the first the poet announces the end of the day; in the second he paints a lonely and threatening river landscape; and in the third he hears death's sorrowful music: "There at the fording in the little boat the unknown man plays upon his lute." Carpenter sets all three stanzas, creating an ABA form. The first section is in a funereal G♯ minor, the vocal line descending to the G♯ below middle C, making this song untypically low for Carpenter. (The composer depicts the lute in the piano part through a technique he long associated with old folk styles, as evidenced by the early Shakespeare settings: an open fifth preceded by a grace note.) The song's middle section effectively portrays the ominous, windswept evening through dotted rhythms, rocking seventh chords, and whole-tone figuration. The final section returns to the G♯-minor lute music, although the texture changes for the last line, about the "unknown man." Here the voice has a tender, pentatonic melody, pianissimo, while the piano states a fragile pentatonic countermelody over a D♯ pedal (ex. 22). Such delicacy prefigures *Water-Colors* and

EXAMPLE 22.   Carpenter, "The Day Is No More," mm. 73–83.

other music from the war years (the lingering Franckian harmonies in the B section notwithstanding).

One early performance of "The Day Is No More" took place in Argentina, where Jessié S. de Pamplin sang it. In 1950 contralto Carol Brice recorded the song for Columbia Records. Reviewing this performance, Philip Miller thought the song "effective."[103]

"The Day Is No More" has a cold, empty sadness that is new for Carpenter. Indeed, the song marks a poignant turning point in the composer's life: it bids farewell to the overflowing joy and hopefulness of *Gitanjali* and *Adventures in a Perambulator* and turns, with a shiver, toward some brave new world.

CHAPTER EIGHT

From the Piano Concertino to *Water-Colors*

1915–1916

Carpenter's 1915 Concertino for Piano and Orchestra is the first score characteristic of the composer's mature work. It lacks the audacity of Carpenter's music from the 1920s and the intimacy of his music from the 1930s, and it exhibits less technical command than many later works, but it contains pages that would not be out of place in *Krazy Kat* (1921) or the Piano Quintet (1934).

The composer thus found his mature voice in the crucible of World War I. Carpenter himself made a connection between the Piano Concertino and the war, writing Ellen, "Oh I started a new thing yesterday—I think it's going to be a piano concerto (with orchestra—you know) quite gloomy and barbaric and wild—but with a return at the end to something peaceful and hopeful—like war & peace."[1]

Carpenter's Piano Concertino also represents a landmark in American concert music quite generally; it sounds, for the first time perhaps, that percussive, riotous, irreverent note that would come to typify twentieth-century American music at its most characteristic. Along with Irving Berlin's "Alexander's Ragtime Band" (1911) and Jelly Roll Morton's "Jelly Roll Blues" (published in 1915 in Chicago), the Piano Concertino announces a new era in American music. "A racy, barbarian fantasy," Eric De Lamarter called it in his review of the 1916 premiere, "involved, enigmatic, mesmeric . . . agonizing to the mid-Victorian ear." George Whitefield Chadwick, hearing it in Boston in 1920, wrote to the composer: "My hat off to you for your bully piece which I have just heard at the Symphony! I call that *real* American music. Without paying tribute to red, black or yellow folk tunes, it breathes of our gay, reckless and optimistic spirit, which is unquenchable in us, if anything is." Stumbling across the piece in Paris in 1920, Otto Luening found it something of a culture shock: "I had never heard any jazz rhythms in a symphonic piece; but the way he used the orchestra was also curious to my ears."[2]

Carpenter worked on the Piano Concertino from July to October 1915. In program notes written for a 1922 performance, he described the work as

> a light-hearted conversation between piano and orchestra—as between two friends who have traveled different paths and become a little garrulous over their separate experiences. The conversation is mostly of rhythms—American, oriental and otherwise. The rules of polite talk, as always, between friends, are not strictly observed—often, in animated moments, they talk both at once, each hearing only what he says himself. Presently the moment comes, as always between friends, when no conversation is necessary.[3]

This description coincidentally resembles Charles Ives's program for his 1913 String Quartet no. 2, characterized as a work "for 4 men—who converse, discuss, argue (in re 'politick'), fight, shake hands, shut up—then walk up the mountain-side to view the firmament." Moreover, both works quote Dan Emmett's "Dixie." And yet the differences are telling: Carpenter's work is a "light-hearted conversation" about varied experiences; Ives's composition depicts political debate and spiritual transcendence. Further, Carpenter's "conversation" does not involve Ives's kind of textural explorations but unfolds traditionally; the dialogue between pianist and orchestra is, if anything, Mozartean.

The Piano Concertino's novelty resides, rather, in its colorful, eclectic ideas. It makes prominent use, above all, of Hispanic idioms, and the allusions to ragtime, waltzes, spirituals, "oriental" (Near Eastern?), and other styles all give way, sooner or later, to Latin inflections. Later in life Carpenter spoke of the "concealed Spanish blood" that irrepressibly bubbled to the surface of his scores, much as Jelly Roll Morton spoke of jazz's "Spanish tinge."[4]

Like jazz's "Spanish tinge," the Piano Concertino's "Spanish blood" is more Latin American than Spanish per se, notwithstanding the prominent use of castanets throughout the work, nor the flamenco-like music twenty-one measures after ③ that resembles de Falla. These Latin allusions can be further distinguished between a Caribbean strain, with its characteristic *cinquillo* rhythm (the kind of 3 + 3 + 2 subdivision found in danzóns, congas, merengues, rumbas, and cha-chas), and a South American strain, with its syncopated habanera rhythms (as found in the Argentinian tango and the Brazilian maxixe and samba). The movement initially explores the former kind of rhythm (ex. 23), moving later toward tangolike passages (ex. 24).

How did Carpenter—a Pilgrim descendant—come by his "Spanish

EXAMPLE 23. Carpenter, Concertino for Piano and Orchestra, first movement, mm. 3–8.

blood"? Spanish music had long attracted non-Spaniards, and Carpenter undoubtedly picked up a few lessons in this regard from such composers as Bizet, Verdi, Lalo, and Debussy. But what about Latin American music? He probably knew something about Gottschalk from Amy Fay, but more im-

EXAMPLE 24. Carpenter, Concertino for Piano and Orchestra, first movement, ⑥, mm. 6–7.

portant he clearly assimilated some Latin American music itself, mostly, one imagines, of a popular nature. Here, again, Chicago played its part.

The first great wave of American interest in Latin America came in the 1840s as a result of the American-Mexican War and resulted in the American success of such Mexican hits as Iradier's "La paloma." According to Robert Stevenson, Chicago and New Orleans became "the two cities in which were published, during the rest of the century, most songs and instrumental pieces by Cuban and Mexican composers."[5] One indication of Chicagoan interest in Mexicana was Frederic Grant Gleason's (1848–1903) three-act opera *Montezuma,* begun one year after the composer arrived in Chicago in 1877 and completed in 1884.

For the 1893 Columbian Exposition, Chicago launched a monumental exploration of music south of the border. The city commissioned works from Brazil, Argentina, Guatemala, Mexico, and Uruguay, whose composers responded with everything from operas to band music. Guatemala even sent a five-octave marimba for display. Latin America's most famous composer, Antônio Carlos Gomes (1836–96), arrived with great fanfare to conduct selections from five of his operas. Some of these discoveries may well have impressed Carpenter the way non-Western music at the Paris Exposition influenced Debussy.

The Spanish-American War of 1898 further intensified American interest in Latin American music. Americans began their century-long infatuation with Caribbean and South American dances, above all, the tango, popularized in 1913 by Vernon and Irene Castle. Irene Castle, in fact, was a personal friend of the Carpenters. On 13 July 1915, even as Carpenter was at work on the Piano Concertino, Irene wrote to Rue, "Do have a good rest and don't drink yourself to death—it's such a sticky finish."[6] Moreover, John McCutcheon mentions in his memoirs that he and his friends—including the Carpenters—took tango lessons from Maurice and Florence Walton before the dance became a national fad, possibly as early as 1908.[7]

Despite its profound indebtedness to Latin American music, the Piano Concertino could not possibly be taken for the work of a Latin American. In the opening page, for instance, the almost mechanically rhythmic drive, the sparse texture, the acerbic minor modality (especially the G# in m. 6) opening up, in measure 7, to a surprisingly whimsical tune in D major with saucy, ragtimelike syncopations—what could be more American? A passage at five after 7, *più animato,* comes especially close to Scott Joplin; indeed, the composer's allusions to the tango and ragtime cannot always be distinguished. Like Scott Joplin's *Heliotrope Bouquet* or W. C. Handy's "St. Louis Blues," the

Piano Concertino fuses Hispanic and American elements in intimate ways.[8]

In short, the Piano Concertino's modern, American flavor can be largely attributed to rhythms derived from Latin American music, but only as filtered through a sensibility shaped by the composer's American identity. This aspect of the work anticipates such composers as Piston, Copland, Gershwin, and Bernstein, who similarly integrated Hispanic elements in distinctly American ways. With the Piano Concertino, we can witness the style in the making.

The three-movement work is conceived as essentially without pause. Carpenter actually writes *attacca* after the slow movement and suggests as much at the end of the first movement by means of a thin-thin double barline followed immediately by the second movement's key and meter signature.

With their changing tempos, tonal surprises, and thematic cross-references, the Piano Concertino's three movements are formally elusive. The composer's own description ("Each movement is in the simplest song form—first subject, second subject, and repetition—except the last movement, which has a short coda based on the first subject in the first movement") seems overly simplistic. The movements conform sooner to the improvised frivolity of a Carpenter costume party than to any conventional ternary design. The composer wears one mask for only so long—gondolier, matador, blues singer, gigolo, sheik of Araby—until he tires of it and tries on another.

The form of the first movement, in fact, can perhaps best be described as ABCA, with A (1 to 2), the Caribbean-like section with its *cinquillo* rhythms; B (2 to 8), the now sultry, now whimsical tango/ragtime section; C (8 to 14), the more romantic, waltzlike section (that hints at "Yankee Doodle" in a brief interlude at eleven after 11); and A (14 to six after 16), the return to the opening theme (with the romantic C theme nostalgically recalled for a brief moment at 15).

On the other hand, the slow second movement forms a clear ternary design. The A section, Largo, $\frac{4}{4}$ (to 19), is related to African American music (though the piano part suggests some relation to the composer's American Indian style as well; see ex. 25). Carpenter originally labeled a sketch of the main theme, played by the cellos, "Berceuse negre," and, further, the music resembles an unpublished violin piece called "Negro Berceuse." According to Percy Grainger, this movement "reflects memories of the singing of Negro stevedores along some tributary streams of the lower Mississippi River."[9] If anyone knew this to be true, Grainger would have; but given the twice-mentioned term *berceuse* and the full context of Carpenter's career, the influence of black women and African American lullaby would seem more pertinent. In any case, Carpenter's pentatonic cello theme updates related

EXAMPLE 25. Carpenter, Concertino for Piano and Orchestra, second movement, mm. 2–7.

melodies by Chadwick and Dvořák. Its rubato rhythms and harmonic movement reflect not only African American folk music but perhaps, in particular, the blues, possibly W. C. Handy's (1873–1958) "St. Louis Blues," published in 1914.

The B section, Largamente (☐19☐ to ten after ☐20☐), in $\frac{5}{4}$ and vaguely Hispanic in style, provides contrast. At ☐20☐ Carpenter begins an impressionistic transition back to A; the piano part contains the marking "in imitation of chimes." At five after ☐20☐ this transition takes on the earmarks of the composer's harmonic work with Ziehn.

The finale's "oriental" main theme savors of the popular Middle Eastern or North African exoticism soon to be exploited in the films of Rudolph Valentino (ex. 26). Carpenter derived this music from the "Prelude" of an unpublished Prelude and Fugue for piano that he presumably wrote as an exercise for Ziehn. One would hardly suspect a neoclassical derivation for this swirling, picturesque music; only on reflection do the driving $\frac{6}{8}$ rhythms seem related to Bach.

The last movement's ternary form is somewhat lopsided: a large $\frac{5}{8}$ section (☐21☐ to ☐29☐) that puts forth the "oriental" theme; a short, waltzlike middle section with themes derived from material stated earlier (☐29☐ to sixteen before

EXAMPLE 26.   Carpenter, Concertino for Piano and Orchestra, third movement, mm. 17–24.

[31]); and a short reprise of the vigorous $\frac{5}{8}$ music (sixteen before [31] to [32]) that involves some new material alternately reminiscent of Dave Brubeck and Manuel de Falla (twelve before [31] to sixteen before [32]). After this comes a long, episodic coda consisting of a poignant, Moderato transformation of the waltz theme in which the composer, as it were, finally removes his mask ([32] to [33]); a joyous Animato affirmation of the waltz ([33] to [34]); and a whimsical Vivo ([34] to the end) that returns to the first movement's opening rhythms.

At thirteen measures before the very end, Carpenter simultaneously quotes "Old Folks at Home" and "Dixie" in the orchestra against a third, vaguely Indianist melody in the piano. Carpenter no doubt borrowed this tricky quodlibet from Irving Berlin's keyboard version of "Alexander's Ragtime Band," a song that he had quoted in *Adventures in a Perambulator*. Consequently, the passage is as much—if not more—a quotation of Berlin as of Foster and Emmett. As with Berlin, Carpenter uses such material—as he also will in *Skyscrapers*—as a joke, in order to highlight the music's jazzy, modern context.[10]

The Piano Concertino's three movements can be said to be in D major, F♯ major, and F♯ minor/A major, respectively. Within each movement, however, Carpenter progresses spontaneously and unpredictably to foreign tonal goals, including those a tritone away. The music's tonal language further involves certain ambiguities, often between the major and minor of a given key, but also between relative major and minor: the slow movement's A sections begin with a low D♯ in the bass, suggesting at once D♯ minor and F♯ major; and the same movement's B section is continuously poised between C major and A minor.

The music spins out fairly square phrase lengths, inclining toward two- and four-measure groupings, often in sequential patterns. Sometimes the music evokes popular *aaba* song forms, complete with "bridge." The main portion of the A section of the slow movement, for instance, comprises one such song form. These procedures point ahead to Gershwin's instrumental works, although Carpenter handles his more occasional use of such forms with greater subtlety. In the first movement, for instance, the return of the main theme after the "bridge" at ☐ leads into a modulatory section, not to a resolution of the theme, as one might expect.

The Piano Concertino's skillful and imaginative orchestral writing, whose novelties struck Otto Luening as "curious," is unconventionally brassy, percussive, and bright, with colorful flickers of piccolo, cymbals, trumpet, tambourine, and glockenspiel. This, too, helps define the work's Americanism. The woodwind sounds that open the slow movement are particularly novel and, combined with the accompanying modal ambiguity, forewarn the composer's attraction to Stravinsky in the years ahead.

Carpenter's Piano Concertino found a loyal champion in composerpianist Percy Grainger (1882–1961). The Australian-born Grainger had recently taken up residence in New York, after a glamorous decade in Europe, where he won the friendship of Grieg, Delius, Busoni, Reynaldo Hahn, Cyril Scott, and Cecil Sharp. After hearing the New York premiere of *Adventures in a Perambulator* on 5 November 1915, he "applauded, shouted bravo, and declared his intention of going back to personally congratulate the composer."[11] Grainger subsequently premiered the Piano Concertino with Stock and the Chicago Symphony on 10 March 1916, in a performance that also featured Grieg's Piano Concerto and Liszt's *Mephisto Waltz*.

Upon leaving Chicago, Grainger looked back "with joy on the artistic and human experiences at 710 Rush."[12] He wrote Delius in 1918: "In 5 or 10 years time it [American music] will be in full blast compositionally. John Alden Carpenter and Howard Brockway are real geniuses to my mind, and there are 3 Negro composers of the real stuff in smaller forms: W N [*sic*] Cook, Dett and Diton."[13]

Carpenter's Piano Concertino did not catch on as quickly as his prewar music had. The critics equivocated; De Lamarter's comment that the work was "agonizing to mid-Victorian ears" suggested the kind of advance over *Gitanjali* and *Perambulator* that made the Piano Concertino less immediately accessible. Significantly, the work began sparking widespread interest only in late 1920, during the first flush of the jazz age; in fact, listeners like Luening, who first heard the piece in the summer of 1920, sensed a connection between the Piano Concertino and jazz.

It took some time before New York and Boston had an opportunity to hear the work. Grainger planned to give the New York premiere with Josef Stransky and the New York Philharmonic on 29 January 1920, but Stransky canceled the performance after the music arrived late. Carpenter himself thought that Stransky had more than enough time to prepare the score, writing to Grainger: "On the occasion of the first performance here in Chicago, Mr. Stock put it into rehearsal on Monday morning for the first time and it was produced, as you know, on the following Friday afternoon. We averaged less than two hours for each of the four rehearsals that were given the piece and Mr. Stock spent no time whatever on a previous study of the score."[14] The work now had to wait until next season.

In the meantime, the French American pianist E. Robert Schmitz (1889–1949) began his notable career as a champion of new American music by giving the Boston premiere of the Piano Concertino (with some changes the composer had made the previous year) with the Boston Symphony under Monteux on 13 February 1920—when Chadwick heard it.[15] The critics—including visiting New Yorkers hearing the piece for the first time—seemed as nonplussed as ever. "Fantastic and Whimsical" and "Audacious and Electrifying" read the subheadings for Olin Downes's review in the *New York Evening Post;* stated Downes, flatly, "It is a strange work." The music reminded H. T. Finck, like Luening, of jazz: "It would hardly be fair to say that the concertino is superior (not super) jazz; but the suggestion was there. The music's American quality, in any case, could not be mistaken by anyone."[16] Carpenter himself admired Schmitz's "surprising understanding of the so-called 'American' elements of the composition."[17]

Carpenter had hoped that Schmitz would give the Piano Concertino's Paris premiere with Damrosch in early May, but Schmitz had already arranged to play the work in Paris with Rhené-Baton and the Pasdeloup Orchestra on 16 June 1920.[18] Otto Luening attended this performance (noting its "jazz rhythms"), as did Rue Carpenter, who sent back to her husband "a full description of the very interesting audience which was present."[19] Rue's letter—like nearly all of the correspondence between herself and her husband—appears to have been lost, but the "interesting audience" included French composers Louis Aubert and Darius Milhaud.[20]

Parisian critics liked the Piano Concertino, at least according to the reviews sent to the composer and those quoted in *Musical Courier.* Louis Vuillemin wrote: "What a pleasure this [the Piano Concertino] was indeed. This work is dashing, lively, rhythmic and colorful. It is picturesque with a luxurious and colorful instrumentation." Jean Poueigh listened "with great sympathy [to] the three parts of this work, where one can easily discover familiar folk tunes." Another critic specifically referred to the second movement's main theme as a "mélodie des plantations."[21] Although the critics wrote of "endless" applause, Carpenter understood from either his wife or Schmitz that the work did not particularly excite the audience—an impression later confirmed by Pitts Sanborn.[22] The composer wrote to Schmitz, "It is not to be expected that this particular type of American music should find at first very much favor in European countries, dealing as it does with an idiom which is unfamiliar and whose spirit is not fully understood."[23]

Schmitz and Monteux planned to introduce the Piano Concertino to New York on 18 March 1920, but the work once again was canceled, this time because of a strike by the Boston Symphony. Schmitz subsequently wanted to play the work in New York in the fall of 1920, but Carpenter thought it only fair that "inasmuch as the failure of the Philharmonic to play the Concertino this winter was in no wise Grainger's fault, and, inasmuch as he was the first pianist to take an interest in the piece, it would not be entirely courteous on my part, if I did not give him the opportunity to present the piece first in New York next season if he wishes to do so."[24] Grainger and Damrosch (not Stransky) finally gave the Piano Concertino's New York premiere on 28 November 1920. Pitts Sanborn, who had heard the Paris premiere, compared the two concerts: "The performance on that occasion . . . suffered from hasty preparation and insufficient rehearsal. . . . The performance yesterday presented the work much more favorably."[25]

Thus, like Milhaud, Copland and Gershwin at least had an opportunity to hear the Piano Concertino in 1920. Copland especially is likely to have attended a performance of the work; by 1919 he understood that fashionable New York considered Carpenter and Griffes outstanding names in American music (though his respect for Rosenfeld might have made him skeptical).[26] Would Milhaud, Copland, or Gershwin have found any inspiration in the music's "jazz" or at least American rhythms?

No evidence suggests as much. In 1922, after stating that American music had influenced European music, Milhaud, when asked by reporters whether he meant MacDowell's or Carpenter's music, answered: "Neither the one nor the other. . . . I mean jazz."[27] Neither Gershwin nor Copland acknowledged any importance to Carpenter's music either; Copland especially would have had reason to do so in, say, his 1927 article "Jazz Structure and Influence."[28] But at the least the Piano Concertino, and even more so Carpenter's *Krazy Kat* of 1921, set the stage for the emergence of Milhaud's *Création du monde,* Gershwin's *Rhapsody in Blue,* and Copland's *Music for the Theatre.*

The Piano Concertino became, in fact, one of America's most popular orchestral works of the 1920s and 1930s, even rivaling the composer's own

Adventures in a Perambulator.[29] Rudolph Reuter and Stock played it in Chicago again on 31 March 1922. Schmitz continued to champion the work, including performances on 22 July 1926, with Emil Oberhoffer at the Hollywood Bowl, where "it met with a very spontaneous success with the 22,000 people composing the audience,"[30] and on 17 December 1926, with Fritz Reiner and the Cincinnati Orchestra.

As part of the 1933 Chicago World's Fair, the black pianist-composer Margaret Bonds performed the work with Stock at a special Chicago Symphony concert on 17 June 1933. This concert featured African American performers and composers and included the premiere of Florence Price's 1932 Symphony in E Minor. Carpenter's possible influence on both Bonds and Price needs to be explored. Bonds's performance of the Carpenter Piano Concertino, for instance, might have influenced Price's own 1934 Piano Concerto; in any case, Price would have sympathized with Carpenter's closeness to African American lullaby.

In the meantime, Grainger continued to perform the "adorable" Piano Concertino nearly every other year or so from 1920 to 1950. In 1939 he played it with Stock and the Chicago Symphony and with Eugene Goossens and the Cincinnati Orchestra. Reviewing the latter performance, Howard Hess recalled Sandburg's lines: "Come and show me another city with lifted head singing so proud to be alive and coarse and strong and cunning."[31] In 1936 Grainger himself wrote, "John Alden Carpenter's works are typical of American music at its best, and, almost overpunctilious as they are in the cleanliness and refinement of their craftsmanship, they show those sharply contrasted moods of wistfulness and sparkling buoyancy that so often delight us in the arts of the New World."[32]

In a 1940 letter to the composer, Grainger further declared the Piano Concertino "the finest work for piano and orchestra since C. Franck's Variations." But the "ridiculous condition" of the conductor's score, which he called "a disgrace to American music," hampered the work's popularity. Grainger, in fact, expressed astonishment that, despite Schirmer's resources and the composer's private wealth, no "decent score" was available.[33] Carpenter answered: "I have struggled constantly with Schirmer over the unsatisfactory condition of the concertino material. To hear now that they are still sending out to conductors for actual use, the illegible published facsimile of my original score, is just one more shock to me as I was under the impression that they had on hand, a full sized photostatic copy of my original score, the original having been lost through some carelessness in their rental department." Carpenter threatened to "go down to New York and plant a bomb on the doorstep of #3 East 43rd Street." As a postscript, he added, "As to riches, I have many blessings, but few dollars."[34]

In response to another complaint from Grainger—this one concerning an upcoming performance with Hans Kindler—Carpenter revised the score while in Carmel during the winter of 1947, "making," in his own words, "very few actual changes, but cleaning up bowing, tempi indications, etc."[35] He also extensively touched up the orchestration, primarily by adding or deleting doublings. In the slow movement, for example, he doubled the opening cello melody with the violins (and embellished it as well); while in the same movement's Largamente section, he removed the string doubling of the piano solo. He also omitted the quotes of "Old Folks at Home" and "Dixie."

On reflection Carpenter further cut fifty-nine measures from before ㉝ in the last movement. "My reasoning is as follows," he explained to Grainger. "It is too close to the end of the work to interrupt the flow of the final drive with a slow and rather sentimental episode such as [rehearsal] 32 to [rehearsal] 33 in which the piano provides nothing but an uninteresting 'plunk-plunk' accompaniment." He proposed, rather, a short bridge and asked Grainger for his opinion. Grainger replied that he thought the cut a mistake, and Carpenter responded, "I shall heed your advice and make no cuts."[36] In fact, the published revised score offered the cut as an option.

In probably the same year, 1947, Carpenter also wrote an optional, unpublished, thirty-seven-measure cadenza for the solo piano beginning one measure after ㉞, just one measure into the final Vivo. The composer likely sought to redress the work's relative lack of virtuosic display (he had, in fact, written a three-measure, cadenza-like passage at this very juncture in a preliminary sketch of the work more than thirty years earlier). In addition, he presumably intended the cadenza's dark A-Phrygian modality, often poised over a dominant pedal, to make the music's eventual resolution in A major sound all the brighter. The end result was stylistically congruent with the rest of the music despite some features more clearly reminiscent of the composer's late music, such as Pedro's Fatal Dance from the revised *Birthday of the Infanta* (1938/40).

By the 1940s the pianist George Roth, something of a Carpenter protégé, had identified himself, like Grainger, with the Piano Concertino. Roth played the work all across the country, sometimes with orchestras, sometimes in his own arrangement for solo piano. After 1947 he adopted the revised version, writing the composer in 1948, "I still say it is *the* American piano concerto and the new orchestra score is a masterpiece."[37]

Marjorie Mitchell, pianist, and William Strickland, conductor, recorded the revised Piano Concertino for Composer's Recordings, Inc., in 1964 (without taking the optional cut and apparently unaware of the optional cadenza).[38] The reviews of this recording were mixed. Alfred Frankenstein wrote, "Like most of Carpenter's music, it begins well, in a witty dialogue of piano and orchestra which sounds like a bit of jazz by MacDowell, but before long the work bogs down in Carpenter's kind of banality." William Flanagan similarly stated, "I would be the last man in the world to hold its lightness or even its innocence against it, but its nineteen-fifteenish view of Impressionism is so strongly naïve that it seems almost to be mocking." On the other hand, Arthur Cohn thought it "enjoyable fare concocted of many eclectic ingredients. . . . Eclectic though it is, there is little academic dust on the score." And Milano found it "a relaxed and atmospheric work; the form is clear and simple and the texture is lightly colorful. The work is very pleasant and while not Carpenter's best, certainly deserves to be revived, now and then, in our concert halls."[39]

Even as Carpenter was applying the finishing touches on the Piano Concertino, the *Christian Science Monitor* of 30 October 1915 published an article that featured Carpenter's thoughts on the much-discussed subject of an "American school of music." Arguing that "all our art is bound to be polyglot, and that does not mitigate against individualism in the accomplishment of large and serious things," Carpenter observes with sympathetic caution the use of Indian and Negro folklore by American composers, a trend he refers to as "this harking back to the elemental to define nationalism." He draws distinctions, however, between the relative usefulness of Indian and Negro music. Citing Busoni's *Indian Fantasy,* which he finds "neither uplifting nor sympathetic," Carpenter states: "The American Indian is elemental, but as a musical inspiration on the basis of his own idea of music he is hard and inflexible. The moment you take him away from his natural and picturesque surrounding he becomes unnatural, unpicturesque—not an object to inspire the music." Negro music, he claims, offers greater potential, "for his idea is harmonious and rhythmical. The Indian music appears denatured and devitalized, but the melodies of the Negro do not lose their felicitous sense of harmony and have a lilt in rhythm that is irresistible. The base of the sound is oriental, from the same shell that echoes the Spanish, Moorish and Russian strain." But he asks, "Why hark back to traditions and forgotten things for thematic treatment?" suggesting, rather, that the American composer take a cue from the songs of George M. Cohan (1878–1942): "The tireless, joyous and enthusiastic George Cohan waves the flag and flings out his simple lilting songs in a way that appears to please the public; our more serious and reserved composers might get a hint concerning the great American idea, from the observation rather than the study of his rhythmical gladness."[40]

In yet another article published about the same time, Carpenter took an even stronger stand against self-conscious nationalism among both critics and composers. "You may lead your creative impulse to our very best American folk-music material," he warned, "but you can't make it drink." (Charles Griffes cut out Carpenter's article and kept it among his papers.)[41] In later years Vernon Duke sarcastically looked back to this credo as a "musical Declaration of Independence No. 3, after similarly emphatic pronouncements by William Fry and Edward MacDowell," and observed that both Carpenter and Griffes "led their creative impulses to the muddy waters of French post-impressionism . . . and drank their fill."[42] In fact, Carpenter's assimilation and subtle evaluation of Indian folklore, Negro music, and contemporary popular song proved unique.

Carpenter wrote two small songs in 1915, one for his wife—"Aged Woman" (words by Rue)—and one for his mistress—"The Mystery" (words by Ralph Hodgson). Rue's "Aged Woman" seems autobiographical; she placidly enjoys flowers, birds, children, and the "peace my youth sought to destroy." Carpenter's gentle, slightly disturbing E-Dorian melody suggests a not altogether easy acceptance of age. The composer never published the song, which he wrote in one day, 7 February.

Carpenter composed the more alluring "Mystery" in May for Ellen Borden, who kept the song hidden among the composer's love letters to her. The verse by Ralph Hodgson (1871–1962)[43] even resembles Carpenter's letters to Ellen:

He came and took me by the hand,
Up to a red rose tree,
He kept His meaning to himself,
But gave a rose to me.

Carpenter depicts the presentation of the rose by a series of chromatic harmonies that are Straussian enough to suggest a kinship, if not actual familiarity, with *Der Rosenkavalier*. "The Mystery" is not as exquisitely wrought or as finely individual as Carpenter's best songs, but it is lovely and deserves to be known.

During the first half of 1916, Carpenter set five Chinese poems translated by the great English orientalist Herbert Giles.[44] He completed "To a Young Gentleman" (a Confucian ode) on 5 January, "The Odalisque" (by Yü-hsi) on 10 January, "Spring Joys" (by Wei Ying-Wu) in March, "On a Screen" (by Li-Po) on 30 April, and "Highwaymen" (by Li-Shé) on 7 May. All except "To a Young Gentleman" (a "National Ode" collected by Confucius in the sixth century B.C.) dated from the Tang dynasty (618–907). Later in 1916 Carpenter published "On a Screen," "The Odalisque," "Highwaymen," and "To a Young Gentleman" as a cycle titled *Water-Colors* ("Spring Joys" remained unpublished).

Carpenter's attraction to Chinese poetry of the Tang period once again reflected an awareness of literary trends. Harriet Monroe and Ezra Pound, in particular, discovered in such poetry the very ideals that they had been promulgating under the banner of imagism: vivid imagery, lucid expression, flexible rhythms. Indeed, *Poetry* published translations of old Chinese poetry by Ezra Pound, Arthur Waley, and Amy Lowell (in collaboration with Florence Ayscough) alongside the latest offerings from Europe and America.[45]

A letter to Ellen Borden suggests that Carpenter originally intended these settings for voice and orchestra: "I think you will like them, I'm going to call them 'Water Colors.' They can't be made very big, but I think they can be made very neat—with lots of little Ming effects in the orchestra."[46] And in fact, although he composed the songs for voice and piano, Carpenter soon after arranged them for voice and chamber orchestra.

Even by Carpenter's own standards, these Chinese settings are particularly sensitive, especially the cycle's first song, "On a Screen." At first, as sketches show, he approached this song fairly conventionally, but the sparse delicacy of Li-Po's three images—the resting tortoise, the nesting bird, and the boatman's daughter—inspired him to drastically pare down the music's texture (ex. 27). Christopher Palmer felt that the result could well be Carpenter's masterpiece: "The music is simple and beautiful; it has all the serenity and limpidity of a Kao K'o-kung landscape, with a pleasing contrast between the mutedly chromatic harmonic inflexions at 'a bird 'mid the reeds' and the diatonic transparency of 'a light skiff propelled.'"[47]

The music's harmonic ambiguity also contributes to the song's evocative atmosphere, specifically, the F-minor/A♭-major shadings of the first image, the A♭-major/minor inflections over a dominant pedal—never resolved—of the second image, the surprising D♭-major tonality of the third image, and the return to F minor/A♭ major for a reprise of the first image, resolving, finally, into a wonderfully calm F major. Enough similarities with "Bruyères"

EXAMPLE 27.   Carpenter, "On a Screen," from *Water-Colors,* mm. 1–9.

suggest that, by this time, Carpenter knew Debussy's *Préludes,* book 2 (1913), and had learned something about landscape painting from it.

The second song, "The Odalisque," is another exquisite bit of chinoiserie, this one full of life and charm. A "gaily dressed" harem girl bewails "the fate that forbids her to roam" and counts the "buds on each flower / while a dragonfly flutters and sits on her comb." The piano's light sixteenth notes depict the fluttering dragonfly, symbol of the harem girl's desire, while the staccato eighth notes suggest her youthful gaiety. The ironically tearful musical setting for "bewailing" and "flower" is delicious, only slightly short of musical comedy. Carpenter enlivens this little song further by arriving at the tonic's secondary dominant at the end of the poem, followed by a short instrumental interlude and a reprise of the poem's last line, which, at last, reaches tonal resolution at the final word, "comb."

According to legend the Chinese poet Li-Shé wrote "Highwaymen" at the insistence of brigands into whose hands he had fallen. In the poem's first four lines, Li-Shé depicts a misty, threatening landscape with hidden highwaymen; but, he says in the last four lines, there is no need to fear, "For more than half the world consists of bigger rogues than they!" The delighted brigands let Li-Shé go.[48]

In his setting Carpenter uses delicate seconds, fourths, and fifths to depict the misty landscape and ominous forest glades; then simple triads, louder dynamics, and faster rhythms for the punch line. He ties the whole together, however, by repeating the punch line, this time with music from the song's introduction.

The cycle's final song, "To a Young Gentleman," is a strophic ballad in three stanzas. In some ways it resembles the composer's 1911 setting of Barnes's "Don't Ceäre." But here the maiden *does* care (1) what her parents would say, (2) what her brothers would say, and (3) what the world would say. Of all these settings, this one makes greatest use of stock Chinese gestures—pentatonic melodies, secondal harmonies, jaunty rhythms, and so on. But the song's subtle form, with its changing tempos, textures, and keys (from D♭ major to B♭ major to C major and back to D♭ major), is distinctive and nicely captures the shifting moods—from concerned to flirtatious to melancholy. "To a Young Gentleman" also provides the cycle with a delightfully whimsical finale.

In the unpublished "Spring Joys," the poet wanders by the riverbank to watch the willow catkins and peach blossoms floating down the river. Carpenter's lovely setting is particularly vivid, as in the rise and fall of the line "I watch the willow-catkins wildly whirled on every side." The song, however, seems less complex and exotic than the other Chinese settings, the vaguely Chinese trillings in the piano notwithstanding; its simplicity and sweetness remind one sooner of the *Improving Songs*. This comparative simplicity may have decided Carpenter against including it with the others.

Carpenter dedicated "Highwaymen" to Tom Dobson, and "To a Young Gentleman" to Maggie Teyte. Teyte and Carpenter had already worked closely together for a few years. On the other hand, the young Tom Dobson had only just emerged on the music scene and must have been a more recent acquaintance.

Tom Dobson probably would be a more familiar name today had he not died two years later, in 1918, at age twenty-eight.[49] Born in Portland, Oregon, in 1890 to an English father and an American mother, he grew up in California and in 1911 settled in New York, where he studied singing, piano, theory, and composition, including lessons with Howard Brockway.

Dobson forged a unique career somewhere between that of a song recitalist and a cabaret entertainer; he would accompany himself at the piano, singing comical songs of his own as well as the latest European and American art songs, all by memory. Reviewing one such concert, a critic for *Musical America* wrote: "Mr. Dobson is one of the very few singers before the public today who can keep an audience merry and keyed up to the point of laughter and at the same time maintain the dignity and standard of a sincere artist. . . . Mr. Dobson sits at the piano, strikes the keys idly as if unconscious of an audience and entertains in an easy, natural manner that has the delightful flavor of intimacy."[50] After Dobson's death, Kate Douglas Wiggin recalled:

> With a voice of no intrinsic beauty he had the power to make the speech of his songs music, and the songs themselves something altogether rare and lovely. . . . When I recall the hours of keen delight this boy's art gave us—

the pure fun, the touch of sympathetic instinct that brought sudden tears, the joy born of the fresh revelation of some fine poem wrought into music, and contrast them with the boredom I have suffered when hearing some academic darling of the critics—I can only reflect that there are voices and other voices, singers and other singers, artists and artisans, and interpreters of all sorts![51]

Rue Carpenter illustrated Dobson's own settings of James Stephens, published posthumously in 1919.[52]

Dobson naturally gravitated toward the Carpenter songs—both the most jocular of the children's songs and the most sensitive of the art songs. At his New York premiere at the Punch and Judy Theatre on 12 April 1916, he sang eight Carpenter songs: four from *When Little Boys Sing* as well as "Le Ciel," "A Cradle Song," and the two Chinese settings that Carpenter had written thus far, namely, "The Odalisque" and "To a Young Gentleman." The Carpenter songs proved the hit of the evening and had to be repeated. Carpenter might well have attended this concert, which also featured songs by Brahms, Grieg, and Hahn, as well as Griffes's setting of Wilde's "Symphony in Yellow."[53] In any case, the dedication of "Highwaymen" quickly followed.

Christine Miller performed the entire *Water-Colors* with the composer at the piano in Chicago on 4 October 1916. She and Carpenter repeated the work in New York at an all-Carpenter concert sponsored by the MacDowell Club on 6 February 1917. Lucille Stevenson also sang *Water-Colors* in Chicago on 7 January 1917.

In early 1918 Carpenter arranged *Water-Colors* for voice and chamber orchestra, apparently in response to a request for a new work by the newly formed Chicago Chamber Orchestra.[54] He auditioned Mina Hager, a young mezzo-soprano from Madison, South Dakota, stationed at the Great Lakes Training Camp, and engaged her for the premiere after hearing her sing, among other things, "Annie Laurie."

Hager "fell in love with *Water-Colors* immediately" and remained a lifelong devotee. On 30 March 1918 Hager, accompanied by the composer, gave a concert entirely devoted to Carpenter's songs, very possibly the first of its kind. She sang the orchestrated *Water-Colors* once again at a 26 December 1925 concert of the Chicago Allied Arts and continued to sing Carpenter's songs—old and new—in the decades ahead.[55] In 1970 she grieved that "so many of his songs are now out of print."[56]

Hager recorded the entire *Water-Colors* with the composer for the Chicago Gramophone Society and, later, "On a Screen" and "The Odalisque" with Celius Dougherty. The clarity, delicacy, and poetry of her singing on these recordings help explain the composer's high regard for her, as evident from this 1941 letter to Virgil Thomson: "It has long been my conviction that Miss Hager has very unusual gifts. Her voice is not extraordinary but she has a rare clairvoyance in her gift of interpretation. She has had some success in a limited way since she left Chicago and established herself in New York some years ago but nothing like the recognition to which, in my judgement, she is entitled."[57]

After *Water-Colors* Carpenter never again set Chinese or any Asian poetry. The work proved part of a trend, like the enormously popular John Golden–Raymond Hubbell 1916 song "Poor Butterfly," inspired by *Madama Butterfly*. But at the same time, the work signaled, for Carpenter, a transition to a leaner, more ironic musical style, comparable, perhaps, to the role the *Japanese Songs* and the *Song of the Nightingale* played in Stravinsky's development.

CHAPTER NINE

From the First Symphony *(Sermons in Stones)* to "Berceuse de guerre"

1916–1918

▍▍▍ Carpenter began work on his First Symphony, subtitled *Sermons in Stones,* on 31 July 1916 and completed it on 6 March 1917. He wrote the work for the Litchfield County Choral Union Festival, one of the time's premier showcases for new American music.

The Litchfield County (Connecticut) Choral Union was founded in 1899 to honor Robbins Battell (1819–95), a highly regarded choral conductor. In the summer of 1900, the Choral Union initiated annual June concerts featuring major works for chorus and orchestra. Rather than sell tickets to these concerts, the union distributed them to choral members and honored guests. The press usually managed to obtain tickets from friends.

In 1906 the festival moved from the Winsted (Connecticut) Armory to a music shed constructed on the Norfolk, Connecticut, estate of Carl Stoeckel (1858–1925), a wealthy patron who had helped conceive and organize the festival. The new Music Shed held 2,000 seats: 30 in the wings, 425 for the chorus, 100 for the orchestra (though only about seventy-five players were usually employed), and the remaining 1,445 for attendants out front.

In 1908 the festival began launching new scores by Horatio Parker, George Whitefield Chadwick, Samuel Coleridge-Taylor, Henry Hadley, and others. Some of these works were for chorus and orchestra; others were just for orchestra. The composer received an honorarium, and the music was promised at least three rehearsals.[1]

Carpenter derived the descriptive title of his three-movement symphony from Shakespeare's *As You Like It,* providing a fuller quotation in the score's flyleaf:

Sweet are the uses of adversity,
Which, like the toad, ugly and venomous,

Wears yet a precious jewel in his head.

And this our life, exempt from public haunt,

Finds tongues in trees, books in the running brooks,

Sermons in stones, and good in everything.

The heroic duke, banished to the Forest of Arden by his brother-usurper, speaks these lines at the start of act 2; how better, he tells his exiled followers, to live in the woods than the "envious court" full of "painted pomp."[2]

Surely the Great War led Carpenter to reflect on this speech. Like the duke, he presumably intended his *Sermons in Stones* to keep up morale during a time of strife and to encourage his compatriots, exiled in their Forest of Arden of rural Connecticut, far from the "envious court" of warring Europe, to find comfort in nature's goodness. Indeed, a letter to Ellen Borden further documents the composer's optimism during these years: "It is awful over there—isn't it? But I think it was absolutely inevitable—that man has played with soldiers so long. . . . And I believe that it will help the world and force the world down from a plain of living that was false and impossible to maintain."[3]

Although optimism in the face of an "awful" war informs the basic mood of *Sermons in Stones,* tracing all the programmatic implications of the duke's speech as it affects this sprawling three-movement symphony would be next to impossible. The first, fairly slow movement itself has four contrasting sections of varying length. The first section immediately puts forth a bitter-sweet, nobly Elgarian theme that well matches the motto's opening line, "Sweet are the uses of adversity" (ex. 28). This theme resembles Carpenter's patriotic anthem "The Home Road," composed later in 1917. But the symphony is more personal and subtle; indeed, this passage contains some modal ambiguity: the E pedal in the bass alludes to both A minor and C major.

Carpenter derives the symphony's other principal themes from this opening one, which we might consequently call the motto theme. A secondary theme, stated by the winds after ⑴, has a pastoral quality in keeping with Shakespeare's imagery. After alternating both themes, sometimes in counterpoint with short, martial brass calls, Carpenter arrives at a third theme, a funeral march in E♭ minor (seven after ⑺), marked *molto espressivo.*

The first movement's second section, in ⁶⁄₈ and marked Moderato, begins at ⑾. Its *dolce* theme, derived from a cadential figure of the motto theme, recalls Carpenter's many lullabies, although the setting is agitated, looking ahead to the composer's song "Berceuse de guerre." This section subse-

EXAMPLE 28.   Carpenter, First Symphony *(Sermons in Stones)*, first movement, mm. 3–13.

quently develops previously stated material against a four-note figure, itself derived from the motto theme's countermelody. Here, however, the figure has whole-tone inflections and resembles the tolling of bells.

After reaching a cadence in D♭ major, the second section ends, and a third (Vivo) section ensues, involving a waltzlike, vaguely Hispanic transformation of the motto theme. Finally, Carpenter returns to the motto theme in a climactic—and now unambiguous—C major for the movement's fourth and last section. The movement concludes with the funeral march transformed into a *molto tranquillo* C major, a Mahlerian gesture not unlike the end of *Songs of a Wayfarer*: "war alles, alles wieder gut" (everything, everything was good again).

The second movement, Allegro, is a straightforward scherzo movement in ABA form. The main theme involves another waltzlike transformation of the motto theme, this one cast in a *Ländler*-like, macabre E minor. The pastoral trio, Lento, begins in G major and concludes in a peaceful D♭ major (⑦ to ⑫). The recapitulation of the A material is in large part literal, although it features, conspicuously, a new, quasi-fugal development of the waltz theme at ⑯. The E-major coda sweetly recalls the pastoral trio theme. Again, the music resembles Mahler, whose symphonies Carpenter would have heard under Stock.

The last movement, arguably in ABCA form, expands on material derived from the first movement. It opens with a Moderato section in A minor, whose stately, Aeolian theme is put forth in the bass clarinet against a pizzicato ostinato in the cellos. A triumphant transformation of the first movement's martial brass calls follows ([2]). At [3] Carpenter introduces a Presto passage in B♭ minor, whose somewhat primitivist style recalls the composer's American Indian and Near Eastern music; the theme itself looks back to the funeral music of the first movement. One might guess that this Presto initiates the finale proper, but, in fact, it represents an episode; the stately opening theme returns in A♭ minor at [6], rounding out this first section.

The finale's second section, Poco più con moto, in $\frac{6}{4}$, begins at [8] and features gossamer transformations of previous themes, set against a luminous D♭ major, a key that Carpenter throughout this work seems to associate with tranquillity. At [13] a third section, Allegro, recapitulates material from the second-movement scherzo.

The symphony climaxes with grand statements of the finale's main theme in A minor ([16]) and the work's motto theme in a discordant, polychordal setting ([17]), before quickly resolving to a quiet G major and an echo of the first movement's pastoral melody, played by the English horn.

While certain aspects of Carpenter's First Symphony recall Franck, Mahler, and Elgar, some new elements—especially its ostinatos and polychords—point, for the first time, to Stravinsky. Contemporary critics often referred to this connection, for instance, the reviewer for the *New York Herald Tribune,* who wrote, "The influence of Stravinsky was apparent."[4] This assimilation of Stravinsky represented an important development in Carpenter's music, comparable to his earlier (not much earlier!) discovery of Debussy. In later years Carpenter named Debussy and Stravinsky as his favorite twentieth-century composers.

Consequently, Carpenter became one of the first Americans—along with Varèse and Griffes—to come under Stravinsky's influence. He probably first encountered Stravinsky's music when the Ballets Russes came to Chicago in 1916 and performed *The Firebird* and *Petrushka.* This tour led to friendships with such Ballets Russes luminaries as dancer Adolph Bolm and conductor Ernest Ansermet that, in turn, presumably led to Stravinsky himself: Stravinsky's son Theodore drew a pencil sketch of John and Rue in Nice sometime in 1917, probably during the spring or summer—right after the completion of the symphony. Stravinsky and Carpenter became fairly good friends, and the two spent considerable time together during Stravinsky's visits to Chicago in 1925, 1935, and 1940.

Stock premiered *Sermons in Stones* on 5 June 1917 before an invited audience at the Music Shed of the Litchfield County Choral Union. The critics deemed the work "the most important of the novelties" presented at that year's festival. "There is something fascinating in the grace of its rhythms and syncopations," wrote one critic, "in the langourous slow episode by which its course is interrupted; in the skill with which material from the first movement is introduced; in the piquancy of its instrumental effects."[5]

Stock and the Chicago Symphony gave a more public premiere in Chicago on 19 and 20 October of the same year. The composer-conductor Eric De Lamarter reviewed the work at some length for the *Boston Evening Transcript,* praising "the majestic opening of the slow movement, the sparkle and the vividness of the scherzo, and the last dozen bars of all." Although the work might be overlong, "there are great depths in the musical idea of the first theme, variety and color and movement, power in the climaxes, wisdom in the staging, and of no subject may it be said that it is trite. For in all that Mr. Carpenter does is the trace of fantasy and of skill. Furthermore, there is no American between our two coasts at the present time to challenge his mastery of the orchestra." Moreover, wrote De Lamarter, Carpenter served American music well by adapting a native musical language to the symphonic form "without studious imitation of a scheme he did not feel instinctively, and without fear of the tradition." The new symphony was "his ranking composition so far."[6]

Other Chicago composers praised *Sermons in Stones* as well. The young Leo Sowerby (1895–1968) cited the work's first movement—along with parts of Carpenter's Piano Concertino—as "distinctively American . . . by virtue of their big sweep, their vigor, their lack of sentimentality, affectation and diffuseness." Borowski, too, remembered the symphony as "a remarkably fine work."[7]

Walter Damrosch, who had attended the Stock performance at the Norfolk Festival, introduced the symphony to New York on 19 April 1918, where it found favor with the New York critics.[8] Damrosch performed the work again in 1920. Unable to attend this performance, Carpenter wrote to the conductor, "I particularly regret not being able to hear your interpretation of the Symphony because I always feel that you have some occult way of making my compositions sound better than they really are."[9] Damrosch reported back to the composer: "We had given it very careful preparation (five rehearsals). It went to perfection, and I think you would have been pleased with the sympathetic way in which the many exquisite beauties of your score were brought out by the men." The audience responded with "enthusiastic applause."[10]

The symphony never caught on, however. According to Borowski it was "scarcely of the type whose beauty is apparent at one hearing," and it "failed to excite the public."[11] De Lamarter similarly reported on the symphony's somewhat uncertain reception:

> What our musical public feels, together with its pride in the exploits of a favorite son, is a certain dismay over an exceedingly clever "enfant terrible's" latest prank, one that passeth comprehension, but not one for which he should be spanked. They demand a reason for the motto, written in a firm, small, precise hand on the fly-leaf of that score, "Sermons in Stones," other than that of the music. "Well and good," they argue, "if there is a story in the symphony, it ought to be suggested. For if this work is measured by the canons of a symphony, it is not one, and that's all there is to it!" They find neither the form nor the spirit, and in the meantime more people are talking about John Alden Carpenter than ever before, which is nourishing comfort to the composer. The more talk, the plumper the halo.[12]

The immediate postwar period was not well disposed toward big, solemn, romantic symphonies, and Carpenter himself turned his energies to ballet and chamber music. But when he issued a drastically revised version of the symphony in 1940, it won a number of new and distinguished friends, including Bruno Walter.

In April 1916 Carpenter wrote two small piano pieces, *Little Indian* and *Little Nigger,* for the pianist Lester Donahue. These pieces verify the composer's interest in America's "elemental" folklore, as discussed in the previous chapter, but as shaped by his own individuality, including his love for popular music. Its pentatonic melodies and open-fifth drones notwithstanding, *Little Indian* is a quiet, exquisite lullaby, as opposed to the kind of heroic Indianist fare by Arthur Farwell, Henry F. Gilbert, and Harvey Worthington Loomis featured in Farwell's Wa-Wan Press. Andrew Stiller notes that the result is "somber and thoughtful—not at all what you'd expect from the title."[13]

Little Indian uses ostinato technique (especially the repeated fifth D♯–A♯) more thoroughly and daringly than any Carpenter piece hitherto. Although the work is essentially in D♯ minor, the emphasis on the minor subdominant—not only at the start (ex. 29) but throughout (as represented by the move to G♯ minor in the middle B section)—provides a dark, unsettled quality. The dominant harmony simply does not appear but once, and then as a B♭-major passing chord. The piece concludes on a rich, moody D♯-minor harmony with an added seventh (C♯); the polymodal spacing—a D♯ deep in the bass, a closed, F♯-major triad in the middle register—recalls

EXAMPLE 29.   Carpenter, *Little Indian,* mm. 2–6.

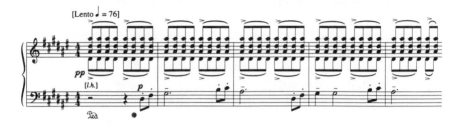

the Piano Concertino but suggests at the same time a growing awareness of Stravinsky. The appearance of the A melody in the midst of the B section (m. 18) evidences a new formal daring as well.

The livelier *Little Nigger* features some ragtime syncopations reminiscent of Debussy's *Golliwog's Cakewalk* (as well as his *Little Nigar,* a work that Carpenter could not have known at the time), but its restrained use of the bass clef makes it as distinctively gentle and soft as *Little Indian.* Moreover, these two pieces (both in ternary form) share a pronounced use of ostinatos; clearly, Carpenter intended them as complementary. *Little Nigger* also bears a close relation to an unpublished violin piece that Carpenter subtitled "Negro Berceuse." Both connections suggest that Carpenter meant *Little Nigger* as a kind of lullaby.

Described in 1917 by Richard Aldrich as "one of the most talented of the young American pianists who have recently come before the public,"[14] Lester Donahue performed *Little Indian* and *Little Nigger* in New York at Aeolian Hall on 23 October 1916. Aldrich found them "interesting": *Little Indian* "shows the characteristic Indian monotony," while *Little Nigger* "has a fascinating rhythm."[15] Donahue played both pieces again in New York on 21 November.

Soon after the November performance, Carpenter started to revise *Little Nigger,* introducing new music just at the return of A. He apparently intended either to delay or to avoid entirely a recapitulation of the main theme, but he started going afield harmonically, at which point he left the revision incomplete. He ultimately renounced the piece altogether.

Instead, Carpenter wrote an entirely new work, *Little Dancer,* in March 1917.[16] He plausibly felt that this energetic, whimsical little piece made a better companion to *Little Indian.* Carpenter presumably composed the piece specifically for Donahue's return engagement at Aeolian Hall on 16 March 1917.

Little Dancer is more complex and adventurous than either *Little Indian* or *Little Nigger*. Carpenter puts forth a very subtle ternary form—if one can call it that. The A section, in A♭ major, modulates to the dominant by the Poco più lento, which introduces a kind of middle section. This middle section remains in the dominant, although its tonal language takes on an ambiguous quality, to the point that the return to A♭ and the main theme at Tempo I comes as something of a surprise.

Indeed, the music's thin, almost bare textures might well obscure the complexity of the harmonic writing. Carpenter derives a number of unusual chords from the whole-tone scale, such as the one at measure 6; the harmony at measure 8—C♭–G♭–B♭♭–D♭–F—is even more evocative (ex. 30). Moreover, the harmonies progress with great freedom and spontaneity. Consider, for example, the return of Tempo I, at which point a dominant seventh chord on B (its D♯ low in the bass) resolves to an A♭-major harmony (with an added sixth) in second inversion—an example, incidentally, of Ziehnian plurisignificance.

Although its title had no ethnic connotations, *Little Dancer* was, at least in part, a substitution for and successor to *Little Nigger*. The music vaguely resembled the earlier work, especially the discarded revisions. These revisions might have inspired *Little Dancer* in the first place. Further, its grace notes, secondal harmonies, and pentatonic inflections anticipated Carpenter's Algerian-inspired Piano Quintet—remembering that the composer himself linked Negro and "Moorish" music.

In any case, *Little Indian* and *Little Dancer* make an attractive pair. According to Andrew Stiller, "Their brevity virtually demands that the two, though composed a year apart, be played together, so they can hold each other up."[17]

On 2 April 1917 Woodrow Wilson went before Congress to ask that a state of war be declared against Germany, and on 6 April the Congress assented almost unanimously.

EXAMPLE 30.   Carpenter, *Little Dancer*, mm. 5–12.

Carpenter responded quickly and decisively. In May he approached John Philip Sousa (1854–1932) about training young bandsmen at the Great Lakes Naval Training Center. Sousa knew and admired Carpenter; earlier that year the bandmaster had predicted that Carpenter was one American composer likely to matter in the years to come.[18] Carpenter arranged a meeting with Sousa; Captain William A. Moffett, commander of the base; Lieutenant James M. Bower, a staffmember (and Sousa's brother-in-law); and himself. As a result, Sousa agreed to enlist as a lieutenant in the navy; he subsequently trained small bands for ships and naval stations and presided over the Band Battalion (the "Jackie" Band), which traveled throughout the United States and Canada, raising more than $21 million for the war.[19]

In September 1917 Carpenter was appointed to the five-member National Committee on Army and Navy Camp Music under the chairmanship of W. Kirkpatrick Brice. The committee's responsibilities included supervising and standardizing the songbooks used in army and navy training camps throughout the country.[20] Carpenter discussed this work with a reporter in early 1918:

> The work that we are doing in the various army and navy training camps has given me one of the biggest musical thrills that you could possibly imagine. What we are working on is simply the idea of mass singing among the soldiers and sailors as a stimulus to military efficiency. We are not interested in the question of music as an art or music as a recreation—these two elements will take care of themselves in due time. What we are trying to do is to help create a spirit and maintain a spirit that will help win the war.[21]

He added that such singing should help "fuse together the many diverse racial elements of our army." And he speculated that the army song might consequently provide the foundation for the emergence of an American school of music.[22] In a later statement Carpenter expanded on this idea to include the whole war experience itself:

> Through the war is to be found that national conscientious basis of the American school of music. The school will be absolutely American, neither Negro nor Indian, but fully American. Americans of the day are only those who lived through a war—the Civil War, for instance. The others, who have since that time immigrated to America, are Americans, but their hearts may or may not be American. Through this war every one here will become truly American, and the music in the camp will stimulate the development of our national music.[23]

Carpenter had the particular responsibility of supervising band music. In this connection he and Sousa attended a meeting in Washington on 7 February 1918. Their principal difficulty, Carpenter told a reporter, was in finding suitable bandmasters: "The bandmaster is the motive-power of the military band. He may or may not be a fine, cultured musician; but he must, to realize the purposes of music for the fighting men of our country, be a man of magnetism, of live emotions; and capable, above all else, of enkindling his men."[24]

In the course of 1918, the Committee on Army and Navy Camp Music also became involved, or rather entangled, in trying to establish a standardized text for "The Star-Spangled Banner." They eventually decided against the "so-called Sonneck-Sousa-Damrosch" version, based on historic authenticity, in favor of their own version, based on oral variants. Carpenter explained to Carl Engel that the committee ruled out "historic authenticity, for the simple reason that the American people have no interest whatever in 'authenticity' and will proceed to sing the song the way they are used to singing it regardless of every document that can be produced to the contrary." By the time Carpenter wrote this, however, the war had ended, and the composer admitted that he was tired of the whole discussion.[25]

In addition, Carpenter composed two songs for the war effort: the patriotic anthem "The Home Road" and the fight song "Khaki Sammy."

Carpenter once discussed the inspiration for "The Home Road": On a hot summer's night in 1917 (presumably in Charlotte, Vermont), he watched a seven-piece band, followed by a group of young inductees, marching along with their suitcases in hand. At first he found the procession amusing, but then he sobered at the thought of what lay ahead for the recruits and immediately wrote the words and music to "The Home Road."[26]

In its published version, "The Home Road" contains two verses, each in simple AB form, with the same B for both verses:

For the long, long road to Tipperary
Is the road that leads me home
O'er hills and plains, By lakes and lanes,
My Woodlands! My Cornfields! My Country! My Home!

The "long road to Tipperary" referred to the 1912 English music hall hit by Jack Judge (1878–1938) and Harry Williams (1874–1924), which had become particularly popular with British and American soldiers during World War I;

the little band Carpenter heard that summer night in 1917 might well have been playing it. Carpenter's setting does not actually quote "Tipperary" but merely echoes it, changing the melody's shape somewhat.

The solemnity of "The Home Road" finds some middle ground between Elgar's *Pomp and Circumstance* marches and Irving Berlin's "God Bless America." At the same time, the song recalls French and American revolutionary anthems of the eighteenth century—perhaps because Carpenter's tune (unlike Elgar's or Berlin's) is thoroughly diatonic. Along with the song's closeness to the "Policeman" music from *Adventures in a Perambulator,* this connection helps define its individuality.

Three versions of the song exist: a preliminary, untitled sketch with only a melody line and a single verse; a fair copy titled "Land of Mine," also with only one verse, and dated 4 August 1917; and Schirmer's 1917 published edition, titled "The Home Road," with two verses, dated July 1917 (the date, apparently, of the original sketch).

Whereas the sketch and the fair copy essentially have the same lyrics, Carpenter extensively rewrote the words for the published version. While the original begins, "Sing a song of freedom! Sing a song of joy! / Sing a song of victory, as our boys march by," the published version begins, "Sing a hymn of freedom! Fling the banner high! / Sing the songs of liberty, Songs that shall not die." The reference to "Tipperary" appears in all three versions. Carpenter first misquoted the song, writing "long road" instead of "long way." He corrected himself in the fair copy and consciously returned to "road" in the published edition.

All three versions contain minor musical differences, but the most interesting variants occur between the sketch and the fair copy. For instance, Carpenter moves the word "joy" ("high" in the published edition) down to G (g^1) rather than up to B♭ ($b♭^1$). More dramatically, he interpolates two additional measures in the fair copy that offer the concrete image of "My Cornfields! My Rivers!" to the abstract concepts of country and home, and that provide a sweeping, asymmetrical cadence. In the published version, Carpenter changes the words of this added phrase to "My Woodlands! My Cornfields," so that the song's climax falls on "Cornfields" rather than "Rivers" (ex. 31).

"The Home Road" enjoyed tremendous popularity both during and immediately after the war. Schirmer published not only the composer's version for voice and piano but arrangements for various choral and instrumental combinations. In a newspaper feature devoted to the song, Karleton Hackett wrote: "It begins to appear that amid the welter of patriotic songs

EXAMPLE 31. Carpenter, "The Home Road," mm. 31–36.

which have been called into being of the present crisis one has caught the spirit of the hour. If one may hazard a guess as to the future it is that 'The Home Road' of John Alden Carpenter will become a part of our folklore."[27] Hackett's article was accompanied by a layout titled "Chicago: Birthplace of Great War Songs" and that featured the sheet music covers for "The Home Road," Henry Clay Work's "Marching through Georgia" (1865), and George Frederick Root's "Battle Cry of Freedom" (1862) and "Tramp! Tramp! Tramp!" (1865).

Victor recorded "The Home Road" twice, once with Ralph Crane and another time with the outstanding German American contralto Ernestine Schumann-Heink (1861–1936), who sang it quite slowly and dramatically. Stock regularly featured the song at his children's concerts, often sung by children's choruses.[28] Today, in fact, "The Home Road" survives most conspicuously in anthologies for schoolchildren.

In contrast to "The Home Road," "Khaki Sammy" is a high-spirited salute of the kind that enjoyed great popularity during World War I. Carpenter wrote both the words and music in August 1917 for Nora Bayes (born Leonora or Dora Goldberg), a vaudevillian renowned for her beautiful voice and sophisticated stage presence. A successor to Lillian Russell, Bayes (1880–1928) rose to stardom in the early 1900s, became a Christian Scientist, and married five times (once more than Russell). According to David Ewen, she "had a low, husky voice and a lively and infectious personality, both of which had a hypnotic effect on audiences. She was a stately figure on the stage. She would stride up and down, swinging her hips, a fine lace handkerchief or a fan in her hand. She would stop center stage to deliver a recitation or a rhymed quip."[29] Douglas Gilbert described Bayes as "the American Guilbert, mistress of effortless talent in gesture, poise, delivery, and facial work. No one could outrival her in dramatizing a song."[30] In 1908 Bayes collaborated with her second husband, Jack Norworth, on a big hit, "Shine on Harvest Moon," which became her signature theme.[31] At the start of World War I, Bayes popularized such pacifist songs as "I Didn't Raise My Boy to Be a Soldier" and "Don't Take My Darling Boy Away." But after America's entry in 1917, she stirred audiences with patriotic numbers, most notably, George M. Cohan's "Over There."[32]

Carpenter's "Khaki Sammy," in fact, seems conscious of Bayes's performance of "Over There." The song's last line even states, "You can gamble on your sammy over there" (Bayes would substitute the word "Sammys" for "Yanks," as her recording of "Over There" reveals).[33]

Unlike "Over There," however, "Khaki Sammy" does not call for "Johnnie" to "get your gun"; rather, Johnnie is already marching off to war, the sun "shining on his gun." The soprano Mabel Garrison (1886–1963) recorded "Khaki Sammy" for Victor, and Nora Bayes presumably sang it to good effect, but the song's subtleties—like the ubiquitous, drawn-out appoggiaturas—probably made it less useful than "Over There" and many other such tunes.

In a more private, war-weary vein, Carpenter wrote two art songs—both lullabies—in 1918: "The Lawd Is Smilin' through the Do'" and "Berceuse de guerre."

Composed in January, "The Lawd Is Smilin' through the Do'" has an unattributed text that is either a traditional African American lullaby or one made up by the composer in that style: "All I'se got, an' all I am, Is you," a mother tells her "lil' black lamb." As in "The Home Road," Carpenter sketched out the entire vocal line before adding any harmonies, which helps explain the music's tuneful spontaneity, suggestive of the syncopated rubato of black folk music.

The last line of each of the song's two verses departs from the music's pervasive pentatonicism and features an expressive chromatic line over a series of major triads (on E, D, C, B♭, and E) in a way that anticipates the ending of Gershwin's "Summertime." Throughout, the piano accompaniment delicately evokes the twang of a banjo.

"Berceuse de guerre" (War lullaby) is a setting of a French poem by Émile Cammaerts (1878–1953), a Belgian writer who settled in England in 1908. Schirmer's published edition provides a composition date of July 1918, but this seems mistaken: the poem itself is subtitled "August, 1918." Indeed, one source reports that Carpenter wrote the song just before the armistice on 11 November 1918, probably in October or early November.[34]

In the poem a mother alternately comforts her child with the traditional

French lullaby "Dodo, l'enfant do" and expresses concern for her husband at the front. By the poem's end one hardly knows whom the mother is trying to cheer—her baby, her lover, herself, or the reader. Carpenter only sets the first three of the poem's four verses, placing the horrific climax, "Or is he lying in some hole, With open mouth and with closed eyes?" nearer to the end.

Carpenter's setting effectively contrasts the lullaby and the interior monologues: the music for the former is modal, restrained, and soft; the music for the latter is chromatic, agitated, and turbulent. Further, the song uses a key signature of one flat for the lullaby portions as opposed to five flats for the monologues. The actual tonal centers are far from clear, however: the lullaby hovers abstractedly between F major and D minor; the monologues move restlessly by tritone, making their occasional references to the lullaby all the more poignant.

In the third stanza the harmonic texture becomes increasingly polytonal; the tension between E♭ and A major leads, finally and unexpectedly, to an E-minor resolution at the words "and with closed eyes?" By war's end we find Carpenter strained to the limit, at the edge of the abyss. He never plunged much deeper, but the experience left its mark.

"Berceuse de guerre" proved especially meaningful in the years following the war. Povla Frijsh performed it in 1922, and Mina Hager recorded it in 1937.[35] In May 1940 Carpenter arranged the song for orchestra as "War Lullaby" in an alternative English setting that he himself adapted from the published translation by Tita Brand-Cammaerts. He also made a few changes in the score, most notably, adding a grand pause just before the words "Mon grand enfant." In addition, he slowed the tempo and deleted the French markings.

Although the instrumentation listed on the flyleaf of the score to "War Lullaby" called for a full orchestra, Carpenter, in fact, only scored this arrangement for oboe, clarinet, bassoon, piano, harp, percussion, and strings. The orchestration itself featured soft and sensitive use of harp, glockenspiel, cymbals, timpani, and gong.

CHAPTER TEN

The Birthday of the Infanta

1918

Carpenter wrote his first ballet, *The Birthday of the Infanta* (1917–18), for the Chicago Opera Association, founded in 1915 as essentially a reorganized Chicago Grand Opera. Garden and Campanini continued to provide artistic leadership, but the company's financial backers, especially Harold McCormick, exerted more say than before. According to Ronald Davis, the McCormicks ran the association "as if it were their private entertainment. . . . [They] probably gave Chicago the best opera the city has ever seen, supporting it in a manner reminiscent of the royal courts of eighteenth-century Europe."[1]

During the 1910s America's opera houses provided a choice avenue for ballet, for they employed the nation's best classically trained choreographers, dancers, and pit musicians; indeed, America had no ballet companies to speak of. But whereas opera houses frequently staged new operas, they rarely commissioned ballets. Carpenter had the luck to draw upon his considerable artistic stature and social position; most other American composers simply did not write ballets.

Why did Carpenter undertake a ballet rather than an opera in the first place? Surely, Garden and Campanini would have gladly produced a Carpenter opera. Popular and critical interest in American opera was at a high point during the 1910s. The Metropolitan Opera, under Giulio Gatti-Casazza, and the Chicago Opera annually premiered works by Walter Damrosch, Victor Herbert, Henry Hadley, Reginald de Koven, and many others. Even smaller cities like Seattle, Cleveland, and Los Angeles staged new American operas during the 1910s, a decade Charles Hamm calls "a golden age for opera in this country."[2] Furthermore, expectations ran high that Carpenter, who had established himself in the field of song and orchestral music alike, would write an opera. His publisher Rudolph Schirmer urged him to do so as early as 1914: "I somehow have the feeling that you have it in you to write an Opera that would vindicate the theory that it is just as possible to produce an Opera in the English language as in any foreign tongue."[3] Carpenter's colleague Ernest Schelling (1876–1939) similarly expected him to write "the long promised great American opera."[4]

Carpenter himself had made some moves toward opera before the war (see chap. 4). But by 1917 he "was inclined to doubt whether opera will play much of a part" in the development of American music, in contrast to ballet, which he claimed to be "the more flexible art form and will be found, I think, to offer richer resources for our composers."[5]

Carpenter remained more or less true to this position in the years ahead. In 1924 he told Eugene Stinson that "contemporary composers were largely led to the mimed dance by the unsatisfactory mode of expression offered in opera, with its 'falsities' and handicap to naturalness."[6] He made this point again in 1926: "The modern composers, Stravinsky and the rest, it will be noticed, are not using the opera form. They do not feel at home in it, apparently. Instead, they write ballets. The ballet is flexible; you can do what you want with it—but not opera." Moreover, opera was incompatible with jazz: "For opera we must choose something poetic and remote. Jazz is very near and real."[7]

During these same years, Carpenter similarly argued for the motion pictures over the theater. In 1929, after criticizing Eugene O'Neill's *Strange Interlude* as three acts too long, he admitted that movies "get through to him," whether they are "good or bad."[8] And in a 1931 discussion of new operas by Deems Taylor *(Peter Ibbetson)* and Hamilton Forrest *(Camille)*, Carpenter concluded that whereas motion pictures "had progressed from the mechanical to the artistic . . . the development in the theatre had been just the opposite."[9] For Carpenter, whereas ballet and motion pictures were alive and viable, opera and theater had become mechanical and inflexible.

Toward the end of his life, Carpenter acknowledged the effectiveness of Menotti, but he remained skeptical toward opera.[10] In 1947 he stated, like Leonard Bernstein after him: "Americans have little interest in opera; it is not their dish. But we will get the American equivalent of opera from Broadway."[11]

Carpenter continually toyed with the idea of composing an opera, nonetheless. In 1922 he considered collaborating with Stark Young and Robert Edmond Jones on an opera titled *Somebody's Saint*.[12] And in the 1940s he thought of writing an opera based on James Barrie's (1860–1937) *Young David*. Indeed, Carpenter might well have written an opera if opera itself had not fallen on such bad times in post-Depression Chicago.

Carpenter's early conversion to ballet—relative to his compatriots—owed much to his susceptibility to Diaghilev's Ballets Russes. By 1917, after all, the Ballets Russes had challenged opera as Europe's premiere musical institution with its productions of Stravinsky's *Firebird* (1910), *Petrushka* (1911), and *The Rite of Spring* (1913); Ravel's *Daphnis et Chloé* (1912); Debussy's *Jeux* (1913); and Satie's *Parade* (1917). While on tour in 1916, Diaghilev confidently told his American audience, "Whom have you writing for opera now? Puccini, who hardly merits consideration, musically, and Richard Strauss." In Diaghilev's opinion ballet was a more revolutionary institution than opera because dancers were younger than opera singers.[13]

The Carpenters may well have seen the Ballets Russes in Paris as early as 1910, but they surely attended the company's two Chicago tours in the mid-teens, including two weeks in late February 1916, at which time the corps danced at the University of Chicago's Auditorium Theatre, offering nine ballets (a large percentage of their repertoire), including *Prince Igor, Scheherazade, Afternoon of a Faun, The Firebird,* and *Petrushka.*

Chicago actually responded less well to these ballets than had many other American cities. The local press complained that Adolph Bolm, Léonide Massine, and Xenia Makletsova were poor replacements for the legendary Vaslav Nijinsky and Tamara Karsavina; that the mimed stagings lacked the thrilling virtuosity of Pavlova and more traditional ballet; and that the sensuality of some productions (interracial in *Scheherazade* and onanistic in the *Faun*) was unseemly. The Carpenters presumably concurred sooner with Charles Collins, however, who wrote, "The enchanted music of Stravinsky, the gorgeous color schemes of Bakst, the inspired choreography of Fokine and the orchestral art of Ansermet are too impressive to permit me to worry about Nijinsky." Collins thought the productions "a revelation."[14]

The Ballets Russes returned to Chicago for a few days in January and February 1917, this time with Nijinsky. They performed mostly the same repertoire, although they offered two new works as well: Bolm's *Sadko* after Rimsky-Korsakov and Nijinsky's *Till Eulenspiegel* after Strauss.

Presumably, the Carpenters not only attended the Ballets Russes's Chicago performances but met and possibly entertained some of the dancers, including Adolph Bolm, who would choreograph the composer's first two ballets. Indeed, Bolm may have precipitated Carpenter's decision to undertake a ballet, for the Russian dancer was apparently in on *The Birthday of the Infanta* from the beginning.[15]

Born in St. Petersburg in 1884, Adolph Bolm graduated a first-prize winner from that city's Imperial Ballet school in 1903. From 1904 to 1911 he danced at the Maryinsky Theatre in St. Petersburg, sometimes partnering Pavlova at home and abroad. He established a reputation primarily as a character dancer, however, making a specialty of the "Spanish Dance" from *Swan Lake*. He began dancing in Paris under Diaghilev in 1909 and joined the Ballets Russes officially in 1911, dancing the Tsarevitch in *The Firebird* at Covent Garden. His greatest roles for the Ballets Russes included the Chief Warrior in *Prince Igor* and Pierrot in *Carnaval,* in which he "created such a tragic figure within the scope of the comedy that he almost stole the show."[16]

Bolm prepared and supervised the Ballets Russes's first American tour, assuming the roles usually danced by Nijinsky. Many Americans who hoped to see the fabled Nijinsky were quick to dismiss Bolm as second-rate. This was not, however, the opinion of Charles Griffes, who met and befriended Bolm during the tour, and who concluded that Bolm was "a far more interesting dancer than Nijinsky."[17] Indeed, when Bolm and Nijinsky both danced on the second tour, some critics expressed, doubtless to their surprise, a preference for Bolm.[18]

During this second tour Bolm suffered an injury, the reason most often cited for his decision to stay in America after the Ballets Russes returned to Europe in March 1917. But he had already announced some such intention a year earlier.[19] In fact, Bolm later admitted that he was tired of "petty quarrels" with Nijinsky and other company members, and that he had become, further, an admirer of America and its people:

> I am fascinated by their spirit. There is a childish, busy zest about life in this young continent. Some humming, growing American city filled with color-hungry citizens will be a fine place to live, to create flashing new ballets bright with the tones of life, symbolic of moods of wistfulness and wonder.
>
> I am grateful for the accident which keeps me here in America after our turbulent little group of dancers has sailed for Europe.[20]

Bolm probably realized—rightfully—that America offered him opportunities not available while he remained in the shadow of Fokine and Nijinsky. And unlike many other Russian dancers, according to George Amberg, he had "an intuitive understanding of this country's essential character, its aesthetic climate and its creative potentialities."[21] True enough, after one month's residence, he suggested a baseball ballet to Charles Griffes.[22]

Bolm had choreographed his own ballets since 1912, including a Diaghilev *Khovanshchina* in 1913. After moving to the United States, he devoted more and more time to choreography. From 1917 to 1919 he worked in New

York, staging Rimsky-Korsakov's *Coq d'or* at the Metropolitan Opera and Victor Herbert's *Miss 1917* on Broadway. He also began his own company, the Ballet Intime, a rather avant-garde concern for which Griffes wrote a short, Japanese-inspired ballet, *Sho-jo*.[23] From 1919 to 1927 Bolm lived in Chicago, where he worked at the Chicago Opera (presumably through Carpenter's intervention) and formed another ballet company, the Chicago Allied Arts (1924–27), often cited as America's first ballet company. In 1926 Samuel Putnam called Bolm "an invaluable asset in any comparative hinterland of the arts. . . . He is peculiarly sensitive to world-currents and rather weirdly circuited with those same currents. Rather, he is himself one of the generating batteries."[24] Bolm finally settled in Los Angeles in 1928, where he lived until his death in 1951. In his later years he choreographed for Hollywood films, the San Francisco Ballet (which he helped found in 1932), and the (American) Ballet Theatre (founded in 1939).

Despite this crucial, pioneering work in New York, Chicago, Los Angeles, and San Francisco, and a catalog of more than thirty ballets, Bolm is remembered today primarily as Ruth Page's mentor. Agnes de Mille recalled, simply, that "Bolm was not a good choreographer."[25] Indeed, Bolm's efforts included two disastrous Stravinsky productions: the original *Apollon musagète* in 1928 and a revival of *The Firebird* in 1945 (though Chagall's sets for the latter became world-renowned). On the other hand, Bolm had considerable success not only with his two Carpenter ballets—*The Birthday of the Infanta* and *Krazy Kat*—but with a 1931 *Ballet mécanique* (music by Mosolov) and a 1940 *Peter and the Wolf* (music by Prokofiev). According to George Amberg, Bolm's *Birthday of the Infanta* claims special attention because it was "the first large-sized ballet of his own in which Bolm showed the measure of his choreographic talent," because it was "a work of style, nobility and beauty such as the American ballet had not produced before," and because it was "the first successful collaboration between a noted Russian choreographer and a group of American artists."[26]

Dance historian Verna Arvey found conflicting evidence concerning this Carpenter-Bolm collaboration. Bolm wrote to her that he had "left Carpenter entirely alone" until the composer began to send "completed parts of the score from time to time." At this point he made some suggestions, for example, he asked that Carpenter shorten his solo, which he felt would tax both himself and the audience (Carpenter subsequently shortened the dance by at least one-half). On the other hand, Carpenter told Arvey that Bolm had suggested groupings and movements from the very beginning. In any case, the collaboration must have been congenial: Bolm even named Carpenter his son's godfather.[27]

The Birthday of the Infanta is based on the 1889 fairy tale of the same name by Oscar Wilde. Apparently inspired by Velázquez, the story is set in seventeenth-century Spain, where the Infanta usually enjoys the company of only a small circle of intimates: her melancholy father, who for twelve years has been mourning the queen's premature death (possibly murder) shortly after the Infanta's birth; her cruel uncle, Don Pedro (possibly her mother's murderer); her stern duenna; and the forbidding grand inquisitor. But because today is her twelfth birthday, children of lesser rank can join her in the day's festivities: a mock bullfight, a French tightrope walker, an Italian puppet show, an African juggler-snakecharmer-magician, a "solemn minuet" danced by young boys, a group of gypsy dancers (with tamed bear), and, finally, a misshapen, ugly Dwarf, recently discovered in the woods and brought to court to entertain the Infanta. After the Dwarf dances, the amused Infanta mockingly throws him a rose and requests that he dance for her again after siesta.

In the story's second half, the Dwarf, thinking that the Infanta loves him, jubilantly runs out into the palace gardens, where the flowers recoil from his ugliness, while the birds and lizards defend him. Fantasizing about his future life with the Infanta in the forest, the Dwarf grows impatient and steals into the palace, going from room to room in awe of its gilded magnificence. After espying his ugly reflection in a mirror, he realizes the Infanta's cruel mockery and collapses in grief. The Infanta and her companions enter, laughing and applauding the Dwarf in his death throes, which they take to be a fine bit of acting. When the Infanta insists that the expired Dwarf dance for her, the chamberlain explains that the Dwarf will never dance again "because his heart is broken." The Infanta curls up her lips, saying, "For the future let those who come to play with me have no hearts."

Wilde's "Birthday of the Infanta" contains many features amenable to ballet, not least its dancing dwarf as a protagonist; indeed, Carpenter and Bolm may well have realized that Franz Schreker had already composed his own mimed version in 1908. The plot itself resembles such romantic ballets as *Giselle, Swan Lake,* and other shattered idylls in which a naif falls in love with fatal consequences. The setting further recalls the world of the Ballets Russes, not only another Velázquez-inspired work, *Las Meninas* (1916, to music by Fauré), but *Petrushka,* with its own pathetic antihero posed against a carnival atmosphere.[28] (Carpenter also evokes *Pagliacci* by stating at the end of his scenario, "The comedy is finished.")

Like Franz Schreker and Alexander Zemlinsky, who adapted "The Birthday of the Infanta" to the operatic stage in 1922, Carpenter must also have realized the story's closeness to the Oscar Wilde–Richard Strauss *Salome,* especially given *Salome*'s tremendous notoriety in Chicago of the 1910s. Salome and the Infanta similarly preside over an exotic and corrupt court; rustic goodness—in the form of Iokanaan and the Dwarf—dies at their hands. At the same time, these two works form a mirror image of each other. One Wilde critic summarizes it this way: "Salomé dies, having come face to face with the reality of a romantic dream built around Iokanaan, while the Dwarf follows the same pattern in relation to the Infanta."[29]

Many other things might have drawn Carpenter, who had been attracted to Wilde as early as 1912, to "The Birthday of the Infanta." His *Sermons of Stones* Symphony, composed only one year earlier, 1917, had explored a similar tension between nature and civilization. Then, too, Carpenter would have liked the Spanish setting. Most important, perhaps, the composer's daughter, Ginny, had just turned twelve herself in 1916. Indeed, the Carpenters photographed her dressed in the fantastic Infanta costume designed for the premiere. Arthur Meeker even remembered Ginny looking "in her childhood like a Velasquez Infanta." (She made a strong impression on Bolm, too; he once wrote to her, "Êtes-vous une réalité ou un rêve?")[30] Carpenter dedicated the ballet to her.

The identification of the Infanta with Ginny sheds light on a principal difference between the original story and the ballet adaptation, whose scenario Carpenter wrote himself. In Carpenter's version the Infanta does not react with cruel indifference to the Dwarf's death but "advances with hesitating step to the little figure on the floor" and, realizing he is dead, "softly steals away."[31] For Wilde the Dwarf's death establishes the Infanta's precocious heartlessness; for Carpenter the death becomes a redemptive lesson in sympathy. The composer similarly lightens the story by eliminating the king, Don Pedro (the Dwarf is now called Pedro), the inquisitor, and the duenna; he more cheerfully represents the court establishment with gardeners, nurses, servants, a cook, and two majordomos.[32]

While sketching out the ballet, Carpenter jotted down a number of short musical ideas that he apparently intended as a working lexicon. Some consisted of a simple motive or melody; others involved a specific harmonic context. In a few instances he indicated some instrumentation or such labels as "Bull Fight," "Dwarf," or "Finale." Only a few of these ideas made their way into the completed ballet, however.[33]

On 20 August 1918 Carpenter completed a 44-page first draft, composed on two and sometimes three staves, that closely approximated the finished product completed later that year. Unfortunately, we lack an authoritative version of this 1918 finished work (as opposed to the much-revised version of

1940). The Library of Congress holds the manuscript of a 45-page condensed piano score and a 182-page orchestral score. Both are working scores, with cuts, emendations, and annotations that do not always agree. Although the orchestral score postdates the condensed score, it does not necessarily supersede it. If nothing else, the condensed score contains more explicit stage directions. The following discussion of the ballet draws upon both sources (though rehearsal numbers refer only to the orchestral score).

Carpenter cast the ballet into two scenes—the first in the palace garden, the second in the palace entrance hall—that correspond to the story's two main parts. The hour-long work requires a fairly large orchestra, including strings, piccolo, two flutes, two oboes, English horn, two clarinets, bass clarinet, two bassoons, contrabassoon, four trumpets, four horns, three trombones, tuba, two harps, piano, celesta, glockenspiel, bells, timpani, bass drum, snare drum, tambourine, castanets, and oriental drum.

The ballet begins with a triple pianissimo E pedal in the timpani and basses, the bells quietly tolling a B♭ tritone that forewarns Pedro's death. The music dramatically shifts to a sunny and lively E♭ major, whose static tonality, quartal harmonies, and folklike vigor apparently derive from *Petrushka*.

When the curtain rises at ④, similar music accompanies the palace gardeners at work. This association with "work" distinguishes Carpenter's music from Stravinsky's; indeed, depicting work becomes a conspicuous and, perhaps, particularly American feature of all three of Carpenter's ballets. In *Krazy Kat* a slightly more goofy version of such "work" music depicts Bill Postem on the job. And in *Skyscrapers* this same idiom in a more strident guise accompanies the actions of construction workers.

The gardeners leave, and for a few moments the stage is empty. Carpenter prepares the entrance of the Infanta with a modulation to an introspective B♭ minor. As the Infanta enters, the composer introduces a foreboding chromatic theme with dramatic triplets (four before ⑧). Subsequently, one hears the Infanta's theme proper (ex. 32), a luminous and gentle theme in D♭ major (⑧) not unlike the Ravel of *Ma Mère l'Oye* (Mother Goose). At ⑨ Carpenter introduces a humorous theme as the Infanta's two nurses enter. Soon after, the other children run into the garden to music at once stately and high-spirited. After some alternation of the nurses' and children's music, the Infanta begins her one solo dance (⑪): a simple but haunting tune in F minor, put forth by a solo oboe and accompanied by harps and strings (short as it is, Carpenter eventually cut one page of this number).

At ⑭ the children resume their merrymaking, and then, at the climax of

EXAMPLE 32.   Carpenter, *The Birthday of the Infanta,* [8], mm. 1–4. Infanta's theme.

their dance, they freeze at the sound of an offstage trumpet signal heralding the arrival of the majordomos ([15]). At [17] the court servants, headed by two majordomos, enter to a delightful, somewhat operetta-like fairy-tale march, with a main theme scored for piccolo, solo flute, and glockenspiel. Each servant carries a platter bearing an enormous box. The Infanta opens three gifts to an exuberant Spanish waltz, with augmented harmonies providing occasional suspense (this gift-opening sequence is not found in Wilde). At [22] the trumpet heralds the arrival of gypsy dancers.

Carpenter subsequently condenses and rearranges Wilde's birthday entertainments into four sections: the gypsies (without tamed bear), the juggler and tightrope walker (together), the mock bullfight, and finally the Dwarf.

The lively, exotic gypsy dance (beginning at [24]) is somewhat comparable—and possibly indebted to—de Falla. Carpenter holds off introducing the castanets until this dance; in addition, he asks that paper be placed on the strings of the piano in order "to produce a quasi-guitarre effect," certainly an early, if not the earliest, example of a prepared piano. The music dramatically modulates between G major and G minor. A middle section, for a solo dancer (beginning at [27]), presents a sultry, modal melody played by the bassoon and accompanied by harp and tambourine. Carpenter elides the gypsy dance's big ending with a soft timpani roll crescendoing to a return to the trumpet call, here played by the strings; he thereby at once creates dramatic closure and musical continuity. Waltzlike music follows as the servants offer the children refreshments.

The juggler and the tightrope walker enter, arguing about who will start. The former begins his brief pantomime at ☒ accompanied by picturesque music filled with grace notes, sweeping arpeggios, and secondal and whole-tone harmonies and featuring the oboe and oriental drum (although neither the stage directions nor the scenario suggest as much, Carpenter is possibly thinking of the juggler's snake-charming abilities). The juggler's music dissolves into the tightrope walker's pantomime, beginning at ☒; a new, comic, waltzlike theme, scored for flute and bassoon two octaves apart, depicts his "fat and pompous preparations." He falls, to the children's uncontrollable laughter. The juggler pushes him aside and resumes his act; the tightrope walker begins and falls once again; the two consult with each other, quarrel, make up, and "depart in high spirits."

Carpenter clearly assimilates aspects of American vaudeville into this particular episode and apparently enjoyed doing so: the pantomime consists of thirty pages of orchestral score, that is, nearly a sixth of the entire ballet. For the first performance, however, Carpenter substantially cut the juggler and tightrope walker scene (though the orchestral and condensed scores do not agree on these cuts).

The trumpet call now signals the mock bullfight, which begins at ☒. This episode similarly fills thirty pages of orchestral score but is replete with such colorful music that Carpenter understandably resisted cutting hardly any of it. Even more than the other entertainments, this one has a dramatic and symbolic function: the mock goring of the bull by the children presages the Infanta's fatal mockery of the disfigured Dwarf.

Carpenter's elaborate re-creation of a bullfight is certainly among the most notable efforts of its kind. The bullfighters enter and march around the arena to a solemn $\frac{2}{2}$ processional in A minor (☒); the Infanta hands down the key to the bullpen, as the flute and celesta put forth the processional theme (☒); the trumpet states the traditional signal for bullfights (twelve before ☒); the attendant fumbles in the lock, and the mock bull charges out, depicted by a low and threatening $\frac{6}{8}$ theme in D♭ minor (☒); and the picadors enter (shortly after ☒), accompanied by snare drum, tambourine, and strong quintal harmonies.

The music then changes to a quick, intense $\frac{4}{4}$ in D minor as banderillero and bull square off (☒) and moves to D major as a second banderillero begins his turn.[34] Carpenter introduces a richly scored passage in G major and $\frac{6}{8}$ as the matador enters the fray (beginning eleven after 56). At the music's climax the bull receives the "coup de grace" (thirteen after 59), depicted by a biting juxtaposition of A major and E♭ major; the tritone relation emphasizes the bull's association with Pedro. The attendants triumphantly drag the bull off as the children, and the music, become more and more excited. At the episode's biggest and last climax, the majordomos suddenly cut off this "turmoil of excitement" with their solemn trumpet call (five after 61).

Soon after (twenty-one after 61), an old woman leads in Pedro—called the "Fantastique" in both the piano and orchestral scores—to his signature theme, a haunting, trilled flute melody in A Phrygian (ex. 33). Pedro immediately begins his dance, which is the ballet's only really large solo, constituting the heart of the work. The dance is rather long—about thirteen pages of orchestral score, a fair amount of it slow. (Carpenter eventually cut the dance by about two pages.) The music changes tempo, meter, key, and mood frequently—from sadness to jest to what might be interpreted as Pedro's passion for the Infanta (eleven after 64), suggested by fortissimo rising fourths in the brass. The solo ends dramatically on a D-minor triad followed by a break that allows, for the first time in the ballet, an obvious moment for applause (twenty-three before 68).

At ten before 68 the Infanta throws Pedro her handkerchief (depicted by cascading piano figuration), and the violins state a new, romantic love theme *(molto espressivo)* that incorporates the Dwarf's passionate rising fourths. The mood changes dramatically at ten before 69, as the cook brings out the Infanta's enormous birthday cake, and as the composer recapitulates fragments of the nurses' music and the fairy-tale march. At eleven after 69 a new, tangolike theme in D♭ major/minor is heard; it soon after provides a recessional for the children and apparently represents siesta time. Before the children actually leave, Carpenter briefly returns to the Spanish waltz for the "game of the candles" (twenty-eight before 70).

Throughout this entire scene, Carpenter takes liberties with the Wilde

EXAMPLE 33.   Carpenter, *The Birthday of the Infanta*, 61, mm. 21–24. Pedro's theme.

story, but at this point a subtle deviation must be emphasized, for it dramatically transforms the meaning of the whole work. In the Wilde original the Infanta asks the Dwarf to dance again after siesta. For whatever reason (and one might be that such information would be difficult to communicate in pantomime), the ballet's Infanta makes no such request; rather, the children simply exit, and Pedro enters the palace on his own initiative. When the Infanta finds the expired Dwarf at the end of Wilde's story, she feels, among other things, disappointment that he will not dance for her again as arranged. In the ballet the Infanta is surprised to discover Pedro and cannot express the kind of petulance voiced by Wilde's heroine. Upon this simple detail hangs a world of difference between the two works.

After the children leave, the music returns to the ominous tritone that opened the ballet. The first scene ends with a pantomime in which Pedro remembers the handkerchief (to the love music, at 71), attempts to enter the palace (eleven after 71), scuffles with the gardeners (twenty-five after 71), and finally climbs into the palace through an open window (thirty-nine after 71). The music, full of tense augmented and diminished harmonies, anticipates American film scores of a later period.

Carpenter originally wrote a very short instrumental entr'acte (he seems to have imagined a simple blackout between scenes 1 and 2) but later appended optional music if the production needed more time for a change of scenery, as apparently was necessary in Chicago.

The lights go up at 73 as Pedro is seen entering a palace room through a window. The remainder of scene 2 consists primarily of a solo pantomime and dance in which Pedro recognizes himself in the mirror and collapses. Because Pedro has a rather lengthy solo at the end of scene 1, Carpenter kept this one relatively short. The whole second scene comprises only fourteen pages of orchestral score.

That Pedro has back-to-back solos is one of the ballet's peculiarities, if not flaws. Wilde himself offset the Dwarf's "solos" with commentaries by the flowers, birds, and lizards. Carpenter might have considered some kind of garden dance—as did Schreker—but he and Bolm opted simply for a short second scene.

At the start of scene 2 (73), Carpenter alternates the Infanta's chromatic foreboding theme and Pedro's trilled signature melody. At seven after 73 Pedro jumps into the room to a falling pizzicato figure in the violins. At the moment of recognition before the mirror, the orchestra puts forth a six-note, completely whole-tone harmony, played clipped and triple fortissimo in the strings (thirty-three after 73). At 74, to the strains of the love theme, Pedro holds up the Infanta's handkerchief to the mirror, and at ten before ⑦⑤ he begins what the condensed score refers to as his "Fatal Dance." This short solo features some of the Dwarf's earlier, jolly music from scene 1 transformed into a slow, pathetic D minor. At the dance's climax, Pedro collapses as a quiet and final statement of his signature theme is heard (⑦⑥). A bare tritone returns as Pedro suffers his final agonies (seventeen after ⑦⑥), and he dies as the bell faintly tolls, triple pianissimo (twenty-one after ⑦⑥). The meaning of the bell is finally clear: it signifies Pedro's death.

Carpenter never resolves the Fatal Dance's D-minor tonality: as "the children dance by the door" (twenty-four after ⑦⑥), the basses arrive at D, but as the support for a I_4^6 chord in G major. In total contrast to the preceding music, the celesta and glockenspiel state a reprise of the Spanish birthday waltz. The children finally dance into the room, unaware of the fallen Pedro, and the music settles down in B major, preparing the ballet's E-major conclusion.

A detailed pantomime follows—spelled out in the condensed piano score—against bits and pieces of the Spanish waltz: the Infanta enters, sees Pedro, and motions the children away (⑦⑦); walks slowly to him, kneels beside him, and attempts to rouse him (sixteen before ⑦⑧); lifts his hand (her handkerchief clutched within), which falls to the floor (seven before ⑦⑧); recoils in horror, as her foreboding motive sounds (four before ⑦⑧); and "slowly and mournfully turns away" (⑦⑧). At this point Carpenter restates the lovely Infanta theme, first heard at ⑧. But the tonality is now E major, not Db major, and the meter is $\frac{4}{4}$, not $\frac{6}{4}$—Carpenter now ends each phrase with a little gasp of two quarter notes. Both the new, sharper tonality and the more disjointed phrase structure effectively suggest that Pedro's death has left Carpenter's Infanta chastened.

Carpenter puts forth an especially sweet and delicate passage as the Infanta's friends come forward to comfort her and as they then "slowly steal out of the room" (ten after ⑦⑧). As the curtain slowly falls, the bell once again tolls a tritone, before the music finally comes to rest on a simple E-major triad.

CHAPTER ELEVEN

The Birthday of the Infanta
Its Premiere and Aftermath

▌▐ The Chicago Opera engaged Robert Edmond Jones (1887–1954), then a
▐▐ young and little-known artist from New York, to design the sets and
costumes for the first performance of Carpenter's *Birthday of the Infanta*.
Jones presumably obtained this commission on the recommendations of Carpenter and Bolm, who naturally knew his designs for Nijinsky's *Til Eulenspiegel*. Carpenter in particular had a knack for discovering and promoting
young talent; he further would have identified with Jones's "unique combination of craftsman, romantic, mystic, and Puritan."[1]

Born in New Hampshire, Jones attended Harvard from 1906 to 1910,
studying art and playing violin in the Harvard Pierian Sodality. He worked
as an instructor in Harvard's Department of Fine Arts, moved to New York
in 1912, studied informally with Max Reinhardt in Berlin, and returned to
New York in 1914. Subsequent commissions—none more so than *The Birthday of the Infanta*—established his reputation as one of America's foremost
scenic designers. Jones became associated especially with productions of
Shakespeare and O'Neill (he designed nearly every O'Neill premiere), although he continued working in opera and ballet as well, including designs
for productions of Carpenter's *Skyscrapers* (1926), Schoenberg's *Die glückliche
Hand* (1930), Berg's *Wozzeck* (1930), and Stravinsky's *Oedipus Rex* (1931). His
brief stint in Hollywood in the mid-1930s proved less successful.

In reviewing the 1922 revival of *The Birthday of the Infanta*, Stark Young
devoted most of his attention to Jones's sets and costumes.[2] Years later,
Young once again wrote about these designs—along with Jones's 1921 *Mac-
beth*, the most "unforgettable" of his entire career—for a 1957 retrospective.[3]
Together, these two pieces provide the fullest discussion of Jones's work for
The Birthday of the Infanta.

Young described the first scene, set in the garden courtyard of the palace,
as follows:

On either side the high walls rise, flat spaces with long, heavy moldings, gray varied to darker, ashen tones. At the head of the steps to the left is a door, very high, with a baroque metal awning across the top, and dark red curtains showing through the glass at the sides. A raised terrace and balustrade cross the middle stage between the two walls, and to the back there is a high iron screen, through which appear the Spanish mountains, violet hardening to blue against the cold gray-rose of the sky. All grave, and austere, and cruel, lovely, elegant, and rich.[4]

He depicted the second-scene hall of mirrors, for its part, as "lofty, with a high door looking out on the same cold-rose sky as before, across a terrace promenade. The scene there in the palace is crimson and grey, dull rose, gold, black. Candlesticks with their huge candles stand ten feet high, and there are two mirrors higher still."[5] Young was not so much impressed with Jones's evocation of the Spanish baroque per se as he was with his "dazzling translation of architecture into theatre terms. The same is true of the costumes. They are Spanish seventeenth-century costumes seen superbly in terms of theatre."[6]

Surprisingly, Young failed to mention the Infanta's costume, described by Richard Aldrich in his review of the ballet as "a delightful expansive scarlet and gold gown such as Velasquez represented, also such a headdress."[7] Young dwelled rather on the visual-dramatic effect of one scene in particular, in which "the princess and her ladies in their citron color, their crimson, saffron, rose and white and gold, silver and black, sit behind the terrace balustrade and the little hunchback, in his drab and green, reaches up his lean hand toward the dazzling splendor of them." At a moment like this, argued Young, the decor conveyed "much of the dramatic idea."[8] Jones presumably designed the props as well, including the three birthday gifts, described by Young as "a chest with a gown, brocade banded with galloons of gold; a huge silver cage with strange birds; a painted casket with a doll in a green farthingale."[9]

Bolm choreographed the ballet somewhat in the style of Fokine and danced the part of Pedro himself. For the other roles he mostly cast dancers associated with either the Chicago Opera or his Ballet Intime, including Caird Leslie as the juggler, Alexander Oumansky as the tightrope walker, Vincenzo Ioucelli as the bull, and Margit Leeraas as the gypsy dancer. For the Infanta, however, he chose an unknown, nineteen-year-old student of his from New York, Ruth Page, who later recalled her response: "Needless to say, I accepted with alacrity; it was a marvelous way to start a career. So I began with a great role; and when the critic Percy Hammond said I was 'perfect in the role of the Infanta,' I thought having a big career as a star was all too easy. Well, I have of course been going down, down, down ever since!"[10]

Ruth Page (1900–1991) grew up in an artistic and well-to-do family in Indianapolis. She studied dance with local teachers and then with the Pavlova Company, who took her on their South American tour in 1918. In 1919 Page began lessons with Bolm in New York. After her debut as the Infanta, she danced in Buenos Aires, Monte Carlo, New York, and Washington (for the first performance of Stravinsky's *Apollon musagète* in 1928) and eventually settled in Chicago, where her prominence as dancer, choreographer, and impresario brought her into renewed contact with Carpenter.

On Tuesday, 23 December 1919, Louis Hasselmans conducted the premiere of *The Birthday of the Infanta,* programmed as a curtain-raiser to a performance of *La sonnambula* with Amelita Galli-Curci, Virgilio Lazzari, and Tito Schipa. The premiere apparently had been slated for the preceding weekend, but the sudden, shocking death of the director of the Chicago Opera, Cleofonte Campanini, from pneumonia on Friday, 19 December, caused a postponement.[11]

The premiere played before a glittering full house in the enormous Auditorium, and the *Daily Tribune* devoted an entire column, "Society at the Opera," to the premiere as a social event:

> Scarcely a loge in the horseshoe was unoccupied, and friends of the composer and his family were visiting their box in a constant stream to offer felicitations on the success of the performance.
>
> Mrs. Carpenter wore a frock of ciel blue satin with a straight tunic of silver fish net bound in silver bullion. A filet of rhinestones was wound about her coiffure. Arriving with her was Mrs. Joseph G. Coleman, her next door neighbor, who was gowned in emerald green brocaded in gold. Miss "Ginnie" Carpenter, the composer's young daughter, was perhaps the most excited member of the party. She wore a simple frock of pink crepe with a band of pink buds in her hair.
>
> "Isn't it the most delightful thing?" Mrs. Arthur Ryerson exclaimed during the promenade. "It is going straight to Paris!"[12]

Indeed, Chicago welcomed the ballet with a burst of excitement and civic pride. "If plaudits are a criterion of success," wrote René Devries, "Carpenter's ballet scored hugely, for the auditors which packed the Auditorium wildly applauded and acclaimed the composer, calling him and the principals before the curtain so many times that one lost count. It won high approval and Chicago is proud to count this able writer its son."[13] "The ballet pantomime made a tremendous success, with its scenery and costumes, with its dancing, with its miming and with its music," reported Maurice Rosenfeld.[14] "One of the finest things in the history of the Chicago Opera association came into existence last night at the Auditorium," wrote Edward Moore. "There was a good deal of an ovation at the end of the piece. For once the audience was stirred out of itself by something other than a singer's high note."[15] And Herman Devries stated, "If . . . Paris exults in its possession of a Gustave Charpentier, Chicago may be proud of her John Alden Carpenter."[16]

Theater and music critics devoted whole columns to the work in all the Chicago dailies and in some national journals as well. Bolm's dancing and miming earned particularly high praise. The noted drama critic Percy Hammond wrote that Bolm "is, to the ultimate movement, the eager, unknowing dwarf, fascinated by the attention of a pretty princess, and dancing his heart out to make her smile. . . . Mr. Bolm is a great actor of pantomime."[17] "The story is in his lean and eloquent body," commented James Whittaker, "and the one thrill of the evening is in the tear with which you silently applaud him when, the picture Princess tossing her kerchief to him as reward for the fun he makes from his ugliness, he takes it and her to his heart. He may catch another tear in that final scene of his heartbreak where he wanders into the hall of mirrors in the palace and sees himself for what he is and what a Princess could never love."[18] W. L. Hubbard concurred: "Adolph Bolm as Pedro the dwarf gave an excellent display of finely proportioned, skillfully detailed, and artistically conceived pantomime. He was grotesque, but never repulsive, and his acting made the tragedy of the poor wretch's sorrow and death poignantly felt." Hubbard also praised the choreography as "of rare attractiveness, little of it being of the extreme wild variety of the Russian school. It was rather of the graceful type, and the pantomimic work was remarkably skilled and eloquent."[19]

Page won acclaim not only from Percy Hammond but from René Devries, who thought her "graceful and charming," and from Felix Borowski, who called her Infanta "a little masterpiece."[20] Devries and others also praised the rest of the cast, Jones's sets and costumes, and Hasselmans, who "conducted with skill and care."

Carpenter's score was almost lost in the hubbub, but it, too, was singled out for praise. Wrote Hubbard: "It is music original, individual, essentially of the today and yet possessing many beauties that make immediate appeal. It is music that catches the unusual fanciful spirit of the play and its mood and time, and reflects it skillfully. There is much of the Spanish flavor as would be expected." Other critics, however, offered some caveat or other. For example, René Devries commented that "although the score is sincere, beautiful— ofttimes brilliant—colorful, striking the keynote of individuality which marks Carpenter's writings, there is a feeling of restraint in the music which seems to miss the excitement of childish moments." And Borowski noted that "it is only toward the end of *The Birthday of the Infanta* that the exacting connoisseur perceives that there is a fly in the ointment. One misses something of the poignancy which should delineate the sufferings and the death of the hapless Pedro."[21]

The only shadow cast on the opening night performance came about through an administrative miscalculation: audiences refused to sit through an hour-long ballet and a full-length opera, and began to leave before the end of *La sonnambula*. The press apparently learned that Galli-Curci was incensed and reported that the great prima donna was not "enthusiastic about attacking high C's with only an audience of ushers, complimentary patrons and stage hands left in the theater."[22] Unfortunately, the Chicago Opera had scheduled the ballet as a curtain-raiser for two more performances with Galli-Curci: a *Don Pasquale* on the following Saturday matinee, 27 December, and another *La sonnambula* on the following Monday night, 29 December. Galli-Curci threatened to strike. The company brought Galli-Curci and Carpenter to arbitration, and they agreed to reverse the order for the 27 December performance but leave the 29 December performance as scheduled. Consequently, many patrons who arrived for the 2:00 P.M. start of *Don Pasquale* never made it to the ballet's 5:30 curtain. "Hours Piled upon Hours at Opera Matinee," read Karleton Hackett's headline for the *Chicago Evening Post*.[23] It was Carpenter's turn to stew.

The dailies subsequently reported that Carpenter and Galli-Curci were angry with each other: "Composer and Diva Clash in 'War of the Roses,'" read a *Chicago Tribune* headline on 29 December. Galli-Curci strongly denied this:

> Heavens, no. Artists may have caprices, but never rage. And certainly not for Mr. Carpenter. I admire him too much. It's the management's fault. . . . It was not my fault some of the audience walk out. Mr. Carpenter, he was the goat. Tomorrow evening the ballet will appear first and I will be the goat. It is not pleasant being the goat, but it is the last time. Some day the management may be the goat.

Carpenter, for his part, eulogized Galli-Curci for ten minutes "as refutation of the rumor."[24]

The Chicago Opera learned its lesson. When the company brought Carpenter's ballet to New York for a single performance on 23 February 1920 at the Lexington Theatre, it sensibly paired the work with Ravel's *L'Heure espagnole,* which had received its first American staging earlier that season in Chicago under Hasselmans. This New York performance was a benefit matinee for the Society for the Prevention and Relief of Tuberculosis. Accordingly, ticket prices were high, reported Pitts Sanborn, and the audience smaller than might have been expected. Richard Aldrich, however, wrote that the "large and brilliant audience" brought the society a large profit, and another reporter confirmed that the "huge audience" included Henry Hadley and other prominent musicians.[25]

The New York reviews were as enthusiastic as Chicago's had been. "America Produces an Artistic Masterpiece," read the banner headline for Hamilton Easter Field's review in the *Brooklyn Daily Eagle.*[26] The *New York Morning Sun* agreed: "The Carpenter ballet came on the wings of very hopeful tidings. Chicago, which heard its premiere, was critically and uncritically kind to it, and hailed its composing in exuberant terms. Yesterday's audience was of like mind in greeting it as a clever and certainly the most charming of any American composer's work yet heard on an operatic stage." The *Sun* further claimed that the ballet's "glittering diffuseness compensates for the loss of O. O'Flahertie Wilde's artistic bitterness. . . . The colors, the juggling of dark little sentiments across fields of brightness, the flashing fingered exquisiteness of luxurious description: all these things which are in Wilde's tales for children . . . are caught with amazing adroitness in these short two acts of ballet."[27] Once again Bolm came in for special praise: "His Pedro is an even more remarkable achievement than his moor in *Petrouchka,*" wrote Max Smith.[28]

New York's leading music critics—Richard Aldrich, Daniel Gregory Mason, and Paul Rosenfeld among them—were naturally most interested in hearing Carpenter's new score. "Mr. Carpenter needs no introduction to New York," began Aldrich, "where his music in a number of forms have [*sic*] long been known and admired. He has not before undertaken anything of a dramatic character; but his imagination, his fine taste and skill in writing for the orchestra have been so fully demonstrated that something uncommonly beguiling was to be expected from his treatment of this subject." The new ballet score fully met Aldrich's high expectations:

Mr. Carpenter has written music filled with fancy, with fantastic imagination, now grotesque, humorous, now picturesque and brilliant: music of subtly suggested realisms, glittering and shimmering with shifting orchestral colors. He has found exactly the right expression for the story. His instrumentation is light, exposed: often expressive in its timbres, ingenious and skilful in the manipulation of all the modern resources. There is naturally a Spanish note in certain passages, as in the dances; a note suggested rather than too obviously emphasized.

The score is fascinating. It would perhaps be saying too much to say that it is highly original. Mr. Carpenter has copied nobody; but he has heard Stravinsky, especially in his "Oiseau de Feu," and has profited by it. And he has written with brilliant and refined skill, as a master.[29]

According to Daniel Gregory Mason, the music's "brilliant and refined skill" held great importance to American music:

Whatever reservations one might wish to make about the originality or the expressive potency of this music, one could not but be deeply impressed by its admirable workmanship, its technical competence. It could bear comparison with any European score in this respect—it did, in fact, hold its own beside Ravel's "L'Heure Espagnole," one of the most diabolically clever products of the modern French school. And sound workmanship . . . is precisely one of the rarest and most precious qualities for us [Americans] that a work can have.[30]

Mason agreed with critics that the work recalled Rimsky-Korsakov and Stravinsky, but this inclined him "to praise rather than to blame its composer. It is not every 'American composer' who can write with the brilliance and decorative vividness of Rimsky and his *enfant terrible* pupil!" Further, he argued, influence had its place in an artist's development:

The itch for originality at all costs has been more of a curse than a blessing to our art: it has canonized as independence and liberty that very amateurishness which is the bane of so much of our music, and which in a true analysis is simply ignorance and ineptitude; it has encouraged that indifference to technical mastery, that abandonment to the mere subjective sense of the unutterable which may feel like originality to a self-centered artist but which sounds very like crude dullness to a candid public; it has hindered the patient study of great models which alone can release true creative personality.

Carpenter's growing originality possibly owed something to his escape "from the Boston-Cambridge rarified atmosphere to Chicago, where business shares his time with music."[31]

Mason continued, "'The Birthday of the Infanta,' at any rate, is vivid, solid, vibrant, picturesque, not too preoccupied with harmonic confectionery, and unashamed of frank contagious rhythm." He singled out for praise the bullfight and Pedro's appeal to the Infanta, which "has something of Bach's manly force of dealing, though used to such different ends." The work, however, "seldom gets below the surface, it rarely penetrates below the decorative of the deeper function of music, in which alone music is most itself, that of emotional interpretation and mood-creation." He wanted more music like the soft, plaintive passage just before Pedro's death ([76]).[32]

In many particulars Rosenfeld agreed with Mason, from whom he may even have derived the idea of "music as decoration." But Rosenfeld came to very different conclusions:

> The music is not the expression of the composer's sensations and ideas. It does not pierce out from some hidden center. One feels it has been "made" rather self-consciously. This is music as decoration. On the whole, it is pleasant enough, but not exciting to the mind. One rather likes the dreamy dances of the first scene and the burlesque *tauro-machia*. One rather dislikes the close of that scene, where the dwarf decides to make his way into the palace, the interlude, and all the rest of the business where Carpenter seeks to be dramatic and passionate. For there, he is helpless. One feels the wish; but the performance is both hectic and banal. He seems incapable of facing the situation, of making it with his own blood; and we are not surprised to find him fumbling with vaguely Debussy-like material.[33]

The Chicago Opera planned a Boston premiere of *The Birthday of the Infanta* on the afternoon of 6 March 1920, on a program with *L'elisir d'amore*. But a blizzard left Bolm and some of the other dancers stranded in New Haven.[34] The company substituted the "Dance of the Hours" from *La Gioconda* at the last minute, and Boston missed its one opportunity to see the Carpenter ballet.

During the 1921–22 season, the Chicago Opera revived *The Birthday of the Infanta* on a double bill with *Pagliacci* (with Carpenter's friend Claire Dux as Nedda). Serge Oukrainsky, Bolm's old rival at the Chicago Opera, played Pedro, and Margit Leeraas, who had danced the gypsy solo in the original, played the Infanta. Van Grove conducted. They gave two performances, one in Chicago on 14 January 1922, and the other in New York at the Manhattan Opera House on 2 February.

New Yorkers came out in full force for this second, more affordable opportunity to view *The Birthday of the Infanta*. Richard Aldrich once again reviewed this "welcome revival" for the *New York Times*. He had not changed his high opinion of the work; in fact, he quoted his previous review nearly verbatim! But this revival also brought new critical insights by composer and music critic Deems Taylor (1885–1966) and the playwright, novelist, and drama critic Stark Young (1881–1963).

Deems Taylor reviewed both *The Birthday of the Infanta* and Carpenter's second ballet, *Krazy Kat* (which had premiered two weeks earlier in New York), for *Vanity Fair* in an article titled "America's First Dramatic Composer." His enthusiasm for *The Birthday of the Infanta* exceeded even that for *Krazy Kat:*

> The score is not only the best thing Carpenter has done, but is probably the best ballet score anyone has done since *Petrushka*. It is written exactly in the spirit of the story, with grace, poetry, and whimsy. There is a touch of courtly artificiality about it that never keeps it from being a poignant and unerring commentary upon the action. It has a fine reticence. The tragedy is only a toy one, after all; and the quiet wistfulness of the music for the final scene has a pathos that no amount of tragic thundering could equal. The score has a faintly Spanish flavour, but that is a suggestion rather than a boresome attempt at local colour.
>
> Above all, it is stage music. It gets over. The ballet made an instant appeal when the Chicago company first produced it, and its revival during the company's New York visit this year revealed its enduring vitality. In Carpenter this country seems at last to have produced a real dramatic composer, one who has the deftness and gift for characterization and sense of the stage that a man must possess if he would write for the theatre.

In Taylor's opinion, Carpenter's theatrical excellence put him in a class with Kern, Berlin, Herbert, and Whithorne.[35]

Stark Young's review for the *New Republic,* as we have seen, concentrated on the set designs. He had this, though, to say about the score: "All this innocent and grotesque sombre, ornate gaiety Mr. Carpenter expressed, so austere is his music at times, so macabre, so hauntingly elaborated, so wistful, and so finely withdrawn. The music of the Infanta has none of the fury of sex in it, for the lives that it reveals have an ironical innocence and formality; but in them and in their music as well there is the shadow of what will mature into passion." In spite of Van Grove's "thin" conducting and Serge Oukrainsky's lack of "dramatic magnetism," continued Young, "the imagination of the music constantly appeared; it sustained a modern quality throughout; it had the excitement of poetic sincerity, and it carried the whole piece toward something that was inescapably drama."[36] Young expanded on some of these ideas in an undated letter to the composer from about this time: "I want to tell you again that I think this Infanta the most distinguished thing I have ever seen in a New York theatre. . . . I liked particularly the dwarf's music before the mirror and I liked the final music before the last curtain."[37]

In 1920 Carpenter adapted the ballet for concert performance. Titled *The Birthday of the Infanta Suite* for orchestra, the music incorporated much of the ballet in its three movements:

I.   Introduction—Entrance of the Infanta—Children's Dance—Arrival of the Guests—The Gypsy Dance
II. The Bull Fight
III. Entrance of the Dwarf—The Fatal Dance—The Tragedy—The End

The only sizable omission was the music for the juggler and tightrope walker.

Stock and the Chicago Symphony premiered the suite on 3 December 1920, and Monteux and the Boston Symphony performed it in Boston on 25 February 1921. The critics thought the suite as effective as the ballet. In Chicago, Karleton Hackett wrote, "The music sounded just as fresh and spontaneous in Orchestra Hall as it did in the Auditorium." In Boston, Olin Downes stated, "Mr. Carpenter's music, designed for the stage, is nevertheless effective in the concert room."[38]

Despite considerable popular and critical success, neither the ballet nor the suite entered the repertory, however. Even by the mid-1920s the work had largely fallen into obscurity. In the early 1930s Borowski and Howard explained simply that tragedy was beyond Carpenter's grasp. Borowski wrote, as he had in his review of the premiere: "Only in the closing scene—the death of Pedro—did one feel that Carpenter had somehow missed the mark at which he aimed. High emotions and tragedy are planes of expression on which his gifts rest somewhat uneasily." Howard possibly borrowed his idea from Borowski when he commented that the composer "may not have been emotionally capable of the tragic heights demanded by Pedro's death."[39] But this explanation fails to accord with reviews by Mason, Taylor, and Young, who all singled out for special praise Carpenter's music for Pedro's death.

Indeed, some original admirers continued to regard the work warmly. In 1930 Olin Downes rated both *The Birthday of the Infanta* and *Skyscrapers* as among the composer's "best works": "In the first score, very notably, is reflected the pomp and the decorative glitter that the scene implies; but this with a dramatic sense, in a manner to throw into stronger relief the emotions of the characters. There is perhaps something of the professedly unemotional brilliancy and laconicism that is so prominent an attribute of the earlier Stravinsky, whose influence is obvious in some technical details of both scores. But there is also the note of the naive and of searching pathos." And in 1932 Marion Bauer remembered *The Birthday of the Infanta* as "one of the most beautiful works of its kind."[40]

In 1929 Carpenter revised his suite from *The Birthday of the Infanta.* Stock and the Chicago Symphony premiered the new version on 4 April 1930, and Howard Hanson conducted it in Rochester, New York, on 14 October 1932. Schirmer's 1932 edition of this suite became the only version of the ballet ever published to date. Like the original suite, the revised version included many of the ballet's highlights, but its three movements—"The Guests," "The Infanta," and "Games"—did not follow the ballet's sequence of events. As Carpenter explained to Koussevitzky (who never performed it): "It is virtually a new composition, as I have employed the original material from the purely musical standpoint without reference to the sequence of the original stage scenario. It has been my purpose to produce a musical composition which will be interesting entirely as music without dependence on any story."[41]

By referring to the original ballet (and its 1938/40 revision), we can supplement Carpenter's vague program notes for the 1929 suite as follows: "The Guests" includes the prologue/gardeners' music (to [5]), the entrance of the guests ([5] to [7]), the opening of the gifts ([7] to [12]), and the gypsy dance ([12] to the end of the movement). "The Infanta" consists of the Infanta's entrance (to [21]), her dance ([21] to [22]), Pedro's dance for the Infanta ([22] to four before [24]), the entrance of the children (four before [24] to [27]), and Pedro's death and the finale ([27] to the end of the movement). "Games" includes the juggler–tightrope walker pantomime (to sixteen after [39]) and the bullfight (sixteen after [39] to the end of the movement).

The newness of the 1929 suite goes far beyond Carpenter's modest claims of having rearranged "the sequence of the original stage scenario." The music for the opening of the gifts, the solo gypsy dance, Pedro's dance for the Infanta, and the entrance of the children is entirely new. In fact, these sections can only be identified as such because Carpenter subsequently incorporated this music into his 1938/40 revision of the complete ballet! This raises the question, When writing this new music in 1929, did Carpenter actually have such specific stage action in mind? Certainly, the new gypsy solo—placed in the midst of the gypsy dance—intentionally replaces the old one. But on the other hand, Carpenter plausibly only meant to evoke the Infanta's high spirits in the music that he later used for the entrance of the children.

Carpenter revised the entire ballet for piano four-hands in 1938 and completed the orchestration in 1940. In a letter to Koussevitzky, he explained that he rewrote the work for a ballet company interested in reviving it.[42] This planned revival might have had something to do with Léonide Massine, for whom the composer apparently revised *Krazy Kat* in 1940.

Although Carpenter revised nearly all his orchestral music during these later years, he reworked *The Birthday of the Infanta* more thoroughly than practically any other score, with the exception of the *Sermons in Stones* Symphony (1917/1940). He made only a few minor adjustments in the ballet's basic structure, however. The Infanta now performs her little solo alone onstage, before the other children enter, and at the very end the Infanta does not exit with her friends, as in the original, but rather returns to the front of the stage and kneels beside Pedro as the curtain falls.

This revision, however, drastically cut the ballet from more than an hour to less than thirty minutes. Carpenter shortened the prologue to a brief anticipation of the scene 2 death music that Mason admired so much. Moreover, he radically condensed much of the pantomime, including the children's entrance, the opening of the gifts, Pedro's attempt to enter the palace, and his subsequent exploration in the hall of mirrors. He also shortened the solo dances for the Infanta and Pedro. And between the 1938 four-hands revision and the 1940 orchestration, he eliminated the entire juggler–tightrope walker episode.

Carpenter introduced new music as well, much of which he adapted from the 1929 suite: syncopated, waltzlike music for the entrance of the children that contrasts better with the procession of the guests to follow (⟨8⟩ in the 1940 orchestral score); a lovely, new theme for an added pantomime in which the Infanta and the children converse (⟨9⟩); a total overhauling for the opening of the gifts (⟨15⟩); a new, tangolike number reminiscent of Ravel's *Bolero* for the solo gypsy dance (⟨31⟩); a jaunty, childlike march tune for the matador (⟨54⟩); a less sentimental, more reserved melody for the throw of the handkerchief (⟨79⟩); and for Pedro's Fatal Dance, something Prokofievian in its wildness (⟨92⟩).

Carpenter also completely reconsidered the orchestration. He reduced the woodwinds from three to two, except for the bassoons; the trumpets from four to three; and the harps from two to one. On the other hand, he expanded the already large percussion battery with the addition of gong,

xylophone, and a quartet of wood blocks (this allows him to save the castanets for Pedro's final dance). He also removed the "quasi-guitarre" piano
effects in the gypsy dance.

Most strikingly, the new score called for a mezzo-soprano voice, whose
evocative, Spanish-inflected vocalises appear periodically throughout the ballet: at the beginning, at the new Infanta theme ([9]), at the solo gypsy dance
([31]), and at the exit of the birthday guests ([81]). Carpenter consistently
doubled the voice part with one or another woodwind; according to the
composer's footnotes, some of these doublings were to be used only for
rehearsal, or for performances in which a singer was unavailable. At [31] Carpenter further noted, "In vocalizing her part, the Singer may be free to
employ such syllables as are 'comfortable' for her voice, aiming at a smooth
and flowing effect which may sound like an unfamiliar tongue." As with
many other aspects of the new orchestration, the addition of the singer
derived from the 1929 suite.

Carpenter shortened and revised the work enough so that the ballet
could easily meet concert performance requirements. Indeed, the score includes a few, minor provisions for such an eventuality. In 1940 he nonetheless
revised the 1929 suite as well, with three movements still titled "The Guests,"
"The Infanta," and "Games." And in 1949 he produced a fourteen-minute
second suite, which included only the "I. Gypsy Dance," "II. Bull Fight," and
"III. Finale Triste." George Szell played what seems to have been the 1940
suite with the Chicago Symphony at Ravinia on 8 August 1943, but like
Carpenter's other revisions and adaptations of *The Birthday of the Infanta,*
these final attempts brought little renewed interest in the work.

If one were to revive *The Birthday of the Infanta* as a ballet today, what
score would one use—the 1918 original or the 1938/40 revision? The original
version has the advantage of having proved itself on the stage; indeed, its
tremendous reception holds a certain compelling historical interest. But the
1940 score is stronger musically: it retains the most exciting music, omits
certain flaccid passages, adds some lovely, new things, and features a more
expert and practical orchestration. More to the point, the 1918 version is
practically indecipherable and fairly unobtainable, whereas one can acquire a
rather clear manuscript of the 1940 revision through G. Schirmer.

CHAPTER TWELVE

Krazy Kat

1921

Composed in the summer of 1921, Carpenter's second ballet, *Krazy Kat,* subtitled *A Jazz Pantomime,* was based on George Herriman's comic strip of the same name. The novelty of a ballet—indeed, any concert music—inspired by the comics and jazz instantly earned the work a certain notoriety. In some ways *Krazy Kat* merely marked a return from the wartime solemnity of the *Sermons in Stones* Symphony and *The Birthday of the Infanta* to the whimsy of *Adventures in a Perambulator* and the Piano Concertino. But the music presented a new face: zany, madcap, even slightly grotesque.

Did Carpenter's decision to write a *Krazy Kat* ballet owe anything to Carl Van Vechten, whose 1920 article "The Cat in Music" included some discussion of Stravinsky's 1917 *Berceuses du chat*?[1] Or to Adolph Bolm, who had proposed a baseball ballet to Griffes? In any case, the composer's daughter Ginny once again played a prominent role in this regard, thanks to her enthusiasm for the Herriman comic strip.

Born in New Orleans in 1880 to Greek immigrants, George Herriman grew up in Los Angeles. He worked as an illustrator for various newspapers in New York and Los Angeles before settling permanently in 1924 in Los Angeles, where he died in 1944. He first introduced the *Krazy Kat* characters as part of a strip that he started in 1910, *The Dingbat Family* (soon after retitled *The Family Upstairs*). Readers enjoyed these characters so that Herriman started a separate *Krazy Kat* strip in 1913. His employer, William Randolph Hearst, ran the strip for the next thirty years, in large part because he liked reading it himself.[2] Indeed, the strip never enjoyed the huge popularity of some other comics, but connoisseurs always regarded it highly. Comics authority Bill Blackbeard writes that nowadays it is "universally acclaimed as the greatest comic strip."[3]

Set in Coconino County somewhere in the American Southwest, *Krazy Kat* featured three principals: Krazy Kat, who is in love with and thoroughly devoted to Ignatz Mouse; Ignatz, whose primary delight is to torment Krazy; and Offisa Pupp, who wants Ignatz behind bars. In the strip's last panel, Ignatz would often hurl a brick at Krazy, who would interpret this as a sign of love. While such vaudevillian cat-and-mouse antics were familiar enough, Herriman's strip contained certain offbeat features, including sharp-edged, angular graphics; surrealistic use of landscape; bizarre language full of American slang, pseudo-Yiddish, Joycean wordplay, and the Queen's English; and provocative story lines touched with religious mysticism, political symbolism, and sexual deviance.

Both Carpenter and Ginny had long admired Herriman. When the composer sought out the cartoonist on a trip to Los Angeles in 1917, he brought along the twelve-year-old Ginny to meet him. "She curtsied prettily when she was introduced," recalled Carpenter, "and said, as she had been taught, 'I'm very pleased to meet you.' Herriman grinned broadly and answered, 'Miss Carpenter, you're very easily pleased.'"[4] The artist presented Ginny with an ink drawing dated 17 December of that year.[5]

Herriman was caught off guard when Carpenter approached him four years later about collaborating on a *Krazy Kat* ballet. He wrote back to the composer: "I've never had any idea that these few humble characters of mine would ever have been asked to mingle with the more aristocratic arts, and I must say it is all very shocking to me. I can't imagine K. Kat, I. Mouse, O. Pupp, and J. Stork cavorting and pirouetting en ballet to save my life. However, let's hope the audience doesn't get their cue from Ignatz and pack a few bricks in with them—with evil intent."[6] Herriman agreed to write the scenario (which appeared in the program in Carpenter's own words) and to design the costumes and scenery.

Carpenter's high regard for Herriman anticipated critical acclaim from such commentators as Gilbert Seldes, who in 1924 regarded the strip as "the most amusing and fantastic and satisfactory work of art produced in America to-day."[7] In fact, it was as a volunteer publicist for the Carpenter-Herriman ballet that Seldes developed not only his interest in this particular strip but the notion that such popular arts as comics, jazz, and motion pictures deserved serious attention, the novel thesis of his 1924 *The Seven Lively Arts,* one of the most influential books of its kind. In 1957 Seldes reflected on how the "appearance of a comic strip character in an art-form as remote and chic as ballet (years before Agnes de Mille and *Oklahoma!* showed us that we were all *balletomanes*) gave me an opportunity to back into my subject. It was as if the ballet had thrown a cloak of dignity around Krazy Kat—which was not the way Carpenter himself felt about it."[8]

Seldes found particularly helpful Carpenter's "brilliant little foreword" to the ballet's first performance:

> To those who have not mastered Mr. Herriman's psychology it may be explained that Krazy Kat is the world's greatest optimist—Don Quixote and Parsifal rolled into one. It is therefore possible for him to maintain constantly at white heat a passionate affair with Ignatz Mouse, in which the gender of each remains ever a delightful mystery. Ignatz, on the other hand, condenses in his sexless self all the cardinal vices. If Krazy blows beautiful bubbles, Ignatz shatters them; if he builds castles in Spain, Ignatz is there with the brick. In short, he is meaner than anything, and his complex is cats.[9]

In 1946 E. E. Cummings praised the strip as an allegorical celebration of democracy, and in 1987 Jay Cantor wrote a highly regarded novel that brought the residents of Coconino County into the postatomic world.[10]

Herriman and Carpenter devised the following scenario for their ballet: As Krazy lies sleeping onstage, Offisa Pupp passes by on his beat, and Bill Postem, a canine relative of Offisa Pupp, posts an advertisement for a grand ball. Krazy wakes, sees the poster, locates a ballet skirt, and begins to dance. Joe Stork enters and leaves behind a mysterious bundle. Krazy opens it and, discovering a vanity case, prepares for the ball. Ignatz enters ominously, but Offisa Pupp chases him away. Krazy, oblivious, finishes his makeup and does a Spanish dance. Ignatz, disguised as a (Mexican) catnip merchant, enters with a catnip bouquet for Krazy. The Kat goes into a "Class A fit" and, further incited by Ignatz, dances a "Katnip Blues." Finally, Ignatz throws the inevitable brick and escapes. The stunned Krazy has a "moment of ecstatic recognition—Ignatz Dahlink" and sinks back to sleep. Offisa Pupp passes—all is well.

This scenario recalled *Adventures in a Perambulator* with its innocent creature (Krazy, the baby) whose love mediates societal restraint (Offisa Pupp, the blue policeman) and subversive activity (Ignatz, the organ-grinder). Moreover, by framing the action with their protagonist waking and falling asleep, both works imparted a cyclic, mythic quality. In tone, however, *Krazy Kat* struck a decadent note closer to *The Birthday of the Infanta*: consider the sadomasochistic overtones of the Ignatz-Krazy relationship; the narcissism implicit in Joe Stork's delivery of a vanity case rather than a baby; the story's overt transvestism (although the scenario refers to the sexless Krazy Kat as "he"—and, indeed, Adolph Bolm danced the role—Krazy puts on ballet skirt and evening gloves, powders his face, and adds rouge); and the Dionysian celebration of catnip (representing alcohol, if not marijuana). Did Carpenter associate Krazy's "Katnip Blues" with Mary Garden's Salome, in which, according to the Chicago police, she "wallowed around like a cat in a bed of catnip"?[11]

Carpenter scaled down his ballet to comic strip size, scoring the ten-minute work for a small, pit orchestra, with an instrumentation reminiscent of the bigger dance bands of the time: flute (piccolo), oboe, clarinet, E♭ saxophone, bassoon, two horns, two trumpets, tenor trombone, percussion, piano, harp, and strings (Carpenter originally specified a 4-4-2-2-1 string contingent but later doubled it to 8-4-4-4-2). From the start he must have intended the ballet for Bolm's small, informal Ballet Intime.

In the short prelude that opens the ballet, two trumpets twice state a fanfare in parallel fourths, recalling the opening of *Adventures in a Perambulator*. Both times, the fanfare begins in D major and moves, accompanied by strings and harp, to D♭ major. As the curtain rises, the stage reveals the sleeping Krazy Kat, his steady breathing depicted by alternating ii and V harmonies in D major. A muted trumpet puts forth Krazy's theme, a descending motive marked "Jazzando" that humorously alludes to Debussy's/ Nijinsky's sleeping faun. Offisa Pupp comes onstage to a somber march in F♯ minor that at one point quotes "Yankee Doodle." After he exits the sleep music returns.

Bill Postem enters to a *giocoso* $\frac{3}{4}$ theme played by piccolo and bassoon in unison and answered by the clarinet, with cymbals on the offbeats. (One review of an early production described Postem as being "drunk on his own paste.")[12] As he puts up a poster announcing a grand ball, snatches of a waltz tune alternate with his theme. Krazy wakes up, reads the poster, and begins to dance to his own waltz tune, this one like the waltz found in the last movement of the Piano Concertino. Carpenter suggests Krazy's uncertain footing by alternating $\frac{3}{4}$ and $\frac{2}{4}$ meters (an idea probably derived from the Moor's clumsy waltz in *Petrushka*); after Krazy puts on a ballet skirt, the music becomes more fluent.

Joe Stork makes a brief appearance, his theme played by oboe and bassoon in unison. Rising chromatics reflect Krazy's curiosity about the bundle that Joe Stork distractedly leaves behind. Krazy triumphantly carries off the bundle to a mock military march. When he opens the bundle and discovers the vanity case, the music suddenly changes mood. An alto saxophone enters with a yearning, romantic melody, accompanied by string tremolos and harp arpeggios (the climax of this melody anticipates Leonard Bernstein's setting of the words "if I can wait" from *West Side Story*'s "Something's Coming," a resemblance all the more striking considering the similarities in the dramatic situation).

Ignatz Mouse enters to a whimsical piccolo melody in an acerbic, occasionally polytonal setting (ex. 34). Offisa Pupp reappears, accompanied by his signature music, and chases off Ignatz, who leaves with a taunting piccolo flourish. The saxophone music returns as Krazy applies the finishing touches to his costume. He then breaks out into a Spanish waltz in C major, accompanied alternately by tambourines and castanets.

Disguised as a catnip merchant, Ignatz enters to a new melody played by piccolo, piano, and snare drum. Krazy sniffs the catnip to his Jazzando chromatic motive and breaks into a "Fox-Trot" whose principal theme derives from the Jazzando motive (ex. 35). This fox-trot, the ballet's musical climax, features jazzy blue notes—flatted thirds and sevenths—as well as a jazzy scoring that includes muted trumpet, trombone glissandi, and drum traps. The dance consists of one strain in F♯ major (during which the flute intrudes, at one juncture, with the opening phrase of "Old Folks at Home") and a contrasting one in B♭ major. A section marked Presto ensues as Ignatz prepares to throw his brick. As the brick hits Krazy, a piano and harp glissando

EXAMPLE 34.   Carpenter, *Krazy Kat*, ⑬, mm. 1–6.

lands on F, the dominant. The music settles back into a Largo in B♭ major, with the Jazzando theme in its original drowsy setting. A short Vivo, which incorporates both the opening fanfare music and the chromatic Jazzando motive, brings the ballet to a jaunty conclusion.

In subtitling *Krazy Kat* "a jazz pantomime," Carpenter became the first composer of concert music to use the word *jazz* in the title of a composition.[13] The term itself had initially gained wide currency in Chicago: first, in 1915, as a smear word, *jass,* aimed at a white band from New Orleans, Tom Brown's Ragtime Band (later Brown's Dixieland Jass Band); then, in 1916, as *jass* or *jaz,* applied to both white and black groups; and finally, in 1917, as *jazz,* as in the Dreamland Cafe's Original Jazz Band.[14]

This new style or something like it had actually taken root in Chicago as early as 1906 with performances by black clarinetist Wilbur Sweatman at the Pekin Inn and other South Side establishments. "People of both races came to hear this [Sweatman's] three piece orchestra play jazz music, although they didn't call it jazz then. They called it 'hot music.'"[15] This "hot music," still called "ragtime" on occasion, surely represented a transition from the ragtime of the 1890s to the jazz of the late teens. Carpenter himself stated in 1924, "I have always felt keenly for jazz."[16] And he probably would have agreed with Clive Bell, who, in a 1922 book that the composer admired (and that spoke of ragtime and jazz as more or less synonymous), claimed, "The [jazz] movement bounced into the world somewhere about the year 1911."[17]

Consequently, Carpenter's quotation of "Alexander's Ragtime Band" in

EXAMPLE 35.   Carpenter, *Krazy Kat,* ⸢17⸣, mm. 9–16.

Perambulator (1914) and use of an exuberant "ragtime" style in the Piano Concertino (1915) possibly represented an incorporation of very early jazz. If so, the composer helped initiate the worldwide trend of "jazz-influenced" concert music.[18] It followed, in any case, that Carpenter would take some interest in jazz in the 1920s, to the point that, in later years, his name would first and foremost be associated with the use of jazz in art music.

Carpenter's interest in jazz would have received encouragement from his wife and daughter. Rue even returned from Europe in 1920 with, to her husband's delight, ragtime pieces by Stravinsky and Satie. (Carpenter subsequently wrote to E. Robert Schmitz, "I thought that they were ingenious, particularly Stravinsky's piece, but I did not feel that either one of them had anything whatever to do with the real spirit of ragtime.")[19] As for Ginny, she eventually befriended her Chicagoan contemporary Benny Goodman.

Frederick Stock would have supported Carpenter's interest in jazz as well. Stock had long advised American composers to reflect their own world, but his enthusiasm for jazz went beyond this, as he even touted jazz to Europeans: When Stravinsky visited Chicago in 1925, Stock took him to an integrated cabaret (or a so-called black-and-tan) where they heard "some excellent music . . . of an order entirely new to Stravinsky. He was very greatly impressed, and I told him that it would be a profitable experience for him if he would live a while in some part of the South where he could get acquainted with the real American Negro songs in their native haunts."[20]

As a Chicagoan, Carpenter was particularly well placed to hear early jazz in all its variety. During the decade 1918–28, the "toddlin' town" or, in Ben Hecht's words, the "jazz baby on the lake" became a leading if not the preeminent center for jazz, thanks in large part to the arrival of scores of musicians from New Orleans and other southern and midwestern towns, including such whites as Tom Brown, Nick LaRocca, and Larry Shields, and such blacks as Jelly Roll Morton, Joe Oliver, Freddie Keppard, Jimmy Noone, and Louis Armstrong.[21]

The principal factor abetting the astonishing growth of jazz in Chicago was the arrival during World War I of thousands of African Americans who left the South to take advantage of Chicago's boom economy. Between 1910 and 1920 the black population of the city more than doubled, from 44,000 to 109,000; by 1930 the black population had more than doubled once again, to 234,000.[22] Concentrated mostly in the city's South Side, Chicago's black community provided a large audience for jazz, which accommodated African American traditions to a new, exhilarating, yet often hostile urban environment.

Furthermore, at a time when Prohibition hampered nightclub life throughout the nation, Chicago's freewheeling mayor, William ("Big Bill") Thompson (who governed almost uninterruptedly from 1915 to 1930), let Chicago—especially the South Side—run wild. Oblivious to laws prohibiting alcohol, drugs, gambling, prostitution, and racketeering, Chicago's clubs and cabarets flourished, and jazz musicians found work plentiful. By the mid-1920s Chicago had many more nightclubs than New York City.

Chicago's white population responded enthusiastically to jazz as well. According to William Howland Kenney, "Jazz functioned to express and channel some of the explosive emotions generated by racial and cultural tensions in Chicago,"[23] which included a bloody and traumatic race riot in 1919. White Chicagoans—from dance-band leaders like Isham Jones and Edgar Benson to novelty musicians like Zez Confrey and Paul Biese to such outstanding soloists as Bix Beiderbecke, Benny Goodman, and Gene Krupa—made huge contributions to the dissemination of jazz in white society. Discussing the attraction that jazz held for Chicago's white musicians, Kenney has written:

The initial desire to play this tension-filled, fast moving music came from their anticipation of the excitement of urban life, their alienation from middle-class Victorian moralism, and a keen appreciation for the artful way South Side musicians played their music under trying cultural circumstances. Blacks, for a variety of specific historical reasons, took the lead in Chicago jazz, but the urge to play jazz music in twenties Chicago came from an inter-racial and polyethnic experience of early twentieth-century urban life.[24]

Chicago jazz was primarily an instrumental music, and often associated with dancing. Jazz bands typically ranged in size from five to fifteen players, with larger groups often called "orchestras." A typical band included trumpet, trombone, clarinet, saxophone (by 1920), tuba (or double bass), banjo (or guitar), piano, and drums. Larger groups had two trumpets, two to four woodwinds (clarinets doubling on saxophone), and one or two violins. Jazz bands played all over town—in the swanky hotels and private clubs in the Near North, like the Drake Hotel and the Casino; in the great Chicago ballrooms on the North and West Side, like the Dreamland Ballroom and the Arcadia Ballroom; at trendy, somewhat risqué clubs and restaurants in the Loop, like the Friar's Inn or the College Inn; in the now legendary cabarets in the Near South, like the Sunset Cafe or Royal Gardens; and in the big theaters and motion picture palaces everywhere.

Discussions of Chicago jazz have traditionally profiled two paradigms: a small, black combo playing a highly improvised "hot jazz" (or "real jazz") for a black audience in a cabaret on the South Side; and a large, white orchestra playing a highly arranged "sweet jazz" (or "pseudo jazz" or "near-jazz" or "jazz-oriented dance music") for a white audience in a ballroom on the North Side. Kenney and others have shown, however, that the Chicago jazz scene was vastly more complex than such pigeonholing suggests. Some white combos played hot jazz; some black orchestras played sweet jazz. Sweet bands sometimes featured hot soloists. Some of the best South Side cabarets were black-and-tans in which "blacks and whites could interact with one another in certain socially stylized ways, talking, flirting, drinking, dancing, and listening to music," and in which black and white musicians even played together occasionally (Willie "The Lion" Smith remembered, "There was a lot more mixing of the races in Chicago at that time than there was in New York").[25] And, finally, certain religious and civic leaders—white and black alike—found jazz of any kind reprehensible.

Safe to say, Carpenter most often encountered the kind of jazz Isham Jones, Edgar Benson, and other prominent white dance bands played in the chic hotels, ballrooms, and mansions in the Near North. In December 1920, for instance, the Carpenters attended—indeed, helped arrange—a masked ball at the Potter Palmer Mansion, where, noted one reporter, "a cotillion, not one of the old fashioned kind, but a decidedly new jazzy sort, was danced or rather 'toddled.'"[26] At such functions couples could fox-trot and shimmy in between tangos, waltzes, and other dances. Some society dance bands further specialized in "nut jazz," a satirical, vaudevillian jazz that featured slapstick humor. Occasionally some hot soloist would overstep the prevailing restraint, and the music would "go Bolshevik." By 1924 some musicians denied that the word *jazz* accurately described such music: Isham Jones championed the phrase "American dance music," and Meyer Davis "sponsored a contest to rename 'jazz' for people who disliked the word's lowlife implications."[27] Most, however, continued to use the word *jazz* for a variety of styles.

At the same time, Carpenter heard some hot jazz as well; indeed, if he explored the black-and-tans on the South Side, as Harriett Welling remembered,[28] he would have heard some of Chicago's best jazz. Chances are he also knew Bert Kelly's Stables at 431 North Rush—only three blocks north of his Rush Street home—where such superior black jazz musicians as "Yellow" Nunez, King Oliver, and Freddie Keppard performed throughout this entire period.[29] Perhaps Carpenter also heard some hot jazz in the Loop, though probably not at Big Jim Colosimo's Café, a favorite haunt not only for the Carpenters but for theater people like Al Jolson, John Barrymore, George M. Cohan, and Sophie Tucker and opera people like Mary Garden, Amelita Galli-Curci, and John McCormack.[30]

Newspapers occasionally quoted Carpenter on the subject of jazz. In 1922 he stated:

> Jazz is the American folklore. It is played everywhere. It can be heard in Europe as well as South America; in India and Alaska. And it appeals to everyone. Not that sensuous, indecent, ugly jazz music that the Broadway cabaret orchestras play. That appeals only to the vile instincts in human beings. I am speaking of the rhythmic, harmonious music of which Irving Berlin and Jerome Kern are such good exponents. It's full of character, of pep, of life. And Krazy Kat is the same sort of thing in art—it's jazz of the best sort.[31]

Two years later, in 1924, he said:

> I have always felt keenly for jazz. I have loved it and felt a great value in it. It is the first really spontaneous American musical expression; and, good or bad, you can't afford to ignore what is spontaneous. It has its roots in the American soil, and it contains certain elements that should be used by musicians. To be sure, it lacks one attribute of great music; it has not the spiritual element. But it has the capability of developing almost every other quality of music as an art. America's rhythmic sensitiveness finds an expression in jazz, and in delineating this, it is unavoidable to fall into the accents of this native form.[32]

In 1926 Carpenter further elaborated: "I am convinced that our contemporary popular music (please note that I avoid labelling it 'jazz') is by far the most spontaneous, the most personal, the most characteristic, and, by virtue of these qualities, the most important musical expression that America has achieved. I am strongly inclined to believe that the musical historian of the year 2000 A.D. will find the birthday of American music and that of Irving Berlin to have been the same."[33] In the same year, 1926, he opined that although jazz possessed "wit, precision, and excitement," it had "none of the aesthetic qualities necessary to fine music"; it lacked "spirituality."[34] These remarks constitute nearly all of Carpenter's recorded statements about jazz; after 1926 he never again discussed the matter publicly.

Taken together, these comments reveal a fairly coherent view of jazz. Like most of his contemporaries, Carpenter used the term to include popular song as well as varieties of sweet and hot jazz performance. He admired jazz's universal appeal as well as its characteristic Americanness and found special, personal value in its spontaneous, rhythmic energy (much as he had previously valued the rhythmic spontaneity of George M. Cohan). Carpenter claimed special distinction for the songs of Kern and especially Berlin. At its best jazz only lacked "spirituality."

As early as 1922 Carpenter distinguished Berlin from the "sensuous, indecent, ugly jazz music that the Broadway cabaret orchestras play," by which he possibly meant hot jazz. By 1926 he concluded, like Isham Jones, that the jazz he preferred and had compared to the comics was best referred to as "contemporary popular music" rather than jazz. Such rankings and qualifications presumably involved extramusical factors, since Carpenter would not have encountered hot jazz on recordings (indeed, very little hot jazz was recorded before 1923) but most likely in black-and-tans, where heavy drinking, drug use, suggestive dancing, and flagrant prostitution were commonplace. Carpenter naturally would not have found this environment as alluring as some classical and jazz musicians twenty to thirty years his junior. In view of all this, the composer's 1926 settings of Langston Hughes, with their sensitive and sympathetic depictions of dancers and jazzmen in a black-and-tan, are all the more amazing.

Even *Krazy Kat* came closer to the jazz of its time[35]—especially the more commercial sweet jazz—than one might assume from the composer's statements about jazz. This included not only the work's instrumentation but such other features as (1) syncopated rhythmic figures, including the division of a $\frac{4}{4}$ meter into units of 3 + 3 + 2 eighth notes (the *cinquillo* rhythm already noted in the Piano Concertino) and, newer still, two bars of $\frac{4}{4}$ divided into units of 1 + 3 + 3 + 3 + 3 + 3 eighth notes; (2) blue notes (alternating major and minor thirds and sevenths); (3) parallel harmonies, including augmented triads and seventh chords, in close position; (4) use of alto saxophone, muted trumpets, trombone glissandi, fortissimo clarinet in its highest register, and drum set; and (5) performance markings like "jazzando" and "traps ad lib." Indeed, early critics like Richard Aldrich complimented Carpenter's mastery of "the principles of jazz."[36]

Moreover, the work's irreverent, exaggerated humor was related to nut jazz and those white society bands who created, in Ralph Berton's words, "a music of burlesque, of caricature, zany humor, rough and violent."[37] Paul Rosenfeld alluded to this in his review of the ballet: "Something of the humor of the jazz-band got into his 'Krazy Kat' score."[38]

Carpenter's incorporation of jazz—for all its limitations—set him apart from other American composers born in the 1870s, such as Farwell, Hill, Mason, Ives, and Ruggles, although Macdonald Smith Moore drew no such distinction in his study of how these "centennial composers" received jazz. Whereas Moore noted aspects of Carpenter that fit the "centennial composer" stereotype—his Puritan heritage, his Congregational background, his Harvard education, his ideas about jazz and "spirituality"—he overlooked features of Carpenter's life and career more pertinent to the subject at hand—his mistrust of New England Puritanism, his high esteem for jazz and popular culture, his music for Paul Whiteman, and his settings of Langston Hughes. Significantly, Moore's conclusions in many instances failed to apply to Carpenter, who acted with exceptional vigor when he assimilated jazz at age forty-four.[39] In this, Carpenter deserves comparison, rather, with his French contemporary Maurice Ravel.

Indeed, *Krazy Kat* might profitably be placed in the context of those brittle, funny, poignant scores coming out of Paris at about this time by Satie, Ravel, Prokofiev, and "Les Six." Its parody, even travesty, of the Ballets Russes and its *Scheherazade* and *Afternoon of a Faun* displayed a dadaist quality, further manifested by the composer's directives for the musical examples in the score's published piano version: "Pizzi-kat-to," "Kurioso," "Kantando," "Villainously," "Without Refinement," and "With a Smile."

True, Carpenter had long shown an inclination to "rag" or "jazz" the great European tradition (as in *Polonaise américaine*), and in this respect *Krazy Kat* more closely resembled the "ragged classics" of Isham Jones than the "symphonic jazz" of Gershwin. Similarly, the dadaist directives smacked of nut jazz. One might even venture the idea that postwar Paris simply caught up with Carpenter, that is, became Americanized. But at the same time, the ballet's acerbic dissonances, mechanical ostinatos, and subtle instrumental shadings suggested some awareness of new Franco-Russian trends, especially the influence of Prokofiev, with whom Carpenter had just recently established a friendship.

Prokofiev first came to America in 1918 under the aegis of Carpenter's neighbor Cyrus McCormick, who had met the Russian composer on a trip to the newly formed Soviet Union. After a few months in New York, Prokofiev arrived in Chicago in December 1918 to perform his First Piano Concerto and conduct his *Scythian Suite* with the Chicago Symphony. Chicago loved him: the Chicago Opera immediately commissioned a work *(Love for Three Oranges),* and the Chicago Symphony an orchestral piece (the Third Piano

Concerto). Prokofiev returned to Chicago in 1920, 1921, 1927, 1933, and 1937. According to one biographer, "New York proved over the years to be less receptive to Prokofiev's music than its midwestern rival, Chicago."[40]

Before leaving New York for Chicago in 1918, Prokofiev probably heard about Carpenter from Adolph Bolm, with whom he was staying (Prokofiev, in fact, made his American debut accompanying Bolm to a dance based on the composer's *Visions fugitives*). Prokofiev soon had the opportunity to meet Carpenter; when the Russian composer arrived in Chicago, McCormick introduced him to "important Chicago cultural and musical figures."[41] By his third trip to Chicago in 1921, Prokofiev, in fact, wrote ahead to Carpenter to inform him of his arrival date, 15 December.[42] (He would have arrived just in time to hear the Chicago Symphony rehearse *Krazy Kat*.) Prokofiev probably met with Carpenter on subsequent trips to Chicago as well.

Krazy Kat contains some general features related to Prokofiev—such as its exaggerated humor—as well as some technical features: the chromatic slipping from one tonality to another, such as the move from D major to D♭ major in the prelude's two phrases; the pungent polychords; and the lean, crisp textures. The bad-boy music for Ignatz Mouse particularly resembles Prokofiev, who, in turn, possibly remembered *Krazy Kat*'s concluding fox-trot while writing the victory march to his own *Peter and the Wolf*.

Stock and the Chicago Symphony gave an initial reading of *Krazy Kat* on 23 December 1921, in a concert that also featured a tribute to Saint-Saëns, who had died the previous week. The reviews were enthusiastic. Paul Bloomfield Zeisler wrote that the work displayed "a rich vein of fantastic and ingenious burlesque, of indigenous humor, or honest strife for something truly and delightfully American. . . . Small stuff, you think? I call it exquisite, of its kind." Another review admired the score's abundant humor: "It has unexpected touches of mirth that tickle one's nerve of risibility, and very often he [Carpenter] plays a joke on the public without cracking a smile—just to see, perhaps, if it reaches us." Edward Moore similarly wrote: "To John Alden Carpenter belongs the credit of having introduced the largest slice of Christmas cheer in music yet discovered. . . . Even Stravinsky himself did no better comedy when he conceived 'Petrouchka.'" Although Moore himself had hoped "for several years" that a concert-music composer would make use of jazz, he correctly predicted some resistance from the musical community.[43]

Listening to the work in concert form, Moore imagined such vaudevillians as Fred Stone and Violet Zell "as the chief parties" (presumably Krazy and Ignatz). In the subsequent months and years, others similarly thought of

Fred Stone (1873–1959) for the part of Krazy Kat (Stone was the loose-limbed comedian best known as the Scarecrow in the musical comedy *The Wizard of Oz;* playing the same role in the 1939 MGM adaptation, Ray Bolger must have known and learned from Stone's performance). Carpenter's contemporaries obviously perceived a connection between *Krazy Kat* and vaudeville, and, indeed, the ballet appeared in the Greenwich Village Follies of 1922 within a year of its premiere.

For the premiere, however, Adolph Bolm choreographed the action and danced the part of Krazy Kat. In a letter to Ginny, Herriman recalled how Carpenter facilitated this production, given the temperaments of Bolm and the other Russian dancers: "Your Pap had an unctious and oleoginous way with him [Bolm] and I must say you've got to have all that, and more, to smooth a ruffled Muscovite."[44] Herriman's costume and set designs included black-and-white cartoons on rollers at the back of the stage; in the tradition of the Chinese theater, one of the ballet dancers rolled up the scenery as the action progressed.[45]

The ballet premiered at New York's Town Hall as part of a concert sponsored by Poldowski's Concerts Internationaux de la Libre Esthétique and Bolm's Ballet Intime. This concert—first given on the afternoon of 20 January 1922, and then again on 22 January—featured Bolm's friends and collaborators from his New York days: French flutist and conductor Georges Barrère and his Little Symphony, Danish soprano Povla Frijsh, clarinetist Fred van Amburgh, and dancer Margit Leeraas.[46] The long and varied program included orchestral works by Polish composers Szymanowski and Poldowski (Lady Dean Paul) and ballets by Prokofiev and Griffes. In addition, Frijsh sang a number of Carpenter's latest songs: "The Odalisque," "The Lawd Is Smilin' through the Do'," "Berceuse de guerre," "Slumber-Song," and "Serenade."

The stylish audience, which included Carpenter's friends John Barrymore and George Arliss (the latter appearing on Broadway in *The Green Goddess*), had come principally to see *Krazy Kat,* which understandably was programmed last. The audience, reported one review, "could not get enough of *Krazy Kat.* They applauded and demanded encores."[47]

The New York notices, however, were generally critical, especially regarding Bolm, whose dancing and choreography (in total contrast to *The Birthday of the Infanta*) was thought to miss the spirit of the work. Carl Engel wrote, "Mr. Bolm, of early Russian ballet fame, was not happily transmuted into the demented feline." Seldes thought that Bolm failed to incorporate something of American dance into his choreography. "As Mr. Bolm danced it," he later wrote, "one felt only the triumph of Ignatz." Henrietta Straus criticized both Bolm and Barrère for failing to capture the work's "peculiarly native flavor": "Their failure was due to no lack of artistry, but merely to the fact that one was a Russian and the other a Frenchman." Many in the audience agreed that Fred Stone should have played Krazy Kat; for Seldes only Charlie Chaplin would do (still others might have imagined Buster Keaton as a fine, deadpan Krazy Kat, complete with ballet skirt and evening gloves).[48]

As for Carpenter's music, the critics were prepared to be skeptical, if not contemptuous, according to Edward Moore and Deems Taylor.[49] Indeed, *Musical America* ran a preview feature that, while admitting that newspaper comics might "develop the American composer's powers of characterization," found the very idea of a comic strip ballet a joke: "Perhaps we shall have even a symphony, at least a theme and variations on 'The Toonerville Trolley That Meets All Trains.'"[50]

Not surprisingly, the reviews of the premiere criticized Carpenter's use of jazz, but for various reasons. Richard Aldrich, for instance, suggested that Carpenter used jazz simply to ensure more performances of his music. Engel offered the fashionably jaded remark that one heard better jazz on Broadway, and Henry Osgood, the pioneer jazz critic, similarly complained that Carpenter's jazz was "too polished."[51] Seldes himself thought the concluding fox-trot deficient and assumed that Irving Berlin or Deems Taylor were more likely to write a *Krazy Kat* ballet worthy of the strip. At the same time, Paul Rosenfeld, no admirer of jazz, complained that the ballet failed to elevate jazz.[52] Both Aldrich and Osgood advised Carpenter to forget jazz and follow the path set out by *The Birthday of the Infanta*, a work they genuinely admired (such advice paralleled critics who urged the neoclassical Stravinsky to return to his Russian ballets).

Writing a few years later, in 1925, Virgil Thomson argued that all jazz-inspired American music—not only *Krazy Kat* but the composer's earlier Piano Concertino, E. B. Hill's *Scherzo,* and George Gershwin's *Rhapsody in Blue*—lacked sincerity. "Mr. Carpenter, in exuberant Chicago style," wrote Thomson, "embraces the popular muse as he might his neighbor's wife, dancing at the country club. Mr. Gershwin, though privately aware of her true character, would put her in an imported corset, give her a feather fan, and take her to Carnegie Hall. Mr. Hill knows only too well that as a New Englander and an academician he would find distasteful any extreme familiarity with one whose race and upbringing are so different from his own."[53] (Had Thomson heard rumors about Carpenter and Mrs. Borden? If not, the reference to "his neighbor's wife" was amazingly perspicacious; if so, it was wickedly cheeky.)

Of the two Carpenter works, Thomson found the Piano Concertino "far the more successful, because it does not limit its Americanism to jazz and because it does not try so hard. *Krazy Kat* failed because the composer bet on a horse he didn't know anything about. The famous *Catnip Blues* in it are got together by pinning little furbelows of rag-time on to a long-winded melody that might just as well have come out of Deems Taylor's pantomime or *Tristan and Isolde.*" Thomson preferred the Americanism of Copland's First Symphony, although Copland had "neither the mature architectural skill of Carpenter nor the melodic gift of Gershwin."[54]

A few reviews regarded *Krazy Kat* much more highly, most notably, Deems Taylor in *Vanity Fair,* Henrietta Straus in *Nation,* and Stark Young in the *New Republic* (this last of the Greenwich Village Follies production). All three emphasized—as Carl Engel had as well—the ballet's distinctively American quality. Taylor wrote: "Perhaps some of us, that afternoon, realized a little more clearly just what 'American' means. No composer of any other nationality would have chosen just that subject, and only Stravinsky, in all the world of music could have written as good a score for it." Straus related "a certain thrill, a certain sense of emancipation in the realization that here at last was a representative work by a representative musician that was neither sectional nor racial in its inspirational sources, yet so purely American that it required a strong national consciousness on the part of its interpreters." Young observed that the work was "entirely—and therefore unprofessedly and never insistently or self-consciously—American." Even Engel agreed that the work was "not without moment for the history of incipient 'American' music."[55]

Taylor, Straus, and Young acknowledged that the work's Americanism owed something to jazz, but they refrained from using this relation as a yardstick with which to measure the work. Whereas Aldrich and Rosenfeld thought that the ballet was—essentially—as bad as jazz, and Engel, Osgood, and Seldes thought it not quite as good, Taylor, Straus, and Young made—in somewhat different ways—the obvious but overlooked point that Carpenter had used jazz for his own purposes. Taylor, for instance, observed that "for all its broad burlesque, its vulgarity, if you like—[the ballet] is a logical, well-developed piece of dramatic composition." Straus praised the composer for turning jazz's "noisy commentaries into philosophical reflections."[56] Young, whose review became the longest and most thoughtful piece on the ballet to date, saw the jazz element as transformed into something like the commedia dell'arte:

Krazy Kat has the story, the vagaries, the music, the gesture that the commedia dell' arte had, the action and movement also, the stream of vitality, the bouyant and incessant rhythm, the excitement of changing line, the bland cruelty and abounding love of life and of oneself, the character of being so intent upon one's own foolish and capricious and inexorable ends. . . . Krazy Kat remains jazz and adds to that a logical and beautiful musical development; it remains cartoon and popular fable, and adds to that the wistfulness and the escape of all great buffoonery, the fluttering and absurd heart of all great clowning. No American material in our theatre this season is apt to achieve a form so right or so promising as do these seven minutes of the Krazy Kat.[57]

Krazy Kat was enough of a hit to be incorporated, later that year, into the Greenwich Village Follies of 1922. Carpenter helped supervise this production. After attending their, in his opinion, disastrous New Haven tryout, he wrote to Ellen: "Such a weird mess! You see the poor old Kat was hurled on the stage for the first time last Monday night at New Haven—without ever having had a *complete rehearsal* with the orchestra and scenery and costumes and lights etc. *all together.*" Carpenter thought it ironic, too, that it was in New Haven that Bolm and his dancers had been stranded two years earlier, forcing the cancellation of *The Birthday of the Infanta* in Boston. But he assured Ellen not to worry: "P.S. I'm all right—just the way you would want me to be. I laugh to myself thinking about Honorary Diplomas and French medals waiting around stage doors—waiting for Jew managers to come out and smile."[58]

Carpenter stayed to oversee rehearsals during the week just before the 24 September opening. "If it doesn't go this time," he wrote Ellen, "it will be *its own* fault."[59] This Greenwich Village Follies production featured Carl Randall as Krazy Kat, Alfred Newman in the pit, and an outer curtain designed by Reginald Marsh. Apparently the choreography for the production was equally undistinguished.

Krazy Kat enjoyed a few other performances. Mark Watkins Stevens danced the eponymous hero in Detroit on 15 February 1923. Two months later, Guy Maier performed the work at a children's concert in Boston, where "obviously the youngsters were enjoying themselves."[60] On 14 April 1928 K. N. Eschman directed a production at Denison University in Granville, Ohio, that used silhouette puppets. But all in all, the ballet—as concert work, dance, or puppet show—received surprisingly few performances, and the work quickly became a vaguely remembered historical landmark.

In 1939 the conductor Fabien Sevitzky (Serge Koussevitzky's nephew) wrote Carpenter about reviving *Krazy Kat* with the Indianapolis Symphony. The composer responded: "This score was written some years ago and I was never satisfied with it. I really think that I would prefer not to have it offered publicly again until I have an opportunity to rewrite it. I feel sure that I can make it more interesting than it is in its present form."[61] Sevitzky persisted, however, and Carpenter accordingly revised the score in 1940.

Carpenter had already reworked the piece somewhat for a party at the Casino Club, at which Guy Maier and Dalies Frantz played the work in a new two-piano version. His extensive 1940 revisions probably drew on this earlier effort.[62] Perhaps in response to earlier criticism, he replaced the concluding two fox-trots with the first and last sections of a 1926 work, *Oil and Vinegar,* that he had written for Paul Whiteman's band (see ex. 41, chap. 16). The first section featured strong syncopations reminiscent of the Charleston; the second section, Lento amoroso, contained a sultry trombone solo, marked, in the *Oil and Vinegar* score, "New Orleans moan." Carpenter obviously felt that this somewhat wilder and jazzier music came closer to Krazy's intoxicated ecstasy. He did not even have to rescore the music much, since the instrumentation of *Krazy Kat* and *Oil and Vinegar* were almost identical, although he transposed the Lento amoroso into C major and wrote new music for Ignatz's final attack. Moreover, he added cascading C-major and Gb-major triads for that moment when Krazy gets hit in the head.

Carpenter also revised Bill Postem's dance, turning its little waltzlike fragments into a slow and static waltz in F# major (possibly meant to depict Postem's insobriety). He similarly made Krazy's first solo—the ballroom waltz—more self-contained and dancelike. Carpenter further replaced Krazy's theme—the Jazzando *Afternoon of a Faun*—with music related to *Oil and Vinegar* (he apparently worked backward in this respect) and took out the quotations of "Yankee Doodle" (which had accompanied Offisa Pupp's entrance) and "Old Folks at Home" (which had popped up in the original fox-trot).

After sending Sevitzky the revised score, Carpenter asked the conductor if he had any additional suggestions; Sevitzky replied that he had none "except perhaps several nuances."[63] Sevitzky and the Indianapolis Symphony gave the first performance of the revised *Krazy Kat* on 15 November 1940. The conductor wrote of its "big success" to Carpenter and added: "I like the work very much. It is colorful and masterly orchestrated, for which I congratulate you."[64]

While working on the revision, Carpenter wrote to his friend Léonide Massine in the hopes of interesting him in a revival of the ballet. Massine had danced and choreographed for Diaghilev (including the original *Parade*), and in later years he had staged many ballets in both America and Europe. Plans went as far as Massine's suggestion that the production include cactus trees that would periodically "come to life" and Carpenter's further idea that the cactus trees might double as "scene shifters and property men, as in the Chinese theatre." But Massine could not find backers for the project.[65]

Schirmer published a piano reduction of the revised score, using the Herriman illustrations (accompanied by principal musical themes) from the original version. (Consequently, in some instances, the illustrated musical themes cannot be found in the score!) Carpenter's old friend, the pianist Rudolph Ganz, championed this revised piano reduction. A Swiss-born pianist, conductor, and composer, Ganz (1877–1972) directed the Chicago Musical College from 1933 to 1954, during which time he established a close friendship with the composer. Ganz performed the new piano reduction at a children's Christmas party at Chicago's Tavern Club on 19 December 1948 with choreography by Walter Camryn. Carpenter, soon to leave Chicago on vacation, wrote Ganz, "It was *perfection*."[66]

Before leaving town, Carpenter located a concern that specialized in lantern slides and had Herriman's illustrations converted to five-inch slides that could be enlarged to any dimension, so that, "synchronized with the progress of the plot," they could be used in concert settings. He sent the slides to Schirmer, hoping especially to interest "conductors specializing in children's programs."[67] Ganz himself used these lantern slides in a 1949 performance of the ballet in Carmel.[68]

The revised *Krazy Kat* was recorded twice: by Richard Korn and the Hamburg Philharmonia Orchestra (1955) and by Calvin Simmons and the Los Angeles Philharmonic (1978).[69] Korn's recording included only excerpts; Simmons's recording consisted of the revised score in its entirety.

The superior Simmons rendition won highly favorable notices. "It is a delight to have the score—so comic, alive, and jaunty—back in the catalog," wrote Paul Kresh. Paul Snook agreed: "This ballet offers a tuneful medley of Carpenter's most prominent characteristics: saucy sweetness, antic whimsy, and a touching naïveté which more often suggests the nursery rather than the cabaret. On its own undemanding terms, this is a lilting and irresistible confection."[70]

Krazy Kat continued, too, to win the occasional revival as both a concert work and a ballet. The Newport Music Festival, for instance, staged it as part of their 1975 summer season, with choreography by Richard Englund. The dancing was "unimaginative" and the score was reduced for two pianos, reported Harold Schonberg, but "enough of the music came through to suggest that 'Krazy Kat' is a delightful period piece—fluffy, amusing, light-weight, and ever so much fun if it is approached for what it is."[71]

The ballet's unusual instrumentation and tiny size possibly discouraged more performances, but unfamiliarity with the comic strip probably became the more daunting obstacle. In his liner notes to the Simmons recording, R. D. Darrell alluded to the necessity of "seeing" the Herriman characters—either onstage or in the mind's eye: "Krazy Kat's failure to hold a place in the orchestral repertory is in large part a consequence of the predominance of its visual over its sheerly sonic appeals. Now that the score has been completely recorded for the first time, it still demands that listeners do it the justice of simultaneously seeing—actually or mentally—the incomparable Herriman scenes and karacters."[72]

This, indeed, would seem the principal challenge toward greater accep-tance of *Krazy Kat*. Critics and historians have focused on the word *jazz* at the expense of the more crucial word *pantomime*. Ultimately, the work's values are theatrical; the ballet has more to do with vaudeville, the silent movies, and, as Stark Young suggested, the commedia dell'arte than with jazz of whatever kind. And the work's genius resides, above all, in its musical portrayals of Krazy Kat, Offisa Pupp, and Ignatz Mouse, portrayals that Herriman claimed did him "honor."[73]

CHAPTER THIRTEEN

The Making of *Skyscrapers*

1924

Carpenter's career climaxed with his third and last ballet, *Skyscrapers: A Ballet of Modern American Life* (1923–24). The ballet enjoyed a successful two-year run at the Metropolitan Opera, a well-received European premiere, and scores of concert performances across the United States, Europe, and Latin America. That *Skyscrapers* was also Carpenter's boldest and brashest work, his *Rite of Spring,* so to speak, was not coincidental: Carpenter wrote it for Serge Diaghilev (1872–1929) and the Ballets Russes.

According to Boris Kochno, "Carpenter admired the Ballets Russes and had long hoped to see a ballet of his listed in the Diaghilev repertoire."[1] In the spring of 1920, Rue set off for Paris in the hopes of negotiating a Ballets Russes Chicago tour under Arts Club auspices, as well as interesting Diaghilev in either staging or commissioning a Carpenter ballet. She brought with her the score and photographs of *The Birthday of the Infanta* as well as a letter of introduction from Pierre Monteux (1875–1964) that read in part: "Monsieur Carpenter is one of the most talented American composers; his tendencies are modern, and I am sure that his ballet, which Madame Carpenter brings to you, will interest you as it interested myself, musically and scenically. It was staged in Chicago by Bolm, and had a great success."[2] Rue's trip to Paris coincided with the European premiere of Carpenter's Piano Concertino, which Diaghilev may have attended. In any case, she left *The Birthday of the Infanta* with Diaghilev, and on 15 April 1921 Prokofiev wrote Carpenter that he was determined to find out Diaghilev's response to the work.[3]

By 1922 Diaghilev had probably learned something about *Krazy Kat* as well, and he and Cocteau were sufficiently impressed to include Carpenter as the only non-French composer in their plans for Plastic Hall, "a kind of international youth theatre in which dance numbers would alternate with experimental films" and that would employ the talents of Satie, Poulenc, Braque, Matisse, and others.[4]

Carpenter's ambitions prompted a trip abroad, and he and Rue spent May through July 1923 in Europe. As he wrote Ellen, the trip's "Original Intention was to get thoroughly shaken up mentally and see what was going on,"[5] meaning, in particular, Diaghilev and the Ballets Russes.

The Carpenters naturally spent most of their time in Paris, where they saw "a lot of the Murphys—they are great fun—and Cole Porter & his wife who is fifteen years older than he."[6] The painter Gerald Murphy and his wife, Sara, were well-to-do Americans (his family owned the Mark Cross Company) who in 1921 moved to Paris and established themselves in the thick of that city's artistic life. The Carpenters possibly knew them before this particular trip or else met them through Stravinsky, Léger, Picasso, or any number of mutual friends. On 4 June the Murphys invited the Carpenters for lunch with Milhaud, Bakst, the princesse de Polignac, and presumably the Porters as well. Not only did Murphy facilitate Carpenter's entrée into Ballets Russes circles, he would leave his stamp on the ballet Carpenter eventually wrote for Diaghilev.

Gerald Murphy (1888–1964) resembled Carpenter in many respects: wealthy, brilliant, a dry wit and elegant dresser, he, too, straddled the worlds of high-bourgeois respectability and bohemian abandon. He began art studies only after viewing some cubist paintings in Paris and for a few years produced some lyrically constructivist canvases (only six survive as of today) that compare favorably with the work of Sheeler and Demuth.[7] Murphy also had some Marxist leanings and enjoyed close friendships, during these years, with such younger American rebels as Dos Passos, Hemingway, Dorothy Parker, Lillian Hellman, and F. Scott Fitzgerald (he and Sara served as Fitzgerald's models—to their dismay—for Dick and Nicole Diver in *Tender Is the Night*).

Murphy's eye impressed all who knew him. Dos Passos once described a walk along the Seine with Murphy and Léger as follows: "Instead of the hackneyed and pastel-tinged Tuileries and bridges and barges, . . . we were walking through a freshly invented world. They picked out winches, the flukes of an anchor, coils of rope, the red funnel of a towboat, half a woman's face seen behind geraniums through the casement window of the cabin of a barge. . . . The banks of the Seine never looked banal again after that walk."[8] Another source reported, "If you climbed the Eiffel Tower with him, he would point out a sight no one had noticed and tell you an amusing story about it into the bargain."[9] Archibald MacLeish wrote, "Murphy's greatest admiration at that period [1920s] was Piero della Francesca, most scientific and precise of fifteenth-century painters, and his passion was not for the abstraction of experience but for experience itself, 'the thing itself'—the 'thing' so like 'itself' that it would become its implications."[10]

Murphy also collected—to the delight and edification of his friends in Paris—jazz recordings (he named his yacht *Weatherbird,* after the Louis Armstrong recording), black spirituals (which he would sing with his wife), and modern gadgets (especially kitchen appliances like the electric waffle iron).[11] Such interests informed the scenario, sets, and costumes that Murphy devised for Cole Porter's 1923 ballet *Within the Quota,* but they achieved, indirectly, fuller and more complete expression in Carpenter's *Skyscrapers.*

Carpenter corresponded with Ellen throughout his three months in Europe (which he referred to as the "Big Test" because they needed to be separated for this long a time). He complained to her about the food (he missed American milk) and about friends who had not "a thought except for food—for wines—for clothes—for things"; he bought some new clothes himself and recommended Clive Bell's "awfully interesting" book *Since Cézanne.*

Carpenter regularly attended concerts and ballets. "It's here awfully interesting and exciting and stimulating and I'm sure that I am going to get a lot of new push and confidence out of it," he wrote Ellen. In late May he met de Falla at a concert "in which he [de Falla] and Milhaud took part." By 5 June he had heard "an extraordinary series of ballets by 'The Six,'" including Honegger's *Skating Rink,* Milhaud's *L'Homme et son désir,* Tailleferre's *Marchand d'oiseaux,* and the collaborative *Les Mariés de la tour Eiffel,* which he thought "killingly funny." In contrast he found Roussel's ballet-opera *Padmâvatî* "rather formidable and dull."[12]

Stravinsky's *Les Noces* (The wedding) overshadowed everything else, however. Carpenter first heard the work at a benefit concert at the home of the princesse de Polignac. "An extraordinary occasion," he wrote Ellen, "such a wonderful house—and such a gather of people that one had always heard about . . . and the new Stravinsky is beyond belief." Then, on 13 June he attended the triumphant public premiere; he himself described the score afterward as "a genuine creation—absolutely new and almost terrifying in its fundamental vigor and austerity." Carpenter surely attended the now legendary champagne dinner on a docked barge on the Seine that Gerald Murphy threw in honor of the occasion. "I think I am going to be commissioned to do something for the Russian ballet," Carpenter wrote the day after the premiere. "There is nothing definite yet—but they seem to be very much interested. Wouldn't it be great sport!"[13]

In late June, Carpenter left for London to get Ginny. While there, he saw Eugene Goossens (1893–1962), whom he "wanted to meet more than any of the other English music boys." He also was "dragged crying to the Duchess of Rutland who was having what seemed to me a most awful kind of party."[14]

On his return to Paris, Carpenter met on 5 July with Diaghilev, who asked him definitely to write something for the Ballets Russes. According to Philip Hale: "Diaghilev suggested a new ballet based on an American subject. Carpenter, returning to this country, thought of a composition which should represent the hurry and din of American life, and its association with jazz." On the other hand, Borowski reported that it was Diaghilev who "proposed that Carpenter should write for him a ballet which should embody the bustle and racket of American life expressed in the terms of the prevalent 'American' musical vernacular." Claudia Cassidy similarly quoted Diaghilev as saying to Carpenter, "Write your score and make it as characteristic as possible of the alternating violence of American life." Madeleine Goss reported further that Diaghilev wanted something about American strikers and suggested the French word for strikes, *"Grèves,"* as a working title. All agreed that Diaghilev told Carpenter not to concern himself with a story but to leave that to Diaghilev and his associates after the composer completed the score.[15]

A letter to Ellen dated 6 July 1923 provides a fuller account of this meeting than we have had hitherto:

> [Diaghilev] actually gave me a subject to work on. And I'm keen about the idea and *if you aren't* I'll be desperate. It's simply the idea of a *Policeman's Strike*. In the beginning there you see a row of fat New York policemen against a background of NY Skyscrapers. Great formality for a few moments—until the Chief of Police comes in and pastes up an announcement that the police dept. has *gone on a strike*. Then begins a gradual crescendo of lawlessness in which all the populace, men, women, & children, and policemen join. *Anything* can happen, and Everything does happen—until at the end—the "strike" is called off and Law & Order is restored. *That's all.*
>
> What D. wants, of course, is something typically American—not a pale copy of some French or Italian or Russian thing—and I'm sure that such a theme could be made effective. Anyway it's an opening wedge—and I'm delighted at the chance. Oh please like it a little,—I know it doesn't give an opportunity for some of the things we love, but we'll do our best with it, anyway, *won't we?*[16]

Diaghilev apparently had in mind Carpenter's portrayals of policemen in *Perambulator* and *Krazy Kat* (which also contains the posting of an announcement). Although he suggested a New York setting, Diaghilev may also have had in mind the Boston police strike of 1919. Unhappy with their salaries and with the city's antiunionism, the Boston police had walked off the job in September 1919, whereupon followed weeks of looting and violence between National Guardsmen and citizens. Finally, Governor Calvin Coolidge retracted the right of policemen to strike and restored order.[17] At the time, Americans widely interpreted this civil unrest as the prelude to a dreaded Bolshevist revolution, and the successful resolution of the work stoppage made Calvin Coolidge a national hero. The strike might have led Diaghilev to consider the extremes of order and lawlessness as "typically American."

Carpenter stayed on in Paris a few more weeks—"Ginny is such tremendous fun to be with," he wrote Ellen. He saw some old friends there, including the Bartletts, Eva Gauthier, George Porter, and "Janet [Fairbank] and her regiment," and he took a heart-wrenching tour of the battlefields at Verdun and Reims, before leaving for Venice in mid-July.[18]

With its exquisite palazzi, picturesque canals, and Lido beach, Venice competed with Paris for the attentions of wealthy, sophisticated Americans during these years. It attracted especially theatrical types, such as the Porters, who might have entertained the Carpenters in their Palazzo Barbaro.[19] In fact, Carpenter planned to be in Venice to meet up with Robert Edmond Jones and the playwright Harrison Garfield Rhodes (1871–1929)—though whether for fun or business we do not know. He also had lunch with Reginald de Koven's widow, the "poor old thing."[20]

Carpenter also presumably spent some time with the Murphys in Antibes, a sleepy town on the Riviera that the Porters had discovered. He apparently visited Antibes on the way to Venice and might have traveled on with Murphy, who spent that summer in Venice working on *Within the Quota* with Porter.

Returning to the States, Carpenter wrote Elizabeth Sprague Coolidge on 5 September, "I heard a lot of interesting new music this summer, and have come back in a 'rage of determination,' as Henry James put it, to produce some myself." He similarly informed Eva Gauthier on 20 September that he was "hard at work on my new ballet and find it very exciting."[21] Carpenter exchanged ideas with Bolm about this new ballet "of American life," which he wanted "to be free, and to have scope and breadth." Bolm visualized a New York back alley as a setting.[22]

Throughout the fall Carpenter referred to the ballet as *The Policeman's Holiday,* but by the time Gerald Murphy visited him in late 1923, Carpenter had discarded the strike idea in favor of "the sounds of metal and machinery."[23] According to Thomas Pierson, this new point of departure was inspired by the noisy construction of the Allerton Hotel just two blocks from the composer's Rush Street home.[24] One senses, too, the influence of Murphy.

In fact, after visiting Chicago, Murphy sent an encouraging letter from New York: "You are thinking in terms of what is real and most American," he wrote Carpenter. "Your thought has been the biggest, most daring and most challenging you've ever had, doubtless. It must not stop there." Murphy warned of two pitfalls, however: the music might not be "as sharp, direct, brilliant, hard and insistent as the idea," or the music might be "too much of all these," as all of Paris deemed *Les Noces*. The letter further advised that Carpenter begin with appropriate instrumental sounds—"The principles behind the sounds of machinery and life are the same as those behind musical instruments, aren't they?"—and suggested, among other possibilities, iron pipes hit with steel hammers, air pumps releasing air, and cymbals hit with steel. "Build for your hearers a towering big structure of riveted steel and stone and then play all the color and ornament on it you want," he concluded. "It means so much to all of us."[25]

Always responsive to new trends, Carpenter surely knew—a few years before Prokofiev's *Leap of Steel* (1925), Converse's *Flivver Ten Million* (1926), and Mossolov's *Factory* (1927)—that composers (in the tradition of the Italian futurists) had begun to find inspiration in modern machinery and industrial sounds. Emerson Whithorne (1884–1958), Leo Ornstein (1892–   ), and George Antheil (1900–1959) had already written airplane pieces for piano, and Arthur Honegger (1892–1955) had provided the machine movement with its biggest hit, *Pacific 231* (1922). Carpenter possibly had some familiarity with Varèse's (1885–1965) own brand of futurism by this time as well.

At this point Carpenter may have already associated his "sounds of metal and machinery" with the construction of skyscrapers (as opposed to airplanes and locomotives, although later evidence suggests he may have been thinking of factories, too), a development related not only to Diaghilev's "background of NY skyscrapers," to the building of the Allerton Hotel, and to Murphy's exhortation to "build . . . a towering big structure," but to the special importance skyscrapers held to Chicagoans. Chicago led the world in the creation and development of skyscrapers—this out of sheer necessity more than anything else: bounded on the north and west by the Chicago River, on the east by Lake Michigan, and on the south by a network of railroads, Chicago's central business area had become more and more costly. By 1890 land in the

Loop demanded close to a million dollars a quarter acre. In the words of one historian, "The only direction to go was up."[26]

Chicago engineer William Le Baron Jenney devised a solution when, in 1884, he designed the world's first steel-framed structure for a downtown office building. In the years following, Chicago witnessed the construction of taller and taller buildings, including the Masonic Temple (at twenty-one stories, the world's tallest in 1892) and the Montgomery Ward Building (again, the world's tallest when it opened in 1900). At the same time, local architects like John Wellborn Root and Louis Sullivan brought the skyscraper to a high level of aesthetic beauty. The English painter Sir John Lavery, looking down Michigan Avenue, told Harriet Monroe in 1911, "These great Olympian buildings strike me as having beauty of a very high order—there had been nothing like it on earth since Egypt built the pyramids."[27]

The skyscraper correspondingly played a large and probably unparalleled part in the city's literary life. Henry Blake Fuller's (1857–1929) novel *The Cliff Dwellers* (1893) was essentially a condemnation of the "materialistic and success-crazed culture" that had given rise to the skyscraper (the book's keynote importance to Chicago's cultural life was evident from the fact that a prominent local arts club named itself after the novel). In later writings Fuller continued to view the skyscraper as a monumental evil. Robert Herrick's (1869–1938) novel *The Common Lot* (1904) similarly criticized skyscrapers as an expression of "the industrial greed and uncoordinated social necessities of a rapidly multiplying and heterogenous people."[28] Other Chicago novels, including *Sister Carrie* (1900) by Theodore Dreiser and *The Pit* (1903) by Frank Norris (1870–1902), also used skyscrapers as a symbol of modern life, though with greater ambivalence, viewing them as at once impressive and threatening.

Chicagoan poets also wrote about skyscrapers, often in a more upbeat manner. In 1912, for instance, Harriet Monroe, who had long "watched with keenest interest the gradual development of the skyscraper," applauded the American architect for taking less "refuge in the past" than other native artists.[29] Carl Sandburg went further. According to one critic: "He saw the skyscraper as the urban community in microcosm and pointed out that its highest purpose was to serve and express the spirit of the people who inhabited it. By the democratic logic Sandburg inherited from Whitman, the individual was most creatively and spiritually alive when he was fully integrated into the life of the skyscraper."[30]

Chicago skyscrapers also intrigued such local humorists as George Ade, who wrote:

Every time the down-town confusion of roofs, chimneys and towers is viewed from some eminence there must come to the mind a query: "When will Chicago reach the era of stability?"

Over there to the northwest a cluster of men no larger than flies are hacking away at a roof from which arises dry clouds of dust. The first blow is struck at the cornice, and the destruction is not to cease until the last foundation stone has been rooted out of the clay.

To the northeast is a right-angled web of steel towering above black roofs and showing like the skeleton of a great monument.

There has not been a time in years when the destruction and construction were not to be seen from the same window, and even the old residents who have watched the ceaseless and marvelous changes of the business district say it is apparently as much unfinished as it was fifty years ago. They may come back in spirit a few centuries hence to view the same old tearing down and building up.[31]

Carpenter's *Skyscrapers* would combine something of the alarm of Fuller and Herrick, the awe of Dreiser and Norris, the exhilaration of Monroe and Sandburg, and perhaps, above all, the whimsy of Ade.

As the symbolic importance of the skyscraper took hold, Carpenter further transformed Diaghilev's idea of a ballet about law and lawlessness into one about work and play. One of Carpenter's earliest discussions of the ballet dated from August 1924:

[*Skyscrapers*] is an attempt to make a musical transcription of contemporary American life. . . . It does not go beneath the surface at all, but treats of what you can't escape, of what hits you right off the street. It is an endeavor to fix the sound of American activity, the sound of industry. After all, organized industry is the thing which is distinctive of America, and it has produced its own sonority and rhythmic life. The ballet will give the character of American work and American play.[32]

The composer would eventually state that the ballet "is simply based on the idea that in this country we work hard and play hard."[33] Presumably thinking of Diaghilev's law–lawlessness–law outline, Carpenter cast his ballet into three parts, in which the outer sections depicted a skyscraper, symbol of work, and the middle section pictured an amusement park, symbol of play.

In the score Carpenter later designated the amusement park as Coney Island or, rather, "any 'Coney Island'" (doubtless in deference to the ballet's premiere at the Metropolitan Opera). He probably had in mind, above all, such popular Chicago amusement parks as the Riverview on the North Side, the Midway and White City on the South Side, and, perhaps, remembrances of the Columbian Exposition. Significantly, these "parks"—which offered visitors no opportunities for the contemplation of nature but rather "the chance to test themselves against the machines that dominated urban life"— arose concurrently with the skyscraper and provided a complementary play-city on a similarly stupendous scale.[34]

At its core, then, the score explored the idea that skyscrapers—with their steel frames, elevators, and noisy construction—and amusement parks—with their roller coasters, Ferris wheels, and popular music—mirrored one an-other. Thus, the ballet could incorporate two principal musical trends of the 1920s: futurism and jazz. Carpenter may have found some inspiration from Clive Bell's association of jazz with Italian futurism.[35] But in more precisely making the association of jazz with skyscrapers, Carpenter rather anticipated later cultural critics such as Le Corbusier, who called Manhattan's skyscrapers "hot jazz in stone or steel," and John A. Kouwenhoven, who, in 1948, viewed jazz and skyscrapers as "the climactic achievements of the vernacular tradition in America."[36] Carpenter explored this dialectic, however, with a subtlety and emotion deeper than simple metaphor or analogy.

In July 1924 Carpenter arrived at the Hotel Excelsior at the Lido, Venice, and presented Diaghilev with a piano score and some orchestral sketches, if not the full score. "I remember it was terrifically hot," Carpenter stated years later, "and we stripped down to our shirtsleeves and went to work looking over my score. I was much encouraged by his reaction to my music and I accepted his suggestion of the title which he intended to use—'Grattes Ciel'—as a French equivalent for 'Skyscrapers.'"[37] Diaghilev and Carpenter apparently agreed on a Monte Carlo production sometime about 1 March 1925.[38]

Diaghilev immediately wrote Boris Kochno: "Happily, his ballet [*Sky-scrapers*] is not as bad as I expected. It's not a 'false-note,' but rather, I'd say, it is American de Falla, with appropriate folklore." He further explained that the ballet no longer dealt with a policeman's strike but rather "an *American factory,* with alarm whistles and workers and such."[39] To Diaghilev's amuse-ment Carpenter had requested that a Soviet artist design the sets, since his score was "not far from Bolshevism."[40] This idea might have been suggested by an exhibition of Soviet art then on display in Venice; in any case, con-temporary Soviet art would have suited Carpenter's depiction of the masses at work and at play in a highly industrial setting.

At the time, Diaghilev was negotiating an American tour with Otto

Kahn and Giulio Gatti-Casazza, codirectors of the Metropolitan Opera; Artur Bodanzky, musical director at the opera; and Morris Gest, a renowned impresario. When Kahn stipulated that the Ballets Russes feature an American ballet, Diaghilev ostensibly played his Carpenter card, for he knew that both Kahn and Gest regarded Carpenter as "a serious and important person."[41] To this day it is unclear whether Diaghilev intended to launch Carpenter's ballet in Monte Carlo, on an American tour, or both.

Before returning to the States, Carpenter stopped in Monte Carlo, where he played his score for Nijinsky's sister, the choreographer Bronislava Nijinska.[42] She likely would have been assigned *Skyscrapers* had Diaghilev staged it that year (Nijinska would leave the Ballets Russes in late 1924, however). Perhaps Carpenter joined the Murphys at Antibes; at least Rue and Ginny did, for in some photographs taken of a 1924 picnic on the plage de la Garoupe on the cape of Antibes, they can be spotted as part of a group that included the Murphys, Picasso and his first wife, Olga (who had danced with Diaghilev), and the count and countess Étienne de Beaumont (described by Calvin Tomkins as "Proustian characters who were great connoisseurs and patrons of the avant-garde").[43] All—except for Picasso—wore wild, fantastic costumes: headbands with pom-poms and tassels, wraps, strings of pearls, beaded bathing suits, enormously tall hats, tutus, and ballet slippers. Rue must have felt very much at home.

In early August, Carpenter returned to Chicago, and by the end of the month, he completed a revised piano score of the ballet based on some changes Diaghilev had suggested. He still had not decided on a title but had narrowed his choices to *Le Chant des gratte-ciel* (The song of the skyscrapers), *Berceuse du gratte-ciel* (Lullaby of the skyscraper), and *Les Grattes-Cielistes* (Skyscrapers). Turning to Ellen for advice, he wrote: "I do think, though, that the Sky-Scraper is a fairly complete symbol of what we are aiming at. 'Berceuse,' of course, is ironique—perhaps too much so."[44] (In 1935 Harry Warren and Al Dubin coincidentally invoked Carpenter's "ironique" title in their "Lullaby of Broadway" for a Busby Berkeley film.) For his working title Carpenter settled on *Le Chant des gratte-ciel*.

Carpenter also redid the orchestration, since Diaghilev opposed the use of singers on the grounds that the effect had been "overdone" in recent years, although Carpenter supposed that the impresario's real concern was "expense and complications of production."[45] Carpenter also decided against using "a combination of two orchestras" (a conventional orchestra with minimal strings and a jazz band),[46] although remnants of this idea survived, apparently, in the German-band music that opened the amusement park sequence.

On 2 September 1924, while at work on the orchestration, Carpenter mailed the revised piano score to Diaghilev. Almost five months later, on 20 January 1925, he wrote Ellen, "Still no word from the unspeakable Diaghileff." A few weeks after that, he had the opportunity to play the score for Nadia Boulanger, whom he described to Ellen as "one of the best living French musicians." Boulanger thought the music "magnificent," and Carpenter wrote Ellen, "Isn't that exciting—oh gee!"[47]

He still had not heard from Diaghilev when Stravinsky arrived in mid-February for concerts with the Chicago Symphony and the Arts Club. Carpenter spent an exhausting week as Stravinsky's tour guide, host, and right-hand man. "I have just come from Stravinsky's room upstairs," wrote Carpenter to Ellen from the Hotel Chicago on 17 February 1925, "where I have been acting as a sort of musical and social advisor and answering telephone calls for him and translating telegrams and getting a splendid view of the intimate workings of genius in its off-hours."[48] Carpenter showed Stravinsky around the Chicago stockyards, threw a party at 700 Rush on 22 February, and helped supervise a reception at the Arts Club on 24 February. "He is the funniest little animal," Carpenter remarked on 19 February. "When he eats pie, he takes it into his arms like a child—and yearns over it. *But* his *brain* is extraordinary." On 21 February, Carpenter once again described Stravinsky as an "extraordinary personality," but one who "requires a degree of concentration." And he thought Stravinsky's Chicago Symphony concert, in which Stravinsky played his recently composed Piano Concerto, "thrilling."[49]

At Stravinsky's request Carpenter played his ballet score for him, as he had for Boulanger. "I think he liked it," he commented to Ellen, "anyway he studied the score with great concentration and made a few very interesting suggestions designed to giving certain places more *kick*—and of course he is the *original* professor Le Kick."[50]

During Stravinsky's week in Chicago, Carpenter finally learned that the piano score to *Le Chant des gratte-ciel* that he had sent Diaghilev had never reached him. After arriving at a few forwarding addresses, it came to rest in Paris, where it had accrued an eighty-dollar storage charge. Carpenter immediately called Gerald Murphy to ask him to hand deliver the score to Diaghilev, but he realized that the ballet would now have to wait for a spring 1926 production. "I'm glad now that I never allowed myself to set too much store on it," he wrote Ellen. "It does make one a little mad though." By April, Carpenter had still not heard from Diaghilev, and he successfully went into negotiations with Gatti-Casazza for a premiere at the Metropolitan Opera. "I don't know if I am doing the best thing or not," he confided to Ellen, "but I'm tired of waiting around for the silent Russian and all the second-hand news I have from that quarter is very discouraging."[51]

On 16 April, Carpenter informed Diaghilev that he had signed a contract with the Metropolitan Opera for the premiere of *Skyscrapers*.[52] He hoped that Diaghilev would consider mounting the European premiere and, in fact, pursued such possibilities for another year or so, but without success.[53]

Indeed, once Carpenter opted for a world premiere in New York, Diaghilev was not likely to settle for a European premiere. But would the Ballets Russes have eventually produced the work otherwise? Perhaps Diaghilev wanted the ballet only as part of an American tour and, once that fell through (which it did), felt no initiative to stage the piece. But didn't Diaghilev originally commission the work independent of an American tour? Did he simply lose interest in Carpenter and the idea of staging a "typically American" ballet? Some evidence suggests as much. Vernon Duke, for instance, reports that the "distinctly urbanistic *Skyscrapers*" was "indignantly turned down by cruel Diaghilev."[54]

Diaghilev's indignation might have involved his growing dislike for Americans and their popular music, an antipathy that deepened in the mid-1920s as Europe came more and more under the influence of American culture. Kochno recalled that Diaghilev "had a horror of jazz" and "was outraged by the jazz invasion of Europe and by its influence on young composers." By 1926 Diaghilev was regularly complaining that jazz and the Charleston were defiling Venice, and he had come to begrudge his friend Cole Porter's success, which he thought "unjustified." As a favor to Porter, he listened to Gershwin play his *Rhapsody in Blue,* but he never even responded to Gershwin's request that he stage it. Such a frame of mind surely turned him against Carpenter's new ballet score.[55] At least Carpenter could take comfort in the fact that he came closer to a Diaghilev production than any other American composer.

Carpenter's contract with the Metropolitan Opera granted him three hundred dollars for orchestra parts and seventy-five dollars for each of a minimum of three performances for the 1925–26 season. The Metropolitan Opera reserved exclusive rights for performances in New York, Brooklyn, Philadelphia, Atlanta, and other cities, excluding (at the insistence of Carpenter) Chicago and points west. Opera management also stipulated the right to renew the contract for the 1926–27 season.

The ballet still had no story per se. In the spring of 1925, Carpenter enlisted the help of Robert Edmond Jones, who had designed the sets and costumes for *The Birthday of the Infanta,* and both men retreated to Charlotte, Vermont, where they spent six months of "gruelling, unremitting labor" hammering out a scenario. Jones later remembered that Carpenter had "expressed the intention to indicate moods of work and play, but beyond this he had not committed himself, not even to a literal locale." The score, however, had five fairly distinct sections, described by Jones as "a short opening passage, a brief transition, a relatively long middle section, another brief transition and again a short passage."[56]

From this structure Carpenter and Jones accordingly devised five scenes, with the first few pages of the score providing an additional setting. They described these six scenes as follows:

SCENE 1   Symbols of restlessness.
SCENE 2   An abstraction of the skyscraper and of the work that produces it—and the interminable crowd that passes by.
SCENE 3   The transition from work to play.
SCENE 4   Any "Coney Island" and a reflection of a few of its manifold activities— interrupted presently by a "throw-back," in the movie sense, to the idea of work, and reverting with equal suddenness to play.
SCENE 5   The return from play to work.
SCENE 6   Skyscrapers.

Using this outline, Jones created five set designs (he used the same design for scenes 3 and 5).

Carpenter did not choose Adolph Bolm to choreograph this ballet; after the experience of *Krazy Kat,* he might have felt Bolm unsuited for this kind of project, saturated, as it was, in the American vernacular. Jones further explained, "It seemed a little devious to say the least, that we should take one of the Europeans who after six months spent watching Florence Mills and other cabaret stars, go home and skilfully apply the borrowed devices of our jazz." Instead, Carpenter and Jones began a "search for an American Adolph Bolm to create the ballet as choreographers do for Diaghilev."[57]

Unable to find an "American Adolph Bolm," however, Carpenter and Jones choreographed some of the dance sequences—for both the laborers in the work scenes and the revelers in the play scenes—themselves. Carpenter jotted these instructions (such as, at one point, "Charleston") directly in the score, along with lighting directions. He and Jones then hired Sammy Lee to stage and choreograph the annotated score.

Along with Busby Berkeley, Seymour Felix, and Bobby Connolly,

Sammy Lee (born Samuel Levy in New York, 1890; died in Woodland Hills, California, 1968) was one of the most celebrated dance-directors of his time. He staged the Broadway productions of Gershwin's *Lady Be Good!* (with Fred Astaire) in 1924, Berlin's *Cocoanuts* (with the Marx Brothers) in 1925, Gershwin's *Oh Kay!* in 1926, and both Kern's *Show Boat* and Berlin's *Ziegfeld Follies* in 1927. In 1929 Lee moved to Hollywood, where he worked for MGM, and where his influence was felt in the work of Busby Berkeley and Fred Astaire.[58]

Skyscrapers posed an unusual challenge for Lee, for he found himself working with the Metropolitan Opera's small, classically trained corps de ballet, augmented by students from the opera company's ballet school. He was surprised at how well these dancers adjusted to "American stage dancing":

> I thought there might be some difficulty in teaching these steps to dancers who had been trained in an entirely different school. But there was not. There is a great difference in these two types of dancers—something which I can hardly explain—but I have had no difficulty in getting these Metropolitan dancers into the intricacies of jazz dancing. As a matter of fact, dancing of that sort can be done by anybody who has a real sense of rhythm.[59]

These dancers were supplemented by a Harlem chorus, under the direction of Frank Wilson, that both sang and danced in the Negro scene (unlike Diaghilev, Gatti-Casazza permitted Carpenter to use singers). According to a recently unearthed document from the Metropolitan Opera's archives, these "twelve colored singers" received $120 for each performance. This apparently was the first time African American singers appeared on the stage of the Metropolitan Opera.[60]

Skyscrapers premiered on 19 February 1926 as the second feature of a triple bill with *Gianni Schicchi* and *Pagliacci*. Louis Hasselmans conducted, and Rita De Leporte, Albert Troy, and Roger Dodge danced the solo roles of Herself, the Strutter, and White-Wings, respectively. The program credited Carpenter, Jones, and Lee as directors and Walt Kuhn as special consultant. Using sketches, photographs, newspaper accounts, and the scenario published in the 1927 Schirmer edition,[61] we can reconstruct a fairly detailed précis of this first production.

Only twenty-one measures long, scene 1 immediately lashes into the cacophonous, frenetic, robotic music that characterizes the "work" portions of the ballet. The colorful, strident orchestration, featuring two pianos, a large percussion battery including cylinder bells, and woodwinds in their high registers, suggests city sounds without recourse to the kind of noises that Murphy advocated. The irregular pounding of the bass drum is particularly effective in suggesting hard, manual labor. The bold use of relentless ostinatos, biting dissonances, loud dynamics, changing and irregular meters, and contrametric patterns also helps evoke hammering, riveting, and urban hustle and bustle. The harmonic texture is static and bitonal: F# dominant seventh and C-major harmonies alternate and clash against a pedal consisting of the common tone E (shades of Ziehnian plurisignificance).

The opening pages clearly reveal the influence of *Les Noces*. This comparison pales by the Coney Island sequence, and even the brightly colored "work" music perhaps comes closer to Dukas's *Sorcerer's Apprentice* or Percy Grainger's *Warriors—Music to an Imaginary Ballet* than to Stravinsky. But the basic impulse behind the work—that blend of cool irony and inexhaustible energy—derives in large part from *Les Noces*.

The music's dense, organic construction plausibly owes something to *Les Noces* as well. In the brief opening scene (more a prelude than a scene per se), Carpenter quickly states some important motives that will dominate much of the work: the Hammer motive,[62] a $\frac{5}{4}$ ostinato made up of repeated notes and jumping octaves (CD track time [tt] .01);[63] a trumpet fanfare at ☐ (tt .21); a jazzy *più animato* (tt .30); and the Work motive, three clipped, highly dissonant chords that often serve as a pickup (tt .39). These static, fragmentary ideas eschew conventional development; rather, they form a collage much like the brittle, mosaicked forms of Stravinsky and the cubist painters.

For the opening scene Jones designed an outer drop curtain consisting simply of alternating black and white diagonal stripes, suggestive of the kind of caution signs found at, for example, railroad crossings. Carpenter called the design a "symbol of danger." In front of the drop Jones placed, on either side of the stage, two stop-sign-shaped posts with blinking red lights, like traffic signals. These light posts remained onstage for the entire ballet; Carpenter treated them as individual instruments, indicating the rhythm of their blinking in the score. This consequently looked forward to the "multimedia" of the 1960s, much as the curtain's design anticipated the "op art" of the same period.

Scene 2 begins at ② (tt .40), just at that moment when the conflicting F# dominant seventh and C-major harmonies resolve to their common tone, E (major). The drop curtain rises to reveal a "huge and sinister skyscraper in course of construction, a tangled mass of red and black shapes." On a scaffold brawny laborers dressed in overalls and wielding sledges, and steel riveters clothed in black, metallic jumpers, hammer and rivet.[64] According to one review, "Patches of over-ripe purple and under-ripe green fall on the workers as they pound, heave, tug and hoist."[65] At the same time, workers in the foreground stand over some opening that spews smoke and "the blue-white fire of an oxyacetylene torch."[66] Above them, men on a scaffold and "others still higher up on the structure"[67] similarly are at work. In the background, behind more girders, sawhorses, and geometric shapes, silhouettes representing "the dreary and endless shadow-procession of the indifferent city crowd" move "listlessly, meaninglessly by."[68]

This scene is also quite short. In addition to the aforementioned fragmentary ideas, the French horns introduce a new, important, lofty theme (the Song of the Skyscrapers, tt .50) whose modal inflections integrate the F♯/C-major harmonies of the opening scene. Vaguely Eastern or American Indian, this theme resembles Stravinsky's "neoprimitivist" melodies, although it recalls much more emphatically the composer's own Indianist music, such as *Little Indian*.

Another quasi-primitivist theme appears at ④ (tt 1.22), one that is closer to children's music: it resembles the taunting tune, "nah-nah-nah-nah-nah," cast, however, in the language of hard hats at work (the Song of the Workers, ex. 36). Some sequential activity brings this second scene to a climactic triple fortissimo, followed by a grand pause.

The transitional scene 3 (⑦ to ⑪) also lasts only a couple of minutes. For this scene Jones designed a plain black curtain with two rounded openings—like tunnel entrances—outlined in white on either side. Jones meant these openings to suggest "the atmosphere of factory egress, of the subway, of the crowded vehicle tearing away from the centers of labor."[69] He emphasized the scene's transitional quality by shading the curtain from dark to light. He also represented the change from work to play by placing a large clock—symbolizing a time-clock—by the opening on the right.

Dressed in their scene 2 work clothes, the laborers "enter from the wings, right—pass with stiff and mechanical step through the first doorway, and reappear almost at once through the other door, now with movement gay and relaxed, and each with his girl on his arm." Deems Taylor referred to these girls as "a bevy of briefly-clad maidens whose looks and costumes suggested that they might be Mr. Ziegfeld's idea of what stenographers should—and seldom do—look like." Another critic reported that a few couples lingered "to embrace and 'jazz' or 'strut' for an instant to Mr. Carpenter's engaging rhythms."[70]

Throughout the transitional scene, the conflict between F♯ and C against

EXAMPLE 36. Carpenter, *Skyscrapers*, 4, mm. 1–3.

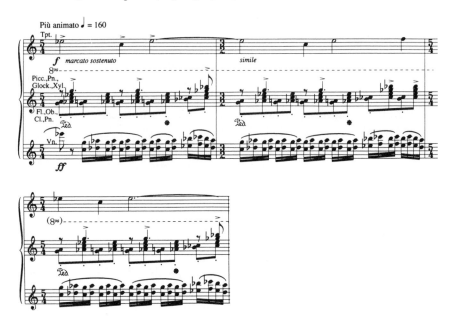

the background of E continues, but the music grows much softer and features a new motive, namely, a sixteenth-note triplet figure (March of the Workers). Although this marchlike passage is less severely mechanical than the previous music, something of the robotic still lingers (like Charlie Chaplin leaving work in *Modern Times*).

At 8 (tt 3.06) the music relaxes further as the Song of the Workers appears in a clear C major with simple triads. At 9 (tt 3.33) the humanizing of the musical texture continues as Carpenter transforms the Song of the Workers (à la Ziehn's order permutation) into a carefree, tuneful melody (ex. 37), complete with banjo and high-hat cymbals, in a clearly defined A♭ major (the tune is a harder, more ironic version of a type later used by Ray Gilbert and Allie Wrubel in their 1946 song for Disney, "Zip-A-Dee-Doo-Dah"). Perhaps this is where some dancers lingered "to embrace and 'jazz' or 'strut.'"

The appearance of a banjo in a symphony orchestra proved one of the score's most memorable novelties, although in later years Carpenter made light of it, saying: "It was confined to one experiment in the score of a ballet of mine called 'Skyscrapers,' in which for three minutes I permitted a banjo player to go on a first class banjo picking binge, to add to the general confusion which was the main theme of my work. It only goes to show that

EXAMPLE 37.   Carpenter, *Skyscrapers*, 9, mm. 1–4.

any doughboy may probably become a hero if he can manage to shoot just one bullet straight."[71] Indeed, Carpenter's use of the banjo was subtle and occasional, providing bits of color rather than important melodic material. But the atmosphere it helped create was as striking, in its own way, as Mahler's use of the mandolin.

The March of the Workers resumes, this time interrupted with staccato major seconds played by two Eb saxophones and two horns accompanied by snare drum, a sound that vividly suggests the blasts of car horns (tt 3.57). At 10 the composer abstracts these "car blasts" into an ostinato figure that accompanies the marchlike triplets, leading directly into scene 4.

Throughout the third scene Carpenter ingeniously metamorphoses his industrial work music into play (or at least nonwork) music: He turns industry's crashing noises into the irreverent dash of jazz's high-hat cymbals; its hectic rhythms into the sassy syncopations of popular music; and its unrelenting, repetitive actions into the impatient beeps of the motorist. This ingeniously underscores one of the ballet's central themes: that American work and American play constitute two sides of the same coin.

Jones's design for scene 4 ("any 'Coney Island'") similarly transforms the girders and sawhorses of scene 2 into roller coasters and circus platforms. (Like so much in this ballet, this conceit parallels and anticipates the animated cartoons of Max Fleischer, for instance, "Granpy's Indoor Outing," in which Granpy amuses Betty Boop and her nephew by transforming a fire escape into a roller coaster.) In addition, one finds, in the foreground, three sideshows with star-studded curtains; farther back, the swinging carriages of a Ferris wheel; and in the distance, an enormous, "preposterous" moon and stylized stars that light up the sky.

This large, episodic fourth scene is best presented in outline form:

1. At ⑩ (tt 4.31) "a little German street-band is discovered surrounded by a crowd of excited pleasure seekers." Carpenter suggests the street band and the crowd by means of a wind band and the full orchestra, respectively. The band quotes the chorus from Brewster and Sloane's 1897 hit "When You Ain't Got No Money Well You Needn't Come Around," often cited as one of the first "ragtime" songs (like the later and more popular "Bill Bailey, Won't You Please Come Home," which it resembles, "When You Ain't Got No Money" is closer to the polka than to real ragtime). The composer's shrill orchestration (with high piccolo and "stridente" trumpet), "wrong" notes, chromatic harmonies, and textural subtleties provide the quotation with an exaggerated and ironic humor.[72]

2. At ⑫ "every dancer is suddenly 'frozen' in the posture of the moment, by a vivid flash of lightning, followed by a roll of thunder and a darkening stage." This is the "'throw-back,' in the movie sense, to the idea of work," and, indeed, at ⑭ workmen once again emerge performing their "stern and mechanical pantomime of labor" to the Hammer motive. At six after ⑭ Carpenter introduces a new and bold theme, which will return near the ballet's conclusion, at ⑤⑤. This theme—which we might call Reminder of Work—has a primitivist quality not unlike the music found in scenes 1 and 2.

3. At ⑯ the action returns to Coney Island. "The eager throng is crowding about a little platform up-stage on which three mechanical dolls are stiffly performing." In the entire ballet this brief passage—only thirteen measures long—is the one that perhaps most forcefully resembles Stravinsky's *Petrushka*. Scenario sketches suggest that Carpenter originally intended this to be children's music and only later interpolated the mechanical-doll idea.[73]

4. From ⑰ to two before ⑳, "there is further diversion in two side-show booths on either side of stage near the footlights, each with a fabulous 'barker' in front, the one offering a snakecharmer, the other the 'Wild Man of Borneo' in chains." (Carpenter may have seen a caged "Wild Man of Borneo" at the 1893 Columbian Exposition.)[74] The sinuous, slightly exotic melody at

five before ⟨18⟩ must be the snake charmer's; the primitivist music at ⟨18⟩, with its alternating $\frac{6}{8}$ and $\frac{5}{8}$ meters (also somewhat Stravinskian), must be the Wild Man of Borneo. The strong similarity between the music for the mechanical dolls and that for the snake charmer and the interpolation of the Hammer motive at six after ⟨17⟩ betray that the score has its own logic independent of the Carpenter-Jones scenario.

5. "General dance movement" follows from ⟨20⟩ to ⟨23⟩. Olin Downes discussed such dancing as follows: "The colors of the dancers are as various and garish as their costumes. Their steps are taken from the American musical comedy stage, the cabaret, the dance hall, but they are far from merely literal imitations or reproductions."[75] These dancers probably included the flappers, sailors, and comic policeman that Oscar Thompson referred to in his review.[76]

6. At ⟨24⟩ (tt 5.58), Grazioso, the ballet arrives at the first of its three solo dances, this one titled "Solo Dance of 'Herself.'" In the tradition of Broadway, Herself enters accompanied by a male chorus line of "followers." Rita De Leporte, who danced the role, "performed in the cabaret or chorus girl style."[77] In her long curls, fanciful hat, and short, ballooned skirt, she resembled Mary Pickford (indeed, her costume sketch by Jones called for a "blonde Mary Pickford wig"). Carpenter and Jones apparently intended this dance to depict the American girl—perky, graceful, flirtatious, and resolute. Did Carpenter originally have a girl's solo in mind for this dance? Had he thought specifically of his daughter Ginny?

Herself's sweet and waltzlike music features a $\frac{3}{4}$ melody accompanied by lilting $\frac{6}{8}$ rhythms, in the manner of Ravel. The melody itself has a sharp, jagged quality. At first it explores, like the Hammer motive from which it derives, only one note. But it eventually grows into a childlike tune in which falling thirds repeat in ever-changing harmonic contexts. A fairly self-contained number in D♭ major, the dance cadences climactically at six after ⟨27⟩, ingeniously preceded by the Work motive. The cadence immediately sputters into a delicate transition that provides exit music for the soloist and that quickly settles on a delicious F seventh harmony (which the composer had prepared all along).

7. A "Merry-Go Round" scene follows. At ⟨28⟩ (tt 7.44) "a group of red-coated attendants wheel in from the wings a fantastic cylinder, covered with mirrors, which they place in the center of the stage, where it slowly revolves, catching and throwing back a thousand lights and colours. In a wide circle around the revolving mirror moves a double file of dancers, giving the effect,

with their prancing step and the nodding plumes on their heads, of the gay manoeuvres of the wooden horses of a Merry-Go-Round." Downes further describes the scene as follows: "A carousel is wheeled into the centre of the stage, and its pillar revolves in one direction while the chorus prances as the horses of the merry-go-round, in the other. The carousel comes slowly to a halt: the horses slow up, droop their heads or remain as if stopped in mid-air."[78] This staging documents Lee's influence on Busby Berkeley. At the same time, Alice Holdship Ware's observation—"the panting hurrying merry-makers peer at their exotic, unwholesome surfaces"[79]—suggests an expressionistic edge that anticipates Bob Fosse's *Cabaret*.

The music for this episode is so picturesque that Carpenter must have had a merry-go-round in mind from the start. The scene's form—from its creaky introduction, with its insistent anticipation of F major (⟨28⟩, tt 7.44), to its abrupt arrival in C major and its medley of tunes (the first at ⟨29⟩, tt 8.05; the second at ⟨31⟩, tt 8.49), to its gradual slowdown (starting at ⟨32⟩, tt 9.21), to its complete stop (ten after ⟨32⟩, tt 9.53)—clearly depicts a carousel ride.

The first carousel tune quotes the verse to Stephen Foster's "Massa's in de Cold Ground" (ex. 38), which offers a silent pun (Foster's lyric begins "Round de meadows am a ringing"). Further, the tune's opening motive has some relation to melodies used earlier in the ballet, such as the Song of the Workers. Carpenter's transformation of Foster's sentimental, "mournful song" into this woodenly mechanical and garishly snazzy version is hilarious, a parody of Victorian sentiment that at the same time suggests the survival of an American tradition in an altogether transformed world.[80]

8. At nine before ⟨33⟩ (tt 9.54), the revolving mirror is quickly removed, and at ⟨33⟩ (tt 10.08) "a short interlude by another small group of dancers" begins. For this interlude Carpenter offers a kind of bustling Street Music centered statically in a modal C major/minor. At ⟨34⟩ (tt 10.38) Carpenter reaches a cadence in C major, followed by a short introduction that sets up the A♭-major tonality of the next solo dance, the Strutter's dance.

9. The Strutter appears on the emptied stage "through a trap in the floor" and begins to dance by himself (tt 10.48). At five after ⟨35⟩ (tt 11.28), four girls join him, and at the cadence one measure before ⟨37⟩ (tt 12.03), he exits with a headlong dive over their bent backs. (In the Metropolitan Opera production, however, he dove "over the backs of a half dozen black, or blacked, comedians," according to Olin Downes.)[81]

The Strutter's music consists of a charming but somewhat grotesque fox-trot—real cartoon music. Everything is a bit distorted and exaggerated:

EXAMPLE 38.   Carpenter, *Skyscrapers*, [29], mm. 1–10.

The eight-measure phrases only allude to popular song forms, the melody insinuatingly hovers on sevenths and ninths, and the orchestration is squeaky and raucous. The music stands midway between the affable wit of Gershwin's "I'll Build a Stairway to Paradise" (1922) and the brittle irony of Weill's "Cannon Song" (1927). Most of all it recalls the whacky humor of the composer's own *Krazy Kat*. The four girls, in contrast, enter to the Street Music.

The original Strutter, Albert Troy, pantomimed and danced in the style of popular comedians of the time,[82] and wore "a costume that outdid any caricature of the newspaper comic strips." This costume included an enormous black top hat, a vest with bare arms (except for large cuffs and cuff links), and bell-bottom trousers. This may have been the costume Carpenter had in mind when he mentioned, in discussing one of the production's costumes, that he had actually seen something like it at Coney Island: "I thought it was part of a masquerade or something of the sort, but I was told that the young fellows actually came to Coney in costumes of that sort."[83]

10. After the Strutter's dance the Street Music returns (at [37], tt 12.04) as "an encounter between two street women" (prostitutes?) unfolds. Others join the

brawl in a passage, clearly indebted to *Petrushka,* that grows more tense and polytonal. At ③⑨ (tt 12.48) a downward xylophone and piano glissando (that arrives at a low, fortissimo G♯) represents, as in *Krazy Kat,* a violent climax, at which point the police enter.

In the passage between ③⑨ and one before ④⓪ (tt 13.26), the police drive the crowd offstage as the English horn faintly echoes the Street Music. The lights slowly dim, and only the Negro street cleaner, White-Wings (the name for janitorial uniforms of the time), remains onstage. (The original White-Wings, Roger Dodge, was a white dancer who wore blackface for this performance.) He finishes his work and reclines against one of the traffic lights to sleep; a spotlight "picks out the whiteness of his costume from the surrounding gloom." Indeed, like the Baby in *Perambulator,* the Dwarf in *Infanta,* and Krazy in *Krazy Kat,* White-Wings is another dreamer-dancer.

11. The ensuing "Negro scene" opens at the pickup to ④⓪ (tt 13.26) with a dream fantasy of the sleeping White-Wings. Behind a gauze curtain, "we see gradually taking shape in the dim light a group of negroes, men and women, half-forgotten types of the poor South. We hear their actual voices, in a song, first slow and soothing, then more animated and rising at last to a fierce religious fervor toward the end of No. 43." In scenario sketches Carpenter refers to this section as a "throw-back to negro plantation life." One critic heard in this music "the song of the moaning sons and daughters of slavery."[84]

This section features a chorus singing nonsense syllables, but ones evocative of African cadence: "Manola Bola, manola monabola. Fiama lo, fiama lo." Carpenter's melody has the kind of pathos Americans—from Stephen Foster to Jerome Kern and beyond—often brought to the subject of poor Southern blacks. The big tune plausibly owes something as well to Gershwin's *Rhapsody in Blue;* whether Carpenter attended its 12 February 1924 premiere, heard the work played on tour, or purchased the Victor recording, he would have naturally encountered this smash hit while working on the ballet. But Carpenter's music, continuing along lines he himself had explored in the slow movement of the Piano Concertino and in "The Lawd Is Smilin' through the Do'," reveals his special sensitivity to black folk traditions. For instance, he cleverly suggests a bluesy, syncopated $\frac{4}{4}$ by casting the main theme in $\frac{6}{4}$.

At ④④ (tt 15.54) the chorus stops singing and begins to dance. "The strong rhythm begins slowly to penetrate the sleeping 'White-Wings'—his legs begin to twitch, he turns and tosses and at last he springs to his feet." An initial theme in C major (four after ④④, tt 16.01) acts as a sort of verse to a second theme in C major (eight before ④⑤, tt 16.17), which functions as the chorus. A contrasting theme in E major (⁴⁵, tt 16.30) marks the point at which White-Wings "springs to his feet." The music returns to the C-major verse (at ⁴⁶, tt 16.48) and chorus (nine after ⁴⁶, tt 17.03), at which point the chorus begins to sing again. This lively dance music bridges the gap between classic New Orleans jazz, like the "Tiger Rag," and Broadway jubilee numbers, like Gershwin's "Clap Yo' Hands" (1926) and Berlin's "Shaking the Blues Away" (1927).

12. At ⁴⁷ "there is a sudden 'black-out' of the lights, followed by a dim greenish obscurity, in which is seen a slow-moving procession of white-masked sandwich-men—a macabre symbol of poverty." According to Ware the Sandwich Men crept "with motions of dazed trying-to-keep-in-line, their white boards seeming to float them on a sea of misery."[85]

This brief Sandwich Men scene contains some of the score's gloomiest music. The polytonal clashes between B♭ dominant seventh and E-minor harmonies pose a dark variation on the F♯ dominant seventh/C-major conflict that opens the ballet. The music grows menacingly louder and then subsides. The soft, widely spaced chords (scored for piano, flutes, and clarinets) that frame this scene intensify the eerie atmosphere.

13. At seven after ⁴⁸ "the last of the sandwich-men has disappeared and the lights flash suddenly up again, revealing the gay 'Coney Island' crowd in the climax of their PLAY." Again, certain similarities between this music and the preceding Sandwich Men scene highlight the ballet's dialectical preoccupations. At two after ⁴⁹ Carpenter introduces a new, playful tune in G major that further suggests the influence of Gershwin. The music after ⁵¹ (tt 17.18) grows more and more frenzied.

The stage blacks out at ⁵² (tt 18.13). Fragments of "Yankee Doodle" and the French ditty "Au clair de la lune" appear in the trumpets and piccolo in a fairly dissonant context. Carpenter presumably intended the "Yankee Doodle"–"Au clair de la lune" pun as a special joke for his intended French audience.

Scene 5—the transition from play to work—begins four measures before ⁵² (tt 18.34). The set design is the same for scene 3, with the action reversed: "The gay crowd of men and girls pour from the wings through one door, and from the other, almost at once, files a stiff and relentless procession of work-men, lock-stepping to their JOB." Carpenter reprises the March of the Workers, interspersed with echoes of the amusement park music from the very top of scene 4, now restlessly treated sequentially and accompanied by wild riffs in the woodwinds.

At ⧈54⧈ (tt 19.03), as scene 6 begins, the curtain rises to reveal, once again, a skyscraper, "stripped now of all non-essentials, a stark and ominous skeleton of black and red." In this design Jones aimed to suggest "the image of a visionary city—a transition from an abstract present to the future."[86] The music takes up the Hammer motive, now shrilly accompanied by the sounds of a factory whistle, depicted by a compressed air whistle doubled by woodwinds in their highest registers. As the hammerers and riveters resume work, another group inches their way "toward the brightening footlights," casting "huge shadows." "Their shadows become more tremendous and more monstrous, till they tower threateningly to the skies. Some of them stretch immense limbs, others open their arms as if in entreaty, and the curtain falls."[87]

The music for this final scene begins with a shortened version of the ballet's first few pages, including restatements of the Song of the Skyscrapers (in its original E tonality), the Song of the Workers, and the Reminder of Work theme. Whereas the Reminder of Work theme—when heard originally in scene 4—had been violently interrupted before reaching its apparent goal of D major, the music now leads directly into a climactic, triple fortissimo restatement of the Song of the Skyscrapers in D major (tt 20.18). Despite the subtle preparation of D major some twenty minutes earlier, this arrival sounds fresh and surprising and provides resonance to Jones's "transition from the abstract present to the future." Carpenter undercuts this grand climax with a jaunty return of the Hammer and Work motives (now in D), suggesting that the work goes on (tt 20.35). The score concludes on a D-major triad with an added, biting B♭.

Skyscrapers consequently moves cyclically from work (the skyscraper) to play (the amusement park) to work (the skyscraper). However, certain aspects—especially scene 4, with its "throw-back," its Negro scene, its Sandwich Men, and other elements that stand outside the basic Coney Island setting—provide a jagged, surreal quality to the three-part design. Indeed, the composer needs to evoke motion pictures to help explain the work's narrative structure. Part of the confusion results from the fact that Carpenter and Jones imposed a scenario on a score that obviously had its own intentions. In any case, the ballet is best viewed as an episodic day-in-the-life of America—with its work, its play, and its dreams. As the Baby says in *Adventures in a Perambulator*, "It is confusing, but it is Life!"

The ballet's tone is as evocative as its form. Carpenter's portrait of modern American life is alternately energetic, noisy, garish, comical, boastful, sentimental, disturbing, violent, and visionary. Over the years this complexity naturally inspired varied interpretations by both critics and choreographers.

CHAPTER FOURTEEN

The Reception of *Skyscrapers*

The Metropolitan Opera premiere of *Skyscrapers* on 19 February 1926 was among the most eagerly awaited events of the New York season. The Chicagoan socialite Janet Fairbank reported to readers back home, "The lovely old theater was crowded, every box was filled, the seats were sold out two weeks in advance, and the standing-room space was jammed from the doors to the roof." She especially relished the effect the work made on the heels of *Gianni Schicchi:* "Everyone in the house sat suddenly erect, thrilled by the clash of the first bars."[1]

Carpenter himself discussed the premiere in a letter to Julius Gold: "I should say that in the main, it went off very well indeed, in fact much better than I expected and it came near enough to the mark that we were shooting at to enable us to see just how much better it might have been and that, I suppose, is the most healthy frame of mind that I could ask for."[2]

The New York dailies were enthusiastic. "This is one of the most interesting of the productions given this season at the Metropolitan, and it is auspicious for the development of a specifically American art form," wrote Olin Downes in the *New York Times*. Downes applauded the choreography and dancing for its "inventiveness," "gusto," and "variety." "And what a pleasure," he wrote, "what an exhilaration, to listen to an American composer of Carpenter's discernment, taste, and his virtuoso mastery of his idiom!"[3]

Reviewing this "remarkably successful" ballet for the *New York Herald Tribune,* Lawrence Gilman praised Jones for his "brilliant and beautiful and often moving notations, searching and poignant and veraciously tragical, veraciously farcical"; Lee for his "fantasy, power and abandon"; and Carpenter for his insight into American life: "It is not parodistic; it is not cruel, this music of his; it is closer to tragic irony, to a richly compassionate understanding, than we had fancied it would be. We are far indeed in this score from mere brainless travesty." The *Evening Post*'s Olga Samaroff similarly claimed that the ballet, unlike Honegger's *Pacific 231,* went beyond the picturesque and parodistic: "Just the reverse seems to me to be the case. The different scenes bring before us the familiar sights and sounds of our everyday American life, but transformed through powerful artistic imagination into something intensely suggestive of all the vital forces that lie beneath external things and that are forming our distinctive national life."[4]

For the most part America's magazines confirmed these assessments. *Musical America*'s Oscar Thompson thought the ballet "an emphatic success" and the score "the work of one who has mastered his materials." Alice Holdship Ware wrote in *Survey,* "The music is thrilling and fresh, the production a summons to the imagination." Only Pitts Sanborn, in his review for *Modern Music,* expressed disappointment; given the ballet's concept and the composer's previous work, "This pantomime-ballet with the towering name ought to have been nothing short of overwhelming, but not for a single little moment did it threaten to bowl me over."[5]

Many critics seemed troubled by the score's relation to Stravinsky, however. Downes's only reservations, for instance, concerned a "lack of a very striking inventiveness" and certain rhythmical procedures that "savor strongly of Stravinsky." Thompson similarly singled out for criticism the music's lack of originality and its resemblance to Stravinsky. Sanborn more harshly spoke of the score's "fatal invitation to imitate *Petrouchka,* and not for the better."[6]

On the other hand, Gilman noted the connection to Stravinsky without any accompanying disapprobation: "Some of the opening pages," he wrote, "are conceived in almost a Stravinskyan vein of mordant grimness." And the reviewer in *Outlook* rebutted the aforementioned criticisms, stating, "There is enough both in the music and in the setting that no Russians or any other people but Americans could have conceived to provide a flavor quite distinctive."[7]

No such controversy marked the score's relation to jazz; indeed, most critics praised the way the composer used jazz and popular materials to suit his own artistic purposes (in striking contrast to the *Krazy Kat* reviews). "This is not literal jazz, but jazz as it has filtered through the mind of a musician who thinks in terms of art," wrote Thompson. "What Mr. Carpenter does in this score of his is to take jazz as he takes the other sounds and movements of American city life and blend it with the rest of his ingredients to make up his musical interpretation," reported *Outlook.* Gilman commented that the music is "steeped in popular idioms, tho not enslaved or shackled by them." Downes, who made a similar point, explained that the composer accomplished this by providing popular idioms within a rhythmic context much more complex than that of simple entertainment music.[8]

While most reviewers clearly felt that the ballet painted a deep, meaningful portrait of American life, they did not necessarily agree as to what kind of portrait it was. Some alluded to a certain fearful or sad quality that belied the work's high spirits. Gilman, for example, emphasized the music's "tragic irony." Downes sensed a dark commentary underlying the ballet's deceptively amusing surface; for him the shadows at the conclusion "become more and more monstrous until they tower threateningly to the skies." Deems Taylor similarly spoke of the traffic lights flashing "malignantly," the Coney Island scene as a "nightmare version of any American amusement park," and the final shadows as "huge and threatening."[9]

In contrast, Thompson saw the work as a healthy depiction of modern America and as a disdainful rebuke to the "tastes of those to whom the age, its dances, its music, its whole outlook on life are a sorry descent into noisy, unbridled animalism." Unlike Downes and Taylor, Thompson spoke of the final shadows as "a Herculean power behind the building of a great city's business edifices."[10]

For her part Ware was unsure how to interpret the ending:

> The music at the end may justify a little grandeur: back of the same clanging workers of the first scene now loom enormous shadows of larger, apotheosized work-rhythms, but are they shadows of glory or of annihilation? Who can tell? To me it all spells despair, terrible and revealing, speaking the truth of America flayed and naked. Here is no languorous ballet, here are challenging hungers fiercely clamorous. Here is exposed the corrosion that lurks indeed beneath our too proud Skyscrapers.[11]

Ware's "despair, terrible and revealing" matched the responses of Gilman, Downes, and Taylor, as well as Carpenter's own "sinister skyscraper"; her "grandeur" and "shadows of glory," on the other hand, came closer to Thompson's "Herculean power" and Jones's "visionary city." Ware seemed more sensitive to the work's ambiguities than most critics.

After the premiere the Metropolitan Opera staged *Skyscrapers* five more times and offered it again the following season for another five performances, giving the work eleven performances in all. *Skyscrapers* again played between *Gianni Schicchi* and *Pagliacci* on 4 March 1926 and as the conclusion of a triple bill with *Petrushka* and *Gianni Schicchi* on 17 March 1926. In all other instances, the ballet followed a full-length opera: *Madama Butterfly* (22 February 1926), *The Bartered Bride* (27 February 1926), *Der Freischütz* (3 April 1926), and so forth. Following the 22 February performance (with *Madama Butterfly*), the *New York Times* reported that Carpenter's new ballet "was again very well received."[12] Its last performance at the Metropolitan Opera (with *Lucia di Lammermoor*) was on 21 January 1927.

Not everyone liked *Skyscrapers*. In a letter to the *New York Times,* one anonymous writer objected that Olin Downes should find this "somewhat boresome and rather ridiculous performance," with its "Russian realism and pure hokum," somehow "'auspicious for the development of a specifically American art form.'" Rather, the work was simply a study "in the bizarre, the queer and the illogical," like the poetry of Gertrude Stein and cubist "paint slingers." The writer further wondered "how mass work and mass play can offer much toward the creation of new form." At best, the ballet "was a mob entertainment for a mob audience, and could not by the wildest stretch of the imagination appeal to an audience of fine sensibilities interested in the creation of a new art form."[13]

Again, neither Gershwin nor Copland evinced any special interest in Carpenter's latest score, but *Skyscrapers* may well have influenced, in particular, Gershwin's *American in Paris* (1928), whose use of taxi horns recalled Carpenter's car-beep sounds.

In late 1927 Carpenter left for Europe to help supervise and attend the ballet's European premiere at the National Theater in Munich. He traveled first to Gibraltar, Genoa, and Florence, before arriving in Munich in early 1928.[14] This German production (under the title *Wolkenkratzer*) featured new choreography by the Munich-born Heinrich Kröller (1880–1930), who had been premier danseur at the Dresden Opera House before establishing himself as one of Germany's leading choreographers.

Kröller, who worked primarily for opera houses in Munich (1917–18), Berlin (1919–21), and Vienna (1922–28), was best known for his collaborations with Strauss and Hofmannsthal in the early 1920s. In 1921 he staged the first German production of the Strauss-Hofmannsthal ballet *The Legend of Joseph* and in 1924 he choreographed the world premiere of another Strauss ballet, *Schlagobers*. According to Hofmannsthal, Kröller's Viennese production of *The Legend of Joseph* was "greatly superior" to Diaghilev's.[15] Both Strauss and Hofmannsthal helped promote Kröller's career.

Kröller's interest in the Carpenter ballet—in stark contrast to Diaghilev's—can be explained in part by the artistic climate of Germany as opposed to France, for the late 1920s witnessed a high tide of German enthusiasm for machines, skyscrapers, jazz, and America.[16] Indeed, the outstanding symbol of this trend, Fritz Lang's 1926 feature film *Metropolis,* contained many images like those found in *Skyscrapers:* futuristic skyscrapers, factory whistles, time clocks, drab workers moving mechanically, gaping holes spewing smoke, gloomy exits and entrances, and in total contrast, madcap, frivolous parties. (The differences, however, were just as instructive: unlike the German film, *Skyscrapers* was not particularly concerned with salvation, evil, and class conflict.)

German interest in jazz and machines had also found its way into the opera house, culminating in such works as Krenek's *Jonny spielt auf* (1927), Weill's *The Czar Has His Photograph Taken* (1928), Hindemith's *News of the Day* (1929), and Max Brand's *Maschinist Hopkins* (1929). *Jonny spielt auf* was particularly successful, with 421 performances in the 1927–28 season alone![17] One German review of *Wolkenkratzer* opened with an imaginary telephone conversation that suggested how commonplace such works had become. "'Hullo? Johnny! Hier ist Teddy. Was machst du?'—'Ich mache Aussehen'— 'Sonst nichts?'"[18]

The previous year Carpenter had in fact attended the 10 February 1927 premiere of *Jonny spielt auf* in Leipzig, and he was instrumental in having the Metropolitan Opera mount it in early 1929.[19] In some ways *Skyscrapers* resembled *Jonny spielt auf* as much as it did Gershwin or Copland, a connection that made sense in light of Carpenter's earlier ties to Wagner, Strauss, and Busoni. In any case, the ballet's machine age imagery and jazz motifs naturally intrigued a public that had flocked to see *Metropolis* and *Jonny spielt auf.*

In choreographing *Wolkenkratzer,* Kröller followed the Carpenter-Jones scenario rather strictly.[20] Further, Leo Pasetti derived his sets and costumes from Jones's originals, although he more clearly identified the ballet's American provenance. He dotted the Coney Island scene, for instance, with waving American flags; in fact, he cleverly established a continuity between the stripes of the American flag, the stripes of amusement park tents, and the stripes of cautionary construction symbols.

Pasetti's costume designs, moreover, provided the ballet with an expressionistic and surreal flavor. Herself appeared in stars and stripes, and the Strutter in cane and monocle, like a cabaret singer. A chorus line of women dressed as sailors similarly provided a distinctly decadent flavor. And in a chilling and ominous gesture, Pasetti costumed the workers in the close-fitting caps and striped, loose-fitting suits of German prisoners.

The Munich Opera gave the first performance of *Wolkenkratzer* on 10 February 1928. Perhaps with the Metropolitan Opera premiere in mind, they programmed *Wolkenkratzer* between Puccini's *Gianni Schicchi* and Joseph Bayer's popular ballet *Die Puppenfee*. Carpenter wrote to Koussevitzky, who had already performed the work in concert form: "The production in Munich . . . came off very well indeed. It was a beautiful performance, scenically and choreographically, and the music was very well played and directed by the young Kappellmeister Schmitz—not with your feeling and understanding, but better than I hoped."[21]

Alfredo Casella (1883–1947) reported that Munich gave the performance a "warm reception"; Kröller and Carpenter were called onstage repeatedly. The Munich papers were also highly laudatory; wrote Josef Ludwig Fischer, for instance, "In his symbolic ballet Skyscraper . . . he [Carpenter] has given a very impressive and sharply outlined sketch of the eternal paradox of the American character and of American life."[22]

This Munich production led to one of the oddest episodes in the composer's career. In 1938 the Nazis officially banned Carpenter's music in their proscriptive guide *Judentum und Musik mit dem ABC jüdischer und nichtarischer Musik beflissener*.[23] Why was Carpenter blacklisted? Unlike most of the banned musicians, he was neither Jewish nor African American (indeed, *Time* wryly commented on the designation "nichtarischer" for this son of the Pilgrims).[24] Moreover, the Nazis only cited the *Improving Songs* and the Violin Sonata, two early and, by the 1930s, barely remembered and thoroughly uncontroversial works. On the other hand, *Skyscrapers* was one of Carpenter's few works to make a stir in Germany and was the kind of piece the Nazis loathed. Presumably, the Nazis remembered the composer's name, and the uninformed henchmen who compiled *Judentum und Musik* simply found a few works to mention.

Hitler himself might have been responsible for the ban. Always a virulent critic of jazz (*Judentum und Musik* also banned Carpenter's associate Paul Whiteman), Hitler was particularly obsessed with the subject in 1928, no doubt because of the kind of interest mentioned above.[25] Since Hitler spent much of 1928 in Munich, he probably knew enough about *Wolkenkratzer* to hate it, whether or not he actually attended a performance.

Even during the ballet's run at the Metropolitan Opera, a *Skyscrapers Suite* began to appear on orchestral programs. The music adapted to a concert setting more readily than Carpenter's previous ballets, partly because the score was conceived without much in the way of specific action, and partly because its half-hour length was neither too long nor too short. Carpenter made certain suggestions for concert performance, nonetheless. He advised that the chorus part be sung by a single soprano and tenor and that the blinking lights be omitted. He also suggested some sizable cuts, most notably, a large chunk of the Coney Island scene (⌞13⌟ to ⌞23⌟), including the music for the flashback, the mechanical dolls, the snake charmer and the Wild Man of Borneo, and some of the general dance music that follows. In addition, he recommended cutting the second half of the merry-go-round episode and the short Sandwich Men scene. With the optional cuts the concert version took only twenty minutes.

Stock and the Chicago Symphony gave the first performance of the *Skyscrapers Suite* on 5 November 1926. In a surprising turnaround, the usually friendly Chicago critics were much more critical than their New York colleagues. In a review titled "Carpenter as Cynic-Realist," Glenn Dillard Gunn wrote, "His picture is true and to me exceedingly unattractive." In another review, this one actually titled "'Skyscrapers' of Carpenter Irks Music Critic," Herman Devries similarly suggested that the work embodied an aesthetic of ugliness: "What a pity that Mr. Carpenter should be so misled by the 'fashion' of today which sees in ugliness the summit of expression!" And Edward Moore confessed, "Without the stage picture it seems a trifle long in both sections, and unrestful without pause."[26]

Why this critical reception from such good friends? Perhaps expectations ran too high. Or perhaps, as Moore argued, the score could not stand on its own without the "stage picture." But given the music's later success with Koussevitzky and others, it simply may not have been well served by Stock.

The suite enjoyed widespread attention during the following 1927–28 season. Fritz Reiner (1888–1963), recently emigrated from Hungary, played the work with the Philadelphia Orchestra on 29 October 1927 and with the Cincinnati Orchestra on 9 March 1928. In Philadelphia, Reiner created a "scandal" among conservatives by using the blinking traffic lights (perhaps this performance prompted Carpenter to specify their omission in the printed edition).[27] "The composition cannot be considered as great music in any sense of the word," wrote one Philadelphia review, "but as a work of a very talented American composer, an effort to portray the spirit of modern America in tonal form. . . . Mr. Reiner's interpretation was exactly in the spirit of the composition. He did not exaggerate nor parody the work, simply letting the music speak for itself, which, with its skillful composition and remarkably fine and effective orchestration, it was well able to do."[28]

An even more successful premiere took place in Detroit, where Victor Kolar and the Detroit Symphony performed it on 5 January 1928. One review, titled "'Skyscrapers' Makes Great Hit with Symphony Fans," reported "lusty whistling from the balcony." "The music bites and thrills," wrote another.[29]

The German-born Alfred Hertz, one of the period's most esteemed albeit forgotten conductors, introduced the *Skyscrapers Suite* to San Francisco on 4 April 1929.

Koussevitzky, yet another émigré, gave the Boston premiere on 9 December 1927. He played the suite, reported one reviewer, "with amazing gusto. The audience seemed ready to join in the delirious revelry." Critic L. A. Sloper agreed with Edward Moore that although the music was "stimulating," it "seemed far less significant" when "deprived of the direct aid of the vivid settings and lighting of the Metropolitan's stage. . . . In the opera house, the action so thoroughly engaged the eye that the ear failed to notice how long drawn out was the use of one of the popular tunes in the 'play' scenes; yesterday we thought it never would be done with."[30] In general, however, the Boston press was more positive than Chicago's.

On 4 February 1928 Koussevitzky introduced the suite to New York. Then, on 7 June, he gave the Paris premiere (of *Les Gratte-Ciel*, as it was called) on a program that included Florent Schmitt's *Rêves*, Albert Roussel's Piano Concerto, and Tchaikovsky's Sixth Symphony. Koussevitzky repeated the program another two times; after the third concert on 10 June, he sent a telegram to the composer declaring the work a "tremendous success."[31] Roger Sessions attended one of these June performances and wrote Copland, "Skyscrapers was much better than I thought—jolly, well orchestrated, and at least superficially American—not a virtue in itself, but lending the music a certain character."[32]

The Parisians loved *Les Gratte-Ciel*. They admired its vigor, its orchestration, and its humor. Like the Germans, they enjoyed its American qualities, so obvious in contrast to the Schmitt and Roussel on the same program. "After all this delicacy," wrote the *Paris Times*, "there seemed something uncouth and strident in John Alden Carpenter's *Skyscrapers*, which is surely an authentic voice from the New World. . . . This had a vitality about it that was overwhelming. There was none of the delicacy and sensitiveness which Florent Schmitt and Albert Roussel had given, but a strength which one feels they are incapable of throwing upon a musical score." Even *Le Figaro*, which complained about the work's vulgarity (most Parisians found Carpenter's use of jazz delightful), admired the music's good humor and high spirits.[33]

In the most insightful and informed review, *Paris-Midi* compared *Skyscrapers* to an elevator ride in which one found, at different levels, Stravinsky, jazz, popular music, and the "shadow of Sousa" ("l'ombre de Sousa"). And yet, on every floor, silhouetted through the elevator window, one always perceived the composer's distinctively ironic profile. Discussing this profile, the review stated: "The music of Carpenter contains an individual humor of the most subtle kind. *Skyscrapers* fulfills the rich promise of the droll *Adventures in a Perambulator* and the jazz-pantomime *Krazy Kat:* a poetic and tender fantasy that yields to its own caprices with an offhand elegance and that adorns its fluent melodies with happy and lively colors. Music of pleasure and quicksilver, music that the joyous fairies must have protected at birth."[34]

The French critics clearly discovered more joy and humor in the music than had their American counterparts, who often spoke of the work's terror and dread! This difference can only partially be explained by the fact that Americans, in many cases, knew the ballet, and the French did not. Whereas many Americans reacted to the music with some insecurity (were they really so crude and garish and violent?), the French viewed the score as an ironic and witty national portrait. This French view had its own distortions. *Le Menestrel,* for instance, wrote that the music confirmed that Americans were not dreamers, when in fact the ballet contained an entire dream sequence! But Carpenter composed *Skyscrapers* specifically for a French audience, and he probably anticipated something more like their kind of charmed and amused response.

Reaction in Mexico was another matter. In October 1928 the twenty-nine-year-old Carlos Chávez performed *Skyscrapers* during his first season as conductor of the Symphony Orchestra of Mexico (Orquesta Sinfónica de México). The local critics were outraged "that so strident and mechanistic a work should have intruded itself into a Mexican orchestral concert." Chávez turned the incident to good advantage by programming the suite again later in the season, this time to a full house.[35] By this time Chávez had written his own machine-music ballet, the 1926 *Horsepower (Caballos de vapor)*.

Walter Damrosch performed *Skyscrapers* in October 1928, during his one year with the New York Philharmonic. "It is with great joy that I send you these lines of congratulations on the great success of your *Skyscrapers,*" Damrosch wrote the composer. "We gave three performances, two in New York and one in Brooklyn, and each time the audience fairly rose with enthusiastic applause at the end. . . . A great many people tell me that the work was infinitely more effective than when danced at the Metropolitan."[36] In December 1931 Damrosch performed the work on his radio show and informed the composer: "Your *Skyscrapers* has made a sensation. We had hardly finished when telephone calls about it began to pour in to the offices of the NBC. Enclosed is a sample of the many letters received. I am very happy about it, as it is the outstanding American symphonic work of our times."[37]

On 29 July 1933 the Hollywood Bowl mounted a new production of *Skyscrapers* under the auspices of the Symphonies under the Stars Foundation.[38] Harold Hecht, a twenty-five-year-old dancer and choreographer, staged the work; Blanding Sloane designed the sets, masks, and lights; Kay Ottesen designed the costumes; and Nathaniel Finston conducted.

Hecht refashioned the work into eight scenes:

1. "Work: The Boss contemplates the construction of his newest skyscraper by the Workers and their foremen, the Robots."

2. "Revolt: The Players incite the Workers to overthrow the Robots."

3. "Victory March: The Workers and Players march off victoriously."

4. "Cabaret: The Workers and Players attend a cabaret, where the Robots work as waiters."

5. "Dream of the Big Boss: The Boss has a nightmare, in which his money comes to life; and a dream, in which he is denied entrance to heaven."

6. "The Prize Fight: The Workers leave the cabaret and attend a prize fight."

7. "Picnic: The Workers hold a festive picnic and are joined by their repentant Boss, who joins in the dancing."

8. "Return to Work: The Workers go back to work."

This scenario, with its rebellious workers and repentant boss, came closer to Fritz Lang's *Metropolis* than to the original *Skyscrapers*. Indeed, it departed so radically from the original that one can only guess at what music was used for each scene. In seeming defiance of the facts, however, the Hollywood Bowl program book stated: "Although Mr. Hecht's conception of the legend is indeed his own, he has not fallen prey, as so many choreographers might very easily, to the pitfall of departing from the original conception of the composer. Mr. Carpenter has been in constant communication with Mr. Hecht and has repeatedly expressed his gratification at the treatment given his best known work."[39] Carpenter may well have "expressed his gratification," but Hecht obviously departed "from the original conception of the composer."

In discussing this Hollywood Bowl production, Tom Van Dycke defended Hecht's adaptation by arguing that the Depression had dated the ballet: "Conditions have changed in these eight years . . . and it is quite probable that the greasy, mustard-covered hot-dog [of the amusement park] has become a meal instead of a sudden whim." Hecht had successfully "provided an interpretation that is definitely 1933 in its outlook." This included casting actors rather than dancers for some of the roles.[40]

In the 1930s critics continued to take *Skyscrapers* seriously, however, despite changing conditions. John Tasker Howard claimed that the ballet's "underlying irony and human pity for the seeming futility of it all" reflected the composer's growing maturity as an artist. According to Marion Bauer, the work's relentless exposé of "our crudities, our humor, frailties and independence" represented "the apogee of the new American realism." Lazare Saminsky favorably compared its "grand entertainment" to Milhaud's *Christophe Colomb*. Although too derivative of Ravel and Stravinsky, and not as persuasive as Copland, the ballet was, according to Guido Pannain, "an ingenuous work, lively and full of rhythmic energy. . . . It has music which sparkles." Even Daniel Gregory Mason gave the ballet his grudging approval.[41]

Another indicator of the ballet's sustained popularity was a 1932 recording of the work by the Victor Symphony Orchestra under Nathaniel Shilkret, Victor's specialist in popular and semiclassical scores. In his review of this recording, R. D. Darrell already found the ballet's work music "a little 'dated,'" but he praised the Coney Island scene for its "color and gusto."[42]

Throughout the 1930s Koussevitzky championed the suite with success. After performances in Boston and New York in the fall of 1939, a flurry of positive reassessments came forth. Edward Downes wrote that the work sounded "as new and vital as when it was first performed at the Metropolitan Opera 13 years ago, or was it again the consummate art of Dr. Koussevitzky and his men that made it seem so?" Olin Downes once again praised the work as a "diverting, silly, bravura piece of writing." And although the work was an "old story," wrote Oscar Thompson, "its verve, its wit, its unabashed tunefulness and brilliant orchestration—bordering on the popular but still essentially symphonic—well justify any conductor in keeping it on the active list. It is music for the theatre but does not lose its zest in the concert hall."[43]

In Koussevitzky's hands the music retained friends like George Henry Lovett Smith, who claimed, "No score better pictures the mid-twenty metropolis," and Elliott Carter, who similarly wrote: "It is always a pleasure to rehear Carpenter's *Skyscrapers,* his best score to date. It was superbly performed at the Boston concert and I mention it now only to say that here is as directly pictorial a work as any critic might want for comparison with other arts in America. In spirit close to the Reginald Marsh and Dos Passos pictures of the American 1920's, it evokes just as keenly as they do that boisterous, brutal era of the mechanical heart."[44] Like Howard and Carter, Hugo

Leichtentritt concluded that the work evidenced "a considerable advance" in Carpenter's "aesthetic maturity." He observed further that "though American materialism and not spirituality inspires the action, the scenery, and the music, this materialism is at least animated."[45]

In her 1941 survey *Choreographic Music*, Verna Arvey devoted more space to *Skyscrapers* (five pages) than perhaps any other work, including those by Tchaikovsky and Stravinsky. "The music accomplished several things," she wrote. "It placed Carpenter in the front rank of American composers, for many believed that his greatest strength lay in composing serious jazz (of this sort) with a view toward dynamic and forceful characterization. It brought him to the attention of musicians as an orchestrator, a producer of rich effects and varied tone colors. . . . In addition, it portrayed the rush and confusion in contemporary America and was frankly based on the cacophony and rhythmic movement in our city streets." In contrast to Leichtentritt, Arvey found a congenially spiritual subtext: the work taught "that pleasures are close to God's creations; work nearest man's ideals." In her opinion the ballet ended "in a burst of glory."[46]

During the early 1940s the work could still be heard in performance: in Rochester, New York, in 1940; by the Sociedad Pro-Arte Musical in Havana, Cuba, on 20 November 1943; and by Désiré Defauw and the Chicago Symphony in Chicago on 15 March 1945 (this concert also featured Copland's *Lincoln Portrait* with Carl Sandburg, narrator). On 4 and 5 December 1947, the Chicago Symphony again performed *Skyscrapers,* this time under the direction of Artur Rodzinski. "We heard Rodzinski last week beat the whey out of that old 'Skyscrapers,'" Carpenter wrote to his granddaughter. "When he finished, it lay quivering on the floor, and I bowed and perspired profusely."[47]

By this time the critical tide had begun to turn, however. In a review of the aforementioned Rochester performance, Arthur Cohn lambasted the work as "noisy and dated . . . with all its bombastic trivialities and 'super-corny' orchestration." Meanwhile, Giulio Gatti-Casazza, looking back on the Metropolitan Opera production he himself launched, wrote, "The ballet had certain qualities, characteristic of the things it set out to do, though in the last analysis, it was not profoundly original."[48]

After 1950, as live performances of *Skyscrapers* became rarer and rarer, interest in the work dropped precipitously, with the exception of such specialized studies as David Ross Baskerville's "Jazz Influence on Art Music to Mid-Century," which argued that the ballet showed a greater understanding of jazz than the earlier *Krazy Kat;* indeed, "in this ballet score he [Carpenter] produces music closer to its jazz models than anything written up to that time by a classical composer. The score may lack the musical value of *L'Histoire du soldat* and *La Création du monde,* but it rings truer to the American sources of its rhythm than these other works." Baskerville wondered if the work had enough "musical substance to last another generation, but it is a remarkably good example of how a classical composer can effectively integrate jazz elements in a larger form." Such sympathies were unusual for the time.[49]

The second half of the century witnessed two more recordings of the ballet, nonetheless: one in 1953 by Meinhard von Zallinger and the Vienna Symphony Orchestra on LP, and the other in 1987 by Kenneth Klein and the London Symphony Orchestra on CD.[50] Neither recording offered the entire score; indeed, neither was as complete as the 1932 Shilkret recording (which included the Sandwich Men music). Moreover, both von Zallinger and Klein lacked Shilkret's authentic, idiomatic ease in the jazzy passages (Shilkret brought this same expertise to his celebrated 1929 recording of Gershwin's *An American in Paris*).

Von Zallinger's performance—slow, studied, and extensively cut—surely did the ballet's reputation more harm than good. For decades the only recording of the work available, the reviews were almost uniformly terrible. Arthur Cohn's earlier feelings were confirmed; the work had properly "fallen into oblivion. . . . It is terribly square, obvious, and sometimes rather embarrassing. *Skyscrapers* makes some noise, but even in this case (representing the symbol of restlessness) it is merely diluted Les Six machine music." Harold Schonberg claimed that "there is little in the musical content of *Skyscrapers* to enable it to hold its own today." Alfred Frankenstein called it "a coarse and careless affair," although he admitted that it still had "some vitality and amusement in it." Oliver Daniel, who was reminded of the "self-conscious overjoy of the roaring Twenties," was more sympathetic: "Roar it does not, but it dances along merrily with snatches of old tunes remembered and bits of jazz discreetly interwoven."[51]

Torn from its dramatic context, dropped from the repertory, and represented only by a poor recording, *Skyscrapers* lost its meaning to postwar America. The superior Kenneth Klein CD at least offered some hope of attracting new friends. In a review for *Fanfare,* John Ditzky called the Carpenter "well worth the having" and cautioned listeners away from the von Zallinger recording. Joseph Stevenson made no apology for the work, which he called "a raucous, post-War (I) romp. . . . The piece is even wild in its orchestration." In another review, Fred Hauptman found *Skyscrapers* a "period piece" but praised its "brilliant" orchestration. Hauptman's interpretation of the ballet, with "the looming skyscraper of the opening and closing serving as a symbol of inhuman toil and the jazz-toned middle portions depicting a frantic but futile attempt at release," echoed Howard and earlier critics who saw the ballet as, essentially, a work of social criticism.[52]

Skyscrapers, however, eludes any such formulaic summation. Within its large, ample, and complex form, the ballet views the world alternately with humor, nostalgia, awe, and other contrasting emotions. Indeed, Carpenter's portrait of a large American city deserves comparison not only with the writings of Dos Passos, as Elliott Carter suggests, but with the works of Carl Sandburg, Theodore Dreiser, and Sinclair Lewis. Like Carpenter, these literary figures, with their urban realism, their need to take the spiritual pulse of modern American life, their somewhat didactic desire to define for their compatriots (and for foreigners, too) what it means to be an American, and their sly humor, were midwesterners writing most prominently in the first third of the twentieth century. Carpenter's *Skyscrapers* offers a musical portrait that matches these authors in ebullience, monumentality, compassion, and, as the French well understood, irony and humor.

Hubbard (left) and John Alden Carpenter (right) pose in their Little Lord Fauntleroy outfits. Like their older two brothers, Hubbard and John were raised as a pair, eventually going to Harvard as roommates. Their parents "had unusual ideas about raising their sons," according to one family member.

Rue Winterbotham in 1896, shortly before her engagement to John Alden Carpenter. "She has always been remarked as being independent and strong-minded," noted a schoolmate at Farmington, "and does just as she wishes irrespective of what people say."

Bernhard Ziehn, Carpenter's last and most important teacher, in February 1904. "A singular blend of the strict pedant and the ultra-modern progressive" (Julius Gold), Ziehn and his students helped make Chicago, in the opinion of Ferruccio Busoni, America's "most musical" city. "In the short period that I worked with him," stated Carpenter, "I learned more and received more inspiration than from all other previous sources."

The Carpenters outside their eighteen-room estate in Park Ridge, a Chicago suburb named by George B. Carpenter (at the left). Elizabeth Greene Carpenter ("that charming and gifted woman," in the words of Maud Powell) holds the family dog. In the foreground, sit (from left to right) the three (of four) sons who would enter George's ship- and railroad-supply business: John Alden, Benjamin, and Hubbard.

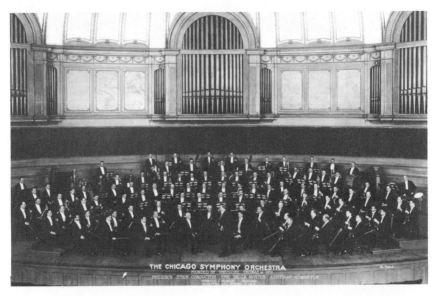

Frederick Stock and the Chicago Symphony Orchestra, in 1926. All of America's major orchestras and most of its great conductors—from Damrosch and Muck in the 1910s to Rodzinski and Walter in the 1940s—played Carpenter's music frequently, but no one more than Stock and the CSO: fourteen works performed more than sixty times, just at subscription concerts. Photograph by Fernand de Gueldre.

Frederick Stock, in 1928. Conductor of the Chicago Symphony Orchestra from 1905 to 1942, Stock steadfastly championed new music from Richard Strauss to John Cage. "I'm just a rabbit that Dr. Stock pulled out of his hat!" said Carpenter. "The great conductor's pushing and encouraging helped me to success." Photograph by Fernand de Gueldre.

Paul Thévenaz's pencil drawing of Rue Carpenter, 1919. As president of the Chicago Arts Club and in other capacities, Rue almost single-handedly brought modern art to Chicago in the period 1915–30. "She was avant-garde when the word was unknown in Chicago," commented Stephen Longstreet.

Glyn Philpot's portrait of John Alden Carpenter, 1918. Rue's friends also painted and sketched husband John and daughter Ginny. Philpot painted this portrait of Carpenter in a single sitting of about three hours. The inscription to Alice Roullier, which reads "A Souvenir of ancient days," reveals Carpenter's sharp and elegant handwriting and his characteristic signature, "J.A.C." Photograph by Frederic Bemm.

The 700 block of Rush Street, in the early 1940s. John and Rue Carpenter lived at 710 Rush (the duplex with the fourth-floor add-on) from 1910 to 1922, and at 700 Rush (the corner home at left) from 1924 to 1932. Remembered Arthur Meeker: "You never could tell whom you were going to meet at the Carpenters'—Stravinsky or Karsavina, Marcel Duchamp or Mrs. Patrick Campbell. But you could be sure, whoever the guests of honour were, they'd not be fussed over tiresomely or placed on a pedestal." J. W. Howlett took this photograph from the Allerton Hotel, whose construction held some importance to the composition of *Skyscrapers*.

Sylvia Moberly-Holland's sketch for *Adventures in a Perambulator*. Walter Disney planned to feature Carpenter's 1914 orchestral hit in a sequel to his 1940 *Fantasia*, but the project never went beyond the storyboard phase. John Canemaker praised Moberly-Holland's preliminary work as "loose and bold in execution." © Disney Enterprises, Inc.

Left to right: John Alden Carpenter, choreographer Adolph Bolm, and set and costume designer Robert Edmond Jones, at work on their 1919 ballet *The Birthday of the Infanta*. According to George Amberg, this ballet represented "the first successful collaboration between a noted Russian choreographer and a group of American artists." Photograph by Maurice Goldberg.

Robert Edmond Jones's sketch for the second and final scene (the Hall of Mirrors) for *The Birthday of the Infanta*. These designs, which Stark Young thought the most "unforgettable" of Jones's entire career, helped establish Jones as one of America's foremost scenic designers. Young marvelled at Jones's "dazzling translation of [Spanish baroque] architecture into theatre terms."

The Infanta discovers the dead Pedro, his hand clutching her handkerchief, at the close of *The Birthday of the Infanta*. Choreographer Adolph Bolm danced Pedro and cast an unknown nineteen-year-old, Ruth Page, as the Infanta. Both garnered raves. "It was a marvelous way to start a career," remembered Page. Photograph by H. A. A. Twell.

Three strips from George Herriman's *Krazy Kat* (12–14 July 1932), clipped out by Carpenter. The Carpenter-Herriman 1921 ballet of the same name led to Gilbert Seldes's conviction that Herriman's strip represented "the most amusing and fantastic and satisfactory work of art produced in America to-day. . . . It was as if the ballet had thrown a cloak of dignity around Krazy Kat—which was not the way Carpenter himself felt about it."

Photographs by
Maurice Goldberg

KRAZY KAT
(Adolph Bolm)

"To those who have not mastered Mr. Herriman's psychology it may be explained that Krazy Kat is the world's greatest optimist—Don Quixote and Parsifal rolled into one. It is therefore possible for him to maintain constantly at white heat a passionate affair with Ignatz Mouse, in which the gender of each remains ever a delightful mystery. Ignatz, on the other hand, condenses in his sexless self all the cardinal vices. If Krazy blows beautiful bubbles, Ignatz shatters them; if he builds castles in Spain, Ignatz is there with the brick. In short, he is meaner than anything, and his complex is kats."—John Alden Carpenter.

OFFICER PUP
(Ulysses Graham)

IGNATZ MOUSE
(Bella Kelvanez)

Two members of the remarkable jazz pantomime ballet written by John Alden Carpenter, and staged by Adolph Bolm of the Metropolitan Opera. Performances were given in Town Hall in New York before distinguished audiences that were nearly, if not quite, as interesting as the ballet. Artists, socially well-known, prominent stage people and notable musicians filled the boxes and the pit.

Coverage of the world premiere of the Carpenter-Herriman ballet *Krazy Kat,* in *Harper's Bazaar* 57 (March 1922): 64. Many viewers cheered the ballet's Americanism: "Perhaps some of us, that afternoon, realized a little more clearly what 'American' means," wrote Deems Taylor. Photographs by Maurice Goldberg.

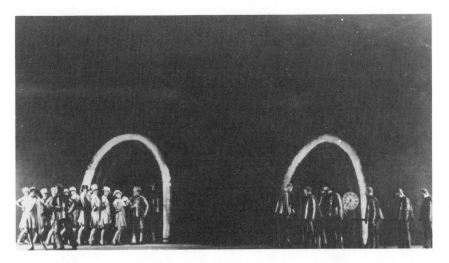

Scene 3 ("The transition from work to play"), from the 1928 German production of *Skyscrapers (Wolkenkratzer)*, choreographed by Strauss's and Hofmannsthal's favorite choreographer, Heinrich Kröller. Workers sullenly exit through tunnels meant to suggest "the atmosphere of factory egress, of the subway, of the crowded vehicle tearing away from the centers of labor" (Jones) and gaily emerge with dates on their arms. This well-received Munich production presumably led to the Third Reich's official ban of Carpenter in 1938.

The principal female lead, Herself, accompanied by a chorus line in the Coney Island scene (scene 4) from *Wolkenkratzer*. Robert Edmond Jones had costumed Herself à la Mary Pickford for the New York premiere, but Munich's costume designer Leo Pasetti used stars and stripes to emphasize the character's American identity.

Robert Edmond Jones's sketch for scene 2 of *Skyscrapers:* "An abstraction of the skyscraper, and of the work that produces it—and the interminable crowd that passes by." First produced by the Metropolitan Opera, the ballet had originally been commissioned by Serge Diaghilev for the Ballets Russes. Wrote Carpenter, "What D. wants, of course, is something typically American—not a pale copy of some French or Italian or Russian thing."

John and Rue Carpenter's only child, Genevieve ("Ginny") Carpenter Hill, en route to her home in Texas in the early 1930s. Remembered Arthur Meeker, Ginny "looked in her childhood like a Velasquez Infanta and, later on, like all the Marie Laurencins you ever saw— least of all, oddly, like the portrait Laurencin did of her." She inspired her father, who adored her, and other artists as well. Asked Adolph Bolm, "Êtes-vous une réalité ou un rêve?"

Ellen Waller Borden and Carpenter in early 1933 on their honeymoon at the Château de la Chèvre d'or in Èze-Village, France. For twenty years prior they had been passionately in love with each other, during which time Ellen inspired many of Carpenter's works: "I want to make some kind of music that will make your mind have happy thoughts," the composer once wrote her.

1020 Lake Shore Drive, the home of John and Ellen Carpenter from 1933 to 1943 (this photograph taken in 1907). Richard Morris Hunt designed this home in the style of a French Renaissance château in 1884 for Ellen's father-in-law by her first marriage, William Borden. "We live as if we were in a hotel," remarked Vera Stravinsky when she and Stravinsky stayed there for two weeks in 1940.

John Alden Carpenter in his later years. "The day of American leadership has dawned," he stated in 1951, "and it is necessary for us to become spiritual leaders. It is not enough to deal with things. In addition, we must express our ideas and ideals. It is the role of music and the arts to be the medium for this expression."

CHAPTER FIFTEEN

Songs from the Jazz Age

1920–1926

|| *Krazy Kat* and *Skyscrapers* overshadowed everything else Carpenter wrote in the early 1920s. This includes thirteen songs written in the period 1920–26: "Slumber-Song" and "Serenade" (1920), both to poems by Siegfried Sassoon; "Thoughts" (1920), to words by Sara Teasdale; "Les Cheminées rouges" (1922) and "Le Petit Cimetière" (1923), both to words by Mireille Havet; "O! Soeur divine" (1923), to words by Emma Calvé; "The Little Turtle" (1926), to words by Vachel Lindsay; "Mountain, Mountain" (1926), to words by Rue Carpenter; and "Shake Your Brown Feet, Honey," "The Cryin' Blues," "Jazz-Boys," "That Soothin' Song," and "Midnight Nan," all to words by Langston Hughes (1926). As a whole, these songs never gained a popularity like that of the composer's prewar songs; indeed, of all these songs, Carpenter published only the two Sassoon settings (as *Two Night Songs*) and four of the Hughes settings (as *Four Negro Songs*).

On 13 April 1920 the Chicago Arts Club hosted the young English poet Siegfried Sassoon (1886–1967), best known for his bitter and satirical antiwar verse. After a large dinner in his honor, Sassoon read some of his poems. Carpenter probably attended this event, in which case he would have sat with the guest of honor. Perhaps Sassoon read the two love lyrics that the composer set later that spring: "Serenade," completed in April 1920, and "Slumber-Song," completed in May. (When he paired the songs, Carpenter placed the slower "Slumber-Song" first.)

In "Slumber-Song" the poet lulls his beloved to sleep with a song that "shall build about your bed / A paradise of dimness." With sleep comes forgetfulness of war: "And there shall be no memory of the sky, / Nor sunlight with its cruelty of swords." For the beloved dreamer, "Time shall be / Only slow rhythmic swaying; and your breath; / And roses in the darkness; / and my love."

The poem consists of a single fourteen-line stanza, but the threefold sequence as described above—from paradisaical song to forgetful dreams to slow breathing—accommodates the composer's penchant for ABA design. This particular ternary form, however, shows unusual formal subtlety and daring. Carpenter concludes the opening D♭-major A section by settling on—as opposed to actually modulating to—a surprising F-major triad at the words "lulled to forgetfulness." He then introduces a syncopated rhythmic figure and a fair amount of tonal instability (dispensing with the D♭-major key signature) for the middle section, which grows climactically toward the phrase "Nor sunlight with its cruelty of swords." In the final section, Poco più lento, Carpenter employs his brand of chromatic sequencing for the beloved's sinking soul, followed by a Straussian repose for time's "rhythmic swaying" and a return to D♭ major at the word "roses." The gorgeous final phrase, "and my love," shows the composer's ripened use of Ziehnian pluri-significance: the piano accompanies the singer's held D♭ with G♭-major, F-minor, E-minor, G♭ seventh, and D♭-major harmonies.

"Slumber-Song" is the culmination (though not the last) of a long series of lullabies. It combines the fairy-dust atmosphere of "The Sleep That Flits on Baby's Eyes," the romantic ardor of "When the Misty Shadows Glide," and the war-torn agony of "Berceuse de guerre." In addition, the song contains a new, provocatively abstract element, in that the text is not so much a lullaby as it is a poem about lullabies. The persona is neither the mother nor the lover but the poet, whose poetry has the magic to comfort. The poetry's free verse emphasizes this abstract quality. While Sassoon deserves much of the credit in providing the composer with a perfectly congenial vehicle, Carpenter's music gives the poem an expressive resonance all its own.

As with "Berceuse de guerre," Carpenter returned to "Slumber-Song" during World War II and arranged it for voice and orchestra in May 1943. The composer elegantly scored the song for a chamber orchestra of woodwinds, horns, harp, celesta, glockenspiel, and strings.

"Serenade" also accommodates Carpenter's preference for ternary form: the serenader (1) imagines the distant beloved, who is falling asleep; (2) hears the rain, which conjures the beloved's "white limbs / And your mouth that stormed my throat with bliss"; and (3) recalls, through song, the beloved "to these arms that were your home."

Carpenter's setting resembles the sultry, Spanish-flavored idiom of *The Birthday of the Infanta;* the flamenco-like rhythms alternate $\frac{6}{8}$ and $\frac{3}{4}$ meters, while the staccato, rolled arpeggios in the piano evoke the guitar (the repeated notes also depict the rain, as in the composer's "Il pleure dans mon coeur"). The song's Spanish qualities owe something to Debussy and possibly de Falla, although as with the *Infanta* its national cut looks ahead to such Americanized Hispanic idioms as Cole Porter's "I Get a Kick Out of You" and Leonard Bernstein's "Maria." Certainly, its two dramatic climaxes—the first at the frankly erotic "And your mouth that stormed my throat with bliss," the second at the words "Recall you to these arms that were your home," with its fortissimo, high A (a^2) on the word "(re)call"—put forth a distinctly American romanticism.

In an extended 1929 analysis of "Serenade," Harry Thorpe argued that Carpenter's handling of the Sassoon poem deserved comparison with Schumann's Heine settings. The composer understood that the poem is no "tuneful ditty beneath the romantic casement; it is a silent serenade to the absent beloved, chanted in the crypt of remembrance and heard only by the listening psyche." In discussing certain rhythmic displacements in measures 25 and 27, Thorpe further wrote, "Mr. Carpenter never falls into the rut of automatism; his artistic invention, always fresh and apparently inexhaustible in its resources, is alert in every bar and beat, creating a wealth of varied detail which materially enriches the tonal texture." The song's ending "is one of the noblest and most stirring in the entire literature of American song."[1]

"Serenade" attracted many singers. Gladys Swarthout, James Melton, and Ethel Casey all recorded it (though not Mina Hager, to whom Carpenter dedicated the song). Today's taste might prefer the more subtle "Slumber-Song," but in any case the two songs make an attractive set.

As with Sassoon, Carpenter's attraction to Sara Teasdale (1884–1933) revealed his continued sensitivity to new, young poets; both Sassoon and Teasdale had become popular only toward the end of World War I. The little Teasdale poem that Carpenter set can be quoted in its entirety:

When I can make my thoughts come forth,

To walk like ladies up and down,

Each one puts on before the glass,

her most becoming hat and gown.

But oh, the shy and eager thoughts

that hide and will not get them dressed,

Why is it that they always seem

so much more lovely than the rest?

For his May 1920 setting, Carpenter uses assertive music with dotted rhythms to portray Teasdale's outward thoughts, and a soft, intimate, and expressive melody for her hidden thoughts. At the end, at the word "rest," the song humorously returns to the dotted rhythms. This little comic gem has some of the simple cheer of Carpenter's songs for children but recalls even more the sly humor of *Water-Colors*.

On 26 August 1920 Carpenter attempted a setting of "The Penitent" by Edna St. Vincent Millay (1892–1950), but he completed only two lines of music. Although more solemn than "Thoughts," this song fragment features a similar intimacy and irony.

Carpenter wrote "Les Cheminées rouges" (Red chimneys) and "Le Petit Cimetière" (The little graveyard) for the French-Canadian mezzo-soprano Eva Gauthier. Born in Ottawa in 1885, Gauthier studied in Paris and Berlin, sang the role of Yniold in London, moved with her husband to Java, and in 1915 settled in New York, where she died in 1958.

Gauthier's recitals provocatively mixed French-Canadian and oriental folk songs, Renaissance and baroque music, modern art songs, and popular hits. On a 1 November 1923 recital at Aeolian Hall that included works by Purcell, Bellini, Bartók, Hindemith, Schoenberg, and Milhaud, George Gershwin accompanied her in a set of songs by himself, Irving Berlin, and Walter Donaldson.[2] Virgil Thomson described Gauthier as "a first-class musician and a great artist. But her voice was not powerful enough for the opera houses, and her distinguished repertory was not for the boob trade."[3]

Gauthier, who probably met Carpenter through Adolph Bolm as early as 1917,[4] sang Carpenter songs throughout the postwar years, including a European tour in 1920 (the composer recommended for this purpose "Le Ciel," "Les Silhouettes," "The Player Queen," "Berceuse de guerre," and *Gitanjali*).[5] In February 1922 Carpenter composed a new song for her, "Les Cheminées rouges" to words by Mireille Havet; in March 1923 he set for her another Havet lyric, "Le Petit Cimetière."

Havet's world-weary but light poems complement each other: "Les Cheminées rouges" is about life, "Le Petit Cimetière" is about death. In the former the red chimneys dance joyously in the infinite blue of the sky, while below men, women, children, and priests pursue their mundane routines. In "Le Petit Cimetière" the symbolism is more oblique: behind a little cemetery a white goat grazes, in front lies a pavement of uneven stones, and in the cemetery itself the dead reunite. Both poems similarly decry the loss of spirituality in the modern world: "Ah! que de gens!" (Ah! what a world!), sighs the poet at the end of "Le Petit Cimetière."

Carpenter's whimsical settings, in French, are uncharacteristically high in their tessitura, this apparently in response to Gauthier's range. Their picturesque piano accompaniments portray the bright sunbeams of "Les Cheminées rouges" and the faint chimings of "Le Petit Cimetière."

Gauthier apparently found the songs arduous or awkward: in October 1923 Carpenter informed her that he had removed some of their "vocal difficulties." A few weeks later he wrote again, expressing delight over her decision to program some Berlin and Gershwin on her upcoming concert of 1 November ("It will do Aeolian Hall a lot of good!"), and recommending "Les Cheminées rouges" as the better of the Havet songs.[6]

In the fall of 1934, Carpenter revised both songs. These revisions, with their greater complexity and chromaticism, provide a particularly good illustration of the composer's evolving style from the 1920s to the 1930s. The original tonal scheme of "Le Petit Cimetière," for example, was simply A major (for the goat and the pavement), C♯ minor (for the graves), and E major (for the reunited souls and the oblivious goat); in contrast, the revised scheme is A major (for the goat), B♭ major (for the pavement), D minor and C♯ minor (for the graves), tonal ambiguity, with some movement toward A♭ major (for the reunited souls), and E major (for the oblivious goat). In addition these revisions are more restrained, less sentimental than their originals.

Carpenter never published these Havet settings in either version, and they do not appear to be among his best songs. "Les Cheminées rouges" nonetheless deserves special attention, for its preoccupation with red chimneys high above the bustling crowds below sheds light on the poetic intentions of the composer's *Skyscrapers*.

In early 1923 the famed French soprano Emma Calvé (1858–1942) sent Carpenter a poem she herself had written, with the request that he set it for one of her upcoming tours. "Mme. Calvé wishes me to add," wrote Calvé's secretary, "that she is a great admirer of your music, and would prefer that you, above all others, should write the musical setting to the words."[7] Carpenter received both Calvé's original French text, "Ma voix," and an English translation by Edwina Davis. In August, Carpenter mailed his setting, titled "O! Soeur divine," to Calvé, who wrote back, in French, "I cried singing your song. . . . It is exquisite, moving, very singable, and with your skilled sense of harmony."[8] Mina Hager sang "O! Soeur divine" as late as 5 May 1933, but the song was never published and is not known to reside in any library; in fact, it remains the only Carpenter song whose whereabouts are unknown.

Vachel Lindsay similarly had long wanted Carpenter to set one of his poems. Carpenter at one time tried his hand at a setting of Lindsay's "Spider and the Ghost of the Fly" but left it incomplete. In November 1926, however, he completed a setting of the 1918 ditty "The Little Turtle," which Lindsay had written for a three-year-old. The "little turtle" snaps at and catches a mosquito, a flea, and a minnow, "but he doesn't catch me." Carpenter's tune is folkish but somewhat jazzed up, with snazzy syncopations in the vocal lines and blue notes in the accompaniment. It is a children's song for the jazz age and one of Carpenter's most delightful.

Also in November 1926 Carpenter composed "Mountain, Mountain" to words by Rue. Short and simple like "The Little Turtle," "Mountain, Mountain" nevertheless evokes a mood of entreaty and despair; the singer implores the mountain ("are you blind, or are you proud?") to hear the voices of the people below.

The song's modality wavers between F♯ minor and D major, finally settling on an F♯-major triad. In deference to the mountain imagery, the piano and voice parts explore their lower ranges. Some syncopations mark the song, almost incongruously, as a jazz-age work. Like Havet's red chimneys, Rue's mountain seems related to Carpenter's skyscrapers.

In March 1926 Carpenter set four lyrics from a recently published volume of poems, *The Weary Blues* (1926), by a virtually unknown, black, twenty-four-year-old poet, Langston Hughes (1902–67): "Jazz-Boys" (Hughes's "Harlem Night Club"), "The Cryin' Blues" ("Blues Fantasy"), "Shake Your Brown Feet, Honey" ("Song for a Banjo Dance"), and "Midnight Nan" ("Midnight Nan at Leroy's"). Carpenter might have heard about Hughes from Vachel Lindsay, who discovered the black poet-busboy in 1925, and who helped arrange for the publication of *The Weary Blues*.

Carpenter was lucky to stumble upon Hughes during these years. On the one hand, Hughes's jazzy vigor and ironic humor perfectly suited the composer's postwar style. At the same time, the poetry's elegant lucidity derived from the sort of imagist poetry—such as Lindsay's—that had long proved congenial to the composer. Little wonder Carpenter's Hughes settings proved the culminating achievement of his jazz period.

Carpenter presumably intended these four songs of March 1926 as a set, in the tradition of *Gitanjali* and *Water-Colors*. But before publishing them in

1927 as *Four Negro Songs,* he replaced "Midnight Nan" with a setting of "That Soothin' Song" ("Misery") from Hughes's second volume of poems, *Fine Clothes to the Jew* (1927), and revised the other three. Consequently, Carpenter composed eight separate Hughes settings: one each for "Midnight Nan" and "That Soothin' Song" and two each for "Jazz-Boys," "The Cryin' Blues," and "Shake Your Brown Feet, Honey."[9] The following discussion refers, in the case of the three latter songs, to the revised versions, unless otherwise indicated.

The five Hughes poems all concern music, specifically (in four out of the five) in relation to black women. Hughes's music poems tend toward two separate categories, however: jazz songs, which depict the joy of jazz, and blues songs, which express the sadness of the blues. "Jazz-Boys" is a jazz song; "That Soothin' Song" and "The Cryin' Blues" are blues songs; and "Shake Your Brown Feet, Honey" and "Midnight Nan" contain elements of both.

In "Jazz-Boys" the poet commands the dancers and musicians in a cabaret to celebrate the moment: "PLAY! / Tomorrow. . . . who knows? / Dance today." Carpenter fashions the text into something like a popular song, with the busy, syncopated piano part suggesting a jazz band. The recurrent rhythm for the words "Jazz-band" and "Jazz-boys" recalls, in particular, the Charleston. The song never ranges far from C major, but some of the harmonies are humorously far-flung chromatically, for example, the C-major triad with added ♯4, ♭6, and ♭7 that ends the song.

Although Carpenter often modified his song texts, he edited Hughes's verse more extensively than was his custom. Not only did he omit and repeat lines, but he actually added words, especially to provide Hughes's short, clipped lines with upbeats. For example, he changed "Dance today!" to "So dance today!" In the revised version of "Jazz-Boys," Carpenter went so far as to expurgate Hughes's images of interracial or, rather, black-white dancing and sexuality. He changed Hughes's "White girls' eyes / Call gay black boys" to "Dark girls' eyes / Call gay black boys"; "Dark brown girls / In blond men's arms" to "Yella girls / In brown men's arms"; and "White ones, brown ones, / What do you know" to "Black ones, brown ones, / What do you know." Carpenter originally set Hughes's words as written; the change may have been made at the request of his publisher or perhaps because of his own sensibilities. In any case, he only had to change the equal quarter notes for "dark brown" into an eighth note and a dotted quarter note for "yella." Today, singers can reverse this process and restore the original words. This would not only be fairer to the poet's and composer's original intentions but would make for a stronger song.

Carpenter's settings of "That Soothin' Song" and "The Cryin' Blues" evoke the twenties' notion of the "blues" (as opposed to its current, folk-based association), even resembling the commercial blues of Tin Pan Alley. At the same time, they are deeply personal art songs of a high order.

In "That Soothin' Song," Hughes's "black gal" asks for a "soothin' song" to help her forget her "no-good man." Carpenter's refined harmonies and displaced rhythms mark his setting as something other than a popular song, despite its tunefulness and foursquare phrasing. More subtly, all of the phrases have a certain monotony, as if the singer can only remember the first phrase of a popular song, or as if its boozy repetitiveness can numb her pain. At the last line, "She's got to hear a blues, Jes' for her misery," Carpenter resolves the D-major tonality—of the "soothin' song," if you will—at the word "blues" and then moves quickly to a C♯-major harmony (with an added G-major triad!) at the word "misery." In this way Carpenter adeptly distinguishes the girl's real "misery" from the playful, ironic sadness of the "soothin' song."

In "The Cryin' Blues" a black girl mourns an unhappy love; she similarly is haunted by the "Hey! Hey!" of the blues singers and their "minor melodies." Carpenter sets only half of the poem and ends with the hopeful line "Sun's gonna shine somewhere again."

"The Cryin' Blues" is arguably among the finest songs Carpenter ever wrote, with the kind of fluid spontaneity that characterizes his best melodies. Numerous felicities abound: the way "Hey! Hey!" poignantly recurs, like some dimly remembered melody; the polyrhythmic accompaniment that suggests, again, some memory of a popular tune; the dramatic contrast between "My man's done left me, chile" and "he's gone away"; the move to a sweet E♭ major at "now those cryin' blues," as if at this point we actually arrive at the haunting tune; the hopeful IV–I progression (used often in traditional blues, though rarely by Carpenter in these songs) for the first statement of "Sun's gonna shine somewhere again"; and the song's disturbing postlude, with its A-major harmony suspended over the tonic E♭ (ex. 39).

"Shake Your Brown Feet, Honey" and "Midnight Nan" both feature a similar ABA design: in their outer sections the poet tells Liza (the "honey") to "shake" her brown feet and Midnight Nan to "strut and wiggle"; their middle sections recall images of death and loneliness, respectively, thus emphasizing the need to dance.

As Hughes indicates in his original title, "Shake Your Brown Feet, Honey" is a "banjo dance," and Carpenter depicts a banjo in the accompaniment by means of broken chords and staccato markings. The dance itself is

EXAMPLE 39. Carpenter, "The Cryin' Blues," from *Four Negro Songs*, mm. 35–40.

in $\frac{3}{2}$, usually broken down into patterns of $\frac{4}{4}$ + $\frac{2}{4}$. The bluesy middle section (whose G major contrasts with the surrounding D major) takes us from dance to song; its tunefulness highlights the conventional wisdom of its verse: "Sun's goin' down this evening, / Might never rise no mo'." After a reprise of Liza's dance, Carpenter returns to the phrase "Might never rise no mo'" for an especially effective coda in which the singer sustains the word "mo'" even after the piano part ends.

Midnight Nan's "strut and wiggle," in E major with jerky figuration in the piano accompaniment, is faster than Liza's "shake." Like the B section in "Shake Your Brown Feet, Honey," however, the middle section of "Midnight Nan," in D♭ major, is slower and more melodic. Carpenter varies the return of the E-major dance music by darkly sprinkling the accompaniment with D♮s, B♯s, E♯s, A♯s, and F𝄪 s. At the very end a held F𝄪 in the piano turns into a G♮ as the composer surprisingly cadences in E minor, not E major.

All five of the Hughes songs have unusual and provocative endings that tend toward tonal surprise and ambiguity. Carpenter apparently intended this to reflect similar practices in blues and jazz. But once having discovered this new freedom, he used it for the rest of his career in many other contexts as well.

Carpenter arrived at these endings only as afterthoughts. The original versions of the three Hughes songs he later revised have much more conventional endings. In the original "Shake Your Brown Feet, Honey," the voice does not sustain the last note after the piano's final chord, and the original "The Cryin' Blues" closes with a comforting E♭-major triad, not a bitonal shudder. Aside from these endings, the revised Hughes songs are much like their originals.

In the fall of 1927, Carpenter apprised Hughes, then on scholarship at Lincoln University, that Mina Hager was to sing his settings (that is, the four original settings including "Midnight Nan") at Aeolian Hall on 25 October 1927. Hughes ran up to hear the concert and wrote to Carpenter, whom he had never met, on 1 November:

> I liked the four songs you've set for me a great deal. The Cryin' Blues and
> Jazz Boys seemed particularly successful in capturing the mood and feeling
> of the poems. They are beautifully done, indeed. . . . The Cryin' Blues sort
> of "brought down the house" and would have been encored twice I'm sure,
> had Miss Hager been granting encores. Jazz Boys and Shake Your Brown
> Feet, Honey were well received, too; but they didn't seem to "get" Midnight
> Nan so well, if one may judge from applause. Miss Hager's interpretation of
> the four songs was splendid and the group certainly made an interesting fin-
> ish for her program. I liked all of them and was agreeably surprised at your
> curious capture of simple racial moods in a modern musical rendering.[10]

Hughes suggested further collaborations, including a setting of one of his blues in the "folk manner." Nothing came of this, although Hughes's report about "Midnight Nan" probably played some part in Carpenter's decision to replace it with "That Soothin' Song."

In discussing prospects for a 1926 Chicago recital, Carpenter also suggested that Eva Gauthier attend the premiere of the Hughes songs: "I have mixed feelings about the songs myself, but I would like very much to have you hear them and advise me what you think of them for your own use in your program out here."[11] Gauthier never gave this particular concert, but she programmed two of the Hughes songs while on tour with composer-pianist Colin McPhee in January 1928.[12]

Over the years *Four Negro Songs* came in for particularly harsh criticism. In 1941 Henry Cowell called "That Soothin' Song" a "commonplace attempt to incorporate Negro feeling into a white man's song," and in 1991 Donal Henahan dismissed "The Cryin' Blues" as "impossibly genteel."[13]

If the songs were performed anything like opera star Vanni Marcoux's 78 rpm recording of "The Cryin' Blues" and "Jazz-Boys," Cowell and Henahan would be justified in their disparagement, as Carpenter would be justified in his doubts.[14] Singers of these songs clearly need to incorporate something from the American vernacular. Mina Hager apparently knew how to sing them, and Philip Miller found a "special poignancy" in Donald Gramm's 1964 recording of "Jazz-Boys."[15] Perhaps if someone like Eileen Farrell had championed them, the *Four Negro Songs* would have rightfully earned a stature more like that of *Gitanjali* or *Water-Colors*.

CHAPTER SIXTEEN

A Postwar Miscellany

1920–1926

On 18 July 1920 Leopold Stokowski wrote to Carpenter: "Next November the landing of the 'Mayflower' will be celebrated everywhere in America, and it seems to be a true and natural subject for a tone-poem which would be very characteristic in style of the American ideal. So I am writing to you in the hope it may interest you."[1] Carpenter accepted the commission and completed *A Pilgrim Vision* in September 1920.

For the premiere Carpenter provided the following program note:

> In order that the purpose of the composer may be made clear, we are asked to imagine the grim little Pilgrim band in a last religious service in England, the march to the sea, the embarkation. We are asked to watch their ship as it sails away and disappears under the edge of the sky. Surely an extraordinary adventure! And surely, at the moment when the sea seems its most tremendous, and the Pilgrim ship its most forgotten, it is easy to think that in that moment the Eye of God rested upon them and smiled. For the sea speeds them on their way and they come at last to the Shore of their Hope. We can share in the exultation of their landing, in the joy of their discovery, and we can feel with them the thrill of the Future America.[2]

A Pilgrim Vision contains a short introduction (Lento), a large section that changes tempo, and a short coda (Molto più lento). The introduction consists simply of a setting for solo organ of psalm tune 100 (Old Hundred) from the Psalter that the Pilgrims brought with them to the New World, namely, Henry Ainsworth's *Book of Psalmes: Englished Both in Prose and Metre* (1612). Carpenter's setting, which comprises only one verse, probably has in mind the opening one: "Showt to Jehovah, al the earth. / Serv ye Jehovah with gladnes: / Before him come with singing-merth. / Know, that Jehovah he God is." This psalm setting presumably represents "the last religious service in England."

The body of the work consists of a free fantasy—in five smoothly connected sections—on motives derived from Old Hundred. The sections seem to correspond with the composer's narrative as follows: (1) Largo, "the march to the sea, the embarkation"; (2) Animato, "it sails away and disappears under the edge of the sky"; (3) Grave, "The Eye of God rested upon them and smiled" (here Carpenter actually writes, in the manuscript copy, "the Eye of God," above the trombone solo); (4) Doppio movimento, "the sea speeds them on their way"; (5) Largo nobilmente, "they come at last to the Shore of their Hope." The work concludes with a short coda, in which Carpenter states his own hymnlike tune to express the "joy" and "thrill" of the Pilgrim landing. At the very end the work quietly recalls bits of Old Hundred.

A Pilgrim Vision thus forms a symmetrical musico-dramatic design with the "Eye of God" at the work's midpoint: Lento (prayer), Largo (embarkment and departure), Animato (at sea), Grave (the eye of God), Doppio movimento (at sea), Largo (arrival and debarkation), Lento (prayer).

Very much a sea piece, Carpenter's music alternately recalls Wagner's *Flying Dutchman* (indeed, one review stated that Wagner was "distinctly reflected at several points"),[3] Debussy's *La Mer,* and MacDowell's *Sea Pieces* (especially "A.D. 1620"). At the same time, the work foreshadows the Americanist movement of the 1930s. In any case, Carpenter's individuality is evident enough, as in the final hymn, which bespeaks the composer of "The Home Road."

Stokowski and the Philadelphia Orchestra premiered *A Pilgrim Vision* on 26 November 1920, in a special Mayflower celebration in honor of the Pilgrim tercentenary. The conductor congratulated Carpenter on his "wonderful imaginative treatment of the 'Pilgrim Vision.' It is a poetic and beautiful work, and I shall enjoy playing it on tour."[4] Stokowski brought *A Pilgrim Vision* to Wilmington, Washington, Baltimore, Harrisburg, Pittsburgh, and New York. Stock and the Chicago Symphony introduced the work to Chicago on 10 November 1922.

After hearing the work in New York in March 1922, Lawrence Gilman praised the music highly: "[Carpenter] has sought . . . to extract the emotional essence of that great adventure of 1620 and state it in terms of musical speech; and he has done this admirably—with gravity, pith, and tenderness; with a rich sense of the nobility and drama of his theme." The work, Gilman concluded, was "as validly and indisputably 'American' as Cape Cod," although he thought this less important than its "distinction and flavor and clear sincerity."[5]

Deems Taylor, on the other hand, chided the same gravity that Gilman admired: "One hears only the voice of those who frowned upon music and love-making and persecuted the Quakers, with never a reminder that the Mayflower also carried spinning wheels, and Peregrin [*sic*] White's mother, and warming pans, and Henry Cabot Lodge's ancestors, and all sorts of jolly people and things."[6]

Critics generally considered the work as, at best, a pleasant occasional piece. One Philadelphia review stated, "The score is interesting, but on the whole uninformed by compelling evidences of inspiration."[7] Felix Borowski later agreed, concluding, "Taken as a whole, 'A Pilgrim Vision,' is not one of the works of which their creator has most reason to be proud."[8] This author hopes, nonetheless, that we will not have to wait for the Pilgrim quadricentennial to hear and reconsider what appears to be a highly attractive and interesting work.

In August 1920 Carpenter wrote a short piano piece titled *Tango américain*. Carpenter had long known and liked the tango, as suggested by his dance lessons with Maurice and Florence Walton, his friendship with Irene Castle, and his use of tangolike materials in the 1915 Piano Concertino. He even composed an untitled song, marked Tempo di tango, that resembled a popular urban tango of the time.[9]

The opening A section of *Tango américain* similarly resembles a popular song in its suave, tuneful melody cast in square eight-measure phrases, although the sharp dissonances and quirky rhythms underscore—as in *Polonaise américaine*—its more personal qualities. Carpenter follows this good-humored A section with a more urgent and improvisatory B section that grows more and more loud, dissonant, and complex, threatening to overwhelm the piece altogether; indeed, its dark, bitonal climax makes the reprise of the whimsical A music something of a surprise. The work's introduction serves, finally, as a humorous codetta.

The *Tango américain* almost duplicated the success of the *Polonaise américaine*. Along with the song "Serenade," of the same year, it became one of Carpenter's last truly popular works. In time many American pianists would associate his name only with this little tango. For Ned Rorem (b. 1923) the piece, as played by his piano teacher, the black pianist and composer Margaret Bonds (1913–72), proved a seductive introduction to "serious" American music. He himself would play it "for anyone who'd listen." (Rorem went on to collect a complete catalog of Carpenter's music and to memorize the score of *Skyscrapers*, which he "loved").[10]

Even more than "Serenade," *Tango américain* might remind listeners of

Cole Porter, who probably knew and admired the piece. Andrew Stiller also notes resemblances to the 1917 hit song by Edgar Leslie and E. Ray Goetz, "For Me and My Gal."[11] Although hardly on the same scale, the *Tango*'s alternately ironic and violent commentary on a prewar dance might profitably be compared, too, to Ravel's *La Valse* (also 1920).

In the fall of 1922, Carpenter wrote a set of six small pieces for piano. Of this set only movements 1, 2, and 6 survive in their entirety; a fragment of the third movement also exists. What remains suggests a collection of waltzes, at once ironic and romantic in tone—a kind of American *Valses nobles et sentimentales* for the 1920s.

This 1922 set became the springboard for the five-movement *Diversions* for piano (1923). Carpenter recycled the set's third movement as *Diversions*'s opening movement and apparently used the set's sixth movement as a model for the new work's fifth movement. The lost movements 4 and 5 might have made their way into the new work as well.

Carpenter possibly rewrote the 1922 set as *Diversions* in the interest of accessibility. Certainly, the later work featured nothing as hermetic or daring as the earlier work's first two movements. At the same time, *Diversions*'s awareness of jazz and European neoclassicism lent it a certain modernist chic.

The first piece, Lento, continues along the path of *Little Indian* in its subtle exploration of ostinato technique. The six-note ostinato F♯–B–F♯–E–B–E continuously encircles the haunting theme (ex. 40), moving through various keys from E minor to its unexpected conclusion in B minor. At measure 25 the ostinato emerges melodically, supported, in turn, by a related ostinato figure. At measure 41 Carpenter develops the material sequentially in what might be called a B section, and at measure 69, after an unstable passage with changing meters and tempos, he returns to the ostinato for an extended reprise of A.

Thomas Pierson and Christopher Palmer both refer to this piece as "impressionistic."[12] Claiming it "as perfect an Impressionist miniature as 'On a Screen,'" Palmer also points out that this movement—along with movements 2 and 5—are "exquisitely-wrought pieces devoid of stereotype." Carpenter's individuality is evidenced in the music's intimate, almost morbid sensitivity, in its cool restraint, and in the Spanish and jazz tinges that anticipate the subsequent movements. The term *postimpressionist* might be a more helpful label; indeed, the music's sharp edges and childlike sweetness recall Satie and Poulenc.

The second piece, Allegretto con moto, also explores an ostinato tech-

EXAMPLE 40.   Carpenter, *Diversions* no. 1, mm. 9–25.

nique: Carpenter puts forth the music's secondal harmonies against the pitch E, which typically sounds on the downbeat of every other measure and is often held, like a drone. The E-major ending is as surprising as the first movement's B-minor conclusion. Palmer's claim that this movement is "impressionistic" in its own right could plausibly alter a rendition like Denver Oldham's, which is rather fast ($\quart$ = 200, as opposed to Carpenter's $\quart$ = 144) and loud (Carpenter's dynamics all read piano or pianissimo, except for one mezzo forte followed quickly by a diminuendo). But again, the word *impressionistic* obscures the piece's own sensibility, which recalls Carpenter's music for Ignatz Mouse.

If the second movement reminds one of Ignatz Mouse, the third piece, Animato—a joyful, somewhat clownish waltz, full of Spanish inflections— evokes Krazy Kat him/herself. The atmosphere is one of Viennese operetta, jazzed up. One hilarious detail is the way the stolid, oompah of the four-measure introduction concludes phrases at measures 11 and 19 and then becomes a subject in its own right at the *giocoso* at measure 33. The more romantic middle section, in E minor, is itself arched; its middle section, Molto con brio, fortissimo, dramatizes the return of the E-minor theme to such an extent that the eventual reprise of the G-major waltz tune comes as a surprise.

The fourth piece, Moderato, in G major, seems specifically Latin American as opposed to Spanish in profile: the light, fanciful theme looks ahead to the kind of patter songs Carmen Miranda would popularize in later decades. When the music now and again entertains a lively, syncopated figure, the music's American quality becomes all the more tangible.

In contrast, the movement's middle section (this fourth piece, like all the others, is in ABA form) evokes American jazz. Carpenter even—and quite uncharacteristically—adheres, at first, to the harmonic and responsorial structure of the blues but then departs from it to mold his melody as he will. He humorously subjects this blues theme's main motive to diminution (mm. 31 and 33), augmentation (m. 38), and inversion (mm. 40–41); finally, he uses it as a cadential formula (m. 44). Ziehn would have been delighted! As for this movement's improbable juxtaposition of Latin music and the blues, Rue Carpenter's fearless advocation of mixing styles comes to mind.

The last piece, Adagio, is the most subtle and unusual of the set and rates among Carpenter's most original works, its small size notwithstanding. The resemblance of the main melody to birdsong suggests that Carpenter intended this as a kind of nature piece. In any case, it merits comparison with Debussy more than most anything else Carpenter wrote. Perhaps it is no coincidence that the melody at measure 18 seems to come right out of *Afternoon of a Faun*.

While some of the last movement's harmonic novelties are impressive even today, the roaming parallel seventh chords at measures 12–15, the long repeats, and the rambling tonal scheme (G major–E♭ major–C major–G major–F♯ minor–G major) seem rather discursive, and the fortissimo climax, with its echoes of the Schumann Piano Concerto, seems mannered. Fortunately, the movement's ending is very effective.

Diversions is Carpenter's largest solo work for piano (aside from the youthful Piano Sonata). Its five movements work well as a set, but like Brahms's intermezzi, they can do nicely on their own or in some other combination. The American pianist and composer Jeanne Behrend (b. 1911) recorded only the first movement for Victor.[13] Numbers 3 and 4 could also profitably be excerpted.

The work's intimacy, charm, and relative technical ease can nicely meet the needs of students and amateurs. Carpenter probably intended *Diversions,* like his other piano music, as much for the home as for the concert hall, and, in fact, the pianist Maurice Dumesnil gave one of its first performances at a private reception for the duke of Alba in Chicago.[14] At the same time, the work could interest professionals as well: Andrew Stiller rightly compared the music's "concisely discursive dreaminess" to Janáček's *On an Overgrown Path.*[15]

Carpenter dedicated his 1923 *Menuet* for flute, violin, cello, and piano to Antonin Barthélemy, the French consul in Chicago. Barthélemy was also a musician who, in the early 1920s, sat on the Music Committee for the Arts Club and even wrote music criticism for Chicago's dailies. On 29 December 1922 Barthélemy joined the Carpenters, the Stocks, and Prokofiev in an Arts Club luncheon for the visiting Vincent d'Indy and his wife. After Carpenter introduced d'Indy, who gave a short talk in French, Barthélemy announced Carpenter a member of the Legion of Honor, and Ginny pinned the decoration on her surprised father.[16] One supposes that in gratitude Carpenter composed this little *Menuet* for Barthélemy and his friends to play.

With its aura of the 1890s salon, the *Menuet* is surprisingly old-fashioned; only some jazzy, shimmering harmonies in the piano (as at the bottom of page 3) betoken the Carpenter of 1923. The composer never published this nostalgic occasional piece, but the work has its charms. It pays stylish homage to the baroque style, with its hemiolas and suspensions (at one point the music even smartly juxtaposes a theme with an augmented version), while blending modern French and popular American features: the rich modal (at times, Phrygian) harmonies recall, appropriately, d'Indy, while the melodies, especially the main tune at measure 17, look ahead to Richard Rodgers.

On 12 February 1924, at Aeolian Hall, Paul Whiteman (1890–1967) and his Palais Royal Orchestra performed an assortment of classical and semiclassical works, arranged for jazz band, in what was billed as "An Experiment in Modern Music." At the time, the idea of arranging the classics and writing new music for jazz band seemed highly promising and revolutionary. Indeed, Whiteman's 1924 "experiment," which included the premiere of George Gershwin's *Rhapsody in Blue,* was an enormous success, and in the course of the 1920s, Whiteman and imitators like Vincent Lopez made notable careers out of "symphonic jazz," as it was sometimes called.[17] By 1930 the trend had run its course, however, and by Whiteman's eighth and last "experiment," on 25 December 1938, many concluded that the whole notion, especially the idea of arranging classical music for jazz band, was passé, if not ridiculous.[18]

In his repeated attempts to duplicate the success of *Rhapsody in Blue,* Whiteman naturally commissioned more music from Gershwin and other American composers. Carpenter responded, in 1925, with *A Little Bit of Jazz* for "jazz orchestra," which he dedicated to Whiteman.

Carpenter's original scoring for *A Little Bit of Jazz* freely deviated from Whiteman's standard orchestra, which, by this time, had grown to twenty-seven musicians: six violins, two violas, two cellos (including William Schuman), one string bass, three trombones, three trumpets, one tuba, four saxophones, one banjo, one guitar, one percussionist, and two pianos.[19] In some contrast, Carpenter called for two French horns, only two trumpets, only one trombone, and no guitar, in addition to an elaborate battery of nine woodwinds to be played by four players: B♭, E♭, and C soprano saxophones, E♭ alto saxophone, B♭ tenor saxophone, E♭ baritone saxophone, oboe, and B♭ and bass clarinet. Carpenter further called on one pianist to double on celesta, and the one percussionist to play bass drum, cymbals, wood block, and timpani.

Whiteman (or more likely his principal arranger, Ferde Grofé) quickly rewrote Carpenter's scoring to better suit the Palais Royal Orchestra.[20] He redid one horn part for third trumpet (or second trombone), the other horn part for third trombone (or euphonium), the bass clarinet part for baritone sax, and the C soprano saxophone part for E♭ soprano saxophone. He then devised an elaborate scheme for woodwind doublings.[21]

Carpenter's score takes itself lightly, ironically. It sounds at times like Kurt Weill or like the evocation of Chicago jazz in John Kander's 1975 musical *Chicago*. At its most distinctive, *A Little Bit of Jazz* looks forward to the composer's Hughes settings of 1926.

The work forms a slightly skewed ABCBA design. After an introduction an A section, in C major, puts forth a slow melody for oboe and violins, with alternating I^7 and $IV^{♭7}$ harmonies in the piano and elsewhere. The rest of the piece is in D major. This includes an Animato B section, a *scherzando* C section with dotted rhythms (reminiscent of Felix Arndt's 1915 hit "Nola"), a Moderato followed by a return to the Animato B music, and a kind of return to the opening A section. A short coda recalls the *scherzando* music, and the piece concludes with the jazzy harmony D–F♯–C–E–G♯.

Whiteman featured *A Little Bit of Jazz* along with Ferde Grofé's *Mississippi Suite* and Leo Sowerby's *Monotony* during his 1925–26 transcontinental tour. One of its earliest performances, if not the premiere, took place in Fort Wayne, Indiana, on 2 October 1925. Whiteman subsequently performed the Carpenter piece in scores of cities and towns throughout the country.

The reviews were mixed. The *Kalamazoo Gazette* considered *A Little Bit of Jazz* among Whiteman's "better offerings," along with Grofé's *Mississippi Suite* and Gershwin's *Rhapsody*. And Glenn Dillard Gunn, reviewing a concert on 11 October at the Auditorium Theatre (that Whiteman played at the 4,200-seat Auditorium indicates the kind of draw he had), wrote: "Mr. Carpenter's 'A Little Bit of Jazz' . . . went over with a bang. It was clever, unpretentious modern dance music wherein great skill was disguised until the musical roughneck never knew he was being high-hatted."[22]

On the other hand, Maurice Rosenfeld thought that even though *A*

Little Piece of Jazz gave further proof of Carpenter's orchestral abilities, "there was nothing that lifted this number above the big output of jazz works that we hear daily and little that was recognizable as coming from the composer of 'The Birthday of the Infanta' or his very clever 'Perambulator Suite.'" John Rosenfield Jr. referred to it as "a laborious effort demonstrating that Mr. Carpenter is not a jazz writer." And Henry O. Osgood called it "an unimportant little thing which suffers from that musical politeness . . . that affects all of Carpenter's jazz."[23]

A Little Bit of Jazz at least fared better than Sowerby's *Monotony,* which Whiteman dropped from his repertoire after a few notoriously unsuccessful performances. Carpenter himself compared Sowerby's "very ambitious piece" to his own "shrinking little piece" and wrote to Ellen, "I have to confess that the audience and critics seemed to prefer Alden's attempt to Sowerby's."[24] But by December 1925 Deems Taylor's *Circus Day* (effectively orchestrated by Grofé) had already supplanted Carpenter's piece as Whiteman's newest novelty. Whiteman did not include *A Little Bit of Jazz* on his spectacular European tour of 1926, nor did he play it again on his return home.

Carpenter continued to take an interest in the jazz band. On 20 November 1925 he completed *The Wrigley Wriggle,* a short, three-staved sketch for a work seemingly intended for a jazz band: the upper voice reads, alternately, "trumpet" and "Eb alto sax"; the music, moreover, resembles *A Little Bit of Jazz.* Carpenter never completed the work as such, but on 14 June 1928 he arranged and expanded it as *The Music Doctor's Blues* for violin and piano, writing, at the end of this unpublished manuscript, "We thank you!"[25]

On 25 June 1926 Carpenter completed his second and last work for jazz band, *Oil and Vinegar.* This work came closer to classic big band scoring than *A Little Bit of Jazz.* The composer dispensed with the oboe and bass clarinet in favor of the English horn and flute. He called for three, not two, trumpets; three, not one, trombones; and no French horns. Carpenter also complemented the celesta with the glockenspiel and substituted the tom-tom for the timpani. He further made greater use of instrumental choirs, including passages for three clarinets and three saxophones in close harmony.

Oil and Vinegar is in four sections: an Animato in G major, a Moderato in C major, a Più lento in Eb major, and a Lento amoroso in Db major. The exuberant, ironic Animato belongs to the world of Fred Waring's 1925 hit "Collegiate" (by Moe Jaffe and Nat Bonx), but transfigured by distinctive and subtle harmony and color (ex. 41). The Moderato is a transcription of Carpenter's Langston Hughes song "Jazz-Boys," written earlier in the year. (Whiteman's musicians are hardly "sleek black boys in a cabaret," but the

EXAMPLE 41.   Carpenter, *Oil and Vinegar*, Animato, mm. 6–14.

association, for Carpenter, is close enough.) The changing meters, pentatonic melodies, and delicate sonorities of the Più lento offer contrast. The Lento amoroso returns to the wit of the opening Animato: Carpenter tells the trombone to play a glissando in the fashion of a "New Orleans 'Moan'" and to play one phrase an octave higher than written "if the player can get away with it." The work concludes with a return to the quiet, delicate Più lento music. *Oil and Vinegar* essentially resembles a medley, like the overture to some exquisitely refined 1920s Broadway musical.

Neither Whiteman nor anyone else apparently ever played *Oil and Vinegar*. In later years Carpenter put the work's obscurity to good advantage: while revising *Krazy Kat* in 1940, he found, in the Animato and Lento amoroso sections, highly suitable music for Krazy Kat's climactic, intoxicated fox-trot.

In the catalog he compiled under the composer's supervision, Felix Borowski mentioned neither *A Little Bit of Jazz* nor *Oil and Vinegar* but rather something titled *Jazz Orchestra Pieces* (1925–26).[26] These "pieces" presumably refer to the two jazz-band works composed for Paul Whiteman (Carpenter possibly thought of them as a set) rather than just *Oil and Vinegar*, as is sometimes assumed.[27]

The *Four Negro Songs* and *Oil and Vinegar* brought Carpenter's jazz period to an end. By 1926 he had begun to regard the popularity of jazz among American composers as somewhat faddish, like the use of the whole-tone scale in the 1910s.[28] Carpenter made a few literal allusions to jazz in his 1927 String Quartet, but thereafter such references became for him a thing of the past.

Carpenter's interest in jazz consequently paralleled jazz's rise and fall in Chicago; indeed, Carpenter possibly abandoned jazz sooner than many other composers because Chicago's great jazz era declined so precipitously. By late 1925 the campaigns of urban reformers and racial segregationists had taken their toll on Chicago's cabaret life, so much so that by late 1926 *Variety* deemed Chicago's nightclub business "a slowly sinking trade." Increasing gangland control of South Side cabarets further alienated many customers. The rise of national radio networks and motion picture sound systems in the late 1920s delivered a final blow. By 1928 many of the city's best jazz musicians had left Chicago, mostly for New York.[29]

During these same years, Carpenter, who often associated jazz with ballet, claimed that the great age of modern ballet was passing. In 1924 he stated that the ballet "may not completely satisfy the creative impulse":

> Stravinsky tells me he has gone as far as he could go with it, and is now turning to absolute music. His final ballet, the "Noces," I heard privately performed, without action, in Europe, some time ago. Later I saw its production as a ballet, and my impression of the absorbing work was that it had really been more beautiful when heard simply as music. I can understand Stravinsky's desire to abandon the ballet form.[30]

Just as Carpenter was one of the first American composers to take up ballet and jazz, he was among the first to put them aside. He was ready for new adventures.

CHAPTER SEVENTEEN

From the String Quartet
to "Young Man, Chieftain"

1927–1931

Carpenter composed his one String Quartet between April and July 1927. Just as he was completing the work, he received a letter from Carl Engel, chief of the Music Division at the Library of Congress, who had heard from Oscar Sonneck that the composer was "at work on a string quartet." Writing on behalf of Elizabeth Sprague Coolidge, Engel asked whether the Rosé Quartet could premiere the work at the Library of Congress as part of the April 1928 Coolidge Festival.[1] (In September 1918 Elizabeth Coolidge, a composer and vigorous patron of new chamber music, had started an annual fall festival of chamber music in Pittsfield, Massachusetts; in April 1925 she inaugurated another such festival, this one a springtime event at the Coolidge Auditorium at the Library of Congress in Washington.)

Carpenter probably had long known Elizabeth Sprague Coolidge (1864–1953), who, like himself, came from an artistic and well-to-do Chicago family. In fact, he had requested Coolidge's help as part of his work for the National Committee on Army and Navy Camp Music during World War I.[2] Coolidge faithfully invited Carpenter to all the Pittsfield and Washington festivals, but he could only rarely attend them: he was usually back at work in September and often abroad or otherwise preoccupied in April.

Carpenter apparently knew and respected Coolidge's own music. Upon hearing some Coolidge at the 1930 Pittsfield Festival, Carpenter sent her flowers; after Coolidge reciprocated with a note of thanks, he replied: "Within certain limitations flowers may be eloquent but I find that there is something more that I want to say. It seems to me that of all the fine works that were offered to us at the Festival the most important was your own creation. In style, in form and in content it was perfection itself."[3]

Carpenter told Engel that he would be delighted to have his String Quartet played at the Coolidge Festival but apprised him of two complications: First, he had already arranged for a private performance of the quartet, under the leadership of violinist Jacques Gordon, "for a few friends" at his home. Second, he planned to take the score with him to Germany in January for possible performance there. "One of my primary ideas in writing a quartet," he explained to Engel, "was to have ready some new piece in smaller form [than *Skyscrapers*], available for performance over there during my visit."[4]

Engel responded that he had no objections to a private performance with Jacques Gordon (nor did he object later when that performance was moved from Carpenter's home to the music rooms of the Arts Club), but he insisted that the first public performance take place at the Coolidge Festival. Engel persuasively reasoned that the Rosé Quartet might well take the work on their subsequent European tour: "Thus Europe, too, would hear the work, and with a delay of only a few months."[5]

Carpenter agreed to Engel's conditions and delicately mentioned the subject of an honorarium: "Whatever it may be, it will be welcome, as I always hope to come out at least whole in these adventures." The request embarrassed Engel. He wrote back that Coolidge should have—or "before long" would have—commissioned a work. But the library had already exhausted "the resources available for this particular purpose on this occasion" by commissioning two other works. Coolidge and Engel might have assumed—as others sometimes did—that with his financial means Carpenter would not attach any importance to honoraria, travel expenses, and the like. If so, they would have been mistaken. But Carpenter was gracious about the whole matter: "I am proud to accept the honor you offer me," he wrote Engel, "which is quite sufficient unto itself."[6]

Carpenter's String Quartet is a rhythmically uninhibited work. Each of its three connected movements (Allegro, Adagio, and Moderato) is full of tempo changes, which the composer advised Engel to omit from the printed program. With Carpenter's approval Engel did not include any tempo markings at all; he simply titled the work "Quartet in three movements (played without pause)."[7]

The quartet's flux exceeds that suggested by the mere mention of tempo changes. The first two movements, for instance, "end" without any tonal resolution. The fast, outer movements have slow sections, and the slow, middle movement has an Allegretto episode. Further, all three movements begin in one key and end in another, and the progress from key to key is sometimes abrupt. In short, the quartet is highly rhapsodic. Familiarity slowly unveils the unity of its design. For one thing the composer makes extensive but subtle use of thematic transformation, including, mostly, fluid development of a few prominent rhythmic motives. And the tonal motion, though unpredictable, is sure of itself.

Carpenter's String Quartet is romantic not only in its rhapsodic form but in its lush, somber harmonies. In the first movement's Moderato section ([8]), for example, dominant seventh and ninth harmonies follow one another in chromatic profusion. Leaner passages, as for example the work's opening, are also richly ambiguous; here, Carpenter wavers between A minor and F major.

Like the first movement of the Piano Concertino, the first movement of the String Quartet comprises four blocklike sections that form an ABCA design. The A section recalls the opening pages of *Skyscrapers,* though Carpenter abstracts the *style mécanique* to the point that the music is far less picturesque than in the ballet. The very opening puts forth a jazzy ostinato constructed out of three semitones (motive *a*); this forms a sort of introduction to a *cantabile* melody, featuring falling and rising fourths, that suggests more clearly a first theme proper ([1]). Before the ostinato returns in its original form at [5], Carpenter states a new, expressive theme that looks back to the opening ostinato and ahead to section B.

Whereas section A hovers between A minor and F major, the slower, more rhapsodic B section ([8] to [15]) revolves around F minor and A♭ major, eventually moving to E♭ major. The brooding, nostalgic duet for first violin and cello (ex. 42) recalls the Nurse-Policeman dialogue from *Perambulator,* now gone, as it were, sour.

Whereas most of sections A and B are in common time, section C ([15] to [22]), Vivo, is in a contrasting $\frac{3}{4}$. This C-major waltzlike music, with its Spanish inflections, could be one of Krazy Kat's dances. The principal thematic material derives from the main theme, with the falling and rising fourths now opening up to fifths.

A transition at [22], in B minor, brings the work back to the main theme in the original key, A minor, but now embellished with the triplet rhythms that Carpenter had introduced in sections B and C. The composer demonstrates his characteristic avoidance of literal repetition by stating another, even more embellished version of the main theme in C minor. Near the end of the movement, Carpenter seems headed for G major, but the music subsides and closes ambiguously, perhaps in E minor. The final, provocative harmonies, like some others in this movement, have an odd similarity to Machaut.

EXAMPLE 42. Carpenter, String Quartet, first movement, ⟦8⟧, mm. 1–8.

The tonal plan of the first movement (if one can speak of such spontaneous music as having a "plan") can thus be outlined as follows:

A (Allegro, mostly $\frac{4}{4}$)   A minor/F major

B (Moderato, mostly $\frac{4}{4}$)   F minor/A♭ major–E♭ major

C (Vivo, $\frac{3}{4}$)   C major (B-minor transition in $\frac{3}{4}$
                                         and $\frac{4}{4}$)

A (Allegro, $\frac{4}{4}$)   A minor–C minor–G major
                                         (E minor?)

Like the slow movements of the Violin Sonata and Piano Concertino,
the String Quartet's Adagio is in ABA form. But unlike the outer sections of
the earlier movements, the A sections of the Adagio are different in key,
theme, meter, even tempo. In fact, a description of this movement as ternary
is justified only by the resemblance of mood and thematic material in the
outer sections (especially in contrast to the middle section). Otherwise, the
last section might be better described as a peroration than a return.

After a brooding introduction, section A features a gentle, bittersweet melody (in $\frac{5}{4}$ and D major) reminiscent of the composer's lullabies. The music modulates to B♭ minor before reaching the contrasting B section, an Allegretto mostly in $\frac{2}{2}$, with a new, rather elusive theme introduced by the cello. Much of this middle section alludes to G minor and B♭ major. The somber introductory material returns at [8] but leads not to the original key and theme but, at [9], to a related $\frac{5}{4}$ theme in F major. This new theme sounds more like the concluding phrase of a long (or interrupted) melody than like some arrival—the ensuing music in $\frac{5}{8}$ sounds, as stated, like a coda. This subtle, almost teasing ambiguity—certainly frustrating to academic expectations—suggests that we cannot simply dismiss Carpenter's asymmetries as mere awkwardness.

The last movement, Moderato, is even less formally clear, as one might guess from the precedent of the Violin Sonata and Piano Concertino. Like the quartet's first movement, this finale essentially comprises four blocklike sections, here forming the design ABCD.

Sections A and B are both scherzolike and popular in character. Section A, in G major, presents three principal ideas: a vaguely Middle Eastern idiom, that is, one related to stock American orientalism ([1]), a cadential tag ([2]), and a songlike melody ([3]). The first two ideas function like the verse to the third idea's chorus. The songlike chorus, in fact, has a melodic cadence right out of Walter Donaldson's 1924 tune "My Blue Heaven," which enjoyed great popularity in 1927, the year of the quartet.[8] Was this an actual quotation, like the snippet of "Alexander's Ragtime Band" in *Perambulator*? Could Carpenter have intended this reference to a song about marital contentment as an ironic allusion to his own teetering marriage to Rue, to whom he dedicated the work?

As in the Piano Concertino, the Middle Eastern idiom gives way, in section B ([6] to four before [13]), to Hispanic inflections. Actually, section B explores two distinct ideas, only the first of which evokes Spanish music: a tango or bolero-like idea (in mixed meter and F♯ major) and a jiglike *scherzando* idea (in $\frac{2}{4}$ and D major). In addition, Carpenter develops introductory material from the slow movement (beginning four before [9]) and the opening movement (five after [10]).

Carpenter leaves off the conflict between F♯ major and D major and abruptly introduces C, a Lento passage in $\frac{2}{2}$ and E♭ major (four before [13] to five after [16]). The cello plays this section's principal theme; a long, expressive melody, it begins in the cello's high register and gradually, calmly descends. The first violin answers the melody at [15].

After a brief transition, Carpenter arrives at the work's final section, D, which recapitulates the first movement's main theme in its original Allegro tempo and A-minor tonality. At ⒄ he smartly modulates back to E♭ major in anticipation of a new, climactic theme at one after ⒅. This theme, stated by the cello, seems the dramatic fulfillment of earlier themes, especially those similarly played by the cello. The music peaks at ⒇, as the first violin and cello play this climactic theme in G major. The tango returns briefly at seven after ⒇, its E tonality preparing the *giocoso* codetta in A minor, an elaboration of the first movement's main theme. The work ends on an A-minor triad.

Whereas we can loosely describe the first movement of the quartet as archlike and the slow movement, similarly, as ternary, the finale defies any formal categorization. Taken as a whole the quartet comprises a sort of rondo, with three statements of the A-minor principal theme, and the rest constituting episodes; but this is far-fetched. Nor can the work be equated with the composer's ballet music, some resemblances aside. Rather, the String Quartet represents its own development of romantic cyclic procedures that go beyond what the composer had already achieved in the Violin Sonata and Piano Concertino.

As planned, Jacques Gordon led a quartet in the first—albeit private—performance of the work. A copy of one score, in fact, bears an inscription from the composer "to Jacques Gordon, who first made this work audible." The Russian-born concertmaster of the Chicago Symphony from 1921 to 1930, Gordon (1899–1948) was widely regarded as one of the foremost violinists of his time. In 1930 he founded the Gordon String Quartet, which performed and eventually recorded Carpenter's quartet for Victor. This lovely 78 rpm recording serves the composer well, aside from a cut of about two pages of music from the finale (from ⒅ to ⒇). This cut arguably throws the work's balance off, thereby suggesting that the score is less casually stitched together than may appear. But because the quartet is as episodic as it is, the cut works fairly well; Carpenter quite possibly suggested it himself.

After attending the Munich premiere of *Wolkenkratzer* in February 1928, Carpenter traveled to Vienna to rehearse the quartet with the Rosé Quartet (Arnold Rosé, Paul Fischer, Anton Ruzitska, and Anton Walter).[9] He arrived in Washington a few days before the 28 April premiere to go over the work with the ensemble once again. At the premiere the Rosé also performed Schubert's D-Minor Quartet and one of the two aforementioned commissioned works, a quartet by Carpenter's Italian contemporary Franco Alfano (1876–1954), best remembered today for completing Puccini's *Turandot*.

Carpenter's String Quartet met with generally favorable reviews. The

Washington Post found it "delightful in conception, with a strong modern trend and yet attention to the tradition of chamber music." Olin Downes was somewhat more negative; although the work was "pleasing for its frank, melodious and often sentimental style . . . the composer tends to lose ground as he progresses. . . . The last movement becomes fragmentary, episodic and over long in spite of 'catchy' themes and rhythms. The score would be better for a ballet than for chamber music. It was, however, very well received."[10]

The Rosé performed Carpenter's String Quartet again in Chicago on 14 May 1928. Eugene Stinson's review described the music as "delightful."[11] Other quartets soon took up the work, including the Pro Arte, who played it in 1933 at the Chicago World's Fair and in 1940 in Buenos Aires, where program notes referred to Carpenter as "one of the most characteristic North American composers."[12] The Chardon Quartet performed the piece in Boston on 18 February 1935, where it came as "a very pleasant surprise" to Theodore Chandler.[13] And the Budapest Quartet played it, along with quartets by Villa-Lobos and Beethoven, on 8 April 1942, at a concert at the Library of Congress in honor of the Music Division of the Pan American Union.

The recording by the Gordon Quartet further made the work known to a larger audience—including New Yorkers. Paul Rosenfeld described as "amiable" the "unanimously mild tone in which the newspapers couched their reports" of the work. His own review was more exacting:

> The grounds of the quarrel with Carpenter's string quartet are equally clear, if not equally cogent [compared with Deems Taylor's opera *Peter Ibbetson*]. Possibly it is a mistake to take any issue with a composition as debonair of spirit, as unpretentious and disarming, as this recent light rhythmical work of the Chicago amateur. His wit and playfulness and cleverness have gone into it more happily than into any of the Concertino's successors: the somewhat Debussyish adagio and the part jazzy, part Spanish moderato are very diverting. For all the eclecticism of the material, the gross opportunism underlying "Peter Ibbetson" is absent: the various stuffs are far more relative to a central idea and interfused with incident, than those of Taylor's opera.
>
> And still, the quarrel with it seems justified. The quartet is insufficiently engaging and substantial. Aiming perhaps at a musical equivalent for light verse, Carpenter has again produced something bordering upon musical *vers de société*. The difference between these two classes of work lies, of course, in the degree of freshness and artistic discipline which the one possesses and the other lacks. Thus, while hitherto puzzled to know precisely what dissatisfied us with this composer's work, today we are perfectly aware that the villain is an incorrigible comfortableness and facility of approach.[14]

In another record review written years later, Colin McPhee echoed these thoughts: "This mild and well-bred music is put together gracefully enough" but "seems a curiously limp work for the period in American music when Varèse and Ruggles were raising their fists to the skies."[15]

On the other hand, Charles Mills qualified Rosenfeld's assessment, writing, "In spite of the highly derivative nature of this work (impressionistic French) it has too much glowing warmth and imaginative invention to be dismissed as amateurish." And Borowski commented: "There can be no doubt that Carpenter has tilled the field of chamber-music with admirable success in this string-quartet, the writing in which is in the modern rather than in the classic vein. The opening of the piece, with its syncopated complexity of rhythm, is more curious than beautiful, but, having had his fling with cross-accents, the composer carries his four instruments into a region of truly alluring charm. . . . The slow movement has moments of striking originality."[16]

Other Carpenter enthusiasts like John Tasker Howard and Thomas Pierson praised the work as well. Howard complimented its "interesting mixture of charm and whimsicality with moments of uncompromising severity." And Pierson thought the music "light, friendly, sometimes sensuous, and always pleasurable," although he felt "a prominence of eclecticism rather out of place in a form of musically pure implications."[17]

Although some of the String Quartet's harmonic and textural refinements apparently owed something to Debussy and Ravel, the music's impassioned rhetoric, spontaneous form, and tonal ambiguity brought it particularly close to Janáček's two contemporaneous quartets (1924, 1928), especially considering their nationalisms as analogous. However, whereas Janáček's quartets drew on an already-established Czech tradition of great stature, Carpenter had small use for the folksiness of Chadwick or Ives. In turn, champions of the 1930s Americana ideal would find it easy to bypass this subtle, jazzy work.

In the last years of the 1920s, Carpenter wrote three songs: "America, the Beautiful" (1928) and "The Hermit Crab" (1929)—both unpublished—and "Young Man, Chieftain" (1929).

For many years now, Katherine Ann Bates's 1895 poem "America, the Beautiful" has served as an unofficial national anthem as sung to Samuel Ward's 1882 hymn tune "Materna." Carpenter composed his own setting on 27 May 1928 (ex. 43). Perhaps as Memorial Day approached, the composer's thoughts turned to the tenth anniversary of the end of World War I, and he set this patriotic poem in commemoration.

Rhythmically, Carpenter's melody is almost identical to Ward's. Occasionally, Carpenter substitutes two quarter notes for a dotted quarter and eighth note, and sometimes vice versa. For example, in the first of its four phrases ("O, beautiful for spacious skies, for amber waves of grain"), Carpenter writes, just the opposite of Ward, two quarter notes for "spacious" and a dotted rhythm for "amber."

Otherwise, Carpenter's setting is very different. The melody, with its smoother shape and expanded range, actually looks on the page like "amber waves" and "mountain majesties." It remains, however, an eminently singable melody; aside from junctures between phrases, leaps larger than a third are found in only two places: "(moun)-tain ma-(jesties)" and "(Ameri)-ca! God (shed his grace)." Further, Carpenter's binary form (a/a') has greater elegance than Ward's rather choppy four-phrase design (aa'a"a'"). He carefully uses high notes to help shape his phrases: phrase 1 reaches an e^2 at the word "am-(ber)"; phrase 2 remains low; phrase 3, like phrase 1, reaches e^2 at the word "shed"; and phrase 4 begins climactically with the song's highest notes, $f\sharp^2$ and g^2, on the words "And crown," and then descends.

As with "The Home Road," the diatonic harmonies make sophisticated use of nonchordal tones, inversion, and harmonic rhythm. Carpenter uses the

EXAMPLE 43.   Carpenter, "America, the Beautiful," mm. 9–16.

tonic harmony more circumspectly than Ward; whereas three of Ward's four phrases cadence in the tonic, Carpenter's first three phrases end on the dominant. And as at the words "O'er hills and plains" in "The Home Road," the composer moves to the submediant at the words "And crown thy good," for a thrill altogether missing in the Ward-Bates version.

The appealing sincerity of Carpenter's setting presumably owes something to its private intentions; indeed, it betokens the composer's increasing interest in prayer. And yet the song would make a splendid patriotic anthem and might well be considered as a candidate in America's long-standing search for an alternative to "The Star-Spangled Banner."

Had Carpenter published the exquisitely delicate "The Hermit Crab," composed in January 1929, Christopher Palmer might well have declared this song "as perfect an Impressionist miniature as 'On a Screen.'"[18] The song's delicacy honors the Robert Hyde text, which is trenchant and finely wrought, like a poem by Li-Po. The poet's identification with the hermit crab, who fills his shell with the stormy sounds of the sea, has an alienated edge unlike Li-Po, however: "And with their songs, I fill my shell, Beneath the swell, beneath the sea."

Carpenter's setting forms a subtle ternary design. The first section, Lento, describes the solemn singing of the sea in a rather static C minor that, near its end, implies a modulation to E♭ major. The second section, Più animato, depicts the storm winds by means of sequential tonal activity. This section leads directly into the third section, Poco più lento, whose textural leanness matches the poetry's introduction of the hermit crab. Far from returning to the opening C minor, this last section is in E major, although the final sonority is an open-ended, A-major harmony (with the voice on the sixth, F♯).

The melodic line is long, spontaneous, fluid. The accompaniment is striking in its harmonic richness: quintal and secondal in the first section, quartal in the second section, and pandiatonic in the third. Like the other quartal and quintal harmonies, the final A-major sonority includes a pile of ascending fourths (C♯–F♯–B–E–A) that nicely matches the sea imagery.

In the same month, January 1929, Carpenter also wrote "Young Man, Chieftain." The text is a Navajo prayer, translated by Mary Austin (1868–1934), the American novelist, playwright, and student of Indian cultures of the American Southwest. This translation originally appeared as "Prayer to the Mountain Spirit" in the January 1917 issue of *Poetry*,[19] and as someone long interested in Indian culture, Carpenter possibly took note of it then. But he surely undertook this particular setting either in anticipation of or, more probably, in response to Mary Austin's visit to the Arts Club, where on 21 January 1928 she lectured on "aboriginal art."

"Young Man, Chieftain" is even more harmonically adventurous than "The Hermit Crab," with dissonant, often bitonal harmonies. Such harmonies serve a very different poetic purpose than in "The Hermit Crab," one closer to Carpenter's 1926 setting of his wife's "Mountain, Mountain." For like many sacred Navajo songs, "Young Man, Chieftain" is a mountain prayer. The mountain pantheistically embodies "young man, chieftain," giver of rain and harvests, keeper of paths and rocks. In its alternations of praise and entreaty, the poem resembles an Old Testament psalm.

The vigorous, four-section form even takes on something of the character of an old New England anthem. The first two sections constitute a prayer for "cleanness": the first section, Lento maestoso, in G, depicts the "keeper of the strong rain"; the second section, Pochissimo più animato, in E♭, describes the "Lord of the small rain." The song's third section, in B♭, and in the original tempo, is a prayer for "fleetness" and "straightness." And the last section, beginning in B♭ and ending in F, prays for "courage" and "staunchness." Throughout, the music often avoids implying a major or minor mode, signaling a new development for Carpenter. The concluding major/minor harmony—consisting of the pitches F, A♭, A, C, and D♭—is particularly daring.

The song's austere and ceremonial style is itself unusual for Carpenter. Only *Little Indian* prefigures it, and this only vaguely. The Phrygian inflections, the grace notes, and the alternations of $\frac{3}{4}$ and $\frac{2}{4}$ suggest some familiarity with the Navajo transcriptions of, perhaps, Alice Fletcher or Natalie Curtis Burlin. That the cosmopolitan Carpenter actually heard Indian singing himself is quite possible; the Arts Club had featured a program of Indian song and dance on 29 January 1923 that Carpenter may well have attended. But the song aims to evoke rather than transcribe Indian music. This attitude brings it, perhaps, closer to Ernst Bloch's *Baal Shem* (1923) or Maurice Ravel's *Chansons madécasses* (1925–26) than to some of the songs by Farwell and Cadman published earlier in the century by the Wa-Wan Press.

Mina Hager gave one of the first performances, if not the premiere, of "Young Man, Chieftain" on 25 January 1929, in Cincinnati with the composer at the piano. She sang it again at an all-Carpenter recital on 5 May 1933 that also included "That Soothin' Song," "Jazz-Boys," and "O! Soeur divine."

As a group, "America, the Beautiful," "The Hermit Crab," and "Young Man, Chieftain" intriguingly parallel three Carpenter works from the period 1916–17: "The Home Road" (1917), "On a Screen" (1916), and *Little Indian*

(1916). They represent the composer's response to his country, to nature, and to Indian culture, respectively. The austerities and ambiguities of the 1928–29 songs mark a ripening of musical thought, and, indeed, these songs help initiate the composer's late period. And yet the correspondences between these early and later works clearly warn against too simple a periodization of Carpenter's career.

Aside from these three austere, private, prayerful songs and a revision of the suite to *The Birthday of the Infanta,* Carpenter composed virtually nothing in the four years from mid-1927 to mid-1931. His creative life came, momentarily, to a practical halt. The 1928–29 songs suggest some kind of spiritual crisis, and, unquestionably, the late 1920s proved a time of great turmoil and hardship for the composer.

First, he had to contend with business problems. His brother Benjamin, who presided over George B. Carpenter and Company, had been in poor health since suffering a stroke in July 1924 (he died on 23 February 1927), and this left the composer with more and more responsibilities. "I can't see anything but a still more definite responsibility for me," he wrote Ellen in August 1924. "And *please—please*—my dearest—don't think it's too awful of me to think how *I* am going to be affected—because I do feel so terribly about it—and so sort of ashamed of having said things—from time to time about Ben." Over the next few years, he tried to disentangle himself from the business, but to no avail.[20]

Such responsibilities came at a time of faltering prosperity and demographic stagnation: between 1927 and 1933 the city's population actually decreased by 165,000.[21] Already by 1925 the poets and jazzmen had left town for greener pastures, and the gangsters had taken over. Carpenter and Company had to contend further with the decline of the railroad- and ship-supply industry caused by the spectacular rise of the truck and automobile industry. "Not a new mile of intercity track had been laid since 1920," wrote one Chicago historian of this period. "All railroads led to Chicago, all roads did not. For the first time since its founding, the city was no longer the essential island, the natural capital of the heartland."[22]

The stock market crash of 1929 took Chicago's shaky economy over the edge. The Depression, notes Alson J. Smith, hit few cities as badly as Chicago:

No town in the country had more unemployment than Chicago; no city had as high a percentage of the population on relief; no community had more spectacular and violent riots and "marches," or more widespread strikes and labor disorders. The proud civic motto "I Will" was thrown into the ashcan. Population growth was almost nil; industrial plant expansion came to a stand-still; skyscraper construction in the down-town section not only ceased but a number of skyline fixtures were actually torn down and converted into parking lots in order to save taxes.[23]

Executives from the Armour Company and Swift Company jumped out of their office windows, hotels and banks failed, people slept in the streets, and there was no money for policemen and teachers. The 1932 collapse of Samuel Insull's Edison Company completed the devastation, bankrupting even the upper classes. Society women went to work; debutante and Twelfth Night balls disappeared; the opera folded. It is sometimes said that Chicago and Vienna were the two great cities that never fully recovered from the Depression.[24]

Hubbard and John seemed ill-equipped to successfully navigate through such changes. At a time when they needed to streamline their operations, they opened a new branch in Kansas City and brought in family members like their nephews Benjamin Carpenter Jr. and Fairbank Carpenter. There were a few bright spots—they provided the 1933 Progress Exhibition all their tent awnings—but by the 1930s they annually operated in the red.[25]

A few of Carpenter's letters during these years intimate, for the first time, economic difficulties. On his return from Asia in June 1931, he wrote to Elena de Sayn that he found himself "very much in arrears not only as regards composition but also in connection with the ordinary material duties of life."[26] And in response to an invitation to Washington to hear a performance of one of his works in 1932, he requested that at least his expenses be covered, explaining, "I am sure you can understand that the good old days are now gone by when I could afford to overlook an item of this sort."[27]

The composer's business responsibilities and economic difficulties not-withstanding, the real hardship Carpenter faced during these years concerned his domestic life, which had become barely manageable.

For most of his marriage to Rue, Carpenter loved another woman, Ellen Borden, the wife of John Borden. From the start their affair had a bittersweet, poignant quality. Carpenter often alluded to his mixed feelings, as in this 1920 letter to Ellen (Carpenter's emphasis here and in subsequent excerpts): "All that I know is that there is something called *Joy*—and another something called *Anguish*—and tonight . . . they are dancing together." But by 1923 the "anguish" had gained the upper hand: during a trip to Europe that summer, he found the separation almost unbearable. During Ellen's travels the following summer, his anxiety increased that much more. On 28 July 1924 he asked, ominously, "Do you suppose that there is danger of our loving each other *too much?*" Then on 12 August he wrote, "I want you back here—I want you so awfully—I want to be close to you—tight close—and just be completely one with you, and not say a single word"; and on 28 August, "The panics I get into when we are separated are exactly the same as the fierce panics of a child left alone. Oh I can't *bear* the thought of anything really keeping us permanently apart. *I love you. I love you. I love you.*"[28]

Ellen's divorce on 12 December 1924 opened up new possibilities. "I dream of bossing you quite a little and interfering *constantly* with your freedom," Carpenter told Ellen on 22 January 1925. At the same time, his separation anxieties only increased. On 16 February he confided: "Every time it gets harder and more unbearable—and this time it's beyond comprehension. If it's good for any one to suffer like this, then I suppose it's all right"; and on 19 February, "I'm so starved when I can't be with you—it's a hunger that grows fiercer every day."[29]

Ellen's divorce brought things at home to a crisis. Rue apparently had known about the affair for some time (how John and Ellen could possibly have hidden their romance—what with regular trysts and a constant flow of love letters—is hard to imagine), but in early 1925 Ginny found out about it as well. Threats and accusations followed. Ginny blamed her father "principally for not speaking out before," so that she and her mother "could have gone one way or the other, when they were five years younger and stronger."[30] Carpenter explained that "for a long time things have not been right and that now we were talking things out openly that had been avoided before." He asked Ginny not to blame Ellen, "that it was *my own persistence* for my own *needs*—that was the driving force." He talked to Ginny, as years later he talked to a friend of Ellen's who had rejected her out of loyalty to John Borden, "about 'keeping the windows open' and never to use the word 'jamais,' and that if we gave them half a chance, all the *important* things and the *true values* will emerge and prevail."[31]

But Carpenter remained with Rue, and things reached a dreadful impasse. On 2 May 1925, from the Ritz-Carlton in New York, Carpenter wrote a letter that would prove typical of his correspondence in the years ahead:

Ellen—Ellen—I am almost *finished.* Thursday and yesterday at Middletown were the cruelest days I have ever had to live—and then, this morning—for two hours—a cruel struggle—on both sides—*to break through the wall.*

"Someone else" [Rue] sees and feels, I *know,* that the *"I"* that is *here* is nothing but a shell—and I could feel at Middletown all the time—how much
more natural and gay and congenial they felt with our host than they ever
had with me. But on the other hand—I couldn't honestly find any signs of
anything else.

Oh darling, my darling—it's such an agony—please be gentle to me in
your mind and in your heart—don't—oh don't try to kill me and our love.
And don't think—really think—that my love for you is the "love of an
idealist" and that it doesn't depend on the "Human Touch." Because, every
minute, day and night, I am crying out for you, every bit of me, for every
bit of you. I hold myself to the road I am travelling, the road that seems to
you so wrong—but I'm sure that *something must happen—something* must
break and give way—*Sometime*—And I *know this*—my darling,—every day
that I wait—every day that passes—*I love you more* and *need you more.* You
can't feel really *"hurt,"* when you know that and all that it means, because
you *possess* me—the *real me*—my body and my spirit—*completely.*

Please oh *please*—send me line to 440 [Wells St.]—and let me know
where I can reach you. I *must know*—and *I* think it would be *wrong* not to
give ourselves *that* much chance, and have that much of a little door open
for the *Sun to Shine Through When it does come out.*[32]

And so it went for six years—"cruel struggles" with Rue, accusations by
Ellen, expressions of guilt, hope, and despair on his part. By June 1927
Carpenter seemed reconciled to the idea that he and Ellen just were not
meant to be together. But in December he told Ellen that he thought of an
upcoming trip abroad with Rue as "an absolute necessity for all of the three
who are concerned,—for me, to do something which I could never be satisfied, later, to have left undone;—for Rue, as a period in which to test the
value of an incomplete relationship, under the most *favorable circumstances,*—
and for you . . . a chance to look at me, and at you-and-me, and at yourself,
with a cool, undisturbed eye . . . the best I can do is not and *cannot be, good
enough.*"[33]

In early 1928 Ellen apparently had had enough and precipitated a break.
She accused Carpenter of "indecision" and later of choosing her as the "one
to hurt." Carpenter tried to explain that "any *other* course *would* in the end
hurt you and me and our love infinitely more" and continued to write sad,
ardent letters to her.[34]

The year 1929 brought a new crisis: Rue needed an operation of some
sort in October, and she and John repaired to Atlantic City at least through
February.[35] Then, in late 1931, Rue died, and Carpenter finally was able to
realize his long-cherished dream of marrying Ellen.

In the course of the 1920s, Carpenter gave his lovesick blues fine expression in his 1926 settings of Langston Hughes. But the emotional burden clearly took its toll on his creativity. He turned to religion for solace.

No evidence suggests that Carpenter ever rejected a belief in God or severed his affiliation with the Congregational Church; indeed, religious themes (though not necessarily Christian ones) often informed his work, most notably, perhaps, his 1913 Tagore settings. In 1919 he expressed to Ellen, on the occasion of her mother's death, a strongly Deist sensibility: "And you must try to be glad, too, that there were only *months* of suffering and not years. Surely there was a Merciful Plan in that. Oh I know how hard it is for you to see any plan at all—any sort of reasonable design. . . . Today I was sure that every tree and every wave understood everything—*Every Plan—Every Design.*"[36]

But in early 1925, just as his personal life was becoming "harder and more unbearable," his letters and writings turned markedly more religious in tone, with "God," "Purpose," "Guide," "Idea," "Light," and "Faith" as key words. On 16 February 1925, for instance, he wrote to Ellen, "Anyway I'm sure there must be a Purpose in it [his suffering] somewhere—and some day, before much longer, I hope we will know—won't we?" A few days later he attended a funeral that only deepened such convictions, and on his forty-ninth birthday, on 28 February, he confided to Ellen:

Everything seems so *mysterious* and *precarious*. We grope along from day to day without the slightest *knowledge* of what the next day may bring. But there is *one tremendous* refuge, and I am finding it more and more, and that is a perfectly *simple*, blind and childlike *Faith*. It may be just weakness on my part, and lack of what is called *Character*, but it is the only defense I can find against the Hurts and Hammerings of Life. And this *Faith* that I have is all based and rooted in Our Love and it is *impregnable*.[37]

During the tumultuous years that followed, Carpenter often expressed such faith in his letters to Ellen: "I am finding some sort of strength and satisfaction in the Idea that has driven me on" (22 November 1926); "Our Guide, whom we trust, has shown the way" (13 June 1927); "I know there is a Guide—and I am following the Light" (1 December 1927); and "I believe in God and miracles, too" (26 October 1928).[38] On 10 September 1930 he wrote Ellen, "My Faith and Conviction are stronger than ever that all of our lives are going to be completely fulfilled," and on the next day he similarly told Julius Gold, "As for me, the cards have been unfavorable for the past year or so—but I am full of hope and I have faith that there will be better pasture over the next hill."[39] And then in a note to Ellen dated 30 December 1931, shortly after Rue's death, he wrote, "God bless and keep you, and help us to do our best, and live our lives as He guides us. Many times each day, this is my prayer."[40]

Some undated letters to Ellen expounding similar ideas probably originate from this time: "And He looks at me from under his closed lids—and he knows so much—and I am glad that he Knows"; and again, "Immortality—I know what that is—*and you know*. We may not be able to *say*—but we know there are things that have no beginning and no end—that shine with a light that it hurts to look at—that grip you in the heart and make you feel superhuman—Immortality is no more incredible than these."[41]

In the few songs that he managed to write during this difficult period, Carpenter gave these feelings direct, sincere expression.

Economic and personal problems notwithstanding, in March 1931 John and Rue left San Francisco on the *Empress of Japan* for a three-month Asian tour that included Tokyo, Peking, Shanghai, Hong Kong, Singapore, Bangkok, and French Indochina. This may not have been Carpenter's first trip to Asia—Rue had traveled to China and Thailand in 1927—but it was his most memorable to date. In Peking he acquired an eighteenth-century k'in made by Li Ts'ang-wu of Ku-ts'un,[42] and in Bangkok he attended a concert at the court of the king of Siam given in his honor.[43] While in Peking, Carpenter also possibly visited Mei Lanfang (1894–1961), the Peking Opera star who had stayed with the Carpenters in Chicago in 1930 on his only tour of the United States (Lanfang, who played mostly female roles, was best known for his portrayal of the "Flowershattering Diva"!).[44]

Carpenter was exhilarated by hearing so much Eastern music. While still in the Orient, he wrote to Carl Engel:

> By the time this reaches N.Y. I suppose you will already have gone to Europe to hear the newest examples of that strange and footless Western music which now sounds so pompous and self-conscious to my new Chinese ears.
>
> It is appalling to find that all of the educated and sophisticated Chinese musicians who have been living and studying in Europe and America, come back to China all aglow with Western music; particularly of the vintage of Schumann and Chopin, and take not the slightest interest in the development of their own marvelous material.[45]

It was "as if, perfectly satisfied that what you had been eating was the most satisfactory cuisine in the world, you began to taste new dishes, and your complete taste mechanism gradually adjusted itself to a new sensation of orderliness and appropriateness," Carpenter explained to Eugene Stinson.[46] The untempered oriental scale reminded him of singing cowboys (an observation that anticipated a statement made years later, namely, that the Chinese are "so much like us, really").[47] Eastern music was "beautiful and a part of life, like religion."[48]

The trip proved a turning point. It confirmed, for Carpenter, the spiritual potential of music—something he had come to feel was missing from jazz and modern art music—and thereby enabled him, one imagines, to undertake his first large-scale composition in years, the 1931 *Song of Faith*. Indeed, the piece's opening unison chorus, accompanied by crashing cymbals, recalled Eastern musics, even though the work was an homage to George Washington.

CHAPTER EIGHTEEN

From *Song of Faith* to *Patterns*

1931–1932

On 1 July 1931 U.S. Representative Sol Bloom, associate director of the George Washington Bicentennial Commission, called upon Carpenter, who had just returned from China, to write a commemorative "ode" in honor of Washington's two hundredth birthday.[1] This commission was part of a wide range of activities sponsored by Congress, including the publication of Washington's writings in twenty-five volumes and the issue of commemorative postage stamps and the new Washington quarter-dollar. Carpenter put aside a work he had begun for the Boston Symphony and composed his Washington tribute, titled *Song of Faith,* between August and October 1931.

After completing *Song of Faith,* Carpenter discussed the personal significance of the work in a letter to Bloom:

> In the writing of this work, I have come to a new realization of the priceless inheritance that has come down to us from George Washington. I have felt, more than ever before, that the enduring value of this inheritance is based not primarily on his military genius, or his contribution to the arts of government, but on the selfless integrity of his character.
>
> It is from that character that we inherit the Great American Dream—the dream which has sustained us through our storms and trials, and which at this very moment we must strive in deepest sincerity to recapture. For the whole world is beset by a dangerous psychology of defeat which for us is but the modern counterpart of the snows of Valley Forge. And it is for our country now to raise its eyes in the Faith of its founders, and lead the way out.
>
> And therefore, if my "Song of Faith" can succeed in lighting one single candle of reaffirmation, I shall be content.[2]

Carpenter scored *Song of Faith* for a four-part chorus of children's (or women's) and men's voices, an unseen narrator (who can be a member of the men's chorus), and orchestra. He wrote the text himself, except for a recitation composed of quotations from Washington's letters and speeches. He further inscribed the score with a Walt Whitman poem celebrating democracy—the fifth poem from the 1860 cycle *Calumus*.[3]

Carpenter's own text—a patriotic one with spiritual overtones—is itself Whitmanesque. It alludes to Abraham ("the father of our fathers") and Jesus ("I feel like a wearied traveler must do. . . . The work is done, the voice of mankind is with me"),[4] and it associates democracy and religious faith with nature ("As a growing river flowing to the sea . . . So his faith abounds"). Moreover, Carpenter emphasizes statements of a religious nature in the Washington recitation, for example, the benedictions "I close this last solemn act of my life by commending the interests of our dearest country to the protection of Almighty God" and "I now make my earnest prayer that He would have you in His holy protection."[5] He further quotes Washington's counsel to "keep alive in our breasts that little spark of celestial fire called Conscience" and "not despair" and remembers Washington's courage in the face of death: "I am not afraid to go." As a whole, this recitation encapsulates the spiritual essence of a man who was actually quite worldly. Only one line—"Let us have a government by which our lives and our liberties shall be secured"—is overtly political.

The *Song of Faith* comprises seven sections. The first, sung by full chorus ("Come now, hear our song!"), invokes the freedom-loving faith of "the father of our fathers." The next four sections recall and describe, respectively, the "young Doodle Dandy" (children's chorus), the "cries of the redmen" (men's chorus), the "old song my mother knew" (full chorus), and "the Yankee band" (full chorus). The sixth section consists of the Washington recitation. The seventh and last section recapitulates the mother's song: "May the hand of God be our stay, / And our guiding star light our way." Thus, the seven sections present, metaphorically, an overview of American history—starting with the source of Washington's faith (1) and moving on to the Revolutionary War (2), the settling of the frontier by men (3) and women (4), and the American Dream (5)—followed by a remembrance of Washington (6) and a lullaby (7).

Carpenter matches these poetic metaphors with appropriate musical styles that can be outlined as follows: hymn (nature/faith), "Yankee Doodle" (the Revolutionary struggle), Indian song (frontiersmen), lullaby (frontier women), and band music (American Dream). Much of this proves familiar Carpenter terrain: the hymn, the Indian music, and the lullaby in particular recall such previous compositions as *A Pilgrim Vision*, "Young Man, Chieftain," and *Perambulator*. At the same time, the work contains new features: the quasi-fugal opening in chorale-prelude style, with its neat suggestion of "a growing river"; the SATB choral writing, often favoring lean unison, two-part, and three-part textures (ex. 44); and the Yankee band music, which combines patriotic and popular styles in a way similar to Gershwin's *Strike Up the Band* (1930) and *Of Thee I Sing* (1931). Throughout, the inspired, sometimes sentimental writing seems to reveal the composer's deepest feelings.

The work's tonal scheme is episodic: Carpenter opens in an ambiguous F minor/A♭ major, moves to F major for "Yankee Doodle," A minor for the Indian song, F major for the lullaby, and C major from the Yankee band to the end. The Washington text is recited over a dominant (G) pedal and is followed by the closing part of the lullaby, now in C major. This closing part of the lullaby itself derives from the opening hymn, thus helping to round out the whole. Near the end of the work, Carpenter recalls a fragment of the hymn (the motive with the raised fourth), now hummed by the men. Then, in a gesture not unlike Ives, he quotes a bit of "Yankee Doodle," played softly by muted trumpets in a somewhat bitonal setting. The piece concludes quietly with a muted B-minor triad in the trumpets against an open quintal harmony, C–G–D, in the lower strings (the B-minor triad possibly sounding like the upper notes of a C-major or G-major harmony).

The Bicentennial Commission apparently thought it appropriate to premiere *Song of Faith* over the airwaves. In December 1931 Koussevitzky expressed interest in conducting this radio premiere, but Carpenter and

EXAMPLE 44.   Carpenter, *Song of Faith*, ③, mm. 1–4.

Schirmer had already made arrangements for Damrosch to give the first performance on 21 February 1932, as part of one of his weekly broadcasts.[6] Just before the premiere, the station featured an interview with Bloom in Washington and Carpenter in Chicago.

Within the next few days and into the spring, orchestras from around the country—including those in Washington, Syracuse, Boston, Chicago, Los Angeles, and Fort Worth—performed *Song of Faith*. Both Stock and Koussevitzky played it on 23 February, the day after Washington's birthday. In Chicago, Carpenter himself narrated (unidentified and offstage), and Noble Cain prepared the chorus; in Boston, Clifton Joseph Furness narrated, and Arthur Fiedler prepared the Cecelia Society. Artur Rodzinski's performance of the work with the Los Angeles Philharmonic marked the start of a close association with the composer.

Many listeners expected something bombastic or trite but found themselves, instead, touched by the music's solemnity and poignance. The work made an especially strong impression in Chicago, not only because the composer was so well known locally, but because Stock performed it twice—at the start and at the end of the program. In fact, the Chicago dailies paid scant attention to the concert's featured soloist, Piatigorsky, in concertos by Saint-Saëns and Bloch.

Eugene Stinson observed that the *Song of Faith* "could never be music of propaganda, but . . . is decidedly music of deep feeling and as such it over-awed yesterday's audience, unprepared for an assault so penetrating and so unostentatious"; the music left the audience "deeply affected." Herman Devries concurred: "Carpenter's 'Song of Faith' has the quality of nobility, of sustained musical sincerity that gives more than ephemeral entertainment." And Eric De Lamarter wrote to the composer, "After a half-dozen hearings, I'm convinced, as I was after the first, that you have done a remarkable thing."[7]

Chicago's enthusiasm for the work climaxed with an editorial in the *Chicago Tribune:* "Without presuming to invade the field of Mr. Moore," the editors stated, referring to their staff music critic, "this department would like to express its admiration for Mr. John Alden Carpenter's 'Song of Faith' and for the spirit of its composer. . . . In this hour of doubting and sacrifice, of struggle and tribulation, an American singer brings us this song of our faith, a song of the quiet hours which make the character of a people."[8]

By April, Victor had recorded and released *Song of Faith* with Noble Cain, conductor, and Carpenter, narrator (although the composer's name did not appear on the recording).[9] Lawrence Gilman gave the work—more so than the recording—a favorable review:

It is significant of Mr. Carpenter's characteristics as an artist—his taste, his tact, his distinction of feeling and of thought, his choice, and fine selectiveness—that he has not debased the moods and emotions implicit in his subject-matter by using them as a pretext for mere patriotic ballyhoo and jingoistic eagle-shrieking. There are no brass bands, no blatant stump-speakers, suggested in this music; no bombs burst in the air from which it takes its breath; and its most impressive moments are moments of an almost devotional quiet and absorption. Rhetoric is absent from its meditative and sober pages. For this is music of faith and love and elevation.[10]

Gilman liked the text less, but he reserved his most severe remarks for the recording's anonymous narrator: "As for the Narrator who speaks the words of Washington that Mr. Carpenter has quoted in the latter part of the work, it must, alas! be said that if anything or any one could impair one's reverence for that immortal Shade, this anonymous declaimer, with his uncultivated voice and diction, would be an almost certain means to that end."[11]

After Gilman's article had gone to press, but before it was actually published, the writer discovered—no doubt to his mortification—that the narrator on the recording was none other than Carpenter. He quickly penned his apologies to the composer: "I should never in my wildest fancies, have imagined that the utterances on the record which I possess were those of John Alden Carpenter."[12] Perhaps Gilman expected the refined and man-nered New England clip of a Franklin Roosevelt; instead, he heard the sort of flat, warm midwestern voice that inspired Copland to choose Henry Fonda for his recording of *A Lincoln Portrait*.

The *Song of Faith* had a few, scattered performances throughout the 1930s, including one with Basil Cameron and the Seattle Symphony on 18 January 1936. On the day of this performance, Cameron wrote to the composer, "I regard the *Song of Faith* as the most inspired expression of national sentiment I have ever encountered in any language, or from any composer."[13]

Cameron's nice letter might have inspired Carpenter to reconsider the work, and he revised *Song of Faith* in February 1936. He reworked it a second time the following year, in 1937. Of these three versions, Schirmer published the 1932 original and the 1937 revision. Although these revisions were fairly substantial, Carpenter left the work's basic structure intact, so much so that he could retain the same rehearsal numbers in all three versions.

Up to ⑮ the 1936 revisions concerned such details as transposing the introduction up an octave, providing an accompaniment for the unison cho-rus at ①, and altering the accompaniment at ⑤. At ⑮, however, the com-poser added text to music that had been purely instrumental. This text prepared the listener for the Yankee band by asking, "Can you hear, far away, can you hear?" Carpenter similarly provided some new words for the long instrumental passage beginning at ⑰. He obviously felt that the instrumental interludes and transitions weakened the work's overall effect. (Carpenter also deleted the line "It is impossible to reason without arriving at a Supreme Being" from the Washington recitative.)

Carpenter continued the process of limiting the role of the orchestra in the 1937 revision, cutting the instrumental passage from two before ⑭ to eleven after ⑭, for instance. More notably, however, he changed the work's ending, replacing the quiet hummed chorus and evocative polychordal harmony with a big crescendo and a fortissimo C-major triad. Carpenter apparently thought that this new ending would make the work more effective, especially in concert.

Song of Faith enjoyed revived interest during World War II. London heard it over the radio in 1941, the *Times* (London) reporting, "It is American in its candour and unselfconsciousness, but it is also music that bears exportation."[14] Vladimir Golschmann programmed it alongside Shostakovich's *Song of the United Nations* for a concert with the St. Louis Symphony on 10 January 1943. And Fabien Sevitzky, who especially admired the work, performed it with Beethoven's Ninth Symphony on 3 February 1945.[15]

Song of Faith had its most spectacular performance, however, at the fifteenth annual Chicago Music Festival at Soldiers' Field on 19 August 1944. That year the festival was dedicated to "America's fighting forces," with an emphasis on "music of a patriotic character."[16] The day before the performance, the festival sponsored a luncheon in Carpenter's honor, and immediately before the performance Carpenter said a few words to the ninety thousand persons in the audience. Then, almost ten thousand singers and instrumentalists performed the work under the direction of Edgar Nelson. Carpenter afterward wrote to John Becker, "Some noise!"[17]

Soon after, Copland's *Lincoln Portrait* came to occupy the kind of position *Song of Faith* enjoyed in the 1930s and early 1940s. These works not surprisingly bore strong resemblances—not so much in style as in feeling and intent. Copland once wrote that he rejected the idea of a Washington tribute because he "couldn't imagine it—too stiff and formal,"[18] suggesting that he was unaware of *Song of Faith*. But Copland spent time with Carpenter in Chicago in 1930 and 1934 and probably had some familiarity with the work.

After World War II, *Song of Faith* found fewer and fewer performances. In his 1962 book *The Choral Tradition*, Percy Young remembered the piece as quintessentially contemporary in its "ruggedness and a sense of purpose" and praised its "fine swinging tunes . . . (a sort of aggregation of melodies which might be folksongs but aren't)."[19]

In 1931 Ginny became engaged to Patrick Hill, an executive in the oil business who had moved to west Texas in the 1920s. (Ginny had some years earlier been engaged to Elliott Cabot, whom her father described as "a fine and manly boy," but she eventually broke off that engagement.)[20] The son of Colonel David Hill of London, Patrick had met Ginny through a mutual friend, Alice Hammond, sister of jazz critic John Hammond and future wife of Benny Goodman. (Ginny and Alice had gone to the Spence School together.) A large Chicago wedding was planned for 21 December 1931.

It would be interesting to know the guest list. Ginny had inherited her mother's charisma and sophistication, along with many of her friends, including George Arliss, Cole Porter, and Arthur Rubinstein. Other close admirers, over time, included Sir William Nicholson, Warren Austin, and Louis Auchincloss. The Stravinskys were also fond of Ginny: they visited her in Washington in 1940,[21] and after Ginny moved to Caracas, they wrote to her, in French, "A little letter would make us very happy."[22]

Two weeks before her wedding, on 7 December, Ginny accompanied her mother, who had a cold, to Dr. Walter Theobald's office on Michigan Avenue. While seated in the waiting room, Rue suffered a massive cerebral hemorrhage and died within minutes. The news shocked Chicago. Rue was only in her early fifties, and few knew how ill she had been over the preceding years.[23]

Rue's obituary in the *New York Times* reported that preparations for the wedding, along with those for a charity ball on 15 December, had caused her some stress. Ginny herself believed that, more than anything else, her father's affair with Ellen Borden was responsible for her mother's stroke. This naturally created some resentment toward her father and especially toward Ellen.[24]

Rather than postpone the wedding, Ginny and Patrick held a small, simple ceremony at the Congregational Church in Charlotte. On the day of their nuptials, 21 December, Carpenter presented Ginny with a little song dedicated to her, "Gentle Jesus, Meek and Mild." This tiny song became Carpenter's only sacred work. Did he intend the song as a wedding gift? a Christmas present? a gesture of condolence? of reconciliation?

Carpenter adapted the text by combining the opening stanzas of two well-known hymns for children: "Gentle Jesus, Meek and Mild" by Charles Wesley (1707–88) and "Jesus, Tender Shepherd, Hear Me" by Mary L. Duncan (1814–40). The "little child" asks "gentle Jesus" to "bless thy little lamb tonight" and "keep me safe till morning light."[25]

Carpenter's setting combines aspects of hymn and lullaby, like Humperdinck's prayer from *Hänsel und Gretel* or Jule Styne's "Tender Shepherd" from *Peter Pan* (characteristically, Carpenter's song finds its own middle ground between these two songs). More specifically, "Gentle Jesus" recalls the last of the *Improving Songs,* "When the Night Comes," in which "mother" sings her "little boy" to sleep. Although mother is now gone, Jesus is there to "keep me safe till morning light."

Nearly the entire song stays rooted in a very diatonic D major; only at the mention of "darkness," near the end, does Carpenter introduce any chromaticism, in this case, a poignant V/vi secondary dominant that resolves, deceptively, to ii–iv–V–I. At the same time, the novel, pentatonic harmonies (one might refer to them as "panpentatonic") have a sweet, luminous elegance all their own and suggest, like the pentatonicism of *Song of Faith,* some relation to Eastern music.

After their wedding the Hills settled briefly in Fort Worth, where Carpenter visited shortly after the event: "It has been wonderful being here," he wrote Ellen, "and I am full of peace and much rested. There has been no talk about 'us,' but there will be at the right time, and I know that God is guiding us all."[26] Ginny and Patrick had one child, Rue, in 1932. In the late 1930s they moved to New Haven, so that Patrick could attend Yale, and they spent the war years in Washington, where Hill worked for the British embassy. After the war Hill became a Shell Oil employee in Caracas and New York before retiring to the Carpenter home in Charlotte. Ginny died in 1984, Patrick Hill in 1991.[27]

Even before Koussevitzky's tenure, the Boston Symphony had established a relationship with Carpenter second only to the Chicago Symphony. Muck had played *Adventures in a Perambulator* and the Piano Concertino in 1915 and 1916; Ernst Schmidt performed *Sermons in Stones* in 1918; and after the war Monteux programmed works by Carpenter—whether *Perambulator* or the concertino or the *Infanta*—nearly every season.

Koussevitzky championed Carpenter with similar zeal. Their relationship began on 9 December 1927, with performances of both *Perambulator* and *Skyscrapers* on the same program. In 1929 Koussevitzky named Carpenter, along with Copland and Sessions, as "America's promising composers."[28] During his years with the Boston Symphony (1924–49), Koussevitzky conducted six Carpenter works in all; this was less than the number of works by

Copland, Bloch, and Dukelsky and the Bostonians Hill, Loeffler, Berezowsky, and Piston, but as many as he conducted by Barber, Harris, Schuman, and many others. Further, Koussevitzky repeated some of these works with unusual frequency and thus helped sustain Carpenter's prominence during the composer's later years.

Koussevitzky naturally thought of Carpenter as he began to commission works for the 1930–31 jubilee season celebrating the fiftieth anniversary of the Boston Symphony. On 28 April 1929 he invited the composer to participate in the celebration: "It would give us the greatest joy, if you wrote a Symphony, Symphonic Poem or whatever you wish, for this occasion."[29] The commission came at a bad time, however; financial and personal problems had practically brought Carpenter's artistic output to a halt. He possibly thought to satisfy this commission with his 1929 revision of *The Birthday of the Infanta Suite,* but Koussevitzky never showed any interest in that particular work and, in any case, would have naturally wanted something brand new.

In March 1930 Carpenter finally began sketches on a new orchestral work, but even so he could not finish it in time for the 1930–31 season. In early 1931 he explained to Koussevitzky, "It has been absolutely impossible during the last six or eight months to devote myself to the completion of the work which I had started for you, owing to all sorts of unfavorable conditions over which I had no control."[30] He hoped at least to have the work ready for the 1931–32 season (like Copland and Ravel),[31] and as late as May 1932, he assured Koussevitzky that he was completing the work, which he described as "bright and cheerful in character and not at all difficult."[32] Carpenter did not finish the composition until July, however, and a performance now had to wait for the 1932–33 season. Indeed, Carpenter did not send the score to Koussevitzky until September 1932, by which time he still had "not yet decided on the title of the new piece." Some weeks later he informed the conductor that he had chosen the title *Patterns.*[33]

Carpenter surely knew that "Patterns" was a famous poem by Amy Lowell—one, perhaps not coincidentally, that concerned the death of a loved one—but he intended his title to carry "no literary or programmatic significance," as he wrote in program notes:

The title "Patterns" has no literary or programmatic significance, but it is my hope that the suitability of the title will be as apparent to the average auditor as it is to me. The piece is in one movement and plays about eighteen minutes. It is not primarily a show piece for the pianist—the strictly "solo" bits are short and infrequent. There is a slow middle section for solo violin with the piano as the principal element in the orchestral support. There is a highly sentimental waltz bit, and short fleeting passages with jazz implications, as well as an absurd bubbling up of my concealed Spanish blood. You can judge from this that the *patterns* are at least various.[34]

The title *Patterns* suggests some acclimation toward contemporary trends (consider, for example, Riegger's 1932 *Dichotomy* or Copland's 1935 *Statements*) and points to the growing abstraction of Carpenter's later works. The chromatic, wedgelike opening statement, played by unison strings, has a certain austere, impersonal quality. That this melody generates much of the subsequent thematic material also reflects a new restraint; indeed, the theme functions somewhat like a row in the Schoenbergian sense.

The piano takes over this rowlike theme and introduces a chromatic motive (F#–G–E#) that has a slightly exotic flavor. The piano and orchestra cadence in B minor, which seems to be the tonality of the opening section (the work begins with a key signature of two sharps). Against the chromatic motive the piano presents another theme, this one quasi-primitivist, with quintal harmonies and melodic tritones. But within a few measures the composer introduces at ② yet another new, *grazioso* idea in $\frac{3}{8}$ and E minor.

This opening section leading to the *grazioso* theme is formally ambiguous. Is it expository? If so, what, if anything, constitutes the main theme: the rowlike motto? the exotic chromatic motive? or the quasi-primitivist theme that follows the arrival of B minor? Is this section simply an introduction? Like the use of the piano as something more than mere color effect, yet something less than full-blown soloist, the work's adventurous form reveals the composer's roots in the late romantic tradition of Saint-Saëns, Franck, and d'Indy.

At ③ the *grazioso* idea develops into a Spanish-flavored section that uses changing meters of $\frac{5}{8}$, $\frac{3}{8}$, and $\frac{2\frac{1}{2}}{8}$ (i.e., $\frac{5}{16}$). At four after ⑤ the music cadences in G, and the composer develops the *grazioso* idea in a free fugal setting. A fortissimo climax brings the music back to the chromatic motive and the original tonality, B minor.

The music never resolves, however, but rather goes on, at four after ⑦, to a passage that has, in Carpenter's words, "jazz implications." A small cadenza for solo piano using the primitivist music ensues, followed by a new, sentimental theme *(molto espressivo)* at ⑪. Much of this music suggests tonal centers of G and E.

A new tempo marking, Molto lento, and the removal of accidentals from the key signature mark the start of section B, in C major. This presumably is the "slow middle section" that Carpenter refers to (though, as we shall see, the work has two slow middle sections!). A solo violin puts forth a sultry, *dolente* melody, while the piano answers with shimmering figuration, the pedal held down; the music resembles Ravel's *Bolero.* This section is relatively short and self-contained, although its last few phrases form a transition to the next section.

The Più animato that follows (⏮ to four after ⏭), which can be labeled C, largely develops material from the first section. The quick-paced modulations, in fact, suggest a kind of development section, although the music quickly winds down in preparation for the next section, D, marked Poco più lento. This second slow section, in D♭ major, is distinctively impressionistic, with rich melodies in the English horn.

Like section C, the ensuing section E is developmental, though in a more decidedly neoclassical manner, with jaunty rhythms, quirky dissonances, and scalar themes. At ㉘ Carpenter introduces a somber jazz-inflected passage (reminiscent of the Sandwich Men from *Skyscrapers*) that offers contrast. At ㉚ Carpenter arrives at a Nobilmente melody in the dominant of the work's concluding tonality, E♭ major. A waltzlike Animato brings the work to an end, like the coda to the Piano Concertino. This coda restates previous material, including the Nobilmente melody and, climactically at the very end, the opening motto, now in E♭ major and over a tonic pedal.

Patterns represents yet a further step from the String Quartet. Whereas both works unfold in one long, rhapsodic movement, *Patterns* makes no concession, as does the String Quartet, to traditional fast–slow–fast format. Nor do the individual sections as outlined above correspond to separate movements; Carpenter rightly refers to them as "short fleeting passages." In some ways *Patterns* resembles a traditional fantasia or ricercar; at the same time, like *Song of Faith,* it plausibly owes something to Broadway overtures and Hollywood film scores.

Carpenter agreed to play the piano solo for the work's premiere. While in rehearsal he gave an interview to the *Boston Traveler* in which he stressed the importance of experimentation for new music: "All living art is experimental, and the progress of all the arts depends upon the success of these experiments." He named Berlin, Kern, Gershwin, Ravel, Stravinsky, Prokofiev, and Hindemith as important and interesting composers. This unusual mix of popular and modernist composers, let alone the notion of the American musical comedy as a kind of experimental music, was unique and highly revealing.[35]

The mention of Hindemith signified a recent development—Carpenter had long expressed his admiration of the other composers he named. He presumably discovered Hindemith through performances by Stock and Koussevitzky, or perhaps through travels abroad. In any case, one can detect Hindemith's influence in *Patterns* and other Carpenter works from the 1930s and 1940s. In 1961 Ellen Carpenter wrote Hindemith, "My husband John Alden Carpenter was a great admirer of your music and of you."[36]

Koussevitzky and the Boston Symphony premiered *Patterns* on 21 October 1932, on a program that also included *Skyscrapers*, Weber's Overture to *Oberon*, and Franck's Symphony in D. They subsequently performed the work in New York as well, while Stock and the Chicago Symphony introduced it to Chicago. Carpenter played the piano part in all of these performances.

Carl Engel further hoped that Hans Kindler and the National Symphony would play *Patterns* for the annual meeting of the Music Teachers' National Association in December 1932, but Kindler could not grant Carpenter's request for a minimum of three rehearsals ("two of these to be devoted to me as soloist"), and so Carpenter and Engel agreed to call off the performance. "It is a very tricky score," Carpenter telegrammed to Engel, "and experience with Boston and Chicago both of whom gave me even more rehearsal than I now ask makes me sure that a performance with less preparation than that suggested would bring no credit to the association or the composer."[37]

The critics reported that audiences in Boston, New York, and Chicago greeted *Patterns* with spirited applause, but they themselves were lukewarm. Cyrus Durgin's *Boston Globe* review was typical of others by Philip Hale, Grace May Stutsman, and Albert Goldberg in holding that, although "lyrical" and "ingratiating," the work was superficial and structurally weak.[38] Carpenter's program note about his "concealed Spanish blood" further provoked the occasional gibe. "For some of us, the Spanish blood was not concealed; it was congealed," stated Philip Hale. And *Time* reported that "*Patterns*, with its sentimental waltz bit, its brief Spanish interlude, its sketchy piano embroidery, was almost anemic, its reception by critics and audience cool."[39]

In the Boston Symphony performances, the work also suffered comparison with *Skyscrapers*. Hale reported that the audience had barely expressed its admiration for *Patterns* when it was "crushed, obliterated" by the ballet. Durgin frankly preferred the old work to the new one: "'Patterns' does not have the vitality, the genial humor, or the intellectual point of 'Skyscrapers.'"[40]

Although Carpenter played the piano part toward the rear of the stage, critics favorably observed his playing. Goldberg noted that "Carpenter played with unsuspected skill—as a pianist, he was a previously unknown quantity—though a more muscular artist might have given the piano a more rightfully prominent place in the ensemble." Irving Weil stated, "Mr. Carpenter played the piano part himself in 'Patterns' and played it very deftly and happily."[41] After attending one performance, Rachmaninoff went backstage to congratulate Carpenter.[42]

A few critics associated *Patterns* with Bach and neoclassicism. Durgin wrote: "It is 'absolute' music, purest of the pure, and its substance is a series of short motives. . . . [One such] is a sturdy phrase which Bach might conceivably have worked out in a fugue." The *Boston Evening Transcript* described the work as an "excellent and individualized example of the so-called 'neo-classicism' now suffusing the European and the American air." The music's "neo-classicism" was plausibly related to the fact that Carpenter wrote the work for Koussevitzky, but few critics other than Grace May Stutsman realized that *Patterns* was a "somewhat tardy contribution to the orchestra's Fiftieth Anniversary celebration."[43]

For all its ingratiating charm, *Patterns* never made it into the orchestral repertory, and for the first time in Carpenter's career, interest in a major work faltered after a first round of performances.

In 1932 Carpenter wrote a short essay titled "Listen to Me," and signed "J. A. C. amateur columnist," that reveals a good deal about his struggles and ideals during these years (see app. C).[44] The essay begins by questioning the relation of the past to the present: "May old thoughts be reconditioned to seem like new? May new thoughts be made intelligible, or are they condemned to tolerance, like the drawings of a child?" One must seek answers for these questions, to "grope unashamed."

Carpenter proposes an aristocracy, a "Guild of Gropers." He contrasts this "guild" with other groups: "the Peaceful and Damned, who have neither evil instincts nor curiosity," "the contortionists who seek to step the rhythms of 1900 to the tunes of '32," and the "Apes, who chatter and multiply."

He further specifies that "the only requirement for [Guild] membership shall be a Cheerful Discontent." "It is possible," he suggests, "that this discontent is the priceless ingredient now seriously lacking in the American character," in that such discontent underpins the "Great American Dream" and its "pursuit of happiness," which is independent of time and place: it can "thrive and flower just as readily on a hot and noisy pavement as in a field of corn."

The essay then asks: "What is this Happiness that we *pursue*? And why, in its *pursuit,* do we pant and labour? Is it not simply a state of spiritual well-being, based on the just perception of the rhythm, the proportions, the perspective, the FORM of our individual lives? Is it not rather to be *invited* than *pursued?*" Carpenter concludes with the hope that "we can tear down the wall between Art and Life. We can study the plumage of the passing birds."

Carpenter's essay itself makes no distinction between art and life. The composer implies, for instance, that the "Peaceful and Damned" have no curiosity about art or life. Similarly, the "contortionists" both dance and think as if they were living thirty years ago. And although the statements about "old thoughts . . . reconditioned to seem like new" and "new thoughts . . . condemned to tolerance" might suggest, say, Stravinsky and Schoenberg, Carpenter seems to have more general trends in mind. Indeed, his one specific reference is not to any artist but to that time when "the ragged remnant of the first American army groped for its existence in the snows of Valley Forge."

At about the same time as this essay, Carpenter set down a poem in free verse on some stationery of the Alice Le Roy Fuller Sanitarium that expressed similar ideas. It is not clear whether Carpenter composed this poem himself or copied it from somewhere, but in any case, the poem is consistent with his other writings from this period: it contends that the "restless irresistible force / That works within me" is the divine will of God. As God guides the birds on "their trackless way," so he guides the fate of men. "In some time— His good time— / I shall arrive! / He guides me—and the bird."[45]

With his "cheerful discontent" led on by a "restless irresistible force," Carpenter continued to balance tradition and novelty, groping his way toward the "Great American Dream," and singing his "Song of Faith" as he searched for new "Patterns."

CHAPTER NINETEEN

Ellen

On 10 January 1933 John Alden Carpenter and Ellen Borden announced their engagement. The *New York Times* reported that the couple planned a spring wedding, but, in fact, they married only twenty days later, on 30 January, at the Boston home of the celebrated Harvard architectural historian A. Kingsley Porter and his wife, Lucy, who was Ellen's aunt; the house itself, Elmwood, had formerly belonged to the poet James Russell Lowell. Carpenter apparently forgot to procure a marriage license, and just before the wedding—in a scatter-brained episode reminiscent, ironically, of his Harvard Glee Club days—he had to rush down to Cambridge City Hall and rush back again.[1]

The Reverend Samuel Eliot (the son of Harvard president Charles William Eliot) of Boston's Arlington Street Church conducted the small, intimate ceremony. Ellen wore a modest traveling suit, and the marriage was witnessed by her two married daughters: Ellen (Mrs. Adlai Stevenson since 1928) and Betty (Mrs. Robert S. Pirie, later Mrs. Ralph Hines).

At the time of this, her second marriage, Ellen Waller Borden (1885–1974) was forty-seven years old, almost ten years younger than John. She, too, descended from an old American family, although the Wallers were Virginia Baptists. Her great-great-grandfather, the Reverend William E. Waller, left Virginia for Kentucky, where his son William S. Waller became a banker.[2] His son—Ellen's grandfather—James B. Waller Sr. moved to Chicago in 1860 and prospered in the city's real estate boom. He founded the suburb of Buena Park, involved himself in local politics, and gave his name to Chicago's Waller Avenue.[3] Ellen's father, James Breckinridge Waller Jr., also managed real estate.

By this time the Chicago Wallers had acquired a reputation for being snobbish and dictatorial, according to David Dangler, whose mother was a Waller.[4] The joke went around that when Waller women came west, the

Indians became nervous. The family also became known for its odd characters—its eccentric misers and the like. Ellen apparently inherited a number of family characteristics—a streak of Baptist asceticism, a strong will, and a passion for politics.

In 1907 Ellen married John Borden, a member of one of Chicago's wealthiest and most colorful families. John Borden's grandfather and father, both lawyers, had made fortunes investing in Chicago real estate and Colorado mining. His grandfather had built a Louis Sullivan mansion on Chicago's South Side, and his father had built a Richard Morris Hunt château on the Near North, two homes that were among Chicago's most renowned showcases until their destruction after World War II.[5] John, too, prospered through smart investments in cab, truck, and oil companies. (In later years Ellen lightly took some credit for the yellow color of American cabs: apparently, she overheard her husband and his associates discussing ways in which cabs could be readily identified and said, "Why don't you paint them the color of my hat, yellow?")[6] John Borden's brother William startled Chicago by becoming a missionary. His sister Joyce married the Croatian violinist Zlatko Baloković, and another sister, Mary, wrote novels. John himself was a sportsman who made well-publicized expeditions to Alaska and the Arctic in 1913, 1916, and 1927.

John Borden and Ellen were unhappily married: John was an alcoholic, and both had extramarital romantic attachments. They finally divorced in 1924.[7] Ellen remained in the Hunt château at 1020 Lake Shore Drive at Bellevue Place, not far from the Carpenters' Rush Street address. When her future son-in-law Adlai Stevenson met her in the 1920s, he estimated her "worth" to be "probably a million."[8]

John Carpenter and Ellen Borden fell in love after the composer returned from a trip abroad in the spring of 1913. Over the next twenty years, they carried on an intense and passionate romance that never abated in ardor and urgency. Carpenter was thoroughly infatuated: he would telephone Ellen at home when she was away just to hear her phone ring, stand outside her empty window, and call out to her while taking solitary walks. "I am thinking of you almost literally every minute whatever I am doing," he once declared. Their frequent absences from Chicago never tempered such feelings: "You seem so near me all the time—no matter how many miles get in between," Carpenter wrote to her in 1931 on his way to Japan.[9]

They often saw each other in public settings and met secretly as well. They seem to have rendezvoused at his place of work and occasionally out of town. Ellen's granddaughter Joan Leclerc believed that their relationship throughout these years was platonic, notwithstanding their apparent physical attraction to each other.[10] In any case, John and Ellen made assignations through the mail; John would write, "Please!!" or "Over-Over-Quick!" followed by a time like "for Monday morning."

As they both traveled from one end of the globe to the other, they sent each other gifts, poems, and books, sometimes pressed with dried flowers. They constantly wrote notes and letters, alternately whimsical and lovesick, but always starry-eyed and poetic. Indeed, the letters focused almost exclusively on their love and hardly ever concerned such mundane matters as business, politics, or social or family gossip.

In their correspondence they used code words: "Hello" and "Goodbye" for "I love you"; "H.D.Y.D." (How Do You Do) for their affair; "George" for their correspondence (after the two-cents postage stamp with George Washington's portrait); "W.H.N." (What's Her Name) for Ellen; "Someone" or "Someone else" for Rue; "Junior" for Ginny; and "440" (440 Wells St.) for George B. Carpenter and Company. Carpenter apparently destroyed all of Ellen's letters, but Ellen saved his and donated scores of them to the Library of Congress, to be opened only ten years after her death. These letters provide a rich, if one-sided, insight into their relationship.

The correspondence itself had enormous importance for Carpenter: "It's such fun writing to you—it makes me so happy," he once wrote.[11] He would often plead for letters: "Help me by writing at least twice a week," he entreated in 1924.[12] He even played cat-and-mouse with her letters: "I put him ['George'] aside—with elaborate carelessness unopened—and pretend (calm outside but inside wild) that he isn't there. Then I steal up on him gradually—When I can't bear it another second, he is opened and I begin."[13] The importance of their correspondence (and something of its quasi-sexual nature) was underscored in a 1913 limerick that Carpenter composed for Ellen:

A sad little stamp named "George"

With feelings abnormally large,

Was sentenced to sit

In a box, until it

Was convenient to grant his discharge.[14]

"George as a Guide and Comforter is beyond anything," he wrote in 1922.[15]

In a long, revealing letter to Ellen (so revealing that he asked her to burn it), Carpenter once discussed his love for her in the form of a children's fable.

There was a "little boy named John," he writes, who was "a perfectly usual little boy as far as one could see, yet with a distinct tendency to be abnormal on the inside," like a mince pie. Little Johnny was devoted to such "items" as public school, raising chickens, his parents, and an "Unfortunately Stout Little Girl" (Rue), but he grew disillusioned with all and turned inward. He discovered "that it is only the inward eye, wandering alone in the strange moonlit places of the mind that can encounter the sweet presences of the shifting forms of Reality." Johnny hoped one day to "encounter Another, who held the same wonderful faith and who by necessity of countless ages would respond thought for thought and tremor for tremor." In the meantime, "he found sure refuge in escape from parents and stuffy books and parlors, to the calm and encouraging regions of fields and woods, where he would sit and gaze unseeing at some friendly star."

While in bed one night, the story continues, little Johnny awakened to a strange voice—"which seemed to him, gay and grave, insistent, kind, reasonably and overwhelmingly appealing"—calling his name. He ran into the woods and heard a "wonderful" song:

Beauty lives for open eyes,
Open hearts. Beauty flies,
Beauty languishes and dies
In a World of stupid lies,—
Beauty lives in April skies.

In a little grassy clearing, he found the singer of the song, a little girl braiding a wreath from grape blossoms. "He knew that here at last was the Reality of his Vision—that he would now cease to be just a little boy, alone in a strange world by himself."

The little girl explained that she had been waiting for him: "I've heard you, out there, for ages,—but I couldn't make you hear *me*." During her wait the clouds "worried across the blue" and then "worried themselves out of sight again." This brought with it the realization "that the sky is always blue if only one can stay above the clouds." Suddenly "sound and sight grew blurred and dim" for Johnny, and he seemed "to fall swiftly for an immeasurable distance." He found himself in bed, listening, in the moonlit night outside, to the "soft singing of the nightingale." Carpenter concluded the story with a quote from Verlaine's "En sourdine": "And when twilight falls, with dark and solemn shadows creeping by, / Voice of our despair, the night-ingale shall sing."[16]

Carpenter clearly found in Ellen Borden a soul mate who could share his spiritual temperament and his sense of isolation from a world of "stuffy books" and "stupid lies." Indeed, his letters to Ellen occasionally chided their friends (they moved, essentially, in the same circles) for their superficial materialism. "Their lives have absolutely no purpose but themselves, and their bodies and their sensations," he asserted in 1925, "they give not one single thing to life. They can be kind and pleasant and easy—but it's a poisonous atmosphere." In another letter he described a party at the Clive Runnells (Chicago socialites): "There was all the usual talk about all the kind of life that I don't know anything about."[17]

Carpenter's alienation only intensified when he found himself at the same social function as Ellen. After one such party, he exclaimed, "That terrible noise—and the sense of separation! I looked at you and wondered—at many things and about many things—and most of all, I was thankful for my Refuge—Our Refuge." Once, at a concert, Ellen threw Carpenter a glance, and the composer "got so excited that I threw my program on the floor and ran." He empathized with the tormented love of John Keats and Fanny Brawne.[18]

Carpenter practically viewed Ellen as his missing half in the Platonic sense. During the summer of 1924, he asked meditatively, "Could you ever dream of a more perfect fit than us, each to each other—inside—outside—mind—body & soul?" and exulted, "Isn't it—excruciating—the *enormous Fun* of being *exactly* alike!" In 1931 he declared, "Everything I see, I see double, with your eyes and mine."[19] With Ellen, Carpenter found someone who could share his interests in spirituality, politics, social welfare, and music.

One friend remembered Ellen as "always spiritual" and especially at-tracted to Theosophy,[20] a movement founded in 1875 in New York largely under the aegis of the American lawyer Henry Steel Olcott and the Russian mystic Helena Blavatsky. Their ideas largely drew upon Buddhist and Hindu concepts of reincarnation and karma, a doctrine of cause and effect. They adapted, too, occultic ideas derived from Zoroaster, Jesus, Lao-tzu, Con-fucius, and Jewish and Islamic mystics. Their guiding precepts included the divinity of man, intercultural understanding, social utopianism, and spiritual leadership. Theosophy exerted worldwide appeal—especially in America, En-gland, Germany, and India during the 1910s and 1920s—to people (often of the upper classes) dissatisfied with established religions.[21]

Carpenter never expressed affiliation with Theosophy; indeed, some of his letters to Ellen intimate a difference between them on particulars of religious thought. In 1927, for instance, he commented that an unnamed book came "near to defining your God as you make *me* feel you have found him, and help me to let Him be my God too," and again, "Seeing and feeling these things in you makes one feel a sort of envy and a need of trying more than ever, me too, to collaborate with God."[22] The only religious literature that he seemed particularly close to was "Saul," which he periodically recommended to Ellen.

On the other hand, Carpenter showed an interest in Asian religions (prompted by Ellen?) that at least dated as far back as *Gitanjali*. The fable cited earlier, with its "necessity of countless ages" and "I've heard you, out there, for ages," suggested Buddhist influence. Carpenter furthermore wrote to Ellen from Peking in 1931: "They say here that *Tao* means 'right road.' If so I know we are good disciples."[23] In any case, the ideals of Theosophy—universalist, utopian, spiritual, heavily Eastern—generally matched the tenor of the composer's writings and interests.

Another of Ellen's "spiritual" interests—Moral Rearmament (or MRA)—was more decidedly Christian in character. The movement was officially founded in 1938 by the American evangelist Frank Buchman (1878–1961), who had promoted similar movements before then. Moral Rearmament counseled a return to the early Christian ideals of absolute purity, honesty, unselfishness, and love. It sponsored group meetings in which members confessed their secret failings and sought guidance from God (MRA directly influenced the founding of Alcoholics Anonymous and related self-help groups). The movement also taught that each individual had the power to transform the world and, in particular, to stem communist expansion.[24]

Ellen might have met Frank Buchman through her friend Halina Rodzinski, who later wrote that Buchman had "something of the simplicity of the Frances [*sic*] who once set Europe ablaze with a renewed and forthright Christian spirit in the Middle Ages." According to Halina, Buchman preached that "God speaks to us if we tune in like a radio."[25] Like many MRA supporters, Ellen and Halina refrained from drinking or wearing any or much makeup (Halina began to wear makeup again after her husband—the conductor Artur Rodzinski—complained that she looked like death).[26] Halina remembered that Ellen defended Buchman to detractors by claiming that he came from a "simple family," and Halina believed that Ellen remained loyal to Buchman her entire life, although Joan Leclerc claimed otherwise.[27]

Carpenter never affiliated himself with MRA, but he attended a party with Adlai Stevenson in Sarasota, Florida, during the winter of 1943–44 at which Frank Buchman was the guest of honor.[28] Whatever interest Carpenter showed MRA seemed in deference to his wife and his close friends Artur and Halina Rodzinski, both of whom had become quite involved with the MRA.[29] Adlai Stevenson Jr., Joan Leclerc, and Robert Pirie all contend that Carpenter had no interest in the movement and, like Artur Rodzinski in later years, found MRA to be "manipulative."[30]

Ellen had quite generally a strong interest in politics and worked diligently on behalf of her son-in-law Adlai Stevenson's campaigns for senator, governor, and president, even after Stevenson's separation and divorce from her daughter.[31] She remained, said Stevenson, an "ardent supporter."[32] (Even Carpenter, who by the 1930s stated his political affiliation as Republican rather than "liberal independent," contributed small amounts to Stevenson's campaigns and hosted parties for him in Chicago.)[33] During World War II, Ellen also won national prominence for relief efforts on behalf of England and France, and later for selling war bonds.[34]

For many years Ellen served, like Carpenter, as a director of the Illinois Children's Home and Aid Society (ICHAS). She also supported the Cradle Society, Chicago's other principal agency devoted to the welfare of orphaned and illegitimate children. In fact, she became a dominant force in Chicago's social welfare for children, pushing for mutual cooperation between ICHAS and the Cradle Society to the point of making it difficult for the professional social workers at ICHAS to pursue their own policies.[35] Ellen's work on behalf of children naturally provided another common bond between herself and Carpenter.

Moreover, Ellen shared Carpenter's interest in music. The pianist Eugene Indjic remembered that Ellen was "very sensitive to music" and that she admired Debussy, Dinu Lipatti, the Boston Symphony, and Carpenter's music, especially *Perambulator* and *Skyscrapers* (Leclerc also recalled her fondness for *Gitanjali* and *Song of Faith*).[36] Honegger personally inscribed a copy of *Rugby* to her when he came to Chicago under Arts Club auspices in 1929. In any case, Carpenter enjoyed sharing feelings about music with Ellen. After hearing *Parsifal* in 1916 (either on 10 January or 17 December, both conducted by Egon Pollak), he wrote: "It is so wonderful. I felt as if I was gradually dwindling to a little green leaf on an enormous tree—with the wind shaking all the branches. And there is one place that always makes me want to cry. It made me think of that night two years ago." And after hearing the Chicago

Symphony play Wagner's "Preislied," he professed, "I went all the way around the world." In later years he would similarly write to Ellen about Stravinsky and others.[37]

Ellen's involvement in music extended, like Carpenter's, to patronage. In early 1933, for instance, she thought of postponing their wedding so that she could complete her work as chair of a committee "seeking $100,000 for the erection of a temple of music at the Century of Progress exhibition before it opens in June."[38] Even before her marriage to Carpenter, she somewhat audaciously joined her rival Rue, in the 1920s, on the boards of the Arts Club and the Allied Arts. After Adlai Stevenson introduced her to Truman and Molotov at the United Nations in 1946, she "went right to work on Vyshinsky and Manuilsky about some Russian music project."[39] And after Carpenter's death, she built a concert shell on the Richard Crane estate in Ipswich, Massachusetts, in her husband's memory. She also helped young musicians like Eugene Indjic.

Ellen's interests in Theosophy and music came together in the person of the French American composer Dane Rudhyar. Ellen probably first met Rudhyar when he visited Chicago in 1925; in any case, she and some other "wealthy patrons" invited him to return to Chicago in November 1928 to lecture on Eastern mysticism and music. Rudhyar recalled that Ellen "was my escort of the time. (She was divorced and had two girls; one of them married Adlai Stevenson. I was there at the marriage.) She asked me to go with her to the opera, and to have dinner at her place—a very elegant, huge mansion—and so on."[40] Ellen presumably experienced something of the thrill felt by the young Chicagoan Ruth Crawford on this same occasion: "I begin to feel his [Rudhyar's] beauty as never before," wrote Crawford in her diary. "Previously when he was here I have admired and stood afar worshipping vaguely, you might say, intellectually, because I was dazzled by his erudition. Now I begin to 'feel' his greatness."[41] Such interests on Ellen's part possibly prompted Carpenter's suggestion to Copland, on the occasion of a 1930 lecture-recital for the Chicago Arts Club, that he devote some time to composers like Rudhyar and Crawford.[42]

Many of Carpenter's letters to Ellen reveal that he often sought her support and advice about his own work. For example, he asked her to read and revise his program notes for *A Pilgrim Vision*. After asking her opinion about possible titles for *Skyscrapers,* he wrote, "Oh darling, you don't know how I love *consulting* you about *everything*." Similarly, on another occasion, he stated, "Oh, my darling, when you don't approve of anything about me—I get completely wild."[43]

More generally, Ellen served Carpenter as muse and inspiration. In 1916 he commented that he wanted to write "something big and fine" to pay his debt to her, "the star that lighted the way. I want to pay and owe again. I want to pay with the brightest, most untarnished coin that I have—I want to drop it in your lap and have nothing left." And in another letter Carpenter expressed his wish

> to make some kind of music that will make your mind have happy thoughts—I want to put you in the very most comfortable chair—and light some sort of fire at your feet that will keep you warm, and light everything around you and make you smile. And I would stand behind your chair and never say a word, unless you wanted me to—a kind of happy old slave—for poking the fire and keeping out draughts—and now and then playing little serenades on a strange instrument of his own. Oh to be able to stand behind the chair![44]

If, for Carpenter, Rue was the "unfortunately stout little girl," and Ellen the "little lady of the grape blossoms," Rue's friends and family saw things differently.[45] Ginny "hated her with a vengeance" and no doubt would have seconded her husband's description of Ellen as "a rather undesirable woman." Carpenter's niece Theodora Brown thought that Ellen was a fool, and the composer's granddaughter Rue found her unpleasantly "rigid," guessing that movements like Theosophy and MRA fed charismatically on her anxiety and guilt.[46]

Ellen's own family regarded her somewhat critically. Joan Leclerc, for instance, admitted that her grandmother was not as sophisticated as Rue, and Adlai Stevenson Jr. similarly doubted that she had much in the way of a formal education. Stevenson further remembered his grandmother as "naïve" and "susceptible to the imprecations of the salesman," recalling the black boxes she kept in order to ward off illness. Robert Pirie thought her a "vain, frivolous, superficial" woman, who was mostly interested in the "social aspects" of concerts. A more distant relative, David Dangler, described her as a "social butterfly" who enjoyed being the center of attention.[47]

Indeed, Ellen's letters suggested a rather overweening personality.[48] Adlai Stevenson's aforementioned phrase, "went right to work," further hinted at a certain overbearing quality in his mother-in-law. Arthur Rubinstein confirmed these impressions in a telling anecdote: Long a devoted friend of Rue and Ginny, Rubinstein stayed with Carpenter on tour in 1937 and discovered that the new Mrs. Carpenter "was an inveterate hostess who gave receptions and parties from morning until night."

The day before the concert, the guests never stopped coming. There were pre-luncheon visits, a large lunch party, some important ladies for tea, a cocktail party of course, a big dinner, and some guest coming after dinner. The hostess was tireless. "Arthur, you must talk to this wonderful man . . . Mrs. X is so keen on meeting you, do sit down with her," and so on and so forth. It was unbearable.

A preconcert lunch party for twelve was the limit. Rubinstein told his hostess: "Helen [*sic*], I cannot lunch with your guests. I shall remain in my room; a cup of coffee would be welcome." The end result of all this was that he barely made the concert on time.[49]

Similarly, when the Stravinskys stayed with the Carpenters in 1940, Ellen hosted a series of formal lunches, teas, and dinners for them. "We live as if we were in a hotel," remarked Vera.[50] The gulf between Rue's easy hospitality ("you could be sure, whoever the guests of honour were, they'd not be fussed over tiresomely or placed on a pedestal")[51] and Ellen's mannered formality must have been striking.

At the same time, Leclerc remembered her grandmother as a bright, vivacious woman with a great sense of fun, and a marvelous hostess in her own right. Pirie and Adlai Stevenson Jr. similarly referred to Ellen as an "amiable" and "lighthearted, cheerful somewhat balmy woman." Conductor Artur Rodzinski's son Richard also admired her warmth and liveliness: "She was a wonderful person to hear chat."[52]

Above all, everyone agreed that Ellen adored Carpenter and treated him with greater deference than had Rue. "I was rather submerged," Carpenter himself told Patrick Hill. "Now, with Mrs. Borden, I am taking the lead."[53] After they married, Ellen traveled with John, entertained his friends, stayed by his side, took pride in his accomplishments. One night, during a horrible bout of food poisoning, she crawled out of bed rather than wake her husband; she explained to an astonished friend that John needed his rest.[54] Even Theodora Brown recalled that Ellen was totally devoted to Carpenter, who, in affairs of the heart, was a "terrific sentimentalist."[55]

After their marriage and an extended honeymoon in Èze-Village, a medieval town on the French Riviera, Carpenter left Rush Street and moved into Ellen's home at 1020 Lake Shore Drive. "A famous example of . . . French Gothic inspired architecture" of the late nineteenth century, the grey limestone mansion designed by Hunt had four floors and a basement with kitchen, laundry, and boiler room.[56] Vera Stravinsky was not exaggerating when she said that staying with the Carpenters was like being in a hotel: 1020 had a huge number of rooms and a large staff that included a housekeeper, maids, cooks, butlers, gardeners, governesses, a laundress, a secretary, and a chauffeur.

In a Chicago social column of the period, such staff members reported that Carpenter liked to wear Chinese shantungs, British tweeds, and Bermuda tropical weights; that he enjoyed simple, elegant food, especially broiled lobster, Boston baked beans, and brown bread; that he liked dogs and, prior to Nicky (his dachshund), had owned a sheepdog; and that for relaxation he played bridge and tennis, took walks, and read books, often on current events or early American history.[57]

Carpenter set up two music rooms at 1020 Lake Shore Drive: a ground floor studio, decorated with the Chinese instruments and vases he had long collected, and a third-floor music room, where he would work every morning with Nicky by his side.

In her diary Vera Stravinsky kept some account of the two weeks (4–17 November 1940) that she and her husband spent at 1020 Lake Shore Drive.[58] On their first night there, Ellen attended the opera (*Tristan und Isolde* with Melchior and Flagstad), while Carpenter remained at home, presumably to dine and chat with Stravinsky. Before the premiere of *Symphony in C* on 7 November, they all attended a dinner at the home of Charlie Swift, whose father had founded the famous meatpacking firm, and whose wife, the German-born soprano Claire Dux, had won critical acclaim for her occasional performances with the Chicago Opera.[59]

The Carpenters hosted dinner again on 8 November and a "big lunch" the following day with the Stocks, "Goodspeed" (presumably Mrs. Charles ["Bobsy"] Goodspeed, who succeeded Rue as president of the Arts Club), "Leyssac" (possibly the Danish actor Paul Leyssac, in the States during these years), and "some university people." After lunch they attended a new work by Prokofiev, *Peter and the Wolf*, at a Ballet Theatre matinee, and met dancers Anton Dolin and Anthony Tudor. On 16 November the Carpenters hosted a tea for the Stravinskys, to which they invited the musicologist Carleton Sprague Smith and Mrs. Rudolph Ganz.

The Carpenters surely attended at least some of the other lunches, teas, and dinners given in honor of the Stravinskys, for instance, those hosted by Ellen's cousin and best friend Mary Langhorne, the wife of Colonel George Langhorne, an army officer decorated for service during the Spanish-American War;[60] Chauncey McCormick, director of International Harvestor and, like the Carpenters, an ICHAS board member; and Edward Ryerson, heir to another great Chicago fortune—this one made by steel and iron—and president of the Chicago Symphony board.

This world of well-heeled politicians, philanthropists, military men, and chairmen of the board marked a change from the days when Rue presided over poets, painters, dancers, and actors at Rush Street. One can only surmise Ellen's influence in this. Surely she did not have the kind of rapport with artists that Rue enjoyed; she came across, rather, as superficial and gushing. But who knows how much the Rush Street scene had appealed to Carpenter in the first place, and whether he himself moved away from it on his own accord? After all, with Ellen, he was finally "taking the lead."

John and Ellen spent less and less time in Chicago, especially after the composer sold the family business in the fall of 1936. By World War II, keeping up their huge Chicago residence had become a troublesome extravagance, and in 1943 they loaned their château to Wesley Hospital,[61] spending their remaining years in Chicago in exclusive apartment buildings on North State Street and Lake Shore Drive.[62]

The Carpenters wanted a summer vacation home but decided against the composer's Charlotte place, largely because they wanted to be close to friends and family in the Boston area. Carpenter consequently left the MacNeil Mansion to Patrick and Ginny, and he and Ellen looked for a new summer home in Massachusetts.

For three summers, from 1933 to 1935, they rented places in Pride's Crossing, a small town outside Beverly on the Massachusetts Bay where Ellen had often vacationed. This general area had long served Boston society as a summer retreat. Henry Clay Frick, Justice Oliver Wendell Holmes, William Howard Taft, and other well-established New England families had had summer residences there. Poet James Russell Lowell wrote, "Find the Yankee word for Sorrento, and you have Beverly—it is only the Bay of Naples translated into the New England dialect."[63] The Carpenters thus could enjoy a close proximity to both friends in Boston and those with summer homes on the North Shore, including Frederic Bartlett, Richard Crane, Archibald MacLeish, Mrs. Graham Houghton, and Mrs. Kingsley (Lucy) Porter.

In 1936 the Carpenters bought their own estate in Beverly, a thirty-room guest house, complete with private beach, indoor pool, tennis court, barn, servants' quarters, and a children's wing, including a children's dining room (the Carpenters naturally turned one of the rooms into a music room). Located at 35 Prince Street in prestigious Beverly Cove, the estate sat majestically on a hill overlooking the bay, with Salem in the distance. The Carpenters called this "wonderful airy summer home" Sunset Hill.[64]

Over the years Sunset Hill suffered some calamities. In 1938 a severe hurricane damaged the grounds, as did a bad storm in 1948. And on 8 July 1940 a fire broke out in the music room, destroying Carpenter's piano and some manuscripts. The blaze swept through the children's wing and all told caused damage estimated at between twenty-five and thirty thousand dollars.[65] Ellen, who lived at Sunset Hill until her death in 1974, considered the fire a blessing in disguise, since with one less wing, she could more easily manage the estate.[66]

Leclerc and Pirie saw more of the Carpenters at Sunset Hill than at 1020 Lake Shore Drive, where children made an appearance only at tea. At Sunset Hill, on the other hand, they knew that their grandparents woke early and had breakfast together on a balcony off their bedroom. By 8:30 Carpenter was in the music room, where he spent the morning "tinkling away" at the piano, with a table and manuscript paper at his right. During this time Ellen worked at her desk—organizing menus, placing phone calls, paying bills, in short, running the household. They all had lunch at 12:30, after which Carpenter took a nap. In the afternoon the Carpenters enjoyed a game of tennis or bridge, and at 3:00 the family gathered for long walks followed by tea and cookies at home. Later, John and Ellen would retire and dress for dinner.

On weekends the Carpenters occasionally went into Boston, but more often they entertained houseguests or friends in the area, including Richard Crane, diplomat and heir to yet another Chicago fortune (this one in plumbing equipment), and his wife, who lived in a huge estate of their own, Castle Hill in nearby Ipswich. Other regular guests included the Langhornes, the McCormicks, the Goodspeeds, the Swifts, and the Bartletts, as well as Boston novelist John Marquand (1893–1960), who had recently won the Pulitzer Prize for *The Late George Apley* (1937), and conductor Sam Barlow and his wife, Ernesta. Joan Leclerc remembered that Carpenter had a special liking for Bartlett and Marquand.[67] On Sundays, Ellen often hosted large, lavish lunches at which Carpenter's whimsical, offbeat humor at the dinner table delighted their guests.[68] "Everyone adored Carpenter," recalled Adlai Stevenson Jr. "He was a sweet, wonderful man."[69]

Whereas the Carpenters summered nearly every year in Beverly (one exception was the summer of 1937, when they traveled to Sweden), they spent the winters in various places—though most of these were fashionable coastal retreats like Beverly. In 1934 they wintered in Algiers; in 1935 they traveled, at John's urging, to Peking; and in 1936 they returned to Èze-Village. After the war broke out, they spent most of their winters either in Florida or California.

*   *   *

After Carpenter's death many subscribed to the notion that Ellen had failed to inspire her husband the way the legendary Rue Carpenter had, and that the quality of his work had declined accordingly. Arthur Meeker, for instance, wrote:

> What I am sure of is that, without the active co-operation of his wife [Rue], his [Carpenter's] artistic career would have been much less successful than it was. She knew how to push him as he couldn't push himself, and was largely instrumental in having his ballets staged at the Munich Opera and the Metropolitan. . . . [Carpenter] mourned her for a year before marrying a nice, kind, rich woman, who made him quite comfortable and happy as long as he lived. But he never composed another vital bar of music. His later works, each given a respectful hearing, have gone the rounds of the symphony orchestras in turn and then fallen into decent oblivion.[70]

This conventional wisdom failed to account for the fact that Carpenter wrote very little during those strained last seven years with Rue that could be compared with the burst of activity that followed his marriage to Ellen; and that his post-1931 compositions proved, in some instances, rather popular, including *Sea Drift,* which Gilbert Chase declared his "most successful" symphonic work.[71] Now we know, further, that Ellen played a preponderant, if secretive, role in Carpenter's creative life as far back as 1913, and that the start of their love affair coincided with *Gitanjali* and *Adventures in a Perambulator*—the composer's first great successes.

CHAPTER TWENTY

Sea Drift

1933

Carpenter began work on *Sea Drift,* his darkest, most solemn work, in February 1933, while on his honeymoon in Èze-Village, France. He completed the composition in Pride's Crossing in September.

In the score's flyleaf Carpenter acknowledged the poetic source of his tone poem: "This music derives its title and has sought inspiration from the noble sea poems of Walt Whitman." Carpenter surely knew that Frederick Delius had set portions of "Out of the Cradle Endlessly Rocking," the first and largest of Whitman's *Sea Drift* poems, in his own *Sea Drift* (1901–3) for baritone, chorus, and orchestra; and that some of Vaughan Williams's *Sea Symphony* (1903–10) similarly used parts of Whitman's collection. One novel feature of Carpenter's work, however, was that it was purely instrumental.

Carpenter first became interested in Whitman upon reading an article from about 1900 by Whitman's assistant, executor, and disciple Horace Traubel (Whitman biographer Justin Kaplan writes that Traubel portrayed Whitman as "the patron saint of American radicalism and socialism").[1] In a letter to Felix Borowski, Carpenter spoke further about the origins of *Sea Drift:*

> Away back around 1915, I experienced my first acute Whitman excitement, and for some time, then, I studied the problem of setting to music in vocal form excerpts from some of the *Sea-Drift* poems. These experiments I could not bring to any result that satisfied me, and I dropped the project.
>
> In February of last year, under the influence of the blue Mediterranean at Eze Village, I took up the old problem again, and abandoned any attempt to make a literal setting of the Whitman verses in a vocal work. I tried to make a composite orchestral record of the imprint upon me of these poems. My hope is that the music makes sense, just as music, with perhaps special meaning for those who love Whitman. My work represents an effort to transcribe my impressions derived from these magnificent poems.[2]

One can imagine Carpenter's hesitancy in setting Whitman, for as a song-writer Carpenter preferred metrical and rhymed verse.

The composer's renewed involvement with Whitman was related to the kind of political and spiritual concerns that had begun to preoccupy him during the late 1920s and early 1930s. Indeed, he had already used a quotation from Whitman as the motto for his 1931 *Song of Faith*, whose text—written by the composer—was itself highly Whitmanesque, as was the composer's 1931 essay "Listen to Me."

Although Carpenter spoke of "poems" in the plural, *Sea Drift*—a slow, one-movement work—took its inspiration primarily, if not exclusively, from "Out of the Cradle Endlessly Rocking." Carpenter even copied down lines from this poem (specifically, parts of the bird's song) onto notepaper.[3] Certainly, the music's melancholic, nostalgic tone matches "Out of the Cradle" better than some of the other poems, including those selected by Vaughan Williams for his *Sea Symphony* (accordingly, Carpenter's work is closer to Delius). Moreover, the work clearly depicts that poem's two principal images, namely, the rocking of the sea and the song of the bird. Indeed, the recently widowed Carpenter might well have found special relevance in the poem's portrayal of a lost mate (although such mournful remembrances of his first wife while on a honeymoon with his second wife seem oddly grim).

Whitman's "Out of the Cradle Endlessly Rocking" concerns the interplay of art, love, and death: At the seashore during an autumn night, the poet remembers, as a boy, watching two birds building their nest on the banks of the Paumanok. He recalls, too, the lonely bird's song of loss, despair, hope, and love after his mate fails to return to the nest. As he listens to the bird, and as the waves of the sea whisper up the word he is seeking, "death," the boy-poet realizes his destiny.

Although Carpenter's music unfolds fluidly, it contains distinct episodes that seem to mirror the poem's basic structure. The composer articulates these episodes with climaxes that typically feature fortissimo or triple fortissimo dynamics and tutti scoring that includes woodwind and brass tremolos or trills, harp and piano glissandi, brass fanfare figures, and cymbal crashes. These climaxes occur at ⑦ (Con bravura), ⑫ (Duramente), four after ⑮, ㉑, and ㉗ (Trionfalmente, followed, at four before ㉘, by Nobilmente). Consequently, the work might be seen as containing five sections, with a short, quiet epilogue.

Each section is distinct enough to suggest some specific relation to "Out of the Cradle." The first section, with its changing meters (from $\frac{9}{8}$ to $\frac{12}{8}$ to $\frac{6}{8}$) and tempos, and its pervasive duplets, clearly evokes the sea, the image that begins—and ends—Whitman's poem. Carpenter's periodic use of such music in later sections resembles the poem's recurrent reminders of the sea.

The second section begins with Scorrendo and Con ardore passages that serve as a transition to a new theme in $\frac{3}{4}$ played by flute and horn (10). This theme, which opens with a prominent motive from the first section in retrograde, has a sad, nostalgic, lullaby-like quality that plausibly relates to Whitman's reminiscence of youth: "A man, yet by these tears a little boy again." Another theme, marked *dolente* and stated initially by the cellos at 11, also evokes the introduction of the lonely, human element into the seascape. Significantly, the theme very much recalls Carpenter's setting of Tagore's "I Am Like a Remnant of a Cloud of Autumn" from *Gitanjali*.

After a short transition, a third section presents a new, pentatonic melody played by the horn and answered by the bassoon. The flute and viola figuration that accompanies these phrases is apparently inspired by the bird story that constitutes the heart of "Out of the Cradle" (13). This music plausibly describes the springtime mating of the birds: "Pour down your warmth, great sun! / While we bask, we two together." Indeed, the question-answer structure suggests a dialogue or duet.

At four before 16 the fourth section begins with an unusual harmony (C♯–D♯–G♯–A) scored for lower strings, harp, and vibraphone, to which the solo English horn soon after adds another pitch, G. The subsequent English horn solo—another *dolente* melody—gives voice to Whitman's grieving bird: "But my love soothes not me, not me." (Delius also used the English horn for this purpose in his *Sea Drift*, although Carpenter's music resembles more Sibelius's *Swan of Tuonela*.) The agitated birdlike music beginning at 17 and continuing through 19 may well depict the bird's ensuing call for his mate: "High and clear I shoot my voice over the waves." And the sadly resigned music that brings this section to its conclusion possibly reflects the bird's final utterances: "O past! O happy life! O songs of joy!" In short, this section matches the bird's "aria" of loss and remembrance.

After another transition, the fifth section recalls the sea music of the opening (23) and the *dolente* theme of the second section (at 25). This fits Whitman's return to the remembrances of the sea and his youth, now informed with new meanings—principally, the poet's destiny. Perhaps the recognition of this destiny—the ecstatic awakening to "the fire, the sweet hell within"—is reflected in the final climax.

Following this climax the initial sea music returns and arrives at a luminous E♭-major cadence, followed by polytonal fragments in the English horn, vibraphone, and French horns. If the music follows "Out of the Cradle" as closely as it appears to, this conclusion surely reflects the poem's ending, in which the sea whispers up to the poet "the word final, superior to all": death.

Whether *Sea Drift* depicts "Out of the Cradle" in the kind of detail outlined above, or represents a more general response to Whitman's poem, the work is a tone poem in the true sense of the word and not, as has often been assumed, a vague musical seascape. The composer's picturesque description of the sea and birds symbolizes shifting and wide-ranging emotions, as in Whitman's poetry; the work's poetic intimacy accordingly deserves comparison with Debussy's *Prelude to the Afternoon of a Faun* perhaps sooner than with *La Mer*.

For all its impressionist atmosphere, *Sea Drift* reveals at the same time an awareness of contemporary trends, including the use of important intervals (as opposed to leitmotifs) to create an organic structure, polytonal and polychordal harmonies, dissonant and polyrhythmic counterpoint (ex. 45), and ostinato techniques. For example, the score's opening two pages paint a picture of the sea, but as with the rowlike melody that begins *Patterns,* the highly chromatic melody put forth by the violas and cellos also provides much of the material for the rest of the work, including the bird's song at [16]. Similarly, the opening juxtaposition of duplets and triplets anticipates the work's extensive and somewhat intricate use of two against three. (Sketches reveal that Carpenter originally conceived this basic idea in $\frac{12}{4}$, with dotted quarters against triplet quarter notes; he later changed it to $\frac{12}{8}$ with duplet quarter notes against groups of three eighth notes.)

Some of these features—for instance, the initial long, chromatic melody in the lower strings—suggest not only the influence of Stravinsky (especially *The Firebird*) but that of such younger composers as Roy Harris, whose *Three Variations on a Theme* (String Quartet no. 2) Carpenter had heard just before writing *Sea Drift* (Carpenter was sufficiently impressed to make a point of attending the premiere of Harris's *Symphony: 1933* in Boston on 26 January 1934). Similar connections could be made to such works as the Estonian composer Eduard Tubin's (1907–61) First Symphony (1934). In short, *Sea Drift* belongs in the context of 1930s neoromanticism, not turn-of-the-century impressionism.

This affinity to 1930s neoromanticism includes the music's tonal language. For example, the opening measures do not establish a clear key or even tonal center, the D pedal point notwithstanding. Only at the unexpected arrival of D♭ major at [1] can one interpret the first six measures as, perhaps, a Neapolitan preparation. Similarly, one hardly expects the arrival of B minor at [2] or, for that matter, any of the other important cadential points. Even the

EXAMPLE 45. Carpenter, *Sea Drift*, ⬜, mm. 7–18.

ending in E♭ major comes as something of a surprise, despite some fore-warning at ⑱ or the climactic arrival of an E♭ pedal at four before ㉘. The music seems headed, rather, for a final cadence in C minor, and one has to listen attentively to the triple pianissimo E♭ in the bass in order to hear the music as ending in E♭ major. Significantly, this is Carpenter's first large-scale work without a key signature.

Within the work's tenuous arrival points, the harmonies move sponta-neously, fluidly. In the twelve measures following the arrival of D♭ major at ⬜ (see ex. 45), for example, a series of slippery, shifting triads can be outlined as follows: D♭–d°–F⁺ (m. 7), D♭–d°–d–G (m. 8), D♭–d–G (m. 9), D♭–E–e–A (m. 10), E♭–f♯–A♭–e–A (m. 11), E♭–f♯–G♯ (m. 12), A–e–F♯⁷ (mm. 13–14), D♯⁺ (mm. 15–16), G♯⁷ (m. 17), b (m. 18). Carpenter further enriches the music's harmonic texture by means of polychordal and even bitonal in-flections, one striking example occurring just before ⑧, as the music rests on an E♭-major triad in the upper strings while suggesting an A-minor triad in the lower strings and bassoon. In another example, at ㉕, the upper strings alternate E-major and F-major harmonies as the bass similarly rocks back and forth between G and C♯! The final measures, too, contain polychordal and bitonal implications; as the strings and horns sustain an E♭-major and C-minor triad, respectively, the vibraphone puts forth a series of three minor triads: A minor, F♯ minor, and C minor.

The use of a vibraphone in an orchestral work (Carpenter introduces it at three before ⑯) was itself somewhat daring, for it marked one of the earliest such instances of its kind. Although not the first score to request a vibraphone (Loeffler earned that distinction in 1930 with his *Evocation* for orchestra and female chorus, first performed in 1931), *Sea Drift*—in anticipation of Milhaud's *L'Annonce faite à Maire* (1933) and Berg's *Lulu* (1934)— might have been the first orchestral work actually to require one (Loeffler allowed the piano to substitute for the vibraphone). Before this, the vibraphone, an American invention of the late 1910s, had been used primarily by jazz bands; consequently, the inclusion of the vibraphone in *Sea Drift* established some continuity with Carpenter's use of banjos and saxophones in his works from the 1920s.

Frederick Stock and the Chicago Symphony premiered *Sea Drift* on 30 November 1933, on a program that included works by Beethoven, Corelli, Mozart, and Moszkowski. Stock performed it again later that season on 23 January 1934. The music's relation to Whitman's poignant poetry eluded Edward Moore, who referred to Carpenter's "pleasant" work as a "tone poem of marine serenity" (Moore's review was even titled "Stock Closes Holiday with Happy Concert"). Nor did Moore find anything—not even the use of the vibraphone—new; rather, the work was "based . . . on [the composer's] earlier technical manner, and developed with the same color and skill which for a long time has been his habit."[4]

Werner Janssen and the New York Philharmonic gave the New York premiere of *Sea Drift* on 8 November 1934 at a historic concert: the first time an American-born conductor led the New York Philharmonic. Having earned good notices in Europe (especially for his Sibelius), Janssen was appointed for one brief season (1934–35) conductor of the New York Philharmonic, along with Toscanini, Klemperer, Lange, Rodzinski, and Walter. Janssen presumably thought it appropriate to offer some American music on the occasion of his New York debut, and *Sea Drift* was a logical choice: a recent work by a leading American composer and one that would naturally interest a Sibelius expert, as the aforementioned resemblance to *Swan of Tuonela* suggests.

According to Lawrence Gilman, the concert was a "triumph" not only for Janssen but for Carpenter: "This music is charged with the sensibility of those dreamers and visionaries who have watched the fading out of the sun from a day that is irrecoverable, and who can tell us of its decrescent loveliness only in music and in words that are charged with a deep nostalgia of the spirit—who, with Whitman, listen 'long and long.'" Leonard Liebling similarly praised the piece as a "work of unusual imagination and power, rich in beauty and effect."[5]

Janssen subsequently performed the work many times. He conducted it in Rochester, New York, in 1934, in Los Angeles in 1937, in Baltimore in 1938, and in Rio de Janeiro in 1941. The reviews were positive. In Rio the *Vanguarda* wrote that *Sea Drift* "enchanted the audience," and the *Diario de noticias* agreed that Janssen projected the work "with intense color, getting everything out of it."[6]

Artur Rodzinski (1894–1958), who may well have heard Janssen's New York debut, performed *Sea Drift* himself with the Cleveland Symphony on 23 and 25 January 1936. During his Cleveland years (1933–42), Rodzinski and his wife, Halina, developed a close friendship with John and Ellen Carpenter, regularly entertaining one another in their respective cities. When Rodzinski gave the American premiere of Shostakovich's *Lady Macbeth of Mtsensk* on 31 January 1935, Halina sat in a box with "friends from Chicago"—the Carpenters and Charlie and Claire Dux Swift. (Did Carpenter chat with George Gershwin, who also attended this performance?) In 1947 Carpenter and Swift helped Rodzinski obtain the directorship of the Chicago Symphony after four stormy years with the New York Philharmonic (1943–47); the Carpenters even arranged for the Rodzinskis to live near them. According to Halina, Ellen Carpenter gave Rodzinski the tour of the Auditorium Theatre that precipitated his attempts to move the symphony out of Orchestra Hall, one of the reasons cited for his dismissal from the orchestra after only one season. The Rodzinskis in no way associated the Carpenters with their various misadventures in Chicago, however. Halina and Ellen, with their mutual interest in Frank Buchman and the MRA movement, remained particularly close, and Rodzinski continued to champion Carpenter, whom he named alongside Copland and Barber as "one of the best" American composers.[7]

Robert C. Marsh's description of Rodzinski resembles Carpenter enough to suggest the kind of common ground between the two men: "Rodzinski was a great musician, a wonderful, imaginative, inspired performer, a champion of all that was new and constructive, and for those who knew and loved him, a powerful force in the cause of selfless artistic integrity. Deeply religious in certain periods of his life, he was convinced that you had to dedicate yourself to something beyond yourself and self-interest. Life acquired meaning if you gave yourself to a cause."[8] A taped performance of Carpenter's *Seven Ages* by Rodzinski and the New York Philharmonic documents the kind of sensitive understanding the conductor brought to Carpenter's music.[9]

Carpenter repeatedly urged Koussevitzky to perform *Sea Drift* in Boston, originally suggesting a December 1933 premiere. Koussevitzky, however, turned down all such requests, usually by asking Carpenter for a "new" work, as in this request of November 1935: "I was hoping that you would have a new work completed, the performance of which you would be willing to entrust to me. Forgive my frankness, but I still hope my 'intuition' has not deceived me." Carpenter persisted nonetheless, and on 14 December 1935 the composer importuned, "I am still hoping and praying for Sea Drift." This seems to have been the end of it, however.[10]

The exchange of letters with Koussevitzky over *Sea Drift* was not the first time Carpenter pressed his cause so hard: he showed similar determination when Diaghilev equivocated about *Skyscrapers* and after Koussevitzky suggested a recording of *Skyscrapers* but never followed through. In fairness to the composer, he was led along in all three instances—or perhaps he just failed to understand a Russian's way of saying no. Why would Koussevitzky—a great Carpenter champion—turn down an orchestral work as accomplished as *Sea Drift*? Perhaps, like Virgil Thomson, he preferred the composer's wittier, more vivacious music.

By the late 1930s Carpenter had begun to think about revising *Sea Drift,* and in 1940 he suggested some cuts to Vladimir Golschmann, who had conducted the work with the St. Louis Symphony Orchestra. "When I was rehearsing 'Sea Drift,'" Golschmann replied, "I had the feeling that a little cut would have detracted in no way from the general impression created by your beautiful composition."[11] Carpenter finally revised *Sea Drift* in 1944. As he did in other—though by no means all—revisions undertaken during the 1940s, the composer made relatively minor alterations, including slight changes of orchestration, and added pickups to themes that had previously started on the downbeat, such as those beginning at ③ and ⑥.

He also made three cuts: (1) the twelve-measure transition, beginning at ⑧, that preceded the work's second section; (2) thirteen measures, from three after ⟨22⟩ to two before ⟨24⟩, in the fifth section; and (3) the Trionfalmente part of the fifth climax (the music picked up with the Nobilmente music at four before ⟨28⟩). As with his abridged "The Lake" from the 1941 revision of *Perambulator,* Carpenter simply stitched the remaining music together without any obvious loss of continuity, though again, one might feel an occasional abruptness.

Unlike the cuts for "The Lake," however, Carpenter could not have had the goal of simply shortening the work, because the cuts were so small, and the piece was not very long to begin with. He obviously was dissatisfied with these passages. Significantly, the first two cuts sequentially developed material in ways that, on reflection, might have sounded like padding. As for the third, much more dramatic cut of a final, triple fortissimo transformation of an important theme, Carpenter possibly thought this passage extravagant and out of keeping with the work's otherwise subdued tone.

The premiere of the revised *Sea Drift* by Rodzinski and the New York Philharmonic on 5 October 1944 introduced the work to many new listeners. Virgil Thomson compared and contrasted it—not unfavorably—with sea music by Debussy and MacDowell:

> It is less . . . the direct rendering of a marine subject, as in Debussy or MacDowell, than the meditations of a gentleman seated by the sea. The work recalls MacDowell in its water-colorish daintiness. . . . But MacDowell had a way of evoking landscape through the rhythmic contour of his thematic material that was more immediate in its communication and more objective than Mr. Carpenter's charming but essentially personal lyricism.[12]

Thomson correctly intuited—as any consideration of the work's relation to Whitman would corroborate—that *Sea Drift* was more "meditation" than "landscape."

Lou Harrison seemed to miss this point when he called *Sea Drift* "regulation ocean music" missing only "the passing pirate ship . . . and the mermaid." The work, he wrote, sounded "vaguely like *La Mer* with the big tunes left out."[13] (Considering the cut Trionfalmente melody, Harrison was closer to the truth than he knew.) Harrison's review suggested that by this time readers of *Modern Music* could be counted on to find Carpenter somewhat ridiculous.

In contrast, Percy Grainger could hardly praise *Sea Drift* enough. In a letter composed one day after the revision's premiere, Grainger expressed his enthusiasm and admiration for the work:

To my ears, it is your most beautiful work; everything that modern music should be—a tally of the moaning, soaring sounds heard in nature, with man's compassionate response to these. It is a perfect mirror of the American soul—tender, musing, wistful; yet not weakened by uncertainty (as sensitive art too often is). On the contrary, it is highly strong, rich and assertive.

To fill a big tonal frame with these soaring, moaning sonorities seems to me one of the hardest of all musical tasks, and one of the most progressive, for to take the voice of nature into man's heart seems to be the instinctive goal of Nordic man. Thus your "Sea-drift" appears to me not merely as a superbly flawless piece of art, but as a deeply up-heartening symbol of the nobility and humanity of its race, age and place.

On the technical side I marvel at its orchestration—orchestration in which no instrument or instrumental group (no color "effects") is outstanding, but in which the composer's consummate skill has sufficed (as Bach's in the first chorus of St. Matthew Passion, for instance) to weld the shrewish orchestra into a blended unity capable of baring the composer's soul.

Grainger further told the composer that he and his wife, Ella, were planning on attending the Sunday matinee in order to "repeat this soul-satisfying experience." *Sea Drift* was, Grainger concluded, "a high-water mark of Nordic soul-revelation and of musical and spiritual progressiveness."[14] Some months later Grainger once again wrote to Carpenter, "I can never fully say what a soul-searching impression I had in hearing your Sea Drift at the Philharmonic and how keenly I look forward to presenting this (in my opinion your noblest orchestral work known to me) masterpiece in Australia as soon as possible."[15]

For Grainger, *Sea Drift* apparently satisfied (among other things) the racial notions he was then cultivating, including the idea that "the best music by Nordic composers (in Germany, Scandinavia, the Netherlands, France, England, America, etc.) seems *to me* better (more complex, more soulful, more peaceable) than the best music of non-Nordic composers."[16] In later years, however, Grainger complained that unlike Grieg, Debussy, Ravel, Fauré, Respighi, and himself, who had all "divorced ourselves from the filthy Sonata-Symphony form," Carpenter and Cyril Scott had joined Sibelius, Nielsen, Parry, and Franck in crawling "on their knees" to the Germans ("the murderers of our young men, not once, *but repeatedly*") by "accepting a German form once more."[17]

The revised *Sea Drift* was also performed by Désiré Defauw and the Chicago Symphony, Vladimir Golschmann and the St. Louis Symphony,

Tauno Hannikainen and the Duluth Symphony, and Werner Janssen and the Janssen Symphony of Los Angeles, where, wrote the conductor, it "made a deep impression."[18]

Leonard Slatkin performed *Sea Drift* with the Chicago Symphony on 1 November 1990 during the orchestra's one-hundredth anniversary season. "When the Chicago Symphony said they wished to present pieces that they had premiered," Slatkin recalled, "I asked for a list and selected this piece. I had never heard it before but found it very rewarding and hope to include it on programs in other places."[19] In their reviews both John von Rhein and Robert C. Marsh deemed the work "lovely" and noted resemblances to Delius. Marsh further thought this performance "an important revival."[20]

Sea Drift was recorded twice: by Karl Krueger and the Royal Philharmonic Orchestra and by Julius Hegyi and the Albany Symphony Orchestra.[21] Paul Snook preferred the latter performance: "Hegyi gets much more pulse and power out of *Sea Drift* than the late Karl Kruger's loving but somewhat limp perusal."[22] Hegyi also followed Carpenter's complex changes of tempo more closely than had Krueger. Neither reading, however, seemed totally convincing in its handling of Carpenter's intricate cross-rhythms and enharmonically drenched harmonies.

Sea Drift remained an esteemed work throughout the second half of the century. In a 1951 overview of Carpenter, Howard Hanson claimed it as his personal "favorite":

> Here Carpenter reveals not only his descriptive powers, of which we are well aware, but an emotional depth of which we had not always been conscious. . . . What sensitive listener who heard it will ever forget that translucent sound at the end where muted horns, low strings, and vibraphone combine the sonorities of four keys with such delicate beauty that one strains one's powers of hearing to prolong the sheer ecstasy of sound. Carpenter's "Sea" may be less sunny and less brilliant than Debussy's, but it is also more profound, more tragic, and more mysterious.[23]

In his 1973 discussion of *Sea Drift,* Christopher Palmer, like Hanson, evoked *La Mer* to make distinctions. He heard "occasional echoes of *La Mer,* but its Impressionism is unashamedly harnessed in the service of romantic nostalgia. The shoreline it delineates is essentially Wagnerian, not Debussian."[24] Noah André Trudeau possibly remembered Palmer when he similarly wrote, "Although the title and rhapsodic mood of this work superficially suggest the influence of Debussy, it is shaped by deeper Wagnerian currents."[25] Given

Carpenter's admiration for Wagner and the romantic love-death imagery of Whitman's "Out of the Cradle" (not to mention the poem's boy hero who can understand birdsong!), some connection with Wagner was perhaps only to be expected.

More like Grainger, Paul Snook noted that "the influence of Carpenter's studies with Elgar can be discerned in its [*Sea Drift's*] quasi-Anglican, post-impressionist evocation of a multi-hued, ever-changing seascape."[26] Nicholas Tawa concluded, however, that "despite the critics' diligent search for hints of Debussy, Delius, and Vaughan Williams, the composition sounds more like itself than like any other work."[27]

CHAPTER TWENTY-ONE

From the Piano Quintet to "Morning Fair"

1934–1935

In the winter of 1934 the Carpenters left for Algeria, sailing from Boston on 27 January and arriving in Algiers in early February. One month later, from his quarters at the Bordj Polignac, Carpenter wrote to Koussevitzky that he and Ellen were enjoying the "marvelous sunshine."[1] They returned to Èze-Village before sailing home from Gibraltar on 14 April.

With its winding streets, dazzlingly white villas, tropical palms, and Moorish architecture, Algiers had long been an exotic, chic retreat for wealthy Europeans and Americans. The 1930s witnessed what has been called the "false apogee" of French colonial rule in Algeria: "Modern hygiene and security were among the benefits introduced, and to the passing observer or the tourist who went to Biskra in the footsteps of Gide, an unruffled prosperity and cartesian order reigned in the midst of exotic mystery and color; by some miracle Versailles had been built in the Garden of Allah."[2]

Algiers and its cosmopolitan mix of Berbers, Arabs, Jews, Turks, and Moors inspired Carpenter. He quickly composed a Quintet for Piano and Strings, writing the first movement between 8 and 26 February, completing the second movement by 4 March, and finishing the last movement on 24 March.

A few days later, on 4 April, Carpenter informed Elizabeth Sprague Coolidge, "I finished last week . . . a new *piano quintette,* which is clamoring to be dedicated to you."[3] Coolidge accepted the dedication and agreed to the composer's suggestion that the work be premiered at the Pittsfield Festival by the festival's South Mountain Quartet, which consisted of Louis Persinger, Edwin Ideler, Conrad Held, and Willem Willeke.

Carpenter hoped that Harold Bauer (1873–1951), the London-born pianist renowned for his performances of piano quintets by Schumann, Franck, and Brahms, would play the piano part. As Carpenter explained to Coolidge, he had met Bauer "once or twice last summer down on the North Shore and he urged me to experiment in the piano quintet form." Bauer's participation—as opposed to his own—would also provide "a much needed opportunity to hear the composition myself in a perfectly detached way."[4] He eventually acquiesced, however, to Coolidge's request that he perform the piano part himself: "I will do the best I can with it but I hope that it will fall on a cool day and my fingers will not stick to the keys."[5]

Carpenter first aired the quintet at a small, informal party in Chicago in June, with himself at the piano and Stock playing the viola part. He apparently made a few changes in the score after arriving at Pride's Crossing in early July, because the score ends with the words "Algiers-Pride's Crossing."

Carpenter's last major chamber work, the Piano Quintet culminated a distinct line of musical thinking that went back to the 1897 Piano Sonata and continued through the 1911 Violin Sonata and the 1927 String Quartet. Its overall form similarly unfolded a pleasant first movement, an introspective slow movement, and a vigorous finale marked by reminiscences of the preceding movements. The quintet's language was more than ever the composer's own, however; the earlier suggestions of Schumann and Chopin, Franck and Busoni, and Berlin and Stravinsky were sublimated to the point that the music sounded particularly individual. Carpenter himself must have recognized the music's quintessential character, for he periodically returned to this work in one way or another for the rest of his life.

Although the Piano Quintet never won much attention from the public or critics, it nonetheless became the subject for the only extensive scholarly analysis of a single Carpenter work, namely, Gregory Burnside Pike's 1981 doctoral thesis on the quintet and its subsequent revisions.[6] Pike's exhaustive analysis of the original 1934 quintet (published by Schirmer in 1937) argues, above all, that the work's melodic ideas—including subsidiary material—derive from a few scant motives, possibly even a single one.[7] The "flow of the melodic line is accomplished by constant intervallic and rhythmic variation," Pike concludes.[8] Indeed, his interpretation of the quintet's three movements as a sonata, variation, and rondo, respectively, demonstrates the difficulty, if not downright futility, of interpreting Carpenter's late music according to classical forms. One cannot even identify principal thematic material, let alone map out a sonata form, with certainty.

Pike's analysis of the first movement as a sonata—a slow introduction in the dominant (A major), consisting of two principal ideas (mm. 1 and 10, respectively); an exposition (☐2 to ☐9) containing a first, second, and closing theme (at ☐2, ☐3, and the piano part four measures after ☐8, respectively); a development (☐9 to ☐14); and a recapitulation (☐14 to the end)—works best until the so-called recapitulation, at which point Carpenter develops material in ways barely distinguishable from the so-called development. Moreover, at four before ⬛16 he arrives at a new syncopated idea—related to his Spanish style—in C♯ major, which he subsequently elaborates and develops, until at ⬛19 it reaches bitonal disintegration. At ⬛20 Carpenter does, indeed, return to the main theme in the tonic, but he recalls only the theme's initial fragment. The whole section, only about forty measures long, is more like a final cadenza or coda than a recapitulation.[9]

This first movement arguably is less like a sonata than like the ABCA movements that open the composer's Piano Concertino and String Quartet. The A section would conform to Pike's exposition, the B to his development, and the C and A to his recapitulation. As in the Piano Concertino and String Quartet, the C section serves as a whimsical, scherzolike interlude, and the return of A provides a coda.

Except for the introduction and conclusion, most of the Piano Quintet's first movement is in $\frac{5}{4}$, although Carpenter occasionally uses $\frac{3}{4}$ and, at one point (⬛18), $\frac{4}{4}$ for added intensity. The composer's expert handling of $\frac{5}{4}$ represents the full flowering of a lifelong fascination with this meter. The movement especially explores the ambiguity generated by changing groupings of 2 + 3, 3 + 2, 1 + 2 + 2, and 2 + 2 + 1; such rhythms help identify the work's American character.

With its swaying $\frac{6}{8}$ rhythms, the Andante that follows is, in contrast, more like a barcarole. Again, the music's form defies schematic interpretation, despite Pike's argument for an elaborate three-part variation form.[10] The slow movements of the String Quartet and other earlier works suggest that Carpenter may well have intended a tripartite design for the quintet's Andante, though of a different and, in a way, simpler kind than that put forth by Pike. This alternative approach would agree with Pike that the first section ends at the Più animato. The second section, however, would consist only of this faster section, and the third section would begin at the Lento, which returns to the mood and tempo of the opening. This results in a somewhat different ABA ternary design: A (up to ⬛25), B (from ⬛25 to four before ⬛27), A (four before ⬛27 to the end, with a coda, initiated, perhaps, after the D♭ cadence two measures after ⬛29).

Two harmonic features of this slow movement warrant special comment. First, Carpenter periodically states a subsidiary theme (at ⬛24, four before ⬛27, and two before ⬛30) that exploits minor seconds. Doubled at the octave and played loudly, these bare minor seconds are rather daring for Carpenter, notwithstanding the rich, triadic chords that soon after enter to clarify their tonal significance. Although related—indeed, derived—from other secondal harmonies (see, for example, the music at [23]), the intensity of these particular seconds helps make this subsidiary theme, in Pike's words, "the musical heart of the entire work."[11] Indeed, Carpenter returns to this theme at the very end of the last movement.

Carpenter's correspondence with the composer John Becker sheds light on these biting, secondal harmonies, so characteristic of the composer's late style. While discussing the sulfa cure prescribed to him for strep throat in 1937, Carpenter wrote, "strep-bugs = C♯, sulfa-cure = C♮." In other letters he identified the minor second, C–C♯, with modern music, telling Becker that he was "hard at work on something new, something extra C–C♯," or that he had "a few C–C♯s inserted for your special benefit." For Carpenter these harmonies accommodated both self-expression and experimentation.[12]

A second noteworthy harmonic feature of the Piano Quintet's slow movement is the final six-note chord, consisting of the pitches D♭–G–F–B(C♭)–B♭–E♭ (ex. 46). The harmony makes sense as a superimposition of the movement's opening G dominant seventh harmony over a tonic D♭, a highly evocative chord that recalls jazz's practice of tritone substitution. But Pike identifies the harmony as a transposition of the famous "mystic chord" (C–F♯–B♭–E–A–D) that underpins many of Scriabin's later works, including *Prometheus* (1910). Carpenter's spacing and doubling seems more jazzy than Scriabinesque, but given the chord's unexpected prominence, one assumes that Carpenter had Scriabin's sonority specifically in mind. Carpenter possibly studied this mystic chord with Ziehn, who was fascinated with the full spectrum of harmonic possibilities. Stock also had a special interest in Scriabin; the Chicago Symphony programmed *The Divine Poem* nearly every year throughout the 1920s and 1930s and performed *Prometheus* in 1914, 1930, and 1937.[13] Considering other aspects of Carpenter's life and work—for instance, his ties to fin de siècle symbolism, his affinity for Russian art, Ellen's attraction to Theosophy and Dane Rudhyar, and the light notation in *Skyscrapers*—a kinship to Scriabin should not surprise.

Ellen Carpenter once stated that the Piano Quintet contains a tune that she and her husband had heard sung by five natives during an after-dinner walk in rainy Algiers.[14] She presumably meant the last movement's quasi-primitivist main theme; initially stated in the piano at measure 9, the theme consists of only four notes (D♯–E♯–F♯–C♯). Carpenter had long featured exotic styles in the finales of his abstract works. This theme is merely a later and more refined example. Moreover, as in the earlier finales, the exotic

EXAMPLE 46.   Carpenter, Piano Quintet, second movement, concluding five measures.

element eventually dovetailed into American styles (which accorded with the composer's ideas about their interrelatedness).

The North African tune, with its C♯–G♯ drone, suggests at times a modal (Mixolydian) C♯ major and, at other times, C♯ minor (ex. 47). (That this C♯-centered portion of the finale has a key signature of four sharps suggests a partiality to C♯ minor.) C♯ major/minor, however, proves only a link from the second movement's D♭ major to the C-major tonality that concludes this final movement. As the Andante moves from the first movement's D major to its own D♭ major, so the finale moves from the Andante's D♭ (C♯) major to its own C major.

Pike's interpretation of this movement as an ABACA rondo is plausible,

EXAMPLE 47.   Carpenter, Piano Quintet, third movement, piano, mm. 9–15.

even though the movement hardly conforms—either thematically or tonally—to the classic rondo. After the exotic C♯-major section, Carpenter introduces, at eight after ⧈35, a slower, more introspective B theme in B minor
that looks back to the first movement's introduction—quite literally, in fact,
at four after ⧈37, at which point Carpenter moves to B major. He abruptly
returns to the African tune in C♯ major at ⧈38 and arrives, via E minor, at G
major for a new *giocoso* theme stated by the cello (theme C) at ⧈42.

Carpenter states the main theme, now in B minor, for the last time (⧈45)
and quickly heads for C major. At ⧈48, in what might be considered a coda, he
returns to the slow movement's impassioned minor-second theme. For the
very end he adds D♭s to the concluding C-major triads, thus incorporating
both the slow movement's minor seconds and the finale's C♯-major/C-major
conflict.

The South Mountain Quartet and Carpenter premiered the Piano Quintet at the opening concert of the 1934 Pittsfield Festival on 19 September.
(Carpenter received five hundred dollars for the performance.) The *New York
Times* thought the quintet "an architectural monument" compared only with
the Sonata for Violin and Piano by Eichheim on the same program, writing
"that the work would have gained had the composer been as consistent in the
choice of the decorative color he applied to its building—its harmonic colors
and idioms—as to its buttresses and timbers." The *New York Herald Tribune*
found the work "somewhat uneven" in its "saliency of inspiration and effectiveness in the treatment of its material." And the *Boston Evening Transcript*
deemed the quintet "amiable music but, in straightforward American, nothing to write home about."[15] Moses Smith contended that the Piano Quintet's
poor reception was due to hasty preparation (though, in fact, Carpenter and
the South Mountain Quartet had been in rehearsal as early as 15 August), but
he praised Carpenter's performance; the composer "played as a virtuoso, not
as one of that curious genre, the 'composer-pianist's."[16]

The work apparently received a better performance some months later
when the Boston String Quartet and Jesús María Sanromá performed it in
Boston on 23 January 1935. The reviews, nonetheless, were only marginally
better; indeed, the *Boston Herald* posted a particularly harsh critique. Although the quintet had "surface charm in spots," it remained "a singularly
commonplace piece. Its imitation of a Spanish atmosphere in the last movement and in part of the first reminds one of some gim-crack Hollywood
hacienda. Moreover it is not at all evident why the composer wrote it for a
piano quintet, since it is not especially suited to the combination. Indeed, its
obviousness might go better in some larger arrangement."[17] Pike suggests

that this particular review might have encouraged Carpenter to arrange the quintet later for orchestra.

Carpenter performed the work again with the Mischakoff Quartet (Mischa Mischakoff, Samuel Thaviu, Milton Preves, and Daniel Saidenberg) on 10 February 1935 at an Arts Club concert. Sanromá also played the work again, this time with the Coolidge Quartet, at a Coolidge-sponsored festival in Mexico City in July 1937. Carpenter regretted having to miss it.[18]

Although Carpenter devoted his later years mostly to revising and arranging earlier works, no other composition preoccupied him—one might even say, obsessed him—like the Piano Quintet. He made extremely minor revisions for its publication in 1937 and then wholly rewrote it as his Second Symphony in 1941–42. In 1946–47 Carpenter revised the quintet, and in 1947 he reworked the Second Symphony. And he left among his papers yet another version of the quintet, this one incomplete. Not counting the changes made for the 1937 publication, this totals four completed versions (two of the quintet and two of the symphony) and one unfinished version of essentially the same work.

Pike's thesis closely compares the completed and incomplete versions of the Piano Quintet. A discussion of these revisions can wait until we have considered the intervening Second Symphony, although we might mention here Pike's conclusion that the published version of the Piano Quintet is superior to its later revisions, along with his hope that "so fine an American work as the original 1934 version will one day earn international acceptance as a vital contribution to the standard chamber music repertoire."[19]

In late 1934 and early 1935, Carpenter composed what were essentially his last songs. In August 1934 he wrote two songs, "Rest" and "The Past Walks Here," that he paired under the title *Songs of Silence*. In December of that year, he set three children's songs: "If," "Worlds," and "The Pools-of-Peace." And in January 1935 he composed his swan song, "Morning Fair."

Carpenter found Mabel Simpson's "Rest" in the September 1925 issue of *Dial*, and Virginia Woodward Cloud's "Past Walks Here" (originally titled "An Old Street") in the *Boston Herald* of 23 August 1934. (Carpenter often clipped out and saved poems.) Both poems featured the kind of melancholic, symbolist imagery that had earlier attracted Carpenter to Lord Alfred Douglas, Paul Verlaine, Mildred Howells, and Helen Dudley: In Simpson's cemetery landscape, the dead keep their secrets and sleep silently as the hedges, willow tree, and "folded rose" share "in the tender dream of death." In Cloud's poem the past walks by noiselessly and alone, "unseen forevermore, save by some heart who, in her half-closed door . . . listening, remembers, half in fear."

Although both songs recall the refined, lush elegance of the composer's prewar songs, they at the same time contain harmonic and tonal novelties, including a preponderance of clusters in the piano accompaniment: not only the ubiquitous seconds of "Rest" but more complex tone clusters of three and even four notes. Moreover, both settings contain modal ambiguities of one sort or another and conclude tremulously in midair; the final harmony of "Rest" (A–B–C♯–E♭–G–F♯) is particularly striking. Stylistically, these songs belong to the world of the composer's 1933 *Sea Drift,* which similarly takes death and remembrance as its subject matter.

"Rest" is the stronger of the two songs and perhaps the most perfect of the composer's late songs. Carpenter's setting of the six-stanza poem betrays only vestiges of his old predilection for ternary form. In the first two stanzas, he depicts the silent cemetery with luminous seventh and ninth chords and the kind of chromatic sequencing long his earmark. In the middle two stanzas, the music becomes more sentimental and diatonic for the willow tree and the rose, with a gentle, syncopated figure in the piano accompaniment to suggest, ostensibly, the wind. And the fifth stanza returns roughly to music more like that of the opening, accelerating to an exquisite climax on the word "heard" (ex. 48). But for the sixth stanza, Carpenter returns to music reminiscent of the middle section, thus linking the tender dream of the rose and the secrets of the dead in a way the poem cannot do by itself.

In contrast, Carpenter matches the one long stanza that makes up "The Past Walks Here" by writing, essentially, one long, highly parlando melody accompanied in the piano by music that portrays the "walking" past. Carpenter's setting nonetheless suggests a modified binary form: the first half, in a modal C♯ minor (the key signature has three sharps), depicts the noiseless past; the slower second half, which begins in A major and then wanders modally until it reaches its surprising conclusion in B major, portrays the rememberer. As in such earlier sad songs as "Il pleure dans mon coeur," Carpenter makes use of pedal tones throughout.

While Carpenter mostly revised Cloud's original text in characteristic ways (changing "knockers are silent" to "the street is silent," adding the word "gentle" to the phrase "some lilac bush a [gentle] breath blows sweet," and, more dramatically, changing "the voiceless street—Looks forth and sighs" to "the voiceless past—Looks forth and sighs"), he took unusual license with the poem's ending by omitting its final, climactic line, *"It is too late for laughter or for love."* The composer might have reasonably felt that this final sigh was

EXAMPLE 48.   Carpenter, "Rest," mm. 25–31.

too melodramatic, but thus edited, the text seems somewhat pointless and the song, for all its exquisiteness, correspondingly unsatisfying. Carpenter himself might have concluded that "The Past Walks Here" was an inferior song, for he never published it. Instead, he published "Rest" initially by itself in 1934 (as *Songs of Silence*, I) and then with "Morning Fair" as *Two Songs for High Voice and Piano* in 1936.

Significantly, both Mabel Simpson and Virginia Woodward Cloud—the poets of "Rest" and "The Past Walks Here"—also wrote children's poetry. Carpenter instinctively or intentionally set verse by poets who—whether Blake, Wilde, Stevenson, or Lindsay—also wrote, as he himself did, for children.

With the three songs "If," "Worlds," and "The Pools-of-Peace," Carpenter actually returned to children's verse. He possibly wrote them specifically for his granddaughter, Rue (b. 1932), whom he adored, and perhaps for some of Ellen's young grandchildren as well.[20] (Indeed, December was a time when the family gathered together for the holiday season.) Apparently he intended these songs as a set—at least Schirmer published them as such.

All three songs explore, with some didactic intention, a child's fantasy world. Mabel Livingston's "If" asks, "Oh, would not it be funny, and would not people stare / If feathers grew on children, and geese had golden hair! / If ships sailed on the meadows and houses on the sea, / And ev'rything were diff'rent / from what it ought, *it really ought to be!*" Aileen Fisher's "Worlds" also depicts two frames of reference: the adult world, which is as "high as a bird can fly," and the child's world, which is as "high as the willowtree." Joan Campbell's more lyrical and introspective "The Pools-of-Peace" similarly juxtaposes the "dusty ways of noon" with the sleepy, nocturnal "pools-of-peace."

With their subtle melodies and rich, Brahmsian accompaniments, these songs—like the *Improving Songs*—could appeal to adults as well as to children. But the days of Kitty Cheatham and Tom Dobson were bygone. Who would sing such songs in concert now? The young composers of children's poetry on the horizon—like Irving Fine—cultivated a more ironic, brittle style and let such older traditions evolve as they would in the Hollywood of Shirley Temple and Judy Garland.

These songs, in fact, highlighted the composer's enduring Edwardian sensibilities. Carpenter even thought about an *Alice in Wonderland* ballet as late as the 1940s, an idea Robert Edmond Jones dissuaded him from by suggesting "something absolutely fresh."[21] Had he written an *Alice* ballet, the music would have had some of the topsy-turvy character of "If," with its insistent motives in free inversion and its tonal contradictions (the final, unexpected B-major triad even has a C♮).

Such a ballet would have also had a sweetness like "Worlds." This song portrays the vast grown-up world by way of, among other things, long notes both high and low. The child's world is slower and softer, with stepwise motion, although Carpenter saves the song's highest note, F♯ (poised over a subdominant harmony), for a climactic depiction of the child's willow tree.

On the other hand, "The Pools-of-Peace" is the stuff of fairies and magic dust (Carpenter forgoes, however, Campbell's stanza about "Winds-of-Dream" and "Elfin lands");[22] it sooner suggests James Barrie than Lewis Carroll. The composer even airs the long-shelved whole-tone scale at the mention of "the minstrels of the Moon."

Like the composer's art songs from the 1930s, these children's songs, as old-fashioned as they are, could not be taken for his prewar music. Their liveliness and vitality have a certain modernity, for example, the jazzy string of seventh chords that so cleverly portray the world's width and length in "Worlds."[23] Perhaps the composer learned something from Shirley Temple, after all.

*   *   *

Carpenter composed his setting of James Agee's "Morning Fair" (originally titled "Sonnet XX") in January 1935. The discovery of Agee was a happy one, for the poet's mystic, romantic bent more or less accorded with the composer's own tendencies. Carpenter discovered the poem in Agee's one book of verse, *Permit Me Voyage,* first published only a few months earlier, in October 1934, when the poet was only twenty-four years old. Carpenter may have learned about Agee from his friend Archibald MacLeish, who wrote the book's laudatory foreword.[24] But as with his earlier attraction to Langston Hughes, Carpenter's immediate response to an unknown poet many years his junior revealed more generally his finely tuned literary instincts. He selected from Agee's volume a sonnet that "can stand comparison with any but the greatest in our language," according to a later pronouncement by Robert Fitzgerald.[25]

A spiritual, disembodied, almost religious love poem, "Sonnet XX"— "Now stands our love on that still verge of day"—resembles Carpenter's love letters to Ellen. The poet compares his love—"new found and unaroused, appareled in all peace and innocence"—to the dawning earth, to "this morning fair." Carpenter's setting seems a little weighed down by the poetry's metaphysics, but Agee's language is so mellifluous and his imagery so lovely that one can hardly blame the composer for his leisurely dwelling on almost every syllable.

The song's spontaneous, unusual form takes its cue from the poem: a first section that arrives, climactically, at the dawn; a second section that describes the "pureleaved air"; and a third section that compares "this morning fair" to the poet's love. Sections 1 and 2 begin with the same melody, which, like a refrain, appears in the third section, but now in the middle of a phrase. The music's far-flung chromaticism (which has its debts to Chopin and Wagner) heightens its elusive form. The first section moves from D major to an ambiguous E major, the second section from D♭ major to E major, and the last section from E major to D♭ major.

Carpenter could not have known that "Morning Fair" was to be his last art song, but it satisfies romantic expectations of what a last song should be: slow, autumnal, full of deep humanity and tenderness. Its broad emotional range encompasses the bold fortissimo climax at the phrase "burnished in the dawn," the heart-melting sentiment of "So stands our love," the almost religious humility of "Appareled in all peace," and the final, emotional outburst at "this morning fair." The song achieves unity by means of relaxed $\frac{3}{4}$ rhythms in the vocal line and two-note, rocking figures in the piano (features that also characterize "The Pools-of-Peace").

"The Past Walks Here," "Rest," and "Morning Fair" all require a larger voice range than do most Carpenter songs, including the 1934 children's songs. Although the tessitura of these songs often lies quite low, just above middle C, at other times it hovers around high G. "Rest" calls, moreover, for an A and B above that (though the composer offers an optional note for the B). Carpenter possibly wrote these songs specifically for his friend, the German American soprano Claire Dux Swift.

None of Carpenter's songs from 1934–35 achieved anything like the popularity of his earlier ones. In contrast, Samuel Barber, who during these years overtook Carpenter as America's foremost art song composer, enjoyed special success with his Agee settings: "Sure on This Shining Night" (1938) and "Knoxville: Summer of 1915" (1948). "Sure on This Shining Night" (also from Agee's *Permit Me Voyage*) even resembled "Morning Fair" in its lyrical $\frac{3}{4}$ melody, its luminous piano accompaniment, and its romantic nostalgia. Carpenter himself recognized Barber as a composer who "exemplifies my own line of musical thinking."[26] And Barber would have been familiar with Carpenter's songs, including those sung by his aunt Louise Homer.

But Barber (and many of his listeners) did not identify with Carpenter's music. Carpenter's atmospheric "Morning Fair" derived from Debussy and Strauss, whereas the lean dissonances and simple triads of "Sure on This Shining Night" (not to mention the canon in the piano accompaniment) spoke a language closer to Poulenc and Distler. Carpenter's setting might well have been the more interesting, but Barber's had an alienated edge that probably came closer to the poet's intentions. In any case, the new generation that MacLeish spoke of in his foreword to *Permit Me Voyage* was Barber's, not Carpenter's.[27]

CHAPTER TWENTY-TWO

Danza and the Violin Concerto

1935–1936

Carpenter especially liked Peking when he toured Asia with Rue in 1931, and in February 1935 he sailed with Ellen across the Pacific to revisit the Chinese capital.[1]

The Carpenters first stopped in Japan, where they contacted some persons recommended by their close Chicago friends George and Mary Langhorne. Iwanaga of Rengo was "not only useful," wrote Carpenter to Mary, "but chummy, and in a strange burst of confidence said—'Yes, Saito is a good man, but he talks too much'" (Makota Saito was prime minister of Japan from 1932 to 1934). Similarly, Prince Iyesato Tokugawa (1863–1942) "was splendid and put me in the way of musical things that may be very useful."[2] After the war, upon hearing that a Tokyo group was interested in producing *The Birthday of the Infanta,* Carpenter fondly recalled this visit to Japan, stating that he had "brought back . . . many happy memories and a deep interest in Japanese cultural values."[3]

In late March the Carpenters reached Peking: "Everything seems more beautiful than ever," the composer wrote to Mary, "and to arrive here in a blaze of warm sunshine with the air full of fruit blossoms, and the hills saying—'To Hell with Japan' in every curve, gives the spinal column something to remember."[4]

In 1935 Peking stood on the edge of cataclysmic change: the Japanese were poised, for the time being, in Manchuria, and the civil war between the nationalists and communists transpired mostly to the south. As with Algiers, Peking's twilight colonial years exerted a strong appeal to Westerners. "Here," observes Barbara Tuchman, "the old mandarin class mingled with venal adventurers, the new China throbbed with plans and hopes of reform, foreigners lived a charmed, hedonistic existence and the silent Altar of Heaven lay in eternal marble perfection open to the sky. . . . Besides diplomatic corps and journalists, educators and missionaries, the capital attracted art collectors and sinologues, travelers who came through and never left, and retired foreigners who settled here from choice because life was gracious and placid and money went far."[5]

Carpenter's friends John Marquand and Harriet Monroe shared the composer's affection for the city. On his arrival in Peking in April 1934, Marquand wrote, "I just got here this morning, but that is long enough to realize, even for a cynic like myself, that Peking is the most beautiful and delightful city in the world." Marquand compared the Forbidden City ("something as strange and dramatically marvelous as anything I have ever seen") to Versailles, and the Temple of Heaven to the Chartres cathedral.[6] Monroe, who also visited Peking in 1934 after an absence of twenty-four years, noted that the city had "a greater awareness of the modern world," yet still,

> for me it was the same grand old town. . . . The crenellated Tartar Wall lift-
> ing its towers, the Chien-men looming up grandly before me with the little
> animals guarding its new-moon curve of yellow roofs, the mixture of races in
> the crowds, the rikshas, bicycles, camels, donkeys, primitive carts, shiny mo-
> tors, threading through the wall's deep archways; then the long drive
> through the streets with their low half-open shops, their sidewalk peddlers
> squatting before little stocks of goods or goodies arranged in rows on the
> papered ground, their peripatetic cooks carrying little ovens full of steaming
> cakes or meats for coolie customers; and finally the narrow *hutung* leading to
> a Chien-Lung home with its flowering courts and beautiful lofty rooms—all
> this brought back the oriental glamor which I had almost lost the scent of.[7]

The Langhornes had suggested that the Carpenters stay at the Tranquil Abode of the Humble Heart, a fashionable Peking establishment operated by Monroe's sister Lucy Calhoun. Calhoun had joined her husband, the diplomat William H. Calhoun, in Peking early in the century. A few years after his death in 1917, she turned "one of the rich old temple palaces of Peking" into a hotel for wealthy, sophisticated visitors.[8] Carpenter affirmed in a letter to Mary Langhorne that "the house and the whole menage are perfect,—full of lovely spirit and comfort. . . . In our entrance court, there is a marble tablet resting on the back of an ancient turtle, and on the tablet is inscribed a Chinese proverb which says:—'Enjoy yourself, for it is later than you think'— which isn't bad medicine, perhaps, for us New Englanders."[9] Lucy Calhoun had moreover furnished his quarters with a Bechstein grand.

While in China, Carpenter met up with Arthur Rubinstein, who gave a concert in Peking (which Rubinstein, like Marquand, thought "one of the most beautiful and interesting cities in the world") before an audience made up entirely of Westerners. After the recital Carpenter showed Rubinstein "everything worth seeing in the old Chinese capital," including the Forbidden City, "previously forbidden during the reign of the Chinese emperors, but now very accessible to tourists." Rubinstein was even more impressed with the beautiful Chinese women with their long skirts slit up on one side "so at every step you saw a well-shaped leg and thigh."[10]

The Carpenters also visited the provisional capital Nanjing, where they were entertained by the American ambassador Nelson Johnson, an unpretentious diplomat who "possessed a wide if not profound knowledge of China."[11] Johnson even hired a hiwa player for the occasion. Carpenter plausibly sympathized with the ambassador's support for Chiang Kai-shek.

Although this was Carpenter's last trip to China, he retained a great interest in the country. "He's especially well informed about conditions in the Far East," commented his tailor in the early 1940s.[12] By 1951 he feared an impending war between the United States and China, stating, "We've always liked the Chinese so much—they're so much like us, really."[13] How fitting that his 710 Rush Street home should survive among the steel and glass of postwar Chicago as a fashionable Chinese restaurant, the Peapod.

According to Rubinstein, Carpenter had taken a home in Peking "to work peacefully on his new compositions." The composer himself informed Mary Langhorne in April that he was "already, for better or worse, back to work."[14] Carpenter further stated in his program notes to his *Danza* for piano (composed in August 1935) that this "little piece was an offshoot from a larger work based on Oriental musical idioms on which I have been engaged ever since a visit to China last spring. In the course of the larger work I found myself toying with the following idea, which seemed to set up such a persistent irritation of its own, that I finally gave it its head and used it as the principal rhythmic germ of *Danza*."[15] In a letter dated 13 November 1935, Carpenter similarly told Koussevitzky, "I have occupied most of my time, since returning from the Orient last spring, on a larger work probably for the stage."[16]

Carpenter never completed this "larger work," however, although it possibly evolved into something like the 1936 Violin Concerto. The only composition that one can trace to his time in Peking is *Danza*.

Danza recalls the traditional Spanish *danza* not only in its melodies and rhythms but in its marked contrasts between vigorous and languorous sections. The composer may well have taken his inspiration from flamenco and other popular Spanish dancing (throughout the 1930s the Chicago Arts Club showed special interest in Spanish and Latin American dance troupes), but he plausibly also learned something from de Falla and Joaquin Turina (1882–1949), whose brilliant *Danzas fantásticas* (1920) were particularly successful. At the same time, *Danza* contains its own kind of jazzy vigor and wit. Carpenter himself considered "the melodic and rhythmic content" to be "a mixture of Spain and America."[17] In the tradition of his two other dances for solo piano—*Polonaise américaine* and *Tango américain*—the composer could have titled the work "Danza américaine." The music presaged, above all, Copland's *Danzón cubano* of 1942.

Danza has some relation to Chinese music as well: its main "idea," after all, derives from a "work based on Oriental musical idioms." This idea is apparently the Allegro brioso motive found in measure 2 in the right hand (after the arpeggiated upbeat). A three-note anapest (E–E–F, soon varied to E–G–F), this motive seems related to Chinese music, though used here, obviously, at the service of a flamenco-like idiom (ex. 49). Chinese touches appear elsewhere as well, as in the pentatonic fourths introduced five measures before the end. The resultant synthesis reflects the unusual circumstances of an American writing a Spanish *danza* based on Chinese materials!

Carpenter introduces his main *brioso* idea boldly, harmonized by the kind of astringent minor seconds previously noted in the Piano Quintet's slow movement. As in the quintet, the ensuing harmonies clarify the composer's tonal intentions, although here the minor second, E–F, is retained even as the harmonic context shifts from D minor to C♯ major/minor, suggesting a new application of Ziehnian plurisignificance. Following this dramatic opening, Carpenter arrives at an *espressivo* melody in D major (beginning in m. 10). One hesitates at labeling this the "main theme," for even though the simultaneous arrival of a tuneful melody and the principal key suggests as much, the work does not subsequently develop this particular idea (in contrast, say,

EXAMPLE 49. Carpenter, *Danza*, mm. 1–3.

to the opening *brioso* motive); indeed, this *espressivo* theme never reappears, although the last three *grazioso* pages contain music somewhat like it.

Less than five minutes in length, the highly compressed *Danza* comprises six sections: a spirited, somewhat rounded Allegro brioso opening, with its dramatic minor-second idea and its *espressivo* theme in D major; a sultry Pochissimo più lento that modulates from D minor to D major; a rhapsodic Più lento, largely in E (Phrygian), that briefly returns to the *brioso* idea at its end; a more romantic Lento version of this melody, interrupted by faster episodes (moving from A major to C minor); a suspenseful Moderato that modulates through E♭ minor and E minor; and a return of the *brioso* idea and, in varied form, the *espressivo* D-major melody, now alternately waltzlike and jazzy. The ubiquitous *brioso* rhythm gives this episodic structure some unity, and with careful attention to the music's melodic flow, *Danza* can sound like an inspired rhapsody.

Carpenter's own assessment of the work was characteristically modest: "I do not think that it is more than a mile deep," he told John Becker, "but I believe that it has a good deal of punch and perhaps some of the thing that you call 'folk quality.'"[18] *Danza* arguably stands as Carpenter's masterpiece for piano nonetheless. Within its small dimensions, it explores a wealth of ideas and sounds. According to Thomas Pierson, *Danza* "distills and sums up" the composer's entire pianistic output.[19]

In September 1935 Carpenter orchestrated *Danza,* using the wood block and castanets, as well as harp and xylophone glissandi, to provide additional "punch." The lovely Pochissimo più lento melody he scored for cellos and oboe doubled at the octave. He also used the piano extensively, although frequently doubled by woodwinds or harp.

Stock and the Chicago Symphony premiered this orchestrated *Danza* on 5 December 1935. Koussevitzky introduced the work to Boston on 17 January 1937; Otto Klemperer gave the work's Los Angeles premiere on 4 March 1938. Stock performed *Danza* as the concluding number of a set that included *Little Dancer* and *Little Indian,* both orchestrated by "an arranger in the employ of Schirmer." Although Carpenter touched up these orchestrations, he could not recommend them to Koussevitzky "excepting as a means of solving what otherwise might be a problem [of programming *Danza*]. A better solution might possibly be to use some short piece of Albéniz, Granados, or some other Spanish composer as a companion piece."[20]

Koussevitzky, however, had his own ideas. He programmed *Danza* at the beginning of the concert's second half, followed by Mendelssohn's

Scherzo from *A Midsummer Night's Dream,* Debussy's *Prelude to the Afternoon of a Faun,* and Wagner's Prelude to *Die Meistersinger von Nürnberg.* The *Boston Globe* commented that the concert proved that "good things come in small packages."[21]

In 1943 Carpenter offered yet another solution to the question of programming *Danza* by orchestrating two other piano pieces: *Polonaise américaine* (in February) and *Tango américain* (in March). Putting the "Polonaise" first, the "Tango" second, and "Danza" third, he titled this new compilation *Dance Suite* (1943).

Hans Kindler and the National Symphony premiered *Dance Suite* on 3 November 1943. After studying the score, Kindler thought the work "superb," although he suggested "a slight Busoni-Paderewski rallentando-crescendo" at the end of the "Polonaise."[22] Carpenter had a chance to argue with Kindler about tempos during rehearsals just before the premiere (the composer wanted them faster). At one point, after Kindler refused his suggestions, Carpenter said, "Perhaps a middle course."[23]

"The suite was enthusiastically received," reported one Washington paper. "The piquancy of themes is matched by original color combinations," stated another.[24] Jerzy Bojanowski, who had already played *Danza* with the Tulsa Symphony in 1940, presided over the Chicago premiere of *Dance Suite* with the Chicago Symphony.

Meanwhile, the original piano version had languished in manuscript. In 1939, upon hearing that Rudolph Ganz had "dusted off my old [Violin] Sonata," Carpenter sent him the unpublished piano version, "which has had some performances in its orchestral arrangements, but has never been used publicly by any pianist. . . . If it should interest you as an encore piece, I would be delighted."[25] Ganz might well have given the original piano version its first public performance. In 1946 pianist Helmut Baerwald began to perform the work from manuscript, including a Town Hall performance on 15 November 1946; he also featured it on an extensive South American tour from April to September 1947. Baerwald told the composer that each time he played *Danza* "it was very effective and was received successfully."[26] He had some suggestions, nonetheless: octave tripling in measures 4–7 and an octave lower for the B♭–D♭ ostinato on page 6.[27] Carpenter incorporated these suggestions for the 1947 Schirmer publication.

Although Carpenter did not extend the "dance suite" concept to his piano originals, recitalists might find it similarly useful and appealing to program the *Polonaise américaine, Tango américain,* and *Danza* as a set. Or they might consider *Danza* as an encore piece, as the composer himself suggested.

*   *   *

In 1936 Carpenter wrote a Concerto for Violin and Orchestra for the Croatian violinist Zlatko Balokovíc (1895–1965). Carpenter started work on the concerto in Èze-Village in March and completed it in Beverly in September. He dedicated the work to Ellen.

Described by Adlai Stevenson Jr. as a "very outgoing, debonair, dashing figure," Balokovíc studied at the Zagreb Conservatory and at the Vienna Meisterschule, where his teachers included the Czech virtuoso Otakar Ševčík. From an early age Balokovíc toured extensively throughout the world, including a New York debut in 1924. Two years later he married Ellen's sister-in-law Joyce Borden amidst suspicions that his motives were largely mercenary.[28]

The Balokovícs settled in New York but often traveled; in fact, the Carpenters may have vacationed in Èze-Village on their recommendation (Ellen kept on good terms with her former sisters-in-law). In 1931 the Balokovícs took a yearlong world cruise from San Francisco to New York skippered by Joyce and a crew of eleven; Balokovíc practiced on board five hours a day and gave concerts along the way. His wife made him presents of two rare Guarneris and a Stradivarius.

Balokovíc was at his height when Carpenter wrote this concerto for him. Notwithstanding an occasional complaint about the smallness of his sound, reviews of the Violin Concerto (which Balokovíc played from Los Angeles to Istanbul) agreed that his performance "was one of winning tone and technical brilliance, very much alive and brimful of enthusiasm."[29] In Los Angeles, Carl Bronson described Balokovíc as a "very great virtuoso."[30]

As with his ballets from the 1920s and his symphonies from the 1940s, Carpenter seemed aware of current trends with his concerto: violin concertos were in the air in the 1930s, as evidenced by those by Stravinsky (1931), Malipiero (1932), Syzmanowski (1933), Berg (1935), Prokofiev (no. 2, 1935), Sessions (1935), Schoenberg (1936), Miaskovsky (1938), Bartók (no. 2, 1938), Hill (1938), Barber (1939), and Piston (1939). Carpenter's foray, however, seemed more like his only other concerto—the 1915 Piano Concertino—than like any of these other works; it similarly unfolded a jazzy first movement, a dirgelike second movement, and a sprightly finale.

The Violin Concerto, however, is so personal and idiosyncratic that even resemblances with the Piano Concertino appear fairly remote; indeed, the work's three principal sections, played without pause, are not separate movements per se. Accordingly, the following discussion refers to these three sections by their principal tempo indications, namely, Allegro, Lento, and

Moderato (measure and rehearsal numbers refer to Schirmer's 1939 arrangement for piano and violin).

The Allegro opens with an introduction that contains two principal motives: the first, *robustamente,* is a vigorous, syncopated, fanfarelike figure cast in two measures of $\frac{3}{4}$ (ex. 50); the second, *gioioso,* is also syncopated but consists of two measures of $\frac{3}{2}$ and $\frac{3}{4}$, respectively (ex. 51). Although the former idea explores rising fourths and the latter idea features repeated notes, both share, as a basic pitch source, a major second and a minor third contained by a perfect fourth (e.g., D–E–G, mm. 7–8). While this pentatonic fragment might well be related to Carpenter's involvement with Chinese music, it also suggests popular American idioms, like Jerome Kern's "Ol' Man River."

Nearly all of the concerto's material derives from the introduction's two related motives. For example, the "main theme" of the Allegro—a *grazioso* melody played by the violin at ②—derives from the *robustamente* motive, while the hemiola accompaniment in the orchestra stems from the *gioioso* idea. Like the main themes of the Piano Quintet and *Danza,* the *grazioso* melody is pointedly understated; that it arrives not in G major as might be expected but in an insouciant Eb major makes it all the more disarming.

The transitional passage that follows the *grazioso* theme (nine after ② to six before ④) illustrates Carpenter's mature use of sequential technique. Although he sequences a four-measure idea six times (each statement consisting, essentially, of two measures of a major harmony and two measures of a diminished harmony), he disguises this sequence so ingeniously that one is hardly aware of it as such. The principal melody—played by the violin—changes from statement to statement, often cumulatively, so that the passage

EXAMPLE 50.　Carpenter, Concerto for Violin and Orchestra, Allegro, mm. 1–3.

EXAMPLE 51.　Carpenter, Concerto for Violin and Orchestra, Allegro, mm. 7–8.

actually sounds like an improvisation. Carpenter further obviates sequential regularity by continually varying the orchestral texture and by unpredictably modulating through double flats and double sharps—from E♭ to F to A to B♭ to B to D♭, before reaching the movement's dominant, B♭. This hypersensitive use of sequence (made more so by dynamic swells, cross-rhythms, and accelerating tempo) imparts a thrilling and somewhat unsettling quality to the music. In the concluding Moderato, indeed, certain sequences—the nine repetitions of the idea stated by the solo violin at ㉙ or the sixteen statements of the orchestra's major thirds at ㊴—seem rather wild.

Similarly, the concerto's larger form takes us to the edge, if not actually over it. Felix Borowski's careful, accurate summation of the work's form into one long paragraph for the Chicago Symphony's program book perforce strikes one like incoherent ramblings.[31] Even more than the Piano Quintet, the Violin Concerto's elaborate nooks and crannies defy clear-cut prose summary.

The Allegro is perhaps best understood as an exploration of the two aforementioned rhythmic ideas—the *robustamente* and the *gioioso*—initially set forth in what we might call the introduction. The material after ②—the Allegro proper—suggests an ABA′ form. The first A section is itself tripartite: the presentation of the *grazioso* main theme and the arrival of the dominant after the sequence described above (to six before ④), a delightful *ben ritmato* contrasting theme (back in the tonic E♭ major) that explores the *gioioso* rhythm (to four after ⑤), and a return of the *grazioso* theme, which moves from the tonic to D major (to ⑦).

The B section (from ⑦ to ⑪), *feroce,* exploits the shifting meters of the *gioioso* motive. The dark, vaguely primitivist music recalls Carpenter's Eastern-inspired music; the orchestration here highlights timpani, snare drum, bass drum, cymbals, and wood block. Much of this section's B♭-major tonality features, moreover, modal inflections.

The reappearance of the *grazioso* theme in E♭ major at ⑪ marks the return of A′. Rather than the extensive sequence described above, Carpenter introduces a new, abbreviated sequence at nine after ⑪, featuring expressive seventh chords in the orchestra. The music, still exploring the *grazioso* idea, moves to G minor (nine after ⑫), A♭ major (⑬), and, finally, C major (⑭ to the movement's end). This C-major coda stands in contrast to the preceding music: the rhythm is more overtly waltzlike, the harmony is much more diatonic, and the sentiment is tender and whimsically childlike. Indeed, this coda suggests a refuge back into childhood. The coda concludes open-endedly with a C augmented triad in the orchestra pitted against the violin's high C (c^3).

Like the Allegro, the Lento, in ABA form, begins with an introduction, made up of a single chromatic line (here scored for English horn and, later, oboe) that is almost twelve-tone. The $\frac{6}{4}$ meter and G♯-minor key signature at five measures after ⟨17⟩ mark the start of the first A section. The doleful ostinato in G♯ minor recalls not only the slow movement of the Piano Concertino but "Bydlo" from Musorgsky's *Pictures at an Exhibition,* while the *dolce,* pentatonic figuration above makes one wonder to what extent the composer's Peking work made its way into this composition.

The solo violin finally enters at ⟨19⟩, at the start of the contrasting B section. This B section, itself arched, consists of one long cantilena in B major (ex. 52). Beautifully suited to the violin, this expressive melody is cast mostly in a gentle $\frac{3}{4}$, accompanied by sweet appoggiaturas in the orchestra not unlike those found in the 1934 children's song "Worlds." The melancholy, G♯-minor A material returns at two before ⟨22⟩, now in $\frac{4}{4}$ (as opposed to $\frac{6}{4}$) and embroidered by a countermelody in the solo violin. The work begins to head back to B major at two after ⟨23⟩ but then dissolves into a kind of far-flung chromaticism reminiscent of late Chopin.

The short Animato that follows in the orchestra (seven before ⟨24⟩ to ⟨24⟩) can be viewed as a codetta to the Lento: like the end of the Piano Quintet's slow movement, this brief Animato brings the Lento to rest quietly with a personal rendering of Scriabin's mystic chord, here using the Russian composer's original pitches (C–F♯–B♭–E–A–D). This second use of the mystic chord confirms its importance to the composer.

The Violin Concerto concludes with a long, complex finale. Carpenter had explored this kind of cyclic ending—in which the finale proper is followed by reminiscences of previous material—as early as the 1911 Violin Sonata (the violin, in fact, appears to have inspired his most rhapsodic and

EXAMPLE 52.   Carpenter, Concerto for Violin and Orchestra, Lento, ⟨19⟩, mm. 1–5.

romantic impulses). But here the finale proper, consisting of the Moderato from ⟨24⟩ to ⟨29⟩, is a mere fraction of the ensuing reminiscences, which constitute nearly one-half of the entire concerto!

The Moderato begins with a cadenza for the solo violin that represents a third version of the music that had introduced the Allegro and the Lento. Arriving first at A major and then at D major, this introduction prepares the finale's main theme, a vigorous, giguelike idea stated by the solo violin in G minor at ⟨25⟩. The polyrhythmic texture—the violin in $\frac{4}{4}$ divided into triplet eighth notes, the orchestra in $\frac{4}{4}$ divided into triplet quarter notes—recalls the hemiola of the earlier *grazioso* theme.

Like the Allegro and the Lento, this Moderato is also in ABA or, at least, rounded form. At ⟨26⟩ the solo violin initiates the B section with a majestic, fortissimo melody in D♭ major derived from the *gioioso* music (m. 7): not the repeated-note motive that Carpenter uses so extensively in the Allegro but rather that motive's countermelody. This grand melody, which can be called the "majestic" theme, plays a crucial role later in the work.

The giguelike music returns at eight after ⟨26⟩ and eventually cadences, at ⟨28⟩, back in G minor. The solo violin follows with a short cadenza, coming to rest on a B♭ trill. Neither the giguelike music nor the G-minor tonality has any particular importance for the remainder of the concerto.

The rest of the concerto consists of varied thematic restatements. Despite the helpful precedence of such cyclic works as his own Violin Sonata, Carpenter's intentions here are especially elusive. Is this concluding section a cadenza? a coda? a recapitulation? a fourth movement? some combination thereof? The sheer size of this section—nearly half the entire concerto, as mentioned—seems to militate against viewing it as a coda or cadenza. And yet the music's quicksilver reminiscences of previous themes—passing impulsively through different tempos and keys—do not suggest a recapitulation or a new movement either.

Whatever one might like to call it, this concluding section can be outlined as follows (to avoid confusion, the work's previous sections—Allegro, Lento, and Moderato—are referred to as the first, second, and third movement, respectively):

1. Lento, ♩ = 60 (⟨29⟩): cadenza-like material derived from the end of the third movement in the solo violin, against fuzzy harmonies related to the mystic chord in the orchestra.

2. Moderato, ♩ = 88 (three after ⟨30⟩): climactic arrival of the mystic chord voiced in anticipation of the bitonal harmony ahead.

3. Allegro molto, $\bullet$ = 160 (five after ③): the *robustamente* motive in a bitonal C-major/G♭-major setting reminiscent, at times, of *Petrushka*.

4. Moderato, $\bullet$ = 72 (③): triumphal statement of the *robustamente* motive in G♭ major.

5. Lento, $\bullet$ = 60 (two before ③): *molto espressivo* version of the majestic theme in C major.

6. $\bullet$ = 80 (③): alternation of the first movement's *feroce* material and the majestic theme, largely in C major.

7. Poco più lento, $\bullet$ = 60 (three after ③): *appassionato* return of the Chopinesque material from the end of the second movement.

8. $\bullet$ = 160 (③): *robustamente* and other first-movement material developed in an exotic setting.

9. Largamente, $\bullet$ = 63 (③): big arrival of the majestic theme in D major.

10. Animato molto, $\bullet$ = 168 (three before ③): brief interruption.

11. $\bullet$ = 63 (two before ③): alternation of the majestic theme and a new *carezzando* melody reminiscent of the composer's *Diversions,* no. 5.

12. Lento, $\bullet$ = 48 (④): calm, broadened version of the majestic theme in A major, followed, similarly, by a *tranquillo* version of the second movement's main theme.

13. Animato, $\bullet$ = 168 (④): development of the first movement's *robustamente* and *grazioso* themes, occasionally with polytonal inflections, moving principally through G♯ major/A♭ major and F♯ major before fragmenting and disintegrating altogether.

14. A tempo, $\bullet$ = 152 (④): the childlike music from the first movement's coda, now in A major, followed by more development of the *robustamente* motive.

15. Con moto, $\bullet.$ = 63 (four after ④): arrival of the *grazioso* theme in its original key, E♭ major.

16. $\bullet$ = 90 (④): sequential development of first-movement material.

17. Molto brioso, $\bullet$ = $\bullet$ (five after ④): climactic version of the *robustamente* motive similar to the Moderato above (no. 4), but now alternately in D♭ major and E♭ major.

18. ♩ = 60 (⟨48⟩): majestic theme in E major.

19. ♩ = 54 (four after ⟨48⟩): brief transition.

20. ♩ = 44 (⟨49⟩): closing melody and a final restatement of the second movement's main theme in C major, with a lingering G♭, played by the vibraphone, against the final C-major triad in the strings that recalls the Scriabinesque and Stravinskian harmonies explored earlier (see nos. 1, 2, and 3, especially).

In addition to the kind of flux suggested by this outline, one finds numerous tempos and meter changes within each of these sections. The concluding portion (no. 20) alone contains nineteen rallentandos (or allargandos), six accelerandos (or stringendos), and no less than seventy changes of meter!

Although such cyclic forms have their origins in late Beethoven and the Romantics, the Violin Concerto takes this tradition so far as to create something extremely personal. More than any other work by Carpenter, this concerto presents something new in the area of form and rhythm. Indeed, its musical "stream-of-consciousness" features an originality comparable to the more highly publicized novelties of *Krazy Kat* and *Skyscrapers*.

The Violin Concerto uses a rather large orchestra: two flutes, two oboes, English horn, two clarinets, two bassoons, four horns, trumpets, three trombones, tuba, celesta, harp, glockenspiel, cylinder bells, piano, vibraphone, timpani, snare drum, oriental drum, bass drum, cymbals gong, and wood block. The composer's inventive orchestration matches his formal daring; he scores one passage (⟨28⟩), for example, for solo violin and oriental drum (an idea that might have stemmed from his interest in Chinese music). Similarly delicate, though more typical, is the long passage from ⟨38⟩ to ⟨42⟩ scored, primarily, for solo violin, harp, celesta, flutes, oboe, clarinets, and strings. Carpenter further controls the number of strings playing at any given time by designating certain passages "tutti" and others "solo" (meaning four desks of first and second violins, three desks of violas and cellos, and two desks of basses).

Before the premiere of the Violin Concerto, the Carpenters spent the summer in Sweden, where they rented the house of some English friends. They returned in late September on the SS *Manhattan* with their friends Artur and Halina Rodzinski. Rodzinski must have told an interested Carpenter about the "remarkable reception" he had just had with the First Symphony of the twenty-seven-year-old Samuel Barber at the Salzburg Festival.[32]

Balokovíc premiered the Violin Concerto with Stock and the Chicago

Symphony on 18 November 1937. The Chicago critics agreed that this was possibly Carpenter's finest work to date. "Carpenter has given the musical world many important symphonic works," wrote Herman Devries, "none more original nor of greater value than his latest output." "The work is one of Mr. Carpenter's strongest, because it has an extreme rhythmic vitality," claimed Eugene Stinson. "To my ears," wrote Claudia Cassidy, just beginning her long career as Chicago's preeminent music critic, "the Concerto shares with 'Adventures in a Perambulator' the distinction of being Mr. Carpenter's finest work. . . . It sings, but not in the broad line of magnificence nor in the flowing gleam of romanticism, but rather in a world of its own, and our own, where a man may brood duskily on life and, at the same time, stand aloof and comment, with some piquant glee, upon his own absurdity."[33]

Thus, Cecil Michener Smith inaccurately represented the work's reception when he stated in *Modern Music* that the piece was "so prolix in form and lacking in freshness of thematic material that its principal favorable publicity in Chicago was on the society pages."[34] By this time, however, the stereotype of Carpenter as a wealthy dilettante had begun to take hold in certain quarters.

Balokovíc proceeded to play the Violin Concerto in numerous cities around the world. He performed it again with Stock in Milwaukee on 6 December 1937, where the local critics gave it rave reviews, and with Otto Klemperer and the Los Angeles Philharmonic on 20 January 1938. Carpenter attended this latter performance, about which one critic reported, "Klemperer's orchestral accompaniment of the Carpenter concerto was superb and Carpenter paid the orchestra many compliments."[35] On 24 February Balokovíc performed the concerto with Rodzinski and the Cleveland Orchestra, prompting a somewhat mixed review from Herbert Elwell: "There are so many attractive things about this concerto that one shrinks from making reservations. . . . It leans a little heavily on the idioms of the international school of ballet composers, whose glamorous epoch in the early part of this century is already dated."[36]

Balokovíc subsequently took the concerto abroad, giving performances in Yugoslavia, Greece, Czechoslovakia, and Turkey. On 10 May 1938, in Belgrade, Yugoslavia's King Peter II awarded Carpenter the Medal of St. Sava (the patron saint of Serbia), thanks, no doubt, to the intercession of Balokovíc and the king's art-loving regent, Prince Paul.

Back in the States, Balokovíc performed the concerto with Koussevitzky and the Boston Symphony both in Boston (on 3 and 4 March 1939) and in New York (9 March 1939), and then with Jerzy Bojanowski and the Tulsa Symphony on 30 July 1940. Carpenter attended the Boston performances, and on the day before the New York premiere, he wrote a short note to Koussevitzky in which he mentioned that he intended no change of tempo at ⁴⁶, and that the tempos at ³⁷ and ⁵⁰ were "a bit too broad." "I hate to speak of these comparatively small things," he continued, "for in all the important details and in general outline and feeling your performances were deeply satisfying to me and I am truly grateful."[37]

The Boston and New York critics tended to be less impressed than those from the heartland. The young Leonard Bernstein, for example, lost patience with the composition:

> The Carpenter work started out as if it were going to be exciting, and got steadily drearier, cloudier, more involved, and fancier (bells, Oriental drum, vibraphone, et al.) until the pianissimo ending found several good friends of modern music asleep in their stalls. The fault lay, probably, in the lack of any significant thematic material, which lack precluded any immediate recognition of thematic development. As the piece progressed (or as time progressed) one was conscious of many small sections which sounded mutually irrelevant, all plunged into a romantic bath perfumed with Debussyan orchestration. There were moments when one sat up, interested, desperately hoping for more of the same, to be rewarded only with some tone-row or other expertly dressed up with nowhere to go.[38]

Musical America similarly reported that considering the music's "one-movement form and lightweight material," the concerto was too long to rivet attention. The *New York Herald Tribune* complained about the music's "discursiveness" and "diffuseness." Even the usually sympathetic Grace May Stutsman faulted the work for diffuseness: "Mr. Carpenter is usually more terse. In this instance he seems to have been unable to point a period to his story when the tale was told." She suggested that he edit it.[39]

Not all the Boston and New York reviews were negative, however. Oscar Thompson considered the work a landmark in the violin concerto repertoire. And in 1946 Hugo Leichtentritt suggested that the work needed "full admission to the rather small repertory of modern concertos of our leading violinists" in order to prove itself, although he predicted that this was not likely to happen: "Even the most famous soloists are not too eager to burden themselves with a new, difficult work of a problematic character, even if such a work should be uncommonly interesting."[40]

CHAPTER TWENTY-THREE

The First and Second Symphonies and Other Revisions and Arrangements

1936–1947

Carpenter had wanted out of George B. Carpenter and Company at least as early as 1924. By the time the Carpenters finally negotiated a sale in 1936, the firm, which had long been losing money, was valued more for its downtown real estate than for anything else.[1] The Astrup Company—a nationwide distributor of awning fabrics and finishing supplies—acquired controlling interest in the company, which kept its old, venerable name until 1978, when it merged with Astrup, becoming one of that company's divisions. At the time of its dissolution, Carpenter and Company was the second oldest corporation in the city of Chicago.[2]

After retiring in the fall of 1936, Carpenter devoted the remainder of his life largely to revising and arranging earlier scores. Described by Ellen as "the most painstaking and meticulous worker in the world—never content with the results of his composition,"[3] he had often wanted to revise one or another work throughout his career. As he told Carleton Smith: "I have never failed to suffer a revulsion after finishing a work. Well, no, that is not altogether true. Most often, however, I am convinced I could do each work better if I could only do it over again."[4] Carpenter only had time, however, to revise a few works, such as his 1934 revisions of *Gitanjali* and the two Havet songs, "Les Cheminées rouges" and "Le Petit Cimetière." Now, with more time on his hands, he looked for every opportunity—typically, some upcoming performance—to rewrite his music, especially his larger works for orchestra. These efforts at revision are listed below chronologically, with the original year of composition in parentheses:

1936   *Song of Faith* (1931)
1937   *Song of Faith* (1931, rev. 1936), Piano Quintet (1934)
1938   *The Birthday of the Infanta* (piano four-hands) (1918)

1940   First Symphony (1917), *Krazy Kat* (1921), *The Birthday of the Infanta*
        (ballet score and Suite no. 1) (1918/1929)
1941   *Adventures in a Perambulator* (1914)
1944   *Sea Drift* (1933)
1947   Piano Concertino (1915), Piano Quintet (1934, rev. 1937), Second
        Symphony (1942)

Aside from the recently completed Violin Concerto (1936), the only major orchestral work that Carpenter did *not* revise during these years was *Skyscrapers*.

In reworking his scores, Carpenter tended toward cutting material, deleting quotations, adding pickups, lightening textures, and fine-tuning details of tempo and dynamics. But his revisions ranged nonetheless from relatively minor alterations (as in *Song of Faith* and the Piano Concertino) to significant cuts (as in *Adventures in a Perambulator* and *Sea Drift*) to extensive rewriting (as in *The Birthday of the Infanta* and *Krazy Kat*).

Schirmer was reluctant to publish these revisions, and relations between publisher and composer became strained.[5] Schirmer would suggest that their well-to-do client help defray the costs for new scores, and the composer—equally, if not more shrewd in business matters—would hold the publisher to this or that contractual clause, becoming sore and frustrated, as evident in a letter to Nathan Broder at Schirmer, dated 20 December 1947:

> For the past *seven* or *eight* years, as our correspondence will show, I had
> been nagging Schirmer for an effective solution of the "Concertino" problem
> [putting out a revised score]. Only recently has any action been taken. The
> resulting new photostat scores will, of course, improve the situation some-
> what, but they are far from a first class job. . . . Furthermore, the cost of do-
> ing this work today is greatly in excess of what it should have been at the
> time I first raised the question. Under all these circumstances I feel strongly
> that I am entitled to a reconsideration by Schirmer of the question of what
> share of the two "Concertino" items above is properly chargeable to me.[6]

In the end Schirmer published only two of Carpenter's revisions—the 1937 *Song of Faith* and a piano arrangement of the 1940 *Krazy Kat*. For the most part they simply made photostats of the revised scores available for rental. Thus, the present confused state of affairs, in which, for the most part, libraries hold the original, published versions, while performances and recordings use the revised manuscripts.

*　　*　　*

In only one instance did a revision result in a thoroughly new work, namely, the revised First Symphony (Schirmer never published this particular work in either version). Deleting the work's original subtitle, *Sermons in Stones,* Carpenter never even referred to his 1940 score as a revision. One might accordingly refer to these two works as *Sermons in Stones* and the First (or 1940) Symphony, respectively (with the understanding that they are not totally different).

Carpenter revised *Sermons in Stones* partly in response to a request from Frederick Stock for a new work to help celebrate the Chicago Symphony's fiftieth anniversary. He started work on the revision in Santa Barbara in January 1940 and completed it in Chicago in April of that year. He returned to this work at a parallel moment in his nation's history—just before America's entry into a world war, offering further evidence that Carpenter originally wrote *Sermons in Stones* with the war in mind. His faith in Shakespeare's message—"strong are the uses of adversity"—remained stalwart, unshattered. He probably hoped once again that America could bring its native optimism to bear on European affairs, which had grown so dark. "At any rate," Carpenter said of the work, "it is peaceful music, and in these days, perhaps that is something."[7]

Carpenter recast the long, three-movement *Sermons in Stones* Symphony into an eighteen-minute, one-movement work. Shortly before the work's premiere, he stated: "Short symphonies, I believe, are in step with our times. As in everything else, people are in a hurry with their music. They can't wait for the old leisurely way of spinning out an idea."[8]

The new, one-movement First Symphony is in ABA form, with A and B containing material from the first two movements of *Sermons in Stones,* respectively. Carpenter barely uses any music from the finale of *Sermons in Stones,* with the exception of the coda, which in a new guise, similarly serves as a coda to the revised First Symphony.

The opening A section is itself tripartite, with sections that roughly correspond to the first, second, and fourth sections of the original first movement. In the first section of the new work, Carpenter uses three basic ideas found in, or at least derived from, the first section of the original first movement: the same first theme (m. 3; measure and rehearsal numbers apply to the score of the revised First Symphony); a new secondary theme, but one similarly pastoral in mood ([2]); and the same Largamente funeral march ([8]). Carpenter further substitutes a new Animato section with triplets ([4]) for the martial brass calls found in *Sermons in Stones.*

The second section begins at ⑭, at which point the composer states the ⁶₈ Moderato melody from the original second section. For the moment he skips the third section (Vivo) and concludes, somewhat like the original fourth section, by recapitulating the motto theme and the funeral march. But he presents them in reverse order: first the funeral march (⑲) in a dark C♯ minor (and not transformed à la Mahler into major) and then the motto theme (㉒) in the foreign key of E major.

Like the middle movement of *Sermons in Stones,* the B section of the 1940 Symphony, beginning at ㉙, is a scherzo with trio. Whereas Carpenter uses essentially the same scherzo theme for both works, he puts forth a new trio theme for English horn (㊷) that has a ripe, nostalgic quality characteristic of his later work (here reminiscent, too, of late Richard Strauss). He also thoroughly rewrites the return of the scherzo (㊿ to ㊽).

At ㊽ Carpenter returns to A by recapitulating that section's first two themes. Like the fourth section of the original first movement, the music is now in a clear C major. The new Animato triplet music returns, followed by the previously skipped-over third section—the Vivo waltz section, now marked Moderato but still *alla breve*. And as stated, Carpenter concludes with the kind of transformation of the motto theme found at the very end of *Sermon in Stones*.

As complicated as all this might appear, it only begins to explain the actual transformation of material from one work to another, for Carpenter essentially retains only themes, or sometimes only their basic shapes or moods. One perhaps best views the original *Sermons in Stones* Symphony as an old and very rough sketch for the 1940 Symphony.

In many ways the revised First Symphony is clearer and leaner than its predecessor, with less recourse to augmented chords, grandiose climaxes, and impressionistic orchestral effects. At the same time, the score is more modern in its choice of harmonies (e.g., the lingering flatted seventh in the glockenspiel at the end) and colors (e.g., the scoring for woodwinds, celesta, and harp in the "trio" section at ㊷). In short, the music belongs wholly to the composer's late style as represented by the Piano Quintet and *Danza*.

Carpenter dedicated the revised First Symphony to Stock, who premiered it on 24 October 1940, the first of ten new works commissioned for the jubilee year. The composer received $125 for the first two performances and $75 for three additional performances. Later in the season, after Stock had introduced the other commissioned works by Casella, Ganz, Harris, Kodály, Miaskovski, Milhaud, Sowerby, Stravinsky, and Walton, and was asked which jubilee works he thought "the most outstanding," he responded,

"They were all fine, but Milhaud, John Alden Carpenter, and Igor Stravinsky seem to have had the most appeal with the audiences."[9]

Time covered the premiere of the 1940 Symphony, complete with a photograph of the "suave, handsome John Alden Carpenter," actually looking rather gaunt but admittedly "smooth and well-dressed." The article disclosed a growing misconception about Stock and the Chicago Symphony: "The peaceful Chicago Symphony has never been notable for its interest in contemporary music," declared the unnamed author in total disregard for the facts. "For 36 years it has played sober classics under the benign baton of white-haired Frederick Stock." As for Carpenter's music, the article went on to state: "Composer Carpenter's new symphony was as smooth and well-dressed as Composer Carpenter himself. Orchestra Hall rang with polite applause; politely Composer Carpenter took three curtain calls. Critics, praising its tuneful themes, its crystal-clear orchestration, were polite too, found it one of the most gentlemanly of symphonies." *Time* further quoted local critics Edward Barry ("The end of the piece contains something as near to an apotheosis as a man of Mr. Carpenter's discretion would ever go. The music becomes broad and majestic and affirmative, only to drop off at the end in a charmingly deprecatory manner") and Claudia Cassidy ("Attractive with no apparent intent to be profound, call it a graceful compliment to the jubilee season") for *Time*'s own purpose, which apparently was to damn with faint praise.[10]

Barry had actually made greater claims for the work than *Time* suggested. The symphony, he wrote, possessed "moderation, urbanity, sensitiveness [and] a certain wistful delicacy," but it also seemed "graver and more profound" than some of Carpenter's earlier music. He especially admired "the remarkable evocative power" of the symphony's thematic material. And although the coda, which prompted applause before the final measure, seemed a miscalculation, he was unsure as to whether to blame the composer or the conductor.[11]

Percy Grainger's enthusiasm for the work, which he heard in Cincinnati, exceeded even Barry's: "It seemed to me," he wrote to the composer, "one of the purest, grandest, noblest, works ever penned. It seemed to me to 'tally' America—the prairies, the sweet tolerance, the grand calm of the USA." He complained only that the work seemed "too short" given its "immense (Walt Whitmanlike) . . . mood," claiming this brevity as characteristic of those countries with the "grandest scenery," like Norway and the United States.[12] Like most listeners, Grainger apparently was unaware of the work's history, but he instinctively put his finger on the music's fundamental contradiction:

the reworking of material from an expansive, romantic work for use in a significantly shorter and more streamlined one.

Stock and the Chicago Symphony brought Carpenter's revised First Symphony to New York on 22 November 1940, and then, in a British War Relief Society Benefit, to Boston on 24 November. The work received another round of good reviews. Francis Perkins observed that although the symphony was based on a much earlier work, it gave "no sense of heterogeneity of style. The idiom is consistent and individual"; this was "sincere and appealing music generous in melodic content, well knit and concise in form, ably wrought in its scoring and in the employment of its ideas."[13] In another New York review, James Whittaker wrote:

> Readily, he can remind you in music of Edna St. Vincent Millay in verse. Both writers have a charming faculty for flirtation with the common, not to say vulgar, without risk to their innate distinctions. Hearing the new and copiously melodic Carpenter symphony is like being dangled for twenty minutes over the edge of Jerome Kern without ever being dropped—though there are moments when only quick work with the rope and one ankle save us.[14]

Whittaker intuited the composer's high regard not only for Jerome Kern but for Edna St. Vincent Millay, whose poems "Renascence" and "God's World" he kept among his papers.

On 5 December 1940, only a few weeks after these New York and Boston performances, Bruno Walter (1876–1962) conducted Carpenter's new symphony with the Los Angeles Philharmonic. Walter had frequently toured the United States throughout the 1920s and 1930s, but now, a refugee from Vienna, he had moved permanently to New York and become a guest conductor at the Philharmonic and the Metropolitan Opera.

Carpenter initially contacted Walter in April 1940, inviting him to conduct opera in Chicago; although the two men had never met, Carpenter mentioned a close mutual friend in his invitation, violinist Zlatko Balokovíc, who spoke of Walter "with such affection and admiration." (Walter turned down the request because he would not have had enough preparation time.)[15] Carpenter subsequently sent Walter the score of his recently completed symphony and invited him to conduct it after Stock premiered the work in the fall. "If it proves interesting to you," Carpenter wrote, "that will be my sufficient reward." A few days later Walter replied to an "overjoyed" Carpenter that he would, indeed, like to perform the symphony.[16]

After he conducted the symphony—from memory!—with the Los Angeles Symphony, Bruno Walter wrote to the composer:

> I am very happy that I can report to you about the sincere magnificent success of your Symphony in both concerts. Not only the public received it with enthusiasm and long and genuine applause, the notices are splendid and what certainly will give you particular satisfaction, the orchestra loved the work and the men are full of praise. I personally can say that I was very earnestly impressed at first sight and my interest, my sympathy and my high appreciation have grown with every new contact; and—no small affair—the mastership of every detail of orchestration was a great pleasure for me.[17]

Considering his general indifference to American and contemporary music, Walter's enthusiasm for Carpenter was unusual. Similarly, Carpenter's letters to Walter revealed a special humility, even reverence; indeed, after the composer's death, Ellen told Walter that her husband had been among his most "ardent admirers."[18] Given certain traits and sensibilities that Walter shared with Stock and Rodzinski (including a high regard for Mahler), it was perhaps only natural that he and Carpenter would develop a similar rapport.[19]

In early 1941 Carpenter proposed that Koussevitzky premiere the revised suite to *The Birthday of the Infanta,* even though the conductor expressed a preference to play the symphony himself: "You know how much I admired it when I heard it done by your Orchestra," he wrote.[20] Koussevitzky never performed either work, however.

Subsequent performances of the revised First Symphony were given by Fritz Reiner and the Pittsburgh Symphony on 17 January 1941 and by Fabien Sevitzky and the Indianapolis Symphony on 20 February 1942. The endorsements of Barry, Whittaker, Grainger, Walter, Koussevitzky, and others suggest that the work might be well worth reviving.

Not only did Carpenter revise a number of older works in his later years, but he arranged others for orchestra, including four songs for voice and orchestra: "Berceuse de guerre" (retitled "War Lullaby") in 1940 and "Blue Gal," "Les Silhouettes," and "Slumber-Song" in 1943. In 1943 he also arranged two piano pieces, "Polonaise américaine" and "Tango américain," which together with "Danza," already orchestrated in 1935, became the 1943 *Dance Suite* for orchestra.

Carpenter's most ambitious adaptation by far, however, was his orchestral transcription of the 1934 Piano Quintet as the 1942 Second Symphony.

He began work on the transcription in Beverly in July 1941 and completed it in Chicago in March 1942. After the war Carpenter revised both the Piano Quintet (in 1946–47) and the Second Symphony (in 1947), thus giving us four versions of essentially the same work, although only the first movement of the 1942 version of the Second Symphony apparently survives as opposed to the complete 1947 version.

The extant movement of the 1942 Second Symphony is surprisingly faithful to its quintet origins, with major changes only at the movement's beginning and end. Carpenter replaces (after mm. 1–7) the original chromatic introduction with a faster, longer, and simpler dominant preparation. As a result, the new introduction omits some important thematic material, making later thematic transformations seem like new ideas! Even more peculiar, the symphony's "main theme" in D major (see ☐2) is the quintet theme heard four measures *after* its own "main theme" in D major. Again, this has almost ghostly implications, in that the symphony's later statements and developments of the unstated main theme lack reference to the exposition. On the other hand, the quintet's main theme had been rather anticlimactic, and one wonders whether the composer always considered the theme stated four after ☐2 to be the quintet's "main theme."

Carpenter also rewrote the movement's ending, starting at four before ☐21 in the quintet. Instead of a brief, introspective passage and a short scherzando codetta, one finds a more extended coda in a very diatonic D major. Perhaps Carpenter considered the original ending too intimate for a symphony. More to the point, this coda, with its clear and extended tonal resolution, balances the new introduction; indeed, both sections use the same newly composed theme.

Other differences between the two versions are more subtle. At a number of junctures—especially at fermatas and pauses—Carpenter adds measures, ostensibly to retain a rhythmic broadening without relying on nuances more appropriate to chamber music. At two points (corresponding to two after ☐15 and four before ☐17 in the quintet), the composer moves directly from one key to another without recourse to some intermediary modulation. He also alters a few time signatures: the quintet's opening $\frac{3}{4}$ to $\frac{3}{2}$ and a rather square $\frac{4}{4}$ (at ☐18 in the quintet) to a more asymmetrical $\frac{5}{4}$ (☐25 in the symphony). Throughout, the symphony's tempos are consistently about one-third faster than those of the quintet.

Texturally, the symphony follows the quintet quite closely; if anything, many passages are thinner than in the original. The strings carry the weight of the argument, often taking over both the quartet's *and* the piano's role.

The frequent unison string writing in the quintet facilitated this; for instance, the dialogue between the piano and unison strings at ⑨ in the quintet becomes a dialogue between the violas and cellos, on the one hand, and the violins, on the other, at ⑩ in the symphony. At other times, however, Carpenter retains a special role for the piano, as at five after ⑤, where the piano, now doubled with clarinets, bassoons, and snare drum, and the strings, now doubled by harp, maintain an exchange similar to that found at five after ⑤ in the quintet.

For the most part, Carpenter uses the winds and brass to color and shade the predominant string line. In the opening three measures, for example, the violin melody is doubled by, at first, the bass clarinet, bassoons, trombones, and harp; then by the English horn and two French horns; and then by the clarinets and the two other French horns. (This technique has some resemblance to Schoenberg's *Klangfarbenmelodie*.) Occasionally, however, Carpenter gives principal themes to such bright alternatives to the string sound as flute, piccolo, and muted trumpet; glockenspiel; and, at the *semplice* piano solo at ⑲ in the quintet, celesta and flutes.

Carpenter sent the completed score of the 1942 Second Symphony to Bruno Walter, who responded, on 11 July 1942, "I am very happy indeed to have found your Second Symphony just as interesting to me and perhaps even more so than the first one."[21] Walter scheduled the work for 22 October 1942, on a program that also included Beethoven's *Leonore* Overture no. 2 and, after intermission, Mahler's First Symphony. By this time Stock, too, had become interested in the work. Because he could offer the composer only a flat fee of forty dollars for each performance, however, he thought it best to defer the premiere to Walter.[22]

Carpenter could not attend the premiere—possibly because of a broken shoulder from a bicycle accident earlier that year—and Walter telegrammed the composer immediately after the concert, "Very Happy To Tell You Of The Great Success Of Your Symphony In Today's Philharmonic Concert. Congratulations."[23]

As with the Piano Quintet upon which it was based, the Second Symphony received somewhat negative reviews. Oscar Thompson described the music as "neatly articulated and the orchestration clear and euphonious. Other than that, this appears to be just another symphony." Olin Downes thought that the symphony "did not, on an initial hearing, appear to be one of Mr. Carpenter's most distinguished utterances. . . . Mahler's First Symphony, a work of wearisome sentimentality and outmoded platitudes, as well as inordinate length, added tedium to the occasion."[24]

Virgil Thomson (who thought the Mahler a revelation) similarly wrote about the Carpenter work with greater respect than enthusiasm:

John Alden Carpenter's Symphony No. 2, which followed [the Beethoven overture] was spread out for us with equal confidence in its values. These are not extraordinary, but they are respectable. It is rich man's music, gentleman's composition. Mr. Carpenter has been to Harvard and Paris; he has traveled in Africa and attended the best musical comedies, remembering both pleasantly. His mind is cultivated and adult. He writes with force and some charm. This work is well woven and contrapuntally alive; it has no empty spots in it. The orchestration is almost too full. I do not mean that it is thick. I mean that it seems to have plenty of instruments available at all times to meet any caprice of the author's musical day. The whole is opulent and comfortable, intelligent, well organized, cultured and firm without being either ostentatious or unduly modest. Beyond these virtues I found little in it to remember.[25]

Thomson's phrase, "It is rich man's music, gentleman's composition," taken out of context, helped shape the composer's postwar reputation.

Stock did not live long enough to conduct Carpenter's symphony; his successor, Désiré Defauw, introduced it to Chicago, where the reviews were similarly tepid. Carpenter "has retired into conservatism," wrote Felix Borowski. The symphony is "a facile and lyrical work," stated Claudia Cassidy, with "an interesting slow movement and a finale reminiscent of some of the composer's more brilliant songs." Remi Gassman, on the other hand, directed his criticism toward the conductor. The performance, he felt, "left much to be desired, since it was perfectly evident that the orchestra was giving it little more than a casual reading. A more integrated work than the First Symphony, it [the Second Symphony] now deserves another hearing on a higher level of conductorial competency."[26]

In 1946 and 1947, while in Beverly, Chicago, and Carmel, Carpenter revised the Piano Quintet. And in 1947 he also reworked the Second Symphony. In addition, he completed four pages (or about one-third of the first movement) of yet another revision of the quintet. "The question as to whether this short segment was composed before or after the revision of 1946–47 . . . remains unanswered," wrote Gregory Pike in his thesis on the three versions of the Piano Quintet.[27] However, the fact that "this short segment" clearly derives from the 1942 Second Symphony strongly suggests a date before 1946.[28] Apparently Carpenter initially attempted a straightforward revision of the quintet based on the Second Symphony and only afterward rejected this in favor of the large-scale revision undertaken in 1946–47.[29]

Carpenter generally retained his revisions from one version of the quintet to the next, so that the evolution from the 1934 Piano Quintet to the 1942 Second Symphony to the 1946–47 Piano Quintet to the 1947 Second Symphony was a gradual one. Consider, for example, the four measures at ⑭ in the 1934 Piano Quintet's first movement, where the "main theme" returns in a chromatic, sequential setting, leading to the arrival of a subsidiary theme (Pike's "closing theme") in G major. In the 1942 Second Symphony (seven after ⑱), Carpenter returns, instead, to new, introductory material (he had done away with the "main theme" as such) accompanied by trills; now six rather than four measures, it prepares the subsidiary G-major theme without any chromatic sequencing. The analogous passage in the 1946–47 Piano Quintet (⑫) retains this new material but prepares G minor, not G major. And the 1947 Second Symphony (⑯) prepares G minor but omits the trills found in the 1942 Second Symphony and the 1946–47 Piano Quintet (opting instead for a chromatic, pizzicato bass part that happens to look back to the original version!).[30]

In general, the four works fall into pairs: the 1934 Piano Quintet and the 1942 Second Symphony represent one general idea, the 1946–47 Piano Quintet and 1947 Second Symphony another. The revised versions tend toward greater clarity of expression: leaner textures, clearer harmonies, more direct motivic development. Their tone, further, is less sentimental; the composer removes the finale's slow, climactic reminiscence of introductory material much as he wanted to take out the slow interlude near the end of the Piano Concertino in 1947 (the change to which Percy Grainger objected). In short, the 1946–47 Piano Quintet and the 1947 Second Symphony come closer to the composer's very late style as represented by *The Seven Ages* and the *Carmel Concerto*.

In his careful comparison of the 1934 and 1946–47 versions of the Piano Quintet, Pike comes down strongly in favor of the former, arguing that the composer's reshuffling of ideas makes the revision baffling to the uninitiated listener. He concludes: "Although the revision reveals changes within the composer's conception that are fascinating when viewed in light of the original, it nonetheless represents a rethinking of the piece that cannot stand purely on its own merits. Although functioning much as an amendment to the original work, the revised 1947 version of the Quintet for Piano and Strings derives its sense of logic from the original 1934 version."[31] In addition, Pike finds the leanness of the 1946–47 version perilously dry, and one would have to admit that the revised piano part is much less interesting than the original.

The revised quintet had at least one performance, namely, by Rudolph Ganz and the Chicago Musical College String Quartet on 15 July 1948.[32] As for the revised symphony, Artur Rodzinski, who in early 1942 had expressed some interest in conducting the original Second Symphony with the Cleveland Orchestra, asked to see the 1947 revision, but he never performed the work in either version.[33] The premiere of the revised Second Symphony fell to the German-born conductor Fritz Busch (1890–1951).

Busch came to the Second Symphony in a roundabout way. He originally planned to conduct Carpenter's *Song of Faith* at the Cincinnati Festival in May 1948 "as it was originally intended—namely, for a chorus of combined *children* and men."[34] When this performance fell through, the conductor's wife, Greta, assured Ellen Carpenter that Busch "appreciates Mr. Carpenter highly as a composer, and loves him as a man," and that he was determined to play something of Carpenter's in Chicago that season.[35] Busch and the Chicago Symphony subsequently scheduled the revised Second Symphony for 24 March 1949, but a few days before the performance, Carpenter learned that the work had been postponed for the summer due to a lack of rehearsal time.[36]

Busch finally premiered the revised Second Symphony at Ravinia on 2 July 1949 to good reviews.[37] (In a letter about this concert, Carpenter said of Ravinia's tent, "You may get the impression that you are attending a circus instead of a symphony performance.")[38] Busch himself wrote admiringly of the work to Carpenter: "The better I come to know the score, the more I like it; I admire the liveliness of invention, your skill in the orchestration and the transparence of the whole composition."[39]

Schirmer never published the revised Piano Quintet but removed the 1942 Second Symphony and substituted it with the 1947 revision. Consequently, today's performer has easy access only to the original 1934 Piano Quintet and the revised 1947 Second Symphony; these are the versions, if any, that are likely to come before the public.

Carpenter's last complete work, the 1948 *Carmel Concerto,* culminated a decade of revising and arranging: It extensively rethought an older composition, like the 1940 First Symphony; it adapted music from one medium to another, like the 1942 Second Symphony; and it incorporated music from an old, forgotten work, like the 1940 *Krazy Kat.* All this naturally made for an essentially new piece, and Carpenter thought of it as such. Our discussion of the work, in any case, awaits a later chapter.

CHAPTER TWENTY-FOUR

From "Blue Gal" to *The Seven Ages*

1941–1945

Throughout the 1930s Carpenter looked upon world events with growing alarm. As a member of the Musicians' Committee to Aid Spanish Democracy, he cosigned, along with Amy Beach, Elizabeth Sprague Coolidge, Aaron Copland, Olin Downes, Alfred Hertz, Daniel Gregory Mason, Wallingford Riegger, and Efrem Zimbalist, a letter of 3 January 1939 urging the U.S. government to lift its embargo "against the legitimate Spanish government. . . . We, as American musicians, believe that passive sympathy will not suffice. In order to preserve the foundations of our own democracy, we must join with those artists who have taken a stand against Fascism."[1]

After World War II broke out later in the year, Carpenter similarly supported the William Allen White Committee, which worked against isolationism. On Memorial Day in May 1941, he further wrote President Roosevelt a stirring letter arguing for intervention. Although he realized that Roosevelt had promised not to declare war unless attacked by a foreign power, the "stark truth," asserted Carpenter, was "that the United States, for the past twelve months or more, has been under steady 'preparatory' attack by both Germany and Italy,—the identical type of 'attack,' without which the fall of France and other European nations would have been impossible." Carpenter encouraged Roosevelt to act accordingly, asking, "Is it not essential that the President of a great republic must be *free* in addressing his people, not only to state his position at any given time, but *free* also to change that position whenever changing circumstances and the security of the country demand such change?"[2]

By this time, indeed as early as June 1940, the Carpenters were leading Chicago's efforts on behalf of British Relief. After America entered the war, Ellen went on to head the city's war bond drives; her committee sold ninety million war bonds in less than a year, winning plaudits from the wife of

Treasury Secretary Henry Morgenthau Jr.[3] In 1943 the Carpenters loaned their huge château at 1020 Lake Shore Drive to Wesley Hospital (which used it as a nurses' home) and sublet an apartment at 1550 North State for $350 a month.[4] In 1945 they moved to another fashionable apartment building at 209 East Lake Shore Drive, and in 1948 they relocated to 999 North Lake Shore Drive, the composer's last Chicago residence.

During the war Carpenter's ongoing revisions and arrangements turned specifically to works that had had some relation to World War I: the First Symphony (1917/1940), the "Berceuse de guerre" (1918/1940), and, less obviously, the two Siegfried Sassoon songs (1920/1943). Also related to the war were three new works from 1941 ("A Song for Illinois" for orchestra, "Blue Gal" for voice and piano, and *Song of Freedom* for orchestra and optional unison chorus) and one from 1942 (*The Anxious Bugler* for orchestra).

"A Song for Illinois" was part of a large, collaborative project: Stock had commissioned twelve Illinois composers to write a variation on the folk song "El-A-Noy" (from Carl Sandburg's *American Songbag*) as a gesture of civic pride and solidarity.[5] David Van Vactor harmonized and orchestrated the theme and composed the first variation; Arne Oldberg, Rossetter G. Cole, Samuel Lieberson, Leo Sowerby, Edward Collins, Florian Mueller, Albert Noelte, Carpenter, Felix Borowski, Rudolph Ganz, and Thorvald Otterström wrote the succeeding variations.

"El-A-Noy" celebrates Illinois's farmland, so rich that Adam would "think it was the garden / He'd played in when a boy." The duple, Aeolian melody, with its pentatonic inflections, represents a familiar type of Anglo-Irish frontier tune. The shape of the melody is arched, with four four-measure phrases that form, roughly, an *abba* design. The last two phrases *(ba)*, repeated, constitute a refrain: "Then move your family westward, / Good health you will enjoy, / and rise to health and honor / In the State of Elanoy."

Composed between 8 and 17 January 1941, Carpenter's variation, "A Song for Illinois," comprises four short sections. The opening section, a $\frac{6}{8}$ Moderato con moto, transforms the entire tune into a jig, with syncopated hemiolas in the accompaniment. At times the music specifically recalls Patrick Gilmore's 1863 "When Johnny Comes Marching Home Again" (a tune that also inspired Roy Harris and Morton Gould during these years). The second section, a $\frac{9}{8}$ Poco più lento, presents a more lyrical version of the song's last two phrases (or, equally, the refrain). After a brief *a tempo,* the *dolce* third section, once again a $\frac{9}{8}$ Poco più lento, develops that fragment of the tune "He'd played in when (a boy)." The last section, back in tempo and $\frac{6}{8}$, returns to the jiglike opening. In short, Carpenter's variation freely mirrors the *abba* structure of the original theme.

At two points in the score, Carpenter asks that the first and second violinists stand and sing. Shortly into the piece, they echo the end of the refrain ("of Elanoy"), singing "For Illinois." And at the variation's conclusion, they stand again to sing, to the composer's own words, "then come away! and come to stay! There's Hell to pay! in Illinois." This last rallying cry functions as the variation's coda and concludes with a bright D-major triad.

Stock and the Chicago Symphony premiered *Variations on an American Folksong* on 17 April 1941 as the finale of a jubilee 1940–41 season that had brought forth many new works, including Carpenter's 1940 Symphony. Claudia Cassidy dismissed the notion that the variations were a "parlor game enjoyed only by the players. They were sound music in which each man mirrored himself." Robert Pollak also admitted that the variations succeeded "in being almost universally intriguing," although he added: "What our local composers have done to the simple tune would probably turn Sandburg's hair black. Their passacaglias, fugues, gigues and andantes are a far cry from the bard and his eloquent guitar." Cassidy singled out for praise the variations by Vactor, Mueller, Borowski, and Ganz, while Pollak selected those by Mueller, Borowski, and Otterström as the "top three contributions."[6]

Carpenter composed the song "Blue Gal" in November 1941. As with his World War I songs "The Home Road" and "Khaki Sammy," he himself wrote the lyrics, which consist of two verse-choruses and three additional choruses. In the two verses, a poor "gal" sorrowfully remembers her man, "far away," and in the two choruses, she looks forward to her man's return and the end of her troubles. The three additional choruses honor the bravery of the "gay beaus" about to send "those Dago's" and "every Nazi" hustling for home.

"Blue Gal" combined the nostalgia of "The Home Road," the spirit of "Khaki Sammy," and the sadness of "Berceuse de guerre." At the same time, it recalled the bluesy, African American flavor of yet another World War I song, "The Lawd Is Smilin' through the Do'," not only in its words—

When a gal is breathin' sorrow,

Cause her man is far away,

And she has to beg and borrow,

Jes' to live another day.

Then, please may the Lawd say,

I'm comin' around, gal, comin' around,

Jes' be care-free,

I'm stayin' around, gal, stayin' around

And some day, some way,

My man'll be home, yes, livin' at home,

And then I'll throw my troubles away.

—but in its syncopated figures, vocal melismas, and modal inflections.

Carpenter wrote and rewrote the lyrics at least three times. In the first version, titled "Blue Gal," both choruses were identical; in the second version, retitled "Breathin' Sorrow," Carpenter introduced the idea of the Lord "hearin' your song, boys, hearin' your song" into the second chorus; and in the third version, once again titled "Blue Gal," he further adjusted the text. Carpenter revised the text once again when he orchestrated the song in May 1943, replacing the two verse-choruses and three optional choruses with four complete verse-choruses. He derived the last two choruses from the optional choruses of the 1941 original but added "Togos" to the list of despised enemies and mentioned the "USA" by name. He orchestrated the song brightly, with a fully scored instrumental tag at the very end.

Carpenter began *Song of Freedom* for orchestra and optional chorus in Beverly in October 1941 and completed it in Chicago that December. A series of working sketches at the Library of Congress document the work's evolution. In October, Carpenter composed a three-staff draft consisting of about five minutes worth of music, alternating a jaunty, $^6_8$ Sousa-like march (with occasional allusions to "When Johnny Comes Marching Home") with a solemn hymn ("for full orchestra and voices(?)") that looked back not only to "The Home Road" but to "Good Ellen" from the *Improving Songs*.

In the following month, November, Carpenter apparently collaborated with Morris H. Martin to find words for the hymn tune. In one early version, they wrote two verses, the first of which began:

Praise all whose hearts are brave and free,

Whose hands are young and strong,

To them we bring our gratitude,

For them we sing our song.

A later version added a verse—very possibly the composer's own—expressing faith in God and the founding fathers. This later version also contains changes in both the melody and the accompaniment.

In late November or early December, Carpenter sketched out a significantly revised *Song of Freedom,* in which he retained the hymn tune along with some of the older march music (including the references to "When Johnny Comes Marching Home," now in triplets) but interpolated new, $\frac{2}{4}$ march music that quotes, at first, a fragment of the composer's "Khaki Sammy" and, later, that same song's entire chorus. This new *Song of Freedom* contains the following design: march music (incorporating new and old ideas) in B♭ modulating to F major, the hymn tune in F major, the "Khaki Sammy" chorus in F major, the march in B♭ major, and the hymn tune in B♭ major.

The final orchestral version, completed in December, only slightly modifies this form: Carpenter expands the introduction, alluding briefly to "Yankee Doodle," and reserves the optional chorus only for the concluding B♭-major statement of the hymn tune (24). (In performances without chorus, the composer indicates a cut of one of the hymn's two verses.) In 1942 Carpenter arranged the work for band and optional chorus.

On 4 March 1942 Stock and the Chicago Symphony premiered *Song of Freedom* at a concert celebrating the one-hundredth anniversary of vocal music in the Chicago public schools. At this first performance, 240 elementary schoolchildren sang the unison choral part. Carpenter also hoped to interest Koussevitzky in the work, which he described to the conductor as "a short (6 minutes) simple, vigorous and direct March tune of typical American character for full orchestra and ending with a new patriotic song for unison chorus."[7] Once again, however, it was not Koussevitzky but his nephew Fabien Sevitzky who took up a new Carpenter work, performing it on 9 May 1942. Edwin Franko Goldman and the Goldman Band played the band arrangement on 4 July 1942.

Song of Freedom failed to duplicate the success of "The Home Road" or *Song of Faith.* Perhaps it too evidently reflected the kind of weariness detected in a comment the composer made shortly after the work's premiere: "I suppose that any composer trying to say something about his country today is just another 'Jongleur,' offering up his bag of tricks as best he may, before an altar."[8] Carpenter himself, however, was pleased with the work's reception.[9]

In 1942 Carpenter declined Claire Reis's invitation to write something for the League of Composers on the occasion of their twenty-year anniversary,[10] but in 1943 he agreed—as did Berezowsky, Cowell, Dello Joio, Hanson, Harris, Herrmann, Ives, Josten, Milhaud, Martinů, Moore, Piston, Porter, Rogers, Sessions, and Still—to write, under League of Composers sponsorship, a short work on a wartime theme to be performed by Artur Rodzinski and the New York Philharmonic and broadcast on radio by CBS. Carpenter completed his contribution, *The Anxious Bugler,* in Beverly in August 1943.

Carpenter explained to Claire Reis that *The Anxious Bugler* attempted to depict the thoughts and feelings of the ordinary soldier: "The 'Anxious Bugler' may stand for any man, anywhere, who finds himself a soldier. He works and sweats, and sometimes he fears. He also has his hopes—with home always in the back of his mind, and at times the stern voice of God in his ears."[11] Perhaps Carpenter's vivid program note—or the picturesque music itself—gave Copland the false impression that Carpenter and William Grant Still "derived their pieces from personal experiences," whereas, in fact, Carpenter (unlike Still) never served in the military.[12]

The Anxious Bugler achieves its highly realistic atmosphere partly through the use of familiar materials: bugle calls for the soldier's work and fears, the Dies Irae for "the stern voice of God," Stephen Foster's "My Old Kentucky Home" for "home always in the back of his mind," and Beethoven's "fate" or "victory" motive from the Fifth Symphony for, plausibly, the Allies' hoped-for victory. These quotations naturally recall Ives, although Carpenter's music more clearly suggests the drama and energy of a World War II documentary sound track.

The work's opening polytonal setting of reveille, for instance, only superficially resembles the ending of Ives's Second Symphony. Carpenter's dissonance, carefully controlled, points to the arrival, at ②, of the work's tonic, B♭ major. At ② the composer states another bugle call, the "Drill Call," also in B♭ major; this call functions somewhat like a first theme. Whereas reveille and "Drill Call" presumably represent the soldier's "work" and "sweat," Carpenter introduces, at four before ③, the element of "fear" by way of a nervous, subsidiary idea consisting of wavering seconds. These two elements—the bugle calls and the fear motive—interact, sometimes in explicitly bitonal contexts, as at ⑤.

At ⑨ the phrase "(Tu)ba mirum spargens sonum" ("The trumpet flings its wondrous sound") from the Dies Irae appears scored for full orchestra, fortissimo, and accompanied by the restless fear motive. The image of a trumpet, now placed in a religious context, suggests some correspondence between the Roman Catholic requiem and American military music, between the sacred and the secular. At the pickup to ⑫, this section climaxes with Beethoven's victory motive, whose falling thirds are related to the bugle calls, the Dies Irae, and the forthcoming Foster quote.

This brief remembrance of Foster's "My Old Kentucky Home" comprises the work's Lento middle section. Carpenter quotes only a fragment of the chorus, "Weep no more, my lady / Oh! weep no more today! / We will sing one song . . . ," leaving off at the words "for the old Kentucky home, For the old Kentucky home far away." At first nostalgic, Carpenter's setting turns darker and more troubled at the words "We will sing one song" (ex. 53). As the quote drifts away, the music vaguely recalls the passage "And there shall be no mem'ry of the sky" from Carpenter's 1920 setting of Sassoon's "Slumber-Song," which he had orchestrated but a few months earlier. The composer might well have thought of "My Old Kentucky Home" as a lullaby.

Carpenter quietly develops the "Tuba mirum" phrase and fear motive (⑭), returns to reveille (⑮), and climactically recapitulates the "Tuba mirum" (⑯) before arriving, at six after ⑯, at a joyous and triumphant coda in the tonic.

Rodzinski premiered *The Anxious Bugler* on 17 November 1943 to favorable reviews. Olin Downes wrote that the quoted materials "merge in Mr. Carpenter's tonal canvas, admirable in its workmanship, unmistakable in its sincerity and with humorous details which point up the essential earnestness of his commentary." Another reviewer described the work as "snatches of native folk lore bristled in a rugged fabric woven around a bugler's nostalgic thoughts of home."[13]

In early 1943 Artur Rodzinski asked some of his favorite composers to write a small piece in honor of the birth of his son Richard on 23 January, and Carpenter obliged with a "Fanfarette-Berceuse" ("for Richard"), completed

EXAMPLE 53. Carpenter, *The Anxious Bugler,* ⑬, mm. 7–14.

in Hobe Sound in February and dedicated to "Halina, Arthur, and Richard. God bless you all."[14] (In her memoirs years later, Halina remembered only the tributes by Barber, Harris, Stravinsky, and Schoenberg; Richard remembered, in addition, those by Martin and Copland.)[15]

Composed for voice, three trumpets, three trombones, timpani, cymbals, and bass drum, the tiny "Fanfarette" contains nine measures of fanfare (Vivo triomphale) and ten measures of lullaby (Lento). The lullaby portion quotes a fragment of the composer's beloved "Dodo, l'enfant do," while throughout, the timpani plays the same rocking figure (A–C) used in "Blue Gal."

Another song, "Canterbury-Bells," a lighthearted tribute to the flowers of the same name, probably dates from about this same time. Carpenter signed the manuscript "Uncle John," suggesting that he wrote it for his step-grandchildren. He presumably intended the song to be sung by children, for he scored it for three voices in close, treble harmony accompanied by piano. The poetry's "swinging" and "ringing" inspired a waltzlike, gently syncopated melody somewhat reminiscent of Brahms's *Liebeslieder* waltzes.

While wintering in Hobe Sound in February 1945, Carpenter wrote to John Becker, "The balmy sunshine down here has caused me to look with disfavor on my embryo violin piece, and I feel my compass seeking a new direction, destination unknown."[16] In this same month Carpenter began *The Seven Ages* for orchestra, a work that would become his only major, completely new work composed after 1936. He worked on it throughout the spring in Chicago and completed it in July in Beverly. Carpenter dedicated the score to his wife, Ellen.

Discussing the origins of *The Seven Ages* with Claudia Cassidy, Carpenter stated:

> Since way back in the early '20s, when I was busying myself in the ballet field, I have carried the conviction that the famous lines of Jacques in "As You Like It" offered a practically foolproof subject, either for ballet or a piece of program music. The theme, I was convinced, "had everything." *All the world* was its *stage*. Into it were woven all the basic symbols of life itself, with room for the play of every fancy of any child, any lover, any toothless old man. All the composer had to do, I told myself, was to "git loose" (as Karleton Hackett used to urge me) and Shakespeare would see him thru.
>
> As the years went by I made two different attempts to get started with the "Seven Ages" theme, first with a symbolistic ballet sketch worked out for me by Natalia Gontcharova, who designed many of Diaghileff's productions

(notably "Les Noces") in the exciting Paris days. Later, I turned to a remarkable abstract movie scenario written for me by Archibald MacLeish. But, alas, neither one of these potent stimulants seemed to ring my bell. So, after a long interval, I decided last year to try to go it alone, so to speak, and the present orchestral suite is the result.

Nothing would be gained by my attempting to provide an analysis of the musical elements of my work, as I am sure they will seem fairly obvious to any listener who troubles to follow my subtitles in the program. If the music still leaves him cold, I become the chief mourner.[17]

Carpenter's "suite" arguably retains something of the ballet and the motion pictures: the former in, say, its depiction of the "schoolboy," and the latter in its portrayal of the "soldier." Such connections with ballet and film, however, seem elsewhere more tenuous, especially toward the end of the work.

Carpenter subtitled the work's seven short movements, of about two to three minutes each, with excerpted phrases from Jacques's speech:

Ia. "All the world's a stage" ["All the world's a stage, / And all the men and women merely players. / They have their exits and their entrances, And one man in his time plays many parts, / His acts being seven ages."]

Ib. "At first, the infant" ["At first the infant, / Mewling and puking in the nurse's arms."]

II. "Then the whining schoolboy" ["Then the whining schoolboy with his satchel / And shining morning face, creeping like snail / Unwillingly to school."]

III. "And then the lover, sighing like a furnace" ["And then the lover, / Sighing like furnace, with a woeful ballad / Made to his mistress' eyebrow."]

IV. "Then a soldier" ["Then a soldier, / Full of strange oaths and bearded like the pard, / Jealous in honor, sudden and quick in quarrel, / Seeking the bubble Reputation / E'en in the cannon's mouth."]

V. "And then the Justice, in fair round belly, with good capon lin'd" ["And then the justice, / In fair round belly with good capon lin'd, / With eyes severe and beard of formal cut, / Full of wise saws and modern instances; / And so he plays his part."]

VI. "The lean and slipper'd pantaloon" ["The sixth age shifts / Into the lean and slipper'd pantaloon, / With spectacles on nose and pouch on side; / His youthful hose well sa'vd, a world too wide / For his shrunk shank, and his big manly voice, / Turning again toward childish treble, pipes / And whistles in his sound."]

VII. "Last scene of all, sans teeth, sans eyes, sans taste, sans everything" ["Last scene of all, / That ends this strange eventful history, / Is second childishness and mere oblivion— / Sans teeth, sans eyes, sans taste, sans everything."]

The work's overall structure conforms roughly to a set of variations; much as man moves through various stages, so the musical material evolves from one movement to the next. Moreover, the individual movements tend to be ternary in shape, with similar contrasting material.

The opening Vivace, Ia, presents a short, introductory fanfare that resembles the "Fanfarette" written on the occasion of Richard Rodzinski's birth. This fanfare puts forth the pentatonic collection of pitches that flavors much of the work. Here, the music outlines an ambiguously modal A minor, and, indeed, this section's concluding sonority suggests both a resolution in A minor and a dominant preparation of C major, the tonality of the ensuing Ib, Andante amabile.

In Ib Carpenter immediately states the lullaby that forms the work's main theme. This theme resembles the mother's lullaby from *Song of Faith,* though as a whole the movement's picturesque portrayal of an infant more readily recalls the composer's *Perambulator.* At four after ③ one even hears, presumably, the baby's "mewling and puking," suggested by minor seconds. These seconds return in each of the subsequent variations at about the same place—with new meanings each time.

The Animato gioco, II, is the work's scherzo movement. It introduces vigorous rhythms and, at ⑪, a rousing melody in G major. The music sensitively portrays a boy's youthful whimsy and good humor.

Movement III, Andantino sentimentale, in D major, begins with an ironic depiction of the lover's sigh (played by clarinet, piano, and glissando trombone). Shakespeare's "woeful ballad" inspires a beautiful principal theme, stated five after ⑯ by the violins and oboe. The middle section—a joyous, waltzlike episode in B♭ major—partakes of Carpenter's Spanish idiom, further documenting the composer's association of Spanish music with love.

The Allegro barbaro, IV, opens in F♯ minor and concludes in F major. Its portrait of a soldier, with discordant harmonies and nervous rhythms, recalls Carpenter's *Anxious Bugler.* Here, however, the composer relieves the pervasive gloom, not by thoughts of home but, at five after ㉘, by some jaunty music derived from the schoolboy movement. And the final victory music is distinctively poignant and reverent, with solemn tolling of bells.

Beginning in a modal B minor and ending in E major, movement V,

Buffo-Pomposo, presents a main theme, at five after ⟨37⟩, for woodwinds (without the flutes) and brass in close harmony, a bandlike sound. The music has a neoclassical flavor (including use of symmetrical inversion) but savors more strongly of the comic juggler and tightrope-walker music from *Infanta*.

The last two movements turn more inward and reflective. Movement VI, Lento dolente, uses glockenspiel, celesta, and harp, together with pizzicato strings and flute, to help impart a sense of fatigue and sadness, with a particularly poignant movement from C♯ minor to A major at ⟨46⟩.

In the last movement, Adagio placido, Carpenter returns to the infant's theme, now effectively rescored—one might say, taken apart—to match Shakespeare's "second childishness." At eight before ⟨51⟩ the music looks back to the ambiguous A-minor modality of the very beginning, now fraught with senility and death. After a brief recapitulation of the opening fanfare, the death music returns, weaker and weaker. Finally, the music dissolves into the A-minor/C-major double-focus that concludes the introduction, followed by one solo gong, pianissimo (ex. 54).

In its strong modal (sometimes bimodal) coloring, its avoidance of clear cadences, and its nontriadic—especially quartal and secondal—harmonies, *The Seven Ages* reveals an assimilation of contemporary trends rather remarkable for a composer approaching seventy years. At ⟨33⟩ Carpenter even puts forth a twelve-tone melody in a setting not unlike Schoenberg. At the same time—and no less adventurous—the work looks decidedly East, especially to Chinese music, what with its extensive pentatonicism, its open parallel fourths, its use of minor seconds (as at six after ⟨53⟩), and its scoring (e.g., the writing for xylophone and pizzicato strings at five after ⟨15⟩).

Rodzinski and the New York Philharmonic premiered *The Seven Ages* on 29 November 1945. Virgil Thomson thought the work, coming on the heels of *Sea Drift* and the Second Symphony, a welcome return to the composer of the *Perambulator*:

EXAMPLE 54.   Carpenter, *The Seven Ages*, last movement, conclusion.

Carpenter's "The Seven Ages" (after Shakespeare's famous passage) is in the vein of his earlier "Adventures in a Perambulator." This is to say that it is music of specific expressive intention in which wit plays the rôle of sharpener to the expressivity. It is Carpenter at his best, which is objective. It describes things. It describes things clearly, using good material and clean workmanship. Criticism is not involved with whether some one else might have described them better. The piece seemed to me a satisfactory communication, if not an especially revealing one, either humanly or musically; and I think the audience was grateful, too. They applauded as if they were, when the composer bowed.[18]

On 2 December, CBS aired the Rodzinski performance in the afternoon. Carpenter notified Elizabeth Sprague Coolidge about the broadcast: "I hope . . . that my little bout with Shakespeare may please you." She wrote back, two days after the program, "It was a great pleasure to listen to your broadcast . . . and I very much enjoyed your 'bout with Shakespeare.'"[19] This broadcast performance did not correspond to the composer's manuscript (Schirmer's rental score) in all particulars. Both the opening fanfare and "the lover" movement, for instance, were somewhat abridged. Carpenter presumably made these revisions after the premiere, perhaps upon consultation with Rodzinski.

Désiré Defauw and the Chicago Symphony played *The Seven Ages* on 4 April 1946. Defauw's performance, the first after the orchestra announced the conductor's reengagement for the 1946–47 season, provided grist for Claudia Cassidy's campaign to oust Defauw. In an article headlined "Conquering Hero Reception Backfires as Defauw Mauls Mozart and Spoils Carpenter Premiere with Dull Performance," she wrote:

> I don't know how you felt about the result, but I wanted to say, "Never mind, Mr. Carpenter, look what happened to Mozart." For this light and graceful setting of the seven ages of man is a score by a composer with a quizzically dry wit; and he suffered the anguish of having his little jokes blown up to bombastic proportions by a conductor without a sense of humor, his little tendernesses dragged into the arena of sentimentality. I heard just enough of the true score to find it tantalizing, and I hope to hear it again under happier circumstances. Meanwhile, I understand perfectly why Mr. Carpenter has preferred to have his more recent music given first performance in New York.[20]

As in New York, however, most Chicago reviews emphasized how well audiences received *The Seven Ages*. Chicago critic C. J. Bulliet, moreover, thought the work "adult and adroit, worthy of an honored place in the vast library of Shakespeare-inspired music."[21]

Subsequently, Eugene Ormandy and the Philadelphia Orchestra played *The Seven Ages* in Philadelphia on 15 November 1946 and took the work on the road to Washington and Baltimore. A few days after the Philadelphia premiere, Ormandy wrote Carpenter, "This is my first opportunity to write and tell you how much joy our orchestra and I have had in performing your *Seven Ages* this past weekend."[22]

Pierre Monteux and the San Francisco Symphony performed the work on 13 February 1947. Before the performance Carpenter declared Monteux "one of the most important and perhaps the greatest conductor in this country today."[23] The composer came up from Carmel for the concert and reported to John Becker: "He [Monteux] has an excellent orchestra and did a good job with my music. Public response, good, critics—50-50."[24] Monteux made two cuts in the score (one of which Carpenter incorporated) for his 29 July 1947 performance of the work with the Chicago Symphony at Ravinia.[25]

By this time Carpenter decided that *The Seven Ages* would make a good ballet after all, and he contacted his longtime friend, the set designer Robert Edmond Jones, who, on the composer's behalf, approached Balanchine about a three-way collaboration. In the meantime, Jones and Carpenter discussed possible stagings, Jones writing to the composer, "There are so many different ways in which the subject could be approached—a 'period piece,' a terrific drama, etc. etc."[26] Carpenter responded by outlining his own ideas for the ballet:

> As a plausible means of providing continuity and variety of movement on the stage, why not action on two levels? Old stuff, but maybe useful for our purposes. This could work out as a "counterpoint" between the principal figures at the front of the stage, with a background group or "chorus" on the upper level, with different lighting, of course, and perhaps a "film" drop in between. The upper level group will help to keep the show in motion, and provide direct references to details of the score, as well as a spoofing commentary on what the chief actors may be pulling off in the foreground, on the lower level.

Carpenter wanted neither a curtain nor set changes between movements, but rather a "'fade-out' during the last few bars of each movement, with complete black-out of a few seconds during the actual pauses in the music."[27] Balanchine, however, ultimately decided not to choreograph *The Seven Ages*, and all plans for another Carpenter-Jones collaboration were put aside.

CHAPTER TWENTY-FIVE

A Friend of the Arts

Carpenter's social position and artistic reputation made him a highly desirable figure in the arts world. The New York Metropolitan Opera even thought, after Campanini's death, that Carpenter should succeed the temperamental Italian as director of the Chicago Opera, according to the newspaper article "New York Opera Folk Boost Carpenter: Business-Artist Combination Just What Chicago Needs, Experts Say."[1] Carpenter never assumed so grand a responsibility but became, nonetheless, a dominant force in Chicago's musical life, especially in the 1920s and 1930s.

Carpenter's involvement in local arts institutions—an inheritance from his mother, as his interest in social welfare stemmed from his father—spanned the Little Room, founded in 1892, to the Choral and Instrumental Association of Chicago, founded in 1944.[2] An informal association of Chicagoan artists, writers, architects, and critics, including Henry Blake Fuller, Hamlin Garland, Lorado Taft, George Ade, Harriet and Lucy Monroe, and John McCutcheon (who would become Carpenter's lifelong friend), the Little Room met at Ralph Clarkson's art studio after the Friday afternoon Chicago Symphony concerts. Those present would "talk and drink tea around the samovar, sometimes with a dash of rum to strengthen it, and every visitor to Chicago who was anybody in any of the arts would be brought to the Little Room by some local confrère. On Twelfth Night, and perhaps another date or two each season, we would have a hilarious play or costume party. There was no lack of wit in the club for concoction of parodies."[3] Like a Montmartre café, the Little Room gave artists an opportunity to congregate and represented a genteel and good-humored rebellion against Chicago's business elite and the city's prevailing materialistic values. Later such Chicagoan institutions as Garland's Cliff Dwellers, Monroe's *Poetry,* and Rue Carpenter's Arts Club could be traced back to the Little Room, which similarly helped set the tone and ideals of Carpenter's music.

The relation of Carpenter's songs to *Poetry* magazine, which the composer helped finance, has already been discussed. Carpenter also supported Garland's Cliff Dwellers, a social club open (pending a club vote) to any man above the age of twenty-five "professionally engaged in literature, painting, sculpture, architecture, music, or the drama, or to lay membership who is a connoisseur and lover of the fine Arts." Founded in 1907, the Cliff Dwellers met in rooms above Orchestra Hall and featured a library and a dining room. Besides Carpenter, other early members included Carpenter's brother Benjamin; his close friend Frederick Bartlett; Garland, Ade, Taft, McCutcheon, and others associated with the Little Room; Robert Herrick; and such musicians as Frederick Stock, Eric De Lamarter, Glenn Dillard Gunn, and Karleton Hackett.[4]

Cliff Dwellers membership was at first limited to 250 and later 300; dues stayed at fifty dollars until the Depression, at which time they went up to seventy-five dollars. More musicians belonged to the Cliff Dwellers than did any other group, and the club regularly honored distinguished musicians: Carpenter himself in 1921, Sowerby in 1922, Respighi in 1926, Cadman in 1927, Koussevitzky in 1928, and Glazunov in 1929.

Carpenter maintained a lifelong association with the Cliff Dwellers; indeed, in 1948 the club offered him an emeritus membership (Carpenter continued to pay the annual dues, nonetheless).[5] In 1910 Carpenter joined the club's Entertainment Committee, and in the 1930s he became one of their directors in addition to regularly serving on the Art Committee. But his involvement with the Cliff Dwellers was not particularly strong, as evident from his omission from Theodore Keane's 1922 *Friendly Libels,* a portrait gallery of the club's lunch regulars.

After World War I, Carpenter devoted considerable time and energy to the patronage and promotion of new music and dance in Chicago. In 1924 he founded and assumed directorship of the Chicago Allied Arts, an organization dedicated to modern ballet. "It is their particular purpose," stated Ruth Page in 1926, "to give Chicago a permanent and growing ballet commensurate with the expense and limitations of a small orchestra and devoted almost entirely to the production of works of living composers of every country."[6]

The Allied Arts brought together the talents, among others, of choreographer-dancers Ruth Page and Adolph Bolm, conductor Eric De Lamarter, costume and scenic designer Nicholas Remisoff,[7] and consultants Rue Carpenter and Frederick Stock—all under Carpenter's leadership. Page explained, "Everyone had such confidence in his [Carpenter's] taste and ability that to raise money all he had to do was to pick up a telephone and call a few friends, and the money came rolling in."[8] Samuel Putnam reported that supporters touted the Allied Arts as a municipal organization, a "civic ballet" on a par with a city's orchestra or opera.[9]

The Allied Arts sponsored performances at the Studebaker Theatre, the Eighth Street Theatre, and the Art Institute's Goodman Memorial Theatre. Their concerts typically opened with a program of instrumental and vocal music, conducted by De Lamarter, followed by a few short ballets and solo dance numbers. When Carpenter attempted—unsuccessfully—to sponsor an Eva Gauthier recital under Allied Arts auspices, he suggested that she devote half of the concert to "classical numbers," and the other half to "contemporary songs, the more startling and experimental the better, and end with one effective and easily absorbed song of a more popular nature." He also explained (with an eye to holding down her fee) that the Allied Arts "depends on a few generous individuals here in Chicago and it loses a good round sum of money on each performance and is organized purely for the development of music in the community."[10]

In a mere three years—1924 to 1927—the Allied Arts performed a number of ballets in Chicago and New York that explored new possibilities for modern dance. Putnam thought it piquant that Bolm, a Russian émigré based in Chicago, should teach America about the "new ballet," which Putnam characterized as "drama, concentrated and sublimated drama, a drama reduced to that simplicity of flowing line which is characteristic of good music and good architecture."[11] Vera Caspary offered a vivid description of one "daring" Allied Arts ballet to music by Scriabin, in which Bolm and Page "represented disembodied emotion floating through space. . . . For most of the time, they lay on black platforms, moving gently as though they floated through space, sometimes singly and at times in amorous and unconventional adagio."[12]

The Allied Arts kicked off their short but brilliant existence in 1924 with stagings of de Falla's *El amor brujo* and Henry Eichheim's *Rivals* ("danced in authentic Chinese costumes"), both choreographed by Bolm and designed by Remisoff.[13] In the particularly rich 1925–26 season, Allied Arts presented four full-length evenings, including ballets to de Falla, Fuleihan, Satie, Schoenberg (a *Pierrot Lunaire* in English, sung by Mina Hager and conducted by Stock),[14] Still, Szymanowski, Tansman, and Vaughan Williams. The shorter 1926–27 season featured a gala performance on 14 November 1926 in honor of Queen Marie, Prince Nicholas, and Princess Ileana of Romania, with ballets to Jeanne Herscher-Clement, Satie, and Scriabin.

The Allied Arts also sponsored Ruth Page's earliest dances, including jazz-inspired collaborations with composer Clarence Loomis that continued along the lines of the Carpenter ballets.[15] After the dissolution of the Allied Arts and Bolm's move to Los Angeles in 1928, Carpenter continued to support Ruth Page, whose ballets from the 1930s—including *Hear Ye! Hear Ye!* (1934) to music by Aaron Copland and *Frankie and Johnnie* (1938) to music by Jerome Moross—owed much to the Chicago composer's financial support, social connections, and artistic sensibilities.[16] Carpenter could do only so much by himself, however. In 1941 he confessed to Page:

> Although I am naturally a chronic optimist I find it hard to be happy over the general outlook for Ballet anywhere. One could laugh if it were not so sad. Here we are with all the important dancers, choreographers, composers, designers and technicians of the world now concentrated in the U.S.A. (together with the best part of the remaining gold supply), and still we seem unable to capitalize and properly organize the opportunity that is slipping by.[17]

When New York's American Ballet Theatre emerged in the 1940s as the best hope for modern American ballet (what with their productions of new works by Copland, Bernstein, Schuman, and others), Carpenter threw his support behind that company, becoming a founder member when Ballet Theatre incorporated in 1947.[18]

As the Allied Arts faded in the late 1920s, Carpenter became more involved in the Chicago Arts Club, whose musical affairs he guided from the club's inception in 1916 to at least the late 1930s. Indeed, the Arts Club would not have been as musically active, one imagines, had Carpenter not been married to the club's president. As it was, the Arts Club emerged in the course of the 1920s and 1930s as the premiere institution for the performance and discussion of new music in Chicago.

Throughout the presidencies of both Rue (1918–31) and Bobsy Goodspeed (1931–40), Carpenter served on the Arts Club's Music Committee. Whether or not he actually chaired the committee, he made and shaped many of its decisions, often in consultation with, above all, Frederick Stock and John Palmer. (Palmer, a composer in his own right, managed the committee's day-to-day business affairs and correspondence, assisted by Isabel Jarvis.) After Carpenter's niece Rue Shaw became president in 1941, Carpenter remained a member of the committee but distanced himself somewhat from its activities, allowing Palmer, Claire Dux Swift, and Felix Borowski to assume the Music Committee's chief decisions.

The Music Committee sponsored three principal types of events: concerts, lectures, and honorary receptions (usually luncheons, teas, or dinners). These functions often overlapped: a musician or lecturer might be honored before a concert or following a lecture. In its early years the committee had an annual budget of from $1,000 to $2,000 (Arts Club members must have been amused when Carpenter insisted on $2,400 for 1926, and his wife held the line at $1,500). Depending on whether the club defrayed traveling expenses, fees for concerts ranged from about $300 to $600 (the $1,200 paid to Stravinsky for a 1935 concert was remarkably lavish by Arts Club standards) and lectures from $50 to $300. Consequently, the club could usually afford a music lecture and a few recitals every year.[19]

As with the fine arts, the Arts Club emphasized developments in modern music. It honored older, distinguished figures like Respighi (1926), Ravel (1928),[20] and d'Indy (1929) and sponsored composers playing their own music: Stravinsky (1925 and 1935), Honegger (1929), Prokofiev (1930), Schoenberg and Alexander Tcherepnin (both 1934), Hindemith (1937), Boulanger and Jean Françaix (1939), Bartók (1940), and Tansman and Cage (both 1942). (Cage won the interest of Frederick Stock, who played recordings of his music for the Arts Club in 1941.)[21] The club regularly featured local composers as well, not only Carpenter but Borowski, Eleanor Everest Freer, Leo Sowerby, and David Van Vactor.

The Arts Club—often in conjunction with the Chicago Symphony— took remarkably quick advantage of the arrivals in America of such men as Stravinsky, Prokofiev, Schoenberg, Hindemith, and Bartók. Carpenter personally wrote Schoenberg in 1933, "In full recognition of the importance to our musical culture of your present sojourn in America, the Arts Club of Chicago is very anxious to organize a special performance of some of your Chamber Music works in connection with a dinner and reception in your honor."[22] Thus, the city heard Chicago Symphony players perform Schoenberg's *Kammermusik* in 1934; Hindemith give the world premiere of his Sonata for Unaccompanied Viola no. 3 in 1937; Nadia Boulanger and Jean Françaix play new two-piano works by Lennox Berkeley, Françaix, and Dinu Lipatti in 1939; and Bartók play Bartók and Kodály in 1940 (the Arts Club unsuccessfully sought to bring Bartók back to Chicago in 1941).[23] Both Schoenberg and Bartók described their time in Chicago as "wonderful."[24]

Prokofiev's 1930 concert featured Russian songs—mostly the composer's own—sung by his wife, Lina Llubera. Carpenter had originally suggested a Prokofiev recital of some sort but was out of town caring for Rue when final arrangements were made. Upon hearing that Llubera was scheduled to sing, he telegrammed Jarvis from Atlantic City, "I favor his [Palmer's] suggestion of February 23 for [Martha] Graham but strongly advise deferring decision on Prokofiev if not too late as I have heard further unfavorable criticism of the assisting singer."[25] Palmer tried wriggling out of the concert, writing Prokofiev about conflicts over the use of club rooms, but it was, in fact, too late: a contract had been signed.[26]

All these concerts were glamorous, well-publicized events, but none more so than the two Stravinsky concerts of 24 February 1925 and 13 January 1935. The former included the suite from *L'Histoire du soldat;* the latter featured the Octet and *Pribaoutki,* which was performed twice: the first time conducted by Eric De Lamarter, the second time by Stravinsky. At the 1935 luncheon in Stravinsky's honor, "Carpenter saluted the noted composer in his most charming, flattering manner," reported an article titled "Intellectuals Now Pivot of Social Whirl."[27]

When the Arts Club booked singers and instrumentalists, as opposed to composers, it typically requested that some modern music be programmed. In advance of an April 1933 concert by the violinist Nathan Milstein, for example, John Palmer asked Arthur Judson to "explain to Mr. Milstein that our club is very much interested in modern and ultra modern trends and that if he would care to include some music by recent composers he would find a very receptive audience" (Palmer suggested the works by Bartók, Stravinsky, and Szymanowski in Milstein's repertoire).[28] Similarly, in 1932 the club requested that the Budapest Quartet play Bartók.

Carpenter went so far as to outline an entire program for another Hungarian quartet, the Roth Quartet:

I.   Beethoven-Haydn-Mozart.
II. Ravel or Debussy.
III. One of the following: Harsanyi, Bartók, Rózsa, Rogister ("Depending primarily on Mr. Stock's or Mr. [Jacques] Gordon's recommendation").[29]

Carpenter also proposed a set of contemporary German songs to Ada Mac-Leish, who duly sang Schoenberg, Berg, and Hindemith on her 1933 recital.[30] The Kolish Quartet similarly honored an Arts Club request by giving the first Chicago performance of Berg's *Lyric Suite* in 1936.

The Arts Club also sponsored folk and non-Western music: Indian classical music by Ratan Devi (1928), a Russian vocal quartet, the Kedroff (1928), Spanish dancing by Argentina (1938) and Carmelita Moracci (1940), Javanese and Balinese dancing, accompanied by gamelan (1939), and Brazilian folk music sung by Elsie Houston (1940). In the 1920s Carpenter hoped to sponsor such African American singers as J. Rosamond Johnson, Paul Robeson, the Hall Johnson Choir, and the Negro Quartet from Fisk University, but without any success, apparently. He similarly failed to get Gershwin for the Arts Club in the early 1930s.

Musical lectures at the Arts Club similarly emphasized modern and, less so, folk and non-Western music. Beginning at 11:30 A.M., the lectures usually lasted an hour and were followed by lunch. Milhaud proved a favorite lecturer: he spoke on modern French music (1927), Debussy (1940), his own theater works (1941), Satie (1942), and Brazilian music (1943). Copland lectured twice: once on young American composers (1930) and later on his collaboration with Ruth Page, *Hear Ye! Hear Ye!* (1934). Other speakers included Jeanne Herscher-Clement on Spanish folk music (1926), Laura Bolton on African music (1932), Olin Downes on Soviet music (1933), Paul Rosenfeld on new American music (1934), Nadia Boulanger on young composers (1939), Nicolas Nabokov on Bach and contemporary music (1940), Roy Harris on new American music (1940), Virgil Thomson on music criticism (1941), Colin McPhee on Balinese music (1942), and Carlos Chávez on Mexican music (1943). Although the selection of lecturers was decided in committee, Carpenter wielded enormous influence over all such decisions, at least until the early 1940s. He personally spearheaded the invitations to Boulanger, Copland, Harris, Thomson, and doubtless others.[31]

Carpenter further took an active part in shaping Copland's initial lecture. Of all Copland's proposals, Carpenter best liked the idea of a lecture-recital on recent works by Antheil, Chanler, Chávez, Harris, Sessions, and Copland himself. He wondered, however, if Copland could in addition include one or two of the following composers: Dane Rudhyar, Virgil Thomson, Carl Ruggles, Adolph Weiss, Ruth Crawford, and Henry Cowell. "In case of necessity," Carpenter wrote Copland, "it might be well to omit Chávez. I know those two sonatinas and they are delightful, but after all he hails from the other side of the Rio Grande."[32]

Carpenter personally extended the invitation to Paul Rosenfeld to come to Chicago in 1934 and lecture about Stravinsky. Rosenfeld proposed, rather, a talk about new American music: "With your leave, I would merely mention the South Americans, and speak at greater length of Ives, Sessions, Copland, Varèse, and Harris." Carpenter thought the idea "splendid." Because Rosenfeld's lecture was scheduled close to Schoenberg's January visit, Carpenter requested that it be rescheduled as late as mid-April, because he would be away for most of the winter: "For purely selfish reasons, I am hoping that you will be willing to defer the date of your lecture until our return."[33]

Carpenter's sponsorship of Rosenfeld represented, perhaps, a height of noble disinterest, since Rosenfeld had long been one of the composer's severest critics. But Carpenter recognized Rosenfeld's importance and abilities, as evident not only from his personal interest in attending the lecture, but in a 1923 letter to Julius Gold: "I agree with you about Rosenfeld, not because he does not approve of me, but because he seems to be lashing himself into certain distortions of perspective which impair his usefulness as a critic. This is a pity, because there are so few writers in the country who can match his natural equipment."[34]

The composer acted as sponsor and impresario in still other capacities. In 1933, for example, he arranged on Elizabeth Sprague Coolidge's behalf three October performances by the Pro Arte Quartet at the Chicago World's Fair. "It seems to me appropriate in celebrating a Century of Progress," Coolidge had notified him the preceding July, "to choose the most conspicuous landmarks in quartet writing during that time." Coolidge suggested specific works by Beethoven and Brahms for the first concert, Franck and Debussy for the second, and Hindemith and Schoenberg for the third. She asked Carpenter to fill out the programs by selecting three American quartets, including his "own fine work."[35]

After consulting with Carl Engel at the Library of Congress, Carpenter recommended quartets by Bloch, himself, and Roy Harris. Coolidge, however, thought that "in order to show historical development," Chadwick or Foote would be a better choice than Bloch, and Carpenter settled on the Chadwick Quartet in D Minor.[36] Not only did Carpenter help settle these repertory questions, he scheduled the 18, 20, and 22 October dates and times at the Goodman Theatre (later moved to Orchestra Hall to accommodate a larger audience), wrangled the Chadwick score from the New England Conservatory, offered advice about ticket sales, arranged receptions for the Pro Arte Quartet and for Roy Harris, and hosted a private lunch for Roy and Johanna Harris, to which he invited Stock, De Lamarter, Borowski, Chauncey McCormick, and Charles Goodspeed.[37] In the end the Pro Arte concerts "made a very deep impression," Carpenter wrote to Carl Engel.[38]

Carpenter helped support the publication of new music. A subscriber to Henry Cowell's *New Music,* he served on their Endorsement Board of Honorary Members, along with Berg, Copland, Ives, Krenek, Milhaud, Poulenc, and Roussel.[39] He was more active, however, with the Society for the Publication of American Music (SPAM).

Founded in the flush of postwar nationalism on 29 April 1919 by a small coterie that included Oscar Sonneck, Daniel Gregory Mason, and Rubin Goldmark, SPAM was a nonprofit organization devoted primarily to the publication of new American chamber music. Once founded, SPAM immediately drafted Carpenter to its Board of Directors, and elected him president from 1919 to 1933.

The Society for the Publication of American Music successfully found a few hundred subscribers willing to pay a five-dollar annual fee to cover their publishing expenses. Out of the large number of scores submitted each year, the board selected five or six works to be performed at their annual meeting in New York; two or three of these works were subsequently chosen for publication. For a few years SPAM brought out orchestral works as well, before dissolving in 1969.

The society primarily intended its publications for home use by cultivated amateurs. Indeed, the 1924 publication of a work by Juilliard's Albert Stoessel became something of a best-seller. By the 1930s SPAM recognized that it represented a somewhat conservative viewpoint, and in 1934 one board member, Burnet C. Tuthill, felt obliged to explain to the public that the society's aim was not to publish works "so cacophonous or difficult to perform as to appeal solely to Left Wing modernists."[40] During Carpenter's tenure, SPAM published, in addition to works by forgotten composers, music by Daniel Gregory Mason, Leo Sowerby, Arthur Shepherd, and Quincy Porter.

With his musical sophistication, business savvy, and social clout, Carpenter offered distinguished leadership to SPAM. His generous sympathies and catholic tastes helped ensure a desirable degree of impartiality and broad-mindedness. Moreover, no one need worry about conflicting interests; his relations with Schirmer made it unnecessary for him to submit his own music for publication. His principal disadvantage was that he often could not attend the annual spring meeting in New York. In 1931 he wrote to Tuthill, "Do you not think that I have been Ghost President of the Society long enough?" Tuthill responded: "You come around with this subject every so often and as regularly it is turned down. I think it will continue to be turned down until you are laid away."[41]

But as SPAM's membership began to fall off during the early days of the Depression, Tuthill agreed that the society needed more active leadership.

Carpenter suggested Rubin Goldmark: "He lives in New York and his name and work are universally known and respected."[42] Tuthill, however, proposed Marion Bauer instead, writing, "It might even be to the advantage of the Society to get some one who is more 'left wing,' for most of our present Directors are pretty much on the right hand side of the center." Carpenter responded: "I . . . agree with you completely that it should be a splendid thing to inject into the working philosophy of the S.P.A.M. a little more of the 'left wing' spirit and bring about what the boys in Washington call a 'controlled inflation.' With that objective in view, I believe that Marion Bauer would be the wisest possible choice, as she has many affiliations in both camps. I am all for it." Other board members apparently raised objections, however, and Carpenter was in fact succeeded in 1933 by another well-known song composer, A. Walter Kramer (Bauer was elected secretary).[43]

Carpenter served the new-music community in other ways. In 1923 he turned over $1,000 he had received from Elizabeth Sprague Coolidge to the American Academy of Rome. In the 1920s he became a member of the International Advisory Committee for E. Robert Schmitz's Pro Musica. And in 1946 he became an incorporator of the Illinois Composers' Guild.[44]

Throughout his career Carpenter also served on various composition and performance juries, including those for the American Academy of Rome and the International Society for Contemporary Music (ISCM). One unusual jury involved sitting through twenty renditions of the Stravinsky Piano Concerto for an upcoming Chicago Symphony performance in the mid-1930s (Carpenter's comment? "Ouch!").[45] Carpenter often turned down such responsibilities, however, for one reason or another. In 1920 he declined to serve on a jury because of business demands.[46] In 1928 a similar request made by Carl Engel drew this different response: "If you and Mrs. Coolidge continue to prod, stimulate and inspire composers, as you continuously do, I am sure you must expect a fair majority of them to prefer to sink or swim as contestants rather than to sit proudly as a judge."[47]

Carpenter helped and supported younger composers in more personal ways. Otto Luening (b. 1900) recalled that Carpenter "was really interested in contemporary music" and that he made a point of introducing himself after a performance of Luening's Sextet in 1921; Carpenter "shook my hand solemnly and commented that the orchestration was beautiful." In fact, Carpenter's recommendations probably led to ISCM performances of music by Luening and another Chicagoan, Henry Eichheim (1870–1942).[48]

Carpenter may have assisted yet another Chicagoan, Leo Sowerby, too, although Ronald M. Huntington's exhaustive research into Sowerby's life has as yet yielded little in this regard. John and Rue Carpenter at least helped sponsor an 18 January 1917 concert of Sowerby's works by the Chicago Symphony and an all-Sowerby concert at the Arts Club in 1920. And as a jury member for the American Academy of Rome, Carpenter probably helped Sowerby obtain the 1921 Rome Prize. But overall, the relationship between Carpenter and Sowerby was surprisingly distant, considering that they were the two most prominent Chicago composers of their day. A conflict between Carpenter and Sowerby over the possible replacement of Felix Lamond as head of the Academy of Rome's Music Department in 1926 might have strained whatever friendship may have existed, although Carpenter eventually supported Sowerby in this matter.[49]

As best he could Carpenter helped other young composers, as in his invitations to Copland, Harris, and Thomson to lecture at the Arts Club. After attending a performance of Copland's *Billy the Kid,* Carpenter congratulated the composer on his work: "I must tell you how keen we were about 'Billy the Kid.' I think it is awfully good from all standpoints, music, choreography and costumes, and they all hang together to perfection,—all fresh and completely on the level. My heartiest congratulations to you and also to Loring both as swell dancer and subtle inventor."[50] Carpenter even encouraged the twelve-year-old Ned Rorem (b. 1923), who early on had become familiar with Carpenter's music through his teacher, Margaret Bonds. In 1936 Rorem recorded some of his own music and mailed the recordings to Carpenter, who wrote back "two letters with avuncular advice, and which I treasured."[51]

Carpenter's correspondence with John Becker and Florence Price more fully reveal his concern and support for younger, American composers.

Becker (1886–1961) was one of the rising stars of the American avant-garde when Carpenter met him in 1934 through Varèse.[52] Later that year Carpenter began a regular correspondence with the Minneapolis composer, and a close friendship ensued. In 1935 Carpenter wrote a series of letters to help Becker obtain financial help through the WPA,[53] and in 1949 he hoped to make the conductor Fritz Busch "Becker-conscious."[54] Becker, in turn, helped bring Carpenter's latest works to Minneapolis.

After her husband's death, Becker's wife recalled, "Mr. Carpenter was aware of their different methods of composing, and would refer to the lightness of his work humorously, and to John's use of dissonances, in like manner."[55] (Carpenter often signed his letters to Becker "C♯–C♮," which became a byword for dissonance and, less literally, newness.)[56] Carpenter's friendship with Becker suggested not only an ironic awareness of differences, however, but real common ground, as further revealed by a comparison of *Skyscrapers* with Becker's 1933 percussion piece *The Abongo.*

Carpenter's correspondence with Florence Price (1888–1953) also began in 1934. According to Eileen Southern, Price was "the first Negro woman to win recognition as a composer."[57] A native of Little Rock, Arkansas, Price had come to Chicago to study at the Chicago Musical College and the American Conservatory of Music. On 15 June 1933 Stock conducted Price's Symphony in E Minor, "the first work by an African-American woman to be performed by a major symphony orchestra."[58] Carpenter undoubtedly knew Price's music when he agreed, in a letter dated 18 December 1934, to "act as proposer" for Price's membership in ASCAP.[59]

Price was encouraged by Carpenter's interest in her "beautiful work." She was particularly delighted by a letter from Carpenter concerning a song of hers that was to be sung by Marian Anderson: "You are certainly to be congratulated on the inclusion of one of your songs in Miss Anderson's programs, for it is undoubtedly, one of the highest goals that any contemporary writer of songs can reach." Price immediately told Anderson about the letter, describing Carpenter as "one of America's most outstanding composers, a man without prejudice—altho he is a millionaire quietly exerting far-reaching influence and power in the world of music. . . . He is very decisive and outspoken in his likes and dislikes."[60]

During and after World War II, Carpenter's attention turned away somewhat from modernist music and dance and focused, rather, on music making for amateurs. He actively promoted the work of Hugh Ross (b. 1898), Schindler's successor as the director of the Schola Cantorum, and later choral conductor at the Manhattan School and at Tanglewood. His work, wrote Carpenter in 1944, was of interest "to all of us who are trying to build up 'Democracy through Education.'"[61]

In 1943 Carpenter joined Ken Carrington in establishing the Office of Civilian Defense (O.C.D.) Committee, whose stated aim was "to provide outdoor concerts in Chicago's parks during the summer months for the relaxation and stimulation of the city's hundreds of thousands of workers in war production plants."[62] With the help of the Chicago Metropolitan Area Office of Civilian Defense, the committee launched a concert series, "Let Freedom Sing!" that featured eleven choral groups performing in three of Chicago's largest parks. The success of these concerts was "phenomenal," remembered Carpenter: "The people wanted the concerts and attended in great crowds. The singers found that they liked singing to these informal audiences who had not paid admission but had gathered because they wanted to sit in beautiful surroundings and listen to good music." It all reminded Carpenter of *The Merchant of Venice:*

How sweet the moonlight sleeps upon this bank!

Here we will sit, and let the sounds of music

Creep in our ears; soft stillness and the night

Become the touches of sweet harmony.[63]

Throughout the fall and winter of 1943–44, the committee sponsored similar concerts at hospitals, servicemen's centers, and park fieldhouses. Soldiers and hospital patients demanded encores. "Chicago recognized this effort to bring good music, well presented, to places where such music is too seldom heard as an important addition to its civic life," wrote Carpenter.[64]

In 1944 the committee incorporated as the nonprofit Choral and Instrumental Association of Chicago, with Carpenter as its president. In addition to concerts in the parks, the association sponsored, in 1945, a Music Week with noontime concerts at the corner of State and Madison Streets in downtown Chicago. Music Week also hosted a Music Conference to discuss amateur music making and related issues.

By 1946 the Choral and Instrumental Association sponsored concerts nearly every day in July and August in six Chicago parks by thirty-eight performing groups, including the First National Bank Choral Association, the Chicago and Northwestern Railway Company Choral Club, and the Aeolian Choral Association. On 4 July an amalgamated group of 250 singers performed at Soldier Field. Carpenter summed up the significance of these concerts: "The importance of these musical events in Chicago cannot be overestimated. Good music is being brought directly into the lives of many, many persons who have had their music only over the radio or from the movie sound tracks. They are, for the first time, realizing that people make up choruses and orchestras, that singing is fun to listen to, and that it is fun to sing." He once again quoted Shakespeare:

The man that has no music in himself,

Nor is not moved with concord of sweet sounds,

Is fit for treasons, stratagems, and spoils;

The motions of his spirit are dull as night,

And his affections dark as Erebus,
Let no such man be trusted.[65]

In 1947, upon hearing of local music institutions on the Monterey Peninsula while in Carmel, the composer further commented: "That's the way it should be. Music must come up through the schools and through the people in order that it be a vital and integral part of living!"[66]

That Carpenter could devote so much time and energy to so many organizations—from the Cliff Dwellers to the Choral and Instrumental Association, from the Allied Arts to SPAM, from the Arts Club to the Illinois Guild of Composers, from the Illinois Children's Home and Aid Society to the U.S. military—was amazing and practically constituted a third career in addition to business and composition. The extent of Carpenter's "far-reaching influence," to use Price's phrase, was hard to fully measure, intimated only by further pieces of evidence: In 1925 he had Oscar Sonneck ask Julius Gold to write a piece on Bernhard Ziehn for *Musical Quarterly*;[67] in 1929 he hoped to do "Boston a service" by getting Koussevitzky to perform Shostakovich's First Symphony, which he thought "an altogether delightful piece of writing";[68] in 1930 he recommended Mina Hager to Walter Damrosch for a broadcast appearance;[69] in 1933 he proposed (unsuccessfully) that Elizabeth Sprague Coolidge be granted an honorary doctorate from the University of Chicago;[70] in 1936 he brought the French musicologist and performer of medieval music Yves Tinayre to the attention of Richard Copley;[71] in 1941 he asked Virgil Thomson to review a performance by Mina Hager;[72] in 1944 he promoted the educational work of Hugh Ross to Elizabeth Sprague Coolidge;[73] and in 1950 he praised Ken Carrington's efforts on behalf of music in the city parks to Chicago's mayor Martin Kennelly.[74] With so many friends in such high places, it was hardly surprising that Carpenter's influence should be "far-reaching."

Carpenter profited from all of these activities as much as anyone. His happiness depended not only on that "state of spiritual well-being" that comes from the "just perception of the rhythm . . . of our individual lives" but in forming a "Guild of Gropers" to share his "Cheerful Discontent."

CHAPTER TWENTY-SIX

Final Years

1946–1951

|||Carpenter typically spent winters abroad, but after war broke out in 1939, he began wintering in either California or Florida: Santa Barbara in 1940, Hobe Sound from 1943 to 1946, Carmel in 1947 and 1948, and Sarasota in 1950 and 1951. These kinds of arty seaside retreats had long attracted him.

Carpenter traveled to Santa Barbara in 1940 possibly in conjunction with the planned revival of *Krazy Kat* with Massine and Herriman. He presumably spent four winters in Hobe Sound, on the other hand, because that was a favored winter retreat for his and Ellen's circle of wealthy, sophisticated, older Americans. He would have at least enjoyed the company of his friend John Marquand, who, in 1945, amusingly described Hobe Sound to his daughter as follows:

> At noon everyone foregathers, as they say in books, at the Beach Club—a sort of semi-enclosed pavilion beside the surf. Here drinks are dispensed from a little bar to tired executives, most of them in their sixties, dressed in schoolboy clothes, and to their women who are either their daughters about your age or reformed chorus girls. Then there is a cafeteria lunch, which means that you have to take your own tray and bring it all by yourself to the table. Lots of women get their diamond bracelets mixed up in the potato salad and break their pearls as they lean over for a piece of black market roast beef. The noise is terrific because everybody is having lots and lots of fun, and thank God, here we all are in the divine Florida sunshine.[1]

With bleaker irony, Marquand wrote to his son in the army: "Dinner dances at the Beach Club, a bar, ocean bathing, music and merriment every minute and nice, nice people—everyone of whom would cut up for $10,000,000. For instance, Vincent Astor is here, and, for example, we are dining tonight with

Ernest Weir, the cruel industrialist without social conscience who crushes the workingman. It is all quite different from Guam and Iwo Jima."[2]

Carpenter shared Marquand's ambivalence: "We got a little fed up with Florida," he told John Becker in late 1946.[3] In 1947 the Carpenters went to Carmel, in part so that they could hear Monteux and the San Francisco Symphony perform *The Seven Ages*. They stayed at the Reginald Inwood house in the Carmel highlands; the following winter they returned to Carmel, renting the Glenburn home. A congenial group of friends awaited them, including Lester Donahue, Rudolph Ganz, Remsen Bird, the Bolms, and San Francisco novelist Martin Flavin and his wife.[4]

A small village on California's Monterey Peninsula, Carmel's rugged beauty had long attracted such writers as Robinson Jeffers, Mary Austin, Sinclair Lewis, and Upton Sinclair. Carpenter agreed that the scenery was splendid but felt, according to one newspaper account, "that the very beauties of California have their dangers; that many of us here are inclined to bask in our own comfort and contentment, and feel ourselves far removed from the problems that beset the rest of the world. 'It might be better for our souls if we weren't so comfortable,' he said."[5]

The Carpenters returned to Florida—specifically, Siesta Key, Sarasota—in 1950 on account of the illness and subsequent death of Ellen's brother James "Monny" Waller; Ellen apparently wanted to be closer to Chicago.[6] The Carpenters sailed in the bay and visited the vacationing Ringling Brothers Circus.

In January 1948, while in Carmel, Carpenter began an orchestral transcription of the 1936 Violin Concerto. He continued work on it after returning to Chicago in April and completed it in Beverly in June. Much of the transcription must have been finished by late February, however, for he informed his granddaughter on 29 February 1948, "I am just finishing a new orchestra piece which sometimes strikes me as being pretty good."[7] Carpenter eventually titled the work the *Carmel Concerto*.

The relation between the *Carmel Concerto* and the Violin Concerto—itself a highly intricate work—is labyrinthine. Carpenter transforms the Violin Concerto's three-movement ABC form—played without pause—into an even smoother, one-movement work that forms an ABCA design. True, the Violin Concerto also returns to A after the C section, but it intersperses such recollections alongside those from sections B and C, in the spirit of an extended cadenza. In the *Carmel Concerto,* A returns more explicitly as a recapitulation, giving the music greater symmetry.

The *Carmel Concerto*'s A section, marked Moderato energico, introduces its main theme, in C major, at ⊡. This theme derives not so much from the Violin Concerto's main theme, stated at ② of that work, but rather from a later transformation of this theme, at nine after ⑫. The subsidiary themes at ③ and ⑥ of the *Carmel Concerto* also correspond to materials from the Violin Concerto.

At ④ Carpenter arrives at a passage that in the Violin Concerto (see ⊡) precedes the main theme, one that, in fact, is introductory! Even more surprising, at ⑦ Carpenter introduces a fairly literal arrangement of his 1916 piano piece *Little Indian* (in D minor, rather than the original C♯ minor). This transcription substitutes for the Violin Concerto's *feroce* passage at ⑦, which is similarly static and primitivist, and which contains a melody—put forth by the solo violin at ⑧—somewhat like that of *Little Indian*.

The *Carmel Concerto*'s B section, Legato tranquillo, is only twenty-seven measures long. Beginning at ⑮ in A major, this tranquil episode subsequently moves to the C♯ minor associated with the Violin Concerto's B section. Essentially, Carpenter reworks only the beginning and ending of the Violin Concerto's ternary B section, omitting the lovely middle part.

The *Carmel Concerto*'s C section, marked Tempo I at ⑲, opens with giguelike material in B♭ major and G minor; the latter music derives from the Violin Concerto's C section, whereas the former is new. Again, bits and pieces of the Violin Concerto reappear in unexpected places. And the composer makes big cuts: at ㉖ in the new work, he jumps, in essence, the more than one hundred measures from ㉙ to ㊳ in the Violin Concerto. At six measures after ㉗, Carpenter introduces a new, Stravinskian melody in the oboe.

At ㉙ the music recalls material from the A section, arriving at a more formal recapitulation in C major at ㉜. Carpenter states a new, impetuous waltz tune in B♭ major (two after ㉞) before returning once more to C major. The surprising G-minor conclusion is, in utter contrast to the Violin Concerto, loud and dynamic.

Carpenter originally intended to title this new work Ballade or Serenade, but Nathan Broder at G. Schirmer suggested, rather, "a non-committal but piquant label on the order of 'Dumbarton Oaks Concerto.'" Carpenter accordingly called the work the *Carmel Concerto Grosso,* later shortened to the *Carmel Concerto.*[8]

In a program note Carpenter explained that the work is a "'concerto for orchestra,' in the contemporary sense, the title serving merely to identify the background against which the work was written."[9] He further implied in an interview with the *Monterey Peninsula Herald* that the work took its inspiration from Carmel: "I feel sure that the locale of the new concerto will identify itself as the magic outlook from our window at Glenburn. Anyone who has seen it can imagine how potent might become the spell of the 'Carmel background' in the consciousness of a composer already deeply under the influence of its charm."[10] Considering the work's derivation from two older compositions, this claimed relation to Carmel is necessarily problematic. Did Carmel's pristine natural beauty, celebrated by Mary Austin, remind the composer of native Indians, hence, the inclusion of *Little Indian* in its pages?

Carpenter and Stokowski arranged for a fall 1949 premiere. On 4 April, Werner Janssen contacted H. W. Heinsheimer at G. Schirmer about introducing the work himself during the summer of 1949 at the Hollywood Bowl, and without consulting Carpenter, Heinsheimer approached Stokowski about deferring the premiere. When Carpenter learned about this from Heinsheimer in a letter dated 3 May 1949, the composer, whose relations with Schirmer (or "Schirmerheimer" as he had begun to call the firm) had soured, was furious—all the more so, no doubt, because Stokowski often declined second performances.[11] An understanding with Stokowski had been reached, Carpenter wrote Heinsheimer back the following day: "Now, out of a clear sky, you are asking him [Stokowski] if he minds yielding up his privilege of *first performance* to another conductor who wishes to introduce the work in the Hollywood Bowl *six months ahead of him!!!*"[12] As usual, Heinsheimer responded apologetically. For his part, Janssen wrote to the composer on 9 May 1949, "You must admit my enthusiasm for the 'Carmel Concerto' ran away with me."[13]

Stokowski premiered the *Carmel Concerto* with the New York Philharmonic on 20 November 1949, a performance broadcast nationwide later that year on 20 December. Carpenter informed John Becker that the premiere "had a greater success than I had hoped for";[14] indeed, Hal Garrott, who heard the Stokowski broadcast, reported "tremendous applause following the finale."[15] Garrott liked the work very much himself and in a burst of cold war patriotism, stated:

> After hearing John Alden Carpenter's "Carmel Concerto" over the radio yesterday, I say, let the Russians keep their Shostakovich and plenty of others. When such music is written by an American, a direct descendent of John Alden, it's time our orchestras played everything he wrote. . . . The piece has an oriental flavor, and at times suggests both Chinese and Indian music. It is modern in spirit and orchestration. The composer never leaves us long with-

out some enchanting melodic figure, interspersed between refreshing rhythms and novel instrumentation. Mr. Carpenter's work will live and grow in public favor because he creates melody—something unknown to most modern composers.[16]

Cecil Smith, on the other hand, was more critical:

The Carmel Concerto, the latest orchestra work of John Alden Carpenter, is a loosely constructed one-movement work, about twelve minutes in duration, employing a conventionally syncopated main theme and a variety of subsidiary materials that are said to be tinged with Oriental and Spanish-American color, although this latter aspect was not conspicuous upon first hearing. The piece is urbane, forthright, and friendly in spirit, but its episodic construction and its tendency to overwork the rather thin subject-matter of the principal theme contribute to a generally labored effect. It is not one of the composer's most successful works.[17]

Both Artur Rodzinski and Tauno Hannikainen implied, however, that Stokowski failed to do the work justice. Rodzinski attributed this failure to insufficient rehearsal: "I wish only that you [Carpenter] were present at the rehearsal because Stokowski is getting very careless lately and during the rehearsals, plays the work once or twice thru and that is all. With all the wonderful and carefully worked out dynamics in your score, it requires a thoro job to prepare it properly." Hannikainen similarly commented, "I noticed that Stokowski, in some places, has not followed John's metronome numbers, [and] in one place has played it exactly twice as slowly as indicated."[18]

On 3 March 1950 Hannikainen and the Chicago Symphony introduced the work to Chicago. Noting a warm audience reception, Seymour Raven further observed: "Mr. Carpenter's work is interesting first because it represents a composer willing in this case to reflect on nature rather than answer it with music. Also it reminds us of the American Indian."[19]

The work failed to find other performances. Rodzinski intended to conduct the piece in 1949 but programmed Vaughan Williams's Sixth Symphony instead, explaining to the composer that he could not afford too many "novelties."[20] Janssen similarly planned to give the West Coast premiere, but his orchestra "folded up." Carpenter turned to Remsen Bird in the hopes that he might intercede on his behalf and interest Alfred Wallenstein, the conductor of the Los Angeles Philharmonic, in the work.[21] Carpenter naturally appealed to Koussevitzky as well, describing the work as "quasi symphonic in structure" with an "emotional content" that "alternates between vigor and repose. Technically it presents no problems."[22]

Carpenter continued to revise older works and contemplate new projects. In February 1946, while in Hobe Sound, he made some sketches for "a serious song for mezzo-soprano, string quartet, harp, and clarinet." Although he never completed the work, it might have provided the basis for another unfinished composition, the *Song of David* for cello and orchestra.[23]

By early 1949 Carpenter had another project in mind, which he referred to as his "Jungle" idea. He discussed the concept with his daughter Ginny, and on 6 April he wrote to her in Caracas, asking her to tell *her* daughter, Rue, what she thought about it. Carpenter explained: "Please understand, that Rue, on receipt of your 'frantic' letter, will psychoanalyze it or me with the help of her Superior Farmington Education (T. S. Eliot and all that!) and thus enable me at least to guess what your real reaction to 'Jungle' may be. This eccentric indirect approach on my part may seem to you to be something like a round robin in a square hole, but in these days of Super Confusion even *robins* may be round."[24] (In this same letter Carpenter told Ginny that he was sending her "a wonderful book," *Cry the Beloved Country*.) Carpenter was still planning this "'jungle' opus" as late as February 1950, while recuperating from a broken hip.[25]

In early 1951 Carpenter informed reporters that he was currently working on a piece for cello and orchestra titled *Song of David,* for the Russian cellist Gregor Piatigorsky.[26] Carpenter explained that he originally had wanted to write an opera after J. M. Barrie's last play, *The Boy David* (1936), but had been unable to obtain the rights. This interest in *The Boy David* was peculiar only in that the play had flopped (indeed, it was widely dismissed by English critics as "a sort of ineffectual Peter Pan for Bible lovers"). Carpenter, however, would naturally have identified with Barrie's work and might well have discerned in this particular play, as did James A. Roy, "a profound tragedy and the supreme expression of Barrie's mystic exaltation, of his communion with the intangible and the eternal."[27]

In August 1950 Carpenter inquired about William Walton's own *Boy David*,[28] although the idea of a *Song of David* for cello and orchestra surely derived from Bloch's *Schelomo,* one of the most widely performed orchestral works of its time. Carpenter probably heard *Schelomo* in Chicago as early as 1923; more recently, he would have heard Leonard Rose perform it under Rodzinski at a 1945 concert that included his own *Seven Ages*.

Carpenter completed only two pages of *Song of David* before he died. Scored for cello, orchestra, and women's voices (four sopranos and four mezzo-sopranos), the manuscript bears an inscription not from Barrie but from Browning's *Saul:* "Here is David, thy servant!" The music's somber pedal, in triple meter with duplets, recalls the composer's Whitman-inspired *Sea Drift,* but its D-Dorian coloring has a distinctive poignance. After the composer's death Ellen sent these two pages of score to Piatigorsky, who wrote back: "I need not tell you how overwhelmed I am to know that he was composing it with me in mind. I do not know of anything that would have given me greater joy than to perform this composition."[29]

In the years following World War II, Carpenter spoke with the full wisdom of his experience about music, art, and society. In a letter to Harvard's president, James Bryant Conant, on 10 September 1945, he stated: "Our postwar world presents to the groping average man so many dilemmas, with a maze of horns pointing in so many directions that he cries aloud for compass and gyroscope. All his natural instincts tell him that he is critically out of balance. . . . It [music] is potent equally for the few and the multitude, both 'Jeffersonian' and 'Jacksonian' in its appeal. It serves indispensably and impartially, as the instinctive voice of despair and triumph and the love of God."[30] In 1947 he similarly professed, "Ideas or inspirations come from God, or from a Divine Origin," and he advised composers to establish "a regular work schedule" and to cut themselves off "from all tradition" ("Get loose! I'm from New England and I know what a Puritanical influence can do").[31]

When asked by one reporter about the postwar music scene, Carpenter approvingly noted that American composers were no longer "running around"; he observed, too, the widespread influence of Stravinsky as opposed to Schoenberg, who "is not an American dish."

> On the other hand, Roger Sessions, a native composer, writes music that is great, profound, and with tremendous workmanship. But, is it communicable? William Grant Still has a very interesting talent. I personally like Gian-Carlo Menotti's operatic pieces, some of which have interesting stage effects; but Samuel Barber exemplifies my own line of musical thinking.

"I'd like to make a prediction," he continued. "The next big move to come in music will come from this country or from Russia; both are the least shackled by tradition."[32]

In a letter to Koussevitzky on the occasion of the conductor's resignation from the Boston Symphony in 1948, Carpenter was less sanguine but still hopeful: "It is perhaps our misfortune that America has become complacently accustomed to *material success,* but we may be thankful that our imagination can still be deeply stirred by the thought of a *great ideal* patiently served and triumphantly achieved through the spirit of devotion."[33] And in 1949 Carpenter assumed a more whimsical tone with his daughter Ginny: "According to my 11th hour, 7th decade credo, if the creative artist is *aware,* he must ask every subject asking for treatment two *heavy* questions: Is it *fun?* Is it (may it be) beautiful?"[34]

Carpenter remained keenly appreciative of some popular music, including, by 1947, Richard Rodgers's *Oklahoma!* and *Carousel.* "Men like Richard Rodgers," he stated, "will give us something to be proud of. Just lift *Oklahoma!* two or three notches, eliminate a few of its crudities, and you have a native dignified art that you don't need to keep alive with a pulmotor like the Metropolitan opera." He expressed admiration for Cole Porter's "tremendous gifts," but Irving Berlin remained his favorite in this area:

> Yes, Berlin is far ahead of even George Gershwin, who was very, very good. Berlin is pure gold. When the musical historian of a century from now goes to work, he may well conclude that American music really began with Irving Berlin. He is one of the world's great composers. He simply has a gift of God—such musical purity, such a melodic sense—the contemporary counterpart of Stephen Foster. And what marvelous ideas Berlin has—ideas that a composer would give his last tooth for![35]

During these final years, Carpenter's health steadily declined. While in New York for the 20 November 1949 premiere of the *Carmel Concerto,* he fell and broke his hip.[36] He spent Christmas at home in bed and then repaired to Sarasota, where he enjoyed some sailing. By March 1950 the doctors had told him that he could "throw away [his] crutches," and by June he felt completely recovered from his "tumble." In early 1951 Carpenter made light of the injury with Irving Sablosky, stating, "Still, it's harder when your ideas give out than when your legs do."[37]

Carpenter's health had been delicate for some time. As early as 1934 Adlai Stevenson referred to "Mr. C's nurse."[38] He was ill for much of December 1936.[39] In late 1937 he developed streptococcus poisoning from neglected teeth and needed to take a sulfa cure for a year, "and that sulfa cure the Docs invented is no joy-ride either," he wrote to John Becker.[40]

In bed with "the grippe" in January 1943, Carpenter was still not well enough in April to travel to the University of Rochester to receive an honorary doctorate.[41] The winter of 1948 also found him "laid up somewhat recently."[42] Indeed, he saw no fewer than thirteen doctors in 1948, including specialists in otolaryngology (ear, nose, and throat), dermatology and syphilology, urology (kidney and urinary infection), internal medicine, and opthamology.[43] He needed the ear and eye specialists for his growing deafness and blindness; by 1949 he was purchasing hearing aids.[44] Indeed, his growing deafness made it hard for him to communicate, remembered Adlai Stevenson Jr., who marveled at his step-grandfather's ability to write finely shaded music nonetheless.[45]

In early February 1951, having recovered from his broken hip, Carpenter suffered a stroke while in Sarasota. Ginny, who had been in New York, flew down to Florida and on 7 February wrote to her husband that it seemed only "a question of hours."[46] Carpenter, however, slowly regained strength. "Now he's conscious," reported the *Chicago Tribune* on 12 February 1951, "able to take solid foods, and is generally so much better that his daughter has gone back to her home in South America."[47]

Carpenter spent his seventy-fifth birthday on 28 February recuperating in Sarasota. His stroke may well have prompted the especially lavish tributes that honored the occasion, including "200 congratulatory wires, flowers and hundreds of letters and cards."[48] Many newspapers featured interviews with the composer. One such included Carpenter's final statement on the importance of art and religion to society:

> Their task is to nourish and sustain people. The day of American leadership has dawned and it is necessary for us to become spiritual leaders. It is not enough to deal with things. In addition, we must express our ideas and ideals. It is the role of music and the arts to be the medium for this expression.
>
> I recommend prayer and a return to religion and art as solution to today's problems. They speak to the best that is in us. These troubled times are not a healthy period for the creator. Artists cannot be afraid of today and afraid for tomorrow and express themselves freely.[49]

Another interview offered the composer's last published thoughts on a subject he had often waffled on—business and music: "For many years until my retirement in 1936 I stole time for music, but I wouldn't give up now what I gained from business. Contacts with people I met there stimulated me and gave me new and richer musical ideas." And he once again discussed the value of popular music: "The composer who ignores the popular music of his own country or neglects the contemporary scene is crazy. George Gershwin left a deep mark on American music; Irving Berlin is a marvel of our own times, and negro spirituals have been an important factor in the making of American music."[50]

In the meantime, Howard Hanson wrote a special appreciation for *Saturday Review* in which he listed the composer's most significant accomplishments: first, along with Chadwick and Gilbert, he broke with the German tradition; second, "He was one of the very first Americans to bring to American music a subtlety and delicacy of expression which had been up to that time generally lacking"; third, he developed a particularly American kind of humor in music; and finally, "though primarily a melodist and colorist, he has remained an interested experimenter in rhythmic techniques."[51]

On the day before the composer's birthday, Rafael Kubelik and the Chicago Symphony performed *Skyscrapers* and the 1940 suite from *The Birthday of the Infanta* (to unenthused reviews).[52] Other birthday celebrations followed: the BBC aired selected works; Eugene Goossens organized a special program with the Sydney Symphony Orchestra; and Marian Anderson, Gladys Swarthout, Kirsten Flagstad, and Mina Hager programmed songs in his honor.[53]

On 3 March 1951 Ellen wrote a concerned John McCutcheon: "John sat up yesterday. We are greatly encouraged."[54] He was soon well enough to leave Sarasota and return to 999 Lake Shore Drive. On 26 April, while at home, his heart failed, and he died. On the next day, services—including performances of some of his own songs—were held at his Chicago home. He was buried in Beverly, followed by another memorial service.

Nearly all of the obituaries—including those in the *Chicago Tribune,* the *New York Times, Variety,* and *Newsweek*—referred to Carpenter as the man Walter Damrosch had called the "most American of composers."[55] The *New York Times* and *Newsweek* similarly cited the composer's most notable achievement as "transferring the spirit and feeling of the jazz idiom to the concert hall" *(New York Times)* and integrating "the jazz idiom and the nervous rhythms of city life into symphonic forms" *(Newsweek).*

An obituary in *Musical America* (written ostensibly by the magazine's editor, Cecil Smith) stood above the rest in breadth and sophistication. "With the passing of John Alden Carpenter," it began, "American music has lost one of its most lucid and humanistic spirits. Carpenter occupied an unusual position among American composers in several respects. He was neither a reactionary nor a revolutionary, but simply an honest artist who accepted the modern era and interpreted it according to his own lights." *Gitanjali* revealed the composer's "sensitive imagination, keen color sense, and romantic aspirations"; *The Birthday of the Infanta* exhibited a "good sense of dramatic atmosphere and a fine, if still somewhat conventional harmonic palette"; *Krazy Kat* belonged to "the jazzy, raucous, humorous, furiously energetic world of modern America"; *Skyscrapers,* a "more searching" work, "mirrored the tensions and drives of the industrial colossus"; and *Sea Drift* "turns from the world of clashing energy, material confusion, and neurotic haste to a world of nature and wild grandeur. . . . It makes one realize the spiritual range of this artist, who could accept the material world without reservation but could also escape from it."[56] Regrettably, future accounts of the composer derived not from this excellent summary but from simpler, more hackneyed sources.

All of the obituaries naturally listed some of the composer's many honors, including an honorary master of arts from Harvard (1922) and honorary doctorates from the University of Wisconsin (1934), the American Conservatory of Music (1936), and Northwestern University (1941). (The University of Rochester also offered him an honorary doctorate in 1943, although, as mentioned, he was too ill to attend graduation ceremonies to the "particular disappointment" of Howard Hanson.)[57] Other honors included membership in the National Institute of Arts and Letters (1918), Chevalier of the French Legion of Honor (1921), the medal of St. Sava (1938), membership in the American Academy of Arts and Letters (1942), and the Gold Medal of the National Institute of Arts and Letters (1947). Carpenter thus became the fourth musician to win the National Institute's Gold Medal; he was preceded by Loeffler (1918), Chadwick (1928), and Damrosch (1938). (After the institute announced its decision, Aaron Copland expressed his congratulations: "As one of the 'runners-up' I particularly want you to know how pleased I am that the honor went to you—and how well merited I think it is." Carpenter replied: "Your note has given me the keenest pleasure. Many thanks! I freely admit that this happening has given this ancient composer an authentic shot in the arm, so if, from now on, I should run a little wild, that will be my alibi.")[58]

A few weeks after Carpenter's death, the *Chicago Tribune* reported that he had left an estate estimated at $100,000. He willed his manuscripts to the Library of Congress, $5,000 to the Chicago Symphony, his royalties to his wife, $5,000 to his granddaughter, and the bulk of his estate to his daughter Ginny.[59]

In 1952 Ellen, with the assistance of friends, built a Carpenter Memorial Theater at Castle Hill, a fifteen hundred acre estate that Mrs. Richard Crane had bequeathed to the state of Massachusetts, and that had become the site of a small, summer music festival in 1950. This Memorial Theater consisted of a small bandshell "painted gray and white with imitation alabaster green columns."[60]

Castle Hill dedicated its new theater on 27 July 1952, with an all-Carpenter program: Mina Hager sang, George Roth performed piano pieces, and the New Music Quartet played the String Quartet.[61] George Roth and the New Music Quartet also participated in a commemorative concert at the Library of Congress on 5 December 1952; this program included the String Quartet, the Piano Quintet, and the Violin Concerto in the violin-piano version, with Broadus Erle playing the violin part.

For the tenth anniversary of the composer's death in 1961, Ellen founded a John Alden Carpenter Memorial Committee, with Carleton Sprague Smith as executive director. The esteemed board of sponsors included Howard Barlow, Leonard Bernstein, Ellen Carpenter, Van Cliburn, Aaron Copland, Howard Hanson, Roy Harris, Olga Koussevitzky, Charles Munch, Eugene Ormandy, Paul Paray, Fritz Reiner, Arthur Rubinstein, Rudolf Serkin, Fabien Sevitzky, Leopold Stokowski, Igor Stravinsky, and Bruno Walter. In accepting his sponsorship, Serkin referred to the composer as "great" and the "master." Harris wrote, "The young have been too long deprived of his beautiful music."[62]

To celebrate this tenth anniversary, Castle Hill held another all-Carpenter concert on 6 August 1961. Eleanor Steber sang *Gitanjali,* and the Fine Arts performed the String Quartet and the Piano Quintet, with Lee Luvisi, piano. On 2 November 1961 a similar commemorative program was given at the Isabella Stewart Gardner Museum in Boston.

The impressive board of the Carpenter Memorial Committee and the distinguished performers at Castle Hill and the Isabella Stewart Gardner Museum did not stem America's growing indifference to the composer. Castle Hill itself was soon after turned over to a land conservation agency, and the Carpenter Memorial Theater was dismantled and forgotten.

Carpenter's music continued to be heard, nonetheless. Schoolchildren still sang "The Home Road," singers continued to perform "When I Bring to You Colour'd Toys" and "The Sleep That Flits on Baby's Eyes," and orchestras occasionally performed and recorded *Adventures in a Perambulator, Krazy Kat, Skyscrapers,* and *Sea Drift.* Still, many works awaited revival, including the charming Piano Concertino, the jazzy String Quartet, the romantic Piano Quintet, the formidable Violin Concerto, the brilliantly scored symphonies, the poetic *Seven Ages,* and dozens of magnificent songs.

Afterword

During the 1940s Charles Ives overtook Carpenter as the preeminent American composer of their generation. By the end of the twentieth century, Ives had so overshadowed all of his contemporaries that any distinction claimed for Carpenter would seem minor and academic to some critics.

Even in his own lifetime, Carpenter never achieved the kind of veneration that Ives won posthumously; he always resisted attributions of greatness. But he was unique among his generation for appealing, during his lifetime, to adventurous conductors, singers, pianists, critics, composers, artists, poets—in short, to many of the same types that after 1940 took an interest in Ives. Even during their lifetime, their music won some of the same friends—performers like Leopold Stokowski, Mina Hager, E. Robert Schmitz, and Eugene Goossens; critics like Olin Downes and Lawrence Gilman; and the composer John Becker.

This Carpenter-Ives reversal happened so suddenly that the literature about Carpenter—most of it from the first half of the century—seemed unaware of Ives, and the newer Ives criticism seemed equally unaware of Carpenter. It was as if Carpenter and Ives lived in separate nations.

At least Carpenter and Ives were aware of each other. Ives took oblique aim at *Perambulator* in his *Essay before a Sonata;* he naturally thought Carpenter mannered and facile, even while acknowledging the composer's wit and talent. Carpenter welcomed Paul Rosenfeld's idea to lecture about Ives, among others, as "splendid"; he at least would have cheered Ives's originality.

Carpenter and Ives had a tremendous amount in common, far beyond the striking fact that both led double lives as businessmen-composers: descended from old Congregational, Republican, New England families, they studied piano and attended New England universities; they shared a high regard for Browning and had overlapping literary tastes; they admired Bach,

Beethoven, Wagner, Bruckner, Dvořák, Debussy, and Strauss yet believed that American music should be distinctive; they loved and incorporated popular musics, including hymns, patriotic airs, Foster, Sousa, and ragtime; they felt unconstrained by academic forms, preferring the song and tone poem; and they emphasized music as a spiritual and social communication.

Indeed, Carpenter and Ives shared ideals related to turn-of-the-century "progressivism": both ridiculed gentility and materialism, took an optimistic and patriotic view of life, restlessly and constantly revised their music, generously supported experimental art, and perhaps above all, derived great inspiration from children.

At the same time, Carpenter and Ives could hardly be more unalike. Ives epitomized the hermetic composer, working in isolation, composing dense, difficult music. Just the opposite, Carpenter wrote lucid, highly accessible music for as wide an audience as possible, including children. Ives's novelty was his complexity; Carpenter's, his straightforwardness.

Ives explored in his creative life his New England background and his childhood in Danbury, Connecticut. Carpenter felt uneasy about his New England heritage—at least its puritanical legacy—and perhaps about his own childhood. He sought ideas from America's other ethnicities (most notably, native Indian, African, Irish, and Russo-Jewish), as well as from the music, dance, and poetry of Latin America, Spain, Africa, the Mideast, India, China, and Japan. Similarly, Ives led a quiet existence, whereas Carpenter traveled all over the world, with friends everywhere. Ives related more to Thoreau, Carpenter more to Whitman.

Moreover, whereas Ives identified with his father—an eccentric small-town bandmaster—and married a woman who shared and nurtured his idealization of his father, Carpenter identified more with his mother—a worldly mezzo-soprano—and, further, looked beyond his parents for guidance: to his first wife, Rue, and her advocacy of modern art, to Bernhard Ziehn and his fearless exploration of nontraditional harmony, to Frederick Stock and his interest in modern music and jazz, to his mistress, Ellen, and her attraction to the occult and Eastern religions, to his daughter Ginny and her love for popular songs and comics, and to numerous artists, writers, dancers, and composers—especially American and Russian ones.

Ives wanted music like a small-town marching band, a revival meeting, a barn dance; Carpenter wanted music like a comic strip, a motion picture, a skyscraper.

All this placed Carpenter in the context of the world-embracing Chicago Renaissance, as opposed to the more New England traditions that Ives inherited. For had not Rue, Ziehn, Stock, Ellen, and Ginny themselves, in their own way, helped shape the Chicago of this time? Did not the city itself love Herriman and Whiteman, Prokofiev and Bolm? And had not Chicago's Carl Sandburg envisioned a music like Carpenter's when he wrote, in 1936:

Who can write the music jazz-classical
    smokestacks-geraniums hyacinths-biscuits
    now whispering easy
    now boom doom crashing angular
    now tough monotonous tom tom
Who has enough split-seconds and slow sea-tides?[1]

So Carpenter and Ives, each responsive to his own traditions, each with his unique sensibilities and abilities, expressed their generation's characteristic ideals in diametrically opposed ways, as evident from a comparison of, say, Carpenter's "Hurdy-Gurdy" from *Adventures in a Perambulator* (1914) with Ives's "Putnam's Camp, Redding, Connecticut" from *Three Places in New England* (1912). Carpenter appealed more to hopeful music lovers of his own time; Ives attracted a similar group in later days. Both embodied the promise and early fulfillment of an art music that, at home and abroad, was recognizably American.

Speech in Honor of Frederick Stock, 5 February 1924
Stock Collection, University of Michigan

Mr. [Arthur Taylor] Aldis, Mr. Stock, and ladies and gentlemen:

On the way over here tonight, the most important member of my family asked me if I was nervous about this evening. I said no, I wasn't nervous, but I was extremely pessimistic. And if you find my remarks in a low key, that will be the reason.

There are one or two things that I think perhaps I am qualified to say from my own observation of the relation of Mr. Stock to native American music. It may be an inelegant characterization, but I don't think it is inaccurate to say that native American music is an incubator baby of rather doubtful parentage. It is a child of low vitality. It has narrow shoulders and long, meager legs, and it is subject to all the inhibitions that float out in all directions from New England.

Now, if that child pulls through, it will be very largely owing to the loving ministrations of Mr. Frederick Stock.

Mr. Stock has been and still is the nurse, the doctor, and the godfather of that child. He picks it up when it falls out of its cradle, and he gives it the proper food and the proper stimulant that it needs, and it may be that eventually, if it can get over a slight tendency to kleptomania, it may achieve a physiognomy of its own. It has one thing to help it. It has the tremendous and deep-seated love and admiration of its godfather.

I have in my pocket here my little miniature score I have to refer to. I am not so gifted as Mr. Stock, who is able to conduct with one hand tied behind his back, without referring to the score.

Another dependent child of Mr. Stock's is musical taste. Mr. Stock is not only a great conductor, but he is a great educator. He has picked up and carried on and developed the organization of his great predecessor; until now that organization may well serve as the standard for all other civic organizations pertaining to educational ideas. He does this, as I look at it, by keeping the door open, not only to the great things of the past but to the current effort and the current achievement—and maintaining this contact is not only essential for current effort and current achievement, but it gives vitality to the organization itself. It cannot keep alive, unless it does keep in touch in that way with what is going on today, and of course, Mr. Stock is the leader because he stays ahead of those whom he leads. You can't lead without being in that attitude.

There is one little story that I want to broadcast about Mr. Stock, because it seems to me it is a symbol, you might say, of the man himself, and his attitude of what he is doing. And this story is in connection with the organization of the student orchestra, what is now called the Civic organization, and that was one of Mr. Stock's ideas. He started that, and has kept it going and has carried it to success, without one penny of reward, on top of an already tremendously full schedule. After the first year of that work, the directors of the Civic Music Association felt that this effort of Mr. Stock's should not go without some reward, and we voted him a nominal reward of one thousand dollars for his work that year. Within two days that check came back with a note from Mr. Stock saying that he could not feel right in that work if he were to accept that check, and wouldn't we use the check in any way we saw fit—perhaps start a fund for the publication of American music. Now, that, ladies and gentlemen, represents Mr. Stock.

I will consult the score again. The miniature score says, "Repeat one-half tone higher." And that very cleverly gives me an opportunity of telling a story.

It is about an event in New York some two weeks ago—an orchestral suite of very high-browed modern music—and after the conductor had finished playing a suite by one of "we moderns," there was meager applause, and the conductor turned around, and he said to the audience, "Now, which part of this suite would you like to have me repeat?" And the audience got its nerve up and said, "All of it," and the conductor turned around and was about to start conducting the piece over again when a voice from the balcony said, "When you play it the next time, play it a half-tone higher."

Well, I think that about all the speech that was in me is now out, and I want to make a very deep bow to our "godfather."

Program for *Adventures in a Perambulator*

Carpenter, *Adventures in a Perambulator* (New York: Schirmer, 1917)

I. EN VOITURE!

Every morning—after my second breakfast—if the wind and the sun are favorable, I go out. I should like to go alone, but my will is overborne. My Nurse is appointed to take me. She is older than I, and very powerful. While I wait for her, resigned, I hear the cheerful steps, always the same, I am wrapped in a vacuum of wool, where there are no drafts. A Door opens and shuts. I am placed in my perambulator, a strap is buckled over my stomach, my Nurse stands firmly behind me, and we are off!

II. THE POLICEMAN

Out is wonderful! It is always different, though one seems to have been there before. I cannot fathom it all. Some sounds seem like smells. Some sights have echoes. It is confusing, but it is Life! For instance; the Policeman; an Unprecedented Man! Round like a ball; taller than my Father. Blue—fearful—fascinating! I feel him before he comes. I see him after he goes. I try to analyze his appeal. It is not buttons alone, nor belt, nor baton. I suspect it is his eye, and the way he walks. He walks like Doom.

My Nurse feels it too. She becomes less firm, less powerful. My perambulator hurries, hesitates, and stops. They converse. They ask each other questions—some with answers, some without. I listen, with discretion. When I feel that they have gone far enough, I signal to my Nurse, a private signal, and the Policeman resumes his Enormous Blue March. He is gone, but I feel him after he goes.

III. THE HURDY-GURDY

Then suddenly there is something else. I think it is a sound. We approach it. My ear is tickled to excess. I find that the absorbing noise comes from a box—something like my music box, only much larger, and on wheels. A dark man is turning the music out of the box with a handle, just as I do with mine. A dark lady, richly dressed, turns when the man gets tired. They both smile. I smile too, with restraint, for music is the most insidious form of noise. And such music! So gay! I tug at the strap over my stomach. I have a wild thought of dancing with my nurse and my perambulator—all three of us together. Suddenly, at the climax of our excitement, I feel the approach of a phenomenon that I remember. It is the Policeman. He has stopped the music. He has frightened away the dark man and lady with their music box. He seeks the admiration of my Nurse for his act. He walks away, his buttons shine, but far off I hear again the forbidden music. Delightful forbidden Music!

IV. THE LAKE

Almost satiated with adventure, my Nurse firmly pushes me on, and almost before I recover my balance I am face to face with new sensation. The land comes to an end, and there at my feet is The Lake. All my other sensations are joined in one. I see, I hear, I feel, the quiver of the little waves as they escape from the big ones and come rushing up over the sand. Their fear is pretended. They know the big waves are amiable, for they can see a thousand sunbeams dancing with impunity on their very backs. Waves and sunbeams! Waves and sunbeams! Blue water—white clouds—dancing, swinging! A white sea-gull in the air. That is *My Lake!*

V. DOGS

We pass on. Probably there is nothing more in the World. If there is, it is superfluous.—*There IS*. It is Dogs! We come upon them without warning. Not *one* of them—*all* of them. First, one by one; then in pairs; then in societies. Little dogs, with sisters; big dogs, with aged parents. Kind dogs, brigand dogs, sad dogs and gay. They laugh, they fight, they flirt, they run. And at last, in order to hold my interest, the very littlest brigand starts a game of "Follow the Leader," followed by all the others. It is tremendous!

VI. DREAMS

Those dogs have gone! It is confusing, but it is Life! My mind grows numb. My cup is too full. I have a sudden conviction that it is well that I am not alone. That firm step behind reassures me. The wheels of my perambulator make a sound that quiets my nerves. I lie very still. I am quite content. In order to think more clearly, I close my eyes. My thoughts are absorbing. I deliberate upon my Mother. Most of the time my Mother and my Nurse have but one identity in my mind, but at night or when I close my eyes, I can easily tell them apart, for my Mother has the greater charm. I hear her voice quite plainly now, and feel the touch of her hand. It is pleasant to live over again the adventures of the day—the long blue waves curling in the sun, the Policeman who is bigger than my Father, the music box and my friends, the Dogs. It is pleasant to lie quite still and close my eyes, and listen to the wheels of my perambulator. "How very large the world is. How many things there are!"

Listen to Me

Carpenter, "Listen to Me," unpublished essay, C-ICN
(J. A. C. amateur columnist, 1932)

Thus do I begin,—with a timid clash of my cymbals and a beating of my drum. I steel my nerves and cross my Rubicon, leaving modesty behind. I stand before you unadorned. I beat my drum,—but within I faint.

Nevertheless,—*Listen to Me*.

Whence come the young ideas? By what plumage shall I know them as they fly by? Where lie the pools of rejected thought, the pools of refuge for the forbidden fingerlings thrown back by Master Columnists? May old thoughts be reconditioned to seem like new? May new thoughts be made intelligible, or are they condemned to tolerance, like the drawings of a child? Thus do I grope before you for fugitive answers. But I grope unashamed.

(Are you still listening?)

As a matter of simple truth, *you* too are groping, or you should be, for the good of your soul. There are, of course, the Peaceful and Damned, who have neither evil instincts nor curiosity. There are also the contortionists who seek to step the rhythms of 1900 to the tunes of '32. There are finally the Apes, who chatter and multiply.

But you and I, are we not of better stuff? Let us then grope frankly together. Let us build up an aristocracy,—a Guild of Gropers. We will have no need of officers or rules, initiations fees or dues, and the only requirement for membership shall be a Cheerful Discontent.

Let us not beat about the bush, but rather acknowledge at once that no good can be born without discontent somewhere in its pedigree. For our purposes, we mean a discontent that hunts failure like a terrier, and pauses at success just long enough to identify it, and push along.

It is possible that this discontent is the priceless ingredient now seriously lacking in the American character. It is possible that we look in the mirror with a dishonest eye and edit the fact to fit our fancy, in the best manner of the successful portrait painter. It is possible, in short, that our salesmanship, with no new fields to conquer, has turned in upon ourselves.

Hardly six generations have passed since the ragged remnant of the first American army groped for its existence in the snows of Valley Forge. And for their sustenance they were given nothing but a Dream. Through the varied drama of the succeeding years that same Dream has fed our hungry souls and led us groping on, through the magnificent pages and ignoble interludes of our history. And at this very moment it may well be that we are making the fateful decision as to whether our Great American Dream shall be realized in spirit or materialized in fact.

In the making of this decision our freedom is complete. Failure can come to us only from vagueness and inertia. Intelligence never denies the spiritual. "The Pursuit of Happiness" is just a phrase without meaning, and therefore dangerous, unless our stoutest hearts and our creative minds can combine on a valid definition. Luckily there are no fashions in Happiness. Its true concept will thrive and flower just as readily on a hot and noisy pavement as in a field of corn. It is just as much at home in our fierce world of industry and invention as ever it was in simpler days. It is unchanging and perennial. It is only our eyes that are dimmed and our sense of values gone astray.

What is this Happiness that we *pursue*? And why, in its *pursuit,* do we pant and labour? Is it not simply a state of spiritual well-being, based on the just perception of the rhythm, the proportions, the perspective, the FORM of our individual lives? Is it not rather to be *invited* than *pursued*?

Thus do I fumble for fugitive answers. But I fumble unashamed. And at least, while fumbling, we may be cheerful and full of promising discontent. We can vigorously grope and examine and reject. We can become conscious students and amateurs of Living. We can begin to master the dangers and the uses of our new and fabulous toys, and lessen the breakage and pandemonium in the nursery.

We can tear down the wall between Art and Life.

We can study the plumage of the passing birds———.

Notes

ABBREVIATIONS USED IN NOTES

AC-ICN	Arts Club Collection, Newberry Library
BW-NN	Bruno Walter Collection, Music Division, New York Public Library
C-DLC	Carpenter Collection, Music Division, Library of Congress
C-ICN	Carpenter Collection, Newberry Library
C-NN	Carpenter Collection, Music Division, New York Public Library
C-RH	Carpenter Collection, Rue Hubert private collection
DLC	Library of Congress, Washington, D.C.
ESC-DLC	Elizabeth Sprague Coolidge Collection, Music Division, Library of Congress
ICN	Newberry Library, Chicago, Ill.
JB-NN	John Becker Collection, Music Division, New York Public Library
JG-DLC	Julius Gold Collection, Music Division, Library of Congress
NN	New York Public Library
OC-DLC	Old correspondence, Music Division, Library of Congress
PG-DLC	Percy Grainger Collection, Music Division, Library of Congress
RG-ICN	Rudolph Ganz Collection, Newberry Library
RH	Rue Hubert
Scrapbook	Carpenter's scrapbooks, Music Division, Library of Congress
SK-DLC	Serge Koussevitzky Collection, Music Division, Library of Congress
WD-DLC	Walter Damrosch Collection, Music Division, Library of Congress
WD-NN	Walter Damrosch Collection, Music Division, New York Public Library

INTRODUCTION

1. Olin Downes, "J. A. Carpenter, American Craftsman," *Musical Quarterly* 16 (October 1930): 443–48.

2. Paul Rosenfeld, *Musical Chronicle (1917–1923)* (New York: Harcourt, Brace, 1923; reprint, New York: Blom, 1972), 167–73.

3. Even in the late 1940s, long after his career had peaked, Carpenter earned more than $6,000 in annual royalties, or about $26,000 in today's currency. How much more money would he have made from his music in the 1920s?

4. Charles Hamm, *Music in the New World* (New York: Norton, 1983); H. Wiley Hitchcock, *Music in the United States: A Historical Introduction,* 3d ed. (Englewood Cliffs, N.J.: Prentice Hall, 1988), 423, 456; Gilbert Chase, *America's Music: From the Pilgrims to the Present,* rev. 3d ed. (Urbana: University of Illinois Press, 1987).

5. Felix Borowski, "John Alden Carpenter," *Musical Quarterly* 16 (October 1930): 449–67.

6. Thomas C. Pierson, "The Life and Music of John Alden Carpenter" (Ph.D. diss., University of Rochester, 1952).

CHAPTER 1. THE CARPENTERS OF CHICAGO

1. Frederic Cople Jaher, *The Urban Establishment: Upper Strata in Boston, New York, Charleston, Chicago, and Los Angeles* (Urbana: University of Illinois Press, 1982), 454, 472–73.

2. Ibid., 453.

3. For general information about Chicago during these years, see Alson J. Smith, *Chicago's Left Bank* (Chicago: Henry Regnery, 1953); Arthur Meeker, *Chicago, with Love* (New York: Alfred A. Knopf, 1955); Stephen Longstreet, *Chicago, 1860–1919* (New York: David McKay, 1973); Perry Duis, *Chicago: Creating New Traditions* (Chicago: Chicago Historical Society, 1976); and David Lowe, *Lost Chicago* (New York: American Legacy Press, 1985). For music in particular, see Annette Fern, "Chicago," *The New Grove Dictionary of American Music,* ed. H. Wiley Hitchcock and Stanley Sadie, 4 vols. (New York: Macmillan, 1986), 1:418–24.

4. For more on Carpenter's genealogy, see C-DLC; C-RH; and Grace Hibbard Reed, "From Pennyville to Park Ridge: The Carpenter Songs," *Park Ridge Herald,* 29 April 1949. For the lineage from John and Priscilla Alden to the composer, see Joan O'Connor, *John Alden Carpenter: A Bio-Bibliography* (forthcoming).

5. Charlotte Brewster to Carpenter, 29 August 1947, and other materials, C-DLC.

6. Reed, "The Carpenter Songs"; see also Albert Nelson Marquis, ed., *The Book of Chicagoans* (Chicago: A. N. Marquis, 1911), 120.

7. At about this same time, one J. Spencer Turner joined the firm as a third partner; he retired in 1870.

8. Josiah Seymour Currey, *Manufacturing and Wholesale Industries in*

Chicago (Chicago: Thomas B. Poole, 1918), 52–55; and *1840–1940: The First Hundred Years* (Chicago: George B. Carpenter and Co., 1940). According to Currey (p. 52), the business began not in 1839 as Huginin and Pierce but in 1840 as Foster and Robb. Fires in 1871 and 1900 destroyed many company records. The in-house, centennial essay *1840–1940* provides a fuller, probably more accurate account of the business's history than does Currey.

9. Isaac D. Guyer, *The North West, Its Commerce and Manufactures* (Chicago: Church, Goodman and Cushing, 1862), quoted in *1840–1940*.

10. Quoted in *1840–1940*.

11. Anita Anderson, letter to author, 20 February 1990.

12. Bessie Louise Pierce, *A History of Chicago*, vol. 3 (New York: Alfred A. Knopf, 1957), 443.

13. Karen A. Shaffer and Neva Garner Greenwood, *Maud Powell: Pioneer American Violinist* (Arlington, Va.: Maud Powell Foundation; Ames: Iowa State University Press, 1988), 54.

14. Katharine was the daughter of the composer's brother George. See Katharine Bermingham to Thomas C. Pierson, 11 January 1977, C-RH.

15. Walter Monfried, "Carpenter, Businessman-Composer," *Milwaukee Journal*, 30 April 1947, 20.

16. Shaffer and Greenwood, *Maud Powell*, 54, 60.

17. Monfried, "Carpenter, Businessman-Composer," 20.

18. Madeleine Goss, *Modern Music-Makers: Contemporary American Composers* (New York: E. P. Dutton, 1952), 34.

19. Mary C. Dalton, "Native Son's Works Earn Special Place in Musical History," *Park Ridge Times-Herald*, 21 October 1987.

20. W. S. B. Mathews, "The Chicago Apollo Musical Club," *Music* 2 (1892): 148–66.

21. Mrs. Theodore Thomas, "The Chicago Amateur Club," *Music* 1 (November 1891–April 1892): 204–11.

22. Shaffer and Greenwood, *Maud Powell*, 138.

23. Minnie Haseman to Katharine Bermingham, received 9 June 1952; Bermingham to Pierson, 11 January 1977. See also Thomas C. Pierson, "The Life and Music of John Alden Carpenter" (Ph.D. diss., University of Rochester, 1952), 1; and Shaffer and Greenwood, *Maud Powell*.

24. R[ené] D[evries], "A Chat with John Alden Carpenter," *Musical Courier*, 4 July 1918, 14.

25. Monfried, "Carpenter, Businessman-Composer," 20.

26. Goss, *Modern Music-Makers*, 34.

27. Carpenter, "Foreword to the Wise," C-DLC.

28. Dalton, "Native Son's Works."

29. Grace Hibbard Reed, "From Pennyville to Park Ridge: And Now It's Our City Hall," *Park Ridge Herald*, 22 April 1949.

30. Haseman to Bermingham, 9 June 1952.

31. Bermingham to Pierson, 11 January 1977.

32. "A Park Ridge Sunday School Class Party Just before the Gay Nineties," *Park Ridge Herald,* 3 November 1933.

33. Reed, "And Now It's Our City Hall"; Haseman to Bermingham, 9 June 1952; Anderson to author, 20 February 1990.

34. Most sources indicate that Carpenter studied with Fay for five years, 1887–91, but Fay left Chicago in 1890 for New York, where she remained until her death.

35. Arthur Loesser, *Men, Women and Pianos: A Social History* (New York: Simon and Schuster, 1954), 538–39.

36. Amy Fay, *Music-Study in Germany,* 15th ed. (Chicago: A. C. McClurg, 1894), 283–352.

37. S. Margaret W. McCarthy, "Amy Fay: The American Years," *American Music* 3, no. 1 (Spring 1985): 54–55.

38. University School report cards for Carpenter, 30 October 1891, 11 December 1891, and 8 January 1892, C-DLC.

39. Mathews, "Chicago Apollo Musical Club," 165.

40. "Chicago Composers: W. C. E. Seeboeck," *Music* 3 (November 1892–April 1893): 332–37.

41. Herma Clark, "Let's Walk along Rush Street," courtesy of James W. Howlett and Sam Mozayani.

42. Goss, *Modern Music-Makers,* 34.

43. Robert P. Casey, "Some Facts about John Alden Carpenter, '97," *Harvard Musical Review* 4, no. 4 (January 1916): 3–5.

44. For symphonic music in Chicago during this period, see Philip Adams Otis, *The Chicago Symphony Orchestra* (Chicago: Summy, 1924). For opera, see Ronald L. Davis, *Opera in Chicago* (New York: Appleton-Century, 1966). The Auditorium Theatre opened in 1889, with President Benjamin Harrison officiating. Teutonic Chicago had a special affection for Wagner and mounted the entire *Ring* cycle during the 1888–89 season.

45. Norman Bolotin and Christine Laing, *The Chicago World's Fair of 1893: The World's Columbian Exposition* (Washington, D.C.: Preservation Press, 1992), 127.

46. Ann McKinley, "Music for the Dedication Ceremonies of the World's Columbian Exposition in Chicago, 1892," *American Music* 3, no. 1 (Spring 1985): 42.

47. Bolotin and Laing, *Chicago World's Fair of 1893;* Adrienne Fried Block, "Amy Beach's Music on Native American Themes," *American Music* 8, no. 2 (Summer 1990): 145; Robert Stevenson, "American Awareness of the Other Americas to 1900," *Essays on Music for Charles Warren Fox,* ed. Jerald C. Graue (Rochester, N.Y.: Eastman School of Music Press, 1979), 202.

48. Reid Badger, *The Great American Fair* (Chicago: Nelson Hall, 1979), 115, 127.

49. Ibid., 21.

CHAPTER 2. EARLY WORKS

1. Hubbard Carpenter [?] to Carpenter, 27 January 1948, C-DLC (Ellen Carpenter thought that Hubbard authored this particular letter).

2. Daniel Gregory Mason, *Music in My Time and Other Reminiscences* (New York: Macmillan, 1938), 46.

3. For music at Harvard in the 1890s, see Walter Raymond Spalding, *Music at Harvard* (New York: Coward-McCann, 1935); and Elliot Forbes, *A History of Music at Harvard to 1972* (Cambridge: Department of Music, Harvard University, 1988).

4. Carpenter, quoted by M. A. DeWolfe Howe, "John Knowles Paine," *Musical Quarterly* 25 (1939): 266.

5. Ibid., 265.

6. Mason, *Music in My Time,* 39.

7. Janet Baker-Carr, *Evening at Symphony* (Boston: Houghton Mifflin, 1977), 37.

8. Richard Aldrich, "Miss Hall and Mr. Wilczek," *New York Times,* 3 April 1903.

9. David Perkins, *A History of Modern Poetry: From the 1890s to the High Modernist Mode* (Cambridge: Harvard University Press, 1976), 87–88.

10. Carpenter remained a very lyrical composer. Thomas C. Pierson argues that Carpenter's "singableness" is due, in part, to the intervallic content of his melodies. According to Pierson's statistical study of representative melodies, 36.2 percent of the intervals are major seconds, 20.4 percent are minor seconds, and 11.3 percent are unisons; whereas 0.7 percent are tritones, and 0.3 percent are major sevenths. Thomas C. Pierson, "The Life and Music of John Alden Carpenter" (Ph.D. diss., University of Rochester, 1952), 40–41.

11. J. Douglas Cook, "The Composer Tells How," *Saturday Review,* 26 June 1954, 54. Over time such traces of gentility repelled Charles Ives, Ezra Pound, Carl Ruggles, and Henry Cowell. Even Paul Rosenfeld, who regarded Carpenter highly, bemoaned the "sickly tenderness in the American breast" that showed itself in Carpenter's music. Paul Rosenfeld, *Musical Chronicle (1917–1923)* (New York: Harcourt, Brace, 1923; reprint, New York: Blom, 1972), 173.

12. Peter van der Merwe discusses the importance of the submediant harmony in the transition from "parlor" to "popular" music; see "The Parlour

Modes," in *Origins of the Popular Style: The Antecedents of Twentieth-Century Popular Music* (Oxford: Clarendon, 1989).

13. Edward A. Berlin, *Ragtime: A Musical and Cultural History* (Berkeley and Los Angeles: University of California Press, 1980), 25.

14. Charles Hamm, *Yesterdays: Popular Song in America* (New York: Norton, 1979), 317–18.

15. Frederic Cople Jaher, *The Urban Establishment: Upper Strata in Boston, New York, Charleston, Chicago, and Los Angeles* (Urbana: University of Illinois Press, 1982), 517. Jaher writes, too, of Chicago's relative lack of careerists in the arts—of obvious import to Carpenter's life—and of the fact that "a specific event gave great impetus to its intellectual and esthetic endeavors." This last point characterizes many of Carpenter's activities, for example, the setting of verse by some poet recently favored by Chicago, or the production of a ballet in the wake of the Ballets Russes's Chicago tour.

16. Quoted by Hamm, *Yesterdays,* 308.

17. George Ade, "The Kind of Music That Is Too Good for Household Use," in *People You Know* (New York: R. H. Russell, 1903), 23–25. Quoted by Lee Coyle, *George Ade* (New York: Twayne, 1964), 44.

18. Andrew Stiller, record review of *Carpenter: Collected Piano Works, Opus,* February 1987, 35; Kyle Gann, record review of *Carpenter: Collected Piano Works, Fanfare* 6, no. 2 (July-August 1986): 115.

19. Stiller, record review of *Carpenter: Collected Piano Works,* 35.

20. Gann, record review of *Carpenter: Collected Piano Works,* 115.

21. Stiller, record review of *Carpenter: Collected Piano Works,* 35.

22. Robert P. Casey, "Some Facts about John Alden Carpenter," January 1916, C-NN.

23. Katharine Bermingham to Thomas C. Pierson, 11 January 1977, C-RH.

24. Mason, *Music in My Time,* 34.

25. After graduating from Harvard in 1896, Edward Knoblock (1874–1945) had a distinguished career as novelist and playwright (he changed the spelling of his last name after college). Carpenter remained friends with him and apparently attempted to fashion Knoblock's 1911 play *The Faun* into an opera.

26. Spalding, *Music at Harvard,* 236–46.

27. Gladys Swarthout to Fred Ryder, 18 March 1938, C-DLC. Swarthout wrote to suggest that Ryder publish the song, long out-of-print.

28. Albert Nelson Marquis, ed., *The Book of Chicagoans* (Chicago: A. N. Marquis, 1911), 119–20.

29. Ben Hecht, *1001 Afternoons in Chicago* (Chicago: Covici-McGee, 1922), 153.

30. *1840–1940: The First Hundred Years* (Chicago: George B. Carpenter and Co., 1940).

31. Walter Monfried, "Carpenter, Businessman-Composer," *Milwaukee Journal,* 30 April 1947, 20.

32. Josiah Seymour Currey, *Manufacturing and Wholesale Industries in Chicago* (Chicago: Thomas B. Poole, 1918), 52–55.

33. *1840–1940.*

34. Monfried, "Carpenter, Businessman-Composer," 20.

35. Madeleine Goss, *Modern Music-Makers: Contemporary American Composers* (New York: E. P. Dutton, 1952), 35.

36. Robert Pollak, "John Alden Carpenter," *Chicagoan,* 11 May 1929, 24.

37. Jaher, *Urban Establishment,* 464, 517.

38. Pollak, "Carpenter," 24.

39. Monfried, "Carpenter, Businessman-Composer," 20.

40. Patrick Hill, interview by author, 15 July 1988.

41. Carlyle M. Scott to Carpenter, 26 March 1913, C-ICN.

42. Monfried, "Carpenter, Businessman-Composer," 20.

43. Virgil Thomson, "Why Composers Write How," in *A Virgil Thomson Reader* (Boston: Houghton Mifflin, 1981), 122–47. Carpenter fits three of Thomson's other pegs as well: the naive composer "who lives by non-musical work" (like Musorgsky, Ives, Satie), the composer who marries into the upper classes (like Debussy), and the successful composer who earns income from his musical works (like Verdi, Gershwin). Moreover, the musical styles that Thomson associates with these four categories all apply, more or less, to Carpenter: The "capitalist" composer "tends to write playful music, to seek charm at the expense of emphasis." The naive composers "derive their melodic material from hymns and canticles, from jazz-ways and darn-fool ditties. They quote when they feel like it." The composer who marries into "big money" is likely to turn to two forms of "capitalistic proletarianism. . . . One is the exploitation of ornamental folklore (somebody else's folklore). The other is a cult of urban populistic theatrical jazz (jazz by evocation) and of pseudo-Viennese waltzes." And the successful composer is "likely to be a theater man." Thomson unwittingly highlighted the multifariousness of Carpenter's life and music.

44. Monfried, "Carpenter, Businessman-Composer," 20.

45. Carpenter to Elizabeth Sprague Coolidge, 5 September 1923, ESC-DLC.

46. Carpenter to Carl Engel, 3 April 1931, Engel Collection, DLC.

47. Carpenter to Elizabeth Sprague Coolidge, 10 April 1933, ESC-DLC.

48. James Strachan, interview by author, 27 February 1993.

49. Quoted in "Symphony to Salute Composer Carpenter," February 1951, Scrapbook.

50. R[ené] D[evries], "A Chat with John Alden Carpenter," *Musical Courier,* 4 July 1918, 14.

51. Carpenter to Elizabeth Sprague Coolidge, 14 October 1920, ESC-DLC.

52. Goss, *Modern Music-Makers,* 34.

53. Pollak, "Carpenter," 24.

54. Carpenter, quoted by Pence James, "Dr. Stock's 'Rabbit' Writes Symphony Called 'Symphony,'" *Chicago Daily News,* 24 October 1940, 9.

55. [Cecil Smith?], "John Alden Carpenter: A Musical Humanist," *Musical America,* 17 May 1951, 12.

CHAPTER 3. RUE WINTERBOTHAM AND SONGS FOR CHILDREN

1. Minnie Haseman to Katharine Bermingham, received 9 June 1952, C-RH. For information about this trip abroad, see C-RH.

2. Albert Nelson Marquis, ed., *The Book of Chicagoans* (Chicago: A. N. Marquis, 1911), 173; C-RH.

3. Lyn DelliQuadri, "A Living Tradition: The Winterbothams and Their Legacy," in *The Joseph Winterbotham Collection* (Chicago: Art Institute of Chicago, 1986), 7.

4. Katharine Bermingham to Thomas C. Pierson, 1 January 1977, C-RH. For the schoolmate's quote and for information about the wedding, see C-RH.

5. Arthur Meeker, *Chicago, with Love* (New York: Alfred A. Knopf, 1955), 171.

6. Stephen Longstreet, *Chicago, 1860–1919* (New York: David McKay, 1973), 227, 325.

7. "Brilliant Figure at Opera," 1922, scrapbook, AC-ICN (the accompanying photograph can be found in Meeker, *Chicago, with Love,* 177); Nancy R., "Arts Club Elects New Directorate at Annual Meeting," *Chicago Tribune,* 21 May 1926, scrapbook, AC-ICN.

8. Theodora (Mrs. Amos) Brown (Carpenter's niece), interview by author, 29 July 1988.

9. Untitled clippings, John Alden Carpenter file, Alice Gerstenberg Collection, ICN.

10. Meeker, *Chicago, with Love,* 164–65; Longstreet, *Chicago, 1860–1919,* 324–25.

11. Rue Carpenter, "Problems in Decoration," *Vogue,* 2 August 1930, 27 ff.

12. Longstreet, *Chicago, 1860–1919,* 325.

13. Rue Carpenter, unpublished lecture, C-RH.

14. John McCutcheon to Rue Carpenter, 5 November ca. 1915, McCutcheon Collection, ICN.

15. Meeker, *Chicago, with Love,* 129–30; Jack Lait and Lee Mortimer, *Chicago Confidential* (New York: Crown, 1950), 227.

16. Rue Carpenter, "Minutes," 1930, AC-ICN.

17. Some years after Rue's death, the club moved to its present location at 109 East Ontario Street.

18. Richard R. Brettell and Sue Ann Prince, "From the Armory Show to the Century of Progress: The Art Institute Assimilates Modernism," in *The Old Guard and the Avant-Garde: Modernism in Chicago, 1910–1940,* ed. Sue Ann Prince (Chicago: University of Chicago Press, 1990), 216: "The Institute offered the [Arts] Club one of its best skylight spaces in the suite of permanent galleries on the second floor."

19. James M. Wells, *Portrait of an Era: Rue Winterbotham Carpenter and the Arts Club of Chicago, 1916–1931* (Chicago: Arts Club of Chicago, 1986), n.p.

20. Brettell and Prince, "From the Armory Show to the Century of Progress," 217.

21. Paul Kruty, "Declarations of Independents: Chicago's Alternative Art Groups of the 1920s," in *The Old Guard and the Avant-Garde,* ed. Prince, 78.

22. Bartlett and Ryerson did not donate their remarkable collections of contemporary art to the Art Institute until 1926 and 1933, respectively. DelliQuadri, "A Living Tradition," 8.

23. Wells, *Portrait of an Era.*

24. DelliQuadri, "A Living Tradition," 8–9.

25. Wells, *Portrait of an Era.*

26. The Brancusi sketch of Ginny is simply titled *Portrait* and bears the inscription "Hommage à Madame Carpenter Presidente du Arts Club," but it appears to be a portrait of Ginny, not Rue.

27. Rue Carpenter, quoted in "See Moscow Players and Keep Up City's Reputation, Plea to Art Lovers," April 1923, scrapbook, AC-ICN.

28. "Resolution for the Establishment of a Memorial Fund," Minutes, 29 January 1932, AC-ICN.

29. Fernand Léger, "Chicago," *Plans,* January 1932, 63–68; English translation, AC-ICN.

30. DelliQuadri, "A Living Tradition," 8–12.

31. Ruth Page, *Page by Page,* ed. Andrew Mark Wentink (New York: Dance Horizons, 1978), 135.

32. Meeker, *Chicago, with Love,* 168–69.

33. Harriett Welling to Thomas C. Pierson, quoted in Thomas C. Pierson to Ginny Hill, 10 September 1981, C-RH.

34. Brown, interview.

35. Meeker, *Chicago, with Love*, 170.

36. Brown, interview.

37. George Arliss to Ginny Carpenter, 24 October 1929; Charles Schwartz, *Cole Porter* (New York: Dial, 1977), 87, 227.

38. Arthur Rubinstein, *My Many Years* (New York: Alfred A. Knopf, 1980), 373; Stella (Mrs. Patrick) Campbell, card to Rue Carpenter, C-RH; Maggie Teyte to Rue Carpenter, 17 January 1919, C-ICN; Hugh Walpole to Rue Carpenter, 7 May 1920, C-ICN.

39. Victoria Sackville-West to Rue Carpenter, 17 April 19??, C-ICN.

40. Schwartz, *Cole Porter*, 87; Gerald Murphy to Carpenter, n.d., C-ICN. Murphy concluded his letter, "What a time you gave us, and how very much we love you."

41. Robert Edmond Jones to Carpenter, 31 December 1931, C-ICN.

42. Longstreet, *Chicago, 1860–1919*, 325.

43. Brown, interview.

44. Meeker, *Chicago, with Love*, 169.

45. Ibid., 165.

46. David Lowe, *Lost Chicago* (New York: American Legacy Press, 1985), 32–33, 107.

47. Herma Clark, "Let's Walk along Rush Street," courtesy of James W. Howlett and Sam Mozayani. The brownstone at 710 survives, broken into apartments since the 1940s; the first floor and basement house a Chinese restaurant, the Peapod.

48. James W. Howlett, interview by author, 8 January 1993.

49. In the years after the death of the Colemans, 712 housed an Actors' Club, a French restaurant, and, most recently, a gay piano bar, Gentry.

50. Clark, "Let's Walk along Rush Street." A PTA building now occupies the space where the old George F. Rumsey home stood.

51. DelliQuadri, "A Living Tradition," 7. On the 1926–27 world tour, see postcards in C-RH. It's uncertain whether Carpenter joined the Winterbothams on their trip to Thailand, which included a concert by a Thai orchestra.

52. *Look around Hinesburg and Charlotte, Vermont* (Chittenden County Historical Society, 1973), 214–15; *Historic Guide to Burlington Neighborhoods* (Chittenden County Historical Society, 1990), 126–29.

53. Thomas C. Pierson, "The Life and Music of John Alden Carpenter" (Ph.D. diss., University of Rochester, 1952), 19.

54. "A New Spirit in American Musical Composition," *Current Opinion* 54 (January 1913): 33.

55. Louis Untermeyer to Carpenter, 18 October 1912, C-ICN. Unter-

meyer sent Carpenter some of his own verse that he hoped the composer might set.

56. Richard Aldrich, *Concert Life in New York, 1902–1923* (New York: G. P. Putnam's Sons, 1941), 169.

57. "Offer Evening of Carpenter's Music," ca. 7 February 1917, Scrapbook.

58. Kate Douglas Wiggin, "In Memoriam," in Tom Dobson, *The Rocky Road to Dublin* (Boston: Oliver Ditson, 1919).

59. Irene Alexander, "Rudolph Ganz to Play Work of Peninsula Composer," *Monterey Peninsula Herald*, 24 March 1949; Walter Monfried, "Carpenter, Businessman-Composer," *Milwaukee Journal*, 30 April 1947, 20.

60. Carleton Sprague Smith, "A Note on Carpenter," *Coronet*, February 1940, 99.

61. Paul Rosenfeld compared Carpenter unfavorably to Debussy and Ravel in this regard; *Musical Chronicle (1917–1923)* (New York: Harcourt, Brace, 1923; reprint, New York: Blom, 1972), 170. See also chap. 7.

62. Carpenter regularly supported a number of other nonprofit organizations. In 1948, for example, he gave donations to the Chicago Red Cross, Harvard Scholarship Fund, Harvard '97 Class Fund, Chicago Natural History Museum, Boy Scouts of America, Art Institute, Women's Aid Society Passavant Hospital, Council of Social Agencies of Chicago, and the Community Fund.

63. The Home and Aid Society was founded in 1883 as the American Educational Aid Society for homeless girls. In 1889 it became the Children's Home Society and then, in 1897, the Illinois Children's Home and Aid Society. In its early years the society emphasized "child-saving," that is, finding kind foster or adoptive parents for "normal" (i.e., physically and emotionally healthy) children under twelve, often orphaned or illegitimate. In 1908 the society started to care for disabled children, and in 1911 it began to emphasize family maintenance, including training for unmarried mothers, as opposed to child saving. By the 1930s the ICHAS had added black children (subject to a one-third quota) and troubled teenagers to its care; by this time, too, conflicts between the well-to-do directors and the paid (or underpaid) professional staff had become highly devisive (see chap. 19 for the board's clash with ICHAS's social workers, in which Carpenter's second wife, Ellen, played a prominent part). Elizabeth White, "The History and Development of the Illinois' Children's Home and Aid Society" (Master's thesis, University of Chicago, 1934); Isabel M. Devine, "Report of Study of Illinois Children's Home and Aid Society" (1935), Chicago Historical Society; Paula F. Pfeffer, "Homeless Children, Childless Home," *Chicago History* 16, no. 1 (Spring 1987): 51–65.

64. Devine, "Report," 2, 14–20.

65. Rue Hubert, interview by author, 15 July 1988; Joan Leclerc, interview by author, 29 May 1991; Robert Pirie, interview by author, 9 July 1991.

66. James Gibbons Huneker, "Music," 24 February 1920, Scrapbook.

67. Carpenter wrote, for example, the following limerick in honor of Robert Hutchins, president of the University of Chicago, who would refer to certain students as "rudderless rabbits": "There was once a young rudder-less rabbit / Whose parents descended from Babbitt; / He steered by the stars / Whether Venus or Mars / It was largely a matter of habit" (Carpenter, limerick in honor of Robert Hutchins, C-DLC). Among his children's poems is "Ode to Progress," written for his granddaughter Rue. The poem began:

> Rue, Rue
> Welcome to you
> The deeper the water
> My only granddaughter
> Is galloping, galloping
> Potter to Porter
> To learn
> To learn
> The lessons she oughter
> The wetter the water
> My cagey granddaughter
> She better had oughter
> Be good
> Be good;

and concluded with the tongue-in-cheek flourish, "For Love! For Yale!! For Culture!!!" Carpenter's offbeat humor is further documented in a 1947 letter to Rue at Farmington, which included the following lines: "I suggest that you resume at once the boxing lessons which you started in Tucson, for you can never tell what may spring out at you from 'neath one of thoses elms,—and with the international situation in its present peculiar state, be sure to get in the first swing"; scrapbook, C-RH.

68. Carpenter, "His Master's Voice" (1918), quoted by Claudia Cassidy, "Symphony to Honor John Alden Carpenter This Week," *Chicago Sunday Tribune,* 25 February 1951, Scrapbook.

69. Meeker, *Chicago, with Love,* 171.

CHAPTER 4. FROM THE *BERCEUSE* TO THE VIOLIN SONATA

1. Philip Adams Otis, *The Chicago Symphony Orchestra* (Chicago: Summy, 1924), 185. The Chicago Symphony was renamed the Theodore

Thomas Orchestra for a few years after the conductor's death (see chap. 7). On Elgar's lukewarm press notices, see Jerrold Northrup Moore, *Edward Elgar: A Creative Life* (New York: Oxford University Press, 1984), 511.

2. Robert Pollak, "John Alden Carpenter," *Chicagoan*, 11 May 1929, 24.

3. Thomas C. Pierson, "The Life and Music of John Alden Carpenter" (Ph.D. diss., University of Rochester, 1952), 4.

4. Michael Kennedy, *Portrait of Elgar* (New York: Oxford University Press, 1987), 224.

5. Percy Young, "John Alden Carpenter," *Musical Opinion* 66 (August 1943): 361–62.

6. Richard Aldrich, review of Carpenter's First Symphony, C-NN; Paul Snook, record review of Carpenter's *Sea Drift*, *Fanfare* 8 (March-April 1985): 361.

7. Pollak, "Carpenter," 24.

8. Hans Moser, *Bernhard Ziehn: Die deutsch-amerikanische Musiktheoretiker* (Bayreuth: Steeger, 1950), translated into English by Keith Lencho (courtesy of Keith Lencho); also, Keith Lencho, interview by author, 7 January 1993.

9. Helen Rudolph Heller, "Bernhard Ziehn: Master of Harmony and Music Theory," in Bernhard Ziehn, *Doric Hymns of Mesomedes* (Chicago: Newberry Library, 1979).

10. Julius Gold, "The Master Is No More—Sic Itur ad Astra," *Musical Courier*, 18 September 1912, 23.

11. Winthrop Sargeant, "Bernhard Ziehn, Precursor," *Musical Quarterly* 19 (1933): 169–77.

12. Thorvald Otterström, untitled discussion of Bernhard Ziehn, April 1926, Ziehn Collection, ICN.

13. Sargeant, "Bernhard Ziehn, Precursor," 173; see also Otto Luening, interview by author, 26 February 1989.

14. Heller, "Bernhard Ziehn." Heller writes that "scores were sent to him from Europe," but even so, writers have been puzzled by how Ziehn—who apparently never left Chicago after settling there in 1868—acquired all his musical sources.

15. Bernhard Ziehn, "Dem Andenken Anton Bruckner" (In memory of Anton Bruckner), *Sonntagsblatt der New Yorker Staatszeitung*, 28 October 1896, trans. Helen Rudolph Heller, Ziehn Collection, ICN. Moser, *Bernhard Ziehn*, considered this article, published only two weeks after Bruckner's death, among Ziehn's "most valuable essays."

16. Lencho, interview.

17. George P. Upton, quoted by Heller, "Bernhard Ziehn."

18. Malcolm MacDonald writes: "The principle that the chromatic scale provides the basic unit of tonality, adumbrated in the 1922 edition of *Harmonielehre*, is independent of the 'twelve-tone method' as such; it had been

partially anticipated by, among others, Busoni and the theorist Bernhard Ziehn (1845–1912). Several music examples in the last section of Schoenberg's *Harmonielehre* are virtually identical with examples in Ziehn's *Harmonie- und Modulationslehre* (1888)." Malcolm MacDonald, *Schoenberg* (London: Dent, 1976), 73 n.

19. Gold, "The Master Is No More," 23.

20. Severine Neff, "Otto Luening (1900–) and the Theories of Bernhard Ziehn (1845–1912)," *Current Musicology* 37/38 (1984): 21–41; idem, "An American Precursor of Nontonal Theory: Ernst Bacon (1898–1990)," *Current Musicology* 48 (1991): 5–26.

21. Anthony Beaumont, *Busoni the Composer* (Bloomington: Indiana University Press, 1985), 162. Beaumont reports that Busoni knew Ziehn in Leipzig, but this seems unlikely given that Ziehn is not known to have returned to Europe after moving to the United States in 1868.

22. Ferruccio Busoni, "Die 'Gotiker' von Chicago, Illinois," in *Von der Einheit der Musik* (Berlin: Max Hesses, 1922), 132–36.

23. Beaumont, *Busoni the Composer,* 161.

24. Ibid., 161–66.

25. Otto Luening, *The Odyssey of an American Composer: The Autobiography of Otto Luening* (New York: Scribner's, 1980), 178, 184.

26. A roman numeral I heads this Largo, but no later movements appear to have survived. Although the Largo is not dated, its harmonic language suggests that Carpenter wrote it after he began studying with Ziehn, perhaps in 1910 or 1911, just before the Violin Sonata.

27. Felix Borowski, "John Alden Carpenter," *Musical Quarterly* 16 (October 1930): 457; John Tasker Howard, *Our Contemporary Composers: American Music in the Twentieth Century* (New York: Crowell, 1941), 35–36; Irving Lowens, record review of Carpenter, *Sonata for Violin and Piano, High Fidelity* 27 (June 1977): 88.

28. Review of Carpenter's Violin Sonata, *New York Times,* Scrapbook.

29. Albert Cotsworth, "Parker and Carpenter," Scrapbook.

30. Deems Taylor, "America's First Dramatic Composer," *Vanity Fair,* April 1922, 59.

31. Carpenter possibly derived the main theme of the Violin Sonata's finale from an incomplete Molto grazioso for piano found among his manuscripts; in any case, the two themes are similar.

32. Dorothy Swainson to Carpenter, undated correspondences, C-ICN.

33. Reviews of Carpenter's Violin Sonata, Scrapbook.

34. Scrapbook.

35. Carpenter to Julius Gold, 10 March 1915, JG-DLC.

36. "A Chicago Composer," *Chicago Evening Post,* 11 March 1913, Scrapbook.

37. Eric De Lamarter, "John Carpenter, Our Musical Insurgent," *Inter Ocean*, 16 March 1913, Scrapbook.

38. John McCormack, quoted in the *Chicago Musical Leader*, 26 October 1916, Scrapbook; Arthur Farwell and W. Dermot Darby, *Music in America*, vol. 4 of *The Art of Music: A Comprehensive Library of Information for Music Lovers and Musicians*, ed. Daniel Gregory Mason et al. (New York: National Society of Music, 1915), 428; Dorothy Swainson to Carpenter, n.d., C-ICN; Charles Cadman to Carpenter, 24 May ca. 1914.

39. Carpenter to Julius Gold, 28 November 1923, JG-DLC.

40. Borowski, "John Alden Carpenter," 457; John Tasker Howard, "American Composers, VI: John Alden Carpenter," *Modern Music* 9, no. 1 (November-December 1931): 12. In this, as in other observations, Howard borrows freely from Borowski.

41. Pierson, "Life and Music of John Alden Carpenter," 20.

42. Carpenter, *Sonata for Violin and Piano*, Eugene Gratovich, violin, and Regis Benoit, piano, Orion ORS-76243.

43. C. Thomas Veilleux, record review of Carpenter, *Sonata for Violin and Piano, American Record Guide*, April 1977, 21; idem, record review of Carpenter, *Sonata for Violin and Piano, New Records*, February 1977, 6; Lowens, record review, 88; Paul Turok, "An American Tragedy," record review of Carpenter, *Sonata for Violin and Piano, Music Journal* 35 (March 1977): 46.

44. Carpenter to Victor Lichtenstein, 10 March 1915, JG-DLC.

45. Robert P. Casey, "Some Facts about John Alden Carpenter, '97," *Harvard Musical Review* 4 (January 1916), C-NN.

46. R[ené] D[evries], "A Chat with John Alden Carpenter," *Musical Courier*, 4 July 1918, 14.

47. Carpenter to Julius Gold, 29 January 1914, JG-DLC.

48. Carpenter to Julius Gold, quoted in William J. Mitchell, review of *Bernhard Ziehn der deutsch-amerikanische Musiktheoretiker*, by Hans Joachim Moser, *Musical Quarterly* 37 (1951): 441.

49. Carpenter to Julius Gold, 14 December 1916, 4 April 1929, JG-DLC.

CHAPTER 5. FROM "TREAT ME NICE" TO "TERRE PROMISE"

1. Felix Borowski, "John Alden Carpenter," *Musical Quarterly* 16 (October 1930): 445. When did Carpenter turn a critical eye to "Treat Me Nice"? Apparently not by 1918, when Schirmer acquired the rights and reprinted it. Throughout his life, however, Carpenter was sensitive about racial issues; he similarly had doubts about his Langston Hughes settings (despite Hughes's own approval). In any case, many still liked the song; in 1932 Schirmer reprinted it again.

2. George Ade, "The Kind of Music That Is Too Good for Household Use," in *People You Know* (New York: R. H. Russell, 1903), 23–25.

3. Philip Adams Otis, *The Chicago Symphony Orchestra* (Chicago: Summy, 1924), 146.

4. William Treat Upton, *Art-Song in America* (Boston: Ditson, 1930), 202.

5. Ibid.

6. The Library of Congress and Joan O'Connor both catalog "The Marshes of Glynn" as complete, but I can only find an incomplete version. The sketches to "The Marshes of Glynn" further reveal that Carpenter's compositional method often involved subtle reworkings. Not happy with his setting of the line "Clamber the forks of the multiform boughs," Carpenter crossed it out and made it twice as fast. After writing an accompaniment for this second version, he decided against this melody, too, and composed a third and final setting for the line. For this version Carpenter retained the accompaniment from the second version and something of the rhythm of that version's melodic line, but with thoroughly new pitches and almost a measure of rest between "Clamber the forks" and "of the multiform boughs." In turn, Carpenter followed this new, third setting with a similar setting for the line "Emerald twilights, Virginal shy lights."

7. The Fine Arts Building also hosted the Studebaker Theatre, boutiques, art galleries, music schools, and the Little Room. Chicago's most prominent figures in the arts—Harriet Monroe, Lorado Taft, Henry Fuller, Hamlin Garland, to name a few—patronized the Fine Arts Building regularly.

8. John T. McCutcheon, *Drawn from Memory* (Indianapolis: Bobbs-Merrill, 1950), 225, 227.

9. Ibid., 225.

10. Carpenter to John T. McCutcheon, 25 November 1927, McCutcheon Collection, ICN.

11. Mina Hager, "Speak for Yourself, John Alden Carpenter!" *Music Journal* 28 (March 1970): 67.

12. Upton, *Art-Song in America,* 202.

13. Thomas C. Pierson, "The Life and Music of John Alden Carpenter" (Ph.D. diss., University of Rochester, 1952), 56.

14. Carpenter, quoted in "Would Have No 'Protective Tariff' to Aid American Music," ca. 1917, C-DLC.

15. John Tasker Howard, "American Composers, VI: John Alden Carpenter," *Modern Music* 9, no. 1 (November-December 1931): 16.

16. Leon R. Maxwell, "America's Contribution to Song Literature," *M.T.N.A. Proceedings* 14 (1919): 159. Upton, *Art-Song in America,* 202, echoed Maxwell's connection between Carpenter and Scott.

17. Otis, *Chicago Symphony Orchestra,* 215.

18. Ronald L. Davis attributes this change in favor of Italian opera to three factors: the higher level of Italian opera under the direction of Toscanini, the acculturation of Chicago's German population, and anti-German political sentiment fueled by Germany's claims in Morocco in 1906. Ronald L. Davis, *Opera in Chicago* (New York: Appleton-Century, 1966), 76.

19. Ibid., 86.

20. Robert C. Marsh, interview by author, 24 November 1992; Davis, *Opera in Chicago,* 86.

21. Davis, *Opera in Chicago,* 89.

22. Alson J. Smith, *Chicago's Left Bank* (Chicago: Henry Regnery, 1953), 120.

23. Arthur Meeker, *Chicago, with Love* (New York: Alfred A. Knopf, 1955), 222.

24. Carpenter translated "En sourdine" into English himself. The other published songs included translations by Henry Chapman and Helen Dudley. The Schirmer songs emphasize the French original, whereas Ditson's "When the Misty Shadows Glide" ("En sourdine") features the English translation.

25. Arthur Farwell, quoted in "A New Spirit in American Musical Composition," *Current Opinion* 54 (January 1913): 33.

26. Upton, *Art-Song in America,* 203.

27. Borowski, "John Alden Carpenter," 455.

28. Upton, *Art-Song in America,* 206.

29. Maggie Teyte, *Star on the Door* (London: Putnam, 1958), 151.

30. Hager, "Speak for Yourself," 67.

31. Ralph Berton, *Remembering Bix: A Memoir of the Jazz Age* (New York: Harper and Row, 1974), 65.

32. Harriet Monroe, *A Poet's Life: Seventy Years in a Changing World* (New York: Macmillan, 1938).

33. Vachel Lindsay to Carpenter, 26 February 1917, C-ICN.

34. By the end of World War I, both the *Dial* and the *Little Review* had moved to New York.

35. Walter Monfried, "Carpenter, Businessman-Composer," *Milwaukee Journal,* 30 April 1947, 20.

36. Rudolph Schirmer to Carpenter, 10 March 1914, C-ICN.

37. Kurt Schindler to Carpenter, 16 August 1912, Scrapbook.

38. Edward Maisel, *Charles T. Griffes: The Life of an American Composer,* rev. ed. (New York: Alfred A. Knopf, 1984); Donna K. Anderson, *Charles T. Griffes: A Life in Music* (Washington, D.C.: Smithsonian Institution Press, 1993).

39. Kurt Schindler, "Composer Who'll Stir the World," *Musical America,* 12 October 1912, 122.

40. Kurt Schindler, quoted in "A New Spirit in American Musical Composition," 33.

41. Arthur Farwell, quoted in ibid.

42. Albert Cotsworth, "Parker and Carpenter," Scrapbook.

43. Philip Greeley Clapp, "An Original American Composer," *Boston Evening Transcript,* 13 November 1912.

44. "Alma Gluck Likes Carpenter's Songs," *New York Times,* 7 October 1912.

45. Maxwell, "America's Contribution to Song Literature," 156.

46. Deems Taylor, quoted in "A Jazz Ballet," *Literary Digest* 73 (15 April 1922): 3.

47. Arthur Farwell and W. Dermot Darby, *Music in America,* vol. 4 of *The Art of Music: A Comprehensive Library of Information for Music Lovers and Musicians,* ed. Daniel Gregory Mason et al. (New York: National Society of Music, 1915), 427.

48. "Alma Gluck."

49. Richard Aldrich, *Concert Life in New York, 1902–1923* (New York: G. P. Putnam's Sons, 1941), 368.

50. McCormack sang "Go, Lovely Rose" in 1916 and again in 1917; see Scrapbook and Anne Rey Simpson, *Hard Trials: The Life and Music of Harry T. Burleigh* (Metuchen, N.J.: Scarecrow, 1990), 82.

51. Julia Culp, quoted in the *Colorado Springs Gazetteer,* 28 March 1914, C-DLC.

52. "John Alden Carpenter's Work," *Opera Magazine,* May 1914, C-NN.

53. Louis Untermeyer to Carpenter, 22 November 1912, C-DLC.

54. Upton, *Art-Song in America,* 197.

55. Carpenter, "Looking-Glass River," on *Songs by American Composers,* Donald Gramm, Desto D411/12.

56. Lucille Mendenhall, "The Songs of John Alden Carpenter" (Master's thesis, North Texas State University, 1952), 53.

57. Hans Nathan, "United States of America," in *A History of Song,* ed. Denis Stevens (New York: Norton, 1960), 426.

CHAPTER 6. FROM *POLONAISE AMÉRICAINE* TO *GITANJALI*

1. Carpenter to Ellen Borden, ca. 1914, C-DLC.

2. Thomas C. Pierson, liner notes to *Carpenter: Collected Piano Works,* New World Records NW 328/329.

3. Krishna Kripalani, *Rabindranath Tagore: A Biography* (New York: Grove Press, 1962); Mary M. Lago, *Rabindranath Tagore* (Boston: Twayne, 1976).

4. Kripalani, *Rabindranath Tagore,* 218.

5. William Butler Yeats, introduction to *Gitanjali,* by Rabindranath Tagore (London: Macmillan, 1913), viii, xiii.

6. Kripalani, *Rabindranath Tagore,* 218–19.

7. Ezra Pound, quoted in Lago, *Rabindranath Tagore,* 72. Indian readers reacted to this "barbarian" business with a mixture of mirth and indignation.

8. Harriet Monroe, *A Poet's Life: Seventy Years in a Changing World* (New York: Macmillan, 1938), 320–21.

9. Humayn Kabir, *Rabindranath Tagore* (London: University of London Press, 1962), 14.

10. Nancy Wilson Ross, *Three Ways of Asian Wisdom* (New York: Simon and Schuster, 1966), 68.

11. Judith Tick, "Ruth Crawford's 'Spiritual Concept': The Sound-Ideals of an Early American Modernist, 1924–1930," *Journal of the American Musicological Society* 54, no. 2 (Summer 1991): 221–61.

12. John Bartlow Martin, *Adlai Stevenson of Illinois* (New York: Doubleday, 1976), 86.

13. One can deduce as much not only from the poetry, which resembles Carpenter's letters to Ellen, but from the fact that Carpenter sketched, on an opposing page, a piece that would become a private love song to Ellen—"The Mystery" of May 1915.

14. In her master's thesis on *Gitanjali,* Arline Hanke still found some of the harmonic movement "too abrupt." Arline Hanke, "A Study of the *Gitanjali* Songs by John Alden Carpenter" (Master's thesis, University of Rochester, 1942), 52.

15. William Treat Upton, *Art-Song in America* (Boston: Ditson, 1930), 210–11.

16. A. H. Fox Strangways, *The Music of Hindostan* (Oxford: Clarendon Press, 1914); Lily Strickland-Anderson, "Rabindranath Tagore—Poet-Composer: An Appreciation," *Musical Quarterly* 10 (October 1924): 463–74.

17. Fox Strangways, *Music of Hindostan,* 92.

18. James Husst Hall, *The Art Song* (Norman: University of Oklahoma Press, 1953), 282.

19. Julius Gold to Carpenter, 9 May 1914, Scrapbook.

20. Henriette Weber, "John Alden Carpenter," *Harper's Bazaar,* May 1920, 78. *Gitanjali* possibly exerted some influence on such mature Griffes songs as *Three Poems by Fiona Macleod* (1918).

21. R. Murray Schafer, ed., *Ezra Pound and Music* (New York: New Directions, 1977), 221. Pound wrote: "The translation of Tagore chosen by J. A. Carpenter is not lyric; it is provided with pseudo-Debussy accompaniment, in the spirit of 'In winter I get up at night,' but even so it might be

taken as an argument that free word cadences offer more to mediocre musicians than the habitual iambic of fourth-rate versifiers. The danger of making 'juice' an homophone for 'Jews' in the last strophe should be overcome by the singer."

22. Kirsten Flagstad to Carpenter, 20 November 1949, C-ICN.

23. Carpenter to Felix Borowski, 1 September 1950, C-ICN.

24. Upton, *Art-Song in America,* 209.

25. Andrew Porter, "Musical Events," *New Yorker,* 23 October 1989, 96.

26. Karleton Hackett, undated review of Carpenter's *Gitanjali,* Scrapbook.

27. Hanke, "A Study of the *Gitanjali* Songs," 4.

28. Claudia Cassidy, "On the Aisle," *Chicago Journal of Commerce,* 15 January 1936, Scrapbook.

29. Carpenter to Serge Koussevitzky, 13 November 1935, SK-DLC.

CHAPTER 7. FROM *ADVENTURES IN A PERAMBULATOR* TO "THE DAY IS NO MORE"

1. Carpenter to Ellen Borden, 29 April 1914, C-DLC.

2. Ibid., n.d., C-DLC.

3. Ibid., n.d., C-DLC.

4. Claudia Cassidy, "Symphony to Honor John Alden Carpenter This Week," *Chicago Sunday Tribune,* 25 February 1951, Scrapbook.

5. Dena J. Epstein, "Frederick Stock and American Music," *American Music* 10, no. 1 (Spring 1992): 36–47.

6. Ezra Schabas, *Theodore Thomas: America's Conductor and Builder of Orchestras, 1835–1905* (Urbana: University of Illinois Press, 1989).

7. Harold C. Schonberg, *The Great Conductors* (New York: Simon and Schuster, 1967), 197.

8. Philip Adams Otis, *The Chicago Symphony Orchestra* (Chicago: Summy, 1924), 185.

9. Schabas, *Theodore Thomas,* 196.

10. Ibid., 234, 245.

11. Philip Hart, *Orpheus in the New World: The Symphony Orchestra as an American Cultural Institution* (New York: Norton, 1973), 41–43.

12. Schabas, *Theodore Thomas,* 232.

13. Otto Luening, interview by author, 26 February 1989; Perry Duis, *Chicago: Creating New Traditions* (Chicago: Chicago Historical Society, 1976), 90.

14. Epstein, "Frederick Stock and American Music," 22.

15. Hart, *Orpheus in the New World,* 44.

16. Stock apparently worked out some arrangement with the orchestra before stepping down, since Carpenter wrote to him in October 1918: "I didn't have a chance today to *really* shake your hand and tell you how glad we are, Rue and I both, that everything has turned out as it has, with you and the orchestra. Your letter was so fine. I think I can imagine the nightmare you have been through and rejoice that now the sun is shining again." Carpenter to Frederick Stock, 8 October 1918, Stock Collection, University of Michigan (Carpenter's emphasis).

17. Hart, *Orpheus in the New World*, 44.

18. Luening, interview.

19. Schabas, *Theodore Thomas*, 256.

20. Epstein argues that Stock's reluctance to tour with the orchestra limited "his chance to be heard by influential Eastern critics, whose verdict was as important to a pre–World War II American orchestra as good European reviews are to an American orchestra now"; Epstein, "Frederick Stock and American Music," 21.

21. Richard Aldrich, *Concert Life in New York, 1902–1923* (New York: G. P. Putnam's Sons, 1941), 656–57.

22. Virgil Thomson, quoted by Epstein, "Frederick Stock and American Music," 21–22.

23. Virgil Thomson, "Chicago's Orchestra," *New York Herald Tribune,* 29 October 1944, C-DLC.

24. Ronald L. Davis, *Opera in Chicago* (New York: Appleton-Century, 1966), 206.

25. Pierre Monteux to Frederick Stock, 21 September 1922, Stock Collection, ICN.

26. Robert C. Marsh, interview by author, 24 November 1992; Phillip Kauffman, interview by author, 25 November 1992. Kauffman and Marsh disagree as to the extent of Stock's reorchestrations.

27. Daniel Gregory Mason, *The Dilemma of American Music and Other Essays* (New York: Macmillan, 1928), 67–70.

28. Alson J. Smith, *Chicago's Left Bank* (Chicago: Henry Regnery, 1953), 112.

29. Nikolai Miaskovsky to Frederick Stock, 29 March 1935, Stock Collection, ICN.

30. Luening, interview.

31. Howard Hanson, "Report of the Committee on American Music," *M.T.N.A. Proceedings* 33 (1938), quoted in Epstein, "Frederick Stock and American Music," 31.

32. Frederick Stock, quoted in Epstein, "Frederick Stock and American Music," 28; Luening, interview.

33. Epstein, "Frederick Stock and American Music," 32, 33, 22.

34. Pence James, "Dr. Stock's 'Rabbit' Writes Symphony Called 'Symphony,'" *Chicago Daily News*, 24 October 1940, 9.

35. Carpenter, quoted in ibid.

36. Carpenter to Ellen Borden, 11 September 1922, C-DLC (Carpenter's emphasis).

37. Carpenter, speech in honor of Frederick Stock, 5 February 1924, Stock Collection, University of Michigan.

38. Claudia Cassidy, "Chicago's Music Circles Mourn Frederick Stock," Scrapbook; Kauffman, interview.

39. Arthur Meeker, *Chicago, with Love* (New York: Alfred A. Knopf, 1955), 221–22; Schonberg, *The Great Conductors;* Michael Steinberg, "Stock, Frederick," *The New Grove Dictionary of American Music*, ed. H. Wiley Hitchcock and Stanley Sadie, 4 vols. (New York: Macmillan, 1986), 4:313–14.

40. Claudia Cassidy, interview by author, 26 April 1991.

41. Otto Luening, *The Odyssey of an American Composer: The Autobiography of Otto Luening* (New York: Scribner's, 1980), 231; Marsh, interview; Kauffman, interview.

42. Franz Schubert, *Symphony No. 9*, Chicago Symphony Orchestra, Frederick Stock, Columbia RL 3008.

43. Epstein, "Frederick Stock and American Music," 26.

44. Carpenter to Frederick Stock, 16 March 1918, Stock Collection, ICN.

45. "On the Other Side of Fame," *Chicago Sun*, ca. 1942, Scrapbook.

46. Mina Hager, "Speak for Yourself, John Alden Carpenter!" *Music Journal* 28 (March 1970): 67.

47. Carpenter to Ellen Borden, 11 September 1922, C-DLC.

48. Carpenter to Ginny Hill, 6 April 1949, C-ICN.

49. B. R., "Carpenter as Musical Humorist," *Musical America*, 13 November 1915, 34.

50. Carpenter cites the four hurdy-gurdy tunes as "Lucia," "Alexander's R. T. Band," "Oh Marie," and "Rip Van Winkle" in an undated letter to Ellen Borden, C-DLC. Did the composer originally choose a tune from *Lucia di Lammermoor* before deciding on one from *Il trovatore,* or did he simply confuse the two operas? Probably the latter. "Rip Van Winkle" plausibly refers to the unidentified waltz tune, perhaps something from Reginald de Koven's *Rip Van Winkle,* although it appears not to come from that score. The tune actually sounds more like Victor Herbert; if the composer could confuse Donizetti and Verdi, he certainly could mistake de Koven for Herbert.

51. Eric De Lamarter, "Chicago Discovers a Merry Tone-Baby," *Boston Transcript,* 27 March 1915, Scrapbook.

52. Karleton Hackett, quoted by Otis, *The Chicago Symphony Orchestra,* 268.

53. Untitled and undated article, C-NN.

54. Carpenter to Walter Damrosch, 11 November 1915, Damrosch-Blaine Collection, DLC.

55. Walter Damrosch, quoted by John Tasker Howard, "American Composers, VI: John Alden Carpenter," *Modern Music* 9, no. 1 (November-December 1931): 10.

56. Carpenter, Christmas card to Walter Damrosch, 19 December 1947, WD-NN.

57. Scrapbook.

58. Oscar Zeigler, "Baby's Ideas of Park Trip Described in Novel Music," *New York Herald Tribune*, 6 November 1915.

59. B. R., "Carpenter as Musical Humorist," 34.

60. Lawrence Gilman, "Drama and Music," *North American Review* 202 (December 1915): 912–14.

61. George Whitefield Chadwick to Carpenter, 17 November 1915, Scrapbook.

62. Ellen Knight, *Charles Martin Loeffler: A Life Apart in Music* (Urbana: University of Illinois Press, 1993), 212.

63. Olin Downes, "Farrar Is Soloist at Symphony," 5 February 1916, Scrapbook.

64. Scrapbook.

65. O[lin] D[ownes?], "Muck Again Plays Carpenter's Suite," *Musical Courier*, 1 January 1916.

66. "Tonal Riot Heard in 'Adventures in Perambulator,'" Scrapbook; Cincinnatues, "Cincinnati Orchestra Plays Carpenter Score," *Musical Courier*, 23 November 1916, 14.

67. "American Music Popular in USSR," Scrapbook.

68. H[enry] T[aylor] P[arker], "Conductor Returned, Composer Applauded, 'Skyscrapers' Heard," 8 December 1927, Scrapbook. See also George Perle, interview by author, 15 February 1994.

69. Carpenter, *Adventures in a Perambulator,* Minneapolis Symphony, Eugene Ormandy, Victor 8455-58/8459-62. In Carpenter's own opinion, "the Ormandy 'Perambulator' recording, from the interpretive standpoint, was perfection," and after the war he attempted to get RCA Victor to rerelease it; Carpenter to Richard Gilbert, 31 August 1948. In this same letter, Carpenter also encouraged Victor to rerelease *Skyscrapers* and *Sea Drift,* which, along with *Adventures in a Perambulator,* "just about tells the whole 'Carpenter' Story."

70. Adeline Fitzgerald, "These Charming People," *Chicago Herald Tribune,* ca. 1940, Scrapbook; John Culhane, *Walt Disney's "Fantasia"* (New York: Abradale, 1983), 120. Disney, however, showed no interest in commissioning new music, even when his staff (unaware that Pierné had died in 1937)

recommended that he "hire Stravinsky or this man Pierné" for *Fantasia*'s mythological episode (Culhane, *Walt Disney's "Fantasia,"* 135). In later years, incidentally, Stravinsky asserted that he granted Disney permission to use *The Rite of Spring* only because Disney's $5,000 offer "was accompanied by a gentle warning that if permission were withheld the music would be used anyway"; Marc Eliot, *Walt Disney: Hollywood's Dark Prince* (New York: Birch Lane, 1993), 134.

71. Culhane, *Walt Disney's "Fantasia,"* 18.

72. Ibid., 109.

73. John Canemaker, "The Fantasia That Never Was," *Print* 42, no. 1 (January-February 1988): 76.

74. Besides *Perambulator,* Disney chose music by Wagner, Sibelius, Weber, Chopin, Brahms, Rimsky-Korsakov, Paul White, and Grieg, as well as an assorted medley from Handel, Mozart, and Brahms (Paul White was the only other American composer selected). On the history of the abandoned project, see Culhane, *Walt Disney's "Fantasia,"* and Canemaker, "Fantasia That Never Was," 77.

75. Carpenter to Felix Borowski, 18 December 1941, C-ICN.

76. Canemaker, "Fantasia That Never Was," 86.

77. Carpenter to Borowski, 18 December 1941, C-ICN.

78. Harvey Taylor, "Miquelle Caps Season with Solo Triumph," *Detroit Times,* 14 February 1947, Scrapbook.

79. Norman Nairn, "Ballet Program Draws Throng at Eastman," *Rochester Democrat and Chronicle,* April 1944, Scrapbook.

80. Olin Downes, *The Lure of Music* (New York: Harper, 1918, 1922), 289; Felix Borowski, "John Alden Carpenter," *Musical Quarterly* 16 (October 1930): 460; Howard, "John Alden Carpenter," 13.

81. Abram Chasins to Carpenter, 27 August 1943, C-DLC.

82. Paul Rosenfeld, *Musical Chronicle (1917–1923)* (New York: Harcourt, Brace, 1923; reprint, New York: Blom, 1972), 170.

83. Charles Ives, *Essays before a Sonata,* in *Three Classics in the Aesthetic of Music* (New York: Dover, 1962), 168.

84. Rita Mead, *Henry Cowell's New Music, 1925–1936: The Society, the Music Editions, and the Recordings* (Ann Arbor: UMI Research Press, 1981), 23.

85. Hugo Leichtentritt, *Serge Koussevitzky: The Boston Symphony Orchestra and the New American Music* (Cambridge: Harvard University Press, 1946), 65.

86. Andrew Stiller, record review of *Carpenter: Collected Piano Works, Opus,* February 1987, 35.

87. Carpenter, *Adventures in a Perambulator,* Vienna State Opera Orchestra, Henry Swoboda, Concert Hall Society H-1640; Carpenter, *Adven-*

tures in a Perambulator, Eastman-Rochester Orchestra, Howard Hanson, Mercury MG-50136.

88. Irving Fine, "Reviews of Records," *Musical Quarterly* 38 (1952): 483.

89. Peter Hugh Reed, "Record Notes and Reviews," *American Record Guide,* May 1952, 267; Arthur Berger, "Spotlight on the Moderns," *Saturday Review,* 31 May 1952, 43. Wayne Shirley recalled: "The young Turks of the mid-1950s knew the work only as a title—a title suggesting exactly the kind of cutesy pieces we disliked: music programmed by conservative conductors so that they could say, 'we do twentieth century music.' None of us could hum a tune from it—or from *Skyscrapers* for that matter." Wayne Shirley, notes to author, 28 September 1992.

90. R. D. Darrell, "The Tape Deck," *High Fidelity* 7 (November 1957): 103; John M. Conly, "Record Reviews," *Atlantic Monthly* 200 (July 1957): 94; Alfred Frankenstein, record review of Carpenter, *Adventures in a Perambulator, High Fidelity* 7 (August 1957): 52; "New Recordings," *Musical America,* July 1957, 28; Trevor Harvey, record review of Carpenter, *Adventures in a Perambulator, Gramophone,* October 1957, 177.

91. James Goodfriend, "Going on Record," *Stereo Review* 37 (October 1976): 60; William D. Curtis, "Guide to Records," *American Record Guide,* November 1977, 38–39.

92. "Cheatham, Catherine Smiley," *The Cyclopedia of American Biography* (New York: Press Association Compilers, 1925).

93. Aldrich, *Concert Life in New York,* 310–11.

94. Kitty Cheatham, "Words and Music of 'The Star-Spangled Banner' Oppose the Spirit of Democracy Which the Declaration of Independence Embodies," *New York Times,* 10 February 1918; *Musical America,* 2 March 1918.

95. Harriet Monroe, *A Poet's Life: Seventy Years in a Changing World* (New York: Macmillan, 1938), 334–39.

96. Curtis Baker Bradford, ed., *W. B. Yeats: The Writing of "The Player Queen"* (Dekalb: Northern Illinois University Press, 1977), 278.

97. Ibid., 20–21, 455.

98. Ibid., 316–17.

99. Carpenter to Ellen Borden, ca. 1914, C-DLC (Carpenter's emphasis).

100. Claudia Cassidy, "On the Aisle," 12 January 1946, Scrapbook.

101. Carpenter to Ellen Borden, n.d., C-DLC.

102. Barnes writes "väice," "fëace," "mid," "woone," and "ees" for, respectively, "voice," "face," "might," "one (whom)," and "yes."

103. Carpenter, "The Day Is No More," Carol Brice, Columbia 17608-10d (in set MM 910), later reissued as Columbia ML 2108. Philip L. Miller, "Voice," *American Record Guide,* June 1950, 337.

CHAPTER 8. FROM THE PIANO CONCERTINO TO *WATER-COLORS*

1. Carpenter to Ellen Borden, ca. 1915, C-DLC.

2. Eric De Lamarter, "Percy Grainger at Orchestra Hall," *Chicago Daily Times*, 11 March 1916, 14; George Whitefield Chadwick to Carpenter, 13 February 1920, C-DLC (Chadwick's emphasis); Otto Luening, interview by author, 26 February 1989.

3. Carpenter, program notes to the Piano Concertino, C-NN.

4. Carpenter, program notes to *Patterns*, C-DLC. For more on the relation of Spanish music to jazz and American popular music, see Alan Lomax, *Mister Jelly Roll* (New York: Duell, 1950); Gunther Schuller, *Early Jazz: Its Roots and Musical Development* (New York: Oxford University Press, 1968); and John Strom Roberts, *The Latin Tinge: The Impact of Latin American Music on the United States* (New York: Oxford University Press, 1979).

5. Robert Stevenson, "American Awareness of the Other Americas to 1900," in *Essays on Music for Charles Warren Fox*, ed. Jerald C. Graue (Rochester, N.Y.: Eastman School of Music Press, 1979), 192.

6. Irene Castle to [Rue] Carpenter, 13 July 1915, C-ICN.

7. John T. McCutcheon, *Drawn from Memory* (Indianapolis: Bobbs-Merrill, 1950), 225.

8. Edward A. Berlin argues that although tango and ragtime have certain melodic gestures in common, the tango has a syncopated bass, whereas ragtime has a straightforward oom-pah-oom-pah bass. Edward A. Berlin, *Ragtime: A Musical and Cultural History* (Berkeley and Los Angeles: University of California Press, 1980), 115–17. In Carpenter's Piano Concertino, however, the allusions to tango and ragtime are usually too enmeshed to be distinguished as such.

9. Percy Grainger, *Seattle Symphony Program Notes*, 9 January 1936, C-DLC.

10. William W. Austin's study of Foster's meanings to hundreds of listeners, performers, and composers—*"Susanna," "Jeanie," and "The Old Folks at Home": The Songs of Stephen C. Foster from His Time to Ours* (New York: Macmillan, 1975)—does not include Carpenter but contains related and helpful discussions of Berlin and Gershwin (p. 331).

11. "Music and Drama," *New York Evening Post*, Scrapbook.

12. Percy Grainger to Carpenter, 2 July 1916, C-ICN.

13. Percy Grainger, quoted in Lionel Carley, "Impulsive Friend: Grainger and Delius," in *The Percy Grainger Companion*, ed. Lewis Foreman (London: Thames, 1981), 39. Howard Brockway (1870–1951) was best known for his arrangements of Appalachian folk song. For information on Cook, Dett, and Diton, see Eileen Southern, *The Music of Black Americans: A History*

(New York: Norton, 1971). Best remembered today as Duke Ellington's mentor, Will Marion Cook (1869–1944), like Carpenter, put Dunbar's words to music. R. Nathaniel Dett (1882–1943) wrote the famous "Juba Dance" and other popular piano pieces, popularized, in part, by Grainger. Carl Diton (1886–1969) was better known as a pianist than as a composer, although Grainger probably knew his *Four Spirituals* of 1914. Grainger naturally gravitated toward composers who, on the whole, were best known for their arrangements of Anglo- and Afro-American folk song. Carpenter apparently represented the exception, and yet this context helpfully contrasts with the standard account of Carpenter as an "impressionist," along with Loeffler, Hill, and Griffes. See H. Wiley Hitchcock, *Music in the United States: A Historical Introduction,* 3d ed. (Englewood Cliffs, N.J.: Prentice Hall, 1988), 157; and Alan Howard Levy, *Musical Nationalism: American Composers' Search for Identity* (Westport, Conn.: Greenwood, 1983), 21.

14. Carpenter to Percy Grainger, 22 January 1920, PG-DLC.

15. Ronald V. Wiecki, "Two Musical Idealists—Charles Ives and E. Robert Schmitz: A Friendship Reconsidered," *American Music* 10, no. 1 (Spring 1992): 1–19. Upon immigrating to the States, Schmitz immediately championed not only Carpenter but Damrosch and Whithorne; writes Wiecki, "Although these composers are today not usually considered to be 'progressive,' at the time they were at the forefront of American music" (p. 2). On Carpenter's changes to the Piano Concertino, see Carpenter to E. Robert Schmitz, 8 October 1918, Schmitz Collection, Yale University.

16. Olin Downes, "New Piano Concerto Fantastic," *New York Evening Post,* 14 February 1920; H. T. Finck, "Music"; and other reviews, Scrapbook.

17. Carpenter to Rosalie Housman, 20 December 1921, Housman Collection, DLC.

18. Carpenter to E. Robert Schmitz, 30 March 1920; E. Robert Schmitz to Carpenter, 3 April 1920, Schmitz Collection, Yale University.

19. Carpenter to E. Robert Schmitz, 24 August 1920, Schmitz Collection, Yale University.

20. "Opinions of the Press," *Musical Courier,* 29 July 1920, 47, courtesy of Keith Lencho.

21. Ibid.; French reviews of Carpenter's Piano Concertino, performed by E. Robert Schmitz and the Pasdeloup Orchestra, Scrapbook.

22. Pitts Sanborn, "Music," *New York Globe,* 29 November 1920, C-DLC.

23. Carpenter to E. Robert Schmitz, 24 August 1920, Schmitz Collection, Yale University.

24. E. Robert Schmitz to Carpenter, 3 April 1920; Walter Damrosch to Carpenter, 9 April 1920; Carpenter to E. Robert Schmitz, 24 March 1920, Schmitz Collection, Yale University.

25. Sanborn, "Music."

26. Aaron Copland and Vivian Perlis, *Copland: 1900 through 1942* (New York: St. Martin's, 1984), 32.

27. Darius Milhaud, *Notes without Music* (New York: Alfred A. Knopf, 1953), 135.

28. Aaron Copland, "Jazz Structure and Influence," *Modern Music* 4, no. 2 (January-February 1927): 9–14. This article mentions Gershwin, Zez Confrey, and a number of European composers.

29. Daniel Gregory Mason, *The Dilemma of American Music and Other Essays* (New York: Macmillan, 1928), 73.

30. E. Robert Schmitz to Carpenter, 22 July 1926, Schmitz Collection, Yale University.

31. Howard W. Hess, "Symphony Concert," Scrapbook.

32. Grainger, *Seattle Symphony Program Notes*, 9 January 1936, C-DLC.

33. Percy Grainger to Carpenter, 6 November 1940, C-DLC.

34. Carpenter to Percy Grainger, 8 November 1940, PG-DLC.

35. Ibid., 14 April 1947, PG-DLC.

36. Ibid., 27 April 1947, 14 May 1947, PG-DLC.

37. George Roth to Carpenter, 25 August 1948, C-ICN (Roth's emphasis).

38. Carpenter, *Concertino for Piano and Orchestra*, Marjorie Mitchell, piano, William Strickland, conductor, Composer's Recordings, Inc., CRI-180.

39. Alfred Frankenstein, record review of Carpenter, *Concertino for Piano and Orchestra*, *High Fidelity* 14 (June 1964): 75; William Flanagan, record review of Carpenter, *Concertino for Piano and Orchestra*, *High Fidelity* 14 (July 1964): 71, 73; Arthur Cohn, record review of Carpenter, *Concertino for Piano and Orchestra*, *American Record Guide*, May 1964, 765; Milano, "The Journal Reviews," *Music Journal*, March 1965, 26.

40. Carpenter, quoted in "Tone Painter Sees Subjects Near at Hand," *Christian Science Monitor*, 30 October 1915, Scrapbook.

41. Edward Maisel, *Charles T. Griffes: The Life of an American Composer*, rev. ed. (New York: Alfred A. Knopf, 1984), 131–32. Walter Piston said something similar during the next world war; Howard Pollack, *Walter Piston* (Ann Arbor: UMI Research Press, 1982), 66.

42. Vernon Duke, *Listen Here!* (New York: Ivan Obolensky, 1963), 53.

43. Hodgson was a fashionable Georgian poet not unlike Ernest Dowson, whose "Terre promise" Carpenter had set in 1913.

44. Herbert Giles, *Gems of Chinese Literature* (Shanghai: Kelly and Walsh, 1883; reprint, New York: Paragon, 1965), may have been a source for these poems. "On a Screen," however, is titled "Snap-Shot."

45. Harriet Monroe, *A Poet's Life: Seventy Years in a Changing World* (New York: Macmillan, 1938), 392.

46. Carpenter to Ellen Borden, ca. 1916, C-DLC.

47. Christopher Palmer, *Impressionism in Music* (New York: Scribner's, 1973), 234.

48. Giles, *Gems of Chinese Literature*, 375.

49. "Dobson, Tom," *The National Cyclopaedia of American Biography* 18 (Clifton, N.J.: J. T. White, 1922): 296. Dobson's death apparently had nothing to do with the war; he died in New York.

50. "New Carpenter Songs on Tom Dobson's Program," *Musical America*, 29 April 1916, C-NN.

51. Kate Douglas Wiggin, "In Memoriam," in Tom Dobson, *The Rocky Road to Dublin* (Boston: Oliver Ditson, 1919).

52. Dobson, *Rocky Road to Dublin*.

53. "New Carpenter Songs"; see also Maisel, *Charles T. Griffes*, 173; and Anderson, *Charles T. Griffes*, 131. According to Anderson: "Strangely, Griffes did not attend Dobson's concert. Instead, he had lunch with Laura Elliot and saw Charlie Chaplin's movie burlesque of *Carmen*." One wonders nonetheless whether Dobson's success with Carpenter's Chinese songs in any way prompted Griffes's *Five Poems of Ancient China and Japan*, which he began work on shortly thereafter.

54. Mina Hager, "Speak for Yourself, John Alden Carpenter!" *Music Journal* 28 (March 1970): 66–67.

55. Bolm Collection, ICN. The 26 December performance, conducted by Eric De Lamarter, possibly featured new orchestrations, for the program indicated "an orchestral version especially arranged for these performances."

56. Hager, "Speak for Yourself," 67.

57. Carpenter to Virgil Thomson, 2 May 1941, Thomson Collection, Yale University. Carpenter wrote this letter to suggest that Thomson review a performance of Hager's with the National Youth Administration Orchestra.

CHAPTER 9. FROM THE FIRST SYMPHONY *(SERMONS IN STONES)* TO "BERCEUSE DE GUERRE"

1. J. H. Vaill, ed., *Litchfield County Choral Union: 1900–1912*, vol. 1 (Norfolk, Conn.: Litchfield County University Club, 1912).

2. Carpenter drew inspiration from *As You Like It* throughout his life. He set the act 5, scene 3, ditty "It was a lover and his lass" ("In Spring") in 1896. And he based one of his last major works, the 1945 orchestral tone poem *The Seven Ages*, on Jacques's famous act 3, scene 7, speech, "All the world's a stage." Shakespeare's bright, brassy heroine, the duke's daughter Rosalind, might have had something to do with the play's appeal; she resembled Rue—and perhaps Ginny, too. In any case, Carpenter surely identified with the

duke's optimism, for a similarly optimistic, even utopian strain characterized his choice of poetry (Blake, Whitman, Stevenson, and Tagore, to take but four examples), his philanthropic work for children, and his personal writings. He even evoked "utopia" in a letter to Ruth Page in 1941: "I hope that we shall discover the brains and good will to work out some sort of constructive Ballet and Opera place in the general direction of Utopia." Carpenter to Ruth Page, 8 June 1941, Dance Division, NN.

3. Carpenter to Ellen Borden, ca. 1916 or 1917, C-DLC.

4. "Three New Works Ably Presented by Litchfield Choral Union," *New York Herald Tribune,* 10 June 1917. See also "New Works at Music Festival," *Christian Science Monitor;* and H. E. Krehbiel, "Time-Tried Music Marks Concert of Symphony Society," *New York Herald Tribune,* Scrapbook. Such statements, which were no more specific than the one cited, probably had *The Firebird* or perhaps *Petrushka* in mind.

5. "New Music Heard in Annual Festival," Scrapbook; "Another Norfolk Festival Provides Musical Laurels," 10 June 1917, Scrapbook.

6. Eric De Lamarter, quoted in "Markedly American," *Boston Evening Transcript,* 18 April 1918, 14.

7. Leo Sowerby, quoted in Babette Deutsch, "America in the Arts," *Musical Quarterly* 7 (July 1921): 305; Felix Borowski, "John Alden Carpenter," *Musical Quarterly* 16 (October 1930): 461.

8. Krehbiel, "Time-Tried Music."

9. Carpenter to Walter Damrosch, 6 January 1920, Damrosch-Blaine Collection, DLC.

10. Walter Damrosch to Carpenter, 23 January 1920, Damrosch-Blaine Collection, DLC.

11. Borowski, "John Alden Carpenter," 461.

12. De Lamarter, quoted in "Markedly American," 14.

13. Andrew Stiller, record review of *Carpenter: Collected Works for Piano, Opus,* February 1987, 35.

14. Richard Aldrich, "Lester Donahue's Recital," *New York Times,* 16 March 1917, 9.

15. Richard Aldrich, "Lester Donahue Plays," *New York Times,* 24 October 1916, 13.

16. This according to the Schirmer edition, in any case. Some evidence suggests that Donahue played a "Little Dancer" in November 1916 (C-DLC), although this might have been the original *Little Nigger* with a new title.

17. Stiller, review of *Carpenter: Collected Works for Piano,* 35.

18. John Philip Sousa, quoted in the *Chicago Tribune,* 11 February 1917, Scrapbook.

19. Paul E. Bierley, *John Philip Sousa: American Phenomenon* (Englewood Cliffs, N.J.: Prentice Hall, 1973), 77–78.

20. "To Unify Music in Army and Navy," 9 September 1917, Scrapbook. The committee was founded at a September 1917 meeting at the offices of Lee F. Hanmer of the Army and Navy Committee on Training Camp Activities.

21. Maurice Rosenfeld, "Chicago Composer Talks of War Music," ca. February 1918, C-DLC.

22. Ibid.

23. R[ené] D[evries], "A Chat with John Alden Carpenter," *Musical Courier,* 4 July 1918, 14.

24. Carpenter, quoted in "Chicago Is Now Metropolis of Martial Music," Scrapbook.

25. Carpenter to Carl Engel, 4 November 1918, Engel Collection, OC-DLC.

26. Rosenfeld, "Chicago Composer Talks of War Music."

27. Karleton Hackett, "'Home Road' Voices Spirit," Scrapbook.

28. Philip Adams Otis, *The Chicago Symphony Orchestra* (Chicago: Summy, 1924), 337, 350.

29. David Ewen, *All the Years of American Popular Music* (Englewood Cliffs, N.J.: Prentice-Hall, 1977), 189.

30. Douglas Gilbert, *American Vaudeville: Its Life and Times* (New York: Whittlesy House, 1940); quoted by Carl H. Scheele in liner notes to *Inventions and Topics in Popular Song, 1910–1929,* New World Records NW 233. Scheele writes that Yvette Guilbert "was a French diseuse and chanteuse celebrated for her distinctive interpretations of folk songs. She is immortalized in Toulouse-Lautrec's sketches and lithographs." Carpenter, who owned collections of Guilbert's songs, possibly made some such connection between Bayes and Guilbert himself.

31. Ruth Etting, impersonating Bayes, successfully revived the song in the 1930s; George Oppenheimer, liner notes to *Follies, Scandals, and Other Diversions,* New World Records NW 215. Etting's wily impersonation—only subtly parodistic—provides a 1930s view of Bayes. For a still later view, see the 1944 Bayes film biography *Shine On Harvest Moon.*

32. Ewen, *American Popular Music,* 189, 232–34. See also Carl H. Scheele, liner notes to *Songs of World Wars I and II,* New World Records NW 222; the album itself includes Bayes's remarkable performance of "Over There."

33. Wayne Shirley suggests that "Sammys," a variant of "Yanks," was "introduced to calm Southern sensibilities" (Shirley, notes to author, 28 September 1992). This accords with Carpenter's song, which mentions soldiers pouring in from, among other states, Arkansas.

34. Undated and untitled article, C-NN.

35. Carpenter, sound recording of "Berceuse de guerre," Mina Hager and Celius Dowgherty, Musicraft 1016.

CHAPTER 10. *THE BIRTHDAY OF THE INFANTA*

1. Ronald L. Davis, *Opera in Chicago* (New York: Appleton-Century, 1966), 108–9. The history of Chicago's opera companies can be summarized as follows: Chicago Grand Opera (1910–15), Chicago Opera Association (1915–22), Chicago Civic Opera (1922–32), and Chicago Lyric Opera (1954–   ).

2. Charles Hamm, *Music in the New World* (New York: Norton, 1983), 447–48.

3. Rudolph Schirmer to Carpenter, 10 March 1914, C-ICN.

4. Ernest Schelling to Carpenter, n.d., C-ICN. Because Schelling died before Carpenter composed his later symphonies, the symphony referred to in this letter is presumably *Sermons in Stones;* consequently, the letter probably dates from about 1917. Ernest Schelling was a well-known composer, pianist, and conductor. His 1923 *Victory Ball* was among the most popular American orchestral works of its time.

5. Carpenter, quoted in "Would Have No 'Protective Tariff' to Aid American Music," ca. 1917, Scrapbook.

6. Eugene Stinson, "New Carpenter Ballet for Monte Carlo Delineates Industrial Activity in U.S.," *Musical America*, 16 August 1924, 27.

7. Carpenter, quoted in the *New York Herald Tribune*, 14 February 1926, and in Carpenter, "Skyscrapers," *Boston Symphony Orchestra Program Notes*, C-NN.

8. Robert Pollak, "John Alden Carpenter," *Chicagoan*, 11 May 1929, 25.

9. "Artist Should Express His Own Period Declares J. A. Carpenter," *Leader*, 23 April 1931, C-ICN. Taylor's *Peter Ibbetson* was performed at Ravinia, which had its own adventurous opera series in the period 1915–31, funded largely by Louis Eckstein, a Chicago businessman. The opera was a big success, according to Ronald Davis. Chicago composer Hamilton Forrest was a protégé of Mary Garden's. The Chicago Civic Opera premiere of *Camille* on 10 December 1931 was among the most publicized events in the history of Chicago opera. The audience liked it, but the critics thought it "a big bore." Garden herself remembered it as "an absolute flop." Davis, *Opera in Chicago*, 189–91, 201. Carpenter told the *Leader* that *Peter Ibbetson* was "well-written" but not interesting to the contemporary composer "because of its constant suggestion of European composers of a former generation." Conversely, he thought *Camille* more interesting but not as well written. Forrest's use of dissonant harmony and jazz would have naturally intrigued Carpenter. See Otto Luening, *The Odyssey of an American Composer: The Autobiography of Otto Luening* (New York: Scribner's, 1980), 240.

10. M. W., "Visits to the Homes of Famous Composers," 1947, C-NN

(excerpts from this article can be found in J. Douglas Cook, "The Composer Tells How," *Saturday Review*, 26 June 1954, 41–42).

11. Walter Monfried, "Carpenter, Businessman-Composer," *Milwaukee Journal*, 30 April 1947, 20.

12. John Pilkington, ed., *Stark Young: A Life in the Arts*, vol. 1 (Baton Rouge: Louisiana State University Press, 1975), 174. C-DLC holds a copy of the Young libretto.

13. Richard Buckle, *Diaghilev* (New York: Atheneum, 1979), 302.

14. Nesta Macdonald, *Diaghilev Observed by Critics in England and the United States, 1911–1929* (New York: Dance Horizons, 1975), esp. 154–60. See also S. L. Grigoriev, *The Diaghilev Ballet* (New York: Dance Horizons, 1957), and Buckle, *Diaghilev*, 300–317.

15. Verna Arvey, *Choreographic Music: Music for the Dance* (New York: E. P. Dutton, 1941), 287.

16. Buckle, *Diaghilev*, 199.

17. Edward Maisel, *Charles T. Griffes: The Life of an American Composer*, rev. ed. (New York: Alfred A. Knopf, 1984), 180.

18. Macdonald, *Diaghilev Observed by Critics*, 200–221.

19. Ibid., 148.

20. Adolph Bolm, "A Dancer's Day," *Dance*, October 1926, 34, Bolm Collection, ICN.

21. George Amberg, *Ballet in America: The Emergence of an American Art* (New York: Duell, Sloan, and Pearce, 1949), 25.

22. Maisel, *Charles T. Griffes*, 193.

23. The Ballet Intime featured, besides Bolm, the Japanese mime artist Michio Ito, the Anglo-Indian dancer Roshanara, and the French-Canadian singer Eva Gauthier; see ibid., 202.

24. Samuel Putnam, "The New Ballet: A Theatric Art," *Drama* 17 (December 1926): 69, Bolm Collection, ICN.

25. Agnes de Mille, *America Dances* (New York: Macmillan, 1980), 75.

26. Amberg, *Ballet in America*, 23.

27. Arvey, *Choreographic Music*, 287.

28. Both Wilde's "Birthday of the Infanta" and Stravinsky's *Petrushka* further feature gypsy dancers and, more important, a puppet show, although Carpenter possibly omitted the story's puppetry and, for that matter, its tamed bear, precisely because these elements were so prominent in Stravinsky's ballet.

29. Rodney Shewan, *Oscar Wilde: Art and Egotism* (New York: Macmillan, 1977), 61.

30. Arthur Meeker, *Chicago, with Love* (New York: Alfred A. Knopf, 1955), 170; Adolph Bolm, signed photograph to Ginny Hill, n.d., C-ICN.

31. Carpenter, "The Birthday of the Infanta," *Manhattan Opera Program Notes,* 2 February 1922, 14, C-NN.

32. In an early draft of the ballet scenario, the Infanta entered first with Don Pedro and the inquisitor, C-DLC.

33. Carpenter also sketched out two openings that he eventually discarded. In the first he imagined the curtain rising quickly, only eight measures into the music. In the second he composed a medley of important leitmotifs.

34. Carpenter uses the term *banderilla,* which is the "barbed dart that the banderillero thrusts into the neck or shoulder of the bull" (*Merriam Webster's Collegiate Dictionary,* 10th ed.), but he apparently means the thruster of the banderilla, namely, the banderillero.

CHAPTER 11. *THE BIRTHDAY OF THE INFANTA:* ITS PREMIERE AND AFTERMATH

1. Lee Simonson, "Legacy," in *The Theatre of Robert Edmond Jones,* ed. Ralph Pendleton (Middletown, Conn.: Wesleyan University Press, 1958), 14.

2. Stark Young, "Translations," *New Republic,* 22 January 1922, 371–72.

3. Stark Young, "Robert Edmond Jones: A Note," in *The Theatre of Robert Edmond Jones,* 3–6.

4. Ibid., 4.

5. Young, "Translations," 371. *The Theatre of Robert Edmond Jones,* 35, contains a black-and-white reproduction of this particular scene.

6. Young, "A Note," 4.

7. Richard Aldrich, "The Opera," *New York Times,* 24 February 1920.

8. Young, "A Note," 4–5.

9. Young, "Translations," 371.

10. Ruth Page, *Page by Page,* ed. Andrew Mark Wentink (New York: Dance Horizons, 1978), 132.

11. Ronald L. Davis, *Opera in Chicago* (New York: Appleton-Century, 1966), 124; W. L. Hubbard, "John A. Carpenter's 'Infanta' Ballet Wins High Approval," *Chicago Daily Tribune,* 24 December 1919, 11.

12. "Society at the Opera," *Chicago Daily Tribune,* 24 December 1919, 11. Nancy (Mrs. Joseph) Coleman was the president of the "Friends of Opera," described by Arthur Meeker as an organization "formed to help advertise the company, and to establish cordial relations between personnel and public." Mrs. Coleman herself was "a woman much on display in the Chicago of her time, the possessor of some truly great qualities—executive ability, friendliness, charm, and a delightful sense of humour. Her only drawback was her husband, a dreadfully dull man who lived to an incalculable age and loved

dining out." Arthur Meeker, *Chicago, with Love* (New York: Alfred A. Knopf, 1955), 239.

13. René Devries, "Chicago Opera Association Revives 'Don Pasquale' Starring Galli-Curci," *Musical Courier*, 8 January 1920, 14.

14. Maurice Rosenfeld, "'Birthday of the Infanta' Scores at Premiere," *Chicago News*, 24 December 1919, Scrapbook.

15. Edward Moore, "Music," *Chicago Daily Journal*, 24 December 1919, Scrapbook.

16. Herman Devries, "Pantomime by Carpenter Rich and Brilliant," 24 December 1919, Scrapbook.

17. Percy Hammond, "The Theaters," *Chicago Tribune*, 28 December 1919, Scrapbook.

18. James Whittaker, "The Ballet," 24 December 1919, Scrapbook.

19. Hubbard, "Carpenter's 'Infanta' Ballet," 11.

20. Felix Borowski, "Mr. Carpenter's Ballet," 2 January 1920, Scrapbook.

21. Hubbard, "Carpenter's 'Infanta' Ballet," 11; R. Devries, "Chicago Opera Association," 14; Borowski, "Mr. Carpenter's Ballet."

22. "Threat of Strike by Galli-Curci Is Arbitrated," *Chicago Herald Examiner*, 29 December 1919, Scrapbook.

23. Karleton Hackett, "Hours Piled upon Hours at Opera Matinee," *Chicago Evening Post*, 29 December 1919, Scrapbook.

24. "Composer and Diva Clash in 'War of Roses,'" *Chicago Tribune*, 19 December 1919, Scrapbook.

25. Pitts Sanborn, "In the Musical World"; Richard Aldrich, "The Opera," *New York Times*, 24 February 1920; "Bolm in Ballet Scores Triumph," Scrapbook.

26. Hamilton Easter Field, "America Produces an Artistic Masterpiece," *Brooklyn Daily Eagle*, 29 February 1920, Scrapbook.

27. Review of Carpenter's *Birthday of the Infanta, New York Morning Sun*, 24 February 1920(?), Scrapbook.

28. Max Smith, "Pantomime by Carpenter a Success," Scrapbook.

29. Aldridge, "The Opera."

30. Daniel Gregory Mason, "Music as Decoration," *Arts & Decoration* 12 (March 1920): 322.

31. Ibid., 322, 362.

32. Ibid., 362.

33. Paul Rosenfeld, *Musical Chronicle (1917–1923)* (New York: Harcourt, Brace, 1923; reprint, New York: Blom, 1972), 171.

34. Carpenter to Ellen Borden, 11 September 1922, C-DLC.

35. Deems Taylor, "America's First Dramatic Composer," *Vanity Fair*, April 1922, 59, 106.

36. Young, "Translations," 371.

37. Stark Young to Carpenter, n.d., Scrapbook. Young's enthusiasm about the ballet led to plans for a Carpenter-Young-Jones opera that never materialized; see chap. 10.

38. Karleton Hackett, "Carpenter Suite at Concert Gives Great Delight"; Olin Downes, "Music of Ballet by Symphony," Scrapbook.

39. Felix Borowski, "John Alden Carpenter," *Musical Quarterly* 16 (October 1930): 463; John Tasker Howard, "American Composers, VI: John Alden Carpenter," *Modern Music* 9, no. 1 (November-December 1931): 14.

40. Olin Downes, "J. A. Carpenter, American Craftsman," *Musical Quarterly* 16 (October 1930): 446; Marion Bauer, *Music through the Ages* (New York: Putnam's, 1932), 443.

41. Carpenter to Serge Koussevitzky, 30 December 1929, SK-DLC.

42. Ibid., 31 January 1941, SK-DLC.

CHAPTER 12. *KRAZY KAT*

1. Carl Van Vechten, "The Cat in Music," *Musical Quarterly* 6 (October 1920): 573–85; reprinted in *Musical Quarterly* 75 (Winter 1991): 37–47.

2. Carpenter presumably took, among other newspapers, Hearst's *Chicago American*.

3. Bill Blackbeard, "Krazy Kat," *The World Encyclopedia of Comics*, vol. 2, ed. Maurice Horn (New York: Chelsea House, 1976), 436.

4. Irene Alexander, "Rudolph Ganz to Play Work of Peninsula Composer," *Monterey Peninsula Herald*, 24 March 1949.

5. George Herriman, ink drawing, C-ICN.

6. George Herriman, quoted in Thomas C. Pierson, "The Life and Music of John Alden Carpenter" (Ph.D. diss., University of Rochester, 1952), 28.

7. Gilbert Seldes, *The Seven Lively Arts* (New York: Harper and Brothers, 1924; rev. ed., New York: Sagamore Press, 1957), 207 (page citations are to the revised edition).

8. Ibid., 3.

9. Carpenter, program notes to *Krazy Kat*, quoted in ibid., 218.

10. E. E. Cummings, "A Foreword to Krazy," in *A Miscellany*, ed. George J. Firmage (New York: Argophile, 1958), 102–6; Jay Cantor, *Krazy Kat* (New York: Collier, 1987). Cummings viewed O. Pupp as the progressive altruist, I. Mouse as the reactionary egoist, and K. Kat as the transcendent embodiment of love, wisdom, and joy: "The meteoric burlesk melodrama of democracy is a struggle between society (Offisa Pupp) and the individual (Ignatz Mouse) over an ideal (our heroine)—a struggle from

which, again and again and again, emerges one stupendous fact; namely, that the ideal of democracy fulfills herself only if, and whenever, society fails to suppress the individual" (p. 105).

11. Ronald L. Davis, *Opera in Chicago* (New York: Appleton-Century, 1966), 89.

12. Stark Young, "Krazy Kat," *New Republic,* 11 October 1922, 175. Because this article reviews a somewhat later production by the Greenwich Village Follies, one cannot say for sure whether Herriman and Carpenter intended Bill Postem to be tipsy. The music, however, seems to support the notion; the quirky flourishes are like musical belches.

13. See David Ross Baskerville, "Jazz Influence on Art Music to Mid-Century" (Ph.D. diss., University of California at Los Angeles, 1965), 341–47 (though Baskerville admits that the jazz in *Krazy Kat* is "tame"); Mary Herron DuPree, "'Jazz,' the Critics, and American Art Music in the 1920s," *American Music* 4, no. 3 (Fall 1986): 291; and Susan C. Cook, *Opera for a New Republic: The "Zeitopern" of Krenek, Weill, and Hindemith* (Ann Arbor: UMI Research Press, 1988), 185–91.

14. William Howland Kenney, *Chicago Jazz: A Cultural History, 1904–1930* (New York: Oxford University Press, 1993), 11, 18, and 67.

15. Dave Peyton, quoted by ibid., 8.

16. Eugene Stinson, "New Carpenter Ballet for Monte Carlo Delineates Industrial Activity in U.S.," *Musical America,* 16 August 1924, 27.

17. Clive Bell, *Since Cézanne* (London: Chatto and Windus, 1922; reprint, Freeport, N.Y.: Books for Libraries Press, 1969), 215; see *infra,* chap. 13.

18. Cook's list of "jazz-influenced" concert works begins with Hindemith, Schulhoff, and other composers of fox-trots (1919) and Milhaud's *Caramel mou* for voice and jazz dance band (1920); Cook, *Opera for a New Republic.*

19. Carpenter to E. Robert Schmitz, 24 August 1920, Schmitz Collection, Yale University.

20. Quoted by Dena J. Epstein, "Frederick Stock and American Music," *American Music* 10, no. 1 (Spring 1992): 32.

21. For discussions of early Chicago jazz, see, above all, Kenney, *Chicago Jazz,* but also Henry O. Osgood, *So This Is Jazz* (Boston: Little, Brown, 1926); Barry Ulanov, *A History of Jazz in America* (New York: Viking, 1957); Thomas J. Hennessey, "The Black Chicago Establishment, 1919–1930," *Journal of Jazz Studies* 2, no. 1 (December 1974): 15–45; and Frank Driggs and Harris Levine, *Black Beauty, White Heat: A Pictorial History of Classic Jazz, 1920–1950* (New York: Morrow, 1982).

22. Nicholas Lemann, *The Promised Land: The Great Black Migration and How It Changed America* (New York: Vintage, 1991), 16.

23. Kenney, *Chicago Jazz,* 169.

24. Ibid., 116.

25. Ibid., 17.

26. "Society Frolics at Arts Club Masked Ball," ca. December 1920, scrapbook, AC-ICN. The article mentions Rue by name, but John probably attended as well.

27. Kenney, *Chicago Jazz*, 61, 80.

28. Thomas C. Pierson to Ginny Hill, 10 September 1981, C-RH, quotes Harriett Welling as follows: "I think they used to go down to the South Side to what was known as 'Black and Tan.'"

29. Kenney, *Chicago Jazz*, 33.

30. Harriett Welling, quoted in Pierson to Ginny Hill, 10 September 1981: "The dance hall on the South Side where they all used to go was Colosimo's." See also Stephen Longstreet, *Chicago, 1860–1919* (New York: David McKay, 1973), 472. Kenney, *Chicago Jazz*, makes no mention of Colosimo's Café, although Longstreet writes that Sophie Tucker's "singing, with *gestures*, of 'Angle Worm Wiggle' caused her arrest by the Chicago cops" (p. 472).

31. Carpenter, quoted by Erich Brandeis, "The Kat That Inspired a Symphony," Scrapbook.

32. Stinson, "New Carpenter Ballet," 27.

33. Carpenter, quoted by Osgood, *So This Is Jazz*, 249–50.

34. Carpenter, quoted in "Jazz Is Assuming Prominence as an American Music Idiom, Declares Sky-Scrapers Composer," *Musical Digest*, 23 November 1926, C-NN.

35. See Robert Kimball, liner notes to *Sissle & Blake's Shuffle Along*, New World Records NW 260; Lawrence Gushee, liner notes to *Steppin' on the Gas: Rags to Jazz, 1913–1927*, New World Records NW 269; and Nat Shapiro, liner notes to *Yes Sir, That's My Baby: The Golden Years of Tin Pan Alley, 1920–1929*, New World Records NW 279.

36. Richard Aldrich, "Music," *New York Times*, 21 January 1922. The scoring for alto saxophone and drum set looks ahead to the use of saxophone and banjos in *Skyscrapers* and vibraphone in *Sea Drift*, and qualifies the composer's remarks, made only a year before, that "I have never used any instrument excepting those in the regular equipment of every modern orchestra nor have any of my scores called for extra players—unless a pianist is regarded as such. I feel that there are so many unexplored regions in the regular orchestra that there is no need of inventing new instruments to express myself." Carpenter to Rose Thomas, 17 March 1920, Rose Thomas Collection, ICN.

37. Ralph Berton, *Remembering Bix: A Memoir of the Jazz Age* (New York: Harper and Row, 1974), 26. This memoir refers also to a jazz-classical contact in the other direction: Berton introduced jazz trumpeter Bix Beiderbecke to the music of Carpenter, whom Berton thought "one of the few

American classical composers worth remembering" (p. 65). Beiderbecke, however, preferred Debussy and Stravinsky to Carpenter and "Les Six."

38. Paul Rosenfeld, *Musical Chronicle (1917–1923)* (New York: Harcourt, Brace, 1923; reprint, New York: Blom, 1972), 169.

39. Macdonald Smith Moore, *Yankee Blues: Musical Culture and American Identity* (Bloomington: Indiana University Press, 1985), 4. Moore's generalizations about the "centennial composers" include (1) "the centennial Yankee generally considered premodern exoticism—Oriental, negro, or medieval—extrinsic to their mission" (p. 9)—oriental and Negro cultures played a central role in Carpenter's work; (2) "Ives agreed with his Yankee peers who balked at suggestions that ragtime might be the characteristically American music" (p. 79)—Carpenter called jazz "the American folklore"; (3) "It comforted Yankees to think that they were of the blood of the Puritans" (p. 44)—Carpenter was critical or at least ambivalent about his Puritan heritage; (4) "Virtually all the centennial composers were antimodernists, though inconsistently. Most despised the avant-garde" (p. 66)—Carpenter's friends included Stravinsky, Prokofiev, Varèse, and John Becker; he promoted performances of Schoenberg in Chicago; he encouraged Copland to include such composers as Cowell, Crawford, and Rudhyar on a planned lecture-recital; and he advised the inclusion of some avant-garde music on recitals; (5) "None seems to have been a Negrophobe, but several were anti-Semitic" (p. 66)—Carpenter's personal friendship with Jews and admiration for such Jewish composers as Bloch and Berlin (especially the notion of Berlin as the quintessentially American composer) precludes serious charges of anti-Semitism, although privately he was not above gibing various ethnicities (his own included).

40. Harlow Robinson, *Sergei Prokofiev* (New York: Viking, 1987), 148.

41. Ibid., 132–70.

42. Serge Prokofiev to Carpenter, 15 April 1921, C-ICN.

43. Paul Bloomfield Zeisler, review of Carpenter's *Krazy Kat,* ca. 1921, C-DLC; "Conductor Stock, Orchestra, in Holiday Mood," 24 December 1921, Scrapbook; Edward Moore, "John A. Carpenter Provides Humor for Chicago Symphony," *Chicago Daily Tribune,* 24 December 1921.

44. George Herriman to Ginny Carpenter, n.d., C-ICN.

45. Young, "Krazy Kat," 176; Alexander, "Ganz to Play Work of Peninsula Composer."

46. Carpenter remained loyal friends with Barrère; see Carpenter to Georges Barrère, 23 March 1942, C-DLC. Ginny's governess, Margaret McNulty, stated that loyalty was one of Carpenter's virtues; he visited her every Christmas ("On the Other Side of Fame," *Chicago Sun,* ca. 1942, Scrapbook).

47. Brandeis, "The Kat That Inspired a Symphony."

48. Carl Engel, "Views and Reviews," *Musical Quarterly* 8 (January

1922): 149; Seldes, *The Seven Lively Arts,* 214; Henrietta Straus, "Marking the Miles," *Nation* 114 (1 March 1922): 292.

49. E. Moore, "Carpenter Provides Humor"; Deems Taylor, quoted in "A Jazz Ballet," *Literary Digest* 73 (15 April 1922): 33.

50. "Comic Strip Music," *Musical America,* 21 January 1922, 292.

51. Aldrich, "Music"; Engel, "Views and Reviews," 148; Osgood, *So This Is Jazz,* 153. Descriptions of Carpenter's "jazz" as being (too) "polite" or "gentlemanly" continued into the 1930s and beyond. See, for example, Cecil Michener Smith's description of Carpenter's "gentleman's jazz" in "Spring Festival, Washington, 1935," *Modern Music* 12, no. 4 (May-June 1935): 198.

52. Seldes, *The Seven Lively Arts,* 215; Rosenfeld, *Musical Chronicle,* 170.

53. Virgil Thomson, "The Cult of Jazz," *Vanity Fair,* July 1925, 54.

54. Ibid.

55. Deems Taylor, "America's First Dramatic Composer," *Vanity Fair,* April 1922, 59; Straus, "Marking the Miles," 292; Young, "Krazy Kat," 176; Engel, "Views and Reviews," 149.

56. Taylor, "America's First Dramatic Composer," 59; Straus, "Marking the Miles," 292.

57. Young, "Krazy Kat," 176.

58. Carpenter to Ellen Borden, 11 September 1922, C-DLC (Carpenter's emphasis). Carpenter occasionally indulged in this kind of ethnic humor; see n. 39 and Carpenter to May Valentine, 2 November 1949, C-ICN, in which Carpenter asked Valentine to smooth things over at Schirmer's and thus "relieve his [Schirmer executive H. W. Heinsheimer's] Jewish anxiety."

59. Carpenter to Ellen Borden, 16 September 1922, C-DLC (Carpenter's emphasis).

60. H[enry] T[aylor] P[arker], "Around to 'Krazy Kat,'" *Boston Evening Transcript,* 21 April 1923, Scrapbook.

61. Carpenter to Fabien Sevitzky, 29 October 1939, Sevitzky Collection, DLC.

62. Carpenter to Henry Kitchell Webster, 19 February 1929, 4 March 1929, Henry Kitchell Webster Collection, ICN.

63. Carpenter to Fabien Sevitzky, 8 November 1940; Fabien Sevitzky to Carpenter, 13 November 1940, Sevitzky Collection, DLC.

64. Fabien Sevitzky to Carpenter, 27 December 1940, Sevitzky Collection, DLC.

65. Carpenter to Léonide Massine, 19 February 1940, C-DLC; Léonide Massine to Carpenter, 7 September [1940?], C-DLC.

66. Carpenter to Rudolph Ganz, 21 December 1948, RG-ICN (Carpenter's emphasis).

67. Ibid., 27 December 1948, RG-ICN.

68. Alexander, "Ganz to Play Work of Peninsula Composer."

69. Carpenter, *Krazy Kat,* Hamburg Philharmonic, Richard Korn, Allegro-Elite 3150; Carpenter, *Krazy Kat,* Los Angeles Philharmonic, Calvin Simmons, New World Records NW 228.

70. Paul Kresh, record review of Carpenter, *Krazy Kat, Stereo Review* 41 (July 1978): 86; Paul Snook, record review of Carpenter, *Krazy Kat, Fanfare* 1 (May-June 1978): 28.

71. Harold C. Schonberg, "Music: Fry's Challenge," *New York Times,* 30 July 1975, 15.

72. R. D. Darrell, liner notes to Carpenter, *Krazy Kat,* New World Records NW 228.

73. Herriman to Ginny Carpenter, n.d., C-ICN.

CHAPTER 13. THE MAKING OF *SKYSCRAPERS*

1. Boris Kochno, *Diaghilev and the Ballets Russes,* trans. Adrienne Foulke (New York: Harper and Row, 1970), 223.

2. Pierre Monteux to Serge Diaghilev, ca. 1920, C-ICN. The French original reads: "Monsieur Carpenter est un des plus talentueuse [*sic*] parmi les compositeurs Americains; ses tendances sont modernes et je suis sur que son ballet, que vous apporte Madame Carpenter, vous interessera comme il m'a interessé moi-même, musicalement et scéniquement. Il a été monté à Chicago, par Bolm et a obtenu un très grand succès."

3. Serge Prokofiev to Carpenter, 15 April 1921, C-ICN.

4. Richard Buckle, *Diaghilev* (New York: Atheneum, 1979), 408.

5. Carpenter to Ellen Borden, 6 July 1923, C-DLC.

6. Ibid., 5 June 1923, C-DLC.

7. William Rubin, *The Paintings of Gerald Murphy* (New York: Museum of Modern Art, 1974); Rick Stewart, *An American Painter in Paris: Gerald Murphy* (Dallas: Dallas Museum of Art, 1986).

8. Dos Passos, quoted by Honoria Murphy Donnelly and Richard N. Billings, *Sara & Gerald* (New York: Times Books, 1982), 224.

9. Andrew Turnbull, *Scott Fitzgerald* (New York: Scribner's, 1962), 155.

10. Archibald MacLeish, foreword to *The Paintings of Gerald Murphy,* by Rubin, 8.

11. Calvin Tomkins, *Living Well Is the Best Revenge* (New York: Viking, 1962), 28.

12. Carpenter to Ellen Borden, 5 June 1923, C-DLC.

13. Ibid., 14 June 1923, C-DLC. For a description of Murphy's party, see Charles Schwartz, *Cole Porter* (New York: Dial Press, 1977), 67.

14. Carpenter to Ellen Borden, 25 and 27 June 1923, C-DLC.

15. Philip Hale, "Skyscrapers," *Boston Symphony Orchestra Program Notes,* C-DLC; Felix Borowski, "Skyscrapers," *Chicago Symphony Orchestra Program Notes,* C-DLC; Claudia Cassidy, "Symphony to Honor John Alden Carpenter This Week," *Chicago Sunday Tribune,* 25 February 1951, Scrapbook; Madeleine Goss, *Modern Music-Makers: Contemporary American Composers* (New York: E. P. Dutton, 1952), 39.

16. Carpenter to Ellen Borden, 6 July 1923, C-DLC (Carpenter's emphasis).

17. Frederick Lewis Allen, *Only Yesterday* (New York: Harper and Row, 1931), 44–45.

18. Carpenter to Ellen Borden, 11 and 14 July 1923, C-DLC.

19. Schwartz, *Cole Porter,* 76.

20. Carpenter to Ellen Borden, 29 May 1923, 20 July 1923, C-DLC.

21. Carpenter to Elizabeth Sprague Coolidge, 5 September 1923, ESC-DLC; Carpenter to Eva Gauthier, 20 September 1923, Gauthier Collection, NN.

22. Verna Arvey, *Choreographic Music: Music for the Dance* (New York: E. P. Dutton, 1941), 290.

23. Gerald Murphy to Carpenter, ca. 1923, C-ICN.

24. Thomas C. Pierson, "The Life and Music of John Alden Carpenter" (Ph.D. diss., University of Rochester, 1952), 29.

25. Gerald Murphy to Carpenter, ca. late 1923, C-ICN.

26. David Lowe, *Lost Chicago* (New York: American Legacy Press, 1985), 124–28.

27. Harriet Monroe, *A Poet's Life: Seventy Years in a Changing World* (New York: Macmillan, 1938), 208.

28. Carl S. Smith, *Chicago and the American Literary Imagination, 1880–1920* (Chicago: University of Chicago Press, 1984), 131–34.

29. Monroe, *A Poet's Life,* 208–9.

30. Smith, *Chicago and the American Literary Imagination,* 128, 136–40.

31. George Ade, "After the Skyscrapers, What?" in *The Best of George Ade* (Bloomington: Indiana University Press, 1985), 184–85.

32. Eugene Stinson, "New Carpenter Ballet for Monte Carlo Delineates Industrial Activity in U.S.," *Musical America,* 16 August 1924, 27.

33. Carpenter, quoted in the *New York Herald Tribune,* 14 February 1926, C-NN.

34. Lewis A. Erenberg, "Ain't We Got Fun?" *Chicago History* 14, no. 4 (Winter 1985–86): 11. Erenberg writes that the "Scenic Railway" at Riverview "was never intended to be scenic. It was a parody of Chicago's elevated railroads that gave riders a chance to take a risk under relatively safe conditions and to enjoy a minor catharsis of the noise and confusion of the industrial world" (p. 12).

35. Clive Bell, *Since Cézanne* (London: Chatto and Windus, 1922; reprint, Freeport, N.Y.: Books for Libraries Press, 1969), 221.

36. John A. Kouwenhoven, *The Arts in Modern American Civilization* (New York: Norton, 1948), 222.

37. Carpenter, quoted by Cassidy, "Symphony to Honor Carpenter."

38. Stinson, "New Carpenter Ballet," 27.

39. Kochno, *Diaghilev and the Ballets Russes,* 223. Although *Skyscrapers* suggests, at one point, factory workers leaving their workplace, it seems puzzling that Diaghilev referred to a factory setting as such and mentioned neither skyscrapers nor amusement parks. Did something get lost in the translation? Or did Carpenter originally intend a factory setting?

40. Buckle, *Diaghilev,* 437.

41. Kochno, *Diaghilev and the Ballets Russes,* 222–23.

42. Fred Austin, "Skyscrapers," *Dance,* April 1926, 24–25. Austin mistakenly refers to Nijinska as Nijinsky's wife. In the context of this mistake, his contention that Nijinska "was to do the choreography" seems even less believable.

43. Tomkins, *Living Well,* 41. Some of these photographs are reprinted in the book's "album."

44. Carpenter to Ellen Borden, 28 August 1924, C-DLC; Arvey, *Choreographic Music,* 289.

45. Carpenter to Ellen Borden, 22 August 1924, C-DLC.

46. Stinson, "New Carpenter Ballet," 27.

47. Carpenter to Ellen Borden, 1 September 1924, 20 January 1925, and 4 February 1925, C-DLC.

48. Ibid., 17 February 1925, C-DLC.

49. Ibid., 19, 21, 23, and 24 February 1925, C-DLC (Carpenter's emphasis). On Stravinsky's tour of the Chicago stockyards, see also Vera Stravinsky and Robert Craft, *Stravinsky in Pictures and Documents* (New York: Simon and Schuster, 1978), 301.

50. Carpenter to Ellen Borden, 19 February 1925, C-DLC (Carpenter's emphasis).

51. Ibid., 25 February 1925, 14 April 1925, C-DLC.

52. Carpenter to Serge Diaghilev, 16 April 1925, Dance Division, NN. Although Carpenter states in this letter that he has "today accepted a proposal by the Metropolitan," the contract actually is dated 14 April.

53. Buckle, *Diaghilev,* 463. For additional sources on the Diaghilev-Carpenter affair, see Lynn Garafola, *Diaghilev's Ballets Russes* (New York: Oxford University Press, 1989), 457 n. 26.

54. Vernon Duke, *Listen Here!* (New York: Obolensky, 1963), 43.

55. Kochno, *Diaghilev and the Ballets Russes,* 222; Buckle, *Diaghilev,* 459, 463.

56. Minna Lederman, "Skyscrapers, an Experiment in Design: An Interview with Robert Edmond Jones," *Modern Music* 3, no. 2 (January-February 1926): 21–22.

57. Ibid., 21–26. Like the better-remembered Josephine Baker, Florence Mills (1901–27) was an African American singer-dancer.

58. Jerome Delamater, *Dance in the Hollywood Musical* (Ann Arbor: UMI Research Press, 1978); Gerald Mast, *Can't Help Singin'* (New York: Woodstock, 1987).

59. Sammy Lee, quoted by Hale, "Skyscrapers."

60. Dorle J. Soria, "Treasures and Trifles," *Opera News* 52 (September 1987): 26.

61. Carpenter, *Skyscrapers* (orchestral score), preface by Carpenter [and Robert Edmond Jones?] (New York: G. Schirmer, 1927). In the following discussion, all uncited quotations refer to this scenario.

62. These labels—the Hammer motive, Work motive, Song of the Skyscrapers, Song of the Workers, March of the Workers, Reminder of Work, Street Music—are of my own devising.

63. Carpenter, *Skyscrapers,* London Symphony Orchestra, Kenneth Klein, EMI compact disc CDC-7 49263 2. Not all the action described can be so identified, since this recording does not include the complete ballet.

64. "Skyscrapers," *Outlook* 142 (3 March 1926): 315.

65. Alice Holdship Ware, "Skyscrapers," *Survey* 56 (1 April 1926): 35.

66. Deems Taylor, "The Musical Event of the Month," Scrapbook.

67. Olin Downes, "'Skyscrapers' Here with 'Jazz' Score," *New York Times,* 20 February 1926.

68. Oscar Thompson, "'Skyscrapers' Acclaimed as Genuinely American," *Musical America,* 27 February 1926, 5.

69. Jones, quoted by Lederman, "Skyscrapers, an Experiment in Design," 22.

70. Taylor, "Musical Event of the Month"; Downes, "'Skyscrapers' Here with 'Jazz' Score."

71. Carpenter to Ashton Steven, *Chicago Herald-American,* ca. 1942, Scrapbook.

72. Henry O. Osgood, *So This Is Jazz* (Boston: Little, Brown, 1926), 31, first noted this quotation. Later in the score Carpenter quotes at least two more melodies, namely, "Yankee Doodle" and Stephen Foster's "Massa's in de Cold Ground." In his review Oscar Thompson also spoke of "fleeting references" to "Dem Goo-Goo Eyes" ("Just Because She Made Dem Goo-Goo Eyes" by John Queen and Hughie Cannon), but he apparently was mistaken in this. See Thompson, "'Skyscrapers' Acclaimed as Genuinely American."

73. Carpenter, draft of a scenario for *Skyscrapers,* C-DLC.

74. Norman Bolotin and Christine Laing, *The Chicago World's Fair of 1893: The World's Columbian Exposition* (Washington, D.C.: Preservation Press, 1992), 152.

75. Downes, "'Skyscrapers' Here with 'Jazz' Score."

76. Thompson, "'Skyscrapers' Acclaimed as Genuinely American."

77. Downes, "'Skyscrapers' Here with 'Jazz' Score."

78. Ibid.

79. Ware, "Skyscrapers," 35.

80. The second carousel tune also sounds like a popular song.

81. Downes, "'Skyscrapers' Here with 'Jazz' Score."

82. Thompson, "'Skyscrapers' Acclaimed as Genuinely American."

83. Carpenter, quoted in the *New York Herald Tribune*, 14 February 1926.

84. "Skyscrapers," *Outlook* 142:315.

85. Ware, "Skyscrapers," 35. Ware implies that White-Wings sleeps by the blinking traffic light during the Sandwich Men scene. Carpenter's scenario suggests, however, that White-Wings exits at the end of the Negro scene. Nor does the score contain light indications at this point.

86. Jones, quoted by Lederman, "Skyscrapers, an Experiment in Design," 22.

87. Downes, "'Skyscrapers' Here with 'Jazz' Score."

CHAPTER 14. THE RECEPTION OF *SKYSCRAPERS*

1. Janet Fairbank, "Carpenter Ballet American, View of Mrs. Janet Fairbank," *Chicago Evening Post*, Scrapbook.

2. Carpenter to Julius Gold, 8 March 1926, JG-DLC.

3. Olin Downes, "'Skyscrapers' Here with 'Jazz' Score," *New York Times*, 20 February 1926.

4. Lawrence Gilman, review of Carpenter's *Skyscrapers*, *New York Herald Tribune*, quoted in "The Descent of Jazz upon Opera," *Literary Digest* 88 (13 March 1926): 25; Olga Samaroff, review of Carpenter's *Skyscrapers*, *New York Evening Post*, quoted in "The Descent of Jazz," 24.

5. Oscar Thompson, "'Skyscrapers' Acclaimed as Genuinely American," *Musical America*, 27 February 1926, 5; Alice Holdship Ware, "Skyscrapers," *Survey* 56 (1 April 1926): 35; Pitts Sanborn, "The 1925–1926 Season," *Modern Music* 3, no. 4 (May-June 1926): 4. Sanborn similarly criticized works as varied as Massenet's *Don Quichotte*, de Falla's *La vida breve*, Respighi's *Pines of Rome*, and Gershwin's *Rhapsody in Blue*.

6. Downes, "'Skyscrapers' Here with 'Jazz' Score"; Thompson, "'Sky-

scrapers' Acclaimed as Genuinely American," 5; Sanborn, "1925–1926 Season," 4.

7. Gilman, review of Carpenter's *Skyscrapers,* 25; "Skyscrapers," *Outlook* 142 (3 March 1926): 315.

8. Thompson, "'Skyscrapers' Acclaimed as Genuinely American," 5; "Skyscrapers," *Outlook* 142:315; Gilman, review of Carpenter's *Skyscrapers,* 25; Downes, "'Skyscrapers' Here with 'Jazz' Score."

9. Gilman, review of Carpenter's *Skyscrapers,* 25; Downes, "'Skyscrapers' Here with 'Jazz' Score"; Deems Taylor, "The Musical Event of the Month," Scrapbook. Although Taylor claimed that the "Metropolitan gave the ballet an elaborate and effective production," he stopped short of any real evaluation of the music other than to say that *Skyscrapers,* "while . . . a serious work of art, is cast in a vein that never evokes the terrifying adjective, 'highbrow.'"

10. Thompson, "'Skyscrapers' Acclaimed as Genuinely American," 5.

11. Ware, "Skyscrapers," 35.

12. "'Skyscrapers' Given Again," *New York Times,* 23 February 1926, 26.

13. "A Dissenter," *New York Times,* 28 February 1926, 6.

14. Carpenter to Ellen Borden, 19 December 1927, C-DLC.

15. *A Working Friendship: The Correspondence between Richard Strauss and Hugo von Hofmannsthal,* trans. Hanns Hammelmann and Ewald Osers (New York: Vienna House, 1952), 350.

16. John Willett, *Art and Politics in the Weimar Period* (New York: Pantheon, 1978).

17. Susan C. Cook, *Opera for a New Republic: The "Zeitopern" of Krenek, Weill, and Hindemith* (Ann Arbor: UMI Research Press, 1988), 217.

18. Review of Carpenter's *Wolkenkratzer* (Skyscrapers), Scrapbook.

19. Cook, *Opera for a New Republic,* 108.

20. Cyril W. Beaumont, *Complete Book of Ballets* (London: Putnam, 1937), 756–57. Beaumont's scenario of *Wolkenkratzer* matches the original *Skyscrapers* (though he mistakenly lists the Munich premiere date as 1929). The scene and cast listings also indicate that the Munich production followed the original scenario.

21. Carpenter to Serge Koussevitzky, 21 February 1928, SK-DLC.

22. Alfredo Casella, "Reflections on the European Season," *Modern Music* 4, no. 4 (May-June 1928): 7; Josef Ludwig Fischer, review of Carpenter's *Wolkenkratzer,* Scrapbook.

23. *Judentum und Musik mit dem ABC jüdischer und nichtarischer Musik beflissener* (Munich: Hans Brückner, 1936), 52.

24. *Time,* 27 June 1938, Scrapbook.

25. Milan Hauner, *Hitler: A Chronology of His Life and Time* (New York: St. Martin's, 1983), 58–60. The Nazis rioted at the Munich premiere of *Jonny spielt auf;* Cook, *Opera for a New Republic,* 105.

26. Glenn Dillard Gunn, "Carpenter as Cynic-Realist"; Herman Devries, "'Skyscrapers' of Carpenter Irks Music Critic"; and Edward Moore, "Stock Gives Carpenter's 'Skyscrapers,'" Scrapbook.

27. "'Skyscrapers' at Symphony Concert,'" Scrapbook.

28. Samuel L. Laciar, "Orchestra 'Plays' Red Traffic Lights," *Philadelphia Public Ledger,* 29 October 1927, 5.

29. Ralph Holmes, "'Skyscrapers' Makes Great Hit with Symphony Fans"; Charlotte M. Torrsney, "New Music Wrecks Symphony Decorum," Scrapbook.

30. "Eighth Concert by Symphony," Scrapbook; L. A. Sloper, "Boston Hears 'Skyscrapers,'" *Christian Science Monitor,* 10 December 1927, 12.

31. Serge Koussevitzky, telegram to Carpenter, 10 June 1928, Scrapbook.

32. Roger Sessions to Aaron Copland, 26 June 1928, Copland Collection, DLC.

33. Parisian reviews of Carpenter's *Skyscrapers: Le Figaro,* 10 June 1928; *Paris Times,* 11 June 1928; *Paris-Midi,* 11 June 1928; *Paris Soir,* 12 June 1928; and *Le Menestrel,* 15 June 1928, Scrapbook. All are in French except for the *Paris Times.*

34. "La musique de Carpenter recèle un humour personnel de la qualité la plus déliée. Elle réalise, en ce 'Gratte-Ciel', les promesses abondantes des cocasses 'Adventures in a Perambulator' et du jazz-pantomime 'Krazy kat': fantaisie poétique et tendre, qui cède, avec une désinvolte élégance, à ses propres caprices, et pare de couleurs heureuses et vives la facilité de ses mélodies. Musique du plaisir et du vif argent, musique dont les fées joyeuses ont protégé la naissance." *Paris-Midi,* 11 June 1928.

35. Robert Stevenson, *Music in Mexico* (New York: Crowell, 1952), 240.

36. Walter Damrosch to Carpenter, 22 October 1928, WD-NN.

37. Ibid., 23 December 1931, WD-NN.

38. The Hollywood Bowl program gives a performance date of 29 July, Hollywood Bowl Archives. Some press accounts, including Joseph Arnold, "Dance Events Reviewed," *American Dancer,* September 1933, 19, say 30 July. The ballet may have been performed both nights, or someone might have entered the date of review as the date of the concert.

39. "The Argument," *Hollywood Bowl Program Notes,* Hollywood Bowl Archives.

40. Tom Van Dycke, "Concerning Mr. Hecht and His 'Skyscrapers,'" Hollywood Bowl Archives.

41. John Tasker Howard, "American Composers, VI: John Alden Carpenter," *Modern Music* 9, no. 1 (November-December 1931): 15; Marion Bauer, *Music through the Ages* (New York: Putnam's, 1932), 433; Lazare Saminsky, "Europe and America in Music Today," *Modern Music* 10, no. 2 (January-February 1933): 93; Guido Pannain, *Modern Composers* (New York: E. P.

Dutton, 1933), 244–45; Daniel Gregory Mason, *Tune In, America* (New York: Alfred A. Knopf, 1931), 164.

42. Carpenter, *Skyscrapers*, Victor Symphony Orchestra, Nathaniel Shilkret, Victor M-130, Victor 11250-52, and Victor (Japanese) ND-313-15; R. D. Darrell, "Analytical Notes and Reviews," *Music Lover's Guide*, September 1932.

43. Edward Downes, "American Festival," Scrapbook; Olin Downes, "American Music Applauded Again," Scrapbook; Oscar Thompson, "Orchestral Concerts in New York," *Musical America*, 10 December 1939, 57.

44. George Henry Lovett Smith, "American Festival in Boston," *Modern Music* 17, no. 1 (November-December 1939): 43; Elliott Carter, "American Music in the New York Scene," *Modern Music* 17, no. 2 (January-February 1940): 96.

45. Hugo Leichtentritt, *Serge Koussevitzky: The Boston Symphony Orchestra and the New American Music* (Cambridge: Harvard University Press, 1946), 65–66.

46. Verna Arvey, *Choreographic Music: Music for the Dance* (New York: E. P. Dutton, 1941), 289–93.

47. Carpenter to Rue (Hill) Hubert, 8 December 1947, C-RH.

48. Arthur Cohn, "Americans at Rochester," *Modern Music* 17, no. 4 (May-June 1940): 256; Giulio Gatti-Casazza, *Memories of the Opera* (New York: Scribner's, 1941; reprint, London: John Calder, 1977), 242.

49. David Ross Baskerville, "Jazz Influence on Art Music to Mid-Century" (Ph.D. diss., University of California at Los Angeles, 1965), 343–47.

50. Carpenter, *Skyscrapers*, Vienna Symphony Orchestra, Meinhard von Zallinger, American Recording Society ARS-37; reissued, Desto D407, DST-6407; Carpenter, *Skyscrapers*, London Symphony Orchestra, Kenneth Klein, Angel compact disc CDC-7 49263 2. The title of the Klein CD, *Skyscrapers and Other Music of the American East Coast School*, complete with a photograph of the Empire State Building, reveals a common misconception about where Carpenter lived and worked.

51. Arthur Cohn, record review of Carpenter, *Skyscrapers*, *American Record Guide*, May 1965, 838; Harold C. Schonberg, "Records: Americans," *New York Times*, 13 December 1953, X15; Alfred Frankenstein, record review of Carpenter, *Skyscrapers*, *High Fidelity* 4 (April 1954): 44; Oliver Daniel, "Americans from Vienna," *Saturday Review*, 26 June 1965, 51–53.

52. John Ditzky, record review of Carpenter, *Skyscrapers*, *Fanfare* 11 (January-February 1988): 277; Joseph N. Stevenson, record review of Carpenter, *Skyscrapers*, *Stevenson Compact Disc Review Guide*, April-May 1988, 2; Fred Hauptman, record review of Carpenter, *Skyscrapers*, *American Music* 7, no. 2 (Summer 1989): 229.

CHAPTER 15. SONGS FROM THE JAZZ AGE

1. Harry Thorpe, "Serenade," *Musical Quarterly* 15 (January 1929): 106–11.

2. Charles Schwartz, *Gershwin* (New York: Bobbs-Merrill, 1973), 75.

3. *Selected Letters of Virgil Thomson,* ed. Tim Page and Vanessa Weeks Page (New York: Summit, 1988), 341.

4. Edward Maisel, *Charles T. Griffes: The Life of an American Composer,* rev. ed. (New York: Alfred A. Knopf, 1984), 202.

5. Carpenter to Eva Gauthier, 19 January 1920, Gauthier Collection, NN.

6. Ibid., 5 and 22 October 1923, Gauthier Collection, NN.

7. Emma Calvé to Carpenter, 5 March 1923, C-ICN.

8. Ibid., 20 August 1923, C-ICN. The French original reads: "J'ai pleuré en chantant votre melodie. . . . Elle est exquise, émouvante, très chantante, et dans votre savante harmonie."

9. The three revised Hughes songs, as well as the new "That Soothin' Song," are dated March 1926 in the Schirmer edition, even though they presumably date from early 1927. Carpenter apparently wanted the published date to reflect the date of his original Hughes settings.

10. Langston Hughes to Carpenter, 1 November 1926, C-ICN.

11. Carpenter to Eva Gauthier, 21 October 1926, Gauthier Collection, NN.

12. Carol J. Oja, *Colin McPhee: Composer in Two Worlds* (Washington, D.C.: Smithsonian Institution Press, 1990), 30.

13. Henry Cowell, "Summer Festivals in the U.S.A.," *Modern Music* 19, no. 1 (November-December 1941): 42; Donal Henahan, "Highbrow, Lowbrow, in Between," *New York Times,* 24 January 1991.

14. Carpenter, sound recording of "The Cryin' Blues" and "Jazz-Boys," Vanni Marcoux, bass, and Pierre Coppola, piano, His Master's Voice DA 988.

15. Philip L. Miller, "American Vocal Music of Today and Yesterday," *American Record Guide,* May 1965, 808.

CHAPTER 16. A POSTWAR MISCELLANY

1. Leopold Stokowski to Carpenter, 18 July 1920, Scrapbook.

2. Carpenter, "A Pilgrim Vision," *Philadelphia Orchestra Program Notes,* 26 November 1920.

3. "Philadelphia Orchestra," *Philadelphia Evening Bulletin,* Scrapbook.

4. Leopold Stokowski to Carpenter, 4 December 1920, Scrapbook.

5. Lawrence Gilman, "Music of the Month," *North American Review* 215 (1922): 692–97.

6. Deems Taylor, review of Carpenter's *Pilgrim Vision*, *New York World*, 15 March 1922, Scrapbook.

7. H. T. C., "Introduce 'Pilgrim' Work of Carpenter," *Musical America*, 4 December 1920, Scrapbook.

8. Felix Borowski, "John Alden Carpenter," *Musical Quarterly* 16 (October 1930): 462.

9. This Tempo di tango apparently predates the *Tango américain;* in fact, it turns up among the composer's sketches from 1912 and 1913. It is not clear whether Carpenter completed this song, since only the instrumental introduction and coda survive.

10. Ned Rorem, *Setting the Tone* (New York: Coward-McCann, 1983), 20, 39, 262 (the book erroneously indexes these pages under "Humphrey Carpenter"); and Ned Rorem, letter to author, 8 February 1993. Rorem remembered that Bonds had played Carpenter's Piano Concertino under the composer's direction.

11. Andrew Stiller, record review of *Carpenter: Collected Piano Works, Opus,* February 1987, 35.

12. Thomas C. Pierson, liner notes to *Carpenter: Collected Piano Works,* New World Records NW 328/329; Christopher Palmer, *Impressionism in Music* (New York: Scribner's, 1973), 234.

13. Carpenter, *Diversions, No. 1,* Jeanne Behrend, Victor 17911.

14. Maurice Dumesnil to Carpenter, 21 June 1942, C-DLC.

15. Stiller, record review of *Carpenter: Collected Piano Works,* 35.

16. "John A. Carpenter Made Member of Legion of Honor," scrapbook, AC-ICN.

17. Henry O. Osgood, *So This Is Jazz* (Boston: Little, Brown, 1926), 152–63.

18. Thomas A. DeLong, *Pops: Paul Whiteman, King of Jazz* (Piscataway, N.J.: New Century, 1983), 232–33.

19. Ibid., 80–81.

20. A manuscript of *A Little Bit of Jazz* at the New York Public Library contains these revisions in pencil. This particular manuscript may be the only extant copy of the score, although there are copied parts at the Whiteman Collection, Williams College, no. 1410.

21. Chester Hazlett played the B♭ and E♭ soprano saxophone parts; Hal McLean played oboe and E♭ alto saxophone; E. Lyle Sharpe played E♭ alto saxophone and B♭ clarinet; and Charles Strickfaden played B♭ soprano saxophone, B♭ tenor saxophone, and E♭ baritone saxophone.

22. Review of Carpenter's *Little Bit of Jazz, Kalamazoo Gazette,* 7 October 1925; and Glenn Dillard Gunn, review of Carpenter's *Little Bit of Jazz,*

Chicago Herald Examiner, 12 October 1925, scrapbook, Whiteman Collection, Williams College.

23. Maurice Rosenfeld, review of Carpenter's *Little Bit of Jazz, Kalamazoo Daily News,* 10 October 1925, scrapbook, Whiteman Collection, Williams College (DeLong, *Pops,* 83, relies on Rosenfeld's critique of the work); John Rosenfield Jr., review of Carpenter's *Little Bit of Jazz, Dallas News,* 22 January 1926, scrapbook, Whiteman Collection, Williams College; Osgood, *So This Is Jazz,* 156.

24. Carpenter to Ellen Borden, 13 October 1925, C-DLC.

25. Carpenter composed yet another small unpublished piece for violin and piano during these years, "Miniature." Its distillation of jazz, mechanistic, and neoclassical elements in a private, almost hermetic way recalls the composer's 1922 piano pieces.

26. Borowski, "John Alden Carpenter," 466.

27. See, for instance, the work list in Gilbert Chase, "Carpenter, John Alden," *The New Grove Dictionary of American Music,* ed. H. Wiley Hitchcock and Stanley Sadie, 4 vols. (New York: Macmillan, 1986), 1:359–60.

28. Carpenter, quoted in "Jazz Is Assuming Prominence as an American Music Idiom, Declares Sky-Scrapers Composer," *Musical Digest,* 23 November 1926, C-NN.

29. William Howland Kenney, *Chicago Jazz: A Cultural History, 1904–1930* (New York: Oxford University Press, 1993), 147–60.

30. Quoted in Eugene Stinson, "New Carpenter Ballet for Monte Carlo Delineates Industrial Activity in U.S.," *Musical America,* 16 August 1924, 27.

CHAPTER 17. FROM THE STRING QUARTET TO "YOUNG MAN, CHIEFTAIN"

1. Carl Engel to Carpenter, 22 July 1927, OC-DLC.

2. Carpenter to Elizabeth Sprague Coolidge, 21 November 1917, ESC-DLC.

3. Elizabeth Sprague Coolidge to Carpenter, 15 October 1930; Carpenter to Elizabeth Sprague Coolidge, 18 October 1930, ESC-DLC.

4. Carpenter to Carl Engel, 2 August 1927, OC-DLC.

5. Carl Engel to Carpenter, 8 August 1927, OC-DLC.

6. Carpenter to Carl Engel, 10 and 19 August 1927; Carl Engel to Carpenter, 15 August 1927, OC-DLC.

7. Carpenter to Carl Engel, 26 September 1927; Carl Engel to Carpenter, 28 September 1927, OC-DLC.

8. David Ewen, *All the Years of American Popular Music* (Englewood Cliffs, N.J.: Prentice-Hall, 1977), 226.

9. Carpenter to Ellen Borden, 31 January 1928, C-DLC.

10. Review of Carpenter's String Quartet, *Washington Post,* 29 April 1928, Scrapbook; Olin Downes, "Washington Hears Quartet by Alfano," *New York Times,* 29 April 1928, Scrapbook.

11. Eugene Stinson, "Music," 14 May 1928, Scrapbook.

12. Program, Carpenter's String Quartet, performed by the Pro Arte Quartet in Buenos Aires, 29 July 1940, Scrapbook.

13. Theodore Chandler, "Music," ca. February 1935, Scrapbook. Chandler wrote, "The element of surprise came from having recently heard the incomparably inferior Piano Quintette by this composer that was given its first performance at the Pittsfield Festival last September."

14. Paul Rosenfeld, "Taylor, Carpenter and Loeffler," *New Republic,* 18 March 1931, 128–29. Ironically, in one of his rare remarks about Carpenter, Wilfrid Mellers equated Carpenter and Taylor: "Of course American music has its own provincialities and its own academicians, such as John Alden Carpenter and Deems Taylor—men who so completely fail to achieve a vernacular adequately expressive of their environment that they accept ready-made a late nineteenth-century European convention which for them is moribund." Wilfrid Mellers, *Music and Society* (New York: Roy, 1950), 204.

15. Colin McPhee, "Records and Scores," *Modern Music* 17, no. 3 (March-April 1940): 180.

16. Charles Mills, "Over the Air," *Modern Music* 19, no. 4 (May-June 1942): 281; Felix Borowski, "John Alden Carpenter," *Musical Quarterly* 16 (October 1930): 466.

17. John Tasker Howard, *Our American Music,* 3d ed. (New York: Thomas Y. Crowell, 1946), 370; Thomas C. Pierson, "The Life and Music of John Alden Carpenter" (Ph.D. diss., University of Rochester, 1952), 31.

18. Christopher Palmer, *Impressionism in Music* (New York: Scribner's, 1973), 234.

19. Mary Austin, "Prayer to the Mountain Spirit," *Poetry* 9, no. 4 (January 1917): 240–41.

20. Carpenter to Ellen Borden, 3 August 1924, 7 May 1925, C-DLC (Carpenter's emphasis).

21. Frederic Cople Jaher, *The Urban Establishment: Upper Strata in Boston, New York, Charleston, Chicago, and Los Angeles* (Urbana: University of Illinois Press, 1982), 540.

22. David Lowe, *Lost Chicago* (New York: American Legacy Press, 1985), 205.

23. Alson J. Smith, *Chicago's Left Bank* (Chicago: Henry Regnery, 1953), 254.

24. Arthur Meeker, *Chicago, with Love* (New York: Alfred A. Knopf, 1955), 272–73; Lowe, *Lost Chicago*, 204.

25. Fairbank Carpenter, interview by author, 18 February 1993; John H. Kirk, interview by author, 22 February 1993; James Strachan, interview by author, 27 February 1993. Fairbank himself claimed that the company suffered from "excessive nepotism." See also "Then . . . the New Deal," in *1840–1940: The First Hundred Years* (Chicago: George B. Carpenter and Co., 1940).

26. Carpenter to Elena de Sayn, 22 June 1931, Sayn Collection, DLC.

27. Carpenter to Carl Engel, 23 September 1932, OC-DLC.

28. Carpenter to Ellen Borden, 28 July 1924, 12 and 28 August 1924, C-DLC.

29. Ibid., 22 January 1925, 16 and 19 February 1925, C-DLC.

30. Ibid., 5 and 7 February 1925, C-DLC. The phrase "five years younger" suggests that Ginny—and possibly Rue, too—believed that Carpenter had been having an affair with Ellen for five years, when actually they had been lovers for twelve years.

31. Ibid., 5 and 7 February 1925, 2 September 1932, C-DLC.

32. Ibid., 2 May 1925, C-DLC.

33. Ibid., 13 June 1927, 1 December 1927(?), C-DLC.

34. Ibid., 27 February 1928, 3 April 1928, C-DLC.

35. George Arliss to Ginny Hill, 24 October 1929, C-ICN; Carpenter to John Palmer, 29 October 1929, AC-ICN; Carpenter, telegram to Isabel Jarvis, 7 February 1930, AC-ICN.

36. Carpenter to Ellen Borden, 1919, C-DLC.

37. Ibid., 16 and 28 February 1925, C-DLC.

38. Ibid., 22 November 1926, 13 June 1927, 1 December 1927(?), and 26 October 1928, C-DLC.

39. Ibid., 10 September 1930, C-DLC; Carpenter to Julius Gold, 11 September 1930, JG-DLC.

40. Carpenter to Ellen Borden, 30 December 1931, C-DLC.

41. Ibid., n.d., C-DLC.

42. Herbert Mueller to Carpenter, 30 October 1931, C-DLC. Mueller certified the instrument's authenticity.

43. Eugene Stinson, "J. A. Carpenter Returns from Study of East," Scrapbook.

44. Mei Lanfang to John and Rue Carpenter, 12 April 1930, C-DLC.

45. Carpenter to Carl Engel, 3 April 1931, Engel Collection, DLC.

46. Stinson, "J. A. Carpenter Returns."

47. Irving Sablosky, "Dean of Chicago Composers Still Active," February 1951, Scrapbook.

48. Stinson, "J. A. Carpenter Returns."

CHAPTER 18. FROM *SONG OF FAITH* TO *PATTERNS*

1. Sol Bloom to Carpenter, 1 July 1931, C-DLC.
2. Carpenter to Sol Bloom, published in "Song of Faith," *Chicago Symphony Orchestra Program Notes,* 25 February 1932, C-NN.
3. In 1867 Whitman revised this poem, and in 1881 he titled it "For You, O Democracy."
4. George Washington to General Henry Knox, 20 February 1784, quoted in Paul F. Boller, *George Washington and Religion* (Dallas: Southern Methodist University Press, 1963), 108.
5. *The Basic Writings of George Washington,* ed. Saxe Commins (New York: Random House, 1948), 498, 504. The former line is from Washington's 1783 Address to Congress on resigning his commission; the latter is from Washington's 1783 Circular to the States. Washington's writings assumed an uncharacteristically religious tone in the period 1783–84, just after the Revolutionary War.
6. Serge Koussevitzky to Carpenter, 11 December 1931; Carpenter to Serge Koussevitzky, 21 December 1931, SK-DLC.
7. Eugene Stinson, "'Song of Faith' Wins Audience by Its Power," 24 February 1932, Scrapbook; Herman Devries, "Song of Faith Praised by Critic," Scrapbook; Eric De Lamarter to Carpenter, 26 February 1932, Scrapbook.
8. "Editorial," *Chicago Tribune,* 25 February 1932, Scrapbook.
9. Carpenter, *Song of Faith,* Chicago A Cappella Chorus and Orchestra, Noble Cain, Victor 1559/60.
10. Lawrence Gilman, "An American Song of Faith," *New York Herald Tribune,* 1 May 1932.
11. Ibid.
12. Lawrence Gilman to Carpenter, 30 April 1932, Scrapbook.
13. Basil Cameron to Carpenter, 18 January 1936, Scrapbook.
14. Review of Carpenter's *Song of Faith, Times* (London), 7 August 1941, Scrapbook.
15. Thomas C. Pierson, "The Life and Music of John Alden Carpenter" (Ph.D. diss., University of Rochester, 1952), 10.
16. "Music Festival Saturday Night," 13 August 1944, Scrapbook.
17. Carpenter to John Becker, 2 September 1944, JB-NN.
18. Aaron Copland, quoted in liner notes to *Aaron Copland Conducts,* Columbia MS 7375.
19. Percy Young, *The Choral Tradition* (New York: Norton, 1962), 314–15.
20. Carpenter to Ellen Borden, 3 April 1928, C-DLC.
21. Robert Craft, ed., *Dearest Bubushkin* (New York: Thames and Hudson, 1985), 114.

22. Igor Stravinsky to Ginny Hill, n.d., C-ICN. The French original reads, "Une petite lettre nous fera un grand plaisir."

23. "Mrs. J. A. Carpenter, Art Authority, Dies," *New York Times,* 8 December 1931, 42.

24. Patrick Hill, interview by author, 15 July 1988; Theodora Brown, interview by author, 29 July 1988; Rue Hubert, interview by author, 15 July 1988.

25. For the original hymns as set, respectively, by Martin Shaw and to an old German melody, see *The Methodist Hymnal* (New York: Methodist Publishing, 1932), nos. 444, 452.

26. Carpenter to Ellen Borden, 9 February 1932, C-DLC.

27. Rue Hubert, interview by author, 14 April 1991.

28. Julia Smith, *Aaron Copland* (New York: E. P. Dutton, 1955), 111–12.

29. Serge Koussevitzky to Carpenter, 28 April 1929, SK-DLC.

30. Carpenter to Serge Koussevitzky, 2 February 1931, SK-DLC.

31. Moses Smith, *Koussevitzky* (New York: Allen, Towne, and Heath, 1947), 218.

32. Carpenter to Serge Koussevitzky, 9 May 1932, SK-DLC.

33. Ibid., 12 September 1932, 3 October 1932, SK-DLC.

34. Carpenter, quoted by Philip Hale, "Patterns," *Boston Symphony Orchestra Program Notes,* C-DLC.

35. "John Alden Carpenter Defends Nation's Music," *Boston Traveler,* 20 October 1932, Scrapbook.

36. Ellen Carpenter to Paul Hindemith, 1961, C-ICN.

37. Carpenter, telegram to Carl Engel, 11 November 1932, OC-DLC.

38. Cyrus Durgin, "Symphony Hall," *Boston Globe,* 22 October 1932; Philip Hale, "Symphony Concert," *Boston Herald,* 22 October 1932; Grace May Stutsman, "New Works Given by Boston Forces," *Musical America,* 10 November 1932, 22; Albert Goldberg, "Novelties Are Featured by Stock," *Musical America,* 10 November 1932, 6.

39. Hale, "Symphony Concert"; "Patterns in Boston," *Time,* 27 October 1932, Scrapbook.

40. Hale, "Symphony Concert"; Durgin, "Symphony Hall."

41. Goldberg, "Novelties," 6; Irving Weil, "Play Carpenter Novelty at Carnegie," 19 November 1932, Scrapbook.

42. Walter Monfried, "Carpenter, Businessman-Composer," *Milwaukee Journal,* 30 April 1947, 20.

43. Durgin, "Symphony Hall"; review of Carpenter's *Patterns, Boston Evening Transcript,* 22 October 1932, C-DLC; Stutsman, "New Works Given by Boston Forces," 22. Even today, standard accounts of these fiftieth-anniversary commissions do not mention Carpenter's work.

44. Carpenter, "Listen to Me," C-ICN. Carpenter apparently wrote this essay for himself, rather than as a lecture or for publication.

45. Carpenter, "How Know I Else Such Glorious Fate My Own," C-DLC. The full poem is:

How know I else such glorious fate my own,
But in the restless irresistible force
That works within me?
Is it for human will
to institute such impulses?
Still less, to disregard their promptings?
Be sure that God
ne'er dooms to waste the strength
He deigns impart!
I go to prove my soul!
I see my way
as birds their trackless way—
I shall arrive!
What time, what circuit first;
I ask not:
In some time—His good time—
I shall arrive!
He guides me—and the bird.

CHAPTER 19. ELLEN

1. "Mrs. Ellen Borden Engaged to Marry," *New York Times,* 11 January 1933, 16; "Mrs. Waller Borden Wed," *New York Times,* 31 January 1933, 21; and "Mrs. Borden Is Married to John A. Carpenter in Old Lowell Home," C-DLC.

2. Henry Waller, *Biography of William S. Waller* (Chicago: n.p., n.d.), courtesy of David Dangler.

3. Herma Clark, "When Chicago Was Young," 8 January 1950, Scrapbook.

4. David Dangler, interview by author, 8 January 1993.

5. David Lowe, *Lost Chicago* (New York: American Legacy Press, 1985), 34, 154; John Drury, "Old Chicago Houses," *Chicago Daily News,* 18 October 1940 and 7 February 1957.

6. Richard Rodzinski, interview by author, 24 November 1992.

7. John Borden married Courtney Louise Stillwell in 1925 and Frances Yeaton in 1933.

8. Walter Johnson, ed., *The Papers of Adlai E. Stevenson,* 8 vols. (Boston: Little, Brown, 1972–79), 1:215. Stevenson—future Illinois senator, governor, and presidential nominee—had independently known the Carpenters, at

whose home he attended a "fancy dress" on 25 April 1926: "Seems funny," he wrote, "a real party on Sunday night. But I suppose that means some stage folk, so it ought to be fun" (p. 195).

9. Carpenter to Ellen Borden, ca. 1924 and 12 March 1931, C-DLC.

10. Joan Leclerc, interview by author, 14 November 1992.

11. Carpenter to Ellen Borden, n.d., C-DLC.

12. Ibid., 6 August 1924, C-DLC.

13. Ibid., 15 August [1924?], C-DLC.

14. Ibid., 22 December 1913, C-DLC.

15. Ibid., 11 September 1922, C-DLC.

16. Ibid., n.d., C-DLC.

17. Ibid., 2 March 1925, 19 August [1924?], C-DLC.

18. Ibid., n.d., and 13 October 1925, C-DLC.

19. Ibid., 26 July 1924, 30 August 1924, and 20 June 1931, C-DLC (Carpenter's emphasis).

20. John Bartlow Martin, *Adlai Stevenson of Illinois* (New York: Doubleday, 1978), 86.

21. See Bruce F. Campbell, *Ancient Wisdom Revived: A History of the Theosophical Movement* (Berkeley and Los Angeles: University of California Press, 1980); Iverson L. Harris, *Theosophy under Fire: A Miniature "Key to Theosophy"* (San Diego: Harris, 1970).

22. Carpenter to Ellen Borden, 12 and 19 September 1927, C-DLC (Carpenter's emphasis).

23. Ibid., 12 April 1931, C-DLC.

24. Basil Entwistle and John McCook Roots, *Moral Re-Armament: What Is It?* (Los Angeles: Pace, 1967), viewed the MRA as it had evolved by the 1960s. For a laudatory account of Buchman, see Garth Lean, *Frank Buchman: A Life* (London: Constable, 1985); for a more critical account, see Tom Driberg, *The Mystery of Moral Re-Armament: A Study of Frank Buchman and His Movement* (New York: Alfred A. Knopf, 1965).

25. Halina Rodzinski, *Our Two Lives* (New York: Scribner's, 1976), 306; Halina Rodzinski, interview by author, 5 January 1992.

26. Ellen's antipathy toward drinking "had nothing to do with MRA, much to do with serious alcoholic problems in her family," according to Joan Leclerc (letter to author, 11 March 1993).

27. Halina Rodzinski, interview; Leclerc to author, 11 March 1993.

28. Lean, *Frank Buchman*, 322.

29. Halina Rodzinski, *Our Two Lives*. The Rodzinskis became friends with Buchman shortly after meeting him in 1941 (p. 207). Whereas Halina remained loyal to MRA, Artur, by the late 1940s, had grown disenchanted with the movement, though not with Buchman personally.

30. Adlai Stevenson Jr., interview by author, 15 April 1993; Joan Leclerc,

interview by author, 29 May 1991; Robert Pirie, interview by author, 9 July 1991 (Stevenson is the son of Ellen's older daughter, Ellen Stevenson; Leclerc and Pirie are the children of Ellen's younger daughter, Betty Borden Pirie Hines). Carpenter's 1950 support of a musical adaptation of Fulton Oursler's *Greatest Story Ever Told* is a bit of evidence that suggests some congruence with MRA aspirations, C-ICN (Oursler [1893–1952] and Henry Denker wrote the book; William Stoess, Zoel Parenteau, and Victor Young collaborated on the music).

31. Martin, *Adlai Stevenson of Illinois*, 276 n, 297 n, 420 ff.

32. Johnson, *Papers of Adlai E. Stevenson*, 6:155.

33. Martin, *Adlai Stevenson of Illinois*, 117, 173, 766. According to Martin the Carpenters donated $150 toward the 1948 gubernatorial campaign, although a list of donations prepared for tax purposes in 1948 cites only $50, C-DLC. They may have donated separate amounts, with the $50 representing Carpenter's share.

34. Johnson, *Papers of Adlai E. Stevenson*, 1:523, 2:68, 69. Ellen's War Bond Committee sold ninety million war bonds in less than a year! See also Robert Craft, ed., *Dearest Bubushkin* (New York: Thames and Hudson, 1985), 117.

35. Paula F. Pfeffer, "Homeless Children, Childless Home," *Chicago History* 16, no. 1 (Spring 1987): 51–65, explored the relationship between ICHAS, the Cradle Society, and prominent Chicago philanthropists like Ellen Borden Carpenter and Chauncey McCormick. According to Pfeffer, Ellen and other volunteers undermined ICHAS's paid social workers from establishing professional standards.

36. Eugene Indjic, interview by author, 15 January 1989; Leclerc to author, 11 March 1993.

37. Carpenter to Ellen Borden, 1916 and n.d., C-DLC.

38. "Mrs. Ellen Borden Engaged."

39. Johnson, *Papers of Adlai E. Stevenson*, 2:339.

40. Dane Rudhyar, unpublished transcript of an interview with Sheila Finch Raynor, 23 May 1975, Oral History of the Arts Archive, California State University, Long Beach; courtesy of Judith Tick.

41. Ruth Crawford, quoted by Judith Tick, "Ruth Crawford's 'Spiritual Concept': The Sound-Ideals of an Early American Modernist, 1924–1930," *Journal of the American Musicological Society* 44, no. 2 (Summer 1991): 233–34.

42. Carpenter to Aaron Copland, 24 January 1930, AC-ICN.

43. Carpenter to Ellen Borden, 25 October 1920, 28 August 1924 (Carpenter's emphasis), and 22 August 1924, C-DLC.

44. Ibid., early 1916 and n.d., C-DLC.

45. Rue and Ellen had their similarities, including a strong crusader's temperament. Indeed, one portrait of Ellen published in a Chicago daily

(framed by her photograph and the question, "Who's Who?") was hardly distinguishable from the kind of tributes Rue had always inspired—at least at a quick glance:

> If she had a dime for every cup
> Of tea she's asked friends to come and sup
> While they helped good causes on their way,
> What an income tax she'd have to pay!
>
> Sometimes it's orphans or China's friends,
> Often it's music, ballet, or trends
> Toward getting votes to save the city,
> Now it's the Op'ra Box Committee!
>
> Stock, Toscanini, Koussevitzky
> L. Massine and V. Nijinsky
> Lin Yu Tang and Wellington Koo
> Many only be names to me and you,
>
> But at one-o-two-o Lake Shore Drive
> They're persona grata with all their tribe
> (Most carpenters labor with wood and nails,
> But hers is concerned with woodwinds and sails).

H. Y., "Who's Who?" ca. 1943, Scrapbook. Rue, however, devoted her life not to "good causes" or "orphans" or "getting votes to save the city" but to art, interior decorating, theater, parties, and balls, to living a glamorous and unconventional life. And if Massine and other artists visited 1020 Lake Shore Drive, they did so often out of loyalty to Rue and the old Rush Street days. Ellen had great respect for Rue, but Rue thought less well of Ellen.

46. Rue Hubert, interview by author, 14 April 1991; Patrick Hill, interview by author, 15 July 1988; Theodora Brown, interview by author, 29 July 1988 ("Ellen had the brains of nothing and was a perfect ass").

47. Adlai Stevenson Jr., interview; Pirie, interview; Dangler, interview.

48. Ellen Carpenter, assorted letters, C-DLC; also Ellen Carpenter to Chauncey McCormick, 28 April 1952, Chauncey McCormick Collection, ICN.

49. Arthur Rubinstein, *My Many Years* (New York: Alfred A. Knopf, 1980), 431–32.

50. Craft, *Dearest Bubushkin,* 117.

51. Arthur Meeker, *Chicago, with Love* (New York: Alfred A. Knopf, 1955), 170.

52. Leclerc, interviews; Pirie, interview; Adlai Stevenson Jr., interview; Richard Rodzinski, interview.

53. Hill, interview.

54. Leclerc, interview, 29 May 1991.

55. Brown, interview.

56. Minutes, 20, 21, and 24 December 1948, AC-ICN; Lowe, *Lost Chicago*, 26, 34. Critics consider 1020 Lake Shore Drive among Richard Hunt's finest designs (Hunt also designed homes for Marshall Field and the Vanderbilts). The house made way for an apartment building in the early 1960s.

57. "On the Other Side of Fame," *Chicago Sun*, ca. 1942, Scrapbook. This article, which featured interviews with Carpenter's secretary, Mary Townsend; tailor, K. A. Haggie; maid, Bertha Canavan; chauffeur, Sven Runquist; and former governess (Ginny's governess), Margaret McNulty, also stated: "He's scrupulous about fan mail" (Townsend); "brown was his favorite color, and he likes casual clothes" (Haggie); and he's "inseparable from his daughter" (McNulty).

58. Craft, *Dearest Bubushkin*, 117.

59. Ronald L. Davis, *Opera in Chicago* (New York: Appleton-Century, 1966), 136–37.

60. Adlai Stevenson Jr. remembered the Langhornes as "pictures of aristocracy: highly ethical, handsome, pillars of the local establishment, mannerly in an old-fashioned way." Adlai Stevenson Jr., interview.

61. Johnson, *Papers of Adlai E. Stevenson*, 2:69.

62. In 1943 and 1944 the Carpenters lived at 1550 North State; from 1945 to 1947 they resided at 209 E. Lake Shore Drive (where Charlie and Claire Dux Swift also lived); and from 1948 to 1951 they lived at 999 North Lake Shore Drive.

63. Brochure for *The Beverly Historical Society and Museum*, Beverly, Mass.

64. Adlai Stevenson Jr., interview.

65. Carpenter, financial statements, C-NN. Joan Leclerc recalled that the fire started in the billiards room (interview, 14 November 1992).

66. "Stevenson's Grandmother Is Dead of a Heart Attack," *Chicago Sun-Times*, 3 November 1974.

67. Leclerc, interview, 29 May 1991.

68. Leclerc to author, 11 March 1993. Leclerc rejected Rue Hubert's claim (Rue Hubert, interview by author, 15 July 1988) that Carpenter's humor sometimes disconcerted Ellen and some of their guests.

69. Adlai Stevenson Jr., interview.

70. Meeker, *Chicago, with Love*, 171. Also, Rue Hubert, interview by author, 19 July 1988; Hill, interview.

71. Gilbert Chase, "Carpenter, John Alden," *The New Grove Dictionary of American Music*, ed. H. Wiley Hitchcock and Stanley Sadie, 4 vols. (New York: Macmillan, 1986), 1:359.

CHAPTER 20. *SEA DRIFT*

1. Scrapbook; Justin Kaplan, *Walt Whitman* (New York: Simon and Schuster, 1980), 41.
2. Carpenter to Felix Borowski, quoted in Borowski, "Sea Drift," *Chicago Symphony Orchestra Program Notes,* C-DLC.
3. C-DLC. Carpenter copied out the following lines:

> Low hangs the moon, it rose late,
> It is lagging—O I think it is heavy with love, with love,
>
> . . . .
>
> O night! do I not see my love fluttering out among the breakers?
> What is that little black thing I see there in the white?
>
> . . . .
>
> High and clear I shoot my voice over the waves,
> Surely you must know who is here, is here,
> You must know who I am, my love.
>
> . . . .
>
> O past! O happy life! O songs of joy!
> In the air, in the woods, over fields,
> Loved! loved! loved! loved! loved!
> But my mate no more, no more with me!
> We two together no more.

4. Edward Moore, "Stock Closes Holiday with Happy Concert," *Chicago Daily Tribune,* 1 December 1933, 17.
5. Lawrence Gilman, quoted by Arline Hanke, "A Study of the *Gitanjali* Songs by John Alden Carpenter" (Master's thesis, University of Rochester, 1942), 9; Leonard Liebling, "Werner Janssen's Triumph Repeated at Philharmonic," Scrapbook.
6. Reviews of Carpenter's *Sea Drift,* Scrapbook.
7. Halina Rodzinski, interview by author, 5 January 1992; Halina Rodzinski, *Our Two Lives* (New York: Scribner's, 1976), 118–19, 295, 378.
8. Robert C. Marsh, "Rodzinski Left His Imprint on CSO," *Chicago Sun-Times,* 22 December 1991, E5.
9. Carpenter, *The Seven Ages,* taped live performance by Artur Rodzinski and the New York Philharmonic, Rodgers and Hammerstein Archive, NN.
10. Carpenter to Serge Koussevitzky, 14 November 1933, 18 and 31 December 1934, 21 November 1935, and 14 December 1935; Serge Koussevitzky to Carpenter, 12 November 1935, SK-DLC.
11. Vladimir Golschmann to Carpenter, 31 January 1940, C-DLC.
12. Virgil Thomson, "Music," *New York Herald Tribune,* 6 October 1944, Scrapbook.

13. Lou Harrison, "First-Time Fashions, New York, 1944," *Modern Music* 22, no. 1 (November-December 1944): 32.

14. Percy Grainger to Carpenter, 6 October 1944, Scrapbook and PG-DLC.

15. Ibid., 21 May 1945, Scrapbook.

16. Percy Grainger to Mrs. Ellen Bull, 5 October 1941, PG-DLC. Grainger's racial ideas included a mix of anti-Semitic and anti-German features.

17. John Bird, *Percy Grainger* (London: Faber and Faber, 1976), 241. It is not clear when or how this change of heart transpired, for Grainger admired Carpenter's revised First Symphony when he heard it in 1940. Percy Grainger to Carpenter, 6 November 1940, C-ICN.

18. Werner Janssen to Carpenter, 30 January 1945, C-DLC.

19. Leonard Slatkin, letter to author, 2 May 1991.

20. John von Rhein, "Slatkin's Departure with 'Pictures' Has Its Gains and Losses," *Chicago Tribune,* 2 November 1990; Robert C. Marsh, "Slatkin Program Fills the Heart—and Mind," *Chicago Sun-Times,* 2 November 1990, Chicago Symphony Archives.

21. Carpenter, *Sea Drift,* Royal Philharmonic Orchestra, Karl Krueger, Society for the Preservation of the American Musical Heritage MIA-142; Carpenter, *Sea Drift,* Albany Symphony Orchestra, Julius Hegyi, New World Records NW 321.

22. Paul Snook, record review of Carpenter, *Sea Drift, Fanfare* 8 (March-April 1985): 361.

23. Howard Hanson, "John Alden Carpenter," *Saturday Review,* 24 February 1951, 51.

24. Christopher Palmer, *Impressionism in Music* (New York: Scribner's, 1973), 234.

25. Noah André Trudeau, "Record Reviews," *Hi Fi/Stereo Review* 35 (April 1985): MA 44.

26. Snook, record review of Carpenter, *Sea Drift,* 362.

27. Nicholas Tawa, liner notes to Carpenter, *Sea Drift,* New World Records NW 321.

CHAPTER 21. FROM THE PIANO QUINTET TO "MORNING FAIR"

1. Carpenter to Serge Koussevitzky, 7 March 1934, SK-DLC.

2. Charles F. Gallagher, *The United States and North Africa: Morocco, Algeria, and Tunisia* (Cambridge: Harvard University Press, 1963), 83.

3. Carpenter to Elizabeth Sprague Coolidge, 4 April 1934, ESC-DLC (Carpenter's emphasis).

4. Ibid., 2 May 1934, ESC-DLC.

5. Elizabeth Sprague Coolidge to Carpenter, 3 May 1934; Carpenter to Elizabeth Sprague Coolidge, 5 May 1934, ESC-DLC.

6. Gregory Burnside Pike, "The Three Versions of the Quintet for Piano and Strings by John Alden Carpenter: An Examination of Their Contrasting Musical Elements Based upon a Formal Analysis of the Original 1934 Version" (DMA thesis, University of Miami, 1981).

7. Pike regards the 1937 Schirmer edition as the "original" score, even though Carpenter slightly revised the 1934 manuscript for publication. These revisions are too minor to warrant much consideration, however.

8. Pike, "Three Versions of the Quintet for Piano and Strings," 117.

9. Pike's analysis of the first movement raises many other questions. Does the introduction, for instance, really have two ideas, or is the second idea merely an outgrowth of the first? (Pike himself points out that the two ideas begin almost identically.) If they are separate themes, what is the importance of the first one? It makes only one brief reappearance (at [14]).

Similarly, Pike's second theme has none of the earmarks of a traditional second theme: it is not prepared by any modulatory activity, it occurs only nine measures into the exposition, and it subsequently alternates with the main theme. Why call it a "second theme"? Indeed, why give so much weight to this particular theme or, for that matter, the so-called closing theme? Why not the cello melody at [5], which is the first theme to really deviate from the tonic key? Or the themes at [7] or at eight measures after [7]?

Moreover, the movement's key scheme deviates from sonata-form analysis: the exposition modulates to the submediant (B minor) rather than the dominant, and the so-called recapitulation arrives on the subdominant (G major) rather than the tonic.

10. Pike outlines the form of this movement as $ABCA_1B_1C_1A_2B_2C_2A_3$. He identifies themes A, B, and C at measure 3, [24], and nine after [24], respectively; A_1, he claims, begins at [25], and A_2 at four measures after [29].

Again, Pike's analysis entails problems. Why downplay the importance of the theme at [23] that is situated between themes A and B? This theme, marked *molto espressivo*, introduces important swaying rhythms as well as a new key signature. If we accordingly revise Pike's interpretation of the first section to read A (cadencing, at two before [23], in C♯ major), B (cadencing in a half-cadence, at one before [24], in B major), C (cadencing, at eight after [24], in E major), and D (leading directly into the second section)—in other words, ABCD rather than ABC—this undermines the neat symmetry of Pike's analysis, for our B theme reappears, as at five after [27], at unexpected places. Further, could the opening theme—differing in many ways from the rest of the movement—be an introductory transition, taking us from the first movement's D major to this movement's C♯ (D♭) major?

(The *attacca* between movements 1 and 2 would support this possibility.)

And what of this slow movement's tonal intentions? After arriving, just before ㉓, in C♯ major, Carpenter introduces a key signature of three sharps for the ensuing five pages. What is the point of this key signature? Except for a fleeting arrival in A major at two after ㉕, the composer never seems to be in either A major or F♯ minor; indeed, at five before ㉗, he arrives climactically at C major, the three-sharp key signature notwithstanding. Eventually, after two lines without any key signature, during which Carpenter modulates through E♭ major and other tonalities, the composer arrives, at ㉙, at a key signature of five flats for a cadence in D♭ major. The rest of the movement is essentially in D♭ major.

In short, the work's tonal design—the quick, momentary, and quite lovely arrival in C♯ major, the movement to nearly every key other than that suggested by the three-sharp key signature, the C-major climax, the modulation to E♭ major and other keys before arriving, finally, at D♭ major—neither supports Pike's analysis nor suggests any obvious alternative.

11. Pike, "Three Versions of the Quintet for Piano and Strings," 61. This is Pike's theme B, my theme C.

12. Carpenter to John Becker, 30 March 1945, 23 November 1945, and 4 February 1950, JB-NN.

13. Dena J. Epstein, "Frederick Stock and American Music," *American Music* 10, no. 1 (Spring 1992): 24; Judith Tick, "Ruth Crawford's 'Spiritual Concept': The Sound-Ideals of an Early American Modernist, 1924–1930," *Journal of the American Musicological Society* 44, no. 2 (Summer 1991): 232.

14. Thomas C. Pierson, "The Life and Music of John Alden Carpenter" (Ph.D. diss., University of Rochester, 1952), 361. Pierson reported that the Carpenters heard "Arabs" in Morocco, but Ellen Carpenter very possibly used the term *Arabs* loosely and heard, in fact, Berbers.

15. H. H., "New Music Marks Festival Opening," *New York Times;* Francis Perkins, "Chamber Music Festival Opens in Berkshires," *New York Herald Tribune;* and Moses Smith, "Franck and Two Americans for the Beginning," *Boston Evening Transcript,* Scrapbook.

16. Smith, "Franck and Two Americans."

17. A. W. W., review of Carpenter's Piano Quintet, *Boston Herald,* 24 January 1935, 28.

18. Elizabeth Sprague Coolidge to Carpenter, 14 October 1936; Carpenter to Elizabeth Sprague Coolidge, 15 October 1936, ESC-DLC.

19. Pike, "Three Versions of the Quintet for Piano and Strings," 120.

20. Ellen's daughter Betty had two children—Bobby and Joan Pirie—and her daughter Ellen had three children—Adlai, Borden, and John Fell Stevenson.

21. Robert Edmond Jones to Carpenter, ca. 1947, C-ICN.

22. Joan Campbell, "The Pools-of-Peace," in *The Open Door to Poetry: An Anthology by Ann Stokes* (New York: Scribner's, 1931), 80.

23. Lucille Mendenhall, "The Songs of John Alden Carpenter" (Master's thesis, North Texas State University, 1952), 103.

24. James Agee, *Permit Me Voyage,* with a foreword by Archibald MacLeish (New Haven, Conn.: Yale University Press, 1934).

25. *The Collected Poems of James Agee,* ed. Robert Fitzgerald (Boston: Houghton Mifflin, 1962), x.

26. M. W., "Visits to the Homes of Famous Composers," 1947, C-NN.

27. MacLeish, foreword to *Permit Me Voyage,* by Agee, 5–7.

CHAPTER 22. *DANZA* AND THE VIOLIN CONCERTO

1. Joan Leclerc, interview by author, 29 May 1991.

2. Carpenter to Mary Langhorne, 1 April 1935, C-DLC.

3. Carpenter to Arthur Vogel, 12 December 1947, C-ICN.

4. Carpenter to Langhorne, 1 April 1935.

5. Barbara W. Tuchman, *Stilwell and the American Experience in China, 1911–1945* (New York: Macmillan, 1970), 65–66.

6. Millicent Bell, *Marquand: An American Life* (Boston: Little, Brown, 1979), 213–17.

7. Harriet Monroe, *A Poet's Life: Seventy Years in a Changing World* (New York: Macmillan, 1938), 444–45.

8. Ibid., 444.

9. Carpenter to Langhorne, 1 April 1935.

10. Arthur Rubinstein, *My Many Years* (New York: Alfred A. Knopf, 1980), 373–74.

11. Tuchman, *Stilwell and the American Experience,* 148; Nelson Johnson to Carpenter, 13 January 1936, C-ICN.

12. K. A. Haggie, quoted in "On the Other Side of Fame," *Chicago Sun,* ca. 1942, Scrapbook.

13. Irving Sablosky, "Dean of Chicago Composers Still Active," February 1951, Scrapbook.

14. Carpenter to Langhorne, 1 April 1935.

15. Carpenter, quoted in "Danza," *Boston Symphony Orchestra Program Notes,* 17 January 1937.

16. Carpenter to Serge Koussevitzky, 13 November 1935, SK-DLC.

17. Carpenter, quoted in "Danza."

18. Carpenter to John Becker, 19 September 1935, JB-NN.

19. Thomas C. Pierson, liner notes to *Carpenter: Collected Piano Works,* New World Records NW 328/329.

20. Carpenter to Serge Koussevitzky, 14 December 1935, SK-DLC.

21. Review of Carpenter's *Danza, Boston Globe,* Scrapbook.

22. Hans Kindler to Carpenter, 11 July 1943, C-DLC.

23. "Composer Carpenter Sets Tunes at Symphony Rehearsal Here," Scrapbook.

24. Review of Carpenter's *Dance Suite;* Alice Eversman, "Rubinstein Superb as Soloist in First Symphony Concert," Scrapbook.

25. Carpenter to Rudolph Ganz, 1 December 1939, RG-ICN.

26. Helmut Baerwald to Carpenter, 15 October 1946, Scrapbook. Town Hall billed the 15 November performance as a premiere, but Baerwald's letter implies previous performances. Perhaps the Town Hall concert was the work's New York premiere.

27. Ibid., 30 October 1946, C-ICN.

28. Adlai Stevenson Jr., interview by author, 15 April 1993.

29. "Carpenter Violin Concerto Played by Balokovic," *Musical America,* 25 March 1939, 10. Barry Edward, "New Carpenter Piece Played by Balokovic," *Chicago Daily Times,* 19 November 1937, 24, alone complained that the violinist "played with a thin tone deficient in character."

30. Carl Bronson, "Philharmonic Orchestra in New Triumph," Scrapbook.

31. Felix Borowski, "Carpenter Violin Concerto," *Chicago Symphony Orchestra Program Notes,* 18 November 1937.

32. "Rodzinski Returns from Salzburg Fete," *New York Times,* 2 October 1937, 18.

33. Herman Devries, "Music in Review"; Eugene Stinson, "Music Views"; Claudia Cassidy, "On the Aisle," Scrapbook.

34. Cecil Michener Smith, "New Works for the Mid-West," *Modern Music* 15, no. 2 (January-February 1938): 107.

35. Bronson, "Philharmonic Orchestra in New Triumph."

36. Herbert Elwell, review of Carpenter's Violin Concerto, *Cleveland Plain Dealer,* 25 February 1938, Scrapbook.

37. Carpenter to Serge Koussevitzky, 8 March 1939, SK-DLC.

38. Leonard Bernstein, "The Latest from Boston," *Modern Music* 16, no. 3 (March-April 1939): 182.

39. "Carpenter Violin Concerto Played by Balokovic"; review of Carpenter's Violin Concerto, *New York Herald Tribune,* 10 March 1939; Grace May Stutsman, "Boston Men Play Carpenter Music," *Musical America,* 25 March 1939, 11.

40. Oscar Thompson, "New Concertos for the Violin," *New York Sun,* March 1939, Scrapbook; Hugo Leichtentritt, *Serge Koussevitzky: The Boston Symphony Orchestra and the New American Music* (Cambridge: Harvard University Press, 1946), 67–68.

CHAPTER 23. THE FIRST AND SECOND SYMPHONIES AND OTHER REVISIONS

1. Patrick Hill, interview by author, 15 July 1988.
2. John H. Kirk, letter to author, 23 February 1993.
3. Irene Alexander, "Rudolph Ganz to Play Work of Peninsula Composer," *Monterey Peninsula Herald,* 24 March 1949.
4. Carleton Sprague Smith, "A Note on Carpenter," *Coronet,* February 1940, 100.
5. Carpenter to H. W. Heinsheimer, Nathan Broder, Felix Greissle, and others, C-DLC.
6. Carpenter to Nathan Broder, 20 December 1947, C-DLC (Carpenter's emphasis).
7. Carpenter, quoted in "Symphony No. 1," *Chicago Symphony Orchestra Program Notes,* 24 October 1940.
8. Carpenter, quoted in Pence James, "Dr. Stock's 'Rabbit' Writes Symphony Called 'Symphony,'" *Chicago Daily News,* 24 October 1940, 9.
9. Frank Siudzinski, "Chicago Now in Top Rank in Music Appreciation: Stock," *Chicago News,* 17 April 1941.
10. "Peaceful Music," *Time,* 4 November 1940, 58.
11. Edward Barry, "New Symphony by Carpenter Wins Acclaim," *Chicago Daily Tribune,* 25 October 1940, 23.
12. Percy Grainger to Carpenter, 6 November 1940, C-ICN.
13. Francis D. Perkins, "Dr. Stock Leads Musicians in New Symphony," *New York Herald Tribune,* 23 November 1940.
14. James Whittaker, "Chicago Orchestra Closes Visit Here," Scrapbook.
15. Carpenter to Bruno Walter, 30 April 1940; Bruno Walter to Carpenter, 6 May 1940, BW-NN.
16. Carpenter to Bruno Walter, 6 and 15 August 1940, BW-NN.
17. Bruno Walter to Carpenter, 7 December 1940, Scrapbook.
18. Ellen Carpenter to Bruno Walter, 7 September 1960, BW-NN. This letter asked Walter to serve as honorary sponsor for a Carpenter Memorial, to which Walter agreed. Bruno Walter to Ellen Carpenter, 12 September 1960, BW-NN.
19. See Roland Gelatt, *Music Makers* (New York: Alfred A. Knopf, 1953); and Harold C. Schonberg, *The Great Conductors* (New York: Simon and Schuster, 1967).
20. Serge Koussevitzky to Carpenter, 4 February 1941, C-ICN.
21. Bruno Walter to Carpenter, 11 July 1942, BW-NN.
22. Frederick Stock to Carpenter, 26 September 1942, Scrapbook.
23. Bruno Walter, telegram to Carpenter, 22 October 1942, Scrapbook.

24. Oscar Thompson, "Walter Conducts Carpenter Work," *New York Sun,* 23 October 1942; Olin Downes, "Philharmonic Led by Bruno Walter," Scrapbook.

25. Virgil Thomson, "Music," *New York Herald Tribune,* Scrapbook.

26. Felix Borowski, "Carpenter's 2nd Symphony Presented First Time Here"; Claudia Cassidy, "Piatigorsky and Defauw Please Large Audience"; Remi Gassman, "Cellist Piatigorsky Makes Rafters Ring," Scrapbook.

27. Gregory Burnside Pike, "The Three Versions of the Quintet for Piano and Strings by John Alden Carpenter: An Examination of Their Contrasting Musical Elements Based upon a Formal Analysis of the Original 1934 Version" (DMA thesis, University of Miami, 1981), 115.

28. This incomplete version not only adds, deletes, and changes material in accordance with the 1942 Second Symphony but varies its textures likewise; so that, for example, where the first violins have an octave passage, divisi, in the symphony, the first violinist plays the same passage in octaves. Like the symphony, this fragment gives more weight to the strings than before.

29. Pike, "Three Versions of the Quintet for Piano and Strings," guesses that the incomplete revision postdated the 1947 revision, even while acknowledging that of the two reworkings, the undated one was closer to the 1934 original. Pike's preference for the 1934 original over the 1946–47 revision seems to have swayed him in the belief that the incomplete revision was an "improvement" over the 1946–47 revision, and reflected the composer's dissatisfaction with that version.

30. Such changes from one version to the next were not always cumulative, however. The 1947 Second Symphony, in particular, sidesteps some revisions found in the 1946–47 Piano Quintet and looks back, at least occasionally, to the 1934 Piano Quintet and the 1942 Second Symphony, as, for example, in the coda of the last movement (the missing two movements of the 1942 Second Symphony would help clarify this matter).

31. Pike, "Three Versions of the Quintet for Piano and Strings," 117.

32. The program (C-ICN) did not specify that the quintet was the revised version, but Carpenter had sent Ganz the revised score nine months earlier. Carpenter to Rudolph Ganz, 19 October 1947, RG-ICN.

33. Artur Rodzinski to Carpenter, 4 November 1942, 11 March 1943, and 26 June 1947, C-ICN.

34. Carpenter to Remsen Bird, 16 April 1947, Bird Collection, ICN (Carpenter's emphasis).

35. Greta Busch to Ellen Carpenter, 21 September 1948, C-ICN.

36. George Kupyer to Carpenter, 21 March 1949, C-ICN.

37. Seymour Raven, "Fritz Busch's 'Tell' Overture Cooking Good," Scrapbook. Raven wrote, "Mr. Busch and the players contributed greatly to the attractiveness of the work."

38. Carpenter to John Becker, 27 June 1949, JB-NN.

39. Fritz Busch to Carpenter, 25 February 1949, C-ICN.

CHAPTER 24. FROM "BLUE GAL" TO *THE SEVEN AGES*

1. Musicians' Committee to Aid Spanish Democracy to Franklin D. Roosevelt, 3 January 1939, Rachmaninoff Collection, DLC.

2. Carpenter to Franklin D. Roosevelt, 28 May 1941, C-DLC (Carpenter's emphasis).

3. Walter Johnson, ed., *The Papers of Adlai E. Stevenson*, 8 vols. (Boston: Little, Brown, 1972–79), 1:455, 523; 2:68–69.

4. Claudia Cassidy, "Won Fame in Career," Carpenter Collection, Chicago Historical Society; Johnson, *Papers of Adlai E. Stevenson*, 2:69. After the war the Carpenters rented 1020 Lake Shore Drive for $500 a month and in 1948 offered it to the Arts Club for $750 a month (a good price), but the Arts Club decided it was not the right space for them. Minutes, 20 and 21 December 1948, AC-ICN.

5. Dena J. Epstein, "Frederick Stock and American Music," *American Music* 10, no. 1 (Spring 1992): 32–33.

6. Claudia Cassidy, "Stock Promises More American Music Next Year as Golden Jubilee Season Closes," *Journal of Commerce*, 18 April 1941; Robert Pollak, "Symphony Ends Jubilee with a 12-Way 'Elanoy,'" *Chicago Times*, 18 April 1941.

7. Carpenter to Serge Koussevitzky, 23 December 1941, SK-DLC.

8. Carpenter, quoted in "Children Sing with Symphony," Scrapbook.

9. Carpenter to Serge Koussevitzky, 9 March 1942, SK-DLC.

10. Carpenter to Claire Reis, League of Composers Collection, NN.

11. Ibid.

12. Aaron Copland and Vivian Perlis, *Copland since 1943* (New York: St. Martin's, 1989), 3.

13. Olin Downes, "'Anxious Bugler' by Philharmonic," Scrapbook; review of Carpenter's *Anxious Bugler*, Scrapbook. In 1952 Thomas Pierson wrote, "The composition [*The Anxious Bugler*] reveals Carpenter's usual sincerity, but is, on the whole, vague and unconvincing," an assessment weakened, however, by the fact that Pierson followed Downes in mistaking the Dies Irae for "Ein feste Burg," and "My Old Kentucky Home" for "Old Folks at Home." Thomas C. Pierson, "The Life and Music of John Alden Carpenter" (Ph.D. diss., University of Rochester, 1952), 37.

14. Halina Rodzinski, interview by author, 5 January 1992; Richard Rodzinski, interview by author, 24 November 1992.

15. Halina Rodzinski, *Our Two Lives* (New York: Scribner's, 1976), 261.

16. Carpenter to John Becker, 10 February 1945, JB-NN.

17. Carpenter, quoted by Claudia Cassidy, "On the Aisle," *Chicago Sunday Tribune,* 31 March 1946. A copy of a MacLeish scenario for a "Moving-Picture Ballet" can be found among Carpenter's papers, C-ICN.

18. Virgil Thomson, review of Carpenter's *Seven Ages,* Scrapbook.

19. Carpenter to Elizabeth Sprague Coolidge, 27 November 1945; Elizabeth Sprague Coolidge to Carpenter, 4 December 1945, ESC-DLC.

20. Claudia Cassidy, "Conquering Hero Reception Backfires as Defauw Mauls Mozart and Spoils Carpenter Premiere with Dull Performance," Scrapbook.

21. C. J. Bulliet, "Carpenter Amusing in 'Seven Ages' Suite," Scrapbook. See also Charles Buckley, "'Seven Ages' Debut Hit," Scrapbook.

22. Eugene Ormandy to Carpenter, 20 November 1946, C-ICN.

23. M. W., "John Alden Carpenter, Composer, Falls under the Spell of the Carmel Coast," *Monterey Peninsula Herald,* 12 March 1947.

24. Carpenter to John Becker, 21 March 1947, JB-NN.

25. Carpenter to Pierre Monteux, 14 April 1947, C-DLC.

26. Robert Edmond Jones to Carpenter, 21 May 1946, C-DLC.

27. Carpenter to Robert Edmond Jones, 10 July 1946, C-DLC.

CHAPTER 25. A FRIEND OF THE ARTS

1. "New York Opera Folk Boost Carpenter: Business-Artist Combination Just What Chicago Needs, Experts Say," scrapbook, AC-ICN. Carpenter responded to this piece with the remark, "I haven't heard a whisper of it."

2. The earliest record I have found of Carpenter's official membership in the Little Room is a letter the composer sent to Ralph Clarkson (6 January 1914, Clarkson Collection, ICN), but Carpenter probably began some association with the Little Room upon his return from Harvard in 1897.

3. Harriet Monroe, *A Poet's Life: Seventy Years in a Changing World* (New York: Macmillan, 1938), 197.

4. Cliff Dwellers yearbooks, 1911–37, ICN.

5. W. W. Kimball to Carpenter, 27 December 1948, C-ICN.

6. Ruth Page, *Page by Page,* ed. Andrew Mark Wentink (New York: Dance Horizons, 1978), 29. Page married the secretary for the Chicago Allied Arts, Chicago lawyer Tom Fisher (p. 135).

7. The Russian-born Remisoff, described by Ruth Page as "a truly great theatre man," donated all his designs, including those for Chicago Allied Arts, to Butler University in Indianapolis. Ibid., 135.

8. Ibid., 134–35.

9. Samuel Putnam, "The New Ballet: A Theatric Art," *Drama* 17 (December 1926): 69, Bolm Collection, ICN.

10. Carpenter to Eva Gauthier, 21 October 1926, 27 October 1925, Gauthier Collection, NN.

11. Putnam, "New Ballet," 70.

12. Vera Caspary, "The Dance Reviewed," 1927, Bolm Collection, ICN.

13. Page, *Page by Page*, 29. The League of Composers presented the New York premiere of the Eichheim-Bolm-Remisoff ballet on 27 March 1927, Tullio Serafin conducting; Eichheim Collection, ICN.

14. This 3 and 5 January 1926 *Pierrot* used an English translation by Henry Meltzer; Stock's daughter Vera Stock Wolfe translated Schoenberg's "Introduction to the Singer"; Bolm Collection, ICN.

15. Page, *Page by Page,* 123.

16. Aaron Copland and Vivian Perlis, *Copland: 1900 through 1942* (New York: St. Martin's, 1984), 235. Copland's interest in modern dance, spurred by his experiences in Chicago, thus owed something—at least indirectly—to Carpenter.

17. Carpenter to Ruth Page, 8 June 1941, Dance Division, NN.

18. "Carpenter, John Alden," *Current Biography* 1947, 96, C-NN.

19. Minutes and Music Series, AC-ICN.

20. For Ravel's visit Carpenter was called upon to negotiate the competing interests and rivalries of the Arts Club, the Chicago chapter of Pro Musica, and La Chorale Française; Music Series, AC-ICN. See also Carpenter to E. Robert Schmitz, 3 and 21 November 1927, Schmitz Collection, Yale University. Carpenter was not on hand for this visit, incidentally, because he and Rue had left for Europe before Ravel arrived in Chicago.

21. John Palmer to Felix Borowski, 6 December 1941, Music Series, AC-ICN.

22. Carpenter to Arnold Schoenberg, 21 December 1933, Music Series, AC-ICN. Carpenter further explained to Elizabeth Sprague Coolidge that the Arts Club had invited Schoenberg "in order to do what we can here to make a suitable gesture in connection with his present sojourn in America"; Carpenter to Elizabeth Sprague Coolidge, 21 December 1933, ESC-DLC. For the Schoenberg dinner, the Arts Club solicited and obtained a fascinating array of congratulatory letters and telegrams from Koussevitzky, Rodzinski, Klemperer, Toscanini, Ormandy, Damrosch, Stokowski, and Reiner that ran the gamut from deep admiration to cool greetings; Music Series, AC-ICN.

23. Andrew Schulhof to John Palmer, 1 February 1941, Music Series, AC-ICN.

24. Arnold Schoenberg to John Palmer, 17 February 1934; Andrew Schulhof to John Palmer, 23 April 1941, Music Series, AC-ICN.

25. Carpenter, telegram to Isabel Jarvis, 7 February 1930, Music Series, AC-ICN.

26. John Palmer to Serge Prokofiev, 11 February 1930, Music Series, AC-ICN.

27. "Intellectuals Now Pivot of Social Whirl," *Chicago Sunday Tribune,* 20 January 1935, Music Series, AC-ICN.

28. John Palmer to Arthur Judson, 2 April 1933, Music Series, AC-ICN.

29. Music Series, AC-ICN. In the end the Roth Quartet performed Mozart, Debussy, and Schumann.

30. Ada MacLeish to John Palmer, 31 January 1933; John Palmer to Ada MacLeish, 15 February 1933, Music Series, AC-ICN.

31. Carpenter brought forward Boulanger's name in a 1924 meeting as "a very talented composer and pianist"; Minutes, 21 November 1924, AC-ICN. He arranged both Copland lectures, the second on behalf of Ruth Page. (When Page once again asked him, in 1937, to "be an angel and see if you can arrange a lecture for Jerome Moross," he had less success; Ruth Page to Carpenter, 15 November 1937; Carpenter to Bobsy Goodspeed, 28 November 1937, Lecture Series, AC-ICN.) Harris simply asked Carpenter if he could lecture (Roy Harris to Carpenter, 13 March 1940, Lecture Series, AC-ICN), and Carpenter duly contacted Goodspeed: "I do hope it isn't too late to arrange a lecture for him [Harris]. I feel sure he would welcome whatever fee the Club can afford, and, of course, he rates high in the musical world, as you well know"; Carpenter to Bobsy Goodspeed, 17 March 1940, Lecture Series, AC-ICN. Carpenter admired Thomson's criticism (he described himself to Thomson as "an inveterate reader of your column in the Herald Tribune"; Carpenter to Virgil Thomson, 2 May 1941, Thomson Collection, Yale University), and he and Ellen hosted a luncheon for Thomson as early as 2 November 1934; Elsie Johns to Virgil Thomson, 10 October 1934; Ellen Carpenter, telegram to Virgil Thomson, 31 October 1934, Thomson Collection, Yale University.

32. Aaron Copland to Carpenter, 16 January 1930; Carpenter to Aaron Copland, 24 January 1930, Music Series, AC-ICN. Copland telegrammed back on 24 March 1930: "Regret Ruggles impossible as no piano composition or arrangement is available." Copland finally decided on a program of Sessions, Harris, Antheil, Weiss, Thomson, and himself; Music Series, AC-ICN.

33. Paul Rosenfeld to Carpenter, 23 December 1933; Carpenter to Paul Rosenfeld, 27 December 1933, 24 January 1934, Lecture Series, AC-ICN. Rosenfeld accommodated Carpenter, partly because the Ballets Russes were in Chicago during the week of 18 April performing the MacLeish-Nabokov ballet *Union Pacific.*

34. Carpenter to Julius Gold, 17 December 1923, JG-DLC.

35. Elizabeth Sprague Coolidge to Carpenter, 11 July 1933, ESC-DLC.

36. Carpenter to Elizabeth Sprague Coolidge, 15 July 1933; Elizabeth Sprague Coolidge to Carpenter, 20 and 21 July 1933; Carpenter to Elizabeth Sprague Coolidge, 21 July 1933, ESC-DLC.

37. Carpenter to Elizabeth Sprague Coolidge, 12 and 18 August 1933, 10 October 1933; Ellen Carpenter to Elizabeth Sprague Coolidge, 5 October 1933; Elizabeth Sprague Coolidge to Ellen Carpenter, 7 October 1933, ESC-DLC.

38. Carpenter to Carl Engel, 26 October 1933, OC-DLC.

39. Rita Mead, *Henry Cowell's New Music, 1925–1936: The Society, the Music Editions, and the Recordings* (Ann Arbor: UMI Research Press, 1981), 65, 72.

40. Burnet C. Tuthill, "Fifteen Years of Service to an American Ideal," *Musical America,* 1934, 5.

41. Carpenter to Burnet C. Tuthill, 14 February 1931; Burnet C. Tuthill to Carpenter, 25 February 1931, Tuthill Collection, DLC.

42. Carpenter to Burnet C. Tuthill, 19 April 1933, Tuthill Collection, DLC. For his part Goldmark had a high regard for Carpenter's music, according to Elizabeth Mitchell, *Music with a Feather Duster* (Boston: Little, Brown, 1941), 99.

43. Carpenter to Burnet C. Tuthill, 14 February 1931, 27 April 1933; Burnet C. Tuthill to Carpenter, 25 February 1931, 18 and 24 April 1933, Tuthill Collection, DLC.

44. Elizabeth Sprague Coolidge, returned personal check to Carpenter, 8 March 1923, ESC-DLC; E. Robert Schmitz to Carpenter, 11 November 1926, Schmitz Collection, Yale University.

45. C-DLC.

46. Carpenter to Elizabeth Sprague Coolidge, 14 October 1920, ESC-DLC.

47. Carpenter to Carl Engel, 8 May 1928, OC-DLC. Carpenter also turned down Alice Gerstenberg's request that he serve on the Advisory Committee of Chicago's Playwrights Theatre; Carpenter to Alice Gerstenberg, 26 October 1933, Gerstenberg Collection, ICN.

48. Otto Luening, *The Odyssey of an American Composer: The Autobiography of Otto Luening* (New York: Scribner's, 1980), 233, 238, 262; Otto Luening, interview by author, 26 February 1989.

49. Ronald M. Huntington, letter to author, 13 October 1991. A series of letters outline the whole Academy of Rome affair, which involved all the 1926 Rome Prize jury members: Carpenter, Sowerby, Walter Damrosch, Walter Spalding, and Richard Aldrich. Originally, Carpenter and Aldrich supported Spalding's attempts to force Lamond's resignation on the basis that he was "not a professional musician." Sowerby countered with arguments that, in Spalding's opinion, showed "signs of ignorance and prejudice." To settle the

question, the entire jury met in New York on 6 December 1926. At the meeting Carpenter, Sowerby, Aldrich, and Damrosch voted to retain Lamond; Spalding alone voted to oust him.

50. Carpenter to Aaron Copland, 27 May 1939, Copland Collection, DLC.

51. Ned Rorem, letter to author, 8 February 1993.

52. Carpenter to Edgard Varèse, 23 January 1934, JB-NN.

53. Carpenter to Walter Roy, 13 August 1935; Carpenter to Norman Alexandroff, 7 October 1935; and Carpenter to Joel Lay, 5 November 1935, JB-NN.

54. Carpenter to John Becker, 11 July 1949, JB-NN.

55. Mrs. John Becker to Thomas C. Pierson, 4 December 1977, JB-NN.

56. Carpenter to John Becker, 23 November 1945, 4 February 1950, JB-NN.

57. Eileen Southern, *The Music of Black Americans: A History* (New York: Norton, 1971), 449.

58. Dena J. Epstein, "Frederick Stock and American Music," *American Music* 10, no. 1 (Spring 1992): 36.

59. Carpenter to Florence Price, 18 December 1934, Price Collection, University of Arkansas.

60. Ibid., 3 March 1950, 13 May 1940, Price Collection, University of Arkansas; Florence Price to Marian Anderson, 14 May 1940, Price Collection, University of Arkansas.

61. Carpenter to Elizabeth Sprague Coolidge, 28 November 1944, ESC-DLC.

62. Carpenter, "Music as Recreation," *Recreation,* October 1946, 352.

63. Ibid.

64. Ibid., 352–53.

65. Ibid., 353, 392–93.

66. M. W., "John Alden Carpenter, Composer, Falls under the Spell of the Carmel Coast," *Monterey Peninsula Herald,* 12 March 1947.

67. Carpenter to Julius Gold, 9 October 1925, JG-DLC. Gold originally hoped that Carpenter would undertake an article or even a monograph about Ziehn; Julius Gold to Carpenter, 31 December 1923, 9 October 1925, JG-DLC. Carpenter also recommended Gold for a Guggenheim Fellowship in 1930. He told Gold: "I cannot help feeling that it puts me in the position of Theodore Roosevelt, the younger, who very complacently gave Lindbergh as he started for Paris on his classic flight, a letter of introduction to the French people." Carpenter to Julius Gold, 11 September 1930, JG-DLC.

68. Carpenter to H[enry] T[aylor] Parker, 5 January 1929, SK-DLC. Carpenter wrote: "Stock played here last week a new symphony by the young

Russian, Shostakowitz, and if you have not already heard it in Boston, you can be doing Boston a service by bringing it to Koussevitzky's attention."

69. Carpenter to Walter Damrosch, 1 December 1930, WD-DLC.

70. Carpenter to Carl Engel, 26 October 1933, OC-DLC.

71. Carpenter to Richard Copley, 5 June 1936, OC-DLC.

72. Carpenter to Virgil Thomson, 2 May 1941, Thomson Collection, Yale University. Rehearsals for an upcoming performance of *Four Saints in Three Acts* prevented Thomson from attending this concert; he further told Carpenter, "I am sorry to have missed hearing Miss Hager and doubly sorry to have missed your song sung by an interpreter whose work you admire." Virgil Thomson to Carpenter, 14 May 1951, Thomson Collection, Yale University.

73. Carpenter to Elizabeth Sprague Coolidge, 28 November 1944, ESC-DLC.

74. Carpenter to Martin Kennelly, 1 September 1950, C-ICN.

CHAPTER 26. FINAL YEARS

1. Millicent Bell, *Marquand: An American Life* (Boston: Little, Brown, 1979), 381.

2. Ibid.

3. Carpenter to John Becker, 23 December 1946, JB-NN.

4. Carpenter to Remsen Bird, 24 September 1949, Bird Collection, ICN.

5. M. W., "John Alden Carpenter, Composer, Falls under the Spell of the Carmel Coast," *Monterey Peninsula Herald,* 12 March 1947.

6. Carpenter to Rudolph Ganz, 4 September 1949, RG-ICN; Carpenter to Remsen Bird, 24 September 1949, 3 January 1950, Bird Collection, ICN.

7. Carpenter to Rue (Hill) Hubert, 29 February 1948, C-RH.

8. Nathan Broder to Carpenter, 19 August 1948, C-ICN.

9. Carpenter, quoted in "Carmel Concerto," *New York Philharmonic Program Notes,* 20 November 1949.

10. Carpenter, quoted by the *Monterey Peninsula Herald,* 14 October 1949, C-ICN. M. W., "Visits to the Homes of Famous Composers," 1947, C-NN, reported that Carpenter loathed the word *inspiration.* (He apparently preferred the term *idea.*) In a letter to Wallace Rice, who had sent him some of his poems, Carpenter nonetheless described a process close to what is commonly thought of as "inspiration": "I never know in advance what happens—but it will be fun to stand with your poems in an exposed place and see if the lightning—some bold young bolt—has a mind to strike us." Carpenter to Wallace Rice, 5 February 1915, Rice Collection, ICN. See also Carpenter's

comment about the "inspiration" he received from Bernhard Ziehn (chap. 4).

11. H. W. Heinsheimer to Carpenter, 3 May 1949, C-ICN. For Carpenter's reference to "Schirmerheimer," see Carpenter to May Valentine, 2 November 1949, C-ICN.

12. Carpenter to H. W. Heinsheimer, 4 May 1949, C-ICN (Carpenter's emphasis).

13. Werner Janssen to Carpenter, 9 May 1949, C-ICN.

14. Carpenter to John Becker, 4 February 1950, JB-NN.

15. Hal Garrott, "Latest Work of Carmel Composer Applauded by Philharmonic Audience," *Monterey Peninsula Herald*, 21 December 1949.

16. Ibid.

17. Cecil Smith, "Carpenter's Carmel Concerto Given Premiere by Stokowski," *Musical America*, 15 December 1949, 8. The phrase "are said to be tinged" referred to Carpenter's own program note: "its moods ranging from vigor to calm, with suggestions of Oriental or Spanish derivations, as well as a bite of *'America' unabashed*."

18. Artur Rodzinski to Carpenter, 3 June 1949; Tauno Hannikainen to John and Ellen Carpenter, 27 March 1950, C-ICN.

19. Seymour Raven, "Carpenter's 'Carmel Concerto' Pleases in Its Chicago Premiere," Scrapbook.

20. Artur Rodzinski to Carpenter, 6 September 1949, C-ICN.

21. Carpenter to Remsen Bird, 24 September 1949, Bird Collection, ICN.

22. Carpenter to Serge Koussevitzky, 10 October 1948, SK-DLC; Carpenter to Artur Rodzinski, ca. October 1949, C-ICN. Koussevitzky expressed a preference for the revised *Adventures in a Perambulator;* Serge Koussevitzky to Carpenter, 26 October 1948, C-ICN.

23. Carpenter to John Becker, 1 February 1946, JB-NN.

24. Carpenter to Ginny Hill, 6 April 1949, C-ICN (Carpenter's emphasis).

25. Carpenter to John Becker, 4 February 1950, JB-NN.

26. Irving Sablosky, "Dean of Chicago Composers Still Active," February 1951, Scrapbook; Felix Borowski, "John Alden Carpenter 75 on Wednesday," *Chicago Sun-Times*, 25 February 1951, Scrapbook.

27. Harry M. Geduld, *Sir James Barrie* (New York: Twayne, 1971), 165.

28. Nathan Broder to Carpenter, 16 August 1950, C-ICN. Walton obviously had a Chicago following, as evident from Stock's commission of the *Scapino* Overture as part of the jubilee season, 1940–41.

29. Gregor Piatigorsky to Ellen Carpenter, 4 December 1951, Scrapbook.

30. Carpenter to James Bryant Conant, 10 September 1945, C-ICN.

31. M. W., "Visits to the Homes."

32. Ibid. Carpenter apparently knew Roger Sessions and met with him when he attended a performance of Sessions's Violin Concerto in Minneapolis in 1947. Andrea Olmstead, *The Correspondence of Roger Sessions* (Boston: Northeastern University Press, 1992), 351.

33. Carpenter to Serge Koussevitzky, 8 May 1948, Scrapbook and SK-DLC (Carpenter's emphasis). Koussevitzky telegrammed back, "Deeply moved by your wonderful letter"; Serge Koussevitzky, telegram to Carpenter, 13 May 1948, Scrapbook.

34. Carpenter to Ginny Hill, 6 April 1949, C-ICN (Carpenter's emphasis).

35. Walter Monfried, "Carpenter, Businessman-Composer," *Milwaukee Journal,* 30 April 1947, 20.

36. Carpenter to John Becker, 4 February 1950, JB-NN. Thomas C. Pierson, "The Life and Music of John Alden Carpenter" (Ph.D. diss., University of Rochester, 1952), 16, writes that a chair collapsed under the composer. Carpenter had something of a history of such mishaps. On 2 September 1924, he ran into a car while crossing the street in Chicago, an accident that again left him on crutches; Carpenter to Ellen Borden, 18 September 1924, 30 December 1924, C-DLC. (He consequently had to cancel plans to attend the Pittsfield Festival that September, explaining to Elizabeth Sprague Coolidge, "I have learned one way how *not* to cross the street among moving automobiles"; Carpenter to Elizabeth Sprague Coolidge, 15 September 1924, ESC-DLC [Carpenter's emphasis].) And in 1942 the composer broke his shoulder in a bicycle accident; Pierson, "John Alden Carpenter," 16; Frederick Stock to Carpenter, 26 September 1942, Scrapbook.

37. Walter Johnson, ed., *The Papers of Adlai E. Stevenson,* 8 vols. (Boston: Little, Brown, 1972–79), 2:203; Carpenter to Rue (Hill) Hubert, 3 March 1950, C-RH; Carpenter to Mina Hager, 1 June 1950, C-ICN; Sablosky, "Dean of Chicago Composers Still Active."

38. Johnson, *Papers of Adlai E. Stevenson,* 1:259.

39. Carpenter to Rudolph Ganz, RG-ICN.

40. Carpenter to John Becker, 9 January 1937, 30 March 1945, JB-NN.

41. Johnson, *Papers of Adlai E. Stevenson,* 2:69; Alan Valentine to Carpenter, 19 April 1943, C-DLC.

42. Carpenter to John Becker, 5 January 1948, JB-NN.

43. I can identify six of these thirteen doctors: Nora Brandenburg (otolaryngology), James Mitchell (dermatology and syphilology), Walter H. Theobald (otolaryngology), Herman Louis Kretschmer (urology), Paul Sternberg (opthamology), and Millard Smith (internal medicine). All practiced in Chicago, except for Smith, who worked in Boston.

44. Carpenter purchased a Paravox Hearing Aid on 24 October 1949, and he apparently obtained a Telex Hearing Aid as well, C-ICN.

45. Adlai Stevenson Jr., interview by author, 15 April 1993.

46. Ginny Hill to Patrick Hill, 5, 7, 8, and 11 February 1951, C-RH.

47. Mildred Bolger, "John A. Carpenter So Much Better Daughter Goes Home," *Chicago Tribune*, 12 February 1951, Scrapbook.

48. "Composer Carpenter 75," *New York Times*, 1 March 1951.

49. Ibid.

50. "Symphony to Salute Composer Carpenter," February 1951, Scrapbook.

51. Howard Hanson, "John Alden Carpenter," *Saturday Review*, 24 February 1951, 50–51.

52. William Leonard, "Carpenter Birthday Observed in Chicago Symphony Season," *Musical America*, 1 April 1951, 21. Leonard wrote that Kubelik "chose a dated pair of compositions that showed neither the composer nor the orchestra at their best."

53. Claudia Cassidy, "On the Aisle," Scrapbook.

54. Ellen Carpenter to John McCutcheon, 3 March 1951, McCutcheon Collection, ICN.

55. Claudia Cassidy, "Won Fame in Career," *Chicago Tribune*, 27 April 1951, Carpenter Collection, ASCAP; "John Carpenter, Noted Composer," *New York Times*, 27 April 1951, 23; "Obituary," *Variety* 182 (2 May 1951): 75; "Obituary," *Newsweek* 37 (7 May 1951): 58.

56. [Cecil Smith?], "John Alden Carpenter: A Musical Humanist," *Musical America*, 17 May 1951, 12.

57. Alan Valentine to Carpenter, 19 April 1943, C-DLC.

58. Aaron Copland to Carpenter, 16 February 1947, Aaron Copland Collection, DLC; Carpenter to Aaron Copland, 21 February 1947, C-DLC.

59. "J. A. Carpenter Will Filed on $100,000 Estate," *Chicago Tribune*, 16 May 1951, Carpenter Collection, ASCAP.

60. Eleanor Page, "J. A. Carpenter Memorial to Be Dedicated," *Chicago Tribune*, 22 July 1952.

61. "Music Stage Dedicated," *New York Times*, 28 July 1952, 12.

62. Rudolf Serkin to Ellen Carpenter, 20 April 1961, C-DLC; Roy Harris to Ellen Carpenter, 16 October 1960, C-ICN.

AFTERWORD

1. Carl Sandburg, *The People, Yes* (New York: Harcourt, Brace, 1936), 44.

Index

Page numbers in italics indicate music examples.

Index

Index

Index

MacDowell, Edward, 12, 15, 16, 18, 96, 140, 143, 144, 148, 261, 325
McEvoy, Ambrose, 37
MacLeish, Ada, 386
MacLeish, Archibald, 38, 40, 41, 211, 314, 339, 340, 376, 386
McNeil, Charles, 42
McNulty, Margaret, 40, 111
MacPhail, Margaret Gilmore, 60
MacPhail, William, 60
McPhee, Colin, 258, 278, 387
MacVeagh, Eames, 35
Maeterlinck, Maurice, 78
Magnard, Albéric, 30
Mahler, Gustav, 106–8, 152, 153, 227, 359, 362, 364–65
Maier, Guy, 206, 207
Makletsova, Xenia, 166
Malipiero, Gian Francesco, 347
Mann, Harrington, 37
Mannes, Clara, 60, 61
Marchesi, Mathilde, 5
Marcoux, Vanni, 259
Marin, John, 37
Markham, Edwin, 18
Marquand, John, 315, 342, 395–96
Marsh, Reginald, 206, 245
Marsh, Robert C., 75, 106, 109, 323, 327
Martin, Morris H., 371, 375
Martinů, Bohuslav, 373, 375
Marx Brothers, 223
Masefield, John, 80
Mason, Daniel Gregory, 14–16, 24, 182–84, 186, 188, 201, 245, 368, 389
Massachusetts, 3, 30, 271, 310; Beverly, 46, 314–15, 347, 363, 365, 371, 373, 375, 396, 404; Boston, 2, 4, 6, 9, 16, 20, 25, 60, 61, 85, 105, 117, 119, 128, 131, 138, 154, 183, 184, 186, 206, 214, 242, 245, 277, 292, 297, 299–300, 301, 303, 313–15, 320, 324, 329, 334, 335, 345, 346, 354–55, 361, 394, 401, 406; Cambridge, 25, 186, 303; Cape Cod, 261; Ipswich, 310, 315, 405, 406; Pittsfield, 271; Plymouth, 58; Pride's Crossing, 128, 317, 330; Tanglewood, 392
Massenet, Jules, 76
Massine, Léonide, 38, 40, 166, 188, 207–8, 395
Masters, Edgar Lee, 1, 37, 82
Matisse, Henri, 39, 70, 210
Maxwell, Leon R., 75, 85
Meeker, Arthur, 34–36, 39–42, 47, 76, 109, 170, 316
Mei Lanfang, 287
Melba, Nellie, 5
Melchoir, Lauritz, 313
Melton, James, 251
Mendelssohn, Felix, 6, 11, 22, 53, 345
Mendenhall, Lucille, 88
Menotti, Gian-Carlo, 165, 401
Metropolitan Opera, 84, 164, 168, 184, 210, 217, 219, 220–21, 223, 230, 235, 237–38, 239, 240, 245, 246, 361, 381, 402
Mexico, 120, 134, 243, 335; Mexico City, 120, 335
Miaskovsky, Nikolai, 107, 347

Middelschulte, Wilhelm, 50, 52–53
Milhaud, Darius, 107, 139, 140, 211, 212, 245, 252, 322, 359, 360, 373, 387, 388
Millay, Edna St. Vincent, 38, 252, 361
Miller, Christine, 87, 148
Miller, Philip, 130, 259
Mills, Charles, 278
Mills, Florence, 222
Milstein, Nathan, 386
Minneapolis, 30, 61, 391
Miró, Joan, 37
Mischakoff, Mischa, 335
Mischakoff Quartet, 335
Mitchell, Marjorie, 143
Mock, Alice, 100
Moffett, William A., 158
Molotov, Vyacheslav Mikhailovich, 310
Monroe, Harriet, 37, 71, 82, 83, 92, 127, 145, 216, 217, 342, 381
Monte Carlo, 179, 218–19
Monteux, Pierre, 106, 120, 139–40, 186, 210, 296, 380, 396
Moody, Mrs. William Vaughan, 92
Moore, Douglas, 373
Moore, Edward, 180, 202, 204, 241–42, 292, 322, 373
Moore, Macdonald Smith, 201
Moore, Thomas, 18
Moracci, Carmelita, 386
Moral Rearmament (MRA), 308–9, 311, 323
Morgenthau, Henry, Jr., 369
Moross, Jerome, 384
Morris, Harold, 304, 371
Morse, Theodore, 19
Morton, Ferdinand "Jelly Roll," 131, 132, 196
Mosolov, Alexander, 168
Moszkowski, Moritz, 322
Mottl, Felix, 105
Mozart, Wolfgang Amadeus, 9–11, 74, 104, 107, 109, 322, 379, 386
Muck, Karl, 85, 117, 119, 120, 296
Mueller, Florian, 369, 370
Mullins, Priscilla, 3
Munch, Charles, 406
Murphy, Gerald, 40, 211–12, 214–15, 220, 224
Musical College (Chicago), 10, 11, 208, 367, 392
Music Teachers' National Association, 300
Musorgsky, Modest, 84, 350

Nabokov, Nicolas, 387
Nathan, Hans, 88
National Institute of Arts and Letters, 405
Neff, Severine, 52, 56
Negro Quartet, 387
Nelson, Edgar, 294
Netherlands, 326
Nevin, Ethelbert, 6, 18
Newman, Alfred, 206
New Music Quartet, 406
New Orleans, 134, 190, 195, 196, 207, 233, 269
New York, 1, 2, 9, 10, 17, 20, 33, 34, 38, 45, 47, 52, 58, 60, 61, 62, 86, 100, 105, 108, 117, 118, 123, 126, 138, 140, 142, 147, 149, 153, 154, 156, 177,

Index

Music in American Life

Juilliard: A History   *Andrea Olmstead*

Understanding Charles Seeger, Pioneer in American Musicology   *Edited by Bell Yung and Helen Rees*

Mountains of Music: West Virginia Traditional Music from *Goldenseal*   *Edited by John Lilly*

Alice Tully: An Intimate Portrait   *Albert Fuller*

A Blues Life   *Henry Townsend, as told to Bill Greensmith*

Long Steel Rail: The Railroad in American Folksong (2d ed.)   *Norm Cohen*

The Golden Age of Gospel   *Text by Horace Clarence Boyer; photography by Lloyd Yearwood*

Aaron Copland: The Life and Work of an Uncommon Man   *Howard Pollack*

Louis Moreau Gottschalk   *S. Frederick Starr*

Race, Rock, and Elvis   *Michael T. Bertrand*

Theremin: Ether Music and Espionage   *Albert Glinsky*

Poetry and Violence: The Ballad Tradition of Mexico's Costa Chica   *John H. McDowell*

The Bill Monroe Reader   *Edited by Tom Ewing*

Music in Lubavitcher Life   *Ellen Koskoff*

Zarzuela: Spanish Operetta, American Stage   *Janet L. Sturman*

Bluegrass Odyssey: A Documentary in Pictures and Words, 1966–86   *Carl Fleischhauer and Neil V. Rosenberg*

That Old-Time Rock & Roll: A Chronicle of an Era, 1954–63   *Richard Aquila*

Labor's Troubadour   *Joe Glazer*

American Opera   *Elise K. Kirk*

Don't Get above Your Raisin': Country Music and the Southern Working Class   *Bill C. Malone*

John Alden Carpenter: A Chicago Composer   *Howard Pollack*

University of Illinois Press
1325 South Oak Street
Champaign, IL 61820-6903
www.press.uillinois.edu